Essential Papers on Suicide

ESSENTIAL PAPERS IN PSYCHOANALYSIS
General Editor: Leo Goldberger

Essential Papers on Borderline Disorders
Edited by Michael H. Stone, M.D.

Essential Papers on Object Relations
Edited by Peter Buckley, M.D.

Essential Papers on Narcissism
Edited by Andrew P. Morrison, M.D.

Essential Papers on Depression
Edited by James C. Coyne

Essential Papers on Psychosis
Edited by Peter Buckley, M.D.

Essential Papers on Countertransference
Edited by Benjamin Wolstein

Essential Papers on Character Neurosis and Treatment
Edited by Ruth F. Lax

Essential Papers on the Psychology of Women
Edited by Claudia Zanardi

Essential Papers on Transference
Edited by Aaron H. Esman, M.D.

Essential Papers on Dreams
Edited by Melvin R. Lansky, M.D.

Essential Papers on Literature and Psychoanalysis
Edited by Emanuel Berman

Essential Papers on Object Loss
Edited by Rita V. Frankiel

Essential Papers on Masochism
Edited by Margaret Ann Fitzpatrick Hanly

Essential Papers on Short-Term Dynamic Therapy
Edited by James E. Groves, M.D.

Essential Papers on Suicide
Edited by John T. Maltsberger, M.D., and Mark J. Goldblatt, M.D.

Essential Papers on Suicide

edited by
John T. Maltsberger, M.D., and
Mark J. Goldblatt, M.D.

NEW YORK UNIVERSITY PRESS
New York and London

Manufactured in the United States of America

Library of Congress Cataloging-in-Publication Data
Essential papers on suicide / edited by John T. Maltsberger and Mark J. Goldblatt.
p. cm. — (Essential papers in psychoanalysis)
Includes bibliographical references and index.
ISBN 0-8147-5549-6 (cloth). — ISBN 0-8147-5550-X (pbk.)
1. Suicide. I. Maltsberger, John T. II. Goldblatt, Mark J., 1955- . III. Series.
RC569.E87 1996
616.85′8445—dc20 96-21405
CIP

New York University Press books are printed on acid-free paper, and their binding materials are chosen for strength and durability.

To
Ann Richmond Seelye
and
Carol, Sasha, and Michael Goldblatt

Contents

Foreword

Edwin S. Shneidman

The paradox is that suicide is alive and well, as this magnificent volume evidences. The field of studying suicide and practicing its prevention celebrates its full academic matriculation, *summa cum laude,* within these pages, which reprint, as the able editors accurately state, the "essential papers" of suicidology.

By their nature, forewords to books are intended to be laudatory, to launch a book on what is hoped to be an auspicious life of its own. Forewords are endorsements, exordia. The reader cannot always believe what is in a foreword, and can rightly suspect elements of hyperbole and even exaggeration.

But what if I came up, in this case, with tangible evidence, demonstrating the sincerity of my beliefs as stated in a quite different venue? The fact is that I have just finished a book of my own, *The Suicidal Mind* (New York: Oxford, 1996), in which, after the main body of the text, there is a section called Recommended Readings where I state: "Given that there are hundreds of books on suicide, even so, after searching my mind, and examining this and that volume in my hands, I have chosen two very special books." One of those two indispensable books is *Essential Papers on Suicide,* edited by Drs. John T. Maltsberger and Mark J. Goldblatt. Here is what I wrote about that book:

> This marvelous volume is both the most recent and by far the most comprehensive "reader" on suicide, the psychological aspects especially. There are 40 selections, technical articles from the psychological and psychiatric literature, from the early 20th century to the most current journals. All the "classical" papers are here. A *must* reference book for the serious student who wishes to review the technical literature.

What are the other indispensable books on suicide? My own favorites are Kate Chopin's *The Awakening,* Gustave Flaubert's *Madame Bovary,* and—if one likes a long read—Leo Tolstoy's *Anna Karenina.* Anyone who reads these wondrous books will know a great deal about suicide. *Essential Papers on Suicide* presents the technical side of the suicidal drama.

Essential Papers in Suicide is truly comprehensive. It spans the period from the early years of this century to the current decade; its contributors represent the suicidal spectrum from Åsberg (brain chemistry) to Zilboorg (the psychodynamic and anthropological aspects of suicide); it contains contributions from several countries, including the United States, England, Sweden, Austria, and Israel; and perhaps best of all, it authoritatively represents the broad multidisciplinary nature of the study of suicide (and of suicide itself) by including the work of top-flight scientists and practitioners.

It is an honor and a privilege for me to be able to lend my (unnecessary) endorsement to this definitive volume, which speaks for itself. New York University Press should be commended for publishing it; Drs. Maltsberger and Goldblatt deserve our gratitude for conceiving of this project and editing the book with such meticulous care.

Introduction

John T. Maltsberger and Mark J. Goldblatt

THOUGH SUICIDE has not one cause, but many, they all flow together into one river whose overwhelming current, mental pain, carries everything before it. Those doomed to it choose death over intolerable suffering that to them seems interminable. Few have better described the anguish that leads to suicide than William Styron (1990), the title of whose autobiographical memoir of near-suicide, *Darkness Visible,* comes from Milton's vision of Hell.[1] Do theological writers draw their vision of damnation from intuitions of depressive suffering? Poets and artists are prey to it (Jamison 1993), but so are multitudes of others. Hundreds of thousands of patients tremble in depressive anguish, and many are carried away into suicide. More than thirty thousand persons commit suicide every year in the United States alone.

Though suicide, after accidents and HIV infection, destroys more young people in the United States than anything else, it is neglected in medical education. Mainstream physicians and surgeons know little more about it than the general public (Murphy 1975). Many psychiatrists have not been well educated about suicide. In psychiatric residents' education considerable biological and psychopharmacological attention is paid to those disorders under whose rubrics suicide is most likely to occur (affective disorders, alcoholism, and schizophrenia), but the clinical phenomena immediately surrounding suicide are scanted. Trainees are taught to tick off items in the *DSM IV* checklist for the major depressive syndromes, but they are not taught how to assess depressive anguish. Indeed, anguish is not even listed among the criteria for diagnosing depression in the standard nomenclature (American Psychiatric Association 1994, 327). There we find "depressed mood" and "diminished interest or pleasure" mentioned, but nothing explicit to direct attention to the howling wind of depressive agony (see Shneidman, chapter 40 below). Unconscious forces in suicide are increasingly neglected in training programs, and so are family dynamics, dreaming, psychotherapeutic treatment, the quality of object relatedness, and careful diagnostic interviewing.

We hope this volume will help clinicians concentrate their attention on those suicide phenomena they may have overlooked, and that it will help readers to come empathically closer to those who are shaken by the terrible forces of suicidal illness.

The study of suicide has eighteenth-century roots, but only in the last thirty-five years has it grown robustly. Jean Esquirol (1772–1840), psychiatrist of the French Revolution, led the way in medicalizing insanity. While working to draw patients out of prison conditions into circumstances of humane care Esquirol devised a classification of mental disorders suggested by the work of Linnæus, the famous plant taxonomist of the Enlightenment. Suicide had a prominent place in Esquirol's studies, claiming a chapter in his *Treatise on Insanity* (1838).

If Esquirol medicalized suicide Émile Durkheim (1858–1917) sociologized it, explicating it in terms of society's tendency to integrate its members (or not), and to regulate the way they think, feel, and act. His celebrated *Le Suicide* (1897) is much cited. A short time later Sigmund Freud and his followers psychologized suicide. A few years after Durkheim's treatise appeared the Vienna Psychoanalytic Society took up the subject. Their 1910 discussions concerning student suicide were subsequently published (Friedman 1967). Freud's (1917) "Mourning and Melancholia" appeared seven years later and concentrated psychiatrists' and psychologists' minds on the unconscious turning of aggression against the self. So strong was the influence of this paper that it overshadowed psychodynamic studies in suicide for the next forty years.

Important as these developments were, the earlier contributions to our understanding of suicide were not frequent, and their appearances were spread over a span of many years. Suicide studies began to be published frequently only a little more than three decades ago, partly because funding for psychiatric research was more freely available at the time, and partly because of the imagination and leadership of Edwin Shneidman, Norman Farberow, Robert Litman, and others who established the Los Angeles Suicide Prevention Center.

The year 1958 was a critical moment in the development of suicide studies. That was when the Los Angeles Suicide Prevention Center (LASPC) opened its doors (Shneidman and Farberow 1965). The energetic core professional staff of the LASPC, a multidisciplinary collaboration, published a number of important papers and accumulated such momentum that more and more people from various portions of intellectual and public-spirited life grew enthusiastic about understanding and preventing suicide. Shneidman invented a new word to suit the times—*suicidology:* the study of suicide and related phenomena.

In 1968, after a Chicago meeting of a number of eminent scholars from different disciplines who were concerned with suicide prevention, Shneidman took the lead in founding the American Association of Suicidology. The Association established a journal devoted to suicide and related subjects *(Suicide and Life Threatening Behavior),* which has served to stimulate interest in and inseminate suicide studies ever since.

In the past thirty-five years what began as a trickle of suicide-related papers has swollen to a flood. The American Suicide Foundation, incorporated in 1987 under the leadership of Dr. Herbert Hendin, now funds suicide research across the United States, and promises much for the growth of suicidology and the future treatment of suicidal patients.

The publication of *Essential Papers on Suicide* comes at a time when the annual publication of suicide material is overwhelming, yet much that appears is clinically remote. It has become difficult to recognize and retrieve many contributions useful in the actual care of suicidal patients. Many good papers molder on the back shelves of libraries. Some of them, having appeared in out-of-the-way journals, are difficult to find. In offering this book we hope to draw attention to some of the best papers and to present them in one volume that will come readily to hand, relieving students of burdensome searching through bookstacks of old bound (and new unbound) volumes when they wish to study or revisit some promising source.

This anthology is not intended to offer a fair sampling of the current literature, a flow continuously supplemented by tributaries from sociology, philosophy, epidemiology, neurochemistry, and other disciplines. We do not underestimate the impressive waters of the suicidological river. For the most part, however, they swirl far from everyday clinical practice. This volume of "essential papers" is intended for clinicians who have no time to swim about looking for what might help them in their work. Specifically, these papers have been selected as aids in *understanding* suicidal patients.

Although there are no psychopharmacological studies here, we do not intend to minimize the value of psychopharmacological and biological contributions. We emphasize, indeed, that adequate treatment of suicidal patients usually involves a broad approach to their problems, one aspect of which is psychopharmacological.

The development of anti-depressant drugs represents the major therapeutic advance in helping suicidal patients in recent years. However, most psychopharmacological papers pertain to the treatment of depression and other psychiatric illnesses in general, and not to suicide specifically.

The controversy that arose concerning fluoxetine (Prozac) soon after it was introduced in the United States seems to have died down (Teicher, Glod, and Cole 1990). All medicines cause some side-effects. The overwhelming majority of psychiatrists believe that anti-depressants are extremely helpful in treating depression. Some depressed patients may worsen while taking antidepressant drugs, either because they develop a certain restlessness known technically as *akathisia,* or because they experience an increase of energy that precedes improvement in their suicidal mood (Rothschild and Locke 1991). In the absence of improved mood, the increased energy may impel a suicide attempt (the depression is getting better, but the suicidal attitude has not improved as fast as the level of energy). No one anti-depressant drug has been proven superior to others in the treatment of suicidal patients. Readers who wish a fuller discussion of the psychopharmacological treatment of depression (most suicidal patients are indeed depressed) may find some of the following references of interest. Herman M. van Praag and his colleagues have edited an excellent volume on the psychobiology of violence and suicide that is of great interest (van Praag, Plutchik, and Apter 1990). The drug treatment of mood disorders has recently been reviewed by Pedro L. Delgado and Alan J. Gelenberg (1995). Mark J. Goldblatt and Alan F. Schatzberg (1990) have reviewed the psychopharmacological treatment of depression as it applies to suicidal patients. There are several outstanding textbooks of psychopharmacology now in print that cover this subject admirably (see, e.g., Schatzberg and Nemeroff 1995).

Our purpose in this collection is to offer an array of papers that are psychologically close to the suicide experience, or else throw light on that experience, whether the papers are biological, chemical, or sociological. Our bias is, in short, psychoanalytic. We believe that a good grasp of the psychology of suicide, and of the special emotional challenges that confront those who treat suicidal patients, is the *sine qua non* for effective clinical work, whatever psychotherapeutic or psychopharmacological tactics one may embrace. If these papers are essential, it is because they deepen our grasp of the texture and color of the inner lives and struggles of suicidal patients and the corollary challenges they pose for those who treat them.

Our arrangement of the papers is chronological. The first seven papers, all of which appeared before 1960, deal with unconscious phenomena in suicidal patients. Ernest Jones's papers (1911, 1912) actually antedate Freud's

"Mourning and Melancholia"; Karl A. Menninger's 1933 paper presents the now famous suicidal triad: the wish to kill, the wish to be killed, and the wish to die. Gregory Zilboorg's papers (1936, 1937, 1975) have much to teach of suicide's symbolism and the thorny personal relationships in which suicidal patients entangle themselves. The ubiquitous equation between sleep and death so common in suicidal cases is described in Kate Friedlander's paper (1940), and Ives Hendrick (1940) presents a case that shows the importance of identification in suicide. Emil A. Gutheil (1948) demonstrates the importance of dreams in understanding the minds of suicidal patients. Viggo W. Jensen and Thomas A. Petty (1958) discuss the almost universal ambivalence suicide attempts express.

The omission of Freud's "Mourning and Melancholia" from this volume is too egregious to escape comment; that paper, after all, overtowers everything else pertinent to suicide in the psychoanalytic literature. We have left it out because it is almost universally available elsewhere and we suffer from constraints of space. We assume the reader's familiarity with it, or at least that the paper will come readily to hand everywhere.

In the 1960s psychoanalytic writers at last turned their attention past the psychological device of "murder turned against the self" as explained by Freud (1917). Leston L. Havens (1965) concentrates on the relationship between the therapist and the patient; Thomas E. Allen (1967) shows the continuity between paranoid states and melancholia, and Robert E. Litman and Charles Swearingen (1972) emphasize the erotic components of suicide and suicide attempts. Stuart S. Asch (1980), in a paper alerting us to the danger of countertransference enactments, draws attention to the operation of murderous introjects in suicide.

The contributions of Gerald Adler, Dan H. Buie, Jr., and John T. Maltsberger after 1970 attend to the immediate subjective experiences of patients and therapists, as well as to the importance of unconscious fantasies about the nature of death. These authors, all Boston psychoanalysts, are former students of the late Elvin Semrad. One of the cornerstones of his teaching was that affect intolerance lies at the heart of psychiatric illness. Another was that to understand and help patients it is necessary to draw empathically close to what they cannot bear. His influence is discernable in their thinking.

Deeper understanding of the psychotherapeutic enterprise is made possible through the contributions of Donald A. Schwartz, Don E. Flinn, and Paul F. Slawson (1974); Herbert Hendin (1981); Edwin Shneidman (1981); and John Birtchnell (1983).

Credit for empirical proof that hopelessness is more closely correlated with suicide than depression belongs to Aaron T. Beck and his colleagues (1975). Anxiety and panic as mental state factors in suicide are demonstrated in the paper by Myrna Weissman and her co-workers (1989). Shneidman has throughout his career emphasized the importance of phenomenology in understanding suicide. We include his recent commentary on "psychache" (1993), where he fixes our attention on mental anguish as the preeminent immediate factor in suicide. The importance of contagion in promoting suicide is addressed by David P. Phillips (1974).

In the past twenty-five years more light has been shone on the problems of child development and child and adolescent suicide. Joseph C. Sabbath's (1969) cases showing the importance of family scapegoating in the promotion of suicide are poignant reminders; his study can be integrated with Joseph Richman and Milton Rosenbaum's (1970) report on the importance of familial hostility and death wishes in suicide. These papers remind us of the late Otto Will's chilling aphorism, "In cases of suicide, ask who wanted the patient dead." We further include Erna Furman's (1984) little known work on masochistic fixations in childhood. Though the paper by Cynthia R. Pfeffer and her colleagues (1986) is written at a remove from individual patient experience (it is essentially epidemiological), we believe it offers an important perspective on the problem of early life suicide. Maurice Friedman and colleagues (1971) address the problem from a developmental point of view in a paper closely related to Jack Novick's (1984).

Some of our later papers are comparatively patient remote, but they are too important to exclude because they give the other selections context. Eli Robins and his colleagues (1959) dispel the entrenched myth that suicide often occurs in the mentally well; they prove the ubiquity of major depressive illness and alcoholism in suicide. This important finding is critical to clinical practice. Marie Åsberg and her colleagues were the first to demonstrate the specific importance of brain chemistry in suicide; their 1976 discussion of the role serotonin plays in suicide has resulted in a sheaf of corroborative investigations. Further, their finding has stimulated new directions in psychopharmacological research. This paper (it has brought suicide into the laboratory) we cannot leave out. Alec Roy's work on suicide in chronic schizophrenia (1982) and family history in suicide (1983) are included for the insightful perspective they offer into severe mental illness and into families where suicide occurs. Alex D. Pokorny (1983) put an important perspective on the prediction of suicide, showing that in the absence of a precise marker prediction is impossible. His paper gives scientific perspective to the universal clinical predicament in suicide: that we must work in half-light, making our way as best we can, forming our judgments and estimates of risk in the ambiguity of shadows. Finally, we reprint the paper by Jan Fawcett and his colleagues from Chicago (1990), who show that there is a difference between predictive suicide risk factors over short periods and long periods of time. This contribution has already begun to shape epidemiological methods for studying risk and will continue to do so in the future.

With the expansion of suicide studies over this century we understand the inner lives of suicidal patients much better than before. The papers gathered here have been selected to reflect this knowledge, to put it into a more general psychiatric perspective, and to provide clinicians with the best possible foundation from which to proceed constructively. We commend them to you and trust you will find them helpful.

NOTE

1. Of Satan's first survey of Hell after the dark angels are cast from Heaven, Milton writes:

> At once as farr as Angels kenn he views
> The dismal Situation waste and wilde:
> A Dungeon horrible, on all sides round
> As one great Furnace flam'd, yet from those flames
> No light, but rather darkness visible
> Serv'd onely to discover sights of woe,
> Regions of sorrow, doleful shades, where peace
> And rest can never dwell, hope never comes
> That comes to all; but torture without end
> Still urges, and a fiery Deluge, fed
> With ever-burning Sulfur unconsum'd.
> —*Paradise Lost,* Book I, ll. 59–69

REFERENCES

American Psychiatric Association. 1994. Diagnostic and Statistical Manual of Mental Disorders. *4th Edition. Washington, D.C.: American Psychiatric Association.*

Delgado, P. L., and Gelenberg, A. J. 1995. Antidepressant and Antimanic Medications. In Gabbard, G. O., ed., Treatments of Psychiatric Disorders. *Washington, D.C.: American Psychiatric Press.*

Durkheim, E. 1897. Le Suicide. *Spaulding, J. A., and Simpson, G., trans.,* Suicide: A Study in Sociology. *Glencoe, Ill.: Free Press, 1951.*

Esquirol, J.E.D. 1838. Des Malades Mentales. *Hunt, E. K., trans.* Mental Maladies, a

Treatise on Insanity. *Philadelphia: Lea and Blanchard, 1845. (The English translation was reissued in a facsimile edition in 1965 by the Hafner Publishing Co., New York.)*

Freud, S. 1917. Mourning and Melancholia. Standard Edition *14:239–260.*

Friedman, P., trans. 1967. Discussions of the Vienna Psychoanalytic Society—1910. On Suicide, with Particular Reference to Suicide among Young Students. *New York: International Universities Press.*

Goldblatt, M. J., and Schatzberg, A. F. 1990. Somatic Treatment of the Adult Suicidal Patient: A Brief Survey. In Blumenthal, S. J., and Kupfer, D. J., eds., Suicide Over the Life Cycle: Risk Factors, Assessment, and Treatment of Suicidal Patients. *Washington, D.C.: American Psychiatric Press.*

Jamison, K. R. 1993. Touched with Fire: Manic-Depressive Illness and the Artistic Temperament. *New York: Free Press.*

Milton, John. 1667. Paradise Lost. *In* The Poetical Works of John Milton, *H. Darbishire, ed. London: Oxford University Press, 1958.*

Murphy, G. E. 1975. The Physician's Responsibility for Suicide. II. Errors of Omission. Annals of Internal Medicine *82:305–309.*

Rothschild, A. J., and Locke, C. A. 1991. Re-exposure to Fluoxetine after Previous Suicide Attempts: The Role of Akisthesia. Journal of Clinical Psychiatry *52:491–493.*

Schatzberg, A. F., and Nemeroff, C. B., eds. 1995. The American Psychiatric Press Textbook of Psychopharmacology. *Washington, D.C.: American Psychiatric Press.*

Shneidman, E. S., and Farberow, N. L. 1965. The LA SPC: A Demonstration of Public Health Feasibilities. American Journal of Public Health *55:21–26.*

Styron, W. 1990. Darkness Visible: A Memoir of Madness. *New York: Random House.*

Teicher, M. H., Glod, C., and Cole, J. O. 1990. Emergence of Intense Suicidal Preoccupation during Fluoxetine Treatment. American Journal of Psychiatry *147:207–210.*

Van Praag, H. M., Plutchik, R., and Apter, A., eds. 1990. Violence and Suicidality. *New York: Brunner/Mazel.*

1. "On 'Dying Together'" and "An Unusual Case of 'Dying Together'"

Ernest Jones

BIOGRAPHICAL NOTE

Ernest Jones (1879–1958), born in Wales and trained in medicine at University College Hospital, London, was the preeminent early leader of the psychoanalytic movement in Great Britain. He was closely associated with Freud and others of his inner circle, the celebrated "Committee." His detailed three-volume biography of Freud is widely known.

The two chapters reprinted here belong to Jones's Toronto period (1908–1913); troubled by accusations and upheavals in his personal and professional life, he left London and worked in Canada for a time, where he was closely associated with the establishment of the American Psychoanalytic Association. Though he described himself as "unhappy in my personal life" at the time (Jones 1959), this was an era of extreme productivity.

COMMENT

In this paper, Jones's erudition and knowledge of mythology, folklore, comparative religion, and other subjects is obvious. "It is known, through analysis," he reminds us, "that the ideas of sex, birth, and death are extensively associated with one another." Suicidally preoccupied patients never fail to prove that this is so. Their conviction that death is a journey that leads to peace is fertile symbolic territory—condensed within it are fantasies of eternal sleep, fusion, sexual (cannibalistic) reunion with the mother, travel, and reverse birth as a passage into paradise.

Ernest Jones, "On 'Dying Together' " (1911) and "An Unusual Case of 'Dying Together' " (1912). From Ernest Jones, *Essays in Applied Psychoanalysis I,* London: Hogarth Press, 1951, pp. 9-21. (These two short chapters had previously been published separately in German, the first in the *Zentralblatt für Psychoanalyse* 1 [September 1911]: 563, and the second in *Zentralblatt für Psychoanalyse* 2 [May 1912]: 455.) Reprinted by permission.

Bernd Heinrich Wilhelm von Kleist (1777–1811) was an unsettled German poet and dramatist, a sometime soldier, law and philosophy student, and possibly a spy, whose eccentricities and restlessness suggest a bipolar disorder. Constantly on the move, he lived in Germany, Switzerland, Paris, and Prague. At the end of his life, poor and embittered by the cool reception given some of his work, he developed a morbid passion for a woman named Henriette Vogel. He shot her to death on the shore of the Wannsee near Potsdam on 21 November 1811 and then shot himself.

The psychology of "dying together" reaches across several suicidal syndromes, including suicide-pacts and murder-suicides. It expresses itself in literature and the arts (Tristan and Isolde are an example).

Jones takes up "dying together" in a case of murder-suicide. Many murders are followed by suicide, especially in Europe. Donald J. West (1967) reported this was true in a third of his cases in England and Wales; in Denmark, it is true in 42 percent. The rate in the United States it is much lower, under 5 percent (Allen 1983; Dalmer and Humphrey 1980). In many of these instances, the murder victim can be shown to have provoked the fatal assault. The same theme expresses itself in suicide-pacts (Santy 1982; Rosenbaum 1983). In some cases, double suicide is the fatal outcome of a fôlie-a-deux (Salih 1981).

REFERENCES

Allen, N. H. 1983. Homicide Followed by Suicide: Los Angeles, 1970–1979. Suicide and Life Threatening Behavior *13:155–165.*

Dalmer, S., and Humphrey, J. A. 1980. Offender-Victim Relationships in Criminal Homicide Followed by Offenders' Suicide, North Carolina 1972–1977. Suicide and Life-Threatening Behavior *10:106–118.*

Jones, E. 1959. Free Associations. *New York: Basic Books.*

Rosenbaum, M. 1983. Crime and Punishment—The Suicide Pact. Archives of General Psychiatry *40:979–982.*

Salih, M. A. 1981. Suicide Pact in a Setting of Folie-a-Deux. British Journal of Psychiatry *139:62–67.*

Santy, P. A. 1982. Observations on Double Suicide: Review of the Literature and Two Case Reports. American Journal of Psychotherapy *36:23–31.*

West, D. J. 1967. Murder Followed by Suicide. *Cambridge, Mass.: Harvard University Press.*

■

I. ON 'DYING TOGETHER'

WITH SPECIAL REFERENCE TO HEINRICH VON KLEIST'S SUICIDE

In a recent interesting monograph on Heinrich von Kleist, Sadger[1] has called attention to a number of considerations bearing on the psychology of the impulse to die together with a loved one, to share death in common. As it is possible in a special journal to pursue an analysis more freely than in writings intended for a lay audience, I wish to comment here on two points in this connection which Sadger—I assume, with intention—left untouched.

Of the general psycho-sexual significance of the idea of death nothing need be added here. Freud, Stekel, and others have fully described the masochistic phantasies in which the idea may become involved, and this is also clearly illustrated in Sadger's monograph. The common mythological and folk-loristic conception of death as a spirit that violently attacks one mainly originates in this source.

The question of 'dying together' is, however, more complicated, the tendency being determined by several motives. The most obvious of these is that underlying a belief in a world beyond, a region where all hopes that are denied in this life will come true. The wish-fulfilment comprised in this belief subserves, of course, a similar function to that operative in the neuroses and psychoses; the consolation it yields, as is well-recognized by theologians, is naturally greater at times when life is filled with disappointment and sorrow. The same is true of the desire to die together with one's beloved, as is well illustrated by the accessory factors that helped to drive von Kleist to suicide.[2] With him, however, as Sadger clearly shows,[3] there was a specific and irresistible attraction toward the act, one which is not at all accounted for by the attendant circumstances. Most psycho-analysts will probably agree with Sadger's conclusions[4] that 'the wish to die together is the same as the wish to sleep and lie together (originally, of course, with the mother)', and that 'the grave so longed for by Kleist is simply an equivalent of the mother's bed'. Von Kleist's own words plainly confirm this: he writes, 'I must confess to you that her grave is dearer to me than the beds of all the empresses[5] of the world'. The idea that death consists in a return to the heaven whence we were born, *i.e.* to the mother's womb, is familiar to us in religious and other spheres of thought.

Deeper motives connect the subject with that of necrophilia. First of these may be mentioned the sadistic impulse, which can be inflamed at the thought of communion with a dead person—partly through the helpless resistlessness of the latter, and partly through the idea that a dead mistress can never be wearied by excessive caresses, can endure without limit, is for ever loyal. The latter thought of the insatiability of the dead often recurs in the literature on vampirism; it is indicated in the verses where Heine, in his dedication to 'Der Doktor Faust', makes the returned Helena say:

Du hast mich beschworen aus dem Grab
Durch deinen Zauberwillen,
Belebtest mich mit Wollustglut—
Jetzt kannst du die Glut nicht stillen.

Press deinen Mund an meinen Mund;
Der Menschen Odem ist göttlich!
Ich trinke deine Seele aus,
Die Toten sind unersättlich.

▪ ▪

(Thou hast called me from my grave
By thy bewitching will;
Made me alive, feel passionate love,
A passion thou canst never still.

Press thy mouth close to my cold mouth;
Man's breath is god-like created.
I drink thy essence, I drink thy soul,
The dead can never be sated.)

In my psycho-analytical experience of neurotics, necrophilic tendencies have further[6] invariably been associated with both coprophilic and birth phantasies. Freud[7] first pointed out the connection between the two phantasies just named, and this has since been amply confirmed by most observers. On the one hand, faecal material is dead matter that was once part of a living body, but is now decomposing, facts that make it easy for an association to be formed between it and a corpse; and on the other hand it is, according to a common 'infantile theory', the material out of which children are made, and, in the form of manure, is a general fertilizing principle. Love for, or undue horror at, a dead body may thus betoken a reversion to the infantile interest and fondness for faecal excrement. This explains the frequency with which the twin motives of (1) a dead woman giving birth to a child, and (2) a living woman being impregnated by a dead husband, occur in folk-lore, literature, mythology, and popular belief.[8] Interesting indications of both, which need not be detailed here, are to be found in von Kleist's short story, 'Die Marquise von O.'. The same combination of coprophilic and birth phantasy probably underlay his remarkable proposal to Wilhelmine von Zenge that they should leave everything else and adopt a peasant's life; as is well known, when she refused to fulfil this 'love condition' he heartlessly broke off their engagement. Sadger quotes the following passage of his in this connection: 'With the Persian magi there was a religious law to the effect that a man could do nothing more pleasing to the gods than *to till a field, to plant a tree, and to beget a child.*[9] I call that wisdom, and no truth has penetrated yet so deeply into my soul as this has. That is what I *ought* to do, I am *absolutely sure.* Oh, Wilhelmine, what unspeakable joy there must be in the knowledge that one is fulfilling one's destiny *entirely* in accord with the will of Nature.' I thus fully agree with Sadger[10] when he maintains that this has a hidden sexual meaning. I have further observed, though I do not know if it is a general rule, that patients having this complex often display an attitude of wonderful tenderness towards the object of their love, just like that of a fond mother for her babe; this was very pronounced in von Kleist's final outburst of 'dithyrambic rapture' towards Henriette, with its 'exchange of pet names that bordered on lunacy'.[11]

Sadger further comments on the 'travelling' significance of dying together. The connection between the ideas of death and travel is primaeval; one thinks at once of the Grecian and Teutonic myths of the procession of dead souls, and of Hamlet's 'undiscovered country, from whose bourn no traveller returns'. The fact, now becoming generally recognized since Freud first called attention to its importance (*Die Traumdeutung,* 1900), that children essentially conceive of death as a 'going away', as a journey, evidently renders this association a natural and stable one. With von Kleist it can be brought into line with his curious mania for travelling, which seemed so objectless and inexplicable to his friends. Two motives in this connection lie fairly near the surface. In the first place, death is conceived of as a voyage of discovery, as a journey to a land where hidden things will be revealed; I have had several religious patients whose curiosity, sexual and otherwise, had been largely transferred on to this idea.[12] Sadger points out how passionate was von Kleist's desire to reach *absolute, certain truth,*[13] and quotes his statement: '*Education* seemed to me the only goal worthy of endeavour, *truth*[14] the only wealth worthy of possession'. When he studied Kant's destructive criticism of the concept of the Absolute, and of a life hereafter, he was shaken to the depths of his being. He wrote: 'And my only thought, which my soul in this utmost tumult laboured on with burning dread, was always this: thy *sole* aim, thy loftiest goal, has declined'. In the second place, a journey can be undertaken in company, and it is significant that in von Kleist's fugue-like escapes this was practically always so. Sadger traces this tendency ultimately to the infantile desire to defy the father and escape with the mother to some distant place where he cannot disturb their mutual relations; therefore dying together can signify in the unconscious to fly with the mother and thus gratify secret desires.[15] The travelling mania is one of many tendencies that may come to expression in flying dreams,[16] and in this connection I should like to throw out a few suggestions. Freud traces the ultimate source of these dreams to the pleasurably exciting chasing of childhood,[17] and has also laid special stress on the relation between bodily movements in general and sexuality.[18] In several psycho-analyses I have found associated with this various anal-erotic motives, which may therefore furnish something towards the later desires. The fact itself that the common expression for defaecation is 'movement', and for faeces 'motion', points to an inner connection between two subjects that at first sight appear to be quite unrelated.[19] I need not here go into the different grounds for the association, but will only remark that when the act of defaecation is especially pleasurable it is apt to acquire the significance of a sexual 'projecting',[20] just as of urine and semen. I have collected much evidence, from both actual psycho-analyses and from folklore, which I hope to detail elsewhere,[21] indicating that *(a)* this connotation of sexual projecting, and of movement in general, is especially closely associated in the unconscious with the act of passing flatus,[22] and *(b)* that this latter act, on account of the idea of penetration to a distance, is sometimes conceived of by children as constituting the essential part of coitus, which thus consists of expelling flatus into the female cloaca. The latter phantasy would, through its association with movement (and therefore flying through a gaseous medium—the air), be particularly well adapted to find expression, together with the other coprophilic, sadistic, and incestuous tendencies referred to above, in the love-condition of dying together, and I would suggest that it might be worth while to investigate future cases of the kind from this point of view.

II. AN UNUSUAL CASE OF 'DYING TOGETHER'

The following dramatic event, which took place here[23] this week, seems to lend itself to some considerations of psycho-analytical interest.

A man and wife, aged thirty-two and twenty-eight respectively, went from Toronto to spend a week-end at Niagara Falls. In company with several other people they ventured on to the great bridge of ice that forms every winter just at the foot of the Falls, and which then joins the American and Canadian shores of the river. The ice-bridge began to crack and drift from its moorings, and a river-man, who knew the locality well and who was on the ice at the time, shouted to the others to make for the Canadian side where there was more chance of getting ashore. The couple in question ignored this advice and rushed towards the American shore, but were soon stopped by open water. They then ran in the other direction (about 150 yards), but when about 50 yards from safety the woman fell down exhausted, crying 'I can't go on! let us die here!' The husband, aided by another man, dragged her onward until they reached the edge. This was 3 yards from the shore, and the intervening water was covered with soft ice. The river-man begged them to cross this, pointing out that the ice would prevent their sinking, and guaranteed to bring them to safety; he demonstrated the possibility of the feat by crossing himself, and later by returning to save another man. The woman, however, declined to take the risk, and her husband refused to go without her. The mass of ice now began to drift down the river, breaking into smaller pieces as it went, and slowly but surely approaching the terrible Rapids that lead to the Niagara Whirlpool. In an hour's time they had drifted to where a railway bridge crosses the ravine, over 60 yards above their heads, and were on the point of being caught up by the swift rapids. A rope, with an iron harpoon at the end, had been lowered from the bridge and this was obviously their last hope of safety. As the ice-floe, now moving rapidly, swept under the bridge, the man successfully seized the rope, but apparently the woman refused to trust to it unless it was fastened around her. At all events the man was seen to be vainly fumbling, with fingers numbed by cold, to tie the rope around his wife's waist. Failing in this in the short time at his disposal before the floe passed onwards, he flung the rope aside, knelt down beside the woman and clasped her in his arms; they went thus to their death, which was now only a matter of seconds.

These are the main facts as published in all the newspapers. The only additional ones I could discover, from a friend of mine who happened to know the couple well, were: that they were devotedly fond of each other, that they had been married for seven years, and that they, the woman in particular, were sad at never having had any children.

The husband's conduct does not call for any special comment, being dictated by sufficiently obvious motives. To these I will only add that he was in the presence of a large audience, the banks of the ravine being lined by thousands of people who had accumulated during the fateful hour, and that it would be difficult or impossible for a man to hold up his head again if he deserted any woman in such a situation, let alone his own wife.

There is, however, more to be said about the woman's conduct, or rather lack of conduct. It is evident that she was throughout overcome by panic and fright, or else convinced of the inevitableness of the fate awaiting her. Her efforts at escape were either paralysed or else *actively hindering,* and she did not respond even to the powerful motive of saving her husband. Now it is known to psycho-analysts, as Freud first pointed out in reference to certain dreams,[24] that emotional paralysis is not so much a traumatic effect of fright as a manifestation of inhibition resulting from a conflict between a conscious and unconscious impulse. A familiar example is that of a woman who cannot protect herself with her whole strength against being raped, part of her energy being inhibited by the opposing unconscious impulse which is on the side of the assailant. The question thus arises whether any such process can be detected in the present case. If so, then the woman's conduct would have to be viewed as expressing an unconscious desire for death, an automatic suicide. The available evidence, as just narrated, is so meagre that any hypothesis of this kind must necessarily be very tentative, but when correlated with psycho-analytical experience in general the probability of its being true is, in my opinion, very considerable.

There is no reason to believe that any desire for death that might have existed could have been other than symbolic; indeed the description I obtained of the woman's state of mind on the day before the calamity makes the idea of any direct suicidal intent highly improbable. We have therefore to ask what other ideas could have been symbolized by that suicide. It is known, through analysis, not only that the ideas of sex, birth, and death are extensively associated with one another, but also that the idea of dying in the arms of the loved one—*'gemeinsames Sterben'*—symbolizes certain quite specific desires of the unconscious. Of these, which have been pointed out especially by Sadger[25] and myself,[26] one in particular may be recalled—namely, the desire to beget a child with the loved one. The unconscious associative connections between this desire and the notion of common suicide are too rich and manifold to discuss here; besides which they are now well enough known to justify one in assuming an understanding of them in informed circles. I will therefore content myself with indicating some of the respects in which the present situation was adapted for supporting this associative connection.

The association between Niagara and death, especially suicide, is one that has been enforced by countlessly repeated experiences. It is not so generally known, however, that the association between it and birth is also very intimate. Niagara is a favourite honeymoon resort—possibly more so for Toronto people than for those of other places in the neighbourhood, on account of the romantic journey thither across the Lake of Ontario. So much is this so that Niagara town is commonly known—in Toronto at all events—as 'the Baby City', from the high percentage of conceptions that date from a visit there. The couple in question were very fond of spending their holidays there, the unconscious attraction being possibly the same as that which drew women of old to the Temple of Aesculapius and which still draws women to various healing waters. They had never been there before in winter-time, a rather strange circumstance, for it is almost as popular with Toronto people in the winter as in the summer because of the beautiful ice effects to be seen at that time. It is conceivable that they were this time drawn by the idea of winter (death, cold, etc.) which was beginning to correspond with their attitude of hopelessness about ever getting a child.

Coming next to the calamity itself we see how similar was the conscious affect investing the two ideas which we suppose became associated; the hope of giving birth to a child was almost as small as that of escaping from the threatened doom. That this doom was one of drowning—in the horrible form of being swept under in an ice-cold whirlpool—is a circumstance of considerable significance in the light of all we know about the symbolic meaning of water in general and of drowning in particular (cf. Freud, Rank, Abraham, Stekel, etc.). If the whole story were told to one as constituting a dream one would have no hesitation in interpreting it as a childbirth fantasy of a sterile woman, the floating *on a block of ice* in a dangerous current of water, in company with the lover, in sight of all the world and yet isolated from it, the threatening catastrophe of drowning, and the rapid movement of being passively swept to and fro (in the paper referred to above I have insisted on the significance of movement in this connection)—all this forms a perfect picture.

Though the actual situation was not a dream but a grim reality, nevertheless the circumstances detailed above are just such as would, especially in a moment of acute emotion, strongly appeal to the latent complex in question and stimulate it to activity. It should be remembered that, in times of despair (defeat, severe illness, danger, enfeeblement, approaching death, and so on), there is a universal tendency to fly from reality by having recourse to the primitive system of thought (Freud's primary *Lustprinzip,* Jung's *phantastisches Denken*), mostly in the form of infantile wishes relating to the mother; indeed I have elsewhere[27] expressed the opinion that the idea of personal death does not exist for the unconscious, being always replaced by that of sexual communion or of birth. We may thus imagine the woman in question as reacting to her frightful situation by rapidly transforming it in the unconscious and replacing reality by the fantasy of the gratification of her deepest desire. The external outcome of this act of transformation illustrates very well the contrast between the practical value of the pleasure principle and that of the reality principle.[28]

One might speculate whether the outcome would have been different if the woman's thoughts concerning childbirth had been more accustomed to assume the common form of the fantasy of saving, or of being saved.[29] It is even possible that this fantasy was operative, and that her objection to being saved by the river-man and by the men who were holding the rope from the bridge was due fundamentally to her excessive marital fidelity, to her determination that no one should save her except her husband. But at this point our speculations become so filmy as to float away into the region of the completely unknown.

NOTES

1. Sadger, *Heinrich von Kleist. Eine pathographisch-psychologische Studie,* 1910.
2. Sadger, *op. cit.* pp. 60, 61.
3. Sadger, *op. cit.* pp. 56–8.
4. Sadger, *op. cit.* p. 60.
5. Empress, like Queen, is a well-known unconscious symbol of the mother.
6. The connection here implied between sadism and coprophilia is discussed at length in a later paper republished as chapter xxxi of the author's *Papers on Psycho-Analysis,* 2nd edition.
7. Freud, *Sammlung kleiner Schriften,* Zweite Folge, p. 168.
8. Numerous examples of this are quoted by Hanusch, *Zeitschrift für deutsche Mythologie,* Jahrgang IV, p. 200; Hock, *Die Vampyrsagen und ihre Verwertung in der deutschen Literatur* (1900), pp. 24, 37, 43; Horst, *Zauber-Bibliothek* (1821), Erster Teil, p. 277; Krauss, *Slavische Volksforschungen* (1908), p. 130; Sepp, *Occident und Orient* (1903), p. 268.
9. The italics are mine (in this instance only).
10. Sadger, *op. cit.* p. 62.
11. Sadger, *op. cit.* p. 59.
12. One of my patients eagerly looked forward to discovering in the next world the authorship of the Letters of Junius!
13. Sadger, *op. cit.* p. 62.
14. On the intimate association between the ideas of truth and nudity see Furtmüller, *Zeitschrift für Psychoanalyse* (1913), Bd. I, p. 273.
15. Sadger, *op. cit.* p. 60.

16. It is perhaps not without interest that the name of the woman with whom von Kleist departed on his endless journey was Vogel (*i.e.* 'Bird').

17. Freud, *Die Traumdeutung,* 2e Aufl., p. 195.

18. Freud, *op. cit.,* 2e Aufl., pp. 53, 54. See also Sadger, 'Haut-Schleimhaut- und Muskelerotik', *Jahrbuch der Psychoanalyse,* Bd. III, p. 525.

19. This association plays a prominent part in the common symptom known as *Reisefieber,* and in the allied 'packing' dreams.

20. It is noteworthy that the common vulgarism for the act is etymologically cognate with the word 'to shoot'.

21. Since the present paper was written this has been done in two monographs published in the *Jahrbuch der Psychoanalyse.*

22. It is noteworthy that the common vulgarism for this both in English and in German singularly resembles the German for travel, 'Fahrt'.

23. *I.e.* Toronto.

24. Freud, *Die Traumdeutung* (1900), p. 228.

25. Sadger, *Heinrich von Kleist* (1910), pp. 59–62.

26. Chapter I of these Essays. [Reprinted as section I above.]

27. *Journal of Abnormal Psychology,* April 1912.

28. See Freud, 'Die zwei Prinzipien des psychischen Geschehens', *Jahrbuch der Psychoanalyse,* Bd. III, p. 1.

29. See chapter x of my *Papers on Psycho-Analysis,* 1918.

2. Psychoanalytic Aspects of Suicide

Karl A. Menninger

BIOGRAPHICAL NOTE

Karl Menninger (1893–1990), whose name is synonymous with the institution the Menninger family developed in Topeka, Kansas, exerted a major influence on American psychiatry. Born in rural America, he studied at Harvard Medical School and the Boston Psychopathic Hospital. He returned to Topeka to participate in the establishment of the Menninger Clinic before undertaking psychoanalytic training in Chicago. This paper, published in 1933, followed the termination of his analysis with Franz Alexander, who read it for Menninger at the Twelfth International Psychoanalytic Congress in Wiesbaden in 1932.

COMMENT

This is the paper that introduced Menninger's suicide triad, "the wish to die, the wish to kill, and the wish to be killed." Implicit here is the idea that no suicide occurs without all three elements coming into play. Many discouraged people wish they might die in their sleep, but do not commit suicide; others may wish to destroy somebody else, and others yet may wish someone would kill them, but without all three components, suicide probably never takes place. Interviews with survivors of suicide attempts who have narrowly escaped death confirms this.

Menninger emphasizes the importance of primitive oral fantasies in suicide, and takes up the symbolism of eating others. He does not address explicitly the wish to be eaten, and alludes only indirectly to hypomanic fantasies in suicide. This paper foreshadows Bertram Lewin's well-known "oral triad" at the heart of the psychology of mania: the wish to eat, the wish to be eaten, and the wish to die.

Karl A. Menninger, "Psychoanalytic Aspects of Suicide." *International Journal of Psychoanalysis* 14 (1933):376–390.

Oddly, Lewin (1950) does not cite Menninger's paper in The Psychoanalysis of Elation, *a book of premier clinical interest in the understanding of suicide. There it is pointed out that Freud (1926) had already discussed the pleasurable fantasy of being eaten. Perhaps beneath Menninger's wish to kill, Lewin would have discerned the wish to eat another, beneath the wish to be killed, the wish to be eaten, and beneath the wish to die, the wish to sleep. Generally speaking, suicide as a hypomanic equivalent has been neglected as an area of study, though C. W. Wahl (1957) touches on it.*

The symbolic meaning of suicide is further addressed in other selections included in this volume, especially in Kate Friedlander's treatment of the sleep-death equation (chapter 6 below), and John T. Maltsberger and Dan H. Buie, Jr.'s "The Devices of Suicide" (chapter 25 below). The reader may also find Jacob Arlow's papers (1955, 1978) and Bettina Warburg's (1938) discussion of suicide fantasies in pregnancy of particular interest in this connection, though these have not been reprinted here because space is limited.

REFERENCES

Arlow, J. A. 1955. Notes on Oral Symbolism. Psychoanalytic Quarterly *24:63–74.*

———. 1978. Pyromania and the Primal Scene: A Psychoanalytic Comment on the Work of Yukio Mishima. Psychoanalytic Quarterly *47:24–51.*

Freud, S. 1926. Inhibitions, Symptoms, and Anxiety. *Standard Edition, 20:75–175.*

Lewin, B. 1950. The Psychoanalysis of Elation. *New York: Psychoanalytic Quarterly.*

Wahl, C. W. 1957. Suicide as a Magical Act. Bulletin of the Menninger Clinic *21:91–98.*

Warburg, B. 1938. Suicide, Pregnancy, and Rebirth. Psychoanalytic Quarterly *7:490–506.*

■

IT IS LOGICAL to expect that a better understanding of how and why man destroys himself would prove of the utmost practical importance. The facile explanations for suicide which are offered daily in the drama and in the newspaper may leave us with an easy satisfaction which of itself should make us suspicious. In real life there is no such evident justice or such naïve simplicity in the workings of fate and retribution. Scientific study of suicide generally falls back upon barren statistical analyses; the general medical literature ignores suicide as if it were scarcely entitled to recognition as a cause of death.

We have reason to expect a clarification of the motives for this phenomenon from an understanding of the unconscious motives, i.e. from psycho-analysis. Yet not since June, 1910, has suicide been a prominent subject of discussion even before psycho-analytical bodies.

It is easy to jump to the generalization that suicide represents in simple form an expression of the instincts toward self-destruction which we now consider as standing opposed to the life instinct. To do so, however, would leave entirely unexplained the extraordinary circumstance that so powerful and universal a principle should come to complete fruition in such a relatively small number of instances. It would also leave unanswered the question of how far external forces and events determine the suicide, a question which in the popular mind admits of answers implying the most astonishing naïveté. If one is to judge by the explanations to be read with monotonous invariability in daily newspaper accounts, life insurance reports, death certificates and statistical surveys, suicide is the logical consequence of circumstances, particularly ill-health, discouragement, financial reverses, humiliation, frustration and unrequited love.

To the psycho-analyst, what is most significant is not that these simple explanations are continually offered in a world where science and everyday experience alike confirm the untrustworthiness of the obvious, but that they are so patiently and unquestioningly accepted. No such lack of curiosity exists, for example, with reference to the motives for murder. The contrast becomes striking if one contemplates the fact that in the mystery and detective stories which are being turned off by the thousand it is rarely the explanation of a *suicide* which is sought but of a murder. Professional indifference in the matter has been equally great. Surely no other mysterious phenomenon of human activity has excited so little scientific investigation.

The conception of self-destruction as a flight from reality, from ill-health, disgrace, poverty and the like, is seductive because of its simplicity. It lends itself to the drawing of parallels between suicide and other regressions such as the taking of vacations, celebrating of holidays, falling asleep, delirium, delusions, drunkenness. Its essential fallacy is one of incompleteness; it lies in the implied assumption that the forces impelling the regression come wholly from without. From the standpoint of analytical psychology the push is more important than the pull, i.e. the ego is driven by more powerful forces than external reality. The paramount factors in determining behaviour are the impulses from within, the motives originating in the individual which express his attempt at adjustment to reality. Innumerable illustrations in history and science could be marshalled to show that for some persons *no* reality can prove unbearable.

For we know that the individual always, in a measure, creates his own environment, and thus the suicidal person must help to create the very thing from which, in suicide, he takes flight. If we are to explain the act dynamically, therefore, we are compelled to seek an explanation for the wish to put oneself in a predicament from which one cannot, except by suicide, escape. In other words if, for one's own unconscious purposes, one brings about an apparent justification in external reality for self-destruction, the unconscious purposes are of more significance in understanding suicide than the apparently simple, inevitable external realities.

This, of course, disposes of those naïve judgements of suicide as either 'brave' (if it seems 'justified' by external circumstances) or 'irrational' (if it does not) and of all such causal explanations as appear in statistical summaries and the like. Psychologically suicide is a very complex act, and not a simple, incidental, isolated act of impulsion, either logical or inexplicable.

THREE ELEMENTS IN THE SUICIDAL WISH

It is not difficult to discover in the act of suicide the existence of various elements. In the German language it is literally a murder of the self *(Selbstmord)*. But it is also a murder *by* the self. It is a death in which are combined in one person the murderer and the murdered. We know that the motives for murder vary greatly—and no less the motives for wishing to be murdered, which is quite another matter. For since in suicide there is a self that submits to the murder and would appear to be desirous of doing so, we must seek the motives of this submission.

In many suicides it is quite apparent that one of these elements is stronger than the other. One sees people who want to die but cannot take the step against themselves; they fling themselves in front of trains, or, like King Saul and Brutus, they beseech armour bearers to slay them. Paradoxically, also, it would seem that many suicidal persons, in spite of the violence of the attack upon themselves, do not seem to be very eager to die.

We must think of suicide, then, as a peculiar kind of death which entails three elements: the element of dying, the element of killing, and the element of being killed. Each element requires separate analysis. Each is an act for which there exist motives, unconscious and conscious. The latter are usually evident enough; the unconscious motives are now our chief consideration.

1. The Wish to Kill

Throughout the universe, of which we are a part, there appear to exist in constant cojacent conflict and opposition the two forces of creation and destruction. Whether this universality of the principle is an inherent property of matter, a subtle adaptation of language or a psychological-philosophical concept to which we are blindly chained by the curious astigmatic limitations of our human mind it is beyond our present powers and purposes to determine.

We can only point to the not unexpected parallel in the findings of depth psychology as to the purposes of the human Unconscious. To create and to destroy, to build up and to tear down, these are the anabolism and katabolism of the psyche no less than of the cells and the corpuscles—the two directions in which the same energies exert themselves.

And just as in the sexual embrace we recognize the concurrence of physical, chemical and psychological forces in the supreme act of creation so we see in murder its direct antithesis, the supreme act of destruction. Psychoanalytic investigations have established beyond any question the murderous destructive wishes which arise in earliest infancy (Klein) and wax and wane repeatedly in the successive periods of childhood. In line with the theory of the death instinct, these destructive tendencies are turned outward from their original engagement or neutralization within the personality. They emerge from the ego and are directed toward an external object in response to stimuli of thwarting or a threat which arouses envy and fear and, therefore, hate.

We know, also, however, the curious propensity of the erotic elements, the sexual element of the life instinct for making the best of a bad situation and of endowing every object relationship with some of its saving grace. Hence in any attack upon an enemy, however strong the wish to kill, we must expect to find in varying quantities an admixture of erotic satisfactions. These act in a dual and contradictory fashion, however; in the erotizing of the cruel sadistic elements they strengthen the murder motif, but at the same time, investing the object of the attack in the form of sympathy, pity, and more especially because of passive dependence upon the powerful rival, they mitigate the severity of the aggression. What the net effect of the erotic component will be varies according to circumstances, i.e. depending upon the relative degree to which the object excites sublimated or unsublimated sexuality in the aggressor.

Introjection

This component of destructive aggression may seem for the moment far afield from the topic of suicide. How is it that these drives in the interests of self-preservation can actually be turned upon the self? The answer is to be found in the phenomenon of *introjection with displacement,* i.e. identification. It is almost axiomatic in psycho-analysis that an object of love or hate which is lost or escapes beyond the reach of the ego can be regained and retained by the process of introjection with the displacement of the emotions appropriate to the original object on to the introjected object, that is, the person within the person. Hence a person unconsciously hated may be destroyed by identifying oneself with that person, or more accurately, identifying that person with the self, and destroying the self.

We must now consider what happens when the attack made by the destructive impulses directed toward an external object are thwarted, and introjection and displacement become necessary. Thwarting may occur under several circumstances: (1) the resistance offered by reality may be too great; (2) the object instead of being overwhelming may be merely elusive; (3) the attack may be inhibited by various internal circumstances, chiefly fear and the sense of guilt; (4) failure of the attack may occur through an undue weakening of its force by the admixture of adventitious erotic elements. This happens regularly in some neurotics, and derives from the failure to make a useful distinction between friend and foe. The result is that the hostility cannot be sublimated by the erotism. The ego consequently must take toward such individuals an oscillating or ambivalent attitude such that the love and hate have alternate expression, or else the hate must be displaced as in the first case.

(5) The exact opposite of (4) occurs when the erotic elements of object relationship are suddenly withdrawn, as for example, by the death of the object. A de-fusion of the instincts takes place, the erotic components are dispersed and the hostile component, since it would otherwise have to be directed against the whole world, is turned inward upon the self.

It is this last-named mechanism which is most commonly observed in melancholia, the condition in which suicide most often happens. The mechanisms of melancholia have been fairly well worked out by Freud, Abraham and others to be schematically as follows: having lost the love object in one way or another the patient is left with uninvested hostilities deeply covered and disguised by the love which is now also uninvested. The destructive or hostile elements acting as the pathfinder, as Freud has suggested, now turn back upon the ego where the beloved object becomes incorporated. The bitter reproaches and attacks unconsciously felt toward the former love object are now consciously directed toward this same object incorporated and disguised within the ego. But now the erotic elements formerly directed toward the love object follow the lead of the hostile tendencies, and one sees the great increase in narcissism which is characteristic of melancholia in paradoxical association with the most extreme self-condemnation. Appropriately, the patient loses all interest in the outside world and until the fires of simultaneous self-love and self-hate have subsided, transferences or any other form of object love are impossible. Were it not for the protection of the narcissism every melancholiac would be determined to commit suicide.

Psycho-analytical literature is replete with illustrations of the phenomena of oral incorporation, introjection and displacement in melancholia, but the following case is so diagrammatic an instance that it may be inserted as a paradigm in this consideration of suicide motivation.

A woman of thirty-five, of unusual capabilities, had manifested all her life tendencies indicative of strong oral-erotic cravings. This cannot be better summarized than in the words of her own sister, who wrote her at one time during her analysis: "You must realise, my dear sister, that you frighten your lovers away by loving so much. Your love is simply engulfing, devouring. You cannot eat your lover like a cake, you know. At least, if you do, you can't expect to go on having him!"

As is so often the case with such individuals, the poor woman had a propensity for selecting lovers whom circumstances made it quite impossible for her ever to possess. One of these, with whom she was deeply in love during a portion of her analysis, had a surname something like Allendorf and was usually referred to as "Al." Shortly after her separation from him (at his instigation) this patient attempted suicide by taking an overdose of the drug allonal. As she later told me, just before the attempt she had had a dream in which she and a group of men which represented the analyst, the lover Allendorf, her father, her brother of whom she was very jealous, and some others were in a car which was wrecked, and all killed except her.

'Yes,' she said, quite offhand, 'they were killed, *Al and all.*' Spoken rapidly in English 'Al and all' sounds exactly like allonal. It was immediately apparent that in attempting to kill herself with the drug allonal she was also carrying out the devouring of her lover and the other disappointing males, which was so apparent in all her actions that even her naïve sister had detected it. Thus she obtained Al, in spite of his flight, by oral incorporation and simultaneously destroyed him by the same method, and *pari passu* she attempted to destroy him in that she had made a destructive attack upon herself in whom Al had been (was being) incorporated.

Gratification of the hostile aggressive wish by introjection is made the more easy by the fact that it seems to the ego to be less dangerous to attack an object of phantasy than an object of reality. But when the object of phantasy is identified with the self, i.e. when the hated-loved person is identified with the ego, the aggression serves two ends, the primary purpose and the secondary one of atonement, to be discussed later. Hence this reflection of the (self) destructive impulses back upon the self appears to be accomplished with an increase in strength, so that the life instincts can no longer hold them in check except by reaction formation (symptoms). If this cannot be accomplished, actual destruction of the self results.

Indirect Aggression

The hostile or destructive aggression against the hated-loved person may be carried out, as is well known, in many ways other than by direct attack. A brief consideration should be given here to these indirect methods of aggression.

The attack upon the hated-loved object is sometimes made, for example, through the destruction of something held dear by the person who is the real object of the attack. It is the greatest torture to a mother to see her child being tortured or killed. In suicide such an aggression can be carried out against the parents by the simple process of self attack; hence, the overwhelming power of the revenge taken by the child who, piqued at some reproach or denial, takes his own life, takes it as it were from his parents. He robs them of their dearest possession knowing that no other injury could possibly be so painful to them.

To a less intense degree the act of suicide is an aggression against those who may in some way be related to the life of the person who kills himself. It may be taken as a reproach against certain individuals or against society as a whole and actually does serve in many instances as an embarrassment or humiliation. Every experienced analyst has been able to observe in the suicidal threats of his patients an intention to alarm the analyst or discredit the analysis. This same motive is undoubtedly active in situations other than the analytic one.

This, then, is an analysis of the *aggressive* component of the suicidal impulse; *it originates in the ego and is reflected upon the ego.*

2. The Wish to Be Killed

We come now to the second element in suicide, the obverse of the killing motive, namely, the wish to be killed. Why, indeed, does anyone wish, not to die or to kill, necessarily, but *to be killed?*

Obviously, being killed is the extreme form of submission, just as killing is the extreme form of aggression. And the enjoyment of submission, pain, defeat, and in the end, death, is the essence of masochism. But it would be a misleading over-simplification to let it go at that. We must understand why satisfactions may be achieved by punishment, that extraordinary phenomenon which we see occurring on all sides, from the persons who enjoy ill-health to those who deliberately put themselves in predicaments in which they suffer.

The result of indulgence in acts of aggression (dictated as we have seen by hate inspired by fear, envy and the desire for revenge) is to bring about a sense of guilt with a corresponding feeling of need for punishment.

It is scarcely necessary, except for purposes of completeness, to point out that a sense of guilt may arise from other than actual aggression; in the unconscious, a wish to destroy is quite equivalent to the actual destruction. One who nourishes murderous wishes must also feel a need for punishment for that sin of a similar sort. From this we see the truth of that statement made by Freud many years ago that *many suicides are disguised murders,* not only, therefore, because of the introjection, which we have discussed above, but for the reason that murder alone justifies in the unconscious the death penalty. Suicide is, therefore, *the death penalty self inflicted.*

In the analysis of compulsion neurotics especially, the tyrannical primitive severity of the super-ego is made manifest. Every analyst could supply scores of illustrations of this phenomenon. One must always remember, however, how the compulsion neurotic disguises the import of his acts and thoughts by the formula of *reductio ad absurdum.* One of my patients, for example, would alternately amuse himself by torturing small animals and then—without any conscious connection—indulge in mutilating, humiliating, abasing or reproaching himself. Sometimes the treatment of the animals and of himself was precisely the same; for example, he would scorch a cat with a burning match, and that afternoon would singe his own hair with a taper. Of course, this did not cause him immediate pain as it did the animals, and he rationalized it by saying that it was done in order to promote the growth of his hair, but as a matter of fact he scorched his hair so irregularly that he gave himself a ridiculous appearance which he knew brought upon him the contempt of his associates. All of this takes on a different aspect if one knows that his dreams and associations made it unmistakable that the animals which he killed were symbolic representations of the analyst and also, of course, of his father. By cutting his hair he gave himself the appearance of a prison convict, as if to act out his phantasies of punishment for his murderous wishes toward me.

Another illustration which might be added is that of a thirty-five-year-old son of a travelling salesman, whose parents had taken him in early childhood on many railroad trips and permitted him to sleep with them in the berth. Riding on the train has always had for him a great fascination and no doubt gratified some incest phantasies in association with the above memories, and also the satisfaction of father identification, his father having made his living by travelling.

At a time when his analysis was in reality progressing very favourably, he one day had the feeling, suddenly, as he rode on the suburban train, that it was senseless, unnecessary, futile, and there came a strong impulse to kill himself, 'because my unconscious plays such tricks on me; I just thought, "Hell! I'll show it! I'll jump out of the train" '. The analytical material of the next few days became chiefly lament and self-reproach for the feeling 'that I have so constantly—*of course* unintentionally—deceived the analyst and tried to fool him and play tricks upon him, all of which reacts only, of course, to my own harm'.

One can see in this impulse to jump from the train, first of all a direct aggressive threat toward the analyst and toward the father whom the analyst represented. Jumping from the train meant the end of the analysis, not only symbolically, but in reality. It was also casting the father out of the train, an obvious symbolic parricide.

The reasons alleged for his contemplated suicide are equally significant. His conscious thought was that his unconscious had played tricks upon him and he would take revenge on his unconscious. Obviously his 'unconscious' was the analyst; he was justifying his attack upon the analyst by charging him with having played tricks. As a matter of fact, however, such an allegation had no basis in reality and was an inverted charge, a charge against himself that he had projected upon the analyst. He had indeed played tricks upon the analyst, as he well knew, and felt guilty about it. He was anxious to shew that these tricks had harmed him and the need for punishment is also fulfilled in the jumping from the train. 'Punishment of the unconscious' represented punishment of himself.

But one can also infer from this (as was clearly brought out in the patient's subsequent material) that he actually wanted the analyst to play these said tricks on him. By playing tricks on him he had unconscious reference, of course, to the erotic motive, i.e. the wish to be homosexually attacked. But against this wish by way of defence (dictated by the super-ego), and against the indignity of the attack (directed by the ego), there arose the outwardly directed destructive tendencies of projection. Thus, 'It is not I who play tricks upon the analyst, it is he who plays tricks upon me. He attacks me. Therefore I hate him, I want to kill him, I do kill him. But for killing him I also feel guilty and must suffer a like fate myself'.[1]

In other words, this man feels guilty for (1) this parricidal wish, (2) his hostile wishes against the analyst, (3) his deception or attempted deception of the analyst, and (4) his homosexual wishes. The guilt for all of these demands punishment of a similar sort, namely, an attack directed against himself. Hence the suicidal impulse.

The Problem of Heredity in Suicide

The question of suicide in families is one which has received almost no competent scientific investigation. Newspaper accounts indicate that in the popular mind the suicidal tendency is hereditary. In my own studies I have come upon several families in which it would certainly appear to be so. For example, one patient came to us at sixty-one on account of strong suicidal propensities which she had several times attempted to gratify. Three of the patient's sisters had killed themselves in an identical manner; the patient's mother, and the patient's mother's mother had also killed themselves in the same way. Moreover, the patient's mother was a twin and the twin brother had also killed himself!

In another instance, a highly regarded family contained five sons and two daughters; the oldest son killed himself at thirty-five; the youngest developed a depression and attempted suicide several times, but finally died of other causes at thirty; a third brother killed himself in a manner similar to that of his oldest brother; still another brother shot himself to death; the oldest daughter took poison successfully at a party. Only two children remain living of the entire family.

I have also on file numerous instances where sisters or brothers have killed themselves. In one instance, three sisters killed themselves simultaneously.

Striking as these illustrations may be, there is no convincing scientific evidence that the suicidal impulse is hereditary, and there is much psycho-analytic evidence to show that these cases of numerous suicides in one family may be explained on a psychological basis. Superficially there is the element of suggestion, but deeper than this is the well-known fact that unconscious death wishes reach their highest development toward members of the family, and when a member of the family dies or kills himself these death wishes are unexpectedly gratified; this produces a sudden and overpoweringly strong wave of guilt feelings which replace the death wish which has been gratified. This wave may be so great and so overwhelming as to make it necessary for the culprit to be punished by death. Sometimes this is done, as every psycho-analyst knows, by dreams of being executed, hanged, killed in some other way, or sentenced to life imprisonment. In other instances, the element of suggestion points the way for the actual self-infliction of the death sentence.

Methods Used in Suicide

A psycho-analytic study of suicide would be incomplete were not some attention given to the unconscious significance of the particular technique selected for the act. That this is strongly determined and over-determined by the unconscious trends of the victim we have good reason to believe on two scores: first, by analogy with similar acts in other patients with less serious outcome; in other words, the established 'general' significance of certain acts; secondly, the much more definite evidence in frustrated suicidal attempts in patients who then, or later, undergo psycho-analytic treatment and study.

A full exposition of this latter evidence would require the inclusion of many individual case studies which the limits both of space and of my experience prohibit. One example is cited above; others have appeared in the literature incidental to the discussion of more general themes.

More general inferences we may readily gain from reading even the daily Press. It is well established statistically, for example, that men more frequently choose shooting and women drowning or the taking of poison or gas. These modes are obviously and clearly related to the masculine and feminine rôles in sexual life.

Extremely suggestive also are such exceptional but authenticated cases as that of suicide by thrusting a red-hot poker down the throat (i.e. fellatio acted out violently and punished with corresponding violence); or that of suicide by lying down before trucks and steam rollers (passive erotic submission); or that of plunging into molten glass, vats of soap, the craters of volcanoes, tanks of blood in packing houses, etc., (the significance of drowning phantasies is one of the earliest of psycho-analytic discoveries); or that of self-crucifixion (Messianic identification). One of my own patients calmly drank raw hydrochloric acid; it was vomited, of course; he tried repeatedly thereafter to accomplish suicide with this agent, diluting it with ginger ale. Finally, after a long period of surgical treatment for œsophageal stricture resulting from the acid burns, and much other treatment (he refused psycho-analysis), he re-established his home and business, and then, about a year later, committed suicide successfully by eating fire-crackers.

Just what these methods may have meant in full detail to these individuals we shall never know, but their similarity to neurotic phantasies and dreams with which we are very familiar in analysis leaves little doubt as to their general significance and reinforces what we have said as to the motives of suicide, viz. that it represents in one act a murder and a propitiation, both of which are erotized. This erotization is conspicuous in the technique of the act.

3. The Wish to Die

Anyone who has sat by the bedside of a patient dying from a self-inflicted wound and listened to pleadings that the physician save a life which only a few hours or minutes before had been attempted, must be impressed by the paradox that one who has wished to kill himself does not wish to die. The popular assumption is that, having yielded to a sudden impulse, the patient has changed his mind. It leaves unanswered why the act should have brought about this change. The pain is usually not great. The prospects of death are actually less than they were before the attempt since 'where there is life there is hope'. One gets the impression that for such people the suicidal act is sometimes a kind of insincere play acting and that their capacity for dealing with reality is so poorly developed that they proceed as if they could actually kill themselves and not die. We have reason to believe that a child has some such conception of death: that it is a going away and that for such goings away there is often a returning. Indeed the concept of a future life which is so real to many people is probably based upon this identification of death and going away.

One must distinguish also between the conscious wish and the unconscious wish to die or not to die, the latter being, as we have seen, the resultant of co-operating and conflicting factors. One sees this unconscious wish not to die in the very frequent attempts at suicide which turn out unsuccessfully because of faulty technique. Many poets and philosophers, including all the pessimists from Schopenhauer down, have been convinced of the desirability of death; yet, being impelled by neither of the other two motives, cannot escape the necessity of living on.

This, to a considerable degree, is perhaps true of many intellectual patients. Oftentimes melancholiac patients of superior intelligence and milder grade of affliction, will marshall unanswerable arguments for the desirability of dying. They will point out with a passionate eloquence and with flawless logic that life is hard, bitter, futile and hopeless; that it entails more pain than pleasure; that there is no profit or purpose in it for them and no conceivable justification for their living on. Of such patients Freud has said: ". . . he has a keener eye for the truth.. . . When in his exacerbation of self-criticism he describes himself as petty, egoistic, dishonest, lacking in independence, one whose sole aim has been to hide the weaknesses of his own nature, for all we know it may be that he has come very near to self-knowledge; we can only wonder why a man must become ill before he can discover truth of this kind'.[2]

The question for us to consider here is to what extent we may associate this conscious wish for death with the death instinct conception. Freud's postulate specifically states that the self-destruction instinct never appears undisguised. Yet, as Alexander points out, nothing else can so well explain the pleasure in exposing one's self unnecessarily to great dangers—as do the mountain climbers, automobile racers, building scalers, or the popular interest in the antics of such movie actors as Harold Lloyd on the sides and tops of skyscrapers, etc. 'The narcissistic gratification derived from one's powers of achievement may indeed play a part here, but no one will fail to see the impulse, completely independent of this . . . to play with death, to expose one's life to serious risks . . . something like a forepleasure . . . to the (ultimate gratification of) the death instinct'.[3]

It is my own view that we may also interpret as some evidence for the activity of the death instinct the observation that the physiological body processes appear to be capable of acting either for or against the personality as a whole. The phenomenon designated by Freud as somatic compliance we may think of as a kind of biological acceptance or rejection of the Id tendencies as modified by the psyche. One frequently sees such a thing as is well illustrated by a case studied by Dr. Catherine Bacon of Chicago. This patient's conscious self-destructive activities went only so far as scratching herself with the deliberate intent of causing a skin infection, with the expressed hope of death. This is common in malingering. But what determines whether or not these infections shall prove fatal? Can we assume with the bacteriologists that it is entirely a matter of quantitative relationships between virulence and resistance, or, in other words, mere chance? Clinical experience certainly leads us to suspect that such infections become serious in just those cases where there are other evidences of strongly active self-destructive tendencies. It is possible that the available strength of the death instinct determines this biological acceptance of the extraneous opportunities for self-destruction.

There is another straw in the wind I wish to mention. It has been suggested that the wish for death may be only another disguise for the frequently observed phenomena commonly interpreted as birth fantasies, or, more accurately, a desire to return to the womb. Suicide by drowning is supposed to be particularly clear in its symbolic suggestion of this tendency. It is not impossible, however, that this interpretation is an exact inversion and that birth fantasies and the various phenomena suggesting a desire to return to the peace of the womb may be only pictorial representations of the unconscious wish for death.

We have seen that the aggressive elements in suicide originate in the ego and the submissive elements in the super-ego; it would conform with Freud's postulate to find that the unconscious wish to die implicit in the death instinct originates in the Id.

To advance this hypothesis, however, we can offer only negative data as I have suggested above. We can show that many individuals in whom the aggressive and submissive elements of self-destruction are strongly operative fail of a successful suicide because of some unwillingness to die, which, while capable of many explanations, certainly lends some support to the view that in such individuals the life instincts are able to maintain their ascendancy over the death instincts. Alexander in a personal communication states that he does not believe that clear psychological representations of the death instinct can be demonstrated. I agree that they have not been, but I do not see why it is *a priori* impossible that they may not be. I think we must recognize, however, that as yet the theory of the death instinct and therefore 'the wish to die' element in suicide is only an hypothesis in contrast to the demonstrated facts of the existence of the other two elements.

RECAPITULATION

So far we have presented the thesis that suicide is a gratification of self-destructive tendencies which upon analysis appear to be composed of at least two elements—an aggressive element—the wish to kill—and a submissive element—the wish to be killed. In addition, it is postulated that a wish to die may be present to a variable degree for which, however, no definite psychological evidence can be offered.

The three components are derived respectively from the ego, the super-ego and the Id. It can be recognized from the clinical phenomena studied that the proportionate strength of these three components varies considerably in various instances, so that in one case the motivation comes most powerfully from the ego, in another from the super-ego, and in still another (perhaps) from the Id.

PARTIAL SUICIDE

This leads us directly to a consideration of those incomplete forms of suicide which deductions and analysis alike show to be directly related to the more successful efforts at self-destruction which we ordinarily call suicide. Self-destruction is, as we shall see, sometimes directly and sometimes indirectly accomplished, sometimes completely and sometimes incompletely. We may well speak of *chronic suicides* as well as *acute suicides;* it is probably not too wide an extension of theory to say that many diseases, both those ordinarily called organic as well as those called functional, may be regarded as various forms of self-destruction—*chronic, indirect* suicide.

For, just as neurotic symptoms may be localized, as in conversion hysteria, or generalized as in major hysteria, so self-destruction may be focalized or generalized. Neurotic syndromes and neurotic character manifestations are similarly focal or generalized. It is not impossible that we may some day be able to show that conversion hysteria and some forms of organic disease represent chronic *focal* self-destructive attacks while ascetism and martyrdom represent chronic *generalized* self-destruction. The ordinary forms of suicide must stand as prototypes of *acute generalized total self-destruction.*

NOTES

1. Cf. Freud: 'The Schreber Case', *Collected Papers,* Vol. III, p. 388.
2. Freud: 'Mourning and Melancholia', *Collected Papers,* Vol. IV, p. 156.
3. Alexander, Franz: 'The Need for Punishment and the Death Instinct', *International Journal of Psychoanalysis,* 1929, Vol. X, p. 256.

3. Differential Diagnostic Types of Suicide

Gregory Zilboorg

BIOGRAPHICAL NOTE

Gregory Zilboorg (1891–1959) was born in Russia and emigrated to the United States following the 1917 revolution. Arriving in poverty, he rose to become one of America's most prominent psychiatrists. He obtained his first medical degree in St. Petersburg and earned another from Columbia University in 1926. After psychoanalytic training in Berlin (1929–1930) he returned to New York City to practice psychiatry and psychoanalysis. A prolific scholar, Zilboorg is known for his papers on postpartum psychosis, criminology, suicide, and "ambulatory schizophrenia." His History of Medical Psychology *was a major contribution. A creative, gregarious man of great energy, he was an expert photographer, woodworker, cook, and an enthusiastic book collector (Braceland 1960).*

COMMENT

Between 1934 and 1938 Zilboorg wrote at least four papers dealing with suicide, three of which are included in this volume. (We omit his anthropological paper [1936], which, though of great interest, seems dated in light of subsequent ethnological advances.)

This first contribution, originally given as a lecture to the New York Neurological Society, acknowledges the importance of Freud's formulation that melancholia expresses anger turned against the self after introjection of an ambivalently loved other. Here Zilboorg discusses a number of cases the thrust of which is to show that Freud's theory of melancholia does not fully explain all suicides. This chapter expanded the dynamic understanding of suicide through examining a variety of patients in diagnostic groups other than melancholia—it addresses suicide in schizophrenia, in "compulsion

---

Gregory Zilboorg, "Differential Diagnostic Types of Suicide." *Archives of General Psychiatry* 35 (1936):270–291. Reprinted by permission.

neurosis," and in what we might today describe as borderline personality disorder.

He asserts that suicide can be an act of revenge against others and argues that it may also express spite. Suicide can arise from identification with the dead. He was wrong in his view that suicide occurs with some frequency in normal persons. (At the time studies showing that suicide is rare outside major mental illness had not been carried out.) Here he emphasizes the ritualistic meaning of suicide, takes into consideration intense Oedipal fixations (hinting at primal scene experiences as a suicide-promoting factor), and suggests that forms of suicide met in "primitive cultures" have much to teach us about contemporary Western suicide.

REFERENCES

Braceland, F. J. 1960. Gregory Zilboorg—A Memorial, 1891–1959. American Journal of Psychiatry *116:671–672.*

Zilboorg, G. 1936. Suicide among Civilized and Primitive Races. American Journal of Psychiatry *92:1347–1369.*

———. *1941.* A History of Medical Psychology. *New York: W. W. Norton.*

■

PREVAILING VIEWS on suicide have been transmitted with comparatively little change from generation to generation for the past one hundred and fifty years. Viewed with awe and a certain psychologic embarassment, suicide appears to the present-day psychiatrist as it did in the past, as an abnormality of mental reactions, or more specifically as an aberration of the instinct of self-preservation, arising from what it has become customary to call undue depressive affects. This point of view, while couched in present-day terms, differs little from that expressed by several generations of medical psychologists, who in turn inherited it from the tradition originated by Saint Augustine.

Saint Augustine was one of the first, if not the first, to postulate that suicide is a sin![1] And sin in those days was a voluntary surrender of one's reason to the pressure of evil, i.e., a sort of intellectual aberration of one's will. The Council of 452 A.D. decreed suicide to be the work of the devil, and as it is well known, many works of the devil have come down to the present in the guise of severe neuroses and psychoses. Hence, the intellectual and moral evaluation of suicide has changed comparatively little, and this estimation, humanized and couched in the scientific terms of modern psychopathology, remains negative; to put it in the words of one of the most recent students of suicide: "It is opposed to the instinct of self-preservation and is therefore a typical perversion."[2] The so-called common sense psychology, while always admitting that suicide is an act of unusual psychologic meaning, tries to explain it by the supposition that it must be an act of despair and possibly one of great courage. However, one hears it as frequently estimated as an act of cowardice. In other words, popular opinion is ambivalent on the subject and views it with a mixture of contempt and admiration. This fact is of more than passing scientific value. One might recall in this connection that on the statute-books of more than one country even today suicide is considered a crime and that Plato almost twenty-five centuries ago was inclined to believe that suicide is a dishonorable act, for a citizen has no right to deprive society of his civic life without the permission of a magistrate. This tradition of disapproval transformed itself in modern times into recognition of an obscure illness and a tendency to limit the suicidal reaction to a group of "insane" persons. That is probably why there has been a constant search for a special pathologic basis for suicide, which some persons see in a singular disturbance of the affective field, others in constitutional predisposition (since many suicides occur in the same family) and still others in specific, although as yet undifferentiated, changes in the brain (in cases of suicide in the involution period of a depression and in those occurring occasionally among persons with arteriosclerotic psychoses and less frequently after severe organic trauma[3]). One therefore frequently hears the inquiry whether it is at all possible for a person to commit suicide without the development of a severe pathologic depression, and one wonders whether the unexpected suicide of some one who appeared normal until the last minute is not, after all, the result of a sudden psychopathologic aberration, which might be called pathologic depression, despair, sense of hopelessness, etc. Be that as it may, it is clear that the problem of suicide from the scientific point of view remains unsolved. Neither common sense nor clinical psychopathology has found a causal or even a strict empirical solution. Most recent statistical studies of suicide have shocked the common sense school by demonstrating that there are more suicides in the community in days of prosperity than in periods of economic depression,[4] and clinical psychiatrists look askance at the fact that, while it is true that patients with depressive psychoses more often commit suicide than other mentally sick persons, a number of suicides occur when the depressed person appears to be convalescing and all but recovered from his depressed state. Moreover, a number of patients who neither are classified as persons with depressions nor behave as such commit suicide at a time when even the experienced clinician had little reason to suspect its possibility. It is hardly necessary to state that neither preventive measures nor scientific causal therapy is at all possible under these circumstances and that only a comparatively small group of patients with severe depressive psychoses can be recognized as potentially suicidal and placed in the protective environment of a hospital.

It is my purpose in this communication to raise and to answer only partially rather than to solve the following questions which suggest themselves: What kind of persons are likely to commit suicide? What is it, i.e., what are the psychologic processes that lead them to suicide? Are there any objective data, signs or manifestations which would lead one to suspect the possibility of suicide before the act is committed? What inferential material has the clinician at hand that might enable him to think in an empirical way of precautionary, if not preventive, measures?

The past twenty-five years have witnessed the development of a deeper insight into the purely psychologic processes of the normal and the abnormal person, and one has learned to view with respect the instinctual drives of man as they present themselves to him, particularly in their unconscious constellations. In other words, a man's development and his instinctual and emotional reactions to the various stages of his development are now recognized as powerful dynamic factors in his life. While the etiology and nature of many of these for the most part unconscious reactions are still obscure, a mass of empirical data has been accumulated which permits one to observe some unconscious processes and to evaluate their respective emotional and dynamic importance in a given case. It would appear logical, therefore, to inquire what the newer psychopathology, which is based on psychoanalysis, has contributed or has to contribute to the problem of suicide.

It is of interest in this connection to quote the words with which Freud summarized the result of a symposium on suicide held in Vienna in 1918:

> Despite the valuable material obtained in this discussion, we have not succeeded in arriving at any definite conclusion. We should like to know above all how it is possible that one overcomes such an extraordinary powerful instinct as the life instinct: is this possible only as a result of disappointment to which the libidinous drives are subjected, or because the ego, pursuing some interest of its own, renounces any self-assertion in life? Perhaps our failure to find an answer to this psychological question is due to the fact that we have no way of obtaining it; by this I mean that in

this problem we are able to utilize as a point of departure only the comparison of the clinically known state of depression with the affect accompanying mourning. However, we are totally ignorant of the affective processes of depressions and of the fate of the libido in this illness; nor is the affect of the mourner yet understood analytically. Let us therefore refrain from forming an opinion until the time comes when experience will have solved the problem.

In other words, the psychoanalytic symposium on suicide at Vienna failed to formulate an adequate answer to the vexing question of what the psychopathology, or rather the psychology, of suicide is. The consensus at that time was that every suicidal person is the victim of strong aggressive impulses which he fails to express outwardly and which he, as a result, turns inward, i.e., on his own self. However, this rather skilful formula, which has since become popular in clinical psychiatric circles, failed to establish a definite clinical or even a theoretical criterion which would throw light on the problem of suicide. Fundamentally the formula was correct, but it was too general to be of any real value, for while it is true that any one who wants to or who does commit suicide suffers from strong aggressive (unconscious) murderous impulses, these impulses are so universal that according to this formula alone the whole world should be in danger of committing suicide, which is obviously not true (Federn).

This unsatisfactory state of understanding was partially ameliorated by the further studies of Abraham, who investigated a number of depressive psychoses, and by Freud, who shortly after the symposium on suicide subjected to careful scrutiny the mental processes of persons with depressions as compared with those of mourners. As a result, a wealth of clinical data was collected, and a better understanding of the depressive psychoses was gained. This understanding can be briefly summarized as follows:

The person suffering from a pathologic depression has a specific set of unconscious fantasies which determine his mood, his whole illness, and a characteristic emotional attitude toward the world which determines his behavior. He identifies himself with another person whom he once loved and then hated; he then loves and hates himself and falls victim to this internal raging battle. The identification, however, in order to produce a depression, is of a special nature, and is based on a particular type of fantasy, a special mechanism. This can be described as follows: The subject is under the dominant influence of a fantasy that he swallowed the once loved and then hated person; he becomes that person and hurls the whole mass of his hostility on this internalized person; the process of being hostile to the internalized person or persons is perceived as depression, self-depreciation and self-hatred, while the act of murder of that person or persons is the act of suicide. As one can readily see, this set of formulations based on the study of the fantasy-life in manic-depressive psychoses is merely an empirical statement of what was observed; it does not, of course, explain suicide. It is of interest to note, by way of illustration, how the aforementioned mechanism of depression can be clinically demonstrated: Thus, it was found that the self-accusations of some depressed persons are frequently literal reproductions of accusations which at one time had actually been directed against the person whom the depressed patient internalized psychologically. Abraham cited the case of a girl who accused herself of being a thief in the same terms which had once been used against her father when, during her young girlhood, he was suspected of having stolen. Moreover, the subject's unusual sadism is taken over by his own conscience, which relentlessly drives him into deeper and deeper depression.

Freud's point of departure was a comparative study of the affects accompanying mourning and depression. His conclusions can be summarized as follows:

In grief which follows an actual loss of a love object, the ego suddenly finds itself in possession of a great amount of free psychic energy which heretofore was bound to the lost object. This free energy cannot naturally reattach itself at once to a new object, for the memories of the lost person keep the subject in a state of tension which cannot at once be overcome. The host of incidents and details related to the lost person, which had been previously perceived as pleasant, become a source of psychic pain, because the object to which love was attached is gone and the psychic energy has to be freed from what was real and has become unreal. The subject at no time loses his capacity for object relationship, but the loss of the object and the psychic energy so painfully freed (made unattached) cause him to withdraw (temporarily) his interest in life. Only after the painful process of weaning from the lost object is completed does the process of reattachment begin and the mourner find his interests in life gradually revived and reestablished. At no time is the sense of loss absent from consciousness.

The inner, affective picture of a pathologic depression is different. Seldom, if ever, does one find a sense of actual loss. To be sure, the death of a loved person may be a precipitating cause of a depressive psychosis, but throughout the depression the complaints of the patient center around other things: He feels dull; he is self-deprecatory and self-accusatory; he has no memory, no mind, no body, etc. The whole trend could be characterized as a complaint that the ego is greatly impoverished; it has lost its tone of life. What happened? Normally, one's ego is turned toward the outside world, and one's psychic energy is bound to it; in a depressive psychosis this energy is withdrawn from reality; this energy, this love for reality, not only becomes free from attachment but renounces any object relationship; it turns toward itself as an object. In other words, it makes its own ego the object; it becomes self-centered, self-loved, self-contained and self-indulgent; that is, it regresses to the earlier level of development known as the narcissistic level. The object or objects which once were ostensibly loved the ego takes into itself, so to speak; it identifies itself with them by way of the mechanism already briefly described and technically known as oral incorporation. The whole process will remain obscure and misunderstood, however, if one does not bear in mind the following fundamental characteristic which is pathognomonic of pathologic depression: The object, the person from whom the depressed person has withdrawn his love, has never been fully loved; unconsciously, and at times half consciously, there always existed a strong undercurrent of dislike, hatred and aggressiveness toward that object. It is this ambivalence, with the negative attitude predominating, which is characteristic of pathologic depression. Consciously the patient may continue to profess love for the object or to project his own aggressiveness, which then appears in the form of anxiety. All psychiatrists have known patients who without apparent rational grounds begin to fear that the husband, wife, child, mother or father might die, might fall a victim to a terrible illness, etc. However, the brunt of the unconscious sadistic hatred and aggressiveness is borne by the ego itself, since it has identified itself with the object and since, in addition, the subject's conscience produces a severe sense of guilt because of the criminal wishes. The result of this structural affective arrangement is a psychic conflict presenting the typical picture of a pathologic depression.

To recapitulate briefly: In a case of a pathologic depression the patient, through identification with a person toward whom his feelings have always been highly ambivalent, loves and hates himself. Since his own ego has become his love object, he feels detached from reality and therefore experiences a sense of poverty of the ego. The unconscious sadism originally directed against the object, reenforced by a sense of guilt, produces the singular phenomenon of the person's becoming sadistic toward himself. Freud[5] stated:

> It is this sadism, and only this, that solves the riddle of the tendency to suicide that makes depressions so interesting and so dangerous. As the primal condition from which the life instinct proceeds, we have come to recognize a self love of the ego which is so immense, and in the fear that rises up at the threat of death, we see

liberated a volume of narcissistic libido which is so vast, that we cannot conceive how this ego can connive at its own destruction. It is true we have long known that no neurotic harbours thoughts of suicide which are not murderous impulses against others redirected upon himself, but we have never been able to explain what interplay of forces could carry such a purpose to execution. Now the analysis of depressive psychoses shows that the ego can kill itself only when the psychic energies, which were originally attached to the object, have been withdrawn upon the ego and the ego can treat itself as an object, when it is able to launch against itself the animosity relating to an object—that primordial reaction on the part of the ego to all objects in the outer world. Thus in the regression to narcissistic object choice the object is indeed abolished, but in spite of all it proves itself stronger than the ego's self.

It is of historical interest to note that the concept of hostility first turned outward against the world and then inward against oneself was the basic idea in the formulations on suicide by the student of a century ago, who sensed it intuitively without being conversant with the mental mechanisms with which modern psychopathology deals. Thus, among others, Tissot in 1840, in his monograph, entitled "De la manie de suicide et de l'esprit de la révolte," postulated that "suicide and revolt are but the double expression of one and the same cause, a double symptom of the same moral malady." Evidently, at least a part of Freud's hypothesis finds its corroboration retrospectively in the sociologic studies of the past. However, despite the considerable insight gained in regard to the mental processes in cases of suicidal depression, the trend observed in prefreudian psychopathology persisted in psychoanalysis also, viz., that suicide is the pathologic outcome of a pathologic state called depressive psychosis. This trend led Freud to state:

> It is remarkable that in contradistinction to depressions, the compulsive neurotic never makes a suicidal attempt; he gives the impression of being immune against the danger of suicide, more so than the hysteric. We understand, of course, that it is the preservation of the object that serves us as a guaranty of security of the ego.

A critical evaluation of all these views is possible only through the examination of clinical material. It is hardly necessary to cite many instances in corroboration of the fact that strong hostilities are operative in cases of depressive psychoses and that these hostilities are characteristically directed by the patients against themselves.

REPORT OF CASES

Case 1. A woman, aged 28, who had always been unusually devoted to her father and whose mother died when the patient was 13, suffered for several years from gastro-intestinal discomfort, periods of irritation and chronic discontent. The only companionship she ever found satisfactory was that of her father. She made many attempts to "be like other girls," but was unable to make herself enjoy the attentions of men. She would take two or three drinks to stimulate herself "to greater courage," but she experienced only disgust when a young man made love to her. One day, a short time before her father was to come home from work, she "decided to end it all"; she put on her prettiest silk brocade kimono and her nicest mules with the conscious intention of looking as attractive as possible; she had a definite wish that her dead body should be pleasing to her father's eye. She turned on the illuminating gas. A short time later she was discovered unconscious by her father. She was taken to a hospital. On recovery from the after-effects of mild gas poisoning, she was transferred for treatment to a hospital for patients with mental disease. She was suffering from depressive neurosis of long standing.

Case 2. A woman in the late thirties, mother of three children, had been in low spirits for some time. In a period of a few months she became increasingly tense, agitated and restless. She complained of insomnia and peculiar sensations in the wrists. Finally, she decided to commit suicide. She slashed her wrists and lost a great deal of blood, but she was saved from death and brought to the hospital. The wounds healed soon, but the emotional state continued with great severity. She wept, groaned, paced the floor and slept little. She professed to have great love for her children and especially for her husband. They were far away in their home in the West. One day, escaping for but a moment the vigilance of the nurse and with a swift, impulsive motion barricading the door by means of her dresser, she broke the window-pane and cut her throat with the glass. As a result of immediate medical attention she failed to die this time also. A few months passed; the patient, while still tense and agitated at times, became more sociable and interested in things outside herself and began to read; she smiled frequently. One day she concealed a piece of glass and in a cheerful, simple manner asked the nurse to bring her a glass of water. While the nurse went out to comply with the request she cut a deep wound in the right side of her neck. A few minutes later she was found cyanotic, almost exsanguinated and gasping. As soon as medical intervention revived her, she began to struggle with surprising violence, demanding that she be allowed to die. However, she recovered, and she was later studied in detail until the drive to suicide receded and then apparently disappeared.

Case 3. A woman, aged 48, had been nervous, tense and dissatisfied for many years. She had always been afraid of pregnancy and was sexually frigid; as a result her marital life was unhappy. She acquired the neurotic habit of consulting many physicians, whom she called on with increasing frequency. She had examinations every time that she suspected she was pregnant. These suspicions and apprehensions she experienced before, during and after the menstrual periods. Although she was a Roman Catholic, she insisted on the use of contraceptives. Yet she remained dissatisfied. She insisted on having curettage done when none was indicated. She insisted that a surgeon tie the uterine tubes. When this was done she began to worry about possible infection. At one time she thought she had syphilis. She had a record of several residences in general hospitals and in institutions for patients with mental diseases. At the age of about 46 she reached the point of general hypochondriasis; she had, she claimed, no movement of the bowels; her intestines were "dried up." She frequently carried a piece of a fragile cake of sand, claiming that this was a piece of her "dried-up intestine"; her brain too was "dried up." She had her own theory of why she looked well physically and gained in weight despite her alleged afflictions. She was agitated and cried. About two years elapsed without bringing appreciable change in her general condition and demeanor. She began to complain in a demanding, aggressive manner that no one was interested in her and that she was abandoned or neglected by every one. On one or two occasions she stated that she was going to die soon. At no time did she express any direct suicidal thoughts—but one evening she suddenly hanged herself.

Case 4. A physician, aged 36, had a particularly great fear of increasing the size of his family and thus the burden of his financial obligations. Being a Catholic, he was equally fearful of the use of contraceptives, and the fecundity of his wife served constantly to deepen and sharpen his conflict. One day, one of his little sons died of an acute illness. He was sad, but his unconscious attitude was betrayed when one day the following exclamation inadvertently slipped from his tongue: "One mouth less to feed!" From that time he fell into a typical suicidal depression. He hanged himself and was revived with difficulty. After he was brought to the hospital, he persistently tried to escape the vigilance of the physicians and nurses in order to kill himself. Long therapeutic talks with his physician revealed an extremely strong unconscious wish that his children should die, a deep sense of guilt because of it, hostility and a murderous attitude toward others whom he thought he loved and a strong ambivalent, incestuous attitude toward his sister. Not only did this patient turn the hostility on himself, actually loving no one, but his deep sense of guilt supplied additional energy for the self-destructive impulses.

Comment

One may postulate that every case of potential suicide must bear clinical evidence of strong unconscious hostility combined with an unusual incapacity for love of others, and if this evidence is found in a case in which depressive features appear suicide becomes a real danger, even though the patient may never express the wish for self-destruction.

The girl in case 1, who attempted to die by gas poisoning, was studied by means of direct psychoanalytic approach. It was as surprising as it was illuminating to find how poor her capacity for love had always been. She was a chronic masturbator; she was unable to (unconsciously she would not) fall in love. She always played the role of a boy and had wished to be one ever since she could remember. She hated her mother. Her father, whom she professedly loved to the exclusion of any one and anything else, she also hated unconsciously. She never forgave him her disappointment when he first preferred her mother and then paid attention to other women after the mother died. She loved him, it appears, merely because he loved her, because "his love was safe," as she put it, i.e., because his love served her as a pretext for not loving others and as a protection against her seeking love elsewhere. Her brother, too, had always been to her the object of envy and hatred because he was a boy and she was not. So far as she played a masculine role in life (hence showing unconscious homosexual leanings), she identified herself with a hated brother and with a father to whom her attitude was extremely ambivalent. She withdrew her love from others and turned her great hostility against herself. Since she had a deep-seated sense of guilt and also hated her mother, with whom she partially identified herself and who was dead, it is clear that there were in this case more than the usual prerequisites for a strong suicidal trend.

The woman in case 2, who attempted suicide three times, was also studied in detail. Her peculiar history also led to the development of a number of extremely exaggerated hostile impulses, which were directed partly against her children but primarily against her husband. Her marriage was not happy. She was the boss, the provider and the brains of the family. She married the man from unconscious spite, although he was inferior to her socially and intellectually. She never loved him. She had always been a tomboy—a mastering, independent, aggressive person. The more intimate history of her childhood and her psychologic development from early childhood through adolescence revealed an increasingly growing hostility toward men (her father and younger brother at first), and her depression and suicidal drive were only an expression of that unbounded sadism which was directed against herself—an ego which had little love to spare for others.

Case 3 is a typical example of the same psychologic orientation. The patient loved no one. She was frigid. She wanted no children. Toward her husband her feelings were strikingly ambivalent. Her sadism, which was turned on herself, found for many years a partial outlet in delusions of being infected and in her frequent self-imposed surgical operations. In a hospital for patients with mental disease her hostility toward the world and other persons found much less outlet than in the outside world. Her demands for surgical treatment remained unheeded; her hatred found expression only in the projection, "No one cares for me." Her incapacity to attach any of her psychic energies to things outside herself was so striking that, while she was not deeply depressed or retarded and was rather active, she was unable to interest herself in any occupational work, a nurse or another patient. She became a separate world in herself within which blind animosity was raging, and she hanged herself.

It is hardly an exaggeration to state that the clinical knowledge of suicide is exhausted at this point, because tradition has emphasized that depression means potential suicide and if a person with apparent absence of depression commits suicide, one believes that one must have lacked in diagnostic acumen and overlooked the "depressive features" in the case. This self-reproach is justified only so far as one has overlooked the suicidal potentialities but not in the questionable diagnosis of depression. The woman in case 1 at no time presented an appearance of classic depression; the condition fell more conveniently under the rubric of neurosis and was nearer the type of obsessional neurosis than any of the other recognized diagnostic appellations. The patient was never retarded, and at no time did she betray the ruminative type of self-accusations. Also, the majority of her symptoms were of a physical nature, consisting of such complaints as "indigestion," constipation, exaggerated menstrual pains and severe abdominal discomfort, which at one time (when her father took another woman home after a social function) became so severe that an operation for appendicitis was performed as an emergency and the appendix was discovered to be normal. Evidently this case was not an instance of a depression, i.e., not one of a depressive psychosis, despite the fact that the patient was suicidal. I shall postpone for a moment the search for diagnostic and prognostic features in this case to bear in mind that in the absence of a typical depression there is no guaranty against possible suicide. In other words, patients with other than typical depressions are likely to commit suicide, and in the light of present-day clinical experience Freud would not subscribe to his original statement that neurotic patients, particularly those with obsessional (compulsive) neuroses, appear to be immune to suicidal impulses.

The same conclusion is reached from a review of case 3. The patient, like the girl in case 1, was not depressed and showed throughout the greater part of her illness an unusually aggressive instead of a depressive mood; she was sarcastic and unpleasant. Both patients gave the impression of having little if any trouble in giving vent to their hostility and rancor, so that one wondered at times whether they had enough hostility left "to turn on themselves" and commit suicide. I shall again reserve judgment until later as to what psychologic dynamic factors were operative in these cases in the direction of self-destruction and shall emphasize that the woman in case 3 had a misophobic, self-indulgent compulsion neurosis of long standing and not a depression.

To add to the illustrative series of suicides by persons who did not suffer from depressive psychoses, case 5 may be cited.

Case 5. A man, aged 52, who was a rather successful and moderately affluent lawyer, was married and had one daughter to whom he was greatly attached when she was a child. His wife was neurotic and frigid. He was a somewhat worrisome, self-centered man, who spent little love on others. He apparently disliked his wife and had unconscious wishes to get away from her, to part from her. He expressed this trend by means of a projection. He became convinced that she was untrue to him with another man, his friend. This was never proved; moreover, there was no presumptive or inferential evidence of the wife's unfaithfulness, except his own assumptive conviction. Acting on this conviction, he established a relationship with another woman, which lasted for years until he came to a hospital for patients with mental disease. Yet his sexual demands were not great; his really gratifying mode of sexual expression appears always to have been masturbation—a habit he had never abandoned since childhood. He started to worry about his health, his heart, his head, the possibility of cancer, etc. His wife (with or without the insistence of the patient but at any rate with his assent) adopted a little girl. The patient liked the child, fondled her and loved her more than would seem normal. He later admitted rather obliquely to having a pedophilic trend. His aggressive impulses soon appeared through the devious path of projection—he became obsessed with the idea that the child might become infected. If a splinter got into her hand or if she stepped on a nail, tetanus might develop; if she was not careful on the fourth of July an explosion of fireworks might burn or infect her, since powder might contain tetanus bacilli. He wrote endless instructions on how to protect her; he changed them presently, for he had forgotten to add an important detail; he then telegraphed home added instructions. He was unable to make up his mind about anything; his ambivalent attitude invaded every field of his activity, so that at times he did not actually know what he wanted, since "yes" and "no," "right" and "wrong," "good" and "bad" appeared almost simultaneously in his conscious attitude toward things. He appeared dull, mildly depressed and preoccupied, even trembling; he stuttered at times, since "to say" and "not to say" were also simultaneous impulses with him.

One day he observed a small hole in the wire screen of a window on the second floor. (His room was on the ground floor.) He became interested in it and made it larger. Little by little, it became large enough for him to crawl out. He recalled that when he saw the hole for the first time a thought passed through his head: "Some one might some day tear it open and get out and injure himself." He crawled out, stood for a moment on the ledge and impulsively jumped off. A few minutes later he was heard calling to a passer-by for help. His voice was peculiarly full of cheerful vigor. While his face was covered with blood, his forehead wounded (the bone was unscathed), his legs wounded and one ankle dislocated, his eyes looked cheerful and almost happy, and he repeated with transparent pleasure: "Now I think I am going to be cured. I am going to get well now." Throughout the period of being bedridden, when he must have suffered a great deal of pain, the patient made no complaints and appeared singularly comfortable. However, the obsessional and depressive symptoms reappeared gradually after complete recovery from the injuries he had sustained.

Comment

This clinical picture leaves no doubt of its being that of a compulsion neurosis, and one may add that, suffering as this patient was from a severe sense of guilt as a result of unconscious hostility and forbidden sexual impulses, he appeared to obtain relief from the self-imposed punishment; this end achieved, he naturally became more cheerful and hopeful. To be sure, the unconscious trend for which he judged himself did not disappear, but it became in some way less unpermissible or more permissible, since he paid for it with his own blood. This psychologic mechanism is met frequently in patients who try unsuccessfully to kill themselves and in some transgressors of the law when they are punished by the State. The same mechanism came to light in the case of the suicidal physician in case 4. After a desperate attempt to commit suicide (by sticking a needle in his heart), he suddenly began to have nocturnal emissions, accompanied by incestuous dreams about his sister. He was greatly attracted to her before he married. Unconsciously, he never abandoned this attachment. His sense of guilt because of this was great, but once he paid for it by means of self-punishment, as a result of which he might have died, his conscience was sufficiently appeased to permit the sinful fantasy to enter his dream.

The sudden recurrence of the incestuous impulse in persons with strong suicidal drives is of paramount diagnostic importance. Hence, one can hardly overestimate the importance of a careful anamnestic study of all direct and indirect evidence and inferences of too great an attachment and too intimate a relationship, no matter how conventionally correct, of the patient to any member of the family which keeps him under the constant strain of having his incestuous wishes stimulated and inhibited at one and the same time. One may recall in this connection the woman in case 1 and her exclusive relationship to her father.

In the light of this clinical evidence that not only depressive psychoses but neuroses are liable to result in suicide. I may also state that schizophrenia does not represent an exception in this respect. Thus, I may mention a case of advanced catatonia of many years' duration.

Case 6. A man, aged 31, was considerably deteriorated socially, intellectually and emotionally. He often indulged for weeks in tearless catatonic whining or manneristic, ceaseless shouting. He defecated and urinated spontaneously like a child. He was fed by a tube for several years; he could not wear clothes except for occasional intervals of a day or two; he gave evidence of a scattered, fragmented, fantastic trend; he heard voices, called for mother incessantly and drooled constantly. With his fingers he loosened teeth and pulled them. Not infrequently he made other attempts to injure himself; he beat his head against the wall or the edge of the bed, cracking his scalp; he plunged from bed head downward. These attempts were vigorous and impulsive. At times he struggled with three or four husky male nurses to get free in order to kill himself. He shouted that he wanted "to die, to go to God." The death impulse was so strong at times that it gave the impression of a wild, insatiable urge.

Comment

While the condition in case 6 may appear too exaggerated to be of common occurrence, one is justified in stating that suicidal trends and acts in a patient with schizophrenia are not unusual. Suicides in these cases are at times among the most difficult to deal with and among the most puzzling. For instance, a patient with acute schizophrenia arrived in the hospital in a somnolent state, which gave the impression of the early stages of stupor; yet he at times aroused himself long enough to reveal a fairly well systematized paranoid trend: His associates were after him; they were all plotting against him; they wanted to deprive him of his job and standing; he thought of them as being mostly Irish Catholics who rose against him, a descendant of an old Protestant Southern family. He tried to castrate himself with a razor. He wished to kill himself, and for a time he presented one of the most difficult problems of management.

The persistence of the impulse to die and its violence are, however, by no means the outstanding clinical features in cases of suicidal schizophrenia. On the one hand, a number of depressions (such as that in the case of the woman who cut her wrists) show the same features, while on the other, the patient with schizophrenia is likely to serve little if any notice of his suicidal intention. For instance, an unmarried man in the early thirties, suffering from paranoid psychosis, displayed extreme jealousy in the acute stages of the psychosis and at the same time an intense flight from any real love for a woman. After several months in a hospital for patients with mental disease he appeared quieted, became apparently more serene and seemed to be convalescent. He showed no external ill effect from the visit of his fiancée one afternoon and continued with the routine of the hospital in his usual manner. He was seen that evening playing billiards with other patients. He greeted the physician with a free, apparently natural smile and retired a little later in good spirits. He was found early in the morning crouched and hanging on his necktie by the bedside.

Evidently, there is no single clinical entity recognized in psychiatry that is immune to the suicidal drive. I may also state, without going into unnecessary details, that while the fundamental mechanism which was described by Freud as characteristic of depressions is met in all instances of apparent depression, in some cases of suicide it is not possible to demonstrate that this mechanism is the only determining factor brought into full play in the act. Moreover, as it has already been stated, the clinician observes a number of patients displaying the operation of this mechanism without the suicidal drive being either directly present or effectively operative when present. Hence, the presence or apparent absence of this mechanism cannot well serve as a reliable diagnostic and prognostic criterion. I shall therefore turn attention to the purely clinical manifestations of some suicidal psychoses and neuroses and try to determine what other features, if any, they possess which could be utilized for diagnostic evaluation.

CLINICAL MANIFESTATIONS OF DIAGNOSTIC VALUE

The woman with a compulsion neurosis, who hanged herself apparently without warning, like many other persons with a similar condition was given to outbursts of anger and was endowed with a bitter and lashing tongue. A few hours before she committed suicide she was her usually surly and aggressively bitter self, which had been familiar to her attendants for many months. However, when the physician failed to pay much sympathetic attention to the "piece of intestine" in the form of a bit of sand cake which she showed to him, she exclaimed that some day she was going to die if no one paid attention to her inner ailments. This was a threat which she carried out impulsively less than three hours later.

This type of suicide appears to be of great clinical importance. It seems to be characteristic of the compulsion neurosis with a suicidal trend. Persons of this type show all the characteristic traits which were described by Freud as anal; they are irritable, persistent, stubborn, cold, contrary, sarcastic, misophobic in various degrees, stingy and spiteful. The well known childish fantasy, "When I am dead they will be sorry," finds its literal expression in their mental life, and their self-murder appears to be an act of aggression against the world, a real act of revenge. The act of suicide appears to have acquired in the fantasy life (mostly unconscious) of these persons a special pleasure value; they libidinize it; it is their supreme expression of hatred. The finer details of their psychic structure have not yet been sufficiently investigated, and the mental processes making such an act possible are still obscure, but there seems to be little doubt that from the clinical point of view they represent a rather treacherous problem, for as has been pointed out, such patients give the impression of constantly ventilating their sadism and one is not infrequently misled into believing that they are too "extraverted" to commit suicide. If they threaten to kill themselves, as this patient did, one is exposed to the danger of falling victim to the common belief that persons who speak of suicide so openly seldom carry out their alleged intentions. As a matter of fact, it is difficult to rid oneself of the impression that spite is a typical cause of suicide and must be seriously taken into account when making a clinical prognostic evaluation in such a case. The presenting symptomatology in cases of this type is rarely that of a depression and almost always that of a compulsion neurosis with agitation and bitter aggressiveness. When one has the opportunity to study more closely the emotional and instinctual reactions of these patients, one can see more clearly the role which a spiteful form of sadism plays in these cases.

Case 7. A woman in the late thirties, mother of five children, three of whom were living, suffered from a compulsion neurosis of many years' duration. She had been treated by many psychiatrists and had acquired a verbal knowledge of various psychiatric terms, but she failed to improve, because she conveniently converted some of her symptoms into a stubborn pattern which she would not abandon; she was in the habit of consulting a physician with the sole (unconscious) purpose of proving to him that he was unable to cure her. Consciously, she applied herself arduously to the task of being treated; she became devoted to her physician and would not leave him or permit him to leave her even for a day. Her restlessness, feeling of diffuse tension, irritability, querulousness at home and restless, almost ill concealed hatred of people in her social contacts all increased as soon as a long week-end or a brief vacation was suggested or planned by her physician. With many variations this pattern was repeated several times in the course of the illness, which covered a period of almost fifteen years. One day, when she appeared to have been functioning comparatively well for many months, her physician declared that he was going away for a brief holiday; the patient wanted to follow him as she had done with two other physicians in the past. This proved impracticable. The patient responded with an almost instantaneous increase of vague restlessness and became too nervous to play her game of golf, which she usually enjoyed. She stated that she would be unable "to stand it," and she expressed the fear that a panic might develop—a name she gave to her states of tension and restless irritability. The day after the holiday began and one day before the physician left the city, the patient took by mouth a considerable quantity of allylisopropyl barbituric acid with aminopyrine and barbital, and about 1 a.m., as she began to sink under the effect of the drugs, she woke her husband and told him what she had done. She remained unconscious for about seventy-two hours, and before completely regaining consciousness she passed through several hours of hyperkinetic agitation. The first words while she was apparently still unconscious were: "I did it out of spite. I did it out of spite." She did not appear to remember this after she regained complete consciousness.

I shall return to this case a little later in connection with another aspect of the problem. For the present attention is centered on the feature of spite. The purely phenomenologic side of the clinical picture was in the main similar to that displayed by the woman in case 3 who hanged herself. Here again one must emphasize that no matter how incomplete or poorly defined the depressive features in cases of compulsion neurosis may be, agitation, sarcasm and mild panicky states definitely tinged with strong aggression and reactions of hate and spite should be taken as danger signals and possible forerunners of an impulsive suicidal act. Consideration of the unconscious mechanisms and the various infantile libidinous constellations is deliberately omitted at this time, because one cannot subject a person to thorough psychoanalysis at a glance, and for practical purposes I must confine myself to drawing on the empirical end-results of psychoanalytic therapy. One may thus utilize the psychologic syndromes which reveal themselves and can be observed from the outside, as it were. These purely external diagnostic or prognostic criteria still await full corroboration. Further psychoanalytic studies in such cases will probably permit one later to subject the data to statistical tabulation and thus facilitate and probably corroborate the work on the clinical typology of suicides. However, these preliminary suggestions should serve not only as a guide for further study but as a purely clinical criterion for the serious evaluation of the spite reaction in persons with severe compulsion neuroses.

ARCHAIC TYPES OF REACTION

As has been suggested, one must bear in mind that the spite reaction briefly described is not yet clearly understood. While its external manifestation is easily observed and its dynamic force is incontestable, it appears that, like all other psychologic reactions, it is intimately woven with a number of other contributing factors of various degrees of importance. Of these factors, one is a frequent part of the psychologic structure of suicidal persons and appears to play a major and probably a decisive role in a number of suicides. This factor is complex, and it is apparently rooted deeply from both the ontogenetic and the phylogenetic point of view. In order to gain a clearer view of it I shall return to the case of the woman who took allylisopropyl barbituric acid with aminopyrine and barbital.

As psychoanalysis in her case proceeded, the patient gave the increasingly convincing impression that the major part of her unconscious fantasy life was preoccupied with thoughts of extreme resentment toward her mother. No matter how strong her hostility toward her father, she always found extenuating reasons for his behavior, because fundamentally she was deeply attached to him. She even forgave him the alcoholism which had caused her a great deal of concern and pain since she was 14 or 15 years of age. There was nothing she could find in her mother that would awaken in her a warm feeling. There was always hovering over her an almost mysterious, although very vague, idea of death. Her mother was still living. The patient became aware of the intense wishes she had for the death of her mother, but her increasing insight failed to alleviate the panicky sense of the ever present idea of some one's death and her deeply repressed but ever rising awareness that she frequently wished to die for some reason that she was unable to explain. Finally, after many months of work, she recalled what appeared to have been one of the most memorable and traumatic incidents of her life. When she was about 3 years of age her mother became pregnant. Her whole fantasy life then became concentrated around that pregnancy. She hated her mother, and her irritability, captiousness and intractability reached a high degree when a baby brother was born. She hated the newcomer and wished that he were taken away. The baby lived for eight months and died of disease. Memories of that period resuscitated in the course of the psychoanalysis disclosed that as a girl of about 4 the patient experienced a period of painful anxiety, which never entirely disappeared throughout adult life. Apparently, she passed through the whole gamut of hostile identification with her little brother who soon died. It was this identification with a dead person that seems to have dominated her psychic life and deeply influenced her emotional attitude toward her own children, in relation to whom she harbored at times deep unconscious wishes for death. Evidently, while she was still very young, a little less than 4, her inner conflicts were stimulated to an unusual degree by the pregnancy of her mother, and her sense of guilt was raised to a high degree of tension by the premature death of the hated little brother. When she was 12, just at the time when menstruation began, she experienced another difficult period of jealousy and anxiety and was never able to overcome her intense hatred of her second brother, who was born at that time—a hatred which soon became conscious and under which she labored with the intense ambivalence that is characteristic of compulsion neuroses.

One is justified in stating that the outstanding feature of this patient's psychologic development was the identification with a dead boy just as she somewhat prematurely reached the height of the oedipus conflict. This conflict, tinged with a strong sense of identification with a dead brother, was acutely revived by the birth of a second brother just as she reached another crucial period of life—puberty.

If one compares this psychologic constellation with that of the woman in case 1, one notes the following features:

This patient too as a girl harbored a strong and conscious hatred against her mother, and just at the time when she began to menstruate and her oedipus conflict thus became revived and accentuated the mother died. Her conscious reaction at the time of the mother's death was one of calm and strange lack of regret and sorrow, but a short time afterward she began to show the first signs of hysterical symptoms and a tendency to mild depressive anxiety. In the course of psychoanalysis, fifteen years later, the patient revived and recognized her great attachment to her mother which lay buried under the conscious hatred. It became clear that after the death of the mother the girl passed through a period of severe unconscious mourning, which found expression in the form of her first clinically defined neurotic symptoms. It was at that time that she experienced identification with her dead mother. Here again is a case of identification which was made at the very time that the patient reached a crucial period in psychologic development—in the midst of an acute revival of her oedipus conflicts. This psychologic constellation was clearly reflected in the suicidal act. The decision to kill herself was reached at a time when the patient was apprehensive that her father might marry again. She was alone in the house awaiting the arrival of her father. She perceived a desire to tidy the house: she swept the rooms; she polished the furniture; in short, she assumed the role of a conscientious and solicitous housewife, thinking all the time that she wanted to die and that she wished her father to find the house in perfect order. As it has been said, she then put on her best pajamas and her favorite kimono and opened the gas-jets. The outstanding thought at that time was that she wanted to look peaceful and attractive to her father when dead; in other words, in the very act of suicide she acted out her identification with her dead mother.

Case 8. A woman, aged 35, who wished to commit suicide by drowning herself with her two little children but who was prevented in time from carrying out her intention, suffered from a series of mild depressions which at times, however, reached considerable severity. The drive to do away with herself appeared at times uncontrollable, and at the time she began psychoanalytic treatment she had been ill clinically for almost nine years. While it would be interesting to review in full the many details in this complex case, which throw considerable light on the origin of the suicidal drives and demonstrate a complex and systematic network of a variety of death wishes, all forming a confluent and cumulative mass of forces that drove the patient to seek death, the clinical aspects in the case will gain in clarity if I limit the review to what appeared the fundamental factor in her psychic economy.

This patient was an only child. When about 6 years of age she discovered a photograph of a little child who was apparently asleep. It was her father's possession and he appeared to cherish it. When she asked him about it he winced and at first gave no answer, but she soon learned that her father had been married to another woman before he married her mother, that that woman had borne him a little son, who died before he reached the age of 1 year, and that the photograph was that of the dead child. Her fantasies took hold of this fact with great avidity. Her father was overheard many times saying that he wished she were a boy, that his first wife's son had died and that about a year after his birth his first wife herself had died in childbirth, the second child being stillborn. They were buried together. The little girl was impressed with these facts at the age of 6, i.e., at the very height of her oedipus problems. Her emotional life was obsessed with this drama; her father loved the dead child more than he loved her; he loved a dead wife and a dead child more than he loved her living mother and his little daughter. An old-fashioned trunk in the house stood at the door of the bedroom of her parents. This trunk was that of the dead wife and was filled with her belongings. The little girl once stole a look into that trunk and discovered a pocketbook with money, dresses and a complete set of baby's clothes—all mementoes which her father cherished. It is impossible, without taking a great deal of space and time, to give a full description of the variety of constellations that grouped themselves with great tenacity in the mind of the little girl around the thought of the dead woman with her dead children. Despite the fact that the patient unconsciously wanted children and although she was happy in her married life, she felt that "for some reason" her children and she should die. The following detail is of decided interest, illustrating the degree of her identification with the dead woman. Her first-born child was a boy, who lived only four hours. Consciously, she reacted to this event with anomalous equanimity; unconsciously, she resented it but never to a great degree. Subsequently she had another child, a girl. She loved this child but wished that it were dead. She did not want any more children, as though she was eager to complete a literal identification with her father's first wife. Her third child, also a girl, was unwanted, but she loved it dearly.

While it is probably a mere coincidence, it should be noted that the patients in all three cases of identification with the dead and in a number of others in my series slept in the bedroom of the parents till very late in childhood. The first patient, who took allylisopropyl barbituric acid with aminopyrine and barbital, slept in the bedroom of her parents until her brother was born; he replaced her till he died, and then she was returned to her old bed. The second patient, who took illuminating gas, slept in the parental bedroom till about the age of 5, and then she was moved into another room which was separated from the main chamber by a thin partition. The third patient slept till the age of 8 or so in a small room which was a sort of alcove of the bedroom of the parents. The mysterious trunk was near-by, at the door.

Proximity to the bedroom of the parents throughout the formative period of late childhood in many cases in which a great variety of clinical pictures are presented later proves to be a source of unusual stimulation of the oedipus wishes of the child and the conflicts resulting from them. It is not difficult to understand that the stronger these wishes and conflicts the more dangerous the situation is in general from the standpoint of future morbidity and the more dangerous it is in particular in the cases in which a morbid identification takes place at one of the crucial periods of the child's development. The clinical data collected since the publication (1905) of Freud's "Three Contributions to the Theory of Sex" brought ample evidence to corroborate his hypothesis of the psychosexual development of man. There are two pivotal periods in the stages of this development which appear to be crucial, particularly in the life of persons who are liable to be driven to identification with a dead person: These are the oedipus period, the so-called phallic phase of which reaches its height at about the age of 6, and the period of puberty, at which time all the conflicts of the phallic period are revived under the pressure of physiologic maturity. The period between these two phases seems to be silent; it is the so-called period of latency, during which the social adjustment of the child takes precedence over any other aspect of its life and the sexual reactions in the genital sense recede to a great extent into the psychologic background.

In cases of the type just considered, as in those of a predominant spite reaction, it is possible to infer from the clinical picture, trend and anamnesis whether real danger of possible suicide exists if one bears in mind what has been said about identification with a dead person. A history of the death of a person close to the child or a circumstance bringing the theme of death into the actual life of the child at one of the two turning-points of the psychosexual development of the child makes suicide a highly probable outcome, particularly if these events occur with the background of strong and constant stimulation of the child's attachment to one of the parents or to their intimate life (such as sleeping in the parents' bedroom until or beyond the age of 6).

I may add, by way of recapitulation, that evidence of a strong oral anlage or fixation or both, which are not difficult to observe clinically, points to a depressive reaction and also to a greater probability of suicidal outcome, regardless of the clinical picture—whether that of depression, obsessional neurosis, hysteria or schizophrenia.

One may state, therefore, that a suicidal drive is not dependent on or derived from any traditional clinical entity found in present-day psychiatric nosology; it is to be viewed rather as a reaction of a developmental nature which is universal and common to the mentally sick of all types and probably also to many so-called normal persons. The very universality of the reaction, and particularly of some of its outstanding characteristics, such as oral incorporation, spite and identification with the dead, leads one to suspect that one may be dealing with an archaic form of man's response to his various inner conflicts, and it would prompt one to seek an answer to the problem in the study of primitive races and their reactions leading to suicide. While this thought opens an entirely different, nonclinical approach, it is perhaps of interest to observe several ethnologic parallels which may throw light on the subject.

ETHNOLOGIC DATA

Ethnologic material is still scarce or scattered, and what material is available remains unsystematized and unsubjected to critical study;[6] hence, that which follows represents nothing but illustrative suggestions.

Many legends of primitive races seem to demonstrate some of the mechanisms of suicide which were met in the clinical cases. Thus, in these legends "a sense of being wronged, even though to us the wrong does not seem very serious, is enough to drive the victim to suicide," stated Seligman,[7] by way of preface to the following Melanesian legend of British New Guinea:

> A girl of Southern Massim prefers the Kanioga root to any other food; her mother and aunt twice eat the Kanioga she had collected for herself. When they ask her to come with them to collect more of the desired root, she refuses; then she laid out all her ornaments and finery and put them on, necklaces of shell heads and quill shell armlets, anklets, and a new grass petticoat; then taking her pet dog in her arms she began to sing slowly: "Because of the lily root, because of the lily root I am going." Presently she went into the bush weeping. . . . When the girl came to a lofty wakola tree which was easy to climb, she climbed it, and her mother running up saw her: "Come down, dear, come down," she said, but the girl answered: "No, no, too late," and then looking down she saw a crocodile in the sea close beneath her. . . . She took off her ornaments one by one and threw them to the crocodile who snapped them hungrily; she then threw her dog, and finally her petticoat, until, when naked, she threw herself down and the crocodile took her.

This legend impresses one as a good symbolic summary of a number of motives and forces which are operative in many suicidal acts of today. It illustrates the ritualistic quality of the act (case 1 of the woman who took illuminating gas, may be compared), and it hints at the deeper dynamics of the wish for death: There is a strong frustration, oral in character, and a deep-seated rejection of further gratification; it is hardly a coincidence that the legend makes the girl die through being eaten by a crocodile; the oral frustration produces a strong reaction of anger (oral sadism) and the culprit dies an oral death.

Another story coming from the Trobiand Islands, related by Malinowski, runs as follows: Kima'i, a boy of 16, had a relationship with his girl cousin, who naturally was forbidden to him by the incest taboo.

> This had been known and generally disapproved of but nothing was done until the girl's discarded lover, who had wanted to marry her, took the initiative. . . . Then, one evening, he insulted the culprit in public, accusing him in the hearing of the whole community of incest and hurling at him a certain expression intolerable to a native. For this there was only one remedy; only one means of escape remained to the unfortunate youth. Next morning he put on his festive attire and ornamentations, climbed a cocoanut palm, and addressed the community, speaking from among the palm leaves and bidding them farewell. He explained the reason for his desperate deed and also launched forth a veiled accusation against the man who had driven him to his death, upon which it became the duty of his clansmen to avenge him. Then he wailed aloud, as is the custom, jumped from the palm some sixty feet high, and was killed on the spot. There followed a fight within the village in which the rival was wounded, and the quarrel was repeated during the funeral.[8]

The deliberateness and the ritualistic quality of this suicide, as of that of the girl of southern Massim, are evident, as is the characteristic method of jumping off a high place. The question of the method used in the act of suicide is of great importance and should present a topic for separate study; it is outside the scope of this communication, however. In regard to the chief points of interest, one can easily see that the motive of incest and the thwarted aggression serve as a legitimate combination for a suicidal outcome; more than that, suicide becomes compulsory under these circumstances. One might state that what is ritualistically compulsory in the primitive community does not disappear from the psychic life of the civilized person; it merely recedes into the background of the unconscious and under proper circumstances of psychologic stress makes its reappearance in the form of irrational impulsiveness, so frequently observed among suicidal persons of the white race. This turning of one's aggression on oneself, legitimatized and honored among the primitive and some civilized races, such as those of ancient Rome or present-day Japan, cannot be passed over without comment. It has obviously great sociologic meaning. It performs a social, preservative function: The individual dies because aggression is forbidden to him, but the community takes care of the business of revenge. One wonders to what extent this aspect of social development may not be responsible for the traditional respect many persons have for suicide and for the idealization of his death wish by the suicidal psychotic or neurotic person. At any rate, it is difficult to rid oneself of the impression that many motivations for suicide which are found among patients are only regressive recrudescences of archaic traditions. This appears to be particularly true of the case of suicide in which identification with a dead person appears to predominate, for one finds that the most powerful motivating determinant of suicide among primitive races is the death of a chieftain or of a husband. Thus, the native women of the Solomon Islands follow their dead husbands impulsively: They die by strangulation, which seems to be the oldest method of choice, next to which comes self-immolation on the funeral pyre, practiced by the ancient Hindus and Slavs.

There are a number of motivations for suicide discernible among primitive peoples as atavistic remnants of a still older past, and strikingly enough, the same and, for that matter, all atavistic reactions appear to be still operating in the psychopathologic conditions which come under clinical observation, particularly the compulsion neuroses and schizophrenia.

These sketchy ethnologic illustrations are given here only in order to indicate that there is an impressive parallelism between the traditions of primitive races relating to suicide and the suicides of today. It appears also that not only do typologic impressions find their counterpart among extant primitive races but the clue to the understanding of the deeper determinants and of the causal constellations leading to suicide must be looked for in anthropologic data which are not yet made available to the clinical psychopathologist.

SUMMARY

The problem of early diagnosis of possible suicidal outcomes in patients is of paramount importance in the treatment and prevention of suicidal trends. Such diagnosis is possible on the basis of observations of mental mechanisms and anamnestic data, which become valuable criteria before the suicidal tendency comes out fully in the trend of the patient. Suicides can be differentiated on the basis of the mental mechanisms, this proving that there are many psychologic types of suicide—a point of diagnostic and therapeutic importance.

NOTES

1. Augustinus, D. Aurelius: De civitate Dei, I, XVI.
2. Achille Delmas: Psychologie pathologique du suicide, Paris, Félix Alcan, 1932.
3. Jankau, V.: Selbstmord nach Unfall, Ztschr. t. d. ges. Neurol. u. Psychiat. 130:148. 1930.
4. Dublin, L. I., and Bunzel, Bessie: To Be or Not to Be: A Study of Suicide, New York, Harrison Smith & Robert Haas. 1933, p. 102.
5. Freud, S.: Collected Papers, New York, 1924–1925, vol. 4, p. 162.
6. The only attempt at a systematic descriptive study of the subject appeared recently by Dr. J. Wisse [Selbstmord und Todesfurcht bei den Naturvölkern, Zutphen, Netherlands, W. J. Thieme, 1933].
7. Seligman, C. G.: Temperament, Conflict and Psychosis in a Stone-Age Population, Brit. J. M. Psychol. 9:187, 1929.
8. Malinowski, B.: Crime and Custom in Savage Society. , New York, Harcourt, Brace and Company, 1926; quoted by Seligman.

4. Considerations on Suicide, with Particular Reference to That of the Young

Gregory Zilboorg

COMMENT

In this wide-ranging discussion of suicide, Gregory Zilboorg opens with a criticism of "common sense" explanations and of medical reductionism. He finds fault with the tendency to explain suicide on "constitutional grounds," a point contemporary readers might well ponder when depression and the suicidal complications associated with it are increasingly viewed in a neurochemical-genetic context. While biological influences are now well understood to be an important part of the underlying constitutional matrix of suicide, they do not fully explain its complexity.

Possibly Zilboorg would have agreed with Edwin Shneidman that suicide is like a tree: its roots correspond to the biological matrix, but the trunk is its psychology. The method, the contents of a suicide note, and the calculated effects on the survivors left behind are the branching limbs, the flawed fruit, and the camouflaging leaves. "But the psychological component, the problem-solving choice—the best solution to the perceived problem—is the main trunk." (Shneidman 1993, 3–4)

In the same vein Zilboorg cautions against facile explanations of suicidal phenomena by attributing them to Freud's metapsychological speculations about the "death instinct." The study of individual cases shows that complex fantasies about death and dying, including permutations of the Oedipus complex, especially in pubertal suicides who have lost their parents earlier, are of critical importance. He identifies spite, fear, and fantasies of escape as important, especially in suicide occurring in the young.

Brian Barraclough (1987) was later to show that the loss of a parent in childhood was no more frequent among a sample of suicides than it was in

---

Gregory Zilboorg, "Considerations on Suicide, with Particular Reference to That of the Young. *American Journal of Orthopsychiatry,* 7(1937):15–31.

his control group. He nevertheless found that the recent death of a parent or spouse was significantly more frequent among the suicides in his sample than among the controls.

There is a contemporary trend to "disindividualize" suicide as researchers have turned in an empirical direction, emphasizing statistical, economic, biological, and sociological investigation. But today, as in the past, suicide cannot be clinically understood, estimated, or prevented without careful psychological study of the individual patient.

REFERENCES

Barraclough, B. 1987. Suicide: Clinical and Epidemiological Studies. *New York: Croom Helm.*

Shneidman, E. 1993. Suicide as Psychache: A Clinical Approach to Self-Destructive Behavior. *Northvale, N.J.: Jason Aronson.*

■

FOR THE SAKE of clarifying the discussion which follows it may be advisable to recapitulate briefly some of the basic findings on suicide expressed during the course of the past few years.[1]

Suicide for many centuries has been considered a sin, a crime, or both. In some regions—in England, for instance, or in the State of New Jersey—it is still illegal to make an attempt at suicide. Statute books thus reflect even today the medieval point of view according to which man is endowed with a free will and, in attempting to kill himself, consciously directs his will toward something forbidden. Obviously, this is one of the left-overs of a theological age—or, more rightly, of the paleozoic age of social psychology.

At the time psychiatry was replacing theology in the field of human psychology, suicide began to be looked upon as the result of a psychopathic state (so-called "temporary insanity") or of an acute psychosis. The old theological tradition continued to linger, however, in the form of man's ethical approach to suicide which kept alive such perennial and unanswerable questions as: Have we a right to commit suicide? Is it selfish to kill one's self? Is suicide cowardly or courageous? It is not difficult to see that the old assumption that man's will is free to choose between good and evil still permeates the soil from which these questions spring. It is almost too obvious to say that whatever drawing-room or academic philosophical interest these questions may have, a scientific study of suicide must disregard them and their possible answers. This last needs emphasis because, on the border-line between parlor psychology and scientific investigation, there is a sort of no-man's-land which is drowned in the fog of a moralistic philosophy and vaguely lit by the twilight of speculative fantasies dressed up in the quasi-scientific cloak of what we are wont to call *common sense.*

How often do we go over the story of an individual who tried to or did kill himself and point out the "self-evident," the "rational" motivations for his act; we speak of the man's despair following a disappointment in love, the loss of a fortune, advancing old age or a serious illness, and we assume that this "common sense" explains the given act of self-destruction. It is hardly necessary to emphasize that such "common sense" testifies to our inherent human superficiality, a superficiality which springs from universal human anxiety, and leads man to grasp at any straw of external plausibility, when faced with the discomfort of looking closer and deeper into the problems of death and life. And if we subject this "common sense" to a partial critical test we are more than likely to stumble upon another traditional obstacle: When it is pointed out that so-and-so was jilted, lost his fortune, failed in some crucially important undertaking, or suffered from a chronic illness or old-age invalidism without so much as an attempt at suicide, we ponder for a moment and then, conjuring up the old standby or "waste-basket" of unsolved problems, we say that there *must* be "something constitutional" about the person who commits suicide. Yet we know that suicide has never been proven to be hereditary, nor in any other way related to congenital characteristics. It is true that we occasionally observe a number of suicides in a series of generations of the same family, but we also observe certain habits of speech, certain familial traits of accent or mannerisms which we have learned to trace rather accurately to the imitative characteristics of the child, i.e., to the process of identification that is particularly potent in children and is responsible for many personality traits normal and abnormal which we observe in the individual's later life. An expert retrospective glance into the nursery will frequently reveal more about a person than a chronic ward of a mental hospital or the morgue.

A careful perusal of clinical material should give a fatal jolt to what we call "common sense," as well as to the constitutionalistic tradition, for neither the one nor the other sheds any true light on the mystery of suicide. No amount of common sense can relieve us of the feeling that the killing of one's self is a mysterious act, running counter as it does to the very essence of the thing to which man is biologically dedicated—life. Springing from the very substance of living, the instinct of self-preservation appears in the suicide to be somehow not only viciated but wholly replaced by an opposite drive as mystifying as it is elemental. The clinician knows all too well how persistent and unreasonable the suicidal drive is at times, how uncontrollable and stormy, for he has seen the so-called "sudden" suicides, the unexpected self-destruction of those patients who appear to have come out of their depressions and to have lost (consciously) their desire to die. Jameison's studies of a number of cases at Bloomingdale Hospital amply bear out this contention.[2]

It is this mystifying characteristic of the phenomenon that has led several research workers to utilize, a bit too freely, the concept of the death instinct and to construct a series of theoretical assumptions which are supposed to explain the phenomenon of suicide. Karl Menninger is, among us, the particular and most able exponent of this point of view.[3] His many observations are of paramount clinical and sociological interest. Valid as they are, one must nevertheless remark that the psychological speculations built around the death instinct as a pivotal point explain comparatively little since these are essentially restatements of the observation that, under certain known and mostly unknown circumstances, the impulse to die becomes greater than the impulse to live, at which time man will injure or kill himself. To say that the death instinct gains the upper hand over the life instinct is merely an elaborate way of stating that man does die or kill himself. By this I do not mean to reject the concept of the death instinct—which may prove a valuable adjunct in the construction of many useful hypotheses or theories—but merely to observe that in clinical psychopathology and pragmatic sociology this particular element of Freudian metapsychology, when applied to the problem of suicide, seems to be rather tautological and either adds to, or at least does not subtract from, our confusion.

In reviewing these theoretical approaches to the clinical psychopathology of suicide, we may note that the psychiatrist's interest in the problem, dictated as it is by his daily contact with clinical material, seems to have led us by silent consent to the assumption that suicide is an act of an abnormal individual, that the suicide is a psychopathic person. This assumption, like that of constitutional or hereditary predisposition, has never been proven. We have drifted into its acceptance as a result of our professional bias, overlooking the fact that it also springs from the old tradition of free will which in modern times appears under the guise of free mind or intelligence; we therefore assume that one must "lose one's mind" in order to want to kill himself. It is questionable, indeed, whether we are here on more solid scientific ground than we were when our psychological theories had for their corner-stone the doctrine of free will.

Under the influence of this silent postulate and with some formal allowance for the importance of what we call *affect,* we have finally developed the tendency to view the whole problem of suicide as an expression of purely pathological conditions. In this we follow the path of academic psychiatry which even psychoanalysis has not as yet fully abandoned. We speak of depressions as causes of suicide, for instance, ignoring the fact that a number of severe depressions never attempt to commit suicide. Individuals suffering from such depressions frequently say that they wish they were dead or possessed the courage to lay hands on themselves, but they never act out their fantasies of achieving death. Too, many hysterias, compulsion neuroses and schizophrenias, even some apparently normal individuals, commit suicide, and this with almost the same frequency as the so-called depressions. Moreover, a clinical condition duly labeled cannot be the cause of self-destruction any more than pneumonia or tuberculosis can be considered the cause of death; it is not pneumonia or tuberculosis as clinical entities that cause death, but the particular pathological processes *certain* pneumonias and *certain* cases of tuberculosis follow which, leading to the destruction of vital organs or to the blocking of various vital functions, cause the cessation of life. If this mode of scientific biological thinking is applied—as it should be—to the study of psychological problems, if we attempt to follow this train of thought in our approach to the problem of suicide, we are at once struck by the fact that we really know almost nothing definite about the specific psychological processes which lead to self-destruction. A truly scientific psychology of suicide is still wanting.

If we discard, because they promise little of scientific validity, these various orientations—the theological, ethical, philosophical and pseudo-biological (i.e. unwarranted conclusions as to heredity)—there remain two methods of approach, two rather broad orientations, which are not mutually exclusive but rather complementary: the sociological and the psychological. Of these, the first engages interest because of its apparent objectivity and the purely impersonal quality of its data. It deals with economic studies and statistics.

As far as the economic factors of suicide are concerned, it is obvious that, important as these appear on occasion, we might fall into the pitfall of onesidedness or run the risk of assuming that "economics is the thing" if these studies were stressed at the expense or to the exclusion of others. How true *is* such an orientation? It is difficult to rid one's self of the suspicion that the well-to-do classes yield proportionally a greater number of suicidal victims than the poorer classes, and to believe that economic depressions do *not* appear to be a contributing factor to the increase of the rate of suicide any more than wars or revolutions. In so far as one can rely on statistics in such matters, it appears that the rate of suicide if anything shows a tendency to drop during social and economic crises.[4] This brings us to the next important aspect of the sociological method of approach, the statistical.

A careful and eager perusal of statistical data on suicide, some of which cover a period of almost one hundred years, led me to concur with the most recent investigators of the subject of suicide[5] who conclude that statistical studies of suicide by themselves are well-nigh useless for our purpose. Unless such statistical data are coupled with a proper study of the individuals lost behind the statistical figures, a study of the life histories and psychological development of those individuals, the figures themselves tell us absolutely nothing. When we review reliable statistical tables on suicide, certain trends do appear to reveal themselves. We learn, for instance, that older people commit suicide in proportion more frequently than younger people, that ratio of suicide per 100,000 population is greater for men than for women, that the ratio of suicide runs inversely to homicide among various races and communities, and that, despite general belief, the number of suicides per given unit of population is not always in proportion to its ratio of "insanity" which latter appears at times to run almost inversely to that of suicide.[6]

Yet all such data suffer from two important defects inherent in the method of approach and it is doubtful whether these can ever be corrected. The first and most important has already been alluded to: The data, dis-individualizing the person as such, concentrate on statistics with the result that we are more than ever removed from the psychology of suicide. The second defect may be briefly stated as follows: Statistical data on suicide are compiled from vital statistics and are therefore never complete since they represent only those cases which lay judgment, i.e. the coroner's, accepts as suicide. One wonders exactly how many genuine suicides fail to find entry in the carefully compiled tables of the conscientious statisticians—those, for instance, who "fall" out of windows instead of jumping out, those who, drunk or sober, are killed in automobile accidents. I knew of a man whose love for alcohol vied with his passion for driving an automobile and whenever intoxicated he could barely control his wish to run over someone—preferably an old woman on the sidewalk—or to drive straight for a lamp post and "be done with it." He finally ran into a post of the elevated railway and incurred serious injuries from which at length he recovered. Had the man died, he would have been classified, on a "common sense" basis, as "death due to injuries incurred while driving an automobile in an intoxicated state." From the psychological point of view, however, this man, dead or alive, is a typical suicide. I also knew a young woman who labored under a great inner need to die. She continued to do her work and to drive her car; after several temptations she finally yielded and ran into a post. She did not die, she was merely bruised; her case could not possibly find its way into the columns of vital statistics, but she was a suicide none the less. These are flagrant examples; there are many "accidents," "illnesses," self-inflicted through a variety of minor slips and mistakes, which on closer investigation prove to be true suicidal reactions carried out carefully and in accordance with a plan which remained unknown not only to the outside world, but to the victims themselves—in other words, suicidal behavior dictated and carried out wholly by factors which never broke through into consciousness.

It seems fair to say, therefore, that statistics, wholly or partially divorced from the study of the pathogenesis and etiology of suicide, are more liable to lead to a misconception than an understanding of the problem. The sociologist himself is not prepared to adopt frankly the same attitude though he seems to have been sensing its inevitability for many years and has gradually turned his attention to individual and social psychology, and to social philosophy, seeking in these branches of thought some light on the subject of suicide. Emile Durkheim[7] in his now classical monograph on suicide gave evidence of this trend as did Enrico Ferri.[8] Almost all of the most recent monographs on the same subject[9] show more of the psychological and less of the purely impersonal and statistical point of view. In general, however, one may say that these psychological essays at understanding the phenomenon of self-destruction continue to remain largely impersonal, i.e. general rather than individual and philosophical rather than psychological, and are inclined to view religion and ideology as determinants in suicidal drives rather than the reverse.

The fact that the Mohammedans, the Jews, the Irish and the Spaniards in old Spain show a comparatively lesser incidence of suicide than the Protestant or the Brahman and Buddhistic races is generally interpreted as a phenomenon in which religious beliefs act either as a deterrent from or a stimulus towards suicide. This point of view is not well founded for it is impossible to be certain which is the cause and which the effect. It is quite thinkable that the self-destructive drives in a given group are responsible for the creation of a given religious orientation rather than the reverse. This is probably true of the Hindu whose propensity towards death may have been more responsible for the elaboration of the ideal of Nirvana than any individually created or traditionally elaborated religious philosophy. It is probably also true of those races who adapted certain religious attitudes suited to their particular balance or dis-balance between aggressive and self-destructive characteristics of life. Hence the Japanese who has the semi-religious tradition of suicide and the Mohammedan who has the religious philosophy of the opposite may perhaps use these philosophies only as an expression of an instinctual attitude which exists in them anyhow, i.e. *before* the corresponding philosophy came to lend it its rationalized or revelatory support. By the same token it is highly questionable whether it is true that the Stoic philosophy contributed a goodly number of suicides; it is perhaps more correct to say that under the influence of many instinctual forces, the nature of which is still unknown to us, the Romans of the last years of the Empire tended towards the development of suicidal trends under the pressure of which both Epicurean and Stoic philosophies served as pseudo-rationalization. We must remember that both the poet of the Epicurean world view, Lucretius, and the father of Stoic philosophy, Zeno, committed suicide. The early Christians, too, committed suicide, in great numbers, though they sought to rationalize their act by seeking martyrdom, soliciting the Cross and the Pyre to take their lives. It was not until the fifth century, under the influence of St. Augustine's dogma, that suicide became a sin.

The question of the genesis of certain ethico-religious ideas on suicide and of the relation these bear to the deeper, instinctual characteristics of man is both important and interesting, but it is doubtful whether a proper solution of this problem will yield more than an explanation of why and how man attempts to express the nature of his destructive and self-destructive drives by means of ethico-religious elaboration. This subject matter belongs to the study of the psychology of culture and not to that of clinical psychology, to the study of the psychology of philosophy and not to that of actual human behavior, though there has been scarcely a monograph on suicide written in the course of the past fifty or sixty years which does not either confuse the philosophical with the truly psychological aspect of the problem or overlook the latter altogether.

If we thus find ourselves drifting back towards clinical psychology in our search for an answer to why suicide, it is because all other departments of psychology seem to present serious defects in scientific method and are therefore unable to offer us more than very general statements of principles and this without the necessary empirical psychological data.

Reference has already been made to the fact that the psychopathologist until recently concentrated his attention on the classificatory aspects of suicide. His trend of thought, expressed schematically, usually ran as follows: This person is depressed; he is *therefore* to be looked upon as a potential suicide; if he finally does commit suicide, all expectations, fears and assumptions are corroborated; but should a patient show definite *schizophrenic* characteristics there is no need to subject him to suspicion of suicide; if suicide occurs in this case, it merely means that what psychopathological jargon terms "the emotional component" has been overlooked. This attitude presents a fair estimate of the usual stencil form of many of our discussions in hospital staff meetings as well as in other clinical conferences which neither clinical nor psychological facts justify, since there is no such thing as an "emotional component." All psychological reactions, normal or abnormal,—and particularly the latter—present *emotional* reactions whether these be obvious or concealed, and whether the clinical picture is that of an agitated depression or of a catatonic stupor. To separate the emotional component and view it as a separate entity is like separating serum from the blood corpuscles. This can be achieved in a test tube but not in any *living* human being. If we turn from this formalistic approach offered by psychopathology towards that presented by psychoanalysis, we find that the latter's contribution to suicide while more enlightening is still insufficient.

It is unnecessary to review here the gradually increasing insight into the problem of suicide which we owe to psychoanalysis. We shall limit ourselves to a simple enumeration of certain points. Like psychiatry, psychoanalysis began by associating suicide with depressions of the manic-depressive type. Freud and Abraham described fully the deeper psychology of these depressions and their major mechanism of oral incorporation combined with the directing of aggression onto one's own self. This series of psychic processes was then described in terms of the topography and the economics of the human personality; psychoanalysis proceeded to show that not only has the act of suicide a definite unconscious meaning, but also that the methods used for carrying out the act of self-destruction are revealing in that they frequently tell of the unconscious infantile content of the act. Thus, suicide by drowning points to an intrauterine fantasy, suicide by jumping out of a window to a birth fantasy, and suicide by shooting to certain aspects of unconscious homosexuality.

This descriptive aspect of psychoanalytic contributions to the problem of suicide proved to be of real value in the understanding of some of the deeper contents of suicide, without, however, explaining its specific dynamics or economics. One felt one had glimpsed something of real value in such facts only to be left without an understanding of why such things occurred genetically. The suicidal drive began to seem more complex than the first dramatic impression had implied. Two aspects of the problem then suggested themselves: first, that suicides differ not only in the method or weapon used for the act of self-destruction but also in the psychological history of the individual and his attitude, conscious and unconscious, towards life and death; second, that the suicidal drive appears to be a real elemental psychic force, universal in nature and apparently confined not alone to human beings. As to the variety of suicidal reactions, the need for an adequate typology of suicide became definitely crystallized, and the typological suggestions as to the *differential* diagnosis of suicide made by this writer elsewhere[10] was the first modest attempt to respond to this need.

The typology as outlined is far from complete; clinical material for a more detailed study is still lacking. It is useful, however, in so far as it discloses that the classical type of killing an incorporated object is not the only type, and that incorporation of an object is in itself not the true cause of suicide; only those individuals who appear to have identified themselves with a *dead* person and in whom the process of identification took place during childhood or adolescence, at a time when the incorporated person was already actually dead, are most probably the truly suicidal individuals. Thus, when a boy or a girl loses a father, brother, mother or sister at the time when he or she is at the height of their oedipus complex or transition to puberty, there is, in case of a neurotic reaction in later life, a true danger of suicide. I found this characteristic in a number of suicidal patients. It is important to note that this point of differentiation might serve as an objective criterion in the study of many individuals who for the time being do not show any suicidal trends. A check-up on a number of suicides as reported in the daily press frequently demonstrates the validity of this contention. One such incident taken from a Boston paper will illustrate this.

A girl of twenty-two was reported to have jumped out of a fourteenth story window. She appeared cheerful the day before, even bought a complete outfit of new clothes. On the next day, Good Friday, she committed suicide; "no motives." She was said to have had a depression about a year previously, and further inquiry revealed that she was more or less always subdued in the spring. ("Seasonal Influence?"—another straw grasped at by many who are preoccupied with the problem.) The girl's mother had died when she was eight years old—an age which frequently presents the last stages of a somewhat delayed oedipus phase though officially it belongs to the latency period. This circumstance alone would not suffice to demonstrate the validity of our assumption that the girl's suicide was the result of a particular kind of accentuated identification with a dead mother, but a further study of the history of the case revealed the striking fact that the girl's mother died fourteen years previously on the same day, i.e., not the same date, but on Good Friday. The girl thus committed suicide on the anniversary of her mother's death. The fact that her depressive moods occurred usually in the spring might be related to an unconscious mourning for her mother at that time, i.e., on Good Friday and for some time thereafter. That this unconscious mourning played a serious rôle in this case is further suggested by the fact that the girl happened to buy new clothes the day before This detail reminds one of the primitive custom of suicide, according to which the person about to commit suicide always first dresses in his or her best clothes—a parallel with our case which seems not entirely accidental.

Such random examples offer added weight to the value of typological studies of suicide and suggest that a mere review of the various "difficulties" our patients happen to endure cannot serve as a criterion of the causation of suicide. Such facts as a sense of inadequacy, complex family relationships, neurotic or psychotic complications, are in themselves of little clinical value in the evaluation and understanding of suicide.

Our allusion to the fact that many primitive people, before committing suicide, dress up in their best ceremonial clothes is of more than passing importance. An intimate study of the details of the how and the when of a suicide—what "little things" occurred or were performed preliminary to the final act of self-destruction—frequently reveals the *ceremonial* quality of a number of self-inflicted deaths and offers a psychological link with the suicides among primitive races. This at once suggests that suicide is far from being the monopoly of civilization—a point of view directly contrary to the universal propensity to emphasize the rôle of current elements of civilization in this problem. It may be considered as almost definitely established that primitive people commit suicide more easily and more frequently than civilized people. The primitive world view has not been abandoned by civilized man and it leads him frequently to appropriate a number of things which are not entirely his own; this is true of suicide also. Thus many primitive people commit suicide either by starving themselves to death or by eating earth. Certain animals, too—for instance, dogs or monkeys—on occasion refuse food and die when mistreated. Biologists have the opportunity to observe such cases of animal suicide by starvation in their laboratories.

We are justified, therefore, in suggesting that suicide is neither a special privilege of civilized man nor even of the human race in general; that it is most probably a universal phenomenon, more biological than purely sociological. This statement, general as it is, has a practical methodological value, for should suicide prove to be a complex biological phenomenon, the clue to the pathogenesis of suicide may rightfully be sought in the instinctual life of man—among primitive people and children. Although substantial data to corroborate these statements are still wanting,[11] the few facts available are highly suggestive and confirmatory of these assumptions.

Let us return for a moment to the available statistical data. It appears that the rate of suicide increases with the age of the group studied, that more old people per unit of population commit suicide than young people. Durkheim's figures, some of which go as far back as 1835, show a sharp rise in the rate of suicide somewhere around the age of fifteen or sixteen. In France, for instance, between 1835 and 1844, the rate of suicide for individuals under sixteen per one million population was 2.2 for boys and 1.2 for girls, while the rate for individuals between sixteen and twenty was 56.5 and 31.7 respectively—an increase of almost twenty-five times the previous rate for boys and girls. The figures for Prussia for the years 1873–1875 show that the relative number of suicides among boys increased eleven times and among girls about fifteen times after the age of sixteen; in Saxony, Italy and Denmark figures show a similar trend. The same phenomenon is observed in this country today—Dublin notes that there were officially 81 suicides of children under the age of fifteen in the United States between 1928 and 1929 as against 926 suicides of adolescents between the ages of fifteen and nineteen—as well as in Argentine[12] where the figures are 286 suicides under the age of sixteen (for the years 1915–1926) and 966 between the ages of sixteen and twenty. The obvious inference drawn from these data is that the age of puberty seems to be the crucial period as far as the development of active self-destructive drives are concerned.

As to the distribution of suicide between the sexes, statistical computations show that among civilized people suicide is more prevalent among men. Dublin's figures would suggest that before the age of sixteen the rate of suicide is lower for boys than for girls but that after this age it is lower for girls. Although older statistics do not seem to bear this out, some data obtained from Argentine[13] appear to confirm the impression. The importance of this detail cannot be overlooked, since the psychic conflicts awakened during the age of puberty are of major significance in the structure and dynamics of suicide, and since the discrepancy in the incidence of suicide between the sexes might serve as an additional clue to the psychological riddle. While suicide among civilized races appears to be a sad prerogative of the male, it is almost monopolized by the female among primitive races. One may, therefore, give expression to the suspicion that the deeper motivations for the suicidal act are not the same in men as they are in women, that man's suicide has more to do with the inner struggles created by passivity and feminine strivings, i.e. by homosexuality. This would perhaps explain why more men shoot themselves than women, shooting having obviously something to do (symbolically) with passive homosexual wishes. The fact that the problems aroused by passive homosexual drives become most acute at puberty may perhaps be the reason why, from puberty forward, more men succumb to suicidal drives than women. The difference in the incidence of suicide in the two sexes cannot be as definite before puberty since the essential differentiation of the unconscious conflicts has not become fully crystallized either psychologically or socially.

There may be some objection to this free use of statistical data which includes age groups of fifteen and sixteen as those having puberty reactions. This can be met in two ways: First, statisticians follow the tradition of subdividing age groups by drawing arbitrary lines to include the ages between birth and sixteen as one group, between sixteen and twenty as a second group and so on, and since the only reason for using these particular subdivisions is one of arithmetical convenience, we are justified—provided we have a valid reason—in lowering the age mark of our first subdivision; and second, since the age sixteen is an arbitrary mark having no specific psychological significance and since it is the only group that includes the pre-puberty group, we have good reason to assume that it is this characteristic that is responsible for the smaller incidence of suicide. So much for our purely theoretical considerations; let us now turn to factual data.

Detailed clinical studies of suicidal children are, as far as I know, still lacking.[14] The impression gained, however, is that youngsters kill themselves more impulsively and with fewer rational motivations than do adults. Childhood attempts at self-destruction are usually results of what appears to be fear or spite or both: girls or boys are afraid they may be punished if they are unduly delayed in returning home and, in their flight from punishment, they "prefer" death; boys or girls, forbidden to do something that they badly want to do, are driven by such frustration to self-destruction. Suicidal reactions based on spite are typical for certain suicidal compulsion neuroses; I know of no adult suicide based on what appears to be external fear or severe spite without the intimate collaboration of a very severe neurosis. On the other hand, fear and spite are frequently the psychological triggers which release the suicidal impulse in the majority of primitive and semi-civilized races. A minor offense, even a remark misconstrued as offensive, is sufficient reason for suicide. Should one express to a Papuan one's surprise at his nose being red, the Papuan's reply is apt to be silent retirement to a quiet spot and summary self-destruction. Frustration of a child brings forth a no less characteristic reaction. Thus, "A girl of Southern Massim prefers the Kanioga root to any other food; her mother and aunt twice eat the Kanioga she had collected for herself. When they ask her to come with them to collect more of the desired root she refuses; 'Then she laid out all her ornaments and finery—necklaces of shell beads, quills, shell armlets, anklets, and a new grass petticoat. She put them all on and, taking her pet dog in her arms, began to sing slowly: Because of the lily root, because of the lily root I am going. Presently she went into the bush weeping. . . .' When the girl came to a lofty wakola tree which was easy to climb she ascended it. Her mother, running up, saw her: 'Come down, deary, come down,' she said, but the girl answered: 'No, no, too late.' Then looking down the girl saw a crocodile in the sea close beneath her. One by one she took her ornaments and cast them to the crocodile who snapped them hungrily; next she threw her dog to the beast, and finally her petticoat. At last, when she was quite naked, she jumped from the tree and the crocodile took her."[15]

Seligmann cites another such example, this one taken from New Guinea: "A boy took a piece of sugar cane but was forbidden by his father to eat it. When finally the father took it away, the boy climbed a cocoanut tree and jumped to his death."[16] The impulsiveness, the ceremonial quality and "naturalness" of suicide as exemplified by these two stories are obvious. As illustrations of suicide of the pre-puberty type, i.e. suicides motivated primarily by infantile oral conflicts—which are, to some extent, also a characteristic of depressive psychoses—these two stories might serve as examples of some of the motivating forces which we can observe clinically in our adult as well as adolescent suicidal individuals. They belong to the type of suicide which results from oral spite or oral aggression. Incidentally, we may conclude from the above examples that jumping off high places was neither invented by nor is it the prerogative of our skyscraper civilization.

The same parallelism may be observed with regard to fear as an apparent motive to active suicide. The classical illustration of suicide out of fear is the self-inflicted death of primitive man at the approach of a victorious enemy. Hardly a primitive tribe exists which does not demonstrate, individually and *en masse,* this preference for death to capture by the enemy. The history of our subjugation of the Indian on this continent, of the Spanish conquest of South America, of the European invasion of Africa and Melanesia, or the history of the epidemics of smallpox among the North American Indians who men, women and children preferred to kill themselves rather than suffer the disease—all these are rich in such material. If primitive man did not kill himself at the approach of the victorious enemy and, taken captive, could not succeed in achieving his own death, he behaved in such a provocative manner that he was executed. Such behavior at times reached mass dimensions; in the West Indies literally over a million people committed suicide out of fear of and spite against an unwelcome invader.

Fear and spite are singularly coupled in these cases as in the suicides of youngsters who kill themselves out of fear of parental punishment. Fear alone produces the usual reaction of flight, but when fear is associated with a sufficient degree of resentment, i.e. aggression, the aggression by some as yet unexplored psychic route turns quickly on itself and the frightened psychological aggressor falls victim of his own hatred. Something akin to the same psychological mechanisms is operative in the suicide of certain criminals who have been convicted to death or who have reason to believe that they may be convicted to death. These psychological processes are largely characteristic of primitive races, very young suicides, apprehended criminals and certain compulsion neuroses, and the impression gained from their observation is that we deal here with a typical and universal reaction.

If we consider the general "common sense" attitude held by the Law to certain aspects of suicide this impression is reinforced. The Law hovers over the doomed criminal with keen and hostile solicitude lest he escape the executioners by committing suicide. The struggle between the Law and the criminal cannot be reduced to that between justice and crime; it is, rather, the battle between two aggressions which, in a state of unequal competition, try to prevent one another from full expression. The criminal seeks to mock at the alleged omnipotence of the Law through suicide—in killing himself he would shear the vindictive Law of its power. The Law resents (unconsciously) this implication and does everything in its ability to protect the narcissistic over-valuation of its power. Sankey, the kidnapper who hanged himself on a tie in a Minnesota prison, said immediately after his arrest that the Law would never "get him." The public, on the other hand, in its identification with the Law, resents the criminal's "cowardly" exodus through voluntary death though it traditionally admires the defender of a city who kills himself rather than surrender to the enemy. This idealization of the hero who dies by his own hand should give us cause to ponder, for whenever we deal with too-long and too-persistent an idealization of certain human acts we must suspect that we deal with a primitive drive in man, a drive which has always dominated mankind, an inner almost biological necessity which man in his evolution had to accept and justify on ethico-philosophical grounds. We idealize maternal attachment to the child and filial love, for instance, as if these were something exceptional and not simply the expression of fundamental biological inter-reactions between female and offspring; many an instinctual need lurks behind the loftiness of a virtue thus idealized. Behind the idealized suicide of the heroic defender of the city there is an unconscious recognition of a set of inevitable, perennial, instinctual urges which are similar to, if not identical with, those which lead the guilty schoolboy to kill himself rather than face an angry parent, and which led Sankey to hang himself in his prison cell.

If we conceive of suicide as an elemental drive with many earmarks of the instinctual, what then is its biological meaning, what—if any—biological function can it conceivably perform? That suicide does perform some sort of function in the biological scheme of things suggests itself by the fact that it appears to be universally at work at various stages of civilization and at the various levels of each individual's development. We may find our answer, perhaps, in the two phenomena which lead, the one to complete physical, the other to complete psychological destruction of the individual.

It is generally accepted that any injury to the peritoneum or to an underlying organ produces a relaxation of the gastro-intestinal tract, a diminution of peristalsis and a lowering of the digestive functions, the result of which is a moderate toxemia. Teleologically speaking, the intestinal tract relaxes in order to give the injured peritoneum a chance to recover from the shock and to institute partial healing. In other words, the intestinal tract "cooperates" with the rest of the organism; it does not insist on continuing its job at normal speed but waits for the peritoneum and the rest of the organism to give the signal that the trouble is overcome. Occasionally, however, the intestinal tract overreaches itself; it remains in its partial slumber in spite of all the signals the organism sends. Gas pains, the excruciating suffering of the patient, enemas and other stimulating medications fail to move it from a stubborn and too literal "understanding" of its biological task. Gangrene finally develops, and the patient dies. Thus the task, so nobly begun, of maintaining or saving life ends in death.

This biological process was once aptly called the dementia praecox of the gastro-intestinal tract,[17] for a similar process is observed in the psychology of dementia praecox. In this psychosis the individual, unable to master reality, first denies its existence and then attempts to restore it by projecting his own fantasies into real life. This process of projection is in itself not pathological—the little boy who calls a match "chu-chu train" and the poet who believes in his fantasies can both be quite normal—for it serves the biological purpose of both mastering and re-creating reality. In dementia praecox, however, the ego overreaches itself to the same extent as do the intestines in the case of paralytic ileus; the individual's ego, to save itself from complete destruction through losing contact with reality, fills that reality with its own projection to such a point that reality is totally abolished. The ego then lives only with its delusions and is itself, therefore, well-nigh abolished: In its attempt to save itself it "chooses" death.

This is the paradoxical process which seems to take place in those suicides the result of fear, spite or frustration. The more primitive, the less developed, the ego organization (i.e., the more narcissistic) the more frequently these psychic mechanisms will be found at work in the active suicidal drive, a fact which explains why this type of suicide is found particularly among the very young, among depressive compulsion neurotics, and among old people. This also explains why suicide before puberty shows infinitely smaller incidence than after the climacterium or in the senium: In childhood the ego organization is still weak, it is in the process of growing, in the process of increasing development of successful mastery of reality; and in the senium, the ego is weakening at a rapid pace and can "save" itself by the paradoxical self-assertion through self-imposed death.

On the basis of the above considerations we may theoretically say that at puberty the task of the ego is to assert itself as quickly and as fully as possible by means of asserting the instinctual drives with which it must make or is inclined to make an unconditional alliance. Should the ego fail in this task the suicidal outcome would offer itself as its paradoxical substitute. It is probably this fact which is largely responsible for the sharp increase in the rate of suicide after puberty. We need not here enumerate the well-known conflicts and their varieties concentrated in urgent and surging mass during puberty. With these in mind, however, we can view as a corroboration of our theoretical conclusion such a typical suicide as the double suicide of a loving couple who are "joined in death" when life refuses them the full consummation of their relationship. In general, the nature of the conflicts during this phase of the individual's development suggests that suicide at, or immediately after, puberty should present, in the light of our present day knowledge, the primitive and impulsive and semi-ceremonial outcome of frustrated *genital wishes* rather than of oral aggressive ones or of spite as we found them in earlier phases.

Clinical material offers ample corroboration of this view, but our studies of this material have not been detailed nor deep enough to trace with clearness and accuracy the psychological texture of the suicidal reactions. Pending further and more thorough study we must limit ourselves first, to inferential evidence and second, to a closer inspection of the suicidal habits of primitive races which may serve as excellent auxiliary guides in clinical work in forming a scientific theory as to the genesis of suicide.

Let us cite an example of the post-puberty type of suicide which, incidentally, also demonstrates how many true suicides are not listed in statistical tabulations: A youth named Hessler lived in a small New Jersey town; he was killed by the brother of the sixteen-year-old girl whom he courted. The case was in the hands of the prosecuting attorney when the following note was discovered among the dead boy's clothing: "To whoever finds this note give it to Miss (here follows the girl's name), the girl I love, to whom I am now giving my life for. I cannot have her so life is not worth living. I know this is a bad thing to do but I don't think God will hold me responsible. So good-by. I love her. I always keep promises." What happened is not clear. All we know is that Hessler called on his girl and was shot by her brother who claimed self-defense. A psychologically trained mind cannot dispose of such a murder and suicidal note as mere coincidence. This type of frustration in love acts psychologically as a prohibition, as a threat to the life of the ego, in brief, as a castration for an oedipus wish; consequently, all cases of suicide among the young present more or less acute explosions of the oedipus difficulties, wrapped particularly in the castration problem and homosexuality (in men).

Anthropological material, in so far as it deals with suicide, gives enlightening support to some of the opinions expressed above; it offers, too, a number of data which may serve to develop further and deeper insight into this problem.

With these considerations in mind, we report here a few incidents taken from the lives and folk-lore of primitive races.

A young lad wounded his comrade in a fight; thereupon he hanged himself out of fear of the elder brother of the victim.[18]

Wisse[19] says that the young men in New Zealand often shoot themselves on the most trifling affront or vexation. One young man who suffered for two days from a toothache cut his throat with a very blunt razor without a handle.

The same author,[20] quoting Kubary, states that young people of the Pelan Islands who find life difficult because of an unhappy love affair, for instance, either refuse to eat and slowly die, or otherwise commit suicide on the spot.

Teit[21] states that among the Thompson-Sudans the girls frequently touch on the head or the arm the man they wish to marry; this gesture in no way obligates the man, but some girls whose wishes are not met commit suicide. The girls of the same tribe also frequently kill themselves when forbidden to marry the boy of their choice.

Seligmann[22] reports the case of a romance between a Melanesian boy and girl. When the boy's mother learned about it she reprimanded him. One day she met the girl and scolded her severely. The girl at once ran into the thicket and hanged herself. Hearing this, the boy climbed a cocoanut tree, stated that his mother would not lose much by the death of such a son, and thereupon leapt to his death.

Neuhauss, who was quoted above, tells us that a father had sexual relations with his daughter in the field. She went to the village, told of what had happened, dressed herself festively, and took poison. Upon hearing this her father also took poison.

Malinowski, in his study of the sexual life among the primitives of the Trobriand Islands, relates among a number of other similar incidents the following legend: A brother and sister had an incestuous relationship; they lay down and knew one another and then they slept; they did not eat, neither did they drink, and that is the reason why they finally died.

There is hardly a primitive country which does not have some rock, crater, or waterfall dedicated to the suicide of lovers, particularly of frustrated girls: We think in this connection of the "Maiden Rock" of the Sioux Indians, of the craters of certain Japanese volcanoes, and of certain waterfalls on the Island of Bali.

These few illustrations give ample evidence of self-destruction on the part of young men and women, self-destruction which not only facts but tradition, legends, sagas, religious parables, relate to the struggle with one's direct or indirect incestuous wishes. Even a cursory review of the ethnological material impresses one with the predominance of suicide among young girls; young men appear, for the most part, to commit suicide either when confronted with the active opposition of a parent—particularly father or brother—or together with their forbidden sexual partner, i.e., in cases of double suicide. In other situations the literature cites mostly girls; the same is true of adult suicide among primitive races. If we recall that the data for civilized races show the reverse relationship as far as sexes are concerned, and that just before or at puberty the number of suicides among boys is usually smaller than or at least equal to the number of suicides among girls, we may conclude that our hypothesis that homosexuality and the concomitant feminine strivings in boys play a paramount rôle in this problem is correct. We may add that these suicides—as far as their unconscious content is concerned—follow closely the patterns of primitive reactions to suicide. As to girls, the problem appears much more obscure and seems to have more to do with oral strivings and oral spite in their genital edition as it were.

This rather prolonged discussion is incomplete despite its length and, in addition to many obvious gaps, it leaves most of the questions open. Its purpose, however, has not been to find any complete answers to these questions, but rather to reformulate the problem in terms of inner psychic relationship and also to add more questions which are not usually asked when we rely on our "common sense," for it is only by seeing clearly the questions imposed upon us by facts that we can hope to be able to look in the proper direction for corresponding answers. The whole problem of suicide, to be solved adequately, requires not only a proper orientation as to "common sense," heredity, psychoses, but primarily a kind of emotional adjustment on the part of the observer and investigator, an adjustment which will enable him to think and see clearly that we gain very little when we give suicide a psycho-pathological label, and that suicide is as much a natural bio-sociological phenomenon as war, or murder, or revolution. Like these phenomena, it cannot be prevented even among the most enlightened amongst us unless it is considered a form of instinctual expression rather than a "mistake" of society, a slip of the mind, or a defect, or a perversion of nature.

NOTES

1. Zilboorg, Gregory. "Suicide among Civilized and Primitive Races," *Am. J. Psychiatry,* 92, 6, May 1936.

2. Jameison Gerald R. "Some Psychiatric Aspects of Suicide," *Psychiatric Quarterly,* April, 1933.

———. "Suicide and Mental Disease: A Clinical Analysis of One Hundred Cases," *Arch. Neurology and Psychiatry,* 36, pp. 1–11, July 1936.

3. Menninger, Karl A. "Psychoanalytic Aspects of Suicide," *Internat. J. Psycho-Analysis,* XIV, Part 3, pp. 376–390, July 1933.

———. "A Psychoanalytic Study of the Significance of Self-Mutilations," *Psychoanalytic Quarterly,* IV, 3, pp. 408–466, July 1935.

———. "Purposive Accidents as an Expression of Self-Destructive Tendencies," *Internat. J. Psycho-Analysis,* XVII, Part 1, pp. 6–16, January 1936.

4. Dublin, L. I. and Bunzel, Bessie. *To Be or Not to Be, A Study of Suicide,* New York, Harrison Smith and Robert Haas, 1933.

5. Achille-Delmas, F. *Psychologie pathologique du Suicide,* Paris, Félix Alcan, 1932.

6. Durkheim, Emile. *Le Suicide, Étude de Sociologie,* Paris, Félix Alcan, 1897.

7. Durkheim, Emile. *Le Suicide, Étude de Sociologie,* Paris, Félix Alcan, 1897.

8. Ferri, Enrico. *La Sociologie Criminelle,* Paris, Félix Alcan, 1914. (Translated from the Italian.)

9. Achille-Delmas, F. *Psychologie pathologique du Suicide,* Paris, Félix Alcan, 1932.

10. Zilboorg, Gregory. "Differential Diagnostic Types of Suicide," *Arch. Neurology and Psychiatry,* 35, pp. 270–291, February 1936. As far as I know this has not been superseded.

11. Data on both primitive people and children are being gathered now under the auspices of the Committee for the Study of Suicide.

12. Bula, Clotilde A. *Analysis Estadistico del Suicidio,* 1934.

13. *Ibid.*

14. Whatever knowledge I have gained on the subject is based more on verbal communications made by colleagues than on written reports. I owe my first data on the subject to Dr. David Levy.

15. Seligmann, C. G. "Temperament, Conflict and Psychosis in the Stone Age Population," *Brit. J. Medical Psychology,* IX, Part 3, 1929.

16. *Ibid.*

17. I owe the word to Dr. Raymond Gosselin.

18. Neuhauss, R. *Deutsch Neu-Guinea,* 1911. Vol. III, p. 92.

19. Wisse, J. *Selbstmord und Todesfurcht bei den Naturvolkern,* Zutphen, Thieme, 1933, p. 62.

20. *Ibid.,* p. 73.

21. Teit, J. "The Thompson Indians of British Columbia," in the report of the Jesup North Pacific Expedition, 1900. Vol. 1, pt. 4, p. 324.

22. Seligmann, C. G. *The Melanesians of British New Guinea,* 1910, p. 572.

5. Some Aspects of Suicide

Gregory Zilboorg

COMMENT

In this article, organized around two case reports—one of them, the "girl in Boston," was mentioned in his 1937 paper (see chapter 4 above)—we find Zilboorg at his practical clinical best. In an informal manner, very close to the patient's experience, he addresses a number of important suicidal phenomena. He takes up the fact that many patients experience a lifting of depression and suicidal resolve after a suicide attempt and explains this in terms of the dynamics of aggressive discharge. He underscores the importance of the revival of Oedipal issues in adolescence and shows its relevance to the clinical experience. He alludes to the suicidal nature of human sacrifice as practiced in ancient cultures, in which the victim (at least to some degree) appears to have been a volunteer, eager to transmigrate to a better life among the dead. The case of the "girl in Boston" offers an opportunity to discuss suicide as a ritual and as an anniversary phenomenon, details often overlooked in contemporary psychiatric practice. He considers the importance of aggressive discharge in protecting suicide-vulnerable individuals from turning against themselves, and concludes his discussion with a protest against Karl Menninger, whom he believed was a reductionist.

■

SOME RANDOM NOTES that I have made from the record and from an interview with one of the patients now in this hospital may serve as a very good illustration of what I might call the speculative approach to suicide.

Gregory Zilboorg, "Some Aspects of Suicide." *Suicide and Life Threatening Behavior,* 5(1975):131–139 (This paper was originally presented as a talk in 1938, but lay unpublished in the Zilboorg-Friedman Archives for many years.) Reprinted by permission.

(You probably know that I am a psychoanalyst, and in certain quarters we psychoanalysts are accused of speculating too much.)

The patient is a lady about 40 years of age. On the 9th of August last without warning she tried to hang herself. According to her own story, every now and then for a few weeks before she made the attempt, a thought would come to her mind that if she wanted to die and if she wanted to kill herself, she would do so by taking a strip of bed sheet and hanging herself. That is the method she had chosen. After the suicide attempt she showed a rather remarkable change in attitude: She appeared clearer, more serene, more in contact with things and more cheerful. At the present moment there is a certain haze over her condition. She seems slightly duller and less in contact with things. A first impression one gains when speaking with her is that she takes up the first word she uses, or even the first sentence, and proceeds to talk around it and weave it into her conversation. It is, I should say, a sort of vague perseveration of ideas. When a patient shows such a perseveration it is very important to note what the things are that she perseverates on, because those are the things over which she apparently has least voluntary control, and therefore those are the things that come directly from the unconscious and may later be connected in a general way with her psychosis. She said she wished to get out of the hospital and be in a quiet place. By "a quiet place" she means work. She would do outdoor work. She would like to do gardening and this would cure her. Noise keeps her weight down. As one listens to the patient and jots these things down, they seem to be more or less reasonable, but if one reproduces the trend, they appear to be what is called euphemistical and irrational. If she were out, she could gain weight, and if she could gain weight she would be well. The thought that accompanied her attempt to commit suicide was that she would save the life of her family if she died. And likewise, as long as she lives, the family in some way loses by it. She returns to the discussion of her weight, or continues to make references to it.

The patient's father was a mill worker but never earned very much. When the patient was a little girl (she was 1 of 11 children, just in the center of the family—the 6th of 11) the family used to help and support themselves. Today her favorite food is fruit. She says she eats meat but was never a meat eater. She dislikes milk, but milk does not disagree with her. We see that under mental stress she has an idea that her health and weight are related, that her mental condition can be cured through some change in her weight, that a lot of noise and people about reduce her weight. She wants to raise vegetables and fruit as if she were a little girl back in her family. She thinks that she is taking food away from other patients in this hospital, and that she would be better out of it. Quite obviously this is a projection of her hostile attitude toward other patients, which expresses itself in the threat of wanting, or unconsciously desiring to take food away from other patients. In brief, we deal here with a case—one of the most difficult cases of suicide—in which there is an element of terrific envy combined with hostility in relation to other people. Envy and hostility have definite oral colorings of eating, gaining weight, taking food away from or leaving food for others.

Further study along these lines shows that when this patient was born there were five older people ahead of her, one of them 14 months older, but then for 3 years there were no children. When she was 3 years old a child came, a brother; when she was 4, a sister; when she was 6, a brother; when she was 7 or 8, another brother; and when she was 8 or 9 years old, another brother. In other words, a great many mouths to feed came in quick succession a short time after her birth, and her ego was probably permanently expressed in terms of orality.

Any old jealousy or any old drives of this nature found in patients may mobilize or stir up so much aggression, so much hatred, so much destructive desires[sic], that should these things be sufficiently repressed, sufficiently put down into the unconscious, sooner or later this aggression will turn on the patient, and the aggression will express itself in the form of a suicidal drive.

It has been observed that the method of committing suicide is not infrequently intimately related to the unconscious conflict. Thus, for instance, a woman who in quick succession had a number of brothers to compete with and who develops severe aggressive masculine drives and desires to be like aggressive men, such a woman will commit suicide; if she does so, or makes an attempt, by cutting her wrists, by stabbing herself, she may fantasy that, if she had a pistol, she would shoot herself. We also find that people with strong oral drives, strong drives to feel jealousy or aggression, show an emotional unconscious, preferential selection of the hanging method, or poison. It is not accidental that immediately after her attempt to commit suicide the patient described above had great difficulty in eating, which brought on numerous disturbances.

This case illustrates an attempt to construct schematically the central mechanism of suicide, and we should ask ourselves a hypothetical question: What must happen to an individual immediately after the attempt at suicide is completed and later if the patient recovers from it? If it is true that suicides in general, and some suicides in particular, are expressions of enormous aggressions turned on the individual himself, then the suicidal act is the supreme manifestation of aggression. Following it an individual must feel exactly like the fellow who is very angry and for a long time decides to remain silent, then suddenly gives way to his passion and calls his interlocutor an SOB and socks him in the jaw. Afterwards he quiets down and patches up the break with him, and they go and have a drink and are better friends than ever before, provided that B is not getting ready to sock the other fellow,

A, back. In other words, what we deal with here is a mechanism in which once this aggressive drive—which is almost an instinctual drive as far as its force is concerned—is expressed, whether by socking somebody in the jaw or by socking the self in the jaw, trying to murder the other fellow or murder the self, when this agression or this drive is gratified to some extent, at that moment peace and serenity set in. The great majority of suicidal individuals feel better, more serene, less aggressive inwardly and outwardly after an attempt at suicide that was particularly serious, especially if they succeeded in reaching a state of unconsciousness and were revived. The patient in the case example showed a remarkable improvement after having attempted suicide, almost as good as the improvement some psychotics of the 15th century showed after they were tortured with red-hot irons, or that psychotics in the 1920s showed after treatment by delirium, or that they show today when they are treated by means of convulsions.

One of the problems of suicide that has puzzled us from the beginning is the problem of mental study. I will not speak of this now. To the other problem, the practical inferences of the study, I should like to devote the remainder of this paper. Using the foregoing as introductory material, I should like to continue with a brief outline of the practical conclusions that we arrived at which have not yet been published; such practical conclusions of necessity will have to be psychiatric.

The first aspect that interests all is how to recognize a suicidal drive. You do not have to be a psychoanalyst or a Freudian to recognize that there is such a thing as an unconscious. To say that the patient is suicidal because she played with a knife seems to be natural, but the superscientist will ask: How do you know, maybe she likes to play with the knife because it is glittering and reflects the light? And the doctors will have to wait until she actually sticks the knife in her throat to say she is suicidal. If we must wait for such proofs, we do not understand anything about these clinical conditions. There are certain inferences drawn ex post facto and in sufficient number to justify our conclusion. It is legitimate, scientifically imperative, and clinically inevitable to recognize threats before they become acts. When a patient says consciously, "I wish I were dead; I want to shoot myself," then it is already an act, like any verbalized threat, even though it has not become an act in the sense that the person draws a pistol and shoots himself. If you make a very hostile speech against a fellow and tell what you think of him, and you even think you want to murder him, you get it off your chest and do not feel so badly. Expressions and words of certain threats are definite, actual substitutes for the motor activity in carrying out the act itself. From this point of view, words and threats of suicide, when they become verbalized, are all acts, and it is too late to make a diagnosis—the diagnosis has been made itself.

What are, therefore, the signs that we could take empirically as signs of potential suicide? There is one interesting sign that you can take as a presumptive bit of evidence of a possible suicidal drive if certain mental conditions prevail, that you could find without examining the patient at all. Take a piece of paper and write the word "Patient," and then account for the history of the patient's family. Line up all the brothers and sisters older than the patient above the patient's name, and all the brothers and sisters younger below the patient, and make +5, meaning 5 years older, or −5 for 5 years younger. The patient becomes the center. Study the number of deaths in the family—father, mother, or a relative who was close to the patient, or a brother or sister—who died a natural death at the time the patient was from 4 to 6 years old or 12 to 14 years old. Remember that this patient is a potential suicidal risk if he develops a psychosis, regardless of whether it is a depression or schizophrenia or a hysterical neurosis. There are good explanations for it. I will give you a very brief outline of this. Between 4 and 6 the patient reaches the height of his or her Oedipus complex. Between 12 and 14, when the patient reaches puberty, the Oedipus complex conflicts which rise to their original intensity are added to the intensity of the puberty conflicts. They are totally revived. At that time there is a wish for the death of a rival, be it father, mother, older brother or sister, or younger brother or sister. If it so happens that the rival actually fulfills the wish of the patient at the time the death conflict is extremely severe and dies, then the identification with the death is terrifyingly strong. This is probably the most primordial cause of suicide in the human breast.

Do not forget that the first suicides, be they in the form of human sacrifice or of voluntary reunion with the dead, were all connected with the death of a father, a chieftain, a husband. Later as civilization grew in complexity the fathers followed their sons into their graves. The famous tradition of believing that human beings were sacrificed was practiced again and again. No human being was ever sacrificed in the sense that animals were sacrificed, namely, apprehended and destroyed on the altar. All the stories and the descriptions of human sacrifice are characterized by the fact that the men or women sacrificed were volunteers. In ecstasy they went to be sacrificed. Actually the word "sacrifice" was invented by our civilization. The original man who went to be sacrificed was not going to be sacrificed, he was entering a better and a glorious life. It is important that the sacrificial ceremony always occurred in connection with a death or the celebration of the memory of a dead person.

The terrific drive to join the dead is so extraordinary that we found a number of our patients attempted or committed suicide exactly on the anniversary of the death of a person who had died during the time the patient was 4 to 6 or 12 to 14 years of age. Let me elaborate on this with a story:

A girl in Boston committed suicide by jumping from a window. She was 21. The story of the relatives was the usual one, as follows: "Who would have thought of it? She appeared perfectly normal, was very cheerful, went out with a friend shopping and bought herself a new dress. One would never have suspected it, and the next day she jumped out of the window."

Here we have a very important inference. If you review a great many suicidal cases, you will find that for 24 to 48 hours before they commit the act there is a tendency on the part of these individuals (and they honestly do not think of suicide) to dress up, to put on their best clothes, to look wonderfully well—and they are very friendly. Merely by way of comparison I will mention that no suicide among primitive races is ever committed in any other than a ceremonial way. Before the act is committed the suicidal boy or girl or the woman or man goes into his tent and puts on ceremonial clothes, occasionally he climbs a tree and makes a speech, and then goes to his death. This girl in Boston bought herself a new dress, and she appeared cheerful. There is a tinge of the ceremonial. If it is true that there is a tinge of the ceremonial in it, then this death must be related to the death of a close relative, because the ceremony of joining in death and jumping on the funeral pyre is well known.

A friend of mine wrote me from Boston about this case. He told me the story and asked, "What ceremony is this?" I asked him to give me the history of the girl, and gradually in about 2 weeks the following was uncovered: The girl's mother died 7 years previously, when the girl was 14. The girl started menstruating at the age of 14, a very short time before her mother died. Toward this information my colleague was very friendly but very scientific. He said that my theory of dates was very interesting but that this girl did not die on the same date that her mother died. He said, "If only this had happened, your theory would have been corroborated." So we went back 7 years and calculated the day of the week when this girl's mother died. We found it was Friday, and, what is more, it was Good Friday. The days of the month did not coincide, but the days of the week did. The girl committed suicide in the following manner: On Thursday she bought herself a dress, and the next day she jumped out of a window, 7 years to the day after her mother's death.

In our study of suicide we have found a great number of such instances. This is probably the most potent type of suicidal drive, and it can only be compared to biological inheritances in human beings. It is the typical suicide of the primitive races. I think we inherit the type. The drive to join one's dead under these particular circumstances is great. Hence when you review the anamnesis, the family history, and make a list of all the children and check up on the death of close relatives, if you find that a death did occur during the periods mentioned, be forewarned and study the individual with intensive accuracy in respect to that, particularly if the individual does not appear depressed, because the distinctive work of suicide is that the individual becomes cheerful and happy 24 hours before; consequently, others are apt to be completely unsuspicious of a possible fatal outcome.

This outstanding characteristic, diagnostic in nature, is an outgrowth of what is recognized in observational psychiatry but to which very little attention has been paid from the standpoint of the analyst. We know of so-called depressed individuals who after being many months in a depression begin to appear well and seem to have no desire to commit suicide, but when careful observation is relaxed they suddenly kill themselves. Even in our textbooks we now find occasional reference to the fact that it is a rather dangerous interval in the patient's recovery, the period immediately following the depression. That is the time when the patient may not be able to withstand the suicidal drive. We forget this frequently. Our desire to identify ourselves with our patients, and be depressed when they are depressed, and be as cheerful as can be because the patient is getting better, is so intense that we lose our objective view. The explanation for this is extremely simple. In the first place, what is a depression? In the strictest sense of the word it is self-chastisement. Whereas in a paranoid schizoid trend, the patient feels that someone in the world ought to be killed or ought to be put in jail, in a depression the patient feels he has committed a sin. Depression is a constant lashing of one's own self, an aggression working overtime 24 hours a day. Why this aggression must turn on one's own self is too complicated a question to answer now. Suffice it to say that empirically we know that this individual is unable to handle his aggression in a normal way and has to turn it on himself. This is the major mechanism of depression.

If I chastise myself a great deal and if I try to cut my throat and if I become unconscious, or if I develop a severe illness like typhoid fever or malaria or the flu, I serve my sentence and I can afford to walk out into the world with a sort of martyrlike satisfaction that I got the licking I deserved. If, however, my depression goes on very nicely, and my doctor is very good to me and says, "Don't think you are so bad, you are not bad at all," and gives me so-called encouragement, the chief therapy we know, then the situation is terrible. It is based on the fact that we ourselves are afraid of our own aggression and when we see how the patient handles it we say, "Shut up; don't tell us. You are not so bad after all. You are good. You were a good mother because you have healthy daughters." But when the patient says she has been a bad mother to her daughter, the patient is thinking in terms of how she hates her daughter as she hated her mother, and wants to kill the daughter the way she wanted to kill the mother. And when you tell her she is good, the only thing she can do is to increase her depression to show that your suggestion that she is good is a devilish insinuation and comes from Lucifer. This is where so-called encouragement in depression is courting suicide. But if you let a depression live itself out, down to its utmost depth, short of letting the patient make a fatal attempt at suicide, that depression having served the sentence will recover gradually and normally. If you let the depression go on with encouragement and adulation so that it becomes, in a sense, a psychological prison sentence, then the individual begins to emerge from the depression with severe charges of hostility that have not been lived out on his own self, and the moment this individual is left alone and wants to kill that environment he has been forced into he will kill himself. We could almost measure the dose of illness in terms of so many cubic centimeters, so many cc's in the degree of hostility almost lived out and so many cc's to be lived out. We can and ought to be aware of this mechanism, to be able to tell the dose of suffering, or self-chastisement, so as not to push the depression out too soon and therefore make the patient a candidate for suicide. So when a patient is profoundly depressed, do not tell him he is not going to be depressed. It is like telling a fasting martyr of the 13th Century that it is perfectly all right, but after a 10-day fast you will give him a good meal. The idea of a good meal will be enough to make him at once go to his father confessor and impose upon himself another 40 days of fasting. You increase the depression. It is paradoxical, as you see, from the standpoint of the fact that our reasonable, rational attitude is totally at variance with, if not contradictory to, the logic of the emotional constellations of the mentally sick individual; but the mentally sick individual is mentally sick because it is an emotional logic disrespective of any rational logic, which forms the weakest link in human relationships.

Now I will illustrate one more practical thing. It is this: There is a tendency, already mentioned without pointing it out deliberately, to believe that suicidal individuals are individuals who in the past showed tendencies to depression and at one time or another might have expressed a desire to die. I claim that the great majority of suicidal cases throughout the history of suicide, inside and outside hospitals, mentally sick and nonmentally sick, are impulsive, not premeditated. By this I mean that the idea of killing oneself and the act of carrying it out may be separated by no more than 24 hours. Hence the psychiatrist cannot be sure that he will see signs of a suicidal drive long in advance, as the drive may not appear until the act is being commited, or perhaps 24 hours before. If the individual survives, he will find for you an excellent explanation for this act that may date back 5 or 6 years. Man restored to himself is a social animal. I think the psychiatrist ought to say that man is an explaining animal and that this explanation would be rationalization.

There is one other sign of the possibility or potentiality of suicide, and that is the degree of aggression that the individual presents and the degree of gratification of this aggression that this individual obtains in life. Take the story of a man who is a big broker, and his tendency all through his career was to be a successful broker and make killings—to make a fortune and lose it and then make another, lose it, and make another. The main thing was to outsmart the other fellow. One broker says, "I had a hunch and tried it; the other fellow said 'No' but I went ahead and did it." In this case there are two different objects: One is to make money, and the other is to make it by killing the fellow who would not do it. You see the element of rivalry. You find a broker who does it nicely and lives constantly on his aggression, then develops stomachaches, which are associated with a drop in the market, and this man becomes a frightened suicidal risk. He has been killing all his life, and suddenly he cannot kill anymore. Chopping wood, shooting, hunting will cure him quicker than putting him into a room at rest. It is very irrational, but that is how it works. Give him a good knife or an ax, and he will take vengeance on the trees and disfigure his garden, and feel better; he will say the physical exercise did it because all his life he has been a broker and sat in the office and that is all it amounts to, and the doctor, who is a good doctor, says, "Use your muscles" and now he feels better. That is the rationalization. You may find an individual who, during most of his life, is passive, quite easy, who takes it on the chin and then goes on placidly again, taking it on. If this individual suffers a loss, you may be almost certain that he will not commit suicide just because he has always been a passive type of individual. But if you go into his history carefully, you will see that his passivity has always been associated with self-punishment, that he would passively develop a throat ache, or headaches, that his passivity was not just a natural passivity of a sleeping child but the passivity of an individual who became passive because he was afraid to kick others but kicked himself by developing headaches and all sorts of other aches. If this man is willfully being taken care of, he will accumulate so much aggression that some day at 5 o'clock in the morning he will hang himself.

And so there is the question of dosing the depression. From this standpoint I would say that there is not a single clinical variety that we know in our psychiatric classifications that springs from suicidal drives, not a single one that springs from actually carrying out suicidal ideas. I will not go as far as Karl Menninger did and speak of all illnesses as full suicides, or partial suicides, and make the whole field of suicide a biological operation. It is rather remarkable that this conception should appear in the mind of a midwesterner, and that I who am a Russian—and the traditional Russian is bent on destruction—should come out with the cheerful and altogether American idea that to attribute all forms of illness to suicidal drives is too Russian for me even though I were in Kansas.

JOURNAL EDITOR'S NOTE

This interesting and instructive paper, presented by Dr. Zilboorg (1890–1959) at Saint Elizabeth's Hospital in Washington, D.C., on August 27, 1938, was found recently by the Editor among the Zilboorg-Friedman Archives. The Archives—a collection of psychoanalytic, anthropologic, and forensic (police) suicidal materials from the 1930s (Friedman, 1967, 1968; Heiman, 1975)—are located at the Laboratory for the Study of Life-Threatening Behavior, University of California at Los Angeles. The paper is printed now not only for its obvious historic interest but also because of its keen heuristic value.

REFERENCES

Friedman, P. Suicide among police: A study of 93 suicides among New York City policemen, 1934–1940. In E. S. Shneidman (Ed.), Essays in self-destruction. *New York: Science House, 1967.*

Friedman, P. A history of the Zilboorg Archives. In N. L. Farberow (Ed.), Proceedings of the Fourth International Conference for Suicide Prevention. *Los Angeles: Delmar Publishing Co., 1968.*

Heiman, M. Police suicides revisited. Suicide, *1975, 5, 5–20.*

6. On the "Longing to Die"

Kate Friedlander

BIOGRAPHICAL NOTE

Kate Friedlander (1903–1949) was born in Austria and obtained the first of three medical degrees at Innsbruck at the age of twenty-four. She soon moved to Berlin where she earned the second, and underwent psychoanalytic training at the Berlin Psychoanalytic Society and Institute. Forced out of Germany because of political developments, she moved to London and sat for her third medical degree in 1936 at Edinburgh.

She was warmly received in the British Psychoanalytic Society, and though productive there, struggled with the Kleinian theory of development. Though she and other continental analysts were grateful to be accepted by the British Society, a tension arose between scientific disagreement on one hand, and indebtedness to the English analysts for hospitality and life-saving assistance on the other. Friedlander presented this paper at the 1938 Paris Congress, apparently to "clarify her own ideas on the death instinct" (Lantos 1966).

Friedlander became an influential figure in the training of child therapists, and in child treatment, especially that of delinquents. She died at the age of forty-six from carcinoma of the lung.

COMMENT

Though Friedlander does not cite Karl Menninger's 1933 paper, she takes up the third vector of his suicidal triad, the wish to die. In the unconscious the wish to die is inextricably entangled with the wish to sleep; a fact reflected in Greek mythology—the gods of sleep and death, Hypnos and Thanatos, were brothers. The child's conception of death is different from that of adults; child study supports the view that at the level of primary process thinking there is no conception of death at all, and that when death occurs in dreams and fantasies, it occurs only symbolically and stands for something else (Rado

Kate Friedlander, "On the 'Longing to Die.'" *International Journal of Psychoanalysis* 21 (1940):416–426. Reprinted by permission.

1933). The wish to sleep in suicide was later elaborated by Bertram Lewin (1950).

For an expanded view of the connection between sleep and suicide see Edwin Shneidman (1967).

REFERENCES

Lantos, B. 1966. Kate Friedlander. In Alexander, F., Eisenstein, S., and Grotjan, M., eds., Psychoanalytic Pioneers. *New York: Basic Books.*

Lewin, B. D. 1950. The Psychoanalysis of Elation. *New York: Psychoanalytic Quarterly.*

Rado, S. 1933. The Psychoanalysis of Pharmacothymia (Drug Addiction). Psychoanalytic Quarterly *2:1–23.*

Shneidman, E. 1967. Sleep and Self-Destruction, a Phenomenonological Approach. In Shneidman, E., ed., Essays in Self Destruction. *New York: Science House.*

■

CONSIDERING that attempts at suicide are not uncommon during analysis and that they represent a very serious complication, it is rather astonishing that the literature on the subject is not more extensive. I am therefore venturing in the present paper to describe the suicidal mechanism of a single case. I do this only because I am of the opinion that this particular mechanism is not uncommon and often actually results in suicide.

In psycho-analytical literature we find at least two ways of approach to the problem of suicide.

The one, which I shall do no more than mention as it has no actual bearing on the problem which I want to discuss here, is the psycho-analytical interpretation of statistics (19), taking into account different cultures and different circumstances. We know that in certain cultures suicide is considered to be a respectable act and that therefore suicide is not necessarily a sign of illness and we also know that in certain circumstances the number of suicides may suddenly increase and include otherwise healthy people. These considerations have not necessarily any bearing on the mechanism of the suicidal act. The fact that in certain circumstances normal people may commit suicide does not exclude the possibility that under these special conditions mechanisms come into play which in normal circumstances are only to be found in neurotic people.

In order to find out what particular mechanism is involved one has to study the mechanism in any given case, and this is the second way of approach to the problem.

The question which I want to examine is whether the melancholic type of suicide is the basis for every suicide committed or whether there are cases or perhaps a whole group of cases in which other mechanisms are the basis for suicide or attempts at suicide.

Before the publication of 'Mourning and Melancholia' (7) it was assumed that various libidinal impulses may lead to suicide. Ernest Jones (14, 15) emphasized that apart from coprophilic, sadistic and incestuous tendencies, certain libidinal phantasies, concerning for instance the anal conception of childbirth, may be acted out in the love-condition of dying together. Jones furthermore expressed the opinion that 'the idea of personal death does not exist for the unconscious, being always replaced by that of sexual communion or of birth'. The question of suicide was also discussed in Vienna in 1910 (25, 5). Various libidinal factors, such as disappointment in love, feelings of guilt, a desire to be punished or revenge, were stated to lead to suicide. Sadger (20) expressed the current opinion very well when he said: 'Nobody will kill himself who has not entirely given up the hope of being loved.' Freud (9) ended the discussion by stating that the main problem had not been solved, namely, what makes it possible for the very strong impulse of self-preservation to be overcome. He was then in doubt whether libidinal disappointment alone would be sufficient to overcome the instinct to live or whether the ego can resign itself out of ego-motives. Freud (7) solved the question two years later in his paper 'Mourning and Melancholia'. The melancholiac who either in reality or in phantasy has suffered the loss of a beloved object is unable to free his libido from the object and its associations. Owing to the prevalent type of narcissistic object-choice, the lost object of the melancholiac becomes introjected. Furthermore, in melancholia regression has taken place to the oral-sadistic phase, so that ambivalence, and with it sadism, are pronounced. The aggression directed against the original object becomes directed against the individual's self or rather against the introjected object. Owing to the severity of the super-ego, in which destructive impulses are prevalent, the patient is forced to destroy himself.

This explanation solved a number of hitherto obscure problems and for years no further advance was made beyond confirmation of the validity of this mode of suicide. Apparently until recently it was assumed that every suicidal act, whether it happens in a melancholic or in a neurotic case, even in hysteria, is based on the same mechanism of aggressions directed against the individual's self and the prevalence of destructive impulses over libidinal ones (2, 3, 4, 13, 17).

In recent years the question has sometimes arisen whether mechanisms other than the melancholic ones may also be responsible for certain types of suicide. Garma (12) stresses the importance of the variable significance of the conception of death in suicide and gives a very valuable scheme in which the libidinal factors involved in suicide are clearly shown. M. Schmideberg (21) emphasizes the importance of libidinal factors and maintains that it is very often 'not the "death instinct" which drives a person to suicide, but strong emotional disturbances—especially anxiety—which interfere with the self-preserving instinct.' It is not quite clear to me whether she believes that in a melancholic case there is also no genuine wish for death, or whether she means that suicidal mechanisms can be different in different cases. No attempt is made to classify the mechanisms in different cases but the various libidinal impulses which may drive to suicide or to substitutes for suicide are explained.

Zilboorg (24) doubts whether all motivations for suicide are to be explained by the classical formula and describes one mechanism which seems to him to be different and for which he finds parallels in the rites of primitive people: namely, the compulsion to become identified with a dead person who has died before the mechanism of identification is completed. Zilboorg's idea is apparently that apart from the classical melancholic type of suicide there is at least this other type in which the active impulse to die is based on a libidinal impulse.

A clinical classification of suicidal cases has been attempted by Federn (5, 6), who points out that there are two groups of abnormal characters found in patients who attempt or commit suicide: people who are inclined to be depressed and people with an inclination to be addicts. To these two groups belong hysterical, obsessional neurotic and neurasthenic patients or even people with no outspoken neurosis at all. To the group of the addicts belong not only really addicted people, but all people who react in the same particular way. The immediate reaction to a frustration is with this type of person an increase of tension until the tension is unbearable. The addict thinks that it is better to die than to go without the thing for which he craves. The suffering is not fictitious but real; it leads to an increased want and death seems to be pleasurable in relieving the unbearable tension. The depression of these people is not as deep as in melancholiacs, but this type is less able to stand tension and suffering which the melancholiac at least partly enjoys. Federn (6) states that the melancholiac has to suffer from that which he has lost, whilst the addict has to suffer for that which he cannot get. Federn's idea apparently is that the reason for suicide is different in these two groups, but it is not clear to me whether he means that the suicidal mechanism is in both groups aggression directed against the individual's self. It seems to me that there is a decisive difference between the mechanisms of the two groups: the addict type wants to die because that seems to him to be more pleasurable than to stand the tension; death is desired in accordance with the pleasure principle.

The case I am going to take has some resemblance to what Federn describes as the addict type. I want to prove that the mechanism which eventually led to the attempts at suicide was due to libidinal impulses.

The patient is a man of twenty-nine years of age in good external circumstances. During the time when the attempts at suicide happened no disturbing external event took place and the patient did not try to give rationalizations in the form of external circumstances as reason for his attempts. He has a masochistic character. The conscious conflict which drives him to attempt suicide is the following. He has a brother who is eight years his senior, and of whom he is jealous: his brother has had so many girls, probably about 200, whilst he, the patient, cannot even get one. His mother therefore respects the elder brother much more than him. He believes that his mother has the same attitude towards him as his brother has: namely, that for him it is not necessary to have a girl. It therefore does not help him just to find a girl, because his brother and his mother would only sneer at him and find the girl not attractive enough. He therefore prefers to stay ill and have no girl at all than to be healthy and be satisfied with a girl who would be inferior to his brother's friends. As he cannot get a girl, he wants to die.

I must point out that behind the Oedipus situation which expresses itself in this conflict lies an oral fixation caused by oral cravings and an oral disappointment in his mother. Hatred against mother and brother are openly expressed with phantasies about their death without any conscious feeling of guilt. The feeling of guilt is compensated by oral and anal frustrations which the patient imposes upon himself. He is extremely ascetic in his food, although he can experience pleasure from eating, and he does not allow himself to spend a penny on pleasurable things. But he gives comparatively large sums of money to a charity, which, interestingly enough, is for buying milk for poor children.

His sexual activities are somewhat limited. He has masturbated since he was fourteen, at times with homosexual and beating phantasies. Occasionally he visits prostitutes.

His first attempt at suicide was, as he called it himself, a staging of a suicide. He closed the windows and door of his room and turned on the gas stove. He had heard that on breathing in gas one becomes drowsy and sleepy, and he intended to go on until he became drowsy and then wanted to stop it. The smell of the gas was noticed by his landlady and he had to interrupt his performance.

Some time later he began to be interested in veronal, as he had heard that it was a drug which could induce sleep without bad after-effects. He studied the action and dosage of the drug carefully from books on pharmacology. He then bought a large amount of it in France, where he could get it cheap and without a prescription. He had read that 40–50 grs., that is 3–4 grm., was the lethal dose. One day he took 28 grs., that is 2 grm., in broad daylight when he was sitting in the park. He did not feel any effect from it. He then took 36 grs., that is 2.5 grm., a little less than what he considered to be the lethal dose. He slept for two days with interruption and felt the after-effects for nearly a week. Some months later he again took 36 grs., that is 2.5 grm., in two doses each of six tablets. Apart from these two serious attempts, he twice took 18 grs., that is, 1.3 grm., in order to sleep over the week-end. Ordinarily he never takes any drugs at all.

The occasions on which he attempted suicide were very similar. The first attempt happened one week-end; the two serious attempts happened at Christmas and at Easter when he would not be coming to analysis for four days. At the same time his brother was away, once on a visit to his mother who lives twelve hours' distance away, and once on a visit to a couple, where the wife was interested in his brother and the patient was slightly interested in her too. On other occasions, when the brother was away on business or I was away on holidays, he did not make any attempt and the thought of suicide did not occur to him.

The psychic situation which induces the patient to make the attempt is in every case the same. Consciously he cannot bear the thought of the time which is in front of him, each time four days, without a girl. The thought of the brother makes him furious and the only way out seems to be for him to go to sleep. He desires to sleep for four days without interruption. He has no conscious thought then that he wants to end his life by taking the drug and actually takes a little less than what is considered to be the lethal dose. He has a vague idea that afterwards everything will be perfectly all right. He has no anxiety and no doubt as to how the drug is going to act. Everything is engulfed in the craving for the drug which will make him sleep and in dwelling on how pleasurable that will be.

Analysis reveals the various mechanisms involved in this attempt at suicide:

(1) By killing himself he can take revenge on his brother, his mother and his analyst. His brother will feel guilty because he has left him alone. His mother, who in reality only cares for his bodily welfare and not for his happiness, will be terribly upset about his death. He can prove by his death to what it is that analysis really leads.

(2) He is able to satisfy his intense oral craving only if it results in death, that is, if he pays for it with his death. The mode of his attempts, namely that he takes drugs, is here significant. His description of his longing to take the drug in this particular situation is very similar to that of an addict.

(3) The act is also a phantasy that by going to sleep he becomes united with his brother as well as with his mother. Probably this union occurs by way of introjection, as various oral phantasies seem to prove.

(4) When he was very small, probably under two years of age, he used sometimes to cry helplessly for his mother to come back, until he fell asleep. When he woke up, his mother was there. This phantasy also shows clearly that what he really wants is not to die but to sleep in order to find his mother when he wakes up again. That is why it is so important to him to take a large amount of the drug and not simply two tablets morning and night. He does not wish to wake up at all during the four days before he can come to analysis again.

(5) There are various phantasies which show that he has great pleasure in imagining what his brother and mother will say when he is dead. Then they will appreciate how much he has suffered and how badly they have treated him. It is significant that at that time he did not want to have a certain amount of money in his name. In case he should commit suicide he does not want his brother and his mother to pay death duties and for that reason to be sorry about his death. He wants to be mourned because mother and brother loved him and for that reason only.

To sum up, the factors involved in this suicidal mechanism are revenge, satisfaction of his strong oral desires, and the phantasy of being saved by his loving mother. As a phantasy, these factors, which are without doubt derived from libidinal impulses only, are by no means rare; on the contrary these elements or some of them, such as taking revenge or the wish to be saved from a dangerous situation, are most common. But patients who very often express such suicidal phantasies may never actually attempt suicide, especially if they become conscious of their libidinal wishes.

The question which has to be solved is, therefore: What special forces are working in this case so that the phantasy is acted out in this dangerous way? In trying to solve the problem which I raised at the beginning, we have to ask the question: Are the forces which drive the man to commit suicide derived from destructive impulses?—which means: Are they aggressions directed against his own self? Does he really want to kill introjected objects or is another mechanism at work?

The patient's aggressions are openly directed against his real love objects, his brother and his mother, and are expressed in many ways. As I have mentioned before, his feelings of guilt are compensated in such a way that he is able to express his hatred against his love objects in phantasy as well as in reality. The patient has no inclination to reproach himself and he does not do so; he does not believe himself to be inferior and therefore not worthy to live. In his moods of depression he reproaches the world and especially his love objects and is waiting for them to give him what he wants. The patient is entirely fixated to his infantile objects, but not only in phantasy. His only real object-relations to-day are those with his relatives, his brother and his mother. Of course both of them have infantile traces and he does not see them as they really are. But it is not only the infantile imago of these people that exists in him; on the contrary, he is still attracted to the living persons. It is significant that he can only have a sexual relationship if his brother and mother are in another town, the further away the better. Apparently he is then able to shift some of his object libido on to other objects.

Furthermore I think it is clear that the patient's ultimate aim is not to destroy himself. He merely wants to sleep in order to wake up to a better life in which all his wishes are fulfilled. Nor does he want to destroy his brother and his mother, since before his attempt at suicide these objects are not introjected, but exist for him in the outside world. In the act of taking in the drug he introjects his beloved objects, but this introjection serves a libidinal aim, namely, union with his mother and not her destruction. Here we see some resemblance between this mechanism and the mechanism of the ecstatic suicide, in which the aim is to be united with the dead lover or with God.

So it seems to be that the force which drives the patient to act out his phantasy is not derived from destructive impulses. To express it in a simpler way, the patient does not want to destroy himself. Actually his attempts at suicide are very pleasurable and when he comes to his analyst after such an attempt he is elated, like somebody who has achieved what he wants and not as if he has failed. If he really wanted to die he would have failed in his purpose.

Nevertheless his attempts are very serious and self-destruction might easily be the result. The astonishing fact is that, although the patient clearly does not want to die, he makes his attempts in a rather dangerous way. He takes a large amount of the drug, which might kill him, especially as he is living alone and might stay in his room for days without being missed.

The question arises why the patient does not take more precautions against dying if it is true that he does not want his attempt to succeed. And now we see the interesting fact that he does take precautions but that these precautions are not sufficient. He takes a little less than the lethal dose. If the lethal dose is 40 grs., he takes 36 grs. He leaves the window open because his mother told him once that fresh air is healthy. When he wakes up after two days he rings up either myself or his medical practitioner. These precautions seem to be and really are childish and incompatible with the high intelligence of the patient. But this strange behaviour becomes clearer if one is aware of the fact that somehow the patient has a conviction that whatever he does his mother is sure to save him. This conviction is so strong that it severely disturbs his sense of reality, and this disturbance of his sense of reality is the one factor which lets the patient act out his phantasy in such a dangerous way. Instead of facing reality he still has an infantile belief in the omnipotence of his parents. The important thing is not what he himself does but what he expects to be his mother's wish.

With this consideration the mechanism of his attempt at suicide becomes clearer; what we see here is a *'Kinderselbstmord'*, the attempt at suicide of a child. In the suicidal phantasies of children the same libidinal factors are at work as we have seen in this case. If we take as an example the suicidal phantasy of Tom Sawyer which was described analytically by Schneider (22), we see that Tom and his friends want to die because they have experienced a disappointment in love. They want to take revenge and are very much interested in the mourning of the grown-ups, who will at last understand what good boys they are. The whole procedure of being alone on the island and having the whole town looking for them is filled with a great amount of libidinal satisfaction. By means of the phantasy of death the lost love relationship is restored again: afterwards everything will be all right. The same mechanism is at the basis of the usual suicidal phantasies of children and also, as we have seen, at the basis of the phantasy of this patient. By means of his death everything will come all right again—of course he will be alive to enjoy it afterwards. Actual suicide in children before puberty is extremely rare. Probably one of the most important reasons for this is not that children do not make attempts at suicide, but that these attempts are such that they do not lead to death, because children are unable to obtain adequate means for it and also because they are looked after and prevented from doing dangerous things. The attempts at suicide made by children usually appear to be in play.

The patient whose attempts at suicide I have described acts out the suicide of a child. As he is grown up, he has adequate means at hand for committing suicide. As his sense of reality is disturbed on account of the fact that he still has an infantile belief that whatever happens his mother will save him, the precautions which he takes are inadequate. His fixation to his strong oral desires, which lead him to this particular mode of suicide, also work in the direction of making the attempts more dangerous.

In summarizing, let me state that, in this particular case, the answer to the problem I raised at the beginning is the following: the 'longing to die' does not express the patient's wish to destroy himself, but serves as the expression of a libidinal phantasy. As mentioned above, the occurrence of such libidinal phantasies has been described by various writers, such as Jones (14, 15), Garma (12), Chadwick (4), M. Schmideberg (21), Bischler (2), Sterba (23). No attempt has so far been made to confront the recognized conception of suicide as the acting out of a libidinal phantasy with the recognized conception of suicide as a depressive mechanism. The mechanism of suicide in melancholia is such that the patient wants to destroy himself because the object with which he is at war is introjected and represented by his own super-ego. Therefore only self-destruction can serve the aim of the melancholiac. In the case which I have described, and also in children who have suicidal phantasies, the conflict lies not with the super-ego but with objects in the outside world. Therefore the aim is not self-destruction, but libidinal gratification by those objects by way of an attempt at suicide. Self-destruction may be the result in the child because it is not yet able to judge reality and in the adult on account of a severe disturbance of his sense of reality.

In my opinion the mechanism I have described is a mechanism not only in one particular case but one which lies at the basis of quite a number of others. The importance of an attempt to classify the various mechanisms of suicide which we meet in our patients is perhaps not so much of theoretical as of clinical interest, since the attitude of the analyst to an attempt at suicide by a patient has to vary according to the mechanism which is at the basis of the given case.

REFERENCES

1. *Bernfeld, S. (1929). 'Selbstmord',* Z. psychoanal. Päd., *3, 355.*
2. *Bischler, W. (1936). 'Selbstmord und Opfertod',* Imago, *22, 177.*

3. *Chadwick, M. (1929). 'Notes upon the Fear of Death',* Int. J. Psycho-Anal., *10, 321.*
4. *Chadwick, M. (1929). 'Über Selbstmordphantasien',* Z. psychoanal. Päd., *3, 409.*
5. *Federn, P. (1929). 'Die Diskussion über "Selbstmord", insbesondere "Schüler-Selbstmord", im Wiener Psychoanalytischen Verein im Jahre 1910',* Z. psychoanal. Päd., *3, 333.*
6. *Federn, P. (1929). 'Selbtsmordprophylaxe in der Analyse',* Z. psychoanal. Päd., *3, 379.*
7. *Freud, S. (1917). 'Mourning and Melancholia',* Coll. Papers, *4, 152.*
8. *Freud, S. (1915). 'Thoughts for the Times on War and Death',* Coll. Papers, *4, 288.*
9. *Freud, S. (1910). 'Schlusswort der Selbstmord-Diskussion',* Ges. Schr., *3, 323.*
10. *Freud, S. (1923).* The Ego and the Id.
11. *Friedjung, J. K. (1929). 'Zur Kenntnis kindlicher Selbstmordimpulse',* Z. psychoanal. Päd., *3, 426.*
12. *Garma, A. (1937). 'Psychologie des Selbstmordes',* Imago, *23, 63.*
13. *Glover, J. (1922). 'Notes on the Psychopathology of Suicide' (Author's Abstract),* Int. J. Psycho-Anal., *3, 507.*
14. *Jones, E. (1911). 'On "Dying Together" ',* Essays in Applied Psycho-Anal., *99.*
15. *Jones, E. (1912). 'An Unusual Case of "Dying Together" ',* Essays in Applied Psycho-Anal., *106.*
16. *Kalischer, H. (1929). 'Leben und Selbstmord eines Zwangsdiebes',* Z. psychoanal. Päd., 2, 363.
17. Klein, M. (1935). 'A Contribution to the Psychogenesis of Manic-Depressive States', Int. J. Psycho-Anal., *16, 145.*
18. *Klein, M. (1932).* The Psycho-Analysis of Children.
19. *Peller-Roubiczek, L. E. (1936). 'Zur Kenntnis der Selbstmordhandlung',* Imago, *22, 81.*
20. *Sadger, I. (1929). 'Ein Beitrag zum Problem des Selbstmords',* Z. psychoanal. Päd., *3, 423.*
21. *Schmideberg, M. (1936). 'A Note on Suicide',* Int. J. Psycho-Anal., *17, 1.*
22. *Schneider, E. (1929). 'Die Todes- und Selbstmordphantasien Tom Sawyers' ',* Z. psychoanal. Päd., *3, 389.*
23. *Sterba, E. (1929). 'Der Schülerselbstmord in André Gide's Roman "Die Falschmünzer" ',* Z. psychoanal. Päd., *3, 400.*
24. *Zilboorg, G. (1935). 'Zum Selbstmordproblem',* Int. Z. Psycho-anal., *21, 100.*
25. *Various Authors (1910).* Über den Selbstmord insbesondere den Schüler-Selbstmord *(Diskussionen des Wiener psychoanal. Vereins, Heft 1).*

7. Suicide as Wish Fulfillment

Ives Hendrick

BIOGRAPHICAL NOTE

Ives Hendrick (1898–1972) trained in medicine at Yale, in psychiatry at the Boston Psychopathic Hospital (later known as the Massachusetts Mental Health Center), in psychoanalysis at the Berlin Psychoanalytic Institute, and then came to Harvard Medical School for thirty-five years until his retirement in 1965 as clinical professor of psychiatry. He was a charter and founding member of the Boston Psychoanalytic Institute, served as its president in 1946–1947, and as president of the American Psychoanalytic Association between 1953 and 1955.

He liked students. Often carelessly dressed, his steel-rimmed spectacles and thick eyebrows shadowed by the smoke of a cigarette, he would relax in his easy chair and listen to the presentation of a case. His skill at promoting discussion in small student groups was extraordinary, and, as the animation rose and understanding deepened, Hendrick would punctuate the air with a characteristic gesture of the hand, as though marking the rhythm of exciting music.

His teaching and his writing centered on the refined observation of clinical detail. With those who spun theories before they studied the patient he had limited patience. In this spirit he published a number of lucidly original articles. His teaching, clinical skill, and writing were all achieved in spite of poor health that burdened him from youth.

COMMENT

In depressed patients who commit suicide, Freud (1915) argued that identification with a lost object lay at the heart of the matter. In this detailed case presentation and discussion, Hendrick suggests another mechanism in suicide: that identification is the purpose *of self-destruction. In contemporary psychoanalytic language, one might say that the aim of suicide can be*

Hendrick, Ives. "Suicide as Wish Fulfillment." *Psychiatric Quarterly* 14 (1940):30–42. Reprinted by permission.

fusion (primary identification, or incorporation) with another (Sandler 1960; Meissner 1981). In cases such as Hendrick's, there is a regressive reactivation of primary fusion and merger of the self-representation with that of an object. (Ordinarily, primary identification is a phenomenon of early childhood which takes place before the capacity for self-object differentiation is developmentally established.) Hendrick suggests that some patients do not attempt suicide because they feel they deserve to die because of their aggression, but that they wish to die in order to escape it. He disagrees with Karl Menninger (see chapter 2 above) that self-punishment is an essential component in every self-destructive act.

Many suicides probably combine Hendrick's regressive phenomenon with the wish to be punished. His perspective, often overlooked, is an important one, inasmuch as the self-object boundaries of many suicidal patients are fluid (Maltsberger 1993).

REFERENCES

Freud, S. 1915. Mourning and Melancolia. Standard Edition, *14:237–260.*

Maltsberger, J. T. 1993. Confusions of the Body, the Self, and Others in Suicidal States. In Leenaars, A., ed., Suicidology: Essays in Honor of Edwin S. Shneidman, *Northvale, N.J.: Jason Aronson.*

Meissner, W. W. 1981. Internalization in Psychoanalysis. *New York: International Universities Press.*

Sandler, J. 1960. On the Concept of the Superego. The Psychoanalytic Study of the Child *15:128–162.*

■

THE SUBJECT of this paper is an unconscious phantasy which was acted out in an almost successful suicidal attempt. The analysis of this phantasy, and of its relationship to a psychotic component of the patient's previous life, disclosed fundamental differences between the mechanism of this suicide and those which occur during depressions.

HISTORY AND ANALYSIS

The patient was an unmarried, professional woman, 38 years of age. Two and one-half years before treatment began, she had taken 20 allonal tablets with suicidal intent and was found asleep in a woods. After a brief hospitalization, she resumed her work and her social activities. Two years later she deliberately "rolled off" a high bridge very late one night into the icy waters of a large river with the intention of drowning herself.

It is the analysis of this second suicidal attempt which primarily concerns us here. An amnesia for the 16 hours which preceded it was nearly complete. The only recollections of this experience were that she had left her home in her automobile early the preceding morning; she had "driven in circles" all day; she had had nothing to eat; late that night she had found herself on this unfamiliar bridge several hundred miles from home, and left her car at the entrance to the bridge. She learned later that a passerby had seen her fall from the bridge. She was rescued, hospitalized for two weeks, and spent the subsequent six months in her mother's home. During this period she had avoided all people, including her family, was mentally unable to resume her work or normal recreations, and had been preoccupied with phantasies, anxieties, and hallucinations of a predominantly schizophrenic type.

The patient had always manifested pronounced schizoid characteristics. In some sharply-limited aspects of her life before the suicidal attempts she had been psychotic, but this had been not at all obvious. She was attractive in superficial relationships, and had achieved a well-deserved success in a profession requiring good adjustment to both children and adults. She had enjoyed a modest amount of social life, chiefly but not entirely among unmarried women, and had demonstrated special ability for artistic sublimation. She had rationalized her unconscious identification with the prohibitive attitudes of a dogmatically religious and very dominant mother, by a rigidly imposed intellectual concept of how life ought to be lived.

The patient was the third of four siblings. A brother, two years older than she, had served as an aviator during the World War, attained the status of "ace," and had been shot down and killed in aerial combat. His heroic death was the final event of an unusually hero-like life. During childhood, school and college, he had been idolized by family and friends, especially by his mother and the patient, not only for his popularity and genuine achievements in scholarship, sports, and leadership among men, but also for his Galahad-like virtues. He had had, so far as his family knew, no love affairs. This had always distressed the patient and she passionately hoped that he had enjoyed relations with women in France before his heroic death. When angered by her mother during the analysis, the patient taunted her viciously by suggesting this possibility.

Her own deeper attitude toward erotic sexuality had, however, closely resembled the asceticism of her brother, although this was intellectually denied. As a young woman she had been engaged four years without a kiss to a pious youth who was highly approved by her mother. But immediately after the news of her brother's death she had renounced him, left home and in a distant city indulged her sexuality promiscuously; during these relationships she always phantasied that her brother had behaved in a similar way in France. In later years, she had seriously considered marrying several lovers, but all these men had seemed to her either intellectually or socially very inferior to herself. Her two strongest affects for men were contempt for those she came to know well, and a constant fear of any superior man's evincing his "male conceit." Her attitude to her kindly but unambitious father had never been free from contempt for his lack of worldly achievement or of authority with her mother.

As soon as these dominant features of her heterosexual life and family attitudes were clear to the analyst, the patient was told: "The only man you have really loved is your brother. You treat those with whom you have tried to make love as though they were your father—not so worthwhile as yourself and not so worthwhile as the rest of the family." Her reaction to this interpretation enabled us to work out some of the repressed phantasies associated with her second suicidal effort. For almost all of this material there had been complete amnesia before the interpretation.

She recalled that before leaving her apartment on the morning before she dropped from the bridge, she had decided to commit suicide in one of two ways: either by repeating the program of her first attempt by going into a woods, taking a lethal drug, and burying herself; or else by taking a boat to Europe and drowning herself in the ocean when exactly half way across. She had prepared herself by donning special clothes including a sweater of a special shade of blue. She had decided to arrange her death so that the family would not learn of it for two months and there would be no funeral. She recalled several forgotten incidents of the 16-hour drive, and very vividly the experience of driving for hours " 'round and 'round in circles." She did not at first recall how or why she finally arrived in the neighborhood of the bridge, but remembered vividly striking the water on her ear.

Her associations during the recovery of these memories showed that many details were reminiscences of the death of her brother. His airplane was reported to have fallen in a woods, and he had been buried there. This had occurred in Europe; and when she had accompanied her mother to Europe, she had refused to visit the brother's grave because she hated her mother's self-glorification of herself for being the mother of a hero (unconsciously her mother's pride that her son was too fine to be sexual). The special clothes she had worn after deciding on suicide were associated with tomboy activities which had been conspicuous traits of her childhood; and the shade of blue of the sweater approximated a shade she adored because it was the color of a sweater worn while playing baseball with her brother. The idea that she would not have her death discovered for two months because she did not wish to be the object of her family's sanctimonious hypocrisy at funerals was a rationalization of the thought that her brother had died without a funeral, and that the family had not learned of his death until exactly two months after it had occurred. Her memories of driving in circles and striking on her ear were now associated with vivid visualizations of the airplane falling in circles and striking diagonally on its wing.

Thus the patient discovered that she had wished to die in the same way her brother had died; that she had dressed in clothes associated with her childhood identification with him in playing baseball; that her two original plans for suicide were derived from the place he died—in the woods in Europe; that the family would learn the news after the same interval of time which had elapsed after the hero's death; and that she had imitated the falling airplane in her 16 hours of driving in circles, and "remembered" striking on her ear because the airplane's wing had struck the ground.

Further work confirmed this amazing clarification of her amnesia. She later recalled with great difficulty passing through a certain town just before she came to the bridge. She remembered that she had been there before. A man she had not previously mentioned in the analysis lived there. She had wanted to telephone him and had stopped off to look up his number. Years previously she had spent several weekends with him. Yet, in contrast to her relations with other men during this period of her life, they never had sexual intercourse ("He was very brotherly!"). A few days after her attempted suicide he had visited her. After his departure she immediately seduced the constant attention of a man living in the hospital, and during this same period developed the obsession that the only way she could resume life among other people would be to become a gangster's woman. These phantasies were associated with a Victory Parade she had witnessed shortly after hearing of her brother's death. She had been watching army airplanes flying overhead; they had recalled her brother, and she was suddenly seized by a feeling of overpowering "lewdness." This experience had led directly to her seeking defloration and a period of sexual promiscuity.

This material showed that the place of the suicidal attempt had been determined by its being the home of a man who had awakened tender conscious feelings she had had for her brother, and the corresponding inhibition of erotic behavior. His reappearance at the hospital had aroused the repressed sexual love for her brother, which was expressed in seductive behavior and phantasies which duplicated those stimulated years before by the airplanes at the Victory Parade. Her suicide phantasies and the behavior which they mobilized were therefore created by her unconscious identification with him, while the site of the attempt was dictated by her repressed desire to seduce him.

This material shows those wishes whose gratification she had sought in suicide and behavior associated with it. But to understand why a wish which could only be gratified by death could dominate her, and how real values and her customary life were suddenly renounced, required an analysis of a critical frustration of her love of women. The patient had had several homosexual love affairs during her adult life. Several years before her first suicidal attempt with allonal, she had become convinced that her hopes for marriage were thwarted, and she had established an overt homosexual relationship with an older woman whom she had later hated. The strongly domineering, possessive and pleasure-denying reactions of this woman provoked constant turmoil and misery for the patient. Her obnoxious traits reminded the patient of the dominating and ascetic personality of both her mother and her older sister and reawakened an intense lifelong resentment for them. The patient could not break off this ambivalent relationship, however, until a younger woman had enticed her and become her partisan against the older woman. Her first attempt to commit suicide by allonal poisoning had been exploited to bind this younger woman and make her an ally against the dominating mother-surrogate. In this way the patient had unconsciously repeated the seduction of her younger sister to an alliance against their mother; this had been an important phase of her adjustment to the emotional problems of her childhood.

Between the first and second suicidal attempts, the patient had rejected the older woman and carried on a love affair with the younger. This sister-surrogate was fun-loving and had men as well as women friends. Her intimacy with the patient was assured by a sort of mutually unconscious make-believe, the sister-surrogate pretending that she was dominant and emotionally dependent on no one, the patient that she was very submissive. Actually the patient controlled the other's choice of apartment, her clothes, recreations, and intellectual pursuits.

For several months preceding the second suicidal attempt, the patient's happiness in this adjustment had been disturbed by fear lest the older woman she had rejected would retaliate by seduction of the sister-surrogate. On the evening before the drive to the bridge, she had seen her "beloved" speaking to this other woman. She had spent that night frenzied with jealousy and hatred, and had phantasied that she was at the door of the older woman's apartment with a pistol in her hand, that when the door was opened she fired. By morning her homicidal phantasy had become a suicidal plan, and before beginning her drive in circles, she had first gone to the beloved's office building to assure herself that the two women were not together. The suicide had therefore been a reaction to her desire to kill the mother-surrogate who threatened to win the sister-surrogate's love.

But it was not only the sudden danger of losing the person of her beloved which precipitated the catastrophe. What she feared still more was the loss of an experience which she had idealized to a superlative degree, and thought of as a "perfect love," the "most precious" experience which life could bring. This ecstatic evaluation of her love affair had developed from erotic experiences in which their usual emotional relationship was reversed; the beloved was then consciously thought of as a dominant man, and unconsciously as both father and brother. The core of these phantasies was that the patient would bear the beloved woman a child. Conceived mutually in their sensual relationships, the phantasy was greatly elaborated at times in their conversations. Thus the patient had attained happiness by the creation of an essentially delusional system of ideas and experiences. There is no evidence that reality-testing of these delusions was ever lost for more than brief and orgiastic periods, yet their vital emotional importance so far transcended their real values as to constitute an unquestionable though limited psychosis which had not affected her every-day activities. The "perfect experience" was therefore based upon a delusion which the mother-surrogate threatened to destroy. The patient was not merely jealous lest she lose a love-partner; she was also unable to cope with the loss of a psychotically created happiness.

Yet there was a still more fundamental determinant of her crisis. At a deeper and even more significant level, the younger woman represented the patient's narcissistic phantasies of herself, both as woman and man. Once during analysis she stood naked before a mirror, phantasied her own image was the beloved's body and adored both its "soft feminine curves" and its "hard boy-like muscles." The patient's associations were that she loved the other's unacknowledged baby-like dependence, her attractiveness to men, her more beautiful breasts; but she also admired her beloved's muscular skill and athletic prowess, and imagined the other girl was a man in their sensual relationships. The patient later dreamed: *I was at a window looking out at a garden; I then came down to the garden and sang up to the window.* Her associations were that the window was that of her beloved's apartment; she actually selected this apartment for the other because of her own phantasy of herself reclining at this window, looking out and enjoying a sensual feeling while she grasped the branches of a tree and drew them in the window. The singer in the dream was associated especially with an experience at the opera when she had visualized her favorite soprano's notes getting larger and larger and higher and higher as they came across the auditorium to her and she had become very excited. The latent content of the dream is therefore similar to her waking phantasies when naked before the mirror; in her beloved's room she can pull the phallus into her and then be like the singer and exhibit a phallically conceived voice before the window herself.

The beloved had become, therefore, not only a baby-sister, a comrade, a sexual partner, and a substitute for a man, but the focus of *all* her libidinal needs. In the reality relationship, the beloved had cooperated to defeat the mother and to take the place of the little sister as that little one whose life and conduct the patient controlled and whose games she shared. In the psychotic relationship, the beloved gratified her incestuous desire and seemed father of her children; and she was also the projection of her own bisexual narcissism. What she most wanted to be herself, feminine woman *[sic]* and masculine exhibitionist, she expressed in the symbols of her dream; these wishes she had projected on the body of her beloved in her mirror phantasies. But the realization of these dominant motives in her love affair had been threatened by the crucial rivalry of the mother-surrogate. The same unconscious phantasies had dominated her return to the man she loved like a brother but rejected sexually, and her identification with the brother by the suicidal attempt.

These were the most powerful motivations of the suicidal act. But associations showed it was at the same time a fulfillment of subsidiary desires. Thus many verbal similarities between her account of "rolling" (not jumping) off the bridge and her description of erotic relations with the beloved disclosed that this relation was also symbolically reestablished. The phantasy of burying herself was associated with lying in water and phantasies of a tender mother. The desire to die like the brother was the consequence of both her love of him and her antagonism. Penis-envy was most intense in her feelings for the hero. It was also shown in such strongly emotionalized phantasies as "my five fingers are like naked boys urinating," "when I am completely happy I like to leap and feel like a penis," and in her contempt for her lovers and her fear of "male conceit." As was shown by her conscious attitude toward what was known of the brother's sexual abstinence and her troubled queries as to why he originally went to France, it was only in his death that he adequately proved his virility to her full satisfaction, and at the same time his power to defy the mother's will. It was therefore only by identification with this act that she was enabled to achieve his phallic omnipotence; but this desire was a full negation of the unusually severe taboos imposed on both by their mother, and so satisfied the infantile need to be stronger than she was. The phallic identification with the brother, as well as the phantasy of possessing her mother's baby and being surrounded by water, are therefore all different means of total mastery of the mother. So the phantasies determining her suicide are also intimately related to her homicidal phantasy of pointing a revolver at the mother-surrogate and shooting; it was a different means of achieving this same goal. The revolver was associated with a penis, and the patient formerly, during the homosexual relationship, deeply resented the mother-surrogate's insistence that the patient, when masturbating her, pretend that the older woman had a penis. In the homicidal phantasy of shooting her, this reality relationship is reversed; and in the phantasy of dying like the brother her own possession of phallic omnipotence and defeat of the mother are at last attained.

DISCUSSION

These fragments of an analysis enable us to understand how this individual failed to find adequate instinctual gratification in normal adult living; the emotional crisis which made her final homosexual adjustment futile and suicide the only release of her tension; and the specific meaning which this suicide had for her. The material is also relevant to important general problems of the theory of psychosis.

Every serious suicidal attempt gives rise to the inevitable question: whatever the rational grounds for escape from life may be, and however pleasant the wishes represented by a mere phantasy of suicide, how is it that the drive to accomplish it can actually supersede the primitive instinct of self-preservation? Our material shows that in this case these extraordinary conditions arose when the only solution to emotional frustration was an act which fulfilled the wish to identify herself with a person who had died. Zilboorg (1) has also reported patients whose suicides repeated psychologically the death of love-objects—in his cases, people who had died during the childhood of the individuals.

But this patient did not wish to identify with a dead brother; she wished to identify herself with him in the act of dying, and that is a very different thing psychologically from the fact of death. Thus she identified with him at the most heroic, virile, and mother-defeating, as well as death-dealing moment of his life. This fact is of special interest in the light of Felix Deutsch's (2) publication of clinical evidence that happiness while dying from organic diseases ("euthanasia") is also in some cases achieved through identification with the previous dying of a love-object. It seems, therefore, that a sufficiently intense drive which can only be gratified by repeating oneself in phantasy the dying of a loved person, may, as in this case, motivate an act which violates one's desire to live; while Deutsch has shown that the inevitability of death from a cause which is not mental may reverse this process, resulting in euphoria and the investiture of the psyche with identification phantasies.[1] The self-preservative function is consequently abolished when the meaning of the suicidal act is supplanted by its libidinal meaning. In this case the libidinal meaning is the desire to be as the other person was when he was dying.

Still more instructive is the clear differentiation of the suicidal mechanism of this basically schizophrenic[2] patient and that of suicides which occur during depressions. Yet in two respects the mechanisms are similar. The precipitating cause, like that of most depressions, is the threatened or actual loss of an ambivalently loved object—in this case, the sister-surrogate. And the sequence of frustrated aggression against the mother-surrogate and the attempt to destroy herself is as clear in this case as in analyzed cases of depression.

But there is no evidence that this patient had identified with the lost object herself, as occurs in typical depression; on the contrary, her identification with the brother-surrogate dominates the picture. In depression, moreover, the effort to die is the consequence of an identification, while here identification is the purpose (the *goal*) of dying, that goal which satisfies all impulses, libidinal and destructive.

Furthermore, she does not, as analyzed cases of depression do, disclose phantasies which may be literally interpreted as a need to punish herself for her aggression. The writer does not favor such a metapsychological assumption here, because it confuses the clear differentiation of schizophrenic and melancholic mechanisms. It implies that the effective drives to destroy oneself in such a case are organized through identification with external authorities in the service of the moral functions. Nor does the writer favor it on empirical grounds because it confuses the guilt mechanisms involved in the frustrations of the patient's normal wishes—to be loved by mother, sister, and brother, and to have a sexual partner and children, with the mechanism of the psychosis itself. There was indeed abundant clinical evidence of guilt associated with her normal sexual phantasies, a very unusual degree of shame for masturbatory impulses and the sexual knowledge of her childhood, her love for the brother-surrogate, and a great deal of fear of moral condemnation by others because she attempted suicide. All these facts definitely indicate a guilt mechanism while she was functioning in a nonpsychotic way. But there was no direct evidence of guilt immediately associated with her wishes to kill the mother-surrogate or to kill herself during the period of psychosis. In contrast to the domination of the ego by the superego, which Freud (4) and Abraham (5) recognized in melancholia, this suicide is a consequence of the domination of the ego by instinctual forces which are organized only to the extent of dictating the specific form of phantasy which is gratified by the suicidal act.

The mechanism is not 'I *deserve* to die for my aggression,' as in depression, but 'I *want* to die in this particular way to escape it.'[3]

I have elsewhere emphasized my opinion that a failure to complete essential identifications during early development is responsible for the inadequacies of the ego which predispose to schizophrenic and schizoid adjustments (9, 10). The absence in psychoanalytic discussion of a clear differentiation between an unconscious need to identify and the characterological consequences of an identification which has been completed is, I think, responsible for the erroneous impression that it is especially in schizoid types of personality that identifications predominate (11). Schizoid people when emotional strive to identify because they feel inadequate; but their inadequacy is largely a consequence of incomplete identification with others during this development. That a tendency of this patient to identify with her brother had been active since early childhood is indeed shown in many ways. She had even completed identifications with some of his superficial traits (ideals, baseball playing, selection of clothes, group leadership) so that childhood activities of the brother had been continued in her own personality as valuable pleasure-giving sublimations. But anything approaching an identification contributing to her basic character organization had not occurred. She had not a masculine character. Her brother was still the object of her heterosexual love as well as her homosexual wish to be like him. The news of his death made her heterosexually promiscuous. On the suicidal day she again sought his surrogate. In contrast to a suicide during depressions, therefore, the suicidal act of this patient is the fulfillment and not the consequence of the identification. And so, in this special case of a wish to identify completely with a person in the act of dying, I think that one may venture a paradoxical truth by saying that the patient attempted to cure the psychosis by dying. When such a cure failed, her subsequent relationships to her total environment became predominantly schizophrenic for the first time in her life.

SUMMARY

To recapitulate: The patient's early efforts for satisfying object-relationships during infancy were thwarted in several directions: her love of the father by his impotent character; her love of the mother by the mother's sadistic morality and the birth of her younger sister. During childhood, these problems were incompletely solved by emotional partnership with her younger sister against the mother, and by her constant play with a group of children led by her brother, whom she adored and imitated in tomboy play. These frustration patterns were repeated in her adult search for love. The incest taboo excluded her brother and all other men whom she admired, although the sexual aspects of her love of him determined her passionate conscious desire that he himself escape erotic inhibitions in France, and her compulsive promiscuity after his death. Her contemptuous reactions to the father, repeated in her feeling for men with whom she had sexual affairs, made marriage impossible. In consequence she sought a tolerable love in homosexuality and repeated her intense ambivalent feelings for her mother in her relationship with the older woman. Her final adjustment originated in a repetition of her love for the baby-sister and alliance with her. This served as an escape from the mother-surrogate, as a gratification of her need to dominate, and as a sensual fulfillment. But the relationship did not fully satisfy her emotional needs until it was supplemented by the delusion that she would become pregnant. The threat of being deprived of this "perfect love" (that is, psychotic love) mobilized all her aggression, and she regressed to the most adequate, although unconscious, object-relationship of her life, her erotic and idealized love of her brother. As she had done in her childhood play, she again attempted to master her aggression against the rest of the world by identifying with him. As he was perfect as a male only in his dying act, it was the symbolic reproduction of this act which represented phallic omnipotence and mastery of the mother, and thus became the immediate goal of all her instincts. This suicidal attempt, in contrast to depressive suicides, represents a different escape from aggression, libidinal frustration, and anxiety, rather than an act of self-punishment. It is not a consequence of identification, but an effort to fulfill the need to solve this terrible crisis in the patient's life by achieving an identification with the act of a hero.

The patient terminated her psychoanalytic treatment after six months, against advice; her understanding of the analytic experience was excellent and she gave as her chief reason for termination her fear of emotional dependence. A year later she resumed normal vocational life, and subsequently married a lifelong friend for whom she had had a romantic attachment since youth, but whose cultural inferiority had previously seemed to her a decisive obstacle to marriage. No information about her marital adjustment is available.

NOTES

1. The reversibility of this mechanism resembles that described by Freud (3) in his discussion of pain: organic pain focuses the libido on the organ, while focusing of libido on an organ in hypochondriasis creates pain. Similarly dying may give rise to euthanasic identification with an object, or the need to identify may create the phantasy of dying.

2. The patient was not in all respects a typical schizophrenic. Reality-testing was not permanently abolished, but it had lost its affective values and regulatory function in the phantasies of being pregnant by the sister-surrogate. Further, her behavior and thought-content during the six months following the suicidal attempt and during portions of the analysis resembled schizophrenia far more closely than other categories of psychosis.

3. In this I differ from the views of some authorities, for example, Karl Menninger (6). Although in many important respects I agree with this author's interpretation of his material, I do not agree that there is psychological material to justify his opinion that self-punishment is a determinant of every self-destructive act, including suicide and psychotic phenomena in general. This seems to me to imply that self-destructiveness is self-punishment by definition, and means that one is using the concept of self-punishment as a redundant synonym for the death-instinct. Compare also Franz Alexander (7), and Herman Nünberg (8).

REFERENCES

1. *Zilboorg, Gregory: Considerations on suicide, with particular reference to that of the young.* Amer. Jour. Orthopsy., Vol. V, *22, 1937.*
2. *Deutsch, Felix: Enthanasia: A clinical study.* Psan. Quart., Vol. V, *347, 1936.*
3. *Freud, Sigmund: On Narcissism. Translated in* Collected Papers, Vol. IV. *Hogarth Press and the Inst. of Psychoanalysis, London, 1925.*
4. *Freud, Sigmund: Mourning and melancholia.* Ibid., Vol. IV, *1914.*
5. *Abraham, Karl: A Short Study of the Development of the Libido. 1924. Translated in* Selected Papers. *Hogarth Press and the Inst. of Psychoanalysis, London, 1927.*

6. *Menninger, Karl:* Man Against Himself. *Harcourt, Brace and Company, New York, 1938.*
7. *Alexander, Franz: Remarks About the Relation of Inferiority Feelings to Guilt Feelings.*
8. *Nünberg, Herman: The feeling of guilt.* Psan. Quart., Vol. III, *589, 1934.*
9. *Hendrick, Ives: Contributions of psychoanalysis to the study of psychosis.* Jour. A. M. A., Vol. 113, *918, 1939.*
10. *Hendrick, Ives: Ego development and certain character neuroses.* Psan. Quart., Vol. V, *320, 1936.*
11. *Hendrick, Ives:* Ibid. *Footnote, page 326.*

8. Dream and Suicide

Emil A. Gutheil

BIOGRAPHICAL NOTE

Emil A. Gutheil, M.D., trained in medicine at the University of Vienna and became first assistant, then colleague, of Wilhelm Stekel. Subsequently he served as the major interpreter of Stekel's "active analysis" and translated Stekel's works into English.

Escaping to America just before the Anschluss, *Gutheil was a founder of the Association for the Advancement of Psychotherapy and the Post-Graduate Center for Psychotherapy. For nearly two decades he served as editor in chief of* The American Journal of Psychotherapy. *His textbooks include* Music and Your Emotions *and* The Language of the Dream. *His most important book,* The Handbook of Dream Analysis, *published in 1951, is still selling actively (Gutheil 1994).*

COMMENT

Dreams afford a valuable window into the minds of suicidal patients, and for that reason are practically important in risk assessment and in psychotherapy with suicidal patients. Nevertheless, little has appeared about the dream in suicide since the publication of Gutheil's paper. Gutheil's contribution is organized around the dreams reported by seven patients. Foreshadowing contributions yet to appear, he touches on a variety of common unconscious suicidal wish-fantasies: the wish to be reborn into a happier life, the wish to punish others, the wish to escape, the wish for reunion. He further uses dream material to demonstrate the immediacy of the two principal suicidal phenomena that Freud described: identification of the ego with someone else leading to the turning of murderous aggression against the self (Freud 1915), and "giving up on oneself" when, in narcissistic exhaustion, all positive investment having been withdrawn from the ego by a repudiative superego,

Emil A. Gutheil, "Dream and Suicide." *American Journal of Psychotherapy,* 2 (1948):283–294. Reprinted by permission of the Association for Advancement of Psychotherapy.

the patient gives up on himself and dies (Freud 1923). In the former case, the self dies as the consequence of an attack; in the latter, from abandonment. It is deserted and left to perish, as it were, on a cold hillside.

Since Gutheil's contribution appeared there have been two reviews of dream phenomena in suicide—the reader may wish to refer to Robert E. Litman (1980) and John T. Maltsberger (1993).

REFERENCES

Freud, S. 1915. Mourning and Melancholia. Standard Edition, *14:237–260.*

———*. 1923. The Ego and the Id.* Standard Edition, *19:1–66.*

Gutheil, T. 1994. Personal communication from Emil Gutheil's son, Thomas Gutheil, M.D.

Litman, R. E. 1980. The Dream in the Suicidal Situation. In Natterson, J. M., ed., The Dream in Clinical Practice. *New York: Jason Aronson.*

Maltsberger, J. T. 1993. Dreams and Suicide. Suicide and Life Threatening Behavior, *23:55–62.*

■

ONE of the most serious concerns of the practicing psychiatrist is that of preventing desperate patients from committing suicide. In many cases such intention is only a passing one, a result of a transient mood, but it may lead to irreversible decisions. It is, therefore, with great interest that the psychiatrist watches the patient's reactions during the treatment. Many of our patients are potential suicides; most of them have, at one time or another, toyed with the thought of self-destruction. Some come to analysis after having made one or more unsuccessful attempts in this direction. In countless cases psychotherapy is able to dispel the patient's gloom and to save his life. Sometimes it loses the race. Unfortunately, we have no absolutely reliable means of preventing suicide, except for our clinical experience and psychological acumen. Not all patients who commit suicide are insane; those who are sane cannot be kept under constant supervision, and the decision to place a non-psychotic patient in a hospital for reasons of a "possible attempt," is not always easy. As a rule, positive transference and the average skill of a trained psychotherapist are sufficient to deliver the patient from extreme despair and to give him hope for recovery.

Better general psychiatric training has made the individual physician able to diagnose depressive conditions more accurately and to differentiate between "harmless" and "dangerous" suicide threats. But of course, mistakes in this respect do occur, and some of them are fatal.

Dreams can be of great assistance in evaluating prognostically a given therapeutic situation. For the impulse to commit suicide, like any other impluse of the patient, manifests itself in dreams. The psychiatrist then has an opportunity to observe it *in statu nascendi* and, if necessary, to intervene effectively to prevent its perpetration. And indeed, since dream interpretation made its decisive progress, the number of suicides committed in the course of treatment has decreased considerably. The chief value of dreams is that they not only indicate the patient's intentions but also usually contain hints as to the deeper mental mechanisms involved.

The whole complex carries such import that it deserves to be studied in detail. Dreams immediately preceding a suicide attempt appear most suitable for an investigation of the dynamics of the case.[1]

The following is a dream of a patient who made a suicide attempt but was rescued. (She drank eight ounces of a bromide solution and cut her wrists.)

Case 1. The patient is a forty-nine-year-old unmarried woman, suffering from menopausal depression. She dreamt:

With a childhood friend (Mary), now dead, I make a trip to the mountains. It is Winter. We are walking together for some time. The landscape is in snow and ice. For some reason our ways separate. She stops while I walk on. But soon I see, there is nothing ahead.[2] *I must go back. The road is very difficult. I can't go on. . . . Suddenly I see,on the other side of a ravine, something like a peaceful summer landscape. I grow weaker and weaker. I hold on to my pointed cane which I am using as a crutch, but then I let myself go . . . and awaken.*

If we attempt to condense the contents of this dream (dreamt one night prior to the suicide attempt), we come, by simplification, to the following formulations:

1. The patient is in company of a person, now dead.
2. The friend's trip ends (she dies) while the patient goes on.
3. The patient encounters insurmountable difficulties. ("There is nothing ahead." Or: "It's no use. . . .") The patient's development (road) is blocked in both directions.

This is the most revealing part of the dream. It is at this point of complete frustration that the patient experiences the vision of peace—"on the other side." The antithesis here is between "this side" and "the other side." This side is cold, wintry—fraught with dangers (picture of the patient's emotional impoverishment caused by withdrawal of object cathexes), while the other side appears promising.

4. She grows weaker and lets herself go—she gives up the struggle.

Psychologically interesting are a few additional details obtained through the patient's associations. Her friend, Mary, was a gay and popular girl. During her lifetime she had had many boy-friends—and did not change her habits even after marriage. Our patient, who spent a rather frustrated life, always secretly envied her friend for her ability to enjoy life without scruples. Entering the change of life she is now reminded in a most definite manner that her own past life was but a series of missed opportunities and unfulfilled hopes (the road back is blocked). Her dream tells her that it is now too late (there is nothing ahead).

The association to the "pointed cane" is also important. The dreamer uses it as a crutch. When asked what came to her mind in connection with this detail of the dream, the patient replied that it reminded her of a shepherd's staff. Then she recalled having seen a picture of Jesus carrying a similar staff. At this point the supposition was expressed that the patient was using her faith as a crutch to surmount her difficulty. She immediately agreed, saying that her religion (Catholic) expressly prohibits the commission of suicide, and that when she decided to take her own life she first prayed for forgiveness.

One of the reasons for the patient's identification with Christ was the fact that her mother, like His, was named Mary. Hidden behind the figure of her friend, Mary, stood the figure of the patient's mother who, incidentally, had also died prematurely. After her mother's death, the patient shared the apartment with her father and took care of his household. During the treatment, after a period of extolling her mother's virtues and blaming herself for not having been a good daughter, she admitted that her relations with her mother had always been strained. There were quarrels and disagreements, particularly because her mother was strict about her contacts with men. When her mother died—the patient was about twenty-eight at that time—she hoped that the main obstacle to her social life had been removed; however, she found herself withdrawing from company, self-conscious, oversensitive (as a result of her feeling of guilt), and so her situation did not improve. Later she appeared to abandon hope for a realistic sexual adjustment and to devote herself exclusively to the care of her father. Analysis established that she hated her mother in particular, because once, when she was about nineteen, she overheard her parents' intercourse. Her first thought was: This woman enjoys her life, but she wants to stop me from enjoying mine. There is reason to believe that in the condensation of the figures of girl-friend and mother, joy of life was the common denominator.

Looking over this dream we can say that its poor prognosis is based upon the complete pessimism pervading its content. The apotheosis of peace appears to the dreamer as a distant view. But no way leads to it (the ravine). The vision occurs simultaneously with expressions of weariness and lack of combative spirit.

BUT WHERE IS THE WISH FULFILLMENT?

Undoubtedly it lies in a distant promise the dream offers. The patient is tired of the struggle; she wants peace at any price—even if it can be obtained "on the other side" only. . . .

If this interpretation is true can we assume that the dream, known to us as a guardian of our mental equilibrium, a warner, an avenger, a fulfiller of our wishes and a bolsterer of our ego, is also capable of easing us into destruction of ourselves?—If we do not accept the idea that the summer scene in the dream has the purpose of conjuring for the dreamer (as a last and desperate attempt to save her life) the potential beauty of life, the warmth and joy of summer that may follow the winter snows—then we must accept the proposition that dreams are indeed capable of easing the individual into accepting death as a solution.[3] Two factors speak against the former of the two possibilities: first, in the dream the peaceful landscape is in fact inaccessible, and secondly, that the patient *did* make a self-destructive attempt despite the dream.

Thus we may assume that under certain pathological circumstances, for instance, in melancholia, in which a so far unknown, probably somatic (toxic) factor affects the structure of the patient's personality, the life-saving function of the dream may fail, and the dream may place itself, as it were, in the service of the death instinct. As an expression of wish fulfillment under the new circumstances, we now find the dream's concern with the elimination of displeasure and suffering. The dream facilitates the reestablishment of perfect peace and harmony, a Nirvana of passivity and wishlessness as maintained in death or before birth. In this way the dream prevents a disorganization of the ego which may be caused by a persistent and insoluble mental conflict. The dream unifies the ego in its customary way, this time by focusing its conative tendencies on the idea of death. It is then an homogeneous ego that perishes in self-destruction.

We know, of course, from the studies of Abraham (1) and Freud (3) that in melancholia the ego (which has become the target of agression and/or destruction) is not a normal one. It is an ego into which an object of primary aggression has been incorporated by narcissistic identification. Freud (loc. cit.) explains the patient's capacity for suicide as follows:

"We have recognized as the primary state, from which the instinctual life originates, such a magnificent self-love of the ego, and, in the anxiety which appears whenever life is threatened, the liberation of such a tremendous amount of narcissistic libido, that we cannot comprehend how that ego can agree to a self-destruction. . . . Now the analysis of melancholia has taught us that the ego can kill itself only if through return of object cathexis it can treat itself as an object; if it can turn against itself a hostility that was meant for an object, a hostility which represents an original reaction of the ego toward the objects of the outer world. . . . In two contrasting situations, extreme infatuation and suicide, the ego is overwhelmed by the object, though in different ways. . . ."

Taking the above factors into consideration, we may assume that in our case it is the hated object of the mother that has been introjected into the patient's ego. (Mother's untimely death increased the patient's impulse for identification.) The thought of destroying this object-laden ego carried with it as a premium the promise of an ultimate union with father. This secret unconscious wish—projected into a distant future, the hereafter, appears fulfilled in the patient's dream as a vision of warmth (libido gratification) in contrast to the cold (loss of libido) maintained in the patient's conscious state. (It is interesting in this connection that Christ was also promised a union with Father after death.)

Summarizing we may say: The interpretation of the above dream enables us not only to reconstruct the pessimistic thought which led the patient onto the path of self-destruction but also to evaluate the specific role of the suicide idea in the dynamics of the depression.

Case 2. The patient is a forty-two-year-old, married woman-physician suffering from manic-depressive psychosis, depressive phase. The following is the last dream she produced before committing suicide by morphine poisoning.

I was accused of having committed ritual murder. The authorities behave as though they exculpated me, but I know this is only a trick. Ultimately they want to put me in jail. I see myself running away, rushing frantically through a maze of rooms and corridors, like through a labyrinth.

If we simplify this dream, we arrive at the following formulations:

1. The patient feels accused of a crime. Since the dreamer is also the author of her dream, it is safe to assume that the accusation represents a self-accusation, such as we commonly see in melancholic conditions.
2. The patient feels that the authorities will ultimately punish her.
3. The dreamer wants to escape punishment by running away, and finds herself in a labyrinth-like maze.

After having thus fixed the skeleton of the dream plot, we may now proceed to the discussion of details.

"Ritual murder," as is known, is the crime of killing a person for ritual purposes. At various times and in various places, followers of various religions accused one another falsely of having perpetrated this crime. The crime consisted in using the blood of the victim for the preparation of ritual meals. Psychoanalytic investigation has thrown light upon this problem. We know now that in this superstition we are dealing with projections of long repressed atavistic drives, particularly of the sadistic and cannibalistic tendencies inherent in man.

It is no coincidence that our patient in her bout of self-accusations happened to select this crime. The oral-cannibalistic root of the manic-depressive psychosis which has been thoroughly investigated by psychoanalysis (1) may account for this detail of our patient's dream. In her case, it is the incorporated figure of a dominating (phallic) mother and the aggression directed against this object which is responsible for the choice of symbolism. In her dream the patient distrusts her self-criticism, she feels the sadistic and destructive character of the superego. It is at this point that she decides to evade the punishing arm of the superego by flight into confusion, insanity, death.

At first glance this dream resembles the nightmare dreams seen so frequently in other individuals who picture themselves as being pursued and fleeing through a maze of rooms. Sometimes it is the awakening that puts an end to the panic experienced in the dream. A closer inspection of this dream, however, makes its special character clear: the dreamer is trapped. The persecutor is not the "villain" we find in dreams of hysterics, but the authority, which calmly awaits the victim's surrender while the latter is still frantically struggling in a sort of mousetrap. The basic emotion in this dream is hopelessness.

Case 3. The dreamer is a forty-year-old clergyman suffering from depression. He has a history of one suicide attempt which he made a few years prior to his treatment. The following dream must be considered "dangerous" from the standpoint of its suicide potential.

I come to mother (who died six years ago) and, crying bitterly, say to her: "Since you died I have not been successful. I wish you were here." And, as an echo—or did my mother answer?—I hear: "I wish you were here." Then it seems as if I fall into a deep pit or down a precipice and I awake feeling queer. It is some time before I become oriented to reality.

The task for the psychotherapist in this case is to counteract the patient's tendency to "join" his dead mother.

The next two cases are presented for the sake of comparison and differential diagnosis.

Case 4. The patient is a forty-three-year-old insurance broker, suffering from reactive depression. He dreams as follows:

Pearl is in the car with me and we are going to Bud's house. I find that I am headed the wrong way and I want to turn in the opposite direction. A sign in the road reads "No U-Turn." I am about to turn anyway, but I see a policeman standing in the roadway, and so I make a right turn into a side street. I am still ahead in the wrong direction, so I turn down another narrow side street. I come to the end of the block and find my way barred by a tall building. I honk the horn and the building disappears. I turn again and I am standing on the edge of a cliff overlooking a river. Suddenly I am entering Bud's apartment. (It seems to be an apartment I had occupied many years ago.) The radio is on very loud and I tell him to turn it down. He says, "No, I don't want the cops to hear it. . . ." Now I am driving down the Parkway, headed toward Bud's house (as though I had not been there yet). A huge pile of sand appears in front of the car, and I swerve sharply to avoid running into it. I straighten out the car and apply the brakes and, as I do so, I see a large tree lying on the ground to my right. I just miss the bare branches as I pass and then come to a full stop. Two cars have been in collision and the one on my side has apparently knocked down the tree. A man is leaning across the hood of the car bleeding profusely. Some other people seem to have been injured. . . .

If we simplify the contents of this dream we find that the dreamer's circuitous route ends with a scene of disaster. We see him frustrated (wrong way, blocked roads), handicapped by his conscience (policemen); we see an expression of mental conflict (collision of cars) with subsequent injury, indicating the possibility of self-injury, since it is the dreamer's own thought that gives the specific color to the dream. And yet—we find here no unequivocal expression of hopelessness or gloom.

Interesting, indeed, are some of the details. In his dream the patient had been to see Bud, his friend, who—significantly—lives in one of the patient's own previous apartments. The patient then behaves as though he had not been there, as though he were trying to get there. . . . He wants to undo something, he wishes he had not done it. And then comes the peculiar statement of the friend; he is playing the radio so loud because he does not want the cops to hear it. A few data of the patient's history may help us understand these obscure passages.

The patient had left his wife and child to follow the lure of a young woman, Pearl, who was at that time his secretary. He soon discovered that she had been having affairs with other men, and among them was his friend, Bud, to whom he had introduced the girl socially. The meeting took place in the apartment mentioned in the dream. When he discovered that the girl betrayed his confidence, he was at first very much upset and wanted to kill her; later he wanted to take revenge on his friend (vision of people bleeding profusely following a crash). He was in a desperate mood and so depressed that he had to be placed temporarily in a sanitarium. After his release he underwent psychotherapy. During his analysis it became clear that the patient regretted having broken up his home in favor of an unworthy woman. He wanted to go back home—but he did not know how to bring about reconciliation. (Analysis helped him to solve the problem.) As stated above, at no place in this dream do we find pessimism or despair. The patient wishes he had never introduced Pearl to his friend; or that he had never left his family. But in his dream he is constantly preoccupied with the idea of getting back on the right road, of readjusting his life. At one place he is even able to employ magic (omnipotence) to remove obstacles. He honks his horn and a building disappears. The patient's associations reveal that the building is the one where his wife and child are living. Whenever he passes it, he is plagued by feelings of remorse. In the dream he erases this painful memory by wishful thinking. The radio which plays so loud reminds him of a scene he once had seen in the movies. A murder was committed, while the loud sound of the radio muffled the noise of the pistol shot. The patient is fighting against an impulse to commit murder—not suicide; but his superego is sufficiently strong to dissipate it.

The repetition of motives, such as we see it in the dream ("headed the wrong way," "no U-turn," "headed in the wrong direction," "my way barred," "standing on the edge of a cliff," "a pile of sand in front of my car," etc.), indicates, generally speaking, a futile effort. This holds true for a dream as well as for a repetition compulsion. The futile effort here is the patient's attempt to reconcile his fateful sexual dependency on the young woman with his sense of loyalty and responsibility.

Case 5. The patient is a woman aged forty-five, suffering from a gastric neurosis. Her dream, quoted below, may be called "harmless."

After another scene with my husband I decide to commit suicide by taking poison. I see a white powder on the table and prepare myself for the last act. Then I see myself in a coffin carried by four men toward the graveyard. My parents (now dead) walk behind our coffin. I commence to weep and awake weeping bitterly because of my own misfortune.

We find a similar mechanism in suicide ideas of children. These ideas are aggressions directed towards other persons (parents). We detect here no identification of the type seen in melancholia. Self-pity expressed in the dream shows her ego strong and fully charged with narcissistic libido.

The analysis of this case proved that the patient had repressed criminal feelings toward her husband. She toyed with the thought of killing him by poison, after she had read about a similar case in the newspaper. Her stomach trouble was found to be a result of self-punishment (identification with the victim).

Her symptom offers her desire for talionic self-punishment an adequate outlet. A real suicide attempt would duplicate this tendency, a fact which is not in keeping with the law of libidinal economy according to which mental processes operate.

Dying, in the dream, does not necessarily represent the dreamer's wish to die. As a matter of fact, this is hardly ever the case. The wish to die in the dream usually appears in a disguise, as we have seen it in the first three dreams presented. The reason for a symbolic expression of death in the dream is not entirely clear; it may be due to the fact that the thought of dying, at first, is resisted by the ego. Be that as it may, experience teaches that most dreams where dying appears in an overt form, are dreams following traumatic incidents rather than dreams forecasting suicide. The war with its plethora of traumatic incidents has produced a great variety of death dreams of the type mentioned. The following few examples are taken from the collection of Kardiner (7):

Case 6. "I was at a party and a fight started. Someone began shooting and shot me dead right through the head. . . ." "I was coming down the elevated stairs. I dropped dead and rolled down the stairs. . . ." "I was on the Woolworth Tower and looked down, and as I did so, I slipped and fell to the ground. I made a hole in the sidewalk and was smashed to bits. . . ." "I was thrown on the tracks. A train came along and ground me up. . . ." "I was swimming and I was drowned."

All these dreams were narrated by the patient eight years after the original trauma. We know now that the psychodynamic purpose of such dreams is to abreact the effect of the trauma. All kinds of threats of annihilation are hallucinated in the patient's dreams and each awakening enhances his feeling of triumph over death and destruction.

The perseveration of death images in the dreams deprives them of their shocking character and lowers their surprise effect (law of diminishing returns). Repetitions of the traumatic experience in dreams are typical for all post-traumatic conditions. In cases where warning dreams have not been available in time to immunize the individual against a possible future shocking experience, that is, in all really surprising accidents, the immunizing work usually performed by the dream through repetition of an anticipated trauma, is made up by a post-traumatic repetition of the shocking experience. This recuperative work may require years. Its objective is the restoration of an intact and well functioning ego, an ego that is again capable of adaptation to and mastery of the outside world as a prerequisite of survival.

Of special interest are dreams of the following type:

Case 7. The patient is a married physician, aged thirty-two, suffering from impotence. In the course of his treatment he had a dream which caused him to awaken with a start:

I see myself dead and laid out in a hall of a funeral chapel. There are many people around, but I recognize no one. I know that I have died from a bite of a poisonous snake. I feel very sad about it and consider the consequences this may have for my wife. The rabbi is speaking with a matter-of-fact voice, rather bored. However, he extols my virtues and finishes his sermon by saying, ". . . and he never cut classes. . . ." The whole audience cries.

Simplifying this dream we may say:

1. The dreamer died following an insidious accident.
2. His virtues are extolled (posthumously) and his previous achievements as a law-abiding individual are praised.
3. The dream carries a strong emotional undertone. He considers the consequences of his ill fortune on his wife and notices a strong general reaction to it by others. ("The whole audience cries. . . .")

Asked for associations to the snake, the dreamer produced very important information. When he was twenty-four, he acquired a luectic infection from a fellow-student who was very promiscuous. He often spoke of her as of a "snake in the grass." The spirochetae he observed in the microscopic specimen also came to his mind in this connection. The traumatic effect of the venereal disease on the patient was exceedingly strong. For a long time he played with the idea of suicide. But the trauma had also another unexpected effect: The patient developed a general sexual inhibition which persisted even after the infection was cured, and most annoying of all was his impotence which had prevented him from consummating his marriage for more than a year prior to his treatment.

Now we understand the dream. It is not the patient's death the dream is portraying so melodramatically; it is the death of his penis, i.e. his impotence. The emotion of the dream gives us a reliable clue: "I feel very sad," "I consider the consequences for my wife," "The whole audience cries." His diminished self-confidence is restored in the dream by the dream's secret recuperative effort: The dreamer may be suspected of being immoral—today—but once, in his past, he used to be a good boy, ". . . and he never cut classes. . . ."

In our attempt to assay which dreams may be considered "harmless" and which "dangerous" as far as the dreamer's suicide plans are concerned, we come to the following conclusions:

Exact rules cannot be established as yet. We are inclined to consider as "dangerous" those dream situations in which the patient's pessimism becomes absolute, i.e. where his ego becomes extremely passive and ready to "give up" (*Case 1:* "I let myself go . . .")[4]; or, where the ego permits other forces to overwhelm it (*Case 2:* "Ultimately they want to put me in jail . . .").

Frustrating experiences as such do not indicate hopelessness. Much depends on the conduct of the ego in the dream. If the dream portrays an actively functioning ego which is capable of mastery, the frustrating dream may be considered "harmless" as far as its suicide potential is concerned.

In "dangerous" dreams death usually appears in symbolic disguise. Overt expressions of death are to be found in dreams of healthy individuals whose ego has suffered an acute indentation through the impact of a potentially death-dealing, *traumatic experience.* The threat of destruction in an individual whose ego has not been properly conditioned to such an experience, leads to a subsequent development of compensatory dream hallucinations of death, followed by recovery (through awakening). This development affords the dreamer a triumphant and uplifting experience of indestructibility. Such dreams, according to Kardiner (loc. cit.), are usually rather fragmentary. Other cases of dreams containing undisguised death expressions can be seen in those "harmless" dreams in which the infantile idea of dying is associated with the *idea of punishing* members of the patient's environment or of gaining sympathy *(Case 5).* Finally, in dreams where the dreamer's death is portrayed as a symbol of another condition, e.g., of his *impotence.* In dreams of this type the dreamer identifies himself with his ineffectual (=dead) genital *(totum pro parte).*

NOTES

1. In my book, *The Language of the Dream* (6) I have presented several examples of such dreams. *Case 3* and *Case 5* were published there.
2. The patient reported this dream in German. She said *"Es geht nicht weiter. . . ."* This sentence can be translated also as meaning "It's no use. . . ."
3. About the death instinct see Freud (4) and Federn (2).
4. "The ego sees itself deserted by its superego and lets itself die." (Freud, *The Ego and the Id,* Hogarth Press, London, 1927.)

BIBLIOGRAPHY

1. Abraham, Karl, Selected Papers on Psychoanalysis, *The Hogarth Press, London, 1942.*

2. Federn, Paul, "The Reality of the Death Instinct," Psychoanalytic Review, XIX, *1932.*

3. *Freud, Sigmund, "Mourning and Melancholia,"* Coll. Papers, Vol. IV, *London, 1924.*
4. *Freud, Sigmund, "Beyond the Pleasure Principle,"* Coll. Papers, *London, 1922.*
5. *Freud, Sigmund,* War, Sex and Neurosis, *Art & Science Press, New York, 1947.*
6. *Gutheil, Emil A.,* The Language of the Dream, *Macmillan, 1939.*
7. *Kardiner, Abram,* The Traumatic Neuroses of War, *Hoeber, New York, 1941.*

9. The Fantasy of Being Rescued in Suicide

Viggo W. Jensen and Thomas A. Petty

BIOGRAPHICAL NOTE

Viggo W. Jensen (b. 1923) and Thomas A. Petty (1918–1993) were both born in Michigan and trained in psychiatry at the Wayne County General Hospital in the late 1940s. They both spent their professional careers in Michigan as psychiatrists and psychoanalysts.

In 1954 during the course of surveying the records of five hundred suicidal patients these authors carried out telephone follow-ups wherever possible. They learned that many of the patients who had planned or carried out serious suicide attempts in the past had been "saved" by someone, in many instances almost inexplicably. Communications, often indirect, were inferred between victim and rescuer. From this study arose their hypothesis of the fantasy of rescue in suicide.

Over the course of their careers these authors continued to study the topic of suicide.

COMMENT

That suicide is always more or less ambivalent is now generally understood (Shneidman 1985). The great majority of cases have some quality of leaving the outcome of attempted suicide to chance. The conscious or unconscious ambivalence of the attempter determines the odds for survival or death, according to its predominant direction. (Russian roulette demonstrates this quality of chance in suicide. Most pistols have six chambers; those who play at that game are attempting suicide with five to one odds for survival.)

Suicide is dyadic; fusion fantasies and self-object confusion lie at its heart, and in almost all instances, a warning is given before the deadly chance is taken. Jensen and Petty show how playing the odds with death almost always

Viggo W. Jensen, and Thomas A. Petty, "The Fantasy of Being Rescued in Suicide." *Psychoanalytic Quarterly,* 27 (1958):327–339. Reprinted by permission.

involves a test for the person who is cast in the role of potential rescuer: "Which is it to be," the attempter unconsciously asks, "Will you save me from death and demonstrate your love, or will you abandon me to death, and demonstrate your aversion?" This phenomenon is of great importance in the treatment of suicidal patients because so commonly the therapist is the chosen rescuer or abandoner, and will almost always be tested in this way at some critical moment of psychotherapy, usually within six to eighteen months of the inception of the treatment.

Erwin Stengel (1964) elaborated on this theme, observing that within every suicide attempt lies an appeal to someone else, sometimes to God or to fate, to choose what the outcome will be. Marilyn Monroe's suicide involved such an appeal, one that went wrong, and so did Sylvia Plath's (Orgel 1974).

REFERENCES

Orgel, S. 1974. Fusion with the Victim and Suicide. International Journal of Psychoanalysis, *55:531–538.*

Shneidman, E. 1985. Definition of Suicide. *New York: John Wiley & Sons.*

Stengel, E. 1964. Suicide and Attempted Suicide. *Baltimore: Penguin Books.*

■

THE ATTITUDE and behavior of the person who attempts suicide express a strong wish not to die. Before and during the act of suicide, a mighty struggle to cling to life conflicts with the self-defeating act. Karl Menninger *(9),* in speaking of the wish to die, drew attention to 'the paradox that one who has wished to kill himself does not wish to die'. He then observed, 'One sees this unconscious wish not to die in the very frequent attempts at suicide which turn out unsuccessfully because of faulty technique'. Stengel *(11)* says, 'There is a social element in most suicidal attempts. Once we look for it we find it without difficulty. There is a tendency to give warning of the impending attempt and to give others a chance to intervene. Those who attempt suicide tend, in the suicidal act, to remain within or to move toward a social group. In most suicidal attempts, irrespective of the mental state in which they are made, we can discern an appeal to other human beings. This appeal also acts as a powerful threat. We regard the appeal character of the suicidal attempt, which is usually unconscious, as one of its essential features.'

Our experience confirms these observations. The 'wish not to die' and the 'appeal character' of the suicidal attempt are acted out in association with a fantasy of being rescued; and this fantasy is expressed in a suicidal attempt so arranged that it provides for the intervention of a particular rescuer to prevent its successful execution. In the preparations for and in the execution of the suicidal act are expressed not only the wish to die but the wish to live and to be saved by this rescuer. A savior is chosen and an opportunity for rescue is provided. If the behavior of the one chosen for the rescue is not what the suicidal person expects or hopes it will be, death is probable or inevitable.

The fantasy and the response of the chosen rescuer are illustrated by the following example.

A desperate young man whose wife was in the final stages of divorce proceedings decided to make a last bid for reconciliation. Without conscious purpose or plan, he loaded his shotgun and put it into the back of his car. Then he called on his sister-in-law, who closely resembled his oldest sister. When troubled he had frequently found solace in her sympathy and understanding. As a result of her encouragement and in a wave of optimism, he rushed to the home of his wife's parents about fifty miles away. But before he left his sister-in-law, he gave her a sealed envelope with the admonition not to open it unless she did not hear from him later than evening.

His wife was not at her parents' home, and while he waited for her to return his optimism waned. His purpose in bringing the gun began to crystallize. If she adamantly refused to consider his plea, he would shoot her and her whole family and commit suicide. As he considered the idea, murder seemed impossible but suicide held an impelling fascination. Finally, after waiting more than half an hour, he decided to commit suicide if his wife did not appear within the next five or ten minutes. However, before she arrived, and before the additional minutes had elapsed, the police appeared and he was taken into custody without a struggle.

His sister-in-law's concern and curiosity had been aroused by his manner and behavior. She had opened the note which suggested suicide without specifically stating that it was intended. She had notified the police.

He had chosen the sister-in-law for his rescuer, provided sufficient provocation to arouse her suspicions and curiosity, and then allowed ample time to elapse for her to save him if she acted promptly.

The following is an example of an unfulfilled wish to be rescued.

A man in his early fifties feared demotion at work and was unhappy about his wife's entry into a professional school. He devoted several weeks to putting the details of his life in order and repeatedly left notes reminding himself to check insurance policies, mortgages, and house repairs. He became more withdrawn than usual, read until early morning instead of sleeping, lost all interest in social activities, and became irritable with his twelve-year-old daughter whom he adored. His wife noticed these changes but did not discuss them with him or anyone else.

One night she went to her regular bridge club meeting and as usual returned home at twelve-thirty. As she entered the house she thought it strange that the light was on in the garage and even stranger that her husband was not in the house. However, supposing that he might have gone on an errand, she sat down to read while she waited for him. The fact that an errand was most improbable at this hour and that if he had used the car for such a reason he probably would have left the garage door open did not occur to her. After glancing through some magazines for half an hour, she decided to investigate the light in the garage. There she found her husband, still breathing, seated on the floor next to the car with its motor running. Next to him was a book of Chekhov's short stories opened to the description of a suicide. This she recognized as a suicide note. However, instead of calling for a doctor, an ambulance, or the police, she called her sister-in-law who instructed her to call the hospital. Her husband was dead on arrival at the hospital. She was grateful for his choice of method 'because it was recorded as accidental'.

It is clear that this man served sufficient warning of his intention and that his warnings were received. By his choice of method and his timing he offered his wife sufficient opportunity to intervene and rescue him. She did not respond. If the fantasy of being rescued underlying the suicidal attempt were to be expressed verbally, it might be: 'If you love me more than you hate me, you will save me. If you will not save me, I shall be dead.' A potential suicide does not become actual unless a possible rescuer, by failing to recognize the significance of the drama unfolding before him or by failing to respond, permits it to occur.

Menninger *(9)* writes that suicide entails three elements: the wish to kill, the wish to be killed, and the wish to die. We suggest a fourth element: an unfulfilled wish to be rescued.

The fantasy of being rescued tends to become conscious in varying degrees. When the wish to be saved is partially or almost wholly conscious, rescue is practically insured by the behavior of the suicidal person. The following case illustrates this point.

A twenty-one-year-old college sophomore told the telephone operator at the university health service department, where he had received almost weekly attention for minor complaints, that he was going to commit suicide. His call was promptly transferred to a social worker who engaged him in conversation while efforts were made to locate the source of the call. Speaking slowly, haltingly, in a barely audible voice, the young man explained that he was going to jump from the twelfth (top) floor of a particular building, that he was calling from a phone booth, that he had no money, no clothes, was in debt, and did not know what to do. Refusing to identify himself or reveal where he lived, he hung up the receiver. In the meantime the call had been traced to one of the booths in the building and a search was under way. Ten minutes later he called back, continued the conversation for several minutes, and then hung up again. By this time every booth in the building had been searched without finding him,—every booth but one in the basement. By the time someone remembered it, he had ended the conversation and left. A watch was put on the roof but he did not go there.

By the next day clues extracted from the conversation provided the means for identifying him, and a social worker went to his room where he was found in bed. The young man had spent the night wandering through the city streets. He was found to be seriously depressed and suicidal, but he had allowed ample opportunity to be rescued. Failure to come to his rescue probably would have been understood by this man as proof of abandonment.

The suicidal person may even become his own rescuer.

An impulsive man in his mid-twenties had lost his job and been put out of his mother's home because of drunkenness. In injured rage he decided to 'end it all'. He chose to jump from a well-traveled bridge that was not very high, into water not very deep, not too far from shore, at an early hour in the evening in late spring when it was not yet dark. The water turned out to be shockingly cold and the idea of dying in such uncomfortable circumstances was unbearable. Since he was a good swimmer he could easily change his mind and save himself. This he did by swimming under the bridge to escape detection. He told no one of his attempt until he related it to his doctor over a year later. The man had rescued himself.

The fantasy of being rescued may, however, be expressed only through slips of the tongue and inadvertent behavior. In such cases, the subject frequently is not aware of or will not acknowledge thoughts of suicide, death, or destruction. If he is aware, and can acknowledge them, he tends to minimize or deny their frequency, intensity, and importance. For such people the thought of suicide is almost inseparable from the act. Initially the suicidal impulse itself may be clinically less obvious than the fantasy of being rescued, which may be acted out as a prelude to and a magical warding off of the impulses of self-destruction.

For example, a woman in her mid-fifties, using a pseudonym because she wanted to keep her visit and identity secret, sought consultation for her adolescent son who had long been a disappointment to her. For weeks she had been unable to sleep or eat, had lost fifteen pounds, and had been mildly hypomanic. Discussing her son, she repeatedly used such colloquialisms as 'I like to died' and 'It'll be the death of me yet'. 'Dead' and 'death' appeared frequently in her speech. However, she adamantly denied thoughts of suicide and insisted she was 'just fine'. During the next few consultations she discussed the possibility of psychoanalysis for her son and provided several clues to her real identity without being aware that she did so.

The night before her next appointment, she terminated the consultations by dropping a note into the doctor's mailbox. She attributed the termination to aggravation of her symptoms, including a number of somatic ones, to a feeling that it was hopeless to try to help herself by talking, and to the conviction that she could now solve her own problem. After verification of her identity she was notified by telegram that her hour would be reserved for her and that she was expected. She kept the appointment and insisted that she had thought of nothing beyond terminating her consultations. However, during the next few weeks after she had begun to sleep, eat, and gain weight, suicidal ideas became conscious and she spoke of them.

After choosing the doctor for a rescuer, alerting him by slips of the tongue and colloquialisms, she told him her real identity without awareness that she was doing so, and then gave warning of her intention with the note and its ominous insistence that she could now solve her own problem.

Even in the suicide attempts of 'borderline', psychotic, and toxic patients a savior seems to be designated, no matter how impersonal and possibly confused the choice, and an opportunity for rescue is provided though that opportunity may be brief. Both designation of the rescuer and the opportunity offered may be so disguised in symbolic terms, so obscure, and so quickly given that the fantasy is almost imperceptible. The following case is typical.

A chronic paranoid schizophrenic patient who had been barely managing to stay out of the hospital had exhausted his financial resources and had been moping for several days in his YMCA room. Late one night he complained of his emotional state to the desk clerk, who promised to drive him to the hospital in a few minutes. However, thirty minutes later when the clerk entered the lobby the patient had disappeared. After waiting briefly for the clerk, he had left and walked to a nearby hotel. Entering the hotel lobby he walked back and forth before the hotel detective, who wondered at this behavior but did nothing. He next rode up and down in the same elevator with the same operator several times. Finally, the operator let him off on the eighth floor and noticed that he seemed to be confused or lost. After a brief delay he committed suicide by jumping from a corridor window.

In succession, this man had chosen a desk clerk whom he knew only slightly and two persons unknown to him to act as his rescuers. Each was presented with a cryptic appeal for help. His own obscurity in communication and the lack of sensitivity in his potential rescuers probably caused his death.

Study of many hundreds of attempts at suicide (including the six hundred or more such cases treated annually at the Detroit Receiving Hospital and the cases among students at Wayne State University, as well as cases reported from private practice) shows us that whenever a reasonably detailed account of the behavior of the suicidal person is available, there is evidence of the fantasy of rescue. Cases cited to disprove the existence of the fantasy have regularly demonstrated it most clearly.

Regardless of the extent to which it has become conscious, the essential features of the fantasy of being rescued are always expressed unconsciously through the acting out of the destructive impulses in the suicide attempt. The voice and its intonations; the gestures and posture; acts done or left undone; habits of eating, drinking, sleeping, and cleanliness; attitudes and emotional responsiveness—all may serve to dramatize the distress of the suicidal person in an infinite variety of ways and to convey both the self-destructive intent and the desire for intervention to the potential rescuer.

The essential features of the fantasy are first perceived unconsciously by the rescuer if he is to fulfil his designated role. This rescuer must be someone who at a particular time responds to the unconscious destructive impulses of the suicidal person as though they were his own; but he must differ from the suicidal one in two essential respects: (1) he must have a surplus of free libidinal energy with which to love the suicidal one and initiate the act of rescue; and (2) he must have sufficient ego strength to deal with the destructive impulses, not only of the one he is to rescue but his own as well, whether they are directed toward himself or the suicidal person.

Thus the rescuer must be among those who at the particular time unconsciously empathize with the suicidal person and simultaneously have sufficient ego strength and libidinal energy for both of them. The prototype for the relationship the suicidal person seeks with the rescuer probably existed originally between the infant and mother at a time when they shared a common ego, chiefly the mother's, and each responded directly to the unconscious of the other as though it were his own; this state is temporarily reinstated by regression in the patient contemplating suicide. Freud *(4)* and Abraham *(1)* have written about children's fantasies of rescuing a parent; such fantasies have an oedipal or reparative meaning. And Glover *(6)* suggested that suicide is due to a sudden confusion of self and external world through projection and introjection.

Moreover, the 'rescue' of the suicidal person is an acting out between him and the rescuer. This is an acting out between parent and child, in its prototype. This kind of acting out has been described by Weiss *(14),* Johnson *(7, 8),* Szurek *(8, 13),* Bird *(2, 3),* and others. Each party in such an acting out responds to the unconscious of the other as if it were his own.

In providing the opportunity for intervention, the suicidal one rarely seems to take into account the possibility that an unforeseen event may delay or prevent the expected behavior of the rescuer. A serious suicidal attempt may be preceded by vague and ambiguous notification and warnings. It may take place just at the time a husband usually arrives home from work or a landlady usually makes a bed,—a time so easily liable to postponement from trivial causes, so exacting in its demand for simultaneity of action between the suicidal one and the rescuer, that successful suicide seems insured. Yet it is most remarkable how seldom an accidental occurrence delays or interferes with the rescuer's fulfilment of his role. But it often happens that a potential rescuer recognizes the role assigned to him yet refuses that role or attempts to transfer it to someone else.

Interference in communication between the suicidal person and the potential rescuer frequently seems to result from certain factors. The rescuer's own unconscious hostility may have been so aroused by the demands, the unpleasantness, and the antagonism of the suicidal person that his predominant unconscious attitude is, 'Do it and be done with it. Good riddance.' This attitude may be one reason why guilt has not seemed to be quite as significant as the ego and libidinal resources in determining the response of the potential rescuer. The denial (both conscious and unconscious) that the suicidal person 'really means it', in spite of obvious evidence that he does mean it, tends to allay the guilt. Later, after the suicide has been committed, nagging guilt frequently sets in. Karl Menninger *(10)* noted that relatives often refuse to see their own part in promoting a suicide. They cannot bear to see how close such behavior is to homicide. Another factor is that the rescuer's ego and libidinal resources may already be taxed by his own affairs so that there is insufficient ego strength and libidinal reserve to deal with the sum of the needs of the two of them.

In 'Mourning and Melancholia', Freud *(5)* says, 'Now the analysis of melancholia shows that the ego can kill itself only when, the object cathexis having been withdrawn upon it, it can treat itself as an object, when it is able to launch against itself the animosity relating to an object—that primordial reaction on the part of the ego to all objects in the outer world. Thus in the regression from narcissistic object choice the object is indeed abolished. . . .' In depression, the ego has been unable to resolve a conflict in relation to the frustrating object. Regression from the narcissistic object choice has therefore taken place, and the conflict has been internalized. The abandonment of the object is the active repetition of the originally passively experienced abandonment of the ego by the primal object (the parent). However, this original abandonment, severe trauma though it was, was not complete and absolute. If it had been the individual would not have lived. This state, however, is regressively reactivated when a situation arises that closely resembles the original trauma or abandonment.

Following the regression and introjection of the object, the object bears the same relationship within the ego to the destructive part of the ego that the originally traumatized helpless infantile ego bore to the originally abandoning primal object. Thus the introjected object and the traumatized infantile ego are in the same position relative to the destructive part of the ego.

If our concept of a fantasy of being rescued in suicide is valid, the suicidal person repeats literally the original trauma and places himself in the position of the originally traumatized infantile ego and in the same position as the introjected object within the ego. Again the ego is literally dependent upon a savior as it was in infancy. Again the ego must be saved, but this time by the surrogate of the primal object *(12)*. Implicit in the wish to be rescued is the wish to save the object and thus to restore the earlier relationship between the ego and its external (loved) object. In other words, the wish to be rescued is an attempt at restitution and implies that the suicidal person must actually be abandoned by the chosen rescuer (who represents the primal object) if suicide is to occur.

Richard Sterba *(12)* elaborated upon the aggression expressed in the fantasy of rescue. 'The content, "rescuing", expressed only a part of the complex fantasy, for the object to be rescued must first have been brought into the danger from which the producer of the fantasy is to save it.' Whereas the rescue fantasy expresses the active wish to save an object brought into danger by the aggression of the producer of the fantasy, the fantasy to be rescued in suicide expresses the passive wish to be saved by an object upon whom the suicidal person has projected a share of his own aggression and whom he unconsciously holds responsible for his impending death. The aggression against the object, or potential rescuer, is expressed passively through the threat of making a murderer of the potential rescuer if the fantasy to be rescued is not fulfilled in reality.

While the fantasy expresses the passive wish to be rescued, the role of the rescuer is an active one and he cannot equivocate if he is to function in his designated capacity. For equivocation will change his function from rescuer to pallbearer. This fact has special importance for psychotherapists and others who by reason of transference are likely to be chosen as rescuers.

The tremendous responsibility implicit in the recognition of the fantasy of being rescued is a powerful deterrent to that recognition. Yet once the potential rescuer becomes conscious of his designated role, failure to accept it may be tantamount to homicide. Specific intervention is necessary. It may range from a telephone call to the imposition of restraint. Simple interpretation may suffice, but usually it does not. Moreover, the rescuer must be prepared to intervene repeatedly or continuously if he is to save the suicidal person. Resort to therapeutic anonymity or passivity by therapist or analyst to avoid the responsibilities of the rescuer is a rationalization at best and will probably end disastrously for the suicidal person and sometimes for the potential rescuer as well.

Just as the preparation for and act of suicide represent a summation of all those forces tending toward self-destruction, so does the fantasy of being rescued represent the summation of those forces tending toward the defeat of the destructive impulses and the continuation of life.

SUMMARY

The fantasy of being rescued from suicide is expressed as a suicidal attempt so arranged that it invites the intervention of a particular rescuer to prevent its successful execution. A wish to be saved is an element in every attempted suicide. The rescuer is chosen from among those who have the capacity to empathize with the suicidal person at a particular time. In 'borderline' and psychotic individuals the choice may be symbolic and vaguely expressed.

The prototype for the relationship the suicidal person seeks with the rescuer probably is that early one between child and parent when they shared a common ego and responded directly to the unconscious of each other. The rescuer must have a surplus of free libidinal energy with which to love the suicidal person and initiate the rescue, and he must have sufficient ego strength to deal with the sum of the suicidal person's and his own destructive impulses. Often a potential rescuer recognizes the appeal to him but disregards it because of his own hostility or lack of ego strength and libidinal resources.

The more conscious the fantasy of rescue, the easier it is for the suicidal person to find and accept a rescuer.

The fantasy is an attempt to restore the original relationship between the primal object and the ego of the suicidal person.

REFERENCES

1. *Abraham, Karl: The Rescue and Murder of the Father in Neurotic Fantasy Formations. In:* Clinical Papers and Essays on Psychoanalysis. Selected Papers, Vol. II. *New York: Basic Books, Inc., 1955.*
2. *Bird, Brian:* Antisocial Acting Out. Symposium 1954. *Amer. J. Orthopsychiatry, XXIV, 1954.*
3. ———*:* A Specific Peculiarity of Acting Out. *J. Amer. Psa. Assn., V, 1957.*
4. *Freud, Sigmund:* Contributions to the Psychology of Love. *Coll. Papers, IV.*
5. ———*:* Mourning and Melancholia. *Coll. Papers, IV.*
6. *Glover, Edward:* On Suicidal Mechanisms. *As quoted by Melitta Schmideberg in A Note on Suicide. Int. J. Psa., XVII, 1936.*
7. *Johnson, Adelaide, M.: Collaborative Psychotherapy: Team Setting. In:* Psychoanalysis and Social Work. *Edited by Marcel Heiman. New York: International Universities Press, Inc., 1953.*
8. ——— *and Szurek, S. A.:* The Genesis of Antisocial Acting Out in Children and Adults. *Psychoanalytic Quarterly, XXI, 1952.*
9. *Menninger, Karl, A.:* Psychoanalytic Aspects of Suicide. *Int. J. Psa., XIV, 1933.*
10. ———*:* Love Against Hate. *New York: Harcourt, Brace and Co., 1942.*
11. *Stengel, E.:* The Social Effects of Attempted Suicide. *Canadian Medical Assn. J., LXXIV, 1956.*
12. *Sterba, Richard:* Aggression in the Rescue Fantasy. *Psychoanalytic Quarterly, IX, 1940.*
13. *Szurek, S. A.:* Notes on the Genesis of Psychopathic Personality Trends. *Psychiatry, V, 1942.*
14. *Weiss, Eduardo:* Emotional Memories and Acting Out. *Psychoanalytic Quarterly, XI, 1942.*

10. Some Clinical Considerations in the Prevention of Suicide Based on a Study of One Hundred Thirty-Four Successful Suicides

Eli Robins, George E. Murphy, Robert H. Wilkinson, Seymour Gassner, and Jack Kayes

BIOGRAPHICAL NOTE

Eli Robins (1921–1995) trained in psychiatry at the Massachusetts General Hospital and McLean Hospital before beginning his work at Washington University in St. Louis. He brought at least three innovations to the study of suicide: he pioneered in the study of substantial numbers of consecutive suicides in the community; he used a wide-ranging semistructured interview to ensure that the same questions were asked in each case; and he paid strict attention to psychiatric diagnosis, using specific and restrictive diagnostic criteria. These innovations were unsympathetic to most academic psychiatrists at the time; more than twenty years elapsed before Robins's approach was widely accepted. His criteria-based diagnostic scheme later formed the background of the current nomenclature, DSM-IV.

George Murphy first began his collaboration with Robins as a third-year psychiatric resident. He writes, "I went on to share with him the case-by-case diagnoses of the 134 suicides and to participate in data analysis and writing for publication. We didn't always agree on diagnoses. When we didn't, Robins never pulled rank. Each of us marshalled his basis for his view. If the data didn't bring about a consensus, the case remained undiagnosed. It wasn't a common attitude at that time, but Robins taught us all that only data, never authority, is a suitable basis for settling disagreement. From that stimulating introduction, I have gone on to devote a substantial part of my career to

---

Eli Robins, George E. Murphy, Robert H. Wilkinson, Seymour Gassner, and Jack Kayes, "Some Clinical Considerations in the Prevention of Suicide Based on a Study of One Hundred and Thirty-Four Successful Suicides." *American Journal of Public Health* 49(1959):888–899. Reprinted by permission.

studies in suicide. Robins's dictum was 'Present your data. Let the reader decide for himself what to think.' "

Murphy, also of Washington University, and Robins, his teacher, shared the Dublin Prize of the American Association of Suicidology for 1995, for outstanding contributions to suicide study.

COMMENT

Before the publication of this paper the distribution of suicide among the different diagnostic groups was little more than conjecture. Indeed, it was still possible to presume, as many writers did, that "normal" individuals without mental illnesses committed suicide. Working at a time when the psychiatric nomenclature was itself extremely muddled (the task force to begin the work that produced The Diagnostic and Statistical Manual of Mental Disorders, Third Edition *was not formed until 1974), these authors had to generate their own rigorous diagnostic criteria. Indeed, much of the impetus for the contemporary revision of the American psychiatric nomenclature came from the Department of Psychiatry at the Washington University School of Medicine in St. Louis, of which Robins was the chairman.*

Peter Sainsbury had recently published an "ecological" study investigating social and economic influences on the suicide rate in greater London. He compared different boroughs and districts, taking into account the special significance of poverty, recent immigration, divorce, and psychological disorder. Through addressing the role of mental illness, he found the extant literature on suicide and mental disorder far from satisfactory. Diagnostic criteria varied from study to study, samples were small, samples were biased, and records were inadequate (Sainsbury 1955, 84–87).

This paper was the first of three English-language efforts to address that problem. Robins and colleagues investigated all the suicides that took place in St. Louis over the course of a year and discovered something remarkable—that 98 percent of them were clinically ill, and that 94 percent had a major *psychiatric illness (none were merely "neurotic"). They established that 68 percent of the total group suffered from either manic depressive disease or chronic alcoholism. What they found was substantially validated by two later studies (Dorpat and Ripley 1960; Barraclough, Bunch, Nelson, and Sainsbury 1974).*

Thus was suicide psychiatrized. Some non-psychiatrists fear the expropriation of the entire topic. Virtually all suicides are psychiatric, but can psychiatry's scope encompass the entire phenomenon? However valuable the psychi-

atric perspective may be, it is necessarily a constricted one. Robins and his colleagues have established some important facts, and suicidologists must deal with them. Yet no one discipline alone can fully explicate the mind and spirit of humanity. "No single learned discipline is sufficient to explain any individual suicidal event" (Shneidman 1993, 8). Suicidal phenomena are too complex, too rich in meaning, too elusive, to be caged in a psychiatric or neurobiological box. They will not be reduced. That suicide is not merely an epiphenomenon of depression is demonstrated by at least two inescapable facts: the majority of depressed patients are not suicidal, and suicide occurs in a substantial number of persons after depression has lifted.

The reader who wishes to pursue the subject of suicide and psychiatric diagnosis further should see the book Robins produced as an expansion of this chapter (1981). Murphy, applying essentially the same methods, has recently published a definitive volume on suicide in alcoholism (1992).

REFERENCES

Barraclough, B., Bunch, J., Nelson, B., and Sainsbury, P. 1974. A Hundred Cases of Suicide: Clinical Aspects. British Journal of Psychiatry *125:355–373.*

Dorpat, T. L., and Ripley, H. S. 1960. A Study of Suicide in the Seattle Area. Comprehensive Psychiatry *1:349–359.*

Murphy, G. E. 1992. Suicide in Alcoholism. *New York: Oxford University Press.*

Robins, E. 1981. The Final Months: A Study of the Lives of One Hundred and Thirty-Four Persons Who Committed Suicide. *New York: Oxford University Press.*

Sainsbury, P. 1955. Suicide in London: An Ecological Study. *London: Institute of Psychiatry/Chapman & Hall.*

Shneidman, E. 1993. Suicide as Psychache. *Northvale, N.J.: Jason Aronson.*

■

A study of suicides that succeeded shows that the majority were mentally ill. The individuals concerned suffered from chronic alcoholism or were in the depressive phase of manic-depressive disease. This study indicates that a practical program of prevention involves diagnosis and hospitalization of such cases.

SUGGESTIONS concerning the prevention of suicide have arisen chiefly from statistical studies of coroners' records *(1)*, from studies of patients who have been hospitalized and who commit suicide in the hospital or shortly after discharge *(2),* from the reports of psychiatrists based on their experiences with their own patients *(5–7),* and from studies of attempted suicide, *(8–10).* These suggestions have, in general, been of value in helping to define more clearly the problem of preventing suicide. In none of these studies, however, have all of the suicides committed within a given geographical area in a specified time period been studied carefully with regard to both the clinical and ecological aspects of suicide. As a result, there are no reported data which can answer the following questions about an unselected (consecutive) group of suicides: (a) What proportion of persons who commit suicide are clinically ill prior to death? (b) What is the nature and frequency of the illnesses from which these persons suffer? (c) Are there other illnesses that, although common, are rarely or never associated with successful suicide? (d) What are some of the factors other than diagnosis that may be helpful in assessing the probability of suicide? (e) In urban United States to what degree is suicide currently a clinical problem, as measured by the proportion of suicides who had been seen by a physician or psychiatrist during their last episode of illness?

Since answers to these questions should be useful in helping to prevent at least some suicides, the present investigation was designed to attempt to gain such information. All suicides occurring in metropolitan St. Louis in a one-year period were studied by means of interviews with relatives, friends, job associates, physicians, and others shortly after each successful suicide.

METHOD

In the one-year period between May 15, 1956, and May 15, 1957, the coroners of the City of St. Louis and of St. Louis County[1] returned a verdict of suicide in the deaths of 134 persons. Of these 134 persons, 119 have been studied by means of a primary interview with close friends or relatives within a few weeks to a few months after the suicide. Of the remaining 15 cases, the relatives refused an interview in 13, and two suicides were transients with no relatives or friends in St. Louis. In addition to the primary interview, interviews were obtained with other relatives, friends, job associates, clergymen, landladies, bartenders, nurses, attorneys, policemen, and physicians. A total of 305 interviews were obtained, including ancillary interviews on the 15 persons for whom no primary interview was obtained. In addition to these interviews, general hospital records, Social Service Exchange records, police records, and mental hospital records were examined.

The primary interview was a systematic one in which over 95 per cent of the responses were scored as yes or no or with a number. Any positive response was pursued with further questions so that there was a minimum of undescribed positive answers. The interview required an average of over two hours to complete. It covered past and present medical and psychiatric history, personal and social history, family history, and details of the successful suicide and the events which lead up to it. The interview will be described in greater detail in other publications.

As will be described later, the great majority of the suicides fell into one or other of two diagnostic groups, manic-depressive depression and chronic alcoholism. For purposes of the present report it is pertinent to describe the way we arrived at these two diagnoses. The diagnosis of manic-depressive depression was based on responses to questions concerning: (a) a previous history of a manic or a depressive episode with complete remission (12 items in the primary interview); (b) discreteness of the present episode (four items); (c) "medical" symptoms, such as insomnia, anorexia, weight loss, and fatigue (37 items); (d) psychological symptoms, such as feeling blue, loss of interest, psychomotor retardation, diminished sexual drive, low expectancy of recovery, and somatic and nihilistic delusions and delusions of poverty and guilt (84 items); and (e) disturbances in social behavior, such as diminished recreational activity and decreased social contacts (20 items). In addition to these items, age of onset and family history of manic-depressive disease were also considered in arriving at the diagnosis. These criteria are based on our clinical experience and on well documented clinical studies *(11,12)*. The diagnosis of manic-depressive disease as used in this study includes the diagnoses of involutional melancholia and psychotic depressive reaction. This use of the term to include these entities has been justified by both clinical *(11,13)* and genetic *(14)* studies. It is our clinical impression that so-called neurotic depressive reaction is in many instances indistinguishable from manic-depressive depression without delusions or grossly apparent retardation, with regard both to symptomatology and clinical course *(15)*. When the neurotic depression is clinically different from a manic-depressive depression the neurotic depression turns out to be merely an episode in a preexisting neurosis, for example, a conversion reaction. The latter diagnosis would then be the primary one. Such secondary neurotic depressions did not occur in any of the 134 cases.

Chronic alcoholism was diagnosed in accordance with the definition of Keller *(16)*, "Alcoholism is a chronic behavioral disorder manifested by repeated drinking of alcoholic beverages in excess of the dietary and social uses of the community and to an extent that interferes with the drinker's health or his social or economic functioning." This definition is in essential agreement with that of the World Health Organization *(17)*. There were 12 items in the interview that were useful in eliciting a history of family, job, social, and medical difficulties related to alcoholism. In addition to these items, age of onset, defined as the age at which the person first got into difficulty because of drinking, and a family history of alcoholism were also considered in making a diagnosis. It is not germane to this report to discuss whether alcoholism is a symptom of different diseases or is a disease entity.

The diagnoses were made by two psychiatrists who reviewed the records independently. If there was an unresolved disagreement with regard to diagnosis or if neither psychiatrist could make a definite diagnosis the person was placed in the undiagnosed group. For a person to be diagnosed as suffering from manic-depressive disease he had to have positive responses in at least three of the five categories (a through e) previously listed, in addition to having the clinical picture of the illness *(11,12)*. To be diagnosed as a chronic alcoholic he had to have at least three positive findings among those listed in Table 4.

RESULTS

Clinical Diagnoses

In this group of 134 suicides, there were 101 persons who were suffering from one of five specific psychiatric illnesses, five who were suffering from a terminal medical illness in whom there was no definite evidence of psychiatric disease, three who were apparently clinically well, and 25 who were probably psychiatrically ill but in whom a specific diagnosis could not be made (Table 1).

In this report only those aspects of clinical diagnosis directly relevant to the possibility of preventing suicide will be discussed. The three most striking findings concerning diagnosis follow. First, 98 per cent of the total group of persons were clinically ill, 94 per cent of them being psychiatrically ill, and 4 per cent only medically ill. Suicide, at least in this urban area, occurs, therefore, almost exclusively in persons who are psychiatrically ill. Second, and more important in so far as prevention is concerned, 68 per cent of all the suicides were found to be suffering from one of two diseases—manic-depressive disease or chronic alcoholism. Excluding the 25 undiagnosed cases, 83 per cent of the remaining 109 cases belonged to one or the other of these two categories (Table 2). Those with manic-depressive disease were

Table 1. Numbers of Persons in Each Diagnostic Group

Diagnostic group	Men		Women		Total group	
Manic-depressive depression	42		18		60	
Chronic alcoholism	27		4		31	
Miscellaneous diagnoses	14		4		18	
Chronic brain syndrome		4		1		5
Terminal medical illness		3		2		5
Schizophrenia		3		0		3
Apparently clinically well		3		0		3
Drug addiction		1		1*		2
Undiagnosed but psychiatrically ill †	20		5		25	
TOTAL	103		31		134	

*Associated with hysteria (conversion reaction).
†Including five patients about whom there was insufficient information.

solely in the depressed phase at the time of their deaths. No person committed suicide while in the manic phase. Third, there was no person in the series who had only an uncomplicated "neurosis" (anxiety reaction, conversion reaction [hysteria], or obsessive-compulsive reaction.[2] This finding is in agreement with that of Jameison who studied hospitalized patients *(3)*. The only person who was given a primary diagnosis of "neurosis" suffered from drug addiction as well as from conversion reaction.

Since the bulk of the suicide problem resides in manic-depressive disease and chronic alcoholism, the first consideration in attempting to prevent suicide is the clinical recognition of these illnesses. Some salient clinical findings among the 60 persons diagnosed as having manic-depressive disease are shown in Table 3. The recognition of manic-depressive disease depends not only upon the elicitation of its symptoms (Table 3, parts d, e, and f and the dagger footnote) but also on the natural history of the disease. Factors in the

Table 2. Proportion of Persons in Each Diagnostic Group

Diagnostic group	Per cent of total group			Per cent of diagnosed group		
	Men	Women	Total	Men	Women	Total
Manic-depressive depression	41	58	45	51	70	55
Chronic alcoholism	26	13	23	32	15	28
Miscellaneous diagnoses	14	13	13	17	15	17
Undiagnosed	19	16	19	—	—	—
Manic-depressive depression + chronic alcoholism	67	71	68	83	85	83

Table 3. Prevalence of Selected Symptoms and Other Historical Data in Persons Diagnosed Manic-Depressive Disease

Item	Per cent
(a) Clinically well, exclusive of attacks of manic-depressive disease	69
(b) Previous episode of manic-depressive disease	46
(c) Discreteness of present attack	
Duration of present attack	
six months or less	57
12 months or less*	87
(d) "Medical" symptoms†	
Insomnia	88
Anorexia	82
Weight loss	80
Low energy, weakness	74
Fatigue	71
Constipation	28
(e) Psychological symptoms	
Blue, depressed, sad	97
Diminished motor activity	77
Loss of interest	72
Diminished sexual interest and activity	61
Undertalkative	59
Low expectancy of recovery; "black" future	53
Feeling of being a burden	44
Indecisiveness	44
Feeling of worthlessness or marked guilt	40
Agitation	38
Personal untidiness	32
Difficulty in thinking and concentration	31
Delusions	27
(f) Disturbances in social behavior	
Decreased social and recreational activity	77
(g) Miscelleaneous items	
Age of onset 40 and over‡	75
Family history of manic-depressive disease	26

*Only 13 per cent of the cases had a duration of the present attack greater than one year. The maximum duration (one case) was four years.

†Other "medical" symptoms, such as headache, palpitation, dyspnea, dizzy spells, abdominal pain, and vomiting, which occur with a high frequency in manic-depressive disease (11, 12), are not listed here because they are less specific in helping to differentiate this illness from other psychiatric diseases. They are, however, important in the recognition of and in the total clinical picture of manic-depressive depression.

‡Age of onset is the age at the time of the first reported attack of manic-depressive disease.

natural history which are important in making a proper diagnosis include a history of being psychiatrically well, exclusive of attacks of manic-depressive disease[3]; a history of a previous episode of manic-depressive disease[4]; a discrete episode of relatively recent onset (Table 3, part c), characterized by the symptoms listed in Table 3 (parts d, e, and f); a family history of manic-depressive disease[4]; and, in half the cases, an onset after the age of 40

(11,13,14,).[5] The importance of this last point is that the other so-called functional psychiatric disorders, anxiety reaction, conversion reaction, obsessive-compulsive reaction, and schizophrenia infrequently or rarely begin after 40 *(11,20–22)*.

The diagnosis of chronic alcoholism may be made when information is obtained that alcohol is used by the patient in such amounts as to interfere with his personal or social relationships, economic welfare, or his health. In attempting to establish this diagnosis it is often important to obtain a history from the family as well as from the patient. In the present series each of these indexes of alcoholism occurred with a high frequency (Table 4).

Factors Other Than Clinical Diagnosis

One of the most striking findings of this study was the high frequency with which these persons communicated their suicidal ideas, by specific statements of intent to commit suicide, by statements concerning their preoccupation with death and desire to die, and by making unsuccessful suicide attempts. These statements were made to family, friends, job associates, and many others. Among the manic-depressives, 68 per cent communicated suicidal ideas, 38 per cent specifically stating they intended to kill themselves; the corresponding figures for the alcoholics were 77 per cent and 61 per cent. In the majority of instances, the suicidal communications were of recent onset (months), repeatedly verbalized and expressed to a number of persons. These communications of suicidal intent have been described in detail elsewhere *(23)*.

The age of the manic-depressives appears to be an important factor in evaluating the probability of suicide. Only five out of 60 cases (8 per cent)

Table 4. Prevalence of Selected Drinking Behaviors and Complications in Persons Diagnosed Chronic Alcoholism

Item	Per cent
Informant thought person drank too much	94
Daily drinking	94
Benders	78
Family objected to person's drinking	78
Arrests related to drinking	66
Medical and psychiatric complications of alcoholism	65
Suicidal person thought he drank too much	62
Job difficulties related to drinking	56
Automobile accidents related to drinking	35

were under 40.[6] This finding appears even more striking when it is remembered that half of unselected (selected without regard to suicide) manic-depressive patients become ill for the first time before 40 *(11)*, yet only 8 per cent of the suicides in the present series were under this age. The latter findings coupled with the fact that half the cases of manic-depressive disease begin before 40 indicates that younger manic-depressives have less tendency to kill themselves than do older ones. The finding that only 13 per cent (two out of 15) of the manic-depressives with an age of onset under 40 killed themselves in their first episode of the disease compared with 68 per cent (30 out of 44) of those over 40 suggests that it is not the number of the attack, but age itself, or its concomitants which somehow increases the tendency toward suicide over the age of 40.

In the manic-depressive group there were 42 men and 18 women, a ratio of 2.3:1. Since manic-depressive disease is said to occur more frequently in women than in men—at least in those hospitalized for the illness *(24,25)*, it appears that there is a special disposition for male manic-depressives to kill themselves.[7] However, the magnitude of the differential rate for suicide between the sexes does not provide additional confidence in predicting the risk of suicide in an individual man or woman.

The duration of the illness in the chronic alcoholics varied from seven to 46 years in the 21 cases where it could be determined with reasonable accuracy, with a mean and median duration of 20 years. The importance of this finding is that suicide infrequently occurs in the early stages of chronic alcoholism. The danger of suicide in alcoholism is, therefore, largely confined to the later periods of the disease. This should not be taken to signify that all these cases were far advanced, in the sense of having serious medical and psychiatric complications or of being completely "down and out." In the 17 cases in whom reasonably definite information was available, 35 per cent did not have any clear evidence of serious complications (Table 4).

Medical and Psychiatric Care

Persons with manic-depressive disease and chronic alcoholism received a substantial amount of medical and psychiatric care in the year preceding their suicides. Almost three-quarters (73 per cent) of the manic-depressives had received care for their manic-depressive disease within one year preceding their suicides and one-half (53 per cent) had received such care within one month of their suicides (Table 5). In contrast, although the chronic alcoholics received substantial care, they received much less than the manic-depressives:

Table 5. Kind of Illness for Which Medical and Psychiatric Care Was Given in the Year Preceding the Suicide

Diagnostic group and kind of illness	Prevalence of care, per cent			
	Time prior to suicide (months)			
	<1	1–3	3–12	Total within 1 year
Manic-depressive disease				
Psychiatric illness only*	44	8	5	57
Psychiatric and medical illness	9	7	0	16
Total care for psychiatric illness†	53	15	5	73
Medical illness only‡	5	2	5	12
Total care for all illness	58	17	10	85
Chronic alcoholism				
Psychiatric illness only*	11	7	7	25
Psychiatric and medical illness	11	4	0	15
Total care for psychiatric illness†	22	11	7	40
Medical illness only‡	11	0	4	15
Total care for all illness	33	11	11	55

*The psychiatric illness referred to throughout the table is manic-depressive disease or chronic alcoholism in each of the diagnostic groups, respectively. The medical illness ranges from care for chronic cardiovascular disease to the treatment for the effects of a suicide attempt.

†The following proportions of each diagnostic group were seen by a psychiatrist within the year: manic-depressive disease, 29 per cent; chronic alcoholism, 11 per cent. The remaining 44 per cent of manic-depressives and 29 per cent of alcoholics who had care for their psychiatric illness within the year were seen by the physicians who did not have special training in psychiatry.

‡It is not definite whether care for the psychiatric illness was to some extent involved here. In every case of chronic alcoholism, the person was suffering from his psychiatric disease as well as from a medical illness.

40 per cent had care for their alcoholism within one year and 22 per cent within one month (Table 5). That the care for both groups was not entirely in the hands of physicians without special training in psychiatry is shown by the findings that 29 per cent of the manic-depressives and 11 per cent of the alcoholics had been examined by a psychiatrist. Additional evidence of the quantity and intensity of care is offered by the findings that 15 per cent of the manic-depressives and 10 per cent of the chronic alcoholics had been in a psychiatric hospital within one year of their deaths, and an additional 11 per cent of the manic-depressives and 6 per cent of the alcoholics had been in general hospitals for symptoms of their psychiatric disease (Table 6).

The difficulties in the psychiatric care of these patients are shown by data concerning the number of persons referred to a psychiatric hospital who did not go, and by the number who killed themselves while still in the hospital or shortly after their discharge. There were 12 manic-depressives (20 per cent of the group) who refused to enter a psychiatric hospital or whose families refused to permit them to enter, shortly before their suicides (Table 6). In

Table 6. Hospitalizations in the Year Preceding Suicide

Hospitalizations for psychiatric disease*	Manic-depressives No.	Manic-depressives Per cent	Alcoholics No.	Alcoholics Per cent
Psychiatric hospital, prior to suicide	7	12	3	10
Suicide while in a psychiatric hospital	2	3.4	0	0
General hospital for psychiatric disease, prior to suicide	5	8	1	3
Suicide while in a general hospital	2	3.4	1	3
Total hospitalizations for psychiatric disease	16	27	5	16
Referred to psychiatric hospital but did not go	12	20	1	3
Total possible hospitalizations for psychiatric disease	28	47	6	19

*Hospitalizations for primarily medical or surgical reasons are not included in these figures.

contrast, only one chronic alcoholic (3 per cent of the group) was referred to a psychiatric hospital and did not go (Table 6). The last figure is low because only three other alcoholics were referred to a psychiatric hospital, and each of them entered the hospital. It is striking that within the year prior to death 47 per cent of the manic-depressives and 19 per cent of the alcoholics had either been hospitalized for their psychiatric disease or had been referred to a psychiatric hospital (Table 6).

There were 10 persons in the two diagnostic groups under discussion who killed themselves within eight months after discharge from a psychiatric hospital. Seven of these persons were manic-depressives, and three were alcoholics. The dangers of premature discharge from the hospital are emphasized by these findings, since each of these patients was in the same episode of illness for which he had been hospitalized. It should be noted that vigilance in the hospital is also necessary since four additional manic-depressives and one additional alcoholic killed themselves while in the hospital (Table 6). Of these five patients, two were in a psychiatric hospital and three in a general hospital.

DISCUSSION

It is our impression that the only generally effective means of reducing the suicide rate is to hospitalize in a closed ward the potentially suicidal person.[8] The problem is one of deciding who is the potentially suicidal person. From the data of the present study, two large subgroups of potentially suicidal persons who are recognizable are those suffering from a manic-depressive depression who communicate their suicidal ideas and those with chronic alcoholism who communicate suicidal ideas. These two subgroups constitute 49 per cent of the total group of 134 suicides. If suicides in these two subgroups (manic-depressives and alcoholics who communicate their suicidal intentions) alone could be prevented, the annual number of lives saved in the United States would be 8,212 (49 per cent of 16,760, the number of persons who committed suicide in the United States in the last reported years)*(27)*.

These findings suggest that, when a person in either of the above two subgroups[9] comes to the attention of a physician, the physician should recommend immediate hospitalization in a closed psychiatric ward. Before physicians should accept this suggestion as a practical recomendation, however, they would need to know the answer to one further question: How many persons with these two diseases communicate suicidal ideas and do not commit suicide, even though they are not hospitalized? That is, how many persons would physicians hospitalize who did not in fact require hospitalization in order to prevent their suicides? The answer to this question is not known and is an area requiring intensive investigation.

It should be pointed out that there appear to be reasons other than potential suicide for hospitalizing manic-depressive patients. These include marked agitation, malnutrition, weight loss, inability to be kept at home, and ill-advised decisions regarding their marital, job, and social lives *(32)*. A recent study suggests that one-quarter of manic-depressive patients makes such ill-advised decisions regarding their lives during their illness *(11)*. There are, therefore, fewer patients hospitalized without justification than would appear from assuming that the only reason for hospitalizing manic-depressive patients is the prevention of suicide.

The difficulties of recommending closed ward hospitalization for all manic-depressives who have communicated their suicidal intentions, without doing a control study of manic-depressives who have not committed suicide, have been discussed above. However, universal hospitalization might nevertheless be considered for the following reasons. First, our results suggest that the elderly male manic-depressive patient who has communicated his suicidal intentions is an especially serious suicide risk, and that perhaps at least all of these patients require hospitalization. Second, there are five studies which indicate that 14.5 per cent of manic-depressives will kill themselves in one or another episode of the disease (Table 7). If the assumption made in the dagger footnote to Table 7 is valid, then it suggests that the risk of suicide in a depressed episode is larger than is usually assumed. Since the mean number of episodes of manic-depressive disease in approximately a 20-year period is 1.8 *(13)*, the chances of suicide are 8 per cent in any given episode. This latter figure may decrease to from 2 to 4 per cent in a given episode if a

Table 7. Death by Suicide in Manic-Depressive Disease: A Summary of Five Follow-Up Studies

Investigator	No. cases	No. dead	Per cent dead	No. dead by suicide	Per cent dead by suicide	Per cent of deaths due to suicide
Langelüddecke *(29)**	341	268	78.8	41	12.0	15.3
Slater *(30)*	138	59	42.8	9	6.5	15.3
Lundquist *(13)*	319	119	37.4	17	5.3	14.3
Schulz *(31)*	2004	492	24.5	66	3.3	13.4
Stenstedt *(14)*	216	42	19.4	6	2.8	14.3
Mean‡						14.5†

*Original article not consulted, reviewed in Stenstedt.[14]

†The figure of 14.5 per cent in the text is this mean. Since there is so little variation in the proportion of deaths by suicide despite the great variation in the proportion who died from any cause, it is assumed that had all patients been followed until their deaths the proportion dead by suicide would have remained near 14.5 per cent.

‡Not weighted for the differing numbers of cases.

whole lifetime instead of 20 years is considered. But even the last figures are too high a death rate to be permitted to occur in manic-depressive disease, which otherwise has such a good prognosis.

There are indications that the possibility of preventing suicide in manic-depressive patients may be even better than in chronic alcoholics. In contrast to the chronic alcoholics, manic-depressives receive more medical and psychiatric care (Table 5); have a discrete episodic illness (Table 3) with a marked and relatively acute behavior change, having a high visibility for concerned relatives; have a short-lived (months) illness with the prospect of a spontaneous (or induced) remission in the vast majority of instances*(3,28);* and, are generally much more amenable to the necessary closed ward hospitalization than are alcoholics.

Is education of the general public concerning the symptoms of manic-depressive disease a part of the answer to the prevention of suicide? In this urban area (St. Louis) 73 per cent of the manic-depressives went to a physician within one year of their suicides for the symptoms of manic-depressive disease. This is a high proportion of the cases and suggests that public education is less needed than are better criteria for hospitalization of such patients when they see a physician. However, the present data have shown that for 20 per cent of the manic-depressives hospitalization was recommended and not accepted by the relatives; therefore, public education along these lines must be considered, and perhaps tried on selected populations. Alcoholism presents a different problem. Although its symptoms are recognizable by the general public, only 40 per cent of these patients had medical or psychiatric care within one year preceding their suicides. This low proportion of the alcoholics seen by a physician is probably related to the chronicity of the disease and to the frequent isolation of advanced alcoholics from their families. If this is the case, public education may not be very helpful in preventing suicide in alcoholics. The high frequency of suicidal communications in the manic-depressives and alcoholics suggests that public education concerning the seriousness of this behavior, at least in the two illnesses under discussion, may be helpful in reducing the suicide rate.

Finally, if we had found that suicide was an impulsive, unpremeditated act without rather well defined clinical limits, then the problem of its prevention would present insurmountable difficulties using presently available clinical criteria. The high rate of communication of suicidal ideas indicates that in the majority of instances it is a premeditated act of which the person gives ample warning. Therefore, there is currently available to the physician information he needs to take an active role in preventing suicide. To take this role, he must be able to diagnose the two illnesses from which the majority of the suicides are suffering and must take a careful history from the family and from the patient as to whether or not the person has communicated suicidal ideas.

SUMMARY AND CONCLUSIONS

1. A study of 134 consecutive successful suicides has been made by means of systematic interviews with family, in-laws, friends, job associates, physicians, ministers, and others a short time after the suicide.

2. Some of the major findings which may be helpful in planning a program of suicide prevention included: (a) 98 per cent of the suicides were clinically ill, 94 per cent of them psychiatrically ill; (b) 68 per cent of the total group were suffering from one of two diseases—manic-depressive depression or chronic alcoholism; (c) there was no patient found with an uncomplicated "neurosis" (anxiety reaction, conversion reaction or obsessive-compulsive reaction); (d) 68 per cent of the manic-depressives and 77 per cent of the alcoholics communicated their suicidal intentions prior to their suicides; (e) 62 per cent of the manic-depressives and alcoholics had had medical and psychiatric care for the illness associated with their suicides within one year of their deaths. The manic-depressives had had even more care than did the alcoholics, 73 per cent versus 40 per cent, respectively.

3. Closed ward hospitalization is suggested as the only currently available effective means of preventing suicide.

4. The decision as to whom to hospitalize was discussed and it was pointed out that for the present it seemed most useful to concentrate on attempting to prevent suicide in two groups—the manic-depressives and alcoholics who communicate their suicidal intentions. Extension of the present work to include manic-depressives and alcoholics who have not committed suicide is necessary in order to establish the over-all frequency of communication of suicidal intent in these diseases.

5. It was emphasized that all physicians should know the diagnostic features of manic-depressive disease and alcoholism, and should ask the patient's family as well as the patient concerning suicidal communications.

NOTES

1. We wish to thank the coroners for the City of St. Louis (Patrick J. Taylor) and for St. Louis County (Arnold J. Willmann and Raymond I. Harris) and their staffs (Mary Alice Quinn, Mildred B. Saemann, and Rose Marie Algarda) without whose cooperation this study would not have been possible.

2. The 25 undiagnosed persons will be discussed in detail in another report. It is only necessary to state here that in no case was there a serious possibility that one of these three "neuroses" was the primary diagnosis.

3. To make the diagnosis of manic-depressive disease it is not essential that the patient be psychiatrically well prior to the onset of the illness or between attacks. This finding, however, greatly increases the likelihood of the diagnosis of manic-depressive disease being correct. In the present study 69 per cent of the persons had no history of other psychiatric illness, 23 per cent had previously used alcohol to excess, and 8 per cent were reported to have been "nervous" all of their lives. Since this last figure is consistent with the reported prevalence of "neurosis" in the general population *(18,19),* it suggests that there is no special relationship to manic-depressive disease. It should be emphasized that the symptoms of lifelong nervousness were not like the symptoms found in the manic-depressive attacks in these "nervous" patients.

4. Although these findings may be expected in only half or less of the cases, their occurrence increases the likelihood of the present episode being manic-depressive disease.

5. In our series, 75 per cent of the cases began after 40. This may be due to some special characteristic of manic-depressives who commit suicide or to the fact that the data were collected in some cases from informants who had not known the suicidal person for his whole life.

6. This difference for the chronic alcoholics was much less striking and therefore of relatively little value in making predictions about individual patients. Nine of the 31 alcoholics (29 per cent) were under 40 at the time they committed suicide.

7. In the present study the ratio of male to female alcoholics is 6:8:1 but this finding is not helpful in deciding about potential suicides in alcoholics, since 6:8:1 ratio is not appreciably different than the estimated 5:5:1 ratio for men to women alcoholics in the United States *(26).*

8. There are no critical data in the literature to support the ideas that drugs, electric shock therapy, or psychotherapy are effective in preventing suicide. Until such data are forthcoming hospitalization seems to be the soundest policy. It is not our purpose to discuss the treatment of the suicidal patient once he is hospitalized except to reemphasize the dangers in discharging such patients too soon.

From the data of this study the ideal way to prevent the majority of suicides appears to be the prevention of manic-depressive disease and alcoholism. Since there is no known way to prevent either of these diseases, this point will not be discussed further.

9. From the findings of this study it is highly suggestive that suicidal communications in the "neuroses" (anxiety, conversion and obsessive-compulsive reactions) do not herald a successful suicide, although they indicate a serious disturbance. As a result, once a proper clinical diagnosis is made, the suicidal communication can be evaluated with a great deal more confidence as to its seriousness or lack of it.

REFERENCES

1. *Parnell, R. W., and Skottowe, I. Towards Preventing Suicide.* Lancet 1*:206–208, 1957.*
2. *Jameison, G. R., and Wall, J. H. Some Psychiatric Aspects of Suicide.* Psychiatric Quart. 7*:211–229, 1933.*
3. *Jameison, G. R. Suicide and Mental Disease: A Clinical Analysis of One Hundred Cases.* Arch. Neurol. & Psychiat. 36*:1–12, 1936.*
4. *Shneidman, E. S., and Farberow, N. L. Clues to Suicide.* Pub. Health Rep. 41*:109–114, 1956.*
5. *Oliven, J. F. The Suicidal Risk. Its Diagnosis and Evaluation.* New England J. Med. 245*:488–494, 1951.*
6. *Eidelman, J. R. Prevention of Suicide.* J. Missouri M. A. 48*:441–446, 1951.*
7. *Bennett, A. E. The Physician's Responsibility in the Prevention of Suicides.* Dis. Nerv. System 15*:207–210, 1954.*
8. *Schmidt, E. H.; O'Neal, P.; and Robins, E. Evaluation of Suicide Attempts as Guide to Therapy. Clinical and Follow-up Study of One Hundred Nine Patients.* J.A.M.A. 155*:549–557, 1954.*
9. *Batchelor, I. R. C., and Napier, M. B. Attempted Suicide in Old Age.* Brit. M. J. 2*:1186–1190, 1953.*
10. *Stengel, E., and Cook, N. G.* Attempted Suicide. Its Social Significance and Effects. Maudsley Monographs No. 4. *London, England: Chapman and Hall Ltd., 1958.*
11. *Cassidy, W. L.; Flanagan, N. B.; Spellman, M.; and Cohen, M. E. Clinical Observations in Manic-Depressive Disease. A Quantitative Study of One Hundred Manic-Depressive Patients and Fifty Medically Sick Controls.* J.A.M.A. 164*:1535–1546, 1957.*
12. *Campbell, J. D. Mild Manic-Depressive Psychosis, Depressive Type: Psychiatric and Clinical Significance.* J. Nerv. & Ment. Dis. 112*:206–236, 1950.*
13. *Lundquist, G. Prognosis and Course in Manic-Depressive Psychoses. A Follow-up Study of 319 First Admissions.* Acta psychiat.et neurol. Suppl. 35*:1–96, 1945.*

14. *Stenstedt, A. A Study in Manic-Depressive Psychosis.* Clinical, Social, and Genetic Investigations. Ibid. 79:*1–111, 1952.*
15. *Ascher, E. A Criticism of the Concept of Neurotic Depression.* Am. J. Psychiat. 108:*901–911, 1952.*
16. *Keller, M. Alcoholism: Nature and Extent of the Problem.* Ann. Am. Acad. Polit. & Social Sc. 315:*1–11, 1958.*
17. *World Health Organization.* Expert Committee on Mental Health, Alcoholism Subcommittee (Second Report). Tech. Rep. Ser. 48:*16 (Aug.), 1952.*
18. *Bremer, J. A. Social Psychiatric Investigation of a Small Community in Northern Norway.* Acta psychiat. et neurol. Suppl. 62:*1–166.*
19. *Cohen, M. E., and White, P. D. Life Situations, Emotions, and Neurocirculatory Asthenia (Anxiety Neurosis, Neurasthenia, Effort Syndrome).* Psychosom. Med. 13:*335–357, 1951.*
20. *Pollitt, J. Natural History of Obsessional States. A Study of 150 Cases.* Brit. M. J. 1:*194–198, 1957.*
21. *Böök, J. A. A Genetic and Neuropsychiatric Investigation of a North Swedish Population with Special Regard to Schizophrenia and Mental Deficiency.* Acta genet. et statist. med. 4:*1–100, 1953.*
22. *Larsson, T., and Sjögren, T. A Methodological, Psychiatric and Statistical Study of a Large Swedish Rural Population.* Acta psychiat. et neurol. Suppl. 89:*1–250, 1954.*
23. *Robins, E.; Gassner, S.; Kayes, J.; Wilkinson, R. H., Jr.; and Murphy, G. E. The Communication of Suicidal Intent: A Study of 134 Cases of Successful (Completed) Suicide.* Am. J. Psychiat. 115:*724–733, 1959.*
24. *Kraepelin, E.* Manic-Depressive Insanity and Paranoia. *Translated by R. M. Barclay. Edited by G. M. Robertson. Edinburgh, Scotland: E. & S. Livingston, 1921.*
25. *Bellak, L.* Manic-Depressive Psychosis and Allied Conditions. *New York, N. Y.: Grune & Stratton, 1952.*
26. *Lisansky, E. S. The Woman Alcoholic.* Ann. Am. Acad. Polit. & Social Sc. 315:*73–81, 1958.*
27. Vital Statistics of the United States, 1955. Vol. II. Mortality Data. *Washington, D. C.: Gov. Ptg. Office, 1957.*
28. *Fetterman, J. L.; Victoroff, V. M.; and Horrocks, J. A Ten-Year Follow-Up Study of Electrocoma Therapy.* Am. J. Psychiat. 108:*264–270, 1951.*
29. *Langelüddecke, A. Über Lebenserwartung and Rückfallshäufigkeit bei Manisch-Depressiven.* Ztschr. Psych. Hyg. 14:*1, 1941.*
30. *Slater, E., Zur Erbpathologie des Manisch-Depressiven Irreseins: Die Eltern und Kindern von Manisch-Depressiven.* Ztschr. Ges. Neurol. u. Psychiat. 163:*1–47, 1938.*
31. *Schulz, B. Sterblichkeit Endogen Geisteskranker und Ihrer Eltern.* Ztschr. menschl. Vererb. -u. Konstitions lehre. 29:*338, 1949.*
32. *Campbell, J. D.* Manic-Depressive Disease. Clinical and Psychiatric Significance. *Philadelphia, Pa.: Lippincott, 1953.*

11. The Anatomy of a Suicide

Leston L. Havens

BIOGRAPHICAL NOTE

Leston L. Havens, clinical professor of psychiatry at the Cambridge Hospital and the Harvard Medical School, was trained at the Massachusetts Mental Health Center in Boston at the time that Elvin Semrad, Ives Hendrick, and Harry Solomon led that institution to its educational zenith. He attributes his interest in psychiatry at least in part to the fact that in his youth his mother attempted suicide. A writer of breadth and unusual scholarship, Havens wrote this paper after he was invited to preside at medical grand rounds at the Massachusetts General Hospital shortly after Marilyn Monroe committed suicide and aroused the interest of physicians in Boston. He recalls that the late Dr. Paul Dudley White, the irrepressible cardiologist, pursued him to the parking lot afterward to tell him, "She wouldn't have done it if she had exercised more."

COMMENT

This case study encompasses in a few pages how we understand suicide, how we may understand or misunderstand a suicidal patient, how we may treat or mistreat her.

Havens opens by pointing out that suicide is not a thing in itself, not a disease, but a syndrome with multiple determinants (Kubie 1967). He shows how psychiatric diagnosis (including the presence of a subtle psychosis), heredity, physical illness, social and religious context, relationships (the need for exterior sustaining resources), and loss play their parts in the development of suicidal states. Character, including the incapacity to renounce loss, also has its role. He shows that empathy and countertransference are at the heart of therapeutic success or failure.

The paper reprinted here (it remains an invaluable teaching tool in train-

Leston L. Havens, "The Anatomy of a Suicide." *New England Journal of Medicine*, 272 (1965): 401–406. Reprinted by permission.

ing programs for mental health workers) should be read with a later essay by Havens (1967) on the psychological examination of suicidal patients. His special emphasis on empathically understanding the hopelessness so characteristic of many of these patients, and not avoiding it, was further developed in a videotaped interview presented at a Cambridge Hospital conference some years later. A transcript of the interview with extensive discussion was subsequently published (Havens 1989).

REFERENCES

Havens, L. L. 1967. Recognition of Suicidal Risks through the Psychologic Examination. New England Journal of Medicine, *267:210–215.*

———*. 1989. Clinical Interview with a Suicidal Patient, with Discussion by L. L. Havens, Sheldon Roth, and John T. Maltsberger. In Jacobs, D., and Brown, H. N.,* Suicide: Understanding and Responding. *Madison, Conn.: International Universities Press.*

Kubie, L. S. 1967. Multiple Determinants of Suicide. In Shneidman, E. S., ed., Essays in Self Destruction. *New York: Science House.*

■

> It is because the physician must deal with situations involving so many independent variables that clinical medicine has remained an art even today—an art based on wisdom and skill derived from experience as much as on scientific knowledge and reasoning. The skill symbolized by the gold-headed cane was not mere charlatanism. It grew in no small part from the physician's awareness—even though ill defined and often subconscious—of the many factors which play a part in the causation and manifestations of disease. It was the fruit of the Hippocratic flowering. Far from being hypnotized by the doctrine of specific etiology, the good physician endeavored, as Pidoux said, to close all the roads through which travels the pathological process.
>
> (René J. Dubos, *The Gold-Headed Cane in the Laboratory.*)

THE PATHOLOGIC PROCESSES that lead to suicide travel on many roads. Like the diseases of everyday concern to the internist, surgeon and pediatrician, the event itself is seldom simply determined. The heart failures that occupy the cardiologist result from intricate convergences of diet, cardiac reserve, exertion, the effects of medication and a host of other factors. Similarly, suicide is the final common pathway of diverse circumstances, of an interdependent network rather than an isolated cause, a knot of circumstances tightening around a single time and place, with the result, sign, symptom, trait or act.

Much in the traditional teaching of psychiatry can, and often does, set our minds against this way of thinking. We are told about diseases, when we seldom have more than syndromes; we are told about single causes whereas we know only about nets of circumstance. Unhappily, traditional diagnostic psychiatry, with its brave talk of schizophrenia and manic-depressive psychosis, was modeled on the bacteriology of syphilis, rabies and cholera, the diseases of prepotent organisms, organisms that *do* sometimes appear to act as over-riding powers, sweeping aside other circumstances to establish unmistakably their diseases. As a result of the power of analogical thinking, this was believed to be the nature of schizophrenic and manic-depressive states; the internal process, unspecified but believed in, would mark its victims forever, drive them down the road to dementia or return again and again in manic or depressive episodes. This does, indeed, seem the way with not a few of the cases, but how far from inexorable the course appears when we take the trouble to inquire into its details!

The case that follows will make this point clear. Its presentation has the goal, too, of clarifying the *way* psychiatrists think about the material and the *facts* that grip their attention, especially one group of facts that concern the patients' relations with others. Furthermore, we shall be searching, in the tradition of clinicopathological conferences, for lessons and mistakes.

The patient came to us when she was fifty-five. This age, and her symptoms, quickly gave us the diagnostic name. She was depressed in mood (she looked it, spoke of it and depressed the interviewer, passing, thereby, all three tests of depressive affect), complained of many shifting and diffuse bodily discomforts, was agitated in her motor behavior and preoccupied with self-depreciatory thoughts and had most of the usual vegetative signs—constipation, weight loss and dry mouth. We could thus easily arrange her symptoms into a syndrome. This labeling procedure, with its resulting diagnosis, agitated depression or involutional melancholia, was plainly no great achievement, but it epitomized the gross examination of the patient. It also pointed our attention in certain directions. Above all, it *warned* us: suicide, attempted or successful, is another part of this syndrome, and although it is attempted more often by women and in a larger percentage of cases successfully completed by men, we had no right to be complacent about the possibility in our patient.

Furthermore, the label tells us what we can expect a patient to have been like before her depression. The name for this premorbid state is compulsive character disorder, and, indeed, she fulfilled our prediction amply. She had been a responsible, conscientious woman, one of the supports of the world, hyperindependent, confided-in rather than confiding, the lady who, at the party, passed around the drinks and the canapés. (How hard it is to talk of a disorder when the outstanding qualities are reserve, integrity and steadiness!) Uncomplaining, she carried great loads. Even her friendships, if meaningful and alive, were shadowed by duty. It is not easy for such patients to fall back on or replace their friends. Here was a second omen of what was to come.

Thirdly, involutional melancholia has, in most studies, a hereditary element. In this case, too, an uncle had committed suicide, just before marriage, and a sister had been clinically depressed. The method of transmission of these inherited traits is unknown. It may be through genetic means, through some psychologic process of identification with family members, or by what could be termed a traumatic mechanism; the incidence of losses of relatives by death in such patients' early years is claimed to be above the average.

Finally, the diagnosis allowed us to predict that something had recently gone wrong in her life. This is a tricky matter, at best difficult to judge. Things are forever going wrong in people's lives. The smoothest, most cork-lined existence does not shut out a steady rain of adverse events, whether catastrophes or pinpricks. At fifty-five death, disease and disappointment are no longer distant rumors; they are regular visitors.

For this reason psychiatrists have never known what to do with the "precipitating event." Some have tried to rest most psychiatric illness on it; others have given it the most epiphenomenal status. Recurrently, mental maladies have been called endogenous or exogenous, depending upon how influential the premorbid happenings appeared. The facts about our patient were particularly ambiguous.

Two years before, she had lost her uterus (because of prolapse). The relatives remembered a transient change of mood after this. One complaint the patient presented to us was perhaps related: "I'm all gone down below."

Six months before she died, there had been a second operation, this time for cystocele. The details of the bladder problem and surgery did not appear, however, to concern her. Instead, she ruminated about breast cancer. The surgeon, before operation, had pointed out an inequality of her breast size;

two friends had recently been hospitalized with breast cancer. Furthermore, she had read one of her nurse-daughter's textbooks, felt a node in her axilla and thereafter could not be reassured.

During the postoperative period she was cared for by the nurse-daughter. Since this daughter appears to be a central figure in the patient's story, we must break off the account of her present illness, which, at first telling, began with the bladder operation, and move back two and a half years.

Three years before she died, the patient and her husband stopped observing their wedding anniversary. The fact was most quietly mentioned, and ostensibly its purpose was to save money. The daughter and a son were away at college. A great-aunt, who had boarded with them, moved out. These were facts suggestive of a rending or a splitting of the once-united home.

A year later, her uterus was removed. Shortly afterward, the daughter met her future husband and became engaged. They intended to marry in September of that year. The patient persuaded them to put it off a year into the following September. Indeed, it was finally put off *two* years, to the September in which the patient died.

All through this story one hears surprisingly little of the husband. He is as historically quiet as he is said to have been in life. In fact, his last act is a non-act: the failure to do something, perhaps for a reason that he himself will suggest.

The marriage was described as amiable—better, it seemed bland, remarkably lacking in passion, unless its end can be called an act of passion. Only one group of family facts stood out. The husband was Catholic; she had been Protestant, a social leader in her church. It appeared that the minister was angry at the marriage. She never returned to her church and never joined the husband in his. The family reversed a common American pattern; she stayed home on Sundays, and he took the children to Mass. Here was one more shrinkage of the possibilities of her confiding; there was one less person to fall back on. We know, from extensive evidence, that it is ministers and priests to whom our citizens go first in times of mental or emotional trouble.

After the bladder operation she became increasingly hypochondriacal. Perhaps partly as a result, another break occurred in her object ties. She missed one appointment with her surgeon because of a head cold; he missed the next owing to infectious hepatitis. They did not come together again. Now, her medical and surgical advisers fell away quickly. Perhaps her hypochondriasis was the reason; we found it exasperating, and others probably did, too. In addition, it was already a little more than hypochondriasis. There were suggestions that she *believed* she had cancer; she had gone from being obsessed to being deluded, a very typical and unfortunate alteration. What made her management even more difficult (although superficially more comfortable for the physician) was that she felt ashamed of her delusion and was only too eager to deny or discount it. I say this made her management more difficult because it obscured the persistence of the delusion. This is more than a difficulty; it is a danger, especially when the patient is, for other reasons, exasperating. As will be seen, I suspect that we were too eager that this woman be well and away, and, like herself, pretended she was well before she was.

In any case, the medical advisers began to give way to psychiatric ones. Typically, this period of transition is marked by two approaches on the part of internists and surgeons. In the first place, the patient was told that her fears were groundless, all in her imagination (one of the worst places to have them), and next, when this had no effect, that she was "overconscious of her body," and that this was wrong. Whether it is *wrong,* I do not know; certainly, it is sick, and in this case, not a sickness to be urged away. Reassurance (as well as drugs given for a few months) had failed, and then exhortation and purgation. Her depression deepened, and she was referred to a psychiatrist.

Much has been written about the family triangle; here was an example of the family quadrangle. There was the quiet husband, by career an engineer, the wife and then the nurse-daughter, the person on whom the mother most depended and who, until her marriage, kept a vigil over the patient. Finally, there was the daughter's boyfriend. Why did the patient not like him? She said he was rich and handsome; no, she said he was "too handsome." Did she mean that he was too handsome for the daughter to resist? Or that she wanted him for herself? The mother effected two postponements of the wedding but could not effect a third.

When the patient came to us, this conflict appeared to be active but largely unconscious. Whether it was unconscious in the psychoanalytical sense of repressed—that is, deeply forgotten—we did not know. It may have been only *denied,* by which is meant kept out of awareness by a continuous conscious act of suppression. She very vigorously denied that the daughter's intended marriage had anything to do with her state.

What right have we to assert that it did? First of all, we have a right to expect that it *should,* especially because we knew that she had made such persistent and active efforts to postpone it. Yet the fact was that, except for a peculiarly embarrassing and isolated crying, it appeared to have *no* effect on her. She was also *joyless* in discussing this superficially splendid match; she was, except for her tears and a barely perceptible sarcasm, emotionally flat. It seemed as if she were not permitting herself any feelings about it at all.

This was her state on admission. She was assigned to a hospital service and a doctor. He set to work caring for her. This was by no means easy. She denied any connection between her symptoms and her life, asked only to go home and politely but firmly resisted his interest. This is one of the most difficult situations in psychiatry. Here was a grown woman, old enough to be the doctor's mother, unaccustomed to confiding, suddenly asked to share secrets with a stranger. She condescended to him, politely questioned his assumptions, talked about leaving, but he held on. (It is often useful to compare psychiatry with surgery, because in both, the *preoperative* period is so important; there is little actual psychotherapy going on in the world—there is mostly preparation for it, arduous but essential.) Gradually, she began to trust him and to talk more. She also slept better, gained a little weight and seemed less depressed. Into this lightening situation entered the first of a series of events that, in retrospect, appear to have hammered down her coffin tight.

The doctor was promoted! He went from being a resident to being a chief resident and had to reduce his case load. She greeted the new doctor coolly. It had been too hard to learn trust of the first to undertake it again, with a second. Nowhere in the field of medicine is it so difficult to change physicians as in psychiatry; continuity of care is almost the first principle of psychiatric treatment. If cases of suicide or relapse are studied breaks in continuity will be found preceding tragedy after tragedy. How was it possible for us to discard our own rule in such a dangerous clinical situation? Or if it had to be discarded, why was the patient not given a more protective environment or electric-shock treatment, which is generally agreed to reduce the risk of suicide?

The pace of this narrative will soon pick up, but it is important to pause here and give what answer we can to these questions. The problem is really one of vigilance, and its maintenance. When the night is long and the day exhausting, if the pressure of danger appears to relax for a moment, the watchman will nod, wander or turn his back on the enemy lines. I suspect it was this way with us. The patient appeared better: she had shown the ability most gratifying to psychiatrists, the capacity to form a relationship; her delusions were less prominent; and the daughter's marriage was imminent and now unavoidable. *In retrospect,* each one of these favorable signs shouts out a warning. The apparent improvement seems now only part of her lifelong effort at a brave face, an effort draining her energies rather than replenishing them. Yes, she had begun a relationship, but how much more ominous this fact becomes when we remember that she had also lost it. True, the daughter's marriage was imminent and unavoidable, but by that amount her own forces had been defeated; she was now *helpless,* and we had not a shred of evidence that she was reconciled.

I wonder if the secret of our mistakes does not lie in a place foreign to the ordinary commerce of medicine, largely unpenetrated by scientific psychology or physiology. A glance in its direction can do no harm and may illuminate the business of psychiatry. The first great task of psychotherapy is to form a relationship. The second is similar to it in difficulty. Many an effort that survives the first fails before the second. This is the task of accepting what the relationship reveals, for it is only after the relationship has been born that we begin to know the deeper nature of the patient's sickness. The most physicianly among us must sometimes quail before what we learn. Deep in our hearts we wish the patients were not sick; indeed, out of this very motive we try to make them better. Especially when the sickness is a sickness of hatred, jealousy, perversity, ambition or passive longings are our receptive powers tried. What I am suggesting is this: we may have hurried our patient toward a false health out of disgust for something we felt in her, all the time largely unaware of what we were doing. I wonder if what disgusted us was not that possessive love of the daughter, with all its power to cling, deaden and destroy.

One week after the changing of the doctors, one week before the patient's death, the nurse-daughter married. The patient left the hospital to attend the wedding, "enjoyed herself," in her words, and returned to the hospital as the daughter flew off on her honeymoon. At home remained the husband and the son, but the patient's watchman was gone. It was the now-married daughter who had done the most.

The following days slipped by with disarming quietness. Symptomatically, she was better, but, as the last week ended, three events occurred. The head nurse on her ward, the staff member closest to the patient, fell ill and remained at home. Her female medical student's period of psychiatry was over; she said good-bye to the patient one day before the patient's death. Finally, the patient was allowed to go home for the weekend.

At home the next afternoon the son and she were discussing a picnic for that weekend. The patient asked where the highest cliff in the neighborhood was, as the best place to hold it. The son subsequently recalled this apparently innocent conversation with dismay, but at the time it seemed the most ordinary question in the world. The patient had an extraordinary gift of making the special ordinary, of turning the remarkable into the commonplace and unobtrusive, but she was already planning no ordinary event. Later that day she took the family car, telling the husband that she planned to visit her mother. This pleased the family, who thought she was better now than ever. She remarked that she would be home soon. But it was not her blood mother she visited, but that larger water home, said to be the starting mother of us all. She went to the highest cliff and, sometime that night, leaped off.

All through this her family slept. At seven on the morning of the next day the patient was found to be not at home. Later, her body washed ashore. The family was strangely quiet, almost expectant. The husband said, "Maybe this was all for the better."

Psychiatric practice, perhaps more than any other specialty, rests on the empathic resources of the doctor. These resources are vital not only to the understanding of each case, but to its treatment as well. Psychiatric treatment consists, to a significant extent, of heightened receptivity.

Surely, an empathic understanding of suicide need not be an isolated possession. Surely, it can grow from an open-minded review and understanding of our own lives, for most people have had suicidal thoughts, perhaps even suicidal impulses. I suppose they are most frequent in adolescence, that great breeding ground of emotional maladies of all sorts, but no time of life is free of them. The crossings into middle age and old age provide ample opportunities, as reality confronts our aspirations with too harsh a stare. The slow compromise, or even surrender, of our fondest hopes is a regular feature of normal human life.

Age is a great advantage to psychiatric understanding, provided it has not discouraged or rigidified a man. One of the main bonuses of a psychiatric residency (perhaps of many other residencies, too) is that it provides a number of years during which a person can grow a little older. For experience, like the poet's touch of nature, makes the whole world kin. The experienced man has the least chance of separating off some people or events as alien; he is the least likely to speak of the psychiatrist's patients as the patients of an alienist. He knows that the maddest madman is, in Harry Stack Sullivan's phrase, "more human than anything else."

Yes, more human than anything else, but *on the surface* not recognizably human, and it is the surface of people that we meet first. Our patient was not joyful at her daughter's marriage, nor was she ostensibly sad or bitter; her response to the event was superhuman or subhuman, depending on one's ideals. If she had come to us and said, "I cannot give my daughter away; I must have her; without her, life means nothing," or, "I am jealous of my daughter; would that my husband had been like hers," we could have more readily understood, but being able to do that, she probably would not have needed us in the first place. It is the very specialness, the indirectness, the very unintelligibility of the patient's reactions that bring the psychiatrist on the scene. He is expected to determine what the patient *really* means. Just as in a physical problem, the practitioner is expected to determine the lesion *behind* the symptom.

I do not want to imply that the patient's whole problem sprang from her relationship with the daughter, or even that it sprang solely from her personal relationships in general. That is not likely to have been true. However, I do believe that the relationship with the daughter was a significant part of the problem and certainly the part we saw most clearly. Even allowing for the many other determinants, we were obliged to use what understanding we had as vigorously as possible. No one at present knows the ultimate causes of diabetes, but no one, for that reason, would refuse the use of insulin to the patient requiring it.

What happened to interfere with our use of what we knew? The patient entered the hospital, gained the attention and concern of a doctor and, soon thereafter, the attention and concern of a nurse and medical student. This momentarily consoled her, perhaps substituted for the daughter she was about to lose. She improved. Then we changed doctors, and, shortly afterward, she was denied the medical student and nurse. During these changes, the daughter married. We did not allow ourselves full realization of the impact of these losses on the patient. We allowed her instead to reassure us. Finally, in permitting this, we may have revealed a *personal* reaction to her that, however understandable, interfered with her care.

First of all, then, I believe we partially cured the case by *substitution*—a kind of artificial or intravenous feeding—of the original doctor, nurse and medical student for the empty spaces in her life. Then, we allowed the patient to go without the feeding, as if the cure were permanent. We did not pay close enough attention to what we might call her social nutrition.

This subject, of people's need for each other, calls for a less apologetic introduction than it did twenty years ago before the animal studies and the great expansion of relevant clinical observation. The psychology of object relations, as it is called, is perhaps the central interest of contemporary psychiatry. Harlow's work on object deprivation in infant monkeys is well known, as are experiments on crowding in rat colonies. Our clinical understanding of object relations has not reached this level of scientific development, but it cannot be ignored. The detailed and attentive inventory of patients' object ties is a vital part of the management of most cases of suicide, as critical as, and very analogous to, the intake-output charts so familiar throughout general medicine. In the object ties, the units cannot be quantified, nor are they readily judged, but estimated they must be.

What stands against their safe estimation? Easily heading the list is the professional person's unwillingness to recognize his own importance. How strange to say of a profession regularly accused of vanity and self-importance! The fact is, however, that many of us allow ourselves to come and go among the patients as if our knowledge and skills were all that counted, our persons not at all. One sees it most vividly with the medical students, who cannot believe in their importance to the people they take care of. Yet, in fact, *we* are the great placebos of our pharmacopeia, and the power of the placebo can be measured by the results of its withdrawal.

Scratch most of us, and you will find one conviction present in some measure. It is the conviction that no one quite understands how much we must put up with. Difficult patients, interminable papers, worries about health, career and family, fatigue and regret may press upon human nature universally, but we only know the full weight on *ourselves.* This weight is heavier in depression, even though, as with our case of suicide, the existence and pain of it were denied. However much they were denied, one can be confident that they were there. To reach behind the false, brave front means reaching that depressive weight and its accompanying conviction of not being understood. How much easier it is to take the patient's bland answer that we have no reason to worry. She told us, "But I have everything in the world to live for," and we were ready to agree. We allowed her to reassure us. We substituted false encouragement for squarely facing the facts. Most of us are too afraid that facing facts with patients will increase the suicidal risk. Not enough of us are willing, for example, to ask the patient if she or he is considering suicide, as if the question itself could bring the result about. Unless our motives are largely and bitterly sadistic, it will not. Instance for instance, feeling understood and discussing what matters are powerful sources of encouragement.

It is not easy to encourage depressed people; most everyday encouragement is not encouraging at all. It says, "Do not have such feelings, hypochondriacal symptoms or thoughts; banish them from your mind—as if you could. I do not want to hear them." I am not suggesting that practitioners go about their business with long faces, wailing with their patients on the consulting-room walls. I imagine patients complain as much about our sober ways as they do about our prices. But ignorant reassurance has contributed far more to suicidal wishes than it has subtracted. Too often, it is our way of saying, "Take your problems elsewhere."

It is possible that we let our patient reassure us and did not notice the sudden object starvation *because we did not want to.* We may not have wanted to admit that there was still a problem beneath the patient's outwardly acquiescent manner, because we did not want the patient. In difficult clinical situations, when choices are not clear and courses of action by no means scientifically proved and directed, semisecret emotions have a field day. The doctor may say that this emotion—this object-tie talk—is all art and no science. A largely pre-experimental field like psychiatry is subject to these tides of disillusionment and ennui. It is like seeing in the semidarkness: vision falls victim to illusion formation and the effects of prejudice.

The anger that we suspect was carried secretly in her may have been conveyed *to us* and been just as secretly present in our clinical decisions. The contagious quality of feelings, if clinical impression rather than experimental fact, is readily observable. We speak of this person as being stimulating, that one as depressing, and one acquaintance as exciting, and another we find ourselves eternally arguing with. Anyone who observes his own reactions closely will find that they are not solely, or even largely, the result of *what* the person says. Manner, attitude, appearance—the great servants of feeling—give their tone not only to social life but to the clinic and consulting room as well. Anger is an extremely contagious feeling, especially when indirect and semisecret. In short, were we reacting to her unspoken anger by becoming angry ourselves? This is the way with the paradoxically quiet situations; the charge is buried, and one must look sharp for the marks of its existence. And the search must be not only of the patients but of ourselves.

There is an old story that very nearly sums up this discussion of suicide. It is a story about generalship and war and, therefore, appropriate to these remarks about treatment and death. It suggests a comparison between the general and the doctor, springing from the amount of pain and fear each has to bear. The French Marshal Turenne, watching his army thrown back and almost defeated, was approached by an aide-de-camp, who wanted to flee before retreat was impossible. The Marshal stood very still. The aide-de-camp asked, "Are you not afraid?"

The great Turenne, considered by Napoleon to have been the greatest of all military leaders, replied, "If you were as afraid as I am, you would run away."

Here is the great challenge of suicide: to stay with the battle and feel, not running from what must be borne.[1]

NOTE

1. I am indebted, for the clinical material, to the discussions of the Massachusetts Mental Health Center Medical Standards Committee, which reviews all suicides and was at that time composed of Drs. William Barnum, Stephen Zaslow, George Heninger and me.

12. Suicidal Impulse in Depression and Paranoia

Thomas E. Allen

BIOGRAPHICAL NOTE

Thomas E. Allen (b. 1936), a native of Milwaukee, attended Princeton University and received his medical degree from Columbia University. His psychiatric training was at Columbia-Presbyterian Hospital and at the New York State Psychiatric Institute.

During his residency he began the work that resulted in this paper. He recalls looking afresh at his case material when it occurred to him that what he had learned was not helpful in understanding the phenomena of paranoid delusions. He asked himself if perhaps delusion formation was an expression of the grief and despair that follows separation. Could the persecutory delusions of a psychotic patient represent a defense against self-destructive impulses?

Allen continues to expand these ideas on the basis of years of clinical work. He is a private practitioner, supervisor, and teacher who lives and works in Towson, Maryland.

COMMENT

In 1508 the English poet William Dunbar wrote,

I that in heill was and gladnèss
Am trublit now with great sickness
And feblit with infirmitie:—
Timor Mortis conturbat me.

Thomas E. Allen, "Suicidal Impulse in Depression and Paranoia." *International Journal of Psycho-Analysis,* 48 (1967):433–438. Reprinted by Permission.

A hypochondriacal fear of death can sometimes warn against impending suicide, a theme Allen addresses in this chapter. He maintains that paranoid thinking and depression are opposite sides of the same coin, and that depression, at the heart of which is a suicidal impulse, underlies paranoid states. He explains the paranoid stance as a defensive effort to ward off self-destruction. This perspective is invaluable in understanding many cases of suicide. This paper, primarily a theoretical contribution, suffers from a want of clinical illustration, but clinical support for his hypothesis is easy to summon.

It is widely understood that patients recovering from paranoid states may abruptly plunge into suicidal depressions. From time to time recovered paranoid patients, hitherto not obviously depressed, abruptly commit suicide after hospital discharge. Such a case has been described by Berman (1992). Sometimes such patients will have expressed, in the course of their psychosis, the fear that they are about to die (Zilboorg 1943). The classical delusion of the influencing machine (Tausk 1933) builds around destructive impulses projected out from the self into inanimate devices that are transparent substitutes for other people—the dreaded influencing machine is an object-substitute. Havens (1962), in a brilliant discussion of hallucinatory phenomena, has shown how recovering psychotic patients experience the movement of spatially distant persecutory voices across the self-object boundary through the skin into the patient's body. At issue is the location of suicide-inviting introjects, whether they lie within the the patient's self-representation (when they are experienced as suicidal impulses) or whether they are projected into objects (when they are experienced as murderous persecution) (Maltsberger 1993). If the deadly introjections are projected into a psychotherapist, the patient may believe the therapist wants to kill him or have him dead (see chapter 24 below). When the projection is incomplete, and is assigned to some part of the patient's body representation split off from the rest of the self, the patient may experience hypochondriachal illusions or delusions, as Allen suggests. Some patients may confuse parts of their bodies with those of others, and attack themselves in psychotic self-defense so that death or serious injury results (Ames 1984). Occasionally patients defend themselves against their own suicidal impulses by projecting them into others: in such an instance the patient fears that others are about to commit suicide, or otherwise to die (Rotov 1970).

The risk of suicide in recovering paranoid patients will be fixed in the mind of the clinician who reads and digests Allen's paper and the corrobora-

tive literature we have cited. This commonly neglected suicide configuration is not only clinically important, but invites further research investigation.

REFERENCES

Ames, D. 1984. Self Shooting of a Phantom Head. British Journal of Psychiatry *145:193–194.*

Berman, A. 1992. Case Consultation: The Suicide of Marigold Perry. Suicide and Life Threatening Behavior *22:396–405.*

Havens, L. L. 1962. The Placement and Movement of Hallucinations in Space: Phenomenology and Theory. International Journal of Psycho-Analysis *43:426–435.*

Maltsberger, J. T. 1993. Confusions of the Body, the Self, and Others in Suicidal States. In Leenaars, A., ed., Suicidology: Essays in Honor of Edwin S. Shneidman. *Northvale, N.J.: Jason Aronson.*

Rotov, M. 1970. Death by Suicide in the Hospital: An Analysis of 20 Therapeutic Failures. American Journal of Psychotherapy *24:216–227.*

Tausk, V. 1933. On the Origins of the "Influencing Machine" in Schizophrenia. Psychoanalytic Quarterly, *2:519–530.*

Zilboorg, G. 1943. The Fear of Death. Psychoanalytic Quarterly, *12:465–475.*

■

SINCE its introduction in 1920, Freud's concept of a death instinct has received sporadic attention and has had its critics, e.g. Fenichel (1935), Pratt (1958) and Horney (Weiss, 1954) and its apologists, Ostow (1958). The prevailing trend has been to view it as a step in the development towards the later dual instinct theory of sex and aggression. But in spite of this it has remained on the psycho-analytic landscape as something of a white elephant, possibly of value and too big to ignore. It is my own view that the concept can play a significant role in understanding depression and paranoia, after some important modifications have been made.

THE DEATH INSTINCT

To understand what follows it is necessary to go into considerable detail to delineate Freud's theory of the death instinct, its derivation and its intended applications. Its development in *Beyond the Pleasure Principle* is not much changed in later restatements (Freud, 1930, 1940) and can serve, therefore, as a means of understanding this concept. A presentation of its development follows in Freud's own language:

> *It seems, then, that an instinct is an urge inherent in organic life to restore an earlier state of things* which the living entity has been obliged to abandon under the pressure of external disturbing forces; that is, it is a kind of organic elasticity, or to put it another way, the expression of the inertia inherent in organic life (p. 36).
>
> If we are to take it as a truth that knows no exception that everything living dies for *internal* reasons—becomes inorganic once again—then we shall be compelled to say that *"the aim of all life is death"* and, looking backwards, that *"inanimate things existed before living ones"* (p. 38).
>
> Seen in this light, the theoretical importance of the instincts of self-preservation, of self-assertion and of mastery greatly diminishes. They are component instincts whose function it is to assure that the organism shall follow its own path to death, and to ward off any possible ways of returning to inorganic existence other than those which are immanent in the organism itself. . . . What we are left with is the fact that the organism wishes to die only in its own fashion (p. 39).

Freud is at great pains to trellis this concept on biological models but actually it is an extrapolation from his pleasure concept of that period, i.e. pleasure is a reduction of internal tension. Thus he writes:

> The dominating tendency of mental life, and perhaps of nervous life in general, is the effort to reduce, to keep constant or to remove internal tension due to stimuli (the "Nirvana principle", to borrow a term from Barbara Low [1920, 73])—a tendency which finds expression in the pleasure principle; and our recognition of that fact is one of our strongest reasons for believing in the existence of death instincts (pp. 55–56).

There was, however, an already felt need for this concept in exploring sadism and masochism thus:

> Is it not plausible to suppose that this sadism is in fact a death instinct which, under the influence of the narcissistic libido, has been forced away from the ego and has consequently only emerged in relation to the object? (p. 54).

and

> The account that was formerly given of masochism requires emendation as being too sweeping in one respect: there *might* be such a thing as primary masochism—a possibility which I had contested at that time (p. 55).

It is, however, precisely in the most important area that Freud backs away, i.e. what is the nature of the subjective phenomenology? Up to this point his description of the phenomenon is behaviouristic although his genius lay in recognizing the importance of understanding the subjective phenomenology in order to understand the behaviour. But on the subjective aspects of the death instincts he is disappointing, for he writes:

> Another striking fact is that the life instincts [Eros] have so much more contact with our internal perception—emerging as breakers of the peace and constantly producing tensions whose release is felt as pleasure—while the death instincts [Thanatos] seem to do their work unobtrusively (p. 63).

This is echoed again in Freud's later writings (1940).

DEPRESSION AND THE DEATH INSTINCT

If one were to begin with the clinical phenomena, rather than with theoretical considerations, perhaps a more useful concept could be evolved. Though Freud's concept has some basic ambiguity there is evidence that at times he is talking about a suicidal impulse which for example in sadism simply gets turned outwards. But certainly suicidal impulses are not a psychic occurrence in most people during non-depressed states, and not even consciously present in most depressed people. Thus maybe the death instinct applies merely to a subclass of depressive states. But would a wider generalization be theoretically valuable and where can one draw the line? It is my feeling that the natural limit of generalization is to all depressed states and consequently it is postulated that a suicidal impulse, often repressed, is a universal concomitant of depression and an indication of latent depression if the impulse is present in the absence of a clinical depression. It is my view that the relationship of the suicidal impulse to the depressive state is like the relationship of sadness or the physiological concomitants of that state. The impulse may be present consciously as a wish or suicide attempt, preconsciously as an obsessional fear, or unconsciously as self destructive behaviour or exaggerated scrupulosity. This impulse is not a part of non-depressed states. It has a phenomenological existence independent of guilt and hostility though it may express them as well as other dynamic possibilities. This view is at marked variance with Freud's (1917) view expressed in his paper on "Mourning and Melancholia":

> We have long known, it is true, that no neurotic harbours thoughts of suicide which he has not turned back upon himself from murderous impulses against others, but we have never been able to explain what interplay of forces can carry such a purpose

through to execution. The analysis of melancholia now shows that the ego can kill itself only if, owing to the return of the object-cathexis, it can treat itself as an object—if it is able to direct against itself the hostility which relates to an object and which represents the ego's original reaction to objects in the external world (p. 252).

There is no doubt that the expressivity, or the proximity to consciousness and to action, of the suicidal impulse in depression is a function of dynamic and analytic considerations such as those of Freud and others (Hendin, 1963), but it is my feeling that these considerations are not the source of this impulse but are rather secondary modifiers of a specific component of the depressive state.

One other consideration deserves discussion and that is a point raised by Arieti (1959) which is that suicide attempts in severely depressed patients most often occur as the patient is emerging from the depths of psychomotor retardation. This cannot be easily explained unless perhaps one views psychomotor retardation as a depressive equivalent of catatonia which in the depressed patient is designed to prevent the carrying out of the suicidal impulse. There may occur in some individuals premature exhaustion of this severe inhibition with resultant loss of control of the suicidal impulse. It is premature because it occurs before the abatement of the depressive state itself. An excellent description of the struggle of the severely depressed patient with the suicidal impulse appears in a paper by Milici (1950).

PARANOIA

This brings me to the main consideration of this paper, the nature of paranoia and its dynamics. But before we can proceed along this line it is first necessary to give a brief account of what ideas have previously been put forth on this subject. Freud gave the first dynamic explanation of paranoia in his paper on the Schreber case (1911) and later wrote two other papers (1915, 1922) on the same subject from different perspectives. However, his basic ideas were contained in the first paper in which he states:

We should be inclined to say that what was characteristically paranoic about the illness was the fact that the patient, as a means of warding off a homosexual wishful phantasy, reacted precisely with delusions of persecution of this kind (p. 59).

and

Nevertheless, it is a remarkable fact that the familiar principal forms of paranoia can all be represented as contradictions of the singie proposition: "*I* (a man) *love him* (a man)", and indeed that they exhaust all the possible ways in which such contradictions could be formulated (p. 63).

Delusions of jealousy contradict the subject, delusions of persecution contradict the verb, and erotomania contradicts the object. But in fact a fourth kind of contradiction is possible—namely, one which rejects the proposition as a whole: . . . "I love only myself." So that this kind of contradiction would give us megalomania, . . . (pp. 64–65).

and

The most striking characteristic of symptom-formation in paranoia is the process which deserves the name of *projection.* An internal perception is suppressed, and, instead, its content, after undergoing a certain kind of distortion, enters consciousness in the form of an external perception (p. 66).

This is an impressive theoretical accomplishment and as Carr (1963) points out "has stood up remarkably well".

The criticism of Freud's view has come from two principle sources. The first were case reports of the coexistence of paranoia and homosexuality (Schmideberg, 1931; Bollmeier, 1938; Hastings, 1941) and the second was from the study by Klein and Horwitz (1949) of eighty patients selected at random from a large sample of formerly hospitalized patients diagnosed as paranoid state or schizophrenia paranoid type. They found that in reviewing the "behaviour, productions, and feelings" of this group of patients only one fifth gave any indication of "homosexual feelings, needs, or conflicts . . . fear of being considered homosexual, fear of being or becoming homosexual, being called terms which might imply it, or fear of homosexual attack" (p. 700). This was reported absent even at the height of their illness when "many patients were too disturbed and disorganized to maintain many defences". There are, of course, some replies to these criticisms and for those the reader is referred to Carr (1963).

Considerations of this kind lead Ovesey (1955) to modify the classical Freudian model by postulating that the homosexual anxiety was made up of anxieties about three separate motivational (wish) components: sex, dependency, and power. The latter two Ovesey regards as giving rise to a pseudo-homosexual anxiety which is misinterpreted by the patient as true homosexual anxiety. These nonsexual wish-components then undergo transformation and projection to various forms of paranoid states. Though this concept does enlarge Freud's original formulation and permits the explanation of the coexistence of paranoia and manifest homosexuality it does not explain any better than Freud the absence of homosexual fears in the majority of paranoid patients. Ovesey, seemingly aware of this, gratuitously adds:

> The table makes clear that the homosexual motivation is in no way exclusive; in fact, I would go so far as to suggest that it is the pure power (aggression) motivation without any pseudohomosexual elaboration that is the constant feature in paranoid phenomena, and that the essential related anxiety is, therefore, a survival anxiety (p. 171).

This will be of interest later.

Working within this general tradition Salzman (1960) offers another solution. He writes:

> Essentially, then, the paranoid development as I see it, is characterized by a grandiose development, frequently messianic in nature, which is an attempt to deal with extreme feelings of worthlessness through a process of denial and reaction formation (p. 680).

and

> Suspicion, hostility, contempt, lack of trust, and delusional formations are an attempt to guard and guarantee the grandiosity (p. 686).

He points out that this is the opposite of the traditional view, i.e. that grandiosity is a "secondary development", for he regards it as the primary "defensive technique", and hostility and delusions as attempts to maintain the grandiosity. He gives up any interpretation along sexual or pseudosexual lines.

There have, of course, been many other ways of viewing paranoid development which cannot be dealt with here and for a broader survey the reader is referred to Cameron (1959). The papers discussed here are felt to represent a train of development towards the present theoretical formulation. The present view is based on the common clinical observation that paranoid thinking and depression are opposite sides of the same coin, which is by way of saying that these two states commonly substitute for one another. Thus in treating a paranoid patient one may find an underlying depression and vice versa. Now as has been previously discussed one feature of depression is a suicidal impulse conscious or unconscious, more or less controlled. It is my view that it is an underlying depression which is always primary and that the paranoia is an attempt to deal with the accompanying suicidal impulse. The paranoid individual projects the suicidal impulse onto the environment so that he can try to deal with it. The logic of his thought is as follows: "I wish to kill (hurt/debase) myself" → "I do not wish to kill myself" → "They wish to kill (hurt/debase) me." Thus it is not he who wishes to kill himself, which the paranoid *could not escape and cannot accept,* but "They" who wish to kill him, someone or something against which he can defend himself. In the grandiose delusion there is an exaggerated denial of the impulse. The logic here is: "I wish to kill myself" → "I do not wish to kill (hurt/debase) myself" → "I want to build myself up, be stronger, better" → "I am stronger, better" → "I am unique" which may progress to "they should know I am unique." At times there is a shifting between the two, i.e. between persecution and grandiosity, and there may even be a third form, i.e. "They see I am unique, they want to save me." This formulation does not cover delusional jealousy or erotomania for which Freud's formulation seems to me to be more adequate.

The paranoid patient is extremely sensitive to the suicidal impulse accompanying depression. In the paranoid patient the impulse is at times too strong to be handled by denial and projection and then an actual serious suicide attempt may be made. If unsuccessful, restitution along the lines of previous projection and denial is made. Occasionally suicidal ideation and grandiose or persecutory delusions may exist concurrently, and in these situations it is the paranoid delusions which are most heavily invested. If the affective investment changes serious risk of suicide is present. The intensity or pressure of the suicidal impulse can frequently be gauged by the degree of elaboration and systematization of the delusions given a reasonably intelligent and integrated individual.

Sullivan (1953) points out the close relationship between hypochondriasis and paranoia which, of course, was originally illustrated in the Schreber case. It is no wonder, for the mechanism is similar. In hypochondriasis there is an exaggeration of minor symptoms in one or another area of the body which is felt by the patient to be a harbinger of a potentially fatal disease. Here there is an attempt to deny the suicidal impulse and deal with it not as a phenomenon of subjective experience and motivation but as coming from some region of the body, a somaticized externalization, rather than a "projected" or "personified" externalization. Hypochondriasis may indeed be the first step towards ultimate paranoid delusional development. Somatic delusions however are of a different nature. Such delusions represent a partial compromise with the suicidal impulse, limiting it to some part of the body, where they take the form of concerns about the death or disappearance of that part. In some cases, of course, there is denial of this attempted compromise and thus concern about a felt exaggerated part. However, such partial compromises as these are rarely sufficient to handle the impulse and the resulting anxiety.

Ideas of reference are phenomenologically distinct from paranoid delusional development as discussed above. Indeed they are derived from a different part of the depressive reaction. It has been common to assume that because of the frequent association of ideas of reference and delusions as well as because of the milder nature of the former that ideas of reference are an intermediate stage in paranoid development. But Bowlby's (1961) discussion of the process of mourning casts a different light on this. He described three phases of the mourning process: (i) "urge to recover the lost object"; (ii) "disorganization" and (iii) "reorganization". He points out that there is disbelief about a loss and: "Coupled with incredulity, however, goes a strenuous effort, usually involuntary and sometimes unconscious, to recover him" (p. 333). And as part of this state there is a similar projected response that the other person is searching for the mourner. Fleischl (1958) came close to this point when in reviewing a case she wrote:

> The ideas of reference are used by her [the patient] as proof that others are still interested in her and paying her some attention (p. 26).

The patient has lost the specificity for the actual lost person and generalizes it to all of the environment. The frustration and irritation at not finding the actual lost one is distorted and projected onto those whom she feels notice her. They are then accused of noticing her for the wrong reasons, but the actual situation is that it is simply the wrong person. The significance of the eye in the drawings of the paranoid may be a related phenomenon.

The last and most difficult question is what makes the paranoid patient so sensitive and terrified of the suicidal impulse arising during a depressive state. There seem to be two potential lines of development. The first is that there may be in paranoid patients a constitutionally stronger set of survival instincts which make it impossible for such an individual to entertain or tolerate an anti-survival wish. It creates such anxiety that he projects it to defend against it. The second possibility is that life as it impinged on the individual has necessitated a hypertrophy of the survival instincts. To a certain extent this is adaptive as it stimulates keener competitive skills. However, it is maladaptive when the death threat comes from the self.

A final note is that this paper has been concerned with the general nature and origin of various aspects of the paranoid development and not the specific content of any given delusion which I feel is derived from the history of the individual and the sociocultural context at the time of their formation.

TREATMENT

What seems therapeutically indicated on the basis of the foregoing discussion is undoubtedly going to seem disappointingly small. However, the major contribution of this paper, it is hoped, will be to the understanding of the paranoid phenomena rather than specific therapeutic applications. The major thrust of treatment should be towards recovering *not* the depression but the trigger of the depression. Perhaps when the relationship is strong enough encouragement of the acceptance of depression is indicated. Interpretation of the origin of the delusions or their content is generally not indicated, which is in accord with observations of Fromm-Reichmann (1950) who states:

> It not infrequently happens that hallucinations and delusions will disappear in the course of the general interpretive psychotherapeutic procedure without having been submitted to direct interpretive endeavour (p. 178).

It should be clear from the above discussions why interpretation of delusions on the basis of their content, confrontations to the patient of their unreality, or explanations are rarely successful.

CONCLUSION

In this paper an attempt has been made to reach a new understanding of depression and paranoia through modifying and limiting Freud's concept of a death instinct. The paper is largely devoted to understanding the phenomena and has limited applications for treatment except insofar as the theoretical understanding makes possible various depth-soundings during the treatment of the patient.

REFERENCES

Arieti, S. (1959). "Manic depressive psychosis." In: American Handbook of Psychiatry I, *ed. Arieti. (New York: Basic Books.)*

Bollmeier, L. N. (1938). "A paranoid mechanism in male overt homosexuality." Psychoanal. Quart., *7.*

Bowlby, J. (1961). "Processes of mourning." Int. J. Psycho-Anal., *42.*

Cameron, N. (1959). "Paranoid conditions and paranoia." In: American Handbook of Psychiatry I, *ed. Arieti. (New York: Basic Books.)*

Carr, A. C. (1963). "Observations on paranoia and their relationship to the Schreber case." Int. J. Psycho-Anal., *44.*

Fenichel, O. (1935). "A critique of the death instinct." Collected papers. *1st Series. (New York: Norton, 1953.)*

Fleischl, M. F. (1958). "A note on the meaning of ideas of reference." Amer. J. Psychother., *12.*

Freud, S. (1911). "Psycho-analytic notes on an autobiographical account of a case of paranoia (dementia paranoides)." S.E., *12.*

——— *(1915). "A case of paranoia running counter to the psycho-analytic theory of the disease."* S.E., *14.*

——— *(1917). "Mourning and melancholia."* S.E., *14.*
——— *(1920).* Beyond the Pleasure Principle. *S.E., 18.*
——— *(1922). "Some neurotic mechanisms in jealousy, paranoia and homosexuality."* S.E., *18.*
——— *(1930).* Civilization and Its Discontents. S.E., *21.*
——— *(1940).* An Outline of Psycho-Analysis. S.E., *23.*
Fromm-Reichmann, F. (1950). Principles of Intensive Psychotherapy. *(Chicago: Univ. of Chicago Press.)*
Hastings, D. (1941). "A paranoid reaction with manifest homosexuality." Arch. Neurol. Psychiat., *45.*
Hendin, H. (1963). "The psychodynamics of suicide." J. nerv. ment. Dis., *136.*
Klein, H. R. and Horwitz, W. A. (1949). "Psychosexual factors in the paranoid phenomenon." Amer. J. Psychiat., *105.*
Milici, P. (1950). "The involutional death reaction." Psychiat. Quart., *24.*
Ostow, M. (1958). "The death instincts—a contribution to the study of instincts." Int. J. Psycho-Anal., *39.*
Ovesey, L. (1955). "Pseudohomosexuality, the paranoid mechanism, and paranoia." Psychiatry, *18.*
Pratt, J. (1958). "Epilegomena to the study of Freudian instinct theory." Int. J. Psycho-Anal., *39.*
Salzman, L. (1960). "Paranoid state—theory and therapy." Arch. Gen. Psychiat., *2.*
Schmideberg, M. (1931). "A contribution to the psychology of persecutory ideas and delusions." Int. J. Psycho-Anal., *12.*
Sullivan, H. S. (1953). The Interpersonal Theory of Psychiatry. *(New York: Norton.)*
Weiss, F. A. (1954). "Karen Horney—her early papers." Amer. J. Psychoanal., *14.*

13. The Suicidal Adolescent— The Expendable Child

Joseph C. Sabbath

AUTOBIOGRAPHICAL NOTE

Joseph Sabbath writes, "In the mid-1960s family therapy and systems theory became popular. People like Ackerman, Bowen, Munuchin, Nagy, Whitaker and Wynne were demonstrating remarkable results. The division of labor in child psychiatry was breaking down—no longer did the psychiatrist always see the child and other workers the parents or other family. When everyone was seen together as part of a total family evaluation new observations and insights were obtained. The mutual interdependent roles of child and parent were clarified as to how each contributed to the frustrations, conflicts, and problems of each other. From these experiences I became aware of the crucial role of the parents in determining the suicidal behavior of the adolescent.

"At the present time I continue with my interests in adolescent and family through private practice and consulting to community clinics in the inner city and Hispanic neighborhoods. The current contribution of psychopharmacology acts as a complement, not a replacement, to the hard-earned insights of the psychodynamics of family therapy."

COMMENT

Scapegoating as a contributing factor to suicide has long been appreciated by clinicians. When suicide or suicide attempts take place in a family context it is usually not difficult to discern ambivalence toward the patient in other members of the family. Hatred and anger may be directed at the patient who is at the same time loved. Sometimes the negative side of the ambivalence is provoked by the emotional barrage of the patient's chronic suicidal threats or behavior. Sometimes the ambivalence seems to have been present from the

Joseph C. Sabbath, "The Suicidal Adolescent—The Expendable Child." *Journal of the American Academy of Child Psychiatry* 8 (1969):272–289. Reprinted by Permission.

suicidal patient's birth. Usually the ambivalence is covert, but in some cases family death wishes directed against the patient are quite explicit.

This paper describes two adolescent suicide attempts and one suicide in which parental rejection played a critical part. By 1969 the importance of this phenomenon had begun to be appreciated in the literature on suicide and depression. Henry I. Schneer and his colleagues alluded to it (1961). A. Schrut (1964) recognized its importance. Robert E. Gould (1965) was aware of it and gave the matter passing mention. It fell to Sabbath to define the problem with unusual clarity and to illustrate it with rich clinical detail in this important contribution.

REFERENCES

Gould, Robert E. 1965. Suicide Problems in Children and Adolescents. American Journal of Psychotherapy, *19:228–246.*

Schneer, Henry I., Kay, Paul, and Brozovsky, Morris. 1961. Events and Conscious Ideation Leading to Suicidal Behavior in Adolescence. Psychiatric Quarterly, *35:507–515.*

Schrut, A. 1964. Suicidal Adolescents and Children. Journal of the American Medical Association, *188:1103–1107.*

■

SUICIDE at any age is an act of desperation. It is a negative answer to the question—to be or not to be. The voluntary act of taking one's own life represents a failure in communication between the individual and his meaningful object relationships, together with an inability to cope with the stresses of life.

Suicide in adolescents is a particularly poignant challenge to those of us in the helping professions, for it points out far too clearly our inability to help a child who by his own actions has made himself nonexistent. He indeed is a "dropout" from life—premature and permanent.

Jacobziner (1965) indicates that suicide occurs more frequently during the adolescent phase than at any earlier age. In the United States in 1962, 102 individuals between the ages of 10 and 14, and 556 between the ages of 15 and 19 committed suicide.

What are the factors responsible for this unfortunate problem in our adolescent population?

This paper proposes the concept of the expendable child to account for one of the multiple factors contributing to adolescent suicidal behavior. It presumes a parental wish, conscious or unconscious, spoken or unspoken, that the child interprets as their desire to be rid of him, for him to die. The pathological disturbance of this child-parent relationship in the cases to be presented reached the critical point in the context of the stresses associated with the developmental phase of adolescence. The parent perceives the child as a threat to his well-being, and the child sees the parents as persecutors or oppressors.

The period of adolescence under discussion is that span of years from the beginning of puberty, around twelve years of age, to college entrance age, eighteen years.

CASE 1

Gail S.—"It Won't Do Any Good"

Gail, an attractive-looking sixteen-year-old high school student, was seen the day following a serious suicidal attempt with sleeping pills. Her manner was detached as she spoke, "Why didn't I die, there's nothing to live for. I took my father's pills, thirty of them; I have been unhappy since age six when I swallowed half a bottle of aspirin." Gail went on to say that it was her parents' fault, that they got what they deserved. "I didn't ask to be born." The night before her suicide attempt Gail had felt depressed. Her mother told her to "snap out of it." At this point Gail said, "Doctor, you just can't do that right away. I felt it was no use, she just didn't understand me. I felt everything was hopeless."

Mrs. S., a depressed appearing middle-aged woman, described her own mother as a strict Victorian type with whom she never felt close or could talk. Both Mr. and Mrs. S. described their marriage as a difficult one. Mr. S. mentioned that a couple of years previously, Gail had been seen at a local private clinic where she was considered "schizophrenic and dangerous," but he disbelieved it. His response to the psychiatrist's recommendation of further hospitalization for Gail following her suicide attempt was, "It won't do any good. I don't want her to spoil it for the other children. You put your time and energy and money on those children that are doing well."

Developmental history revealed that Gail was a planned child, the third of four children with two older and one younger brothers. Her mother claimed that she was born "depressed." At age seven months, the child developed diarrhea, diagnosed as coeliac disease, following an attempt to toilet train her. There was much disagreement over her diet, with mother claiming that father gave her extra food that "irritated her colon."

Mrs. S. stated that the day she came home from the hospital with her last child, Gail, who was two years of age, merely looked up from the table for a moment and then went right on eating her cereal. Mrs. S. could not control the girl's temper tantrums, while her husband felt she was a genius and on this basis excused much of her misbehavior. Gail was enuretic until the time of menarche at age twelve. At this time she was sent to an out-of-town boarding school for two years. On her return home her problems with her parents became more severe than ever. Although her schoolwork improved, Mrs. S. complained of Gail's friends being of the beatnik type. Mrs. S. had frequently referred to Gail as "little fella" and her youngest son as being a little girl. During the past several years, Mrs. S. had turned to her dog for companionship and Gail often referred to the dog as "mother's fifth child."

During Gail's hospitalization Mrs. S was cooperative, while her husband accused the doctors of failure and threatened several times to send Gail to the state hospital. He continued to reiterate, "If there is a rotten apple in the barrel, get rid of it." He believed that by sending his oldest sons away to school he had saved them from his wife's overprotectiveness.

Psychiatric sessions with Gail brought out a picture of a very bright, lonely, perplexed teenager who saw herself as a lying, jealous, ugly, and hateful person. She felt she should not live, that she could never be happy. One time she said, "Two principles ruined my life—everything is either all or nothing, and I'm afraid to try anything because I'm afraid I can't do it." She would admit her mother loved her, but add, "It's because I am her daughter, not because I'm me." About her father she asked, "Why didn't he do anything about my suicide threats?" She complained that when her father recently gave her a piece of jewelry he held it out a distance when presenting it to her. "He is a drug addict, taking all those pills. Why won't he see a psychiatrist?" Then again, "My parents wanted to make me perfect; they failed, and therefore they want to get rid of me."

Formulation

Mrs. A. identified Gail with her own mother, thus using her daughter to continue, in a repetitive, compulsive manner, this former frustrating relationship. In addition, she contributed to her daughter's confusion over her sexual identity, by inferring a reversal of the girl and the youngest son.

The adolescent revival of the struggles against the oedipal and preoedipal ties which had been postponed during Gail's absence at boarding school began to reach a crescendo upon her return home. She became alternately depressed and provocative and accusatory toward her parents. Gail's claim that her parents wanted to make her perfect, and then, having failed, wanted to be rid of her, could have been in part a projection, and in part a fact. The father who had looked upon her as a genius during the latency years could now no longer tolerate her increasing misbehavior and struggles for autonomy. He had disregarded a diagnosis of her being dangerous and schizophrenic the year before, and then later her suicidal threats. He was satisfied to have saved his sons. To Gail, this could have meant either that he had given up hope for her, or that he was implying his consent for her to carry out her suicidal intention. The mother was unable to communicate with her. Both child and parents had succeeded in alienating one another.

It was during this period that Gail became the expendable child. Although she was able at times to perceive some positive feelings from her parents' attitudes, she had to devalue them; e.g., that her mother loved her for being a daughter but not for herself. In any case, for Gail, it was not enough. She felt her mother cared more for the dog than for her. Her philosophy of all or nothing allowed for no compromise. Either she had not developed or she had pushed away any other sources of support, and was left with no alternative but to feel abandoned. The estrangement between her parents and herself was complete. She had given up hope for herself, and apparently turned her anger and self-hatred against her physical self and the ambivalent parental introjects, the same method she used as a six-year-old. As the instrument of self-destruction, she took something that belonged to her father, his sleeping pills. We see in Gail a double negative identification with her "drug addict" father and depressed mother. Through her suicidal act, Gail complied with her father's wishes to be rid of her.

CASE 2

Bill A.—"You're Driving Me Crazy"

Bill A., a sixteen-and-a-half-year-old high school student, was seen once before his death in a car accident. The interview had been suggested by the psychiatrist who was treating his father. He reported that his son was becoming increasingly tense and withdrawn at home, and refused to see any other doctor.

Mr. A., a businessman of forty-six, had been in psychotherapy for the previous six months. The presenting complaint had been feelings of depression and excess intake of alcohol and dexedrine pills.

Mr. A. was an only child. His father drank, hardly made a living, and there was apparently little contact with him. He remembers his father's throwing his report card at him across the room whenever he did not receive an A at school. His mother was described as unaffectionate and having once beaten her son so badly that a neighbor had to intervene.

Mrs. A. was a conscientious but passive, long-suffering wife and mother. She mentioned that Bill, her second son, was an unplanned child and that her husband had expected a girl.

Mr. A. had his sons call him "Captain." He was strict with the boys and frequently "belted" them. His alcoholic brother-in-law's three-year-old son was destructive at home. Mr. A.'s comment was, "I'd kill a kid like that." As the boys grew in size, he became afraid to hit them and would place his wife in the center of the arguments, requiring her to choose between him or them. He was proud of their athletic accomplishments, expecting them to become all-American athletes. The older of the sons said, "He was always trying to put us in a showcase." One day Mr. A. mentioned that Bill had suffered a concussion in a basketball game while he was watching. The coach had put him back in the game as soon as he regained consciousness. Mr. A. commented apologetically, "I know the coach was tough and incompetent, but I was reluctant to interfere." It turned out that Bill had had previous concussions.

The older son, home on leave, had recently become involved in an automobile accident similar to one he had had two years previously. The car he slammed into belonged to a doctor who wrote a note saying, "Your son, if he doesn't kill someone else, will get himself killed one day." The boy on both occasions had had something to drink. Mr. A. was unable to say "no" when his son asked to borrow his car the next evening. He admitted that both his older boy and Bill drove too fast.

Mr. A. complained, "Bill is tough on me. Criticizes the way I eat, the way I breathe, my drinking—but I guess I bother him too—I care too much, like telling him to wear his gloves. I take out the barrels at 5:00 in the morning just to remind him that he has forgotten." The doctor decided to see Mr. and Mrs. A. and their son together because of increasing tension between them.

Bill spoke of his concern over his father's health and mentioned that his drinking upset the whole family. Looking at his father he said, "I think he feels sorry for himself; at times I feel like belting him." Bill refused the suggestion to seek further psychiatric treatment.

Several months after the interview with the son, Mr. A. and his wife's family attended Bill's athletic banquet. When they went to congratulate him for his awards, he turned his back and walked away. At home that evening, Mr. A. followed him around the house asking what happened. Bill retorted, "You're driving me crazy. I can hardly stand living with you any more." This infuriated the father who responded that he was tired of trying not to hurt his feelings. Mrs. A. said that her son was upset at the banquet because he was not given the all-round sportsman's award and hated to have his father brag about him.

Three weeks later the doctor received a midnight call from Mr. A. saying that his son had been killed in an automobile accident. The story that emerged was that Mr. A. had come home drunk the night before and had confessed to his wife that he had slept with another woman. Bill overheard this and the next evening asked to borrow the car to visit a friend. On his return, his car went into an abutment instead of taking the turnoff leading to his home. The police report indicated no evidence that the car brakes had been used, but that the auto went straight for the concrete pillar over the dividing line, "as though it had been purposely aimed." Mr. A. reacted to the event by taking an overdose of drugs and driving to the scene of the accident two days later. He has continued to preoccupy himself with the question of whether or not he was to blame for the tragedy. Some time later, while visiting his own father in the hospital, he just happened to notice his father's profile and said, "You know, it looks just like Bill's." The death of Bill came as a surprise and shock to the community; a newspaper article stressed the "wonderful" relationship between Mr. A. and his sons.

Formulation

The anger and indifference that Mr. A. sensed from his own parents seem to have been visited in large measure upon his own sons. After the death of Bill, his remark about the similarity of profiles clarified the role his son played of the hated father. On the other hand, he saw the boys as the idealized masculine extension of himself through their athletic abilities. The reaction formation against hurting Bill, such as reminding him to wear gloves, contrasted with the unconscious wish for him to be seriously injured or perhaps killed by allowing the coach to put him back into the basketball game after his concussion. He needed the reflected glory of Bill's achievements regardless of the dangers to his son's health. Mr. A. disregarded his sons' dangerous driving. In this way he avoided having to face his intense ambivalence toward them.

If the father saw Bill as an attacker, his son certainly perceived the father in a similar role. Mr. A.'s, "I'm tired of trying not to hurt you" could have meant to Bill that his father was having trouble in hiding his hate for him. Bill had received a serious blow to his narcissism in not receiving the top athletic award.

His father's renewed drinking and infidelity could have been the final disappointment to whatever hope Bill had of an intact family and a respectable self-image. This insult to his mother could have aroused his own wish to hurt her because of her weakness and submission to his father. If so, the resulting guilt would have been overwhelming. He was afraid to identify with his masochistic mother in a homosexual submission to his father. Bill's increasing withdrawal was the sign that communication between him and his father had ceased. It seemed that of the alternatives available to cope with the accumulating rage of so many years, he could either go crazy, "belt" his father, i.e., kill him, or turn the anger against himself. Bill manifestly, in an identification with the aggressor, chose the latter, and in this act also carried out his father's wish for him to be seriously injured or to die.

CASE 3

Sally T.—"Drop Dead"

Sally T., a fifteen-and-a-half-year-old high school sophomore, was seen at a clinic at the request of her mother who claimed she had taken an overdose of aspirin.

Mrs. T. revealed that Sally's conception was unplanned and that while she was pregnant her husband threw her down a flight of stairs. One year after the birth of her second child, a son, her husband deserted her. Sally was two at the time.

Mrs. T. remarried when Sally was age six, and gave birth to a son one year later. Her husband made it clear that he openly favored this boy and that his wife's place in the home was second to that of his son. Sally's own brother, now thirteen, at Mr. T.'s insistence, was placed in a group home because of the boy's uncontrollable behavior.

Sally had been in continual conflict with her mother for the past several years, lying, stealing, and showing "little guilt." The previous year she had taken her stepfather's contraceptives and given them to some boys at school. The caseworker felt that Sally had a certain degree of feeling for the stepfather, but realized that she was a poor second to his son, and the "most dispensable" member of the family. In anger, Mrs. T. frequently told Sally to "drop dead." Mrs. T. and her husband wanted the girl out of the house because of her defiance and unwillingness to cooperate. They objected as well to her boyfriend who was a delinquent.

In the psychiatric interview Sally was mostly concerned with her boyfriend, Al, whom her parents initially accepted and later did not want around. Consequently, one night she ran away to his house. Her stepfather gave her an ultimatum to return. When they arrived home, he forbade her to see her boyfriend any more. She went to her room and swallowed twenty-five aspirin tablets. "I called my girlfriend; I guess I must have sounded kind of drunk because she said she was going to come over. When she arrived she gave me some coffee and saved my life." Later she added, "I was not taking my life because I was angry at my mother but because I had lost Al who had meant the world to me. . . . I feel my mother is too strict, thinks of me as a slave and baby-sitter."

Formulation

The never-ending conflict between Sally and her mother resulted in symptoms of an increasing degree of severity following the onset of adolescence—from enuresis, lying, and stealing, to running away and a suicidal attempt. Her mother, having disposed of her first son, now was working toward getting rid of her daughter. Sally's behavior, which could just barely be tolerated when she was in latency, now became threatening to the parents' marital relationship.

Sally's repertoire of coping methods was running out, as the strength of her conflicting needs was increasing. Revival of the oedipal conflict at adolescence brought a need to defend herself against an underlying attachment to mother and an attraction to stepfather. Through her boyfriend, Al, she was able to find an extrafamilial object that could make her feel like a grown woman, no longer dependent on her parents. However, she chose someone in her own image—a delinquent who was soon denied to her by her mother and stepfather. This threatened her heterosexual defense against her fears of a regressive submission to mother, e.g., "Mother thinks I am a slave." This loss occurring against a background of being frequently told to "drop dead," and feeling the most dispensable member in the family, all brought about feelings of worthlessness and abandonment that culminated in her suicide attempt. Through this action she tried to comply with her mother's wish to be rid of her and for her to die. Sally had become an unnecessary liability to her family.

DISCUSSION

Anna Freud's (1958) paper on adolescence gives a clarifying description of how the adolescent attempts to deal with the anxieties aroused by his attachment to his parents. "They can displace the libido onto objects outside the family and turn the emotions felt toward them into their opposites. This reversal of affect, e.g., love into hate, may then be projected onto the parents who then become the adolescents' main oppressors and persecutors. . . . Conversely, the full hostility and aggression may be turned away from the objects and employed inwardly against the self. In these cases the adolescents display intense depression, tendency to self-abasement and self-injury, or even carry out suicide wishes." The case histories that have been presented illustrate many of these psychodynamic factors. In addition, they indicate the increasing pathological relationship that developed between the adolescent and his parents. The current literature on adolescent suicide emphasizes the importance of understanding the interrelated roles of the child and parents.

Schneer and Kay (1961) speak of the parents engendering a sadomasochistic attitude in the child who, when he encounters rejection again in adolescence, turns to suicide to end his struggle with frustration.

Glaser (1965) discusses the "emotionally detached" parents and the absent father who are not available as resources of love and support in times of stress.

Gould (1965) writes, "For many reasons the parent(s) may wish the child did not exist . . . [and] basically feel they would be happier without children. The child who picks up these clues, and this may be communicated nonverbally as well as verbally, and unconsciously as well as consciously, may try to follow his parents' unconscious (or conscious) wishes and attempt suicide if this is the only way to gain their approval and love." Schrut (1964) in a similar vein writes that in more than half of the nineteen children studied, a basic feeling directed toward the child of being a burden was conveyed unconsciously by the significant parent or parents, clearly from infancy in ten cases. He mentions the struggle in both mother and child "against coming to consciousness—the demand that he be nonexistent."

Teicher and Jacobs (1966b) state that 88 percent of the adolescent suicide attempts in their study occurred in the home, often with the parent(s) in the next room. They believed that this was an indication of the extent of the adolescents' alienation from their parents at the time of the suicide attempt. Another interpretation would be that it was indicative of the parents' need to avoid and deny this destructive behavior in a child who is no longer wanted.

In all of the cases presented the onset of adolescence leads to what Teicher and Jacobs (1966a) call the "escalation stage," where an intensification of the past behavioral problems between child and parent takes place. The past efforts of the parents to control their children's behavior and contain their own ambivalent feelings toward them began to fail. Their adolescents' continuing provocative behavior, changeable moods, periods of withdrawal, and secretiveness added to the parents' feeling helpless, frustrated, and shut out. Parents and children became estranged from each other and the lines of reason and understanding broke down. Now another form of communication, of a different order, came through: the nonverbal and unconscious kind that gave a message to the adolescent of his being no longer wanted; of his parent's (or parents') wish to be rid of him and for him to die.

In Gail's case this communiqué was transmitted through her father's disregarding her suicidal threats and previous diagnosis of being seriously disturbed emotionally. Bill's father allowed the coach to put him right back into the game after a concussion. In addition, he did nothing about either of his sons' dangerous driving, and finally he told Bill, "I'm tired of trying not to hurt you." With Sally there was an overt directive to drop dead, in addition to her own realization that she was the most dispensable one in the family.

When the situation develops in which the parents either consciously or unconsciously, verbally or nonverbally, wish for the adolescent to die, the child is faced with an actual loss which is tantamount to being abandoned. He has become expendable and he knows it, as evidenced by his subsequent suicidal behavior. The expendable child refers to one who no longer can be tolerated or needed by his family. He ceases to be useful either as an object of affection or as the vicarious fulfiller of the needs of his parents. This latter situation is seen in the delinquent, the daughter who is illegitimately pregnant, the child who is the object of incest, the schizophrenic, the juvenile homicide. All these children serve a specific need for the specific psychopathology of each parent, and help to maintain the precarious equilibrium within the family structure. Vogel and Bell (1960) describe such a child as the scapegoat, the object through whom the parents deal with family and personal tensions. These children may become expendable at a certain point in time when they are no longer of use, or when they become a positive threat to the sanity, the marital stability, and the very existence of the parents. Once this situation develops, one or both parents communicate to the child, through verbal or nonverbal behavior, or by conscious or unconscious actions, their wanting to be rid of the child in some way, including the wish for the child to die. This is a degree of rejection carried to a potentially tragic extreme.

The roots of expendability go back at times to birth or even before conception. The child may be unwanted and unplanned for, or, if there is planning, this may quickly give way to a disappointment in the product. With this as a beginning, there is little chance for an early confident mother-child relationship to develop. The consequences are interferences with the healthy development of the ego and its functions. The infant sooner or later develops a specific meaning for the parent, representing a cold mother, rejecting father, or hated sibling. Meanwhile, the parents themselves may have their own special problems and adjustments which may either contribute to or at times ameliorate their difficulties in relating to the child. It is clear from the cases presented how the adolescents' behavior rearoused their parents' own feelings about their unresolved family ties as well as their erotic and hostile drives. The parents are as much victims of their own pasts as they are the contributors to their children's current predicaments.

The concept of the expendable child may be extended to that of the expendable patient. The implication here is that there are factors within the social structure of a mental hospital similar to those of the child-parent interaction, or of the doctor-patient relationship, which may contribute directly or indirectly to the patient's suicidal attempt. Havens (1965) speaks of this point in discussing the hospital staff's reaction to a patient who had been released prematurely and later committed suicide, "We may have hurried our patient toward a false health out of an unaware disgust for something we felt in her" and later—"maybe we did not want the patient."

Once this condition of becoming the expendable child in a family has developed, it is only a question of time until an episode of felt rejection sets off the suicide attempt.

Teicher and Jacobs (1966a) state, "Already alienated from his parents the adolescent may find the closeness of a primary relationship in a romance." In Sally's case her romance was broken up by her stepfather. This loss could very well have revived memories of earlier losses, including that of her father at age two.

There can be no absolute certainty that Bill's car accident was a voluntary act of suicide. Schechter (1957) reports somewhat similar cases. Tabachnick et al. (1966), in their comparative psychiatric study of accidental and suicidal death, state that the people who had died by accident had encountered no clear traumatic situations just preceding their deaths. Those who died by suicide had either experienced the loss of an important person, or a feeling of failure, or being unloved just prior to their deaths. Bill may have felt that his father's earlier comment about being tired of trying not to hurt him and his father's infidelity to his mother destroyed any hope of understanding or support from him. In this context of feeling abandoned he could have turned to suicide.

Gail's suicide attempt followed a quarrel with her mother. She felt that her mother just did not understand her. Her feelings of being abandoned were further reinforced by her father ignoring her suicide threats.

Rochlin (1965) clarifies the dilemma of the "expendable" child who feels abandoned. In writing about the aggressive feelings evoked by object loss he states: "the self is then . . . in the greatest danger from its own attacks, which are often expressed as suicidal wishes and impulses. This suggests that to entertain destructive wishes toward a meaningful object cannot be endured. In the presence of such wishes the self must take the abuses even though its recourse is to project the source of hostility onto another. The object must be spared."

The object is indeed spared—but sometimes at the expense of the adolescent's becoming a dropout from the family or from life itself.

SUMMARY

Three cases are presented which focus on the role of parental attitudes as one of the many factors involved in adolescent suicidal behavior. In each instance there was a background history of significant problems beginning early in the parent-child relationship and reaching a crisis during the developmental stresses of adolescence. The child's attempts at coping with the difficulties of growing up rearoused many of the parents' own unresolved adolescent conflicts, e.g., their sexual and aggressive drives, and struggles with their own ambivalent ties to their respective parents. As a consequence the adolescent and his parents built up an increasing misunderstanding and resentment toward each other, culminating in the parent's perceiving their child's sexuality and hostility as a *threat* to their sanity, marital stability, and even their very existence. The adolescent in turn saw his parents as oppressors and persecutors. The parents responded to this intolerable threat by wishing to be rid of their child, by wishing him dead. The wish was conveyed explicitly through words spoken in anger, e.g., "drop dead," or tacitly, as when the parents disregarded the suicidal threats and gestures that had already been made by their child. The adolescent interpreted these signs as an indication that his parents wanted to be rid of him, indeed wanted him to die—that he could be dispensed with for the sake of everyone else's welfare. He had become *expendable.*

In the three cases described, the adolescents' reaction of feeling abandoned and the subsequent compliance with this felt parental wish appeared to be an important factor leading to their suicide attempt. This appeared to occur at the time when the adolescent's ego, already compromised by previous developmental faults and/or current narcissistic injuries and losses, succumbed to the felt parental wish for them to die.

REFERENCES

Beckett, P. G. S. et al. (1956), Studies in schizophrenia at the Mayo Clinic, I. The significance of exogenous traumata and the genesis of schizophrenia. Psychiatry, *19:137–142.*

Freud, A. (1958), Adolescence. The Psychoanalytic Study of the Child, *13:255–278. New York: International Universities Press.*

Glaser, K. (1965), Attempted suicide in children and adolescents: psychodynamic observations. Amer. J. Psychother., *19:220–227.*

Gould, R. E. (1965), Suicide problems in children and adolescents. Amer. J. Psychother., *19:228–246.*

Havens, L. L. (1964), Psychosis and the concept of ego defect. Presented before the American Psychoanalytic Association, New York.

——— *(1965), The anatomy of a suicide.* New Eng. J. Med., *272:401–406.*

Jacobziner, H. (1965), Attempted suicides in adolescence. J. Amer. Med. Assn., *191:7–11.*

Johnson, A. M. et al. (1956), Studies in schizophrenia at the Mayo Clinic. II. Observations on ego function in schizophrenia. Psychiatry, *19:143–148.*

Rochlin, G. (1965), Griefs and Discontents: The Forces of Change. *Boston: Little, Brown, p. 27.*

Schechter, M. D. (1957), The recognition and treatment of suicide in children. In: Clues to Suicide, *ed. E. S. Shneidman & N. L. Farberow, New York: McGraw-Hill, p. 181.*

Schneer, H. I. & Kay, P. (1961), The suicidal adolescent. In: Adolescents, *ed. S. Lorand & H. I. Schneer. New York: Hoeber, pp. 180–201.*

Schrut, A. (1964), Suicidal adolescents and children. J. Amer. Med. Assn., *188:1103–1107.*

Tabachnick, N., Litman, R. E., Osman, M., Jones, W. L., Cohn, J., Kasper, A., & Moffat, J. (1966), Comparative psychiatric study of accidental and suicidal death. Arch. Gen. Psychiat., *14:60–68.*

Teicher, J. D. & Jacobs, J. (1966a), Adolescents who attempt suicide. Amer. J. Psychiat., *122:1248–1257.*

——— *(1966b), The physician and the adolescent suicide attempter.* J. School Health, *36:406–415.*

Vogel, E. F. & Bell, N. W. (1960), The emotionally disturbed child as the family scapegoat. In: A Modern Introduction to the Family, *ed. N. W. Bell & E. F. Vogel. Glencoe, Ill.: Free Press, pp. 382–397.*

14. Sigmund Freud on Suicide

Robert E. Litman

BIOGRAPHICAL NOTE

Robert E. Litman is clinical professor of psychiatry, University of California (Los Angeles) School of Medicine, and a training and supervisory analyst at the Southern California Psychoanalytic Institute. With Edwin Shneidman and Norman Farberow he was a founder of the Los Angeles Suicide Prevention Center, where he served as chief psychiatrist for thirty-one years. He is a founding member and past president of the American Association of Suicidology.

Litman points to his identification with his father, a North Dakota country doctor, as the source of his interest in pathology and his long collaboration as deputy coroner with three successive Los Angeles chief medical examiners. The "psychological autopsies" he carried out with Thomas Noguchi, M.D., author and "coroner to the stars," were especially memorable.

COMMENT

This essay, a discussion of the evolution of Freud's thinking on the subject of suicide, is unique in the literature. As Litman shows, Freud not only developed the theory of anger turned upon the self, but addressed guilt over death wishes toward others, identification with a suicidal parent, the incapacity to renounce, suicide as revenge, suicide as an escape, suicide and masochism, and suicide as an expression of the controversial death instinct.

This chapter provides an excellent overview that will help the reader place Freud's perspectives on suicide in context with other contributions in this book, many of which develop and elaborate his ideas.

Robert E. Litman, "Sigmund Freud on Suicide." In *The Psychology of Suicide,* E. S. Shneidman, N. L. Farberow, and R. Litman, eds. New York: Science House, 1970, pp. 565–586. Reprinted by permission.

■

> The fateful question for the human species seems to me to be whether and to what extent their cultural development will succeed in mastering the disturbance of their communal life by the human instinct of aggression and self-destruction.[1]
>
> —Sigmund Freud

According to Sigmund Freud, commenting on man's fate in 1930 toward the end of his own long career, suicide and war are different aspects of a unitary problem. They are expressions in human beings of instinctual aggression and instinctual destruction which in turn are interchangeable elements of the death instinct. Furthermore, the process of civilization, which offers the only possibility of deferring the end of mankind by group violence, undermines the psychic health of the individual members of the group and threatens each of them with suicide.[2]

In this essay I shall review the clinical experience and theoretical steps that led Freud to his various conclusions about suicide. My purpose is to abstract from the totality of Freud's writings his pertinent observations and to evaluate the contribution they make to an understanding of suicide and of suicide prevention in our own time, a full generation after Freud's death. The reader who follows me in this task will, I am afraid, encounter difficulties in his path from time to time, although I will try to mark the way as clearly as I can. Unfortunately, Freud never synthesized his views on suicide into an organized presentation. There is no paper on suicide comparable to Freud's dissertations on war.[3] His many clinical observations, inferences, and speculations, which illuminate multiple aspects of suicide, are scattered through numerous papers concerned primarily with other issues and other goals.

In its general outline this review will trace the theme of suicide in Freud's writings from 1881 to 1939, at points deviating from a strictly temporal progression for special topical development. The first section deals with Freud's earlier observations, mostly personal and clinical. The second section is concerned with Freud's later contributions, mostly theoretical and speculative. The third section includes my attempt at synthesis and evaluation. To avoid unnecessary complications, the source material will be limited to Freud's writings and Ernest Jones' biography of Freud.

EARLY EXPERIENCES: 1881–1910

It would be a mistake to assume that Freud's experience with suicide was only theoretical or philosophical. On the contrary, Freud had considerable clinical experience with suicidal patients. There are, for example, references to suicidal symptomatology in all of the case histories that Freud published except that of Little Hans, a five-year-old child.

Suicidal behavior was an important aspect of the symptoms of Josef Breuer's patient, Fraulein Anna O. Breuer discovered the cathartic method of treatment which constituted the beginning stage of the treatment approach that Freud later developed into psychoanalysis. Anna O. at times displayed complete psychic dissociation with two entirely distinct states of consciousness and for awhile spoke only in English. She became suicidal after the death of her father. On the doctor's recommendation and against her will, she was transferred (in June, 1881) to a country house in the neighborhood of Vienna, because of the danger of suicide. The move was followed by three days and nights completely without sleep or nourishment and by numerous attempts at suicide, by smashing windows and by other methods. After this she grew quieter and even took chloral at night for sedation.[4]

Although Freud described this case several times, he did not refer particularly to the suicidal elements. Very early in his career as a psychoanalyst, however, Freud was aware of the importance of guilt over hostile impulses against parents causing symptoms, especially after the parents' death. In May, 1897, in a letter to Wilhelm Fleiss, Freud wrote: "Hostile impulses against parents (a wish that they should die) are also an integral part of neuroses. . . . They are repressed at periods in which pity for one's parents is active—at times of their illness or death. One of the manifestations of grief is then to reproach oneself for their death. . . ."[5]

Possibly Freud's most intense personal experience with suicide occurred in August, 1898. "A patient over whom I had taken a great deal of trouble had put an end to his life on account of an incurable sexual disorder." The suicide of the patient, according to Freud, stirred up in Freud certain painful fantasies connected with death and sexuality, which he more or less successfully repressed. Several weeks later, still under the influence of these unconscious fantasies, Freud was unable to recall the name of Signorelli, creator of magnificent frescoes about the "Four Last Things"—Death, Judgment, Hell, and Heaven. Freud tried to visualize the frescoes and the artist and felt the inadequacy of his associations as a source of inner torment. With great effort he reconstructed his conversation with a traveling companion immediately before the forgetting. The topic was foreign customs, the Turks, their confidence in doctors, their resignation to fate, even death. Freud had thought of telling an anecdote. "These Turks place a higher value on sexual enjoyment than on anything else, and in the event of sexual disorders, they are plunged in a despair which contrasts strangely with their resignation toward the threat of death." A patient (Freud's?) once said, "Herr (Signor), you must know that if *that* comes to an end, then life is of no value." Feeling suddenly uncomfortable, Freud suppressed the anecdote, deliberately diverted his own thoughts from death and sexuality, and changed the subject to the famous frescoes. But in his unconscious effort to continue to forget the suicide, Freud now forgot the painter's name, which joined the memory of the suicide in Freud's repressed unconscious, until someone else suggested the correct name. Freud recognized it instantly and used it to recall the repressed fantasies and reconstruct the mechanism of forgetting. Freud reported the episode immediately to his friend, Fliess,[6] and published an account of it several months later,[7] omitting in these first two reports, however, the fact that the specific unpleasant news which precipitated the forgetting was a patient's suicide. Later, when Freud rewrote the material as the first example in his book *The Psychopathology of Everyday Life* (1901) he included the fact of the suicide.[8]

Ernest Jones says of this incident, "As I hope to expound in a revised edition of Volume I of this biography, it was connected with a significant episode which must have played an important part in the inception of Freud's self-analysis."[9] Unfortunately, Jones died before revising the biography. We are left with an intriguing biographical mystery and an important scientific problem. We ask, Who was this patient? What happened in the analysis? Did Freud describe fragments of the case, even heavily disguised, somewhere in his writings? Or was the history of the patient totally repressed from the memory of science? Why did Jones, who has so much to report about Freud's work and his patients, choose to postpone the illumination of the suicide incident? The important scientific problem is this: Is the taboo on suicide so intense that even psychoanalysts are reluctant to expose their case materials and personal experiences in this area? But here, and many times hereafter, I must restrict digressions or this essay will be a book.

Hopefully, other biographers will supply the missing episode that Jones omitted. My guess is that it related to Wilhelm Fliess, Freud's close friend during the 1890s. Freud began his self-analysis as a systematic project in July, 1897. Why exactly then? For approximately ten years he had been listening to patients, developing and improving his ability to interpret dreams and free associations, including his own. From this material he was being forced to draw some strange and disturbing inferences. Repeatedly and consistently, the stories from his patients forced him to conclude that sexual abuse by the fathers was responsible for the patients' illnesses. He was becoming convinced of the disagreeable reality of rivalries, death wishes, and incest in families. The death of his aged father (October 23, 1896) affected Freud deeply. "At a death the whole past stirs within one. I now feel as if I had been torn up by the roots."[10] Freud's dreams revealed hostility to and guilt feelings about, as well as admiration for, his father. Apparently, some of Freud's unconscious reactions toward his father were transferred to Fliess. Freud found himself becoming irritable with his friend. Freud's dreams and associations connected Fliess with Italy, travel, and Italian art.[11]

Freud was moody, anxious, and depressed for several years after the death of his father. He worked his way back to health through his self-analysis and his writing. There is no evidence that Freud was suicidal during this period, although a possible guiding fantasy was that of death and rebirth. In a letter dated June 12, 1897, he wrote, "I have been through some kind of neurotic experience, with odd states of mind not intelligible to consciousness—cloudy thoughts and veiled doubts, with barely here and there a ray of light. . . ." Freud continued the letter with a paragraph describing a new case, a 19-year-old girl whose two older brothers shot themselves, and then concluded, "Otherwise I am empty and ask your indulgence. I believe I am in a cocoon, and heaven knows what sort of creature will emerge from it."[12] During this whole period, Freud was struggling most particularly with painful feelings of guilty rivalry with his father and with Fliess.

As far as I know, Freud's only overt suicide threats occurred during his long, passionate, and stormy engagement. In 1885, he wrote to his fiancée Martha, whom he eventually married, his decision to commit suicide should he lose her. A friend was dying, and in this connection Freud wrote, "I have long since resolved on a decision (suicide), the thought of which is in no way painful, in the event of my losing you. That we should lose each other by parting is quite out of the question. . . . You have no idea how fond I am of you, and I hope I shall never have to show it."[13] So Freud could understand how someone, like the Turks of the censored anecdote, or his deceased patient, could turn to death when frustrated sexually. "One is very crazy when one is in love."[14] Many years later, Freud was to comment that the two situations of being most intensely in love and of suicide are similar, in that the ego is overwhelmed by the object.[15] In his early theory the claims of love (libido) and self-preservation were opposed, and he consistently maintained that to love is dangerous (acknowledging always that not to love poses an even greater peril). "We behave as if we were a kind of Asra who die when those they love die."[16] (The Asra were a fictitious tribe of Arabs who "die when they love.")

The histories reported by Freud's psychoanalytic patients contain numerous accounts of suicidal behavior. For example, the only sister of Freud's most celebrated patient, the Wolf Man (so called because of his childhood phobia of wolves), committed suicide by poisoning herself. The patient's strange lack of grief over the sister's death aroused Freud's special interest until the psychoanalysis clarified the complicated processes of displacement of the mourning reaction in this patient.[17] The dramatic case of Dr. Schreber's paranoia (1911) included descriptions of Schreber's longing for death. "He made repeated attempts at drowning himself in his bath and asked to be given the 'cyanide that was intended for him.' "[18]

The first of Freud's longer case reports (1905) described fragments of the analysis of an 18-year-old female hysteric whom he called Dora. She pressured her parents into obtaining treatment for her by writing a letter in which she took leave of them because she could no longer endure her life and leaving the letter in a place where they would be sure to find it. Just when Freud's hopes for a successful treatment were highest, she unexpectedly broke it off. Dora was not the first person in the family to talk of suicide. Her father once told the story that he had been so unhappy at a certain time that he made up his mind to go into the woods and kill himself, but Frau K., a friend, recognizing his state, had gone after him and persuaded him by her entreaties to preserve his life for the sake of his family. Dora did not believe the story. No doubt, she said, the two of them had been seen together in the woods having an affair, and so her father had invented this fairy tale of the suicide to account for the rendezvous.

From this case we learn about suicide as a communication, attention getter, cry for help, method of revenge, and as a partial identification, in this case with the father. Also, obscurely, there is in Dora's behavior a deep theme of sadism and aggression; possibly she is doing to others, including Freud, what she believes others have done to her (stirred up false hopes, lied to her, abandoned her cruelly).[19]

Additional insights appear in Freud's 1909 case history of a man with severe obsessional neurosis, whom Freud sometimes called "the man with the rats" because of one dramatic feature of the neurosis, a special fantasy about rats. The patient's many obsessions and compulsions included suicidal impulses and commands. In the analysis, numerous examples of these suicidal commands were identified as punishments for rage and jealousy toward rivals. Freud said, "We find that impulses to suicide in a neurotic turn out regularly to be self-punishment for wishes for someone else's death."[20] Freud was well aware that suicide is not a great danger in obsessive neurotics. The patient said that he might actually have killed himself on several occasions were it not for his consideration for the feelings of his mother and sister. The same sister, incidentally, had told him once when they were very young that if he died she would kill herself. He knew that his own death would pain his mother terribly because a cousin had killed himself eighteen months before, because of an unhappy love affair, it was said, and the man's mother, the patient's aunt, was still miserable.[21]

In *The Psychopathology of Everyday Life* (1901), Freud cited numerous clinical observations that convinced him of the important part played in mental life by an instinct for self-destruction.

> There is no need to think such self-destruction rare, for the trend to self-destruction is present to a certain degree in very many more human beings than those in whom it is carried out. Self-injuries are, as a rule, a compromise between this instinct and the forces that are still working against it, and even when suicide actually results the inclination to suicide will have been present for a long time before in less strength, or in the form of an unconscious and suppressed trend. . . . Even a *conscious* intention of committing suicide chooses its times, means, and opportunity; and it is quite in keeping with this that an *unconscious* intention should wait for a precipitating occasion, which can take over a part of the causation and by engaging the subject's defensive forces, can liberate the intention from their pressure.[22]

The clinical examples include an officer who had been deeply depressed by the death of his beloved mother. When forced to take part in a cavalry race, he fell and was severely injured. A man shot himself in the head "accidentally" after being humiliated by rejection from the army and being jilted by his girl friend. A woman injured herself out of guilt for an abortion. After the injury she felt sufficiently punished.[23]

Despite his many clinical observations concerning suicide, Freud was unable to organize them systematically into his psychoanalytic theory of instincts. On April 20 and 27, 1910, there was a discussion of the Vienna Psychoanalytical Society on the subject of suicide. On this occasion, Adler and Steckel talked at great length and in great detail, emphasizing the aggressive aspects of suicide. Freud, by contrast, said very little, contenting himself with these concluding remarks:

> I have an impression that in spite of all the valuable material that has been brought before us in this discussion, we have not reached a decision on the problem that interests us. We are anxious, above all, to know how it becomes possible for the

extraordinarily powerful life instinct to be overcome; whether this can only come about with the help of a disappointed libido or whether the ego can renounce its self-preservation for its own egoistic motives. It may be that we have failed to answer this psychological question because we have no adequate means of approaching it. We can, I think, only take as our starting point the condition of melancholia which is so familiar to us clinically and a comparison between it and the affect of mourning. The affective processes in melancholia, however, and the vicissitudes undergone by the libido in that condition are totally unknown to us. Nor have we arrived at a psychoanalytic understanding of the chronic affect of mourning. Let us suspend our judgment until experience has solved this problem.[24]

Actually, in 1910, Freud knew a great deal about suicide. He had identified many important clinical features: (1) Guilt over death wishes toward others, especially parents; (2) identification with a suicidal parent; (3) loss of libidinal gratification, or more accurately, refusal to accept loss of libidinal gratification; (4) an act of revenge, especially for loss of gratification; (5) escape from humiliation; (6) a communication, a cry for help; and finally (7) Freud recognized the intimate connection between death and sexuality. Sadism and masochism were obviously the deepest roots of suicide. Freud could not decide, however, where to assign such overwhelming sadism and masochism in his theoretical framework. According to Freud, human behaviors are derived ultimately from needs to satisfy instinctual drives. In his early theory the basic, conflicting instinctual drives were thought to be libido (sensuality, sexuality) and self-preservation (hunger, aggressive mastery). How could suicide satisfy the needs either of sexuality or self-preservation?

THEORIES AND SPECULATIONS: 1911–1939

Eventually, Freud revised his theory of the instincts in order to provide appropriate recognition of the importance of self-destructiveness. In 1932, reviewing his life's work, Freud commented, "Sadism and masochism alike, but masochism quite especially, present a truly puzzling problem to the libido theory; and it is only proper if what was a stumbling block for one theory should become the cornerstone of the theory replacing it."[25] More accurately, the new concept of a death instinct supplemented rather than replaced libido theory.

In considering the totality of Freud's writings, one must view his various contributions against the background of the time in which the writing was done. Up until 1910, the formulations on suicide were in the framework of the libido theory. After 1920, they were in the framework of the death-instinct theory. The articles written in 1914 and 1915 form a transition chapter.

In "Mourning and Melancholia" (written in 1915, published in 1917), Freud followed his own suggestion and took as his starting point a special type of patient, melancholics who express great guilt and self-reproach:

> We see how in him one part of the ego sets itself over and against the other, judges it critically and in a word takes it as its object. Our suspicion that the critical agency which is here split off from the ego might also show its independence in other circumstances will be confirmed by every other observation.[26]

How does this splitting-off occur? The explanation in terms of psychic energy (libido) is quite complicated. Energy withdrawn from a lost object of love is relocated in the ego and used to recreate the loved one as a permanent feature of the self, an *identification* of the ego with the abandoned object. "Thus, the shadow of the object fell upon the ego, and the latter could henceforth be judged by a special agency as though it were an object, the forsaken object."[27] "Shadow" objects existing as structures in the ego (identifications) obviously are not fully integrated into the total personality. A demarcation zone, or fault line remains, along which ego splitting occurs.

Also significant was Freud's speculation that certain ways of loving are less stable than others. Narcissistic love of another, for example, is especially vulnerable to disorganization and regression toward immature and primitive stages of the libido, especially sadism.

> It is this sadism alone that solves the riddle of the tendency to suicide which makes melancholia so interesting and so dangerous. So immense is the ego's self love, which we have come to recognize as the primal state from which instinctual life proceeds, and so vast is the amount of narcissistic libido, which we see liberated in the fear that emerges at a threat to life, that we cannot conceive how that ego can consent to its own destruction. We have long known it is true that no neurotic harbors thoughts of suicide which he has not turned back upon himself from murderous impulses against others, but we have never been able to explain what interplay of forces can carry such a purpose through to execution. The analysis of melancholia now shows that the ego can kill itself only if, owing to the return of the object-cathexis, it can treat itself as an object—if it is able to direct against itself the hostility which relates to an object and which represents the ego's original reaction to objects in the external world. Thus, in regression from narcissistic object-choice, the object has, it is true, been gotten rid of, but it has nevertheless proved more powerful than the ego itself. In the two opposed situations of being most intensely in love, and of suicide, the ego is overwhelmed by the object, though in totally different ways.[28]

The above excerpt is quoted frequently in the literature concerned with suicide, most often with misplaced emphasis on the aspect of the original hostility and murderous impulses. In my opinion, the more important creative concepts are those of regression, disorganization, and ego-splitting, pathologic processes which allow a portion of the ego to initiate action while disregarding the interests of the remainder. Moreover, the positive, didactic quality of the isolated paragraph quoted is misleading in that the impression is created that Freud was making assertions about all suicides, which was not his intention. The tenor of the article as a whole is modest and tentative; and in the first paragraph Freud specifically disclaims general validity for findings based on the analysis of a few specially selected melancholics.

Within a few years Freud had discovered that the process of establishing objects as identifications in the ego was very common. In fact, the ego is made up in large part of identifications. Freud did not carry the theory of identifications much further, but a consistent development of his concept has led to our modern notion that the original representation of most loved objects is split into several parts, good and bad, in both the ego and the superego. These multiple object-identifications, plus the need for establishing defenses and maintaining repressions, result in splits and fissures in every ego. In the 1920s, Freud developed a structural model of mental activity (id, ego, superego) and assigned various functions to the different parts of the model.[29] He stated that the very earliest identifications play a special role in the total self, in that they are more completely split off from the rest of the ego and become the superego, which includes conscience and ideals, has the functions of loving, supporting, judging, and punishing the ego, and may become diseased on its own account. Concepts or images of suicide appear only in the ego and superego, for the id knows nothing of its own death. "In the unconscious everyone of us is convinced of his own immortality."[30] Indeed, even consciously, it is impossible to imagine our own death. "Whenever we attempt to do so we can perceive that we are in fact still present as spectators."[31]

Freud paid little attention to the role (spectator, participant, rescuer, or betrayer) of others in a suicide. He recorded the observations but had no room for them in his theory. For example, he wrote briefly in 1921 about a young man who was tormenting his mistress. He was trying unconsciously to drive her to suicide in order to revenge himself on her for his own suicide attempt several years before in connection with a different woman.[32] In 1916, Freud discussed the characters of the play *Rosmersholm*. In this drama a poor wife, Beata Rosmer, is psychologically poisoned by her rival, Rebecca Gamvik. The wife commits suicide as a reaction to abandonment by her husband and her own sense of worthlessness.[33] Suicide is not a direct theme of either of the papers, which are concerned respectively with telepathy and with guilt over success. Another literary analysis (1928) concerns the story of a mother who tries unsuccessfully to rescue a young gambler from suicide.[34]

The last of Freud's longer case reports, "The Psychogenesis of a Case of Homosexuality in a Woman," was published in 1920. Freud used it to develop further his views on homosexuality, female sexuality, and some technical aspects of psychoanalytic therapy. The patient was an 18-year-old girl, who was brought to Freud by her father about six months after she made a suicide attempt. What disturbed the family was not so much the suicide attempt as the girl's homosexual attachment to a woman about ten years her senior. The woman had not greatly encouraged the girl, and when they were walking together one day and met the father, who gave them a furious look, the woman told the girl they must now certainly separate. Immediately the girl rushed off and flung herself over a wall down the side of an embankment onto the suburban railway line which ran close by. Although fortunately little permanent damage was done, the girl was in bed for some time, and Freud felt that the attempt was undoubtedly serious.

> After her recovery she found it easier to get her own way than before; the parents did not dare to oppose her with so much determination, and the lady, who up until then had received her advances coldly, was moved by such an unmistakable proof of serious passion and began to treat her in a more friendly way.[35]

It seemed to Freud that much of the girl's behavior was a reaction to the birth of her third brother three years previously. It was after that event that she turned her love away from children toward older women. Concerning the suicide attempt, Freud said,

> The analysis was able to disclose a deeper interpretation beyond the one she gave (despair over loss of the lady). The attempted suicide was, as might have been expected, determined by two other motives besides the one she gave: It was the fulfillment of a punishment (self-punishment), and the fulfillment of a wish. As the latter it meant the attainment of the very wish which, when frustrated, had driven her into homosexuality—namely the wish to have a child by her father, for now she fell through her father's fault. From the point of view of self-punishment the girl's action shows us that she had developed in her unconscious strong death wishes against one or the other of her parents—perhaps against her father out of revenge for impeding her love, but more probably against her mother, too, when she was pregnant with the little brother. Analysis has explained the enigma of suicide in the following way: Probably no one finds the mental energy required to kill himself unless, in the first place, in doing so, he is at the same time killing an object with whom he has identified

himself and, in the second place, is turning against himself a death wish which had been directed against someone else. Nor need the regular discovery of these unconscious death wishes in those who have attempted suicide surprise us (any more than it ought to make us think that it confirms our deductions), since the unconscious of all human beings is full enough of such death wishes against even those they love. Since the girl identified herself with her mother, who should have died at the birth of the child denied to herself, this punishment-fulfillment itself was once again a wish fulfillment. Finally, the discovery that several quite different motives, all of great strength, must have cooperated to make such a deed possible is only in accordance with what we should expect.[36]

In a footnote Freud noted "that the various methods of suicide can represent sexual wish fulfillments has long been known to all analysts. (To poison oneself = to become pregnant; to drown = to bear a child; to throw oneself from a height = to be delivered of a child.)"

The most significant of the ideas expressed above is the discovery that suicide is multiply determined by the interaction of several motives. The emphasis is on ego-splitting and identifications. The suicidal act is explained as a reenactment, by a split-off ego identification with mother, of the delivery of the brother. The murderous look the father gave the girl is mentioned. Allusion is made indirectly to the theme of death and rebirth (rescue). The effect of a suicidal act as a communication that changes the environment is recorded. Erotic and masochistic elements of the suicide attempt are specially noted. Death wishes are described as the source of the energy required for suicide, yet death wishes are not limited to suicides but are typical of all human beings.

Evidently, from Freud's later writings, the announcement of a solution of the enigma of suicide was premature. Many questions and uncertainties remained. For example: Was it true that in most suicides the ego murdered the object? Or, more often, did the incorporated object murder the ego? Freud continued to feel that his theoretical explanations were incomplete for several major clinical phenomena associated with self-destructiveness.

The most important of these for psychoanalysis is the "negative therapeutic reaction."[37] Some neurotics inevitably respond to good news, congratulations, or progress in analysis, by increased anxiety, depression, or self-injury.

Judged by all their actions the instinct of self-preservation has been reversed. They seem to aim at nothing other than self-injury and self-destruction. It is possible, too, that the people who in fact do, in the end, commit suicide, belong to this group. It is to be assumed that in such people far-reaching diffusions of instinct have taken place, as a result of which there has been a liberation of excessive quantities of the destructive instincts directed inward. Patients of this kind are not able to tolerate recovery toward treatment and fight against it with all their strength. But we must confess that this is a case which we have not yet succeeded completely in explaining.[38]

Also unexplained was the problem of masochism. Why should many people require pain, punishment, humiliation, and degradation as prerequisites for sexual pleasure? In 1920 Freud proposed for speculative consideration that there might be an instinctual drive toward death.[39] His arguments were partly on clinical grounds (traumatic neuroses, repetitive actions) and partly biological and philosophical. Although at first the new ideas were advanced tentatively and cautiously, Freud soon came to accept them fully and with increasingly complete conviction.[40]

After long hesitancies and vacillations we have decided to assume the existence of only two basic instincts, *Eros* and *the destructive instinct.* The aim of the first of these basic instincts is to establish even greater unities and to preserve them thus—in short, to bind together; the aim of the second is, on the contrary, to undo connections and so to destroy things. In the case of the destructive instinct, we may suppose that its final aim is to lead what is living into an inorganic state. For this reason we call it the *death instinct* . . . In biological functions the two basic instincts operate against each other or combine with each other. Thus, the act of eating is a destruction of the object with the final aim of incorporating it, and the sexual act is an act of aggression with the purpose of the most intimate union. This concurrent and mutually opposing action of the two basic instincts gives rise to the whole variegation of the phenomena of life . . .[41]

The dangerous death instincts are dealt with in individuals in various ways; in part they are rendered harmless by being fused with erotic components; in part they are diverted toward the external world in the form of aggression and, to a large extent, they continue their internal work unhindered.

When the superego is established, considerable amounts of the aggressive instincts are fixated in the interior of the ego and operate there self-destructively. This is one of the dangers to health by which human beings are faced on their path to cultural development. Holding back aggressiveness is, in general, unhealthy and leads to illness . . .[42]

The death-instinct concept was a major theoretical construction. It has, however, received relatively little acceptance among psychoanalysts. Why was Freud so convinced of its usefulness? Ernest Jones suggests that there were subjective motives and reports insightfully on Freud's intense, complicated, personal, daily fantasies about death.[43] However, Freud's own explanation is logically consistent. Freud said he accepted the death-instinct theory because he needed it to explain masochism (and suicide). How then do suicide and masochism appear from this viewpoint?

> If we turn to melancholia first, we find that the excessively strong superego which has obtained a hold upon consciousness rages against the ego with merciless violence . . . What is now holding sway in the superego is, as it were, a pure culture of the death instinct and in fact it often enough succeeds in driving the ego into death . . .[44]

> In melancholia the ego gives itself up because it feels itself hated and persecuted by the superego instead of loved. To the ego, therefore, living means the same as being loved by the superego, so that the death by suicide symbolizes or reenacts a sort of abandonment of the ego by the superego. It is a situation similar to separation from the protecting mother.[45]
>
> The original quantity of internalized death instinct is identical with masochism. The individual tries to externalize this energy as aggressiveness or sadism. Where there is a cultural suppression of the instincts, the destructive instinctual components are turned back into his superego. Now we see a helpless, masochistic ego in relationship with a sadistic superego. The modality of the relationship is punishment. In order to provoke punishment the masochist must do what is inexpedient, must act against his own interests, must ruin his prospects, and perhaps destroy himself. But since there is always some fusion of the erotic and destructive instincts; there is always an obvious erotic component in masochism, so that even the subject's destruction of himself cannot take place without libidinal satisfaction.[46]

Due to the prolonged, extreme biological and social helplessness of the human infant, who cannot unaided satisfy his vital needs or regulate his own destructive instincts, each individual must incorporate controlling, coercing, and punishment components into his superego.[47] By this process the instincts are tamed, and the child can participate in family life and education. By an anthropological analogy, Freud viewed civilization as a group superego development. In civilized man, extra aggression is channeled into the superego and turned against the ego. It is now felt as unconscious guilt, masochism, a need to be punished, or an obscure *malaise* and discontent. The price we pay for our own advance in civilization is a loss, to some degree, of the possibilities of happiness.[48] "We owe to that process (civilization) the best of what we have become, as well as a good part of what we suffer from."[49]

To Freud, suicide represented a symptom of what we suffer from, a product of man and his civilization, a consequence of mental trends which can be found to some degree in every human being.

SYNTHESIS AND EVALUATION

Experience has confirmed Freud's statement that each suicide is multiply determined by the interaction of several motives. Suicide is by no means a homogeneous or unitary piece of human behavior. On the contrary, suicide comprises a variety of behaviors with many important aspects—historical, legal, social, and philosophical, as well as medical and psychological. The psychoanalytic explanations of the psychopathology of suicide are complex, multidimensional and, at some points, ambiguous and redundant.

There are, according to Freud, *general features* of the human condition, at least in Western civilization, which make each individual person somewhat vulnerable to suicide. These general features include: (1) The death instinct, with its clinical derivatives, the aggressive instinct directed outward and the destructive instinct directed inward; (2) The splitting of the ego; this is inevitable because of the extreme helplessness of the human ego in infancy when it is unable to master its own instincts and must conform to the parents or perish; and (3) The group institutions, family and civilization, which require guilty compliance from every member of the group.

The above general features only begin to account for any individual suicide. Individual suicides involve certain *specific suicide mechanisms.* All of them involve a breaking down of ego defenses and the release of increased destructive, instinctual energy. Examples are: (1) loss of love objects, especially those who have been loved in certain dangerous ways; (2) narcissistic injury, symbolically through failure or by direct physiological injury through fatigue or toxins; (3) overwhelming affect: rage, guilt, anxiety, or combinations; (4) extreme splitting of the ego with decathexis of most elements and a setting of one part against the rest; and (5) a special suicidal attitude and plan, often based on an identification with someone who was suicidal.

Finally, there are a great number of *specific predisposing conditions* that more or less favor suicide, although they are not precipitating mechanisms of suicide. These include: (1) a disorganized or disharmonious ego structure which splits up under relatively low conditions of stress; (2) a tendency of the libido to be fixated at preoedipal positions, especially strong tendencies toward sadism and masochism; (3) disease of the superego due to cruel parents, dead parents, parents that wished the person dead, or some constitutional inherited superego trait of excessive destructiveness; (4) strong attachment of the libido to death, dead loved ones, or a fantasy of being dead; (5) vivid erotic fantasies which symbolize and cover up death wishes; for example, the fantasy of bearing a child by father, symbolically actualized as a fall from a height; and (6) a chronically self-destructive living pattern, expressed, for example, as gambling addiction or homosexuality.

The following evaluative comments are based on my several years' experience as chief psychiatrist in a multidisciplinary project of research, training, and clinical service for suicide prevention. My experience is in agreement with Freud's general schematic view. Deep down, there is a suicidal trend in all of us. This self-destructiveness is tamed, controlled, and overcome through our healthy identifications, ego defenses, and constructive habits of living and loving. When the ordinary defenses, controls, and ways of living and loving break down, the individual may easily be forced into a suicidal crisis. At such times he feels helpless, hopeless, and abandoned and may or may not be aware of a great deal of unexpressible, aggressive tension.

However verbalized, most of the therapeutic actions of therapists at the Suicide Prevention Center are aimed at reinforcing the ego defenses, renewing the feeling of hope, love, and trust, and providing emergency scaffolding to aid in the eventual repair and healing of the splits in the patient's ego. Direct psychological techniques for turning the aggression outward have not been particularly successful in our experience. Frequently, we try to deal with the emotional turmoil directly with drugs. Hopefully, we may eventually move into the future predicted by Freud: "The future may teach us to exercise a direct influence by means of peculiar, particular chemical substances on the amounts of energy and their distribution in the mental apparatus." He added, "It may be that there are other still undreamed-of possibilities of therapy, but for the moment we have nothing better at our disposal than the technique of psychoanalysis. For that reason, despite its limitations, it should not be despised."[50]

In my opinion, we still have nothing better at our disposal than psychoanalysis or psychoanalytic psychotherapy as remedies for many of the chronic neurotic reactions and weaknesses which, if uncorrected, may eventually lead toward suicide but are not in themselves precipitating mechanisms of suicidal crises. The years have brought innovations based directly or indirectly on psychoanalytic principles that greatly expand our therapeutic range. These include various brief psychotherapy techniques, psychotherapy in groups, and environmental therapy in hospitals and clinics. All of these approaches, and others, are effective when they are employed at the suitable moment in the appropriate case.

Many of Freud's perceptive inferences have been explored and consolidated by later workers. For example, Freud often referred to certain dangerous ways of loving, in which the ego is "overwhelmed" by the object. Typically, the psychic representations of the self and other are fused, and the other is experienced as essential for survival. Modern writers have termed these attachments "symbiotic," making explicit the analogy to the primitive dependent relationship between a baby (or fetus) and its mother. Freud's observation that symbiotic love is a potential precursor of suicide still holds true.

Freud's dictum that suicide starts with a death wish against others, which is then redirected toward an identification within the self, has been overly accentuated among some psychotherapists, in my opinion, and has become a cliché. Freud is quoted as support of a relative overemphasis on aggression and guilt as components of suicide, with underemphasis of the helplessness, dependency, and erotic elements. Often, however, the suicidal drama reproduces not so much guilt for the unconscious wish of the child to murder the parent but rather a reaction of abandonment on the part of the child to the parent's unconscious wish for the child's death. The mechanism of regression and the themes in suicide of helplessness, constriction, and paranoid distrust have made the deepest impression on me.

Freud pointed out that infantile helplessness is the essential circumstance which creates masochism, but Freud was accustomed to using his concept of the oedipal complex as his reference point for psychopathology. From that viewpoint, guilt over rivalry with parents, especially the father, looms large. At the Suicide Prevention Center, I am more accustomed to using the mother-child preoedipal relationship as a reference concept. Further research, hopefully, will clarify this issue.

It is remarkable that Freud said so little about the all-important attitude of the mother in instilling into a child the desire for life. It is remarkable because Freud was well aware of the influence of his own mother in instilling in him a feeling of confidence and zest for living.[51] Moreover, he had found in his patients and in himself, as a reason for continuing to live, the idea that his premature death would be painful to his mother. When his mother died in 1930, aged 95, Freud noticed in himself a feeling of liberation. "I was not allowed to die as long as she was alive and now I may."[52]

Freud's personal attitude toward death, according to the sharp eye of his biographer Jones, was altogether a rich and complex one with many aspects. "In the world of reality he was an unusually courageous man who faced misfortune, suffering, danger, and ultimately death itself with unflinching fortitude. But in fantasy there were other elements." There was at times a curious longing for death. "He once said he thought of it every day of his life, which is certainly unusual."[53]

In three essays on war and death, Freud expressed himself as a cautiously hopeful realist. Horrified and depressed by the cruelty, fraud, treachery, and barbarity of World War I, he tried to extract some value out of discarding his illusions about civilization and facing disagreeable truths (1915). "To tolerate life remains, after all, the first duty of all living beings. Illusion becomes valueless if it makes this harder for us." And, characteristically, he added, "If you want to endure life prepare yourself for death."[54] Freud described himself as a pacifist (1933). "We pacifists have a constitutional intolerance of war . . . whatever fosters the growth of civilization works at the same time against war."[55] Perhaps some of the psychotherapists whose work exposes them continuously to affects of violence, sadism, and death gain in confidence and flexibility by partially identifying with the complex personality of Freud.

Freud had a few recommendations for society. Possibly, he thought, there would be less suicide if society permitted more sexual and aggressive freedom to its members, though one could not be sure. He thought there was an advantage in providing at intervals opportunities for mass release from inhibitions as, for instance, in carnivals or the ancient Saturnalia. Certainly, Freud saw in our present civilization and its future extensions the only hope for mankind.

> Civilization is a process in the service of Eros, whose purpose is to combine single human individuals and after that families, then races, peoples and nations into one great unity, the unity of mankind. Why this has to happen, we do not know. The work of Eros is precisely this: These collections of men are to be libidinally bound to one another. Necessity alone, the advantages of work in common, will not hold them together, because man's natural aggressive instinct, the hostility of each against all and all against each, opposes this program of civilization. Now I think the meaning of the evolution of civilization is no longer obscure to us. It must present the struggle between Eros and death, between the instinct of life and the instinct of destruction as it works itself out in the human species. This struggle is what all life essentially consists of, and the evolution of civilization may therefore be simply described as the struggle for life of the human species.[56]

This philosophy of joining together and of enjoying each other has, I believe, played a large part in the forming of the spirit of the Suicide Prevention Center. The group spirit has in turn supplied a great deal of the constructive energy required to continue effective work in an area so full of destructive attitudes and hazardous outcomes. The injurious effect on the suicidal person of separation and alienation from the other persons who have loved him was indicated but not emphasized by Freud. We find that in helping a suicidal individual through a crisis, therapists often enlist the cooperation of many people. The goal is to reduce the patient's withdrawal and self-preoccupation and involve him once again in the common interactions of the living.

In our day-to-day therapy of suicidal crises we pay little attention to theory, particularly such deep abstractions as the death instinct. In speculative moments, however, we wonder if perhaps Freud's ominous correlation of suicide and war may not have been a fateful forecast. What if nuclear war were to be precipitated not by accident or policy but by a suicidal individual willing to kill "the others" with him? We encounter potential destroyers of their worlds at our Center fairly often. We take care to leave a door open and not to box them in. In such emergencies, of course, we work not from theory but with intuition and judgment, seeking words, gestures, or actions that will relieve tension and establish communication. The key might be an understanding look, a shared feeling, or a cup of coffee.

Freud was well aware of the difference between philosophic speculations about the general causes of man's misery and the requirements of practical life to do something about it. In a letter to Einstein (1933) on the problem of preventing war, he commented, "The result, as you see, is not very fruitful when an unworldly theoretician is called in to advise on an urgent practical problem. It is a better plan to devote oneself in every particular case to meeting the danger with whatever means lie at hand."[57] Freud applied the same advice to his own clinical endeavors. In 1926, discussing a young patient, Freud wrote, "What weighs on me in his case is my belief that unless the outcome is very good it will be very bad indeed; what I mean is that he would commit suicide without any hesitation. I shall therefore do all in my power to avert that eventuality."[58] That last could well be the motto of the Suicide Prevention Center.

NOTES

1. S. Freud, *Standard Edition of the Complete Psychological Works* (London: Hogarth Press, 1953–1965), Vol. 21, p. 145.
2. *Ibid.,* Vol. 22, pp. 110–111; Vol. 23, pp. 148–150.
3. *Ibid.,* Vol. 14, pp. 289–300; Vol. 22, pp. 213–215.
4. *Ibid.,* Vol. 2, p. 28.
5. S. Freud, *The Origins of Psycho-Analysis* (New York: Basic Books, 1954), p. 207.
6. *Ibid.,* pp. 264–265.
7. Freud, *Standard Edition,* Vol. 3, pp. 290–196.
8. *Ibid.,* Vol. 6, pp. 1–6.
9. E. Jones, *The Life and Work of Sigmund Freud* (New York: Basic Books, 1953–1957), Vol. 2, pp. 333–334.

10. Freud, *The Origins,* pp. 170–171.
11. *Ibid.,* pp. 193–195.
12. *Ibid.,* p. 211.
13. Jones, *op. cit.,* Vol. 1, p. 122.
14. *Ibid.*
15. Freud, *Standard Edition,* Vol. 14, pp. 247–252.
16. *Ibid.,* pp. 289–300.
17. *Ibid.,* Vol. 17, pp. 21–23.
18. *Ibid.,* Vol. 12, p. 14.
19. *Ibid.,* Vol. 7, pp. 3–122.
20. *Ibid.,* Vol. 10, pp. 153–318; Vol. 13, p. 154.
21. *Ibid.,* Vol. 10, pp. 153–318.
22. *Ibid.,* Vol. 6, pp. 178–185.
23. *Ibid.*
24. *Ibid.,* Vol. 11, p. 232.
25. *Ibid.,* Vol. 22, p. 104.
26. *Ibid.,* Vol. 14, pp. 247–252.
27. *Ibid.*
28. *Ibid.*
29. *Ibid.,* Vol. 19, pp. 3–66.
30. *Ibid.,* Vol. 14, pp. 289–300.
31. *Ibid.*
32. *Ibid.,* Vol. 18, pp. 191–192; Vol. 22, pp. 45–46.
33. *Ibid.,* Vol. 14, p. 325.
34. *Ibid.,* Vol. 21, pp. 191–194.
35. *Ibid.,* Vol. 18, pp. 147–172.
36. *Ibid.*
37. *Ibid.,* Vol. 19, p. 49.
38. *Ibid.,* Vol. 23, pp. 180–182.
39. *Ibid.,* Vol. 18, pp. 3–64.
40. Jones, *op. cit.,* Vol. 3, pp. 275–280.
41. Freud, *Standard Edition,* Vol. 23, pp. 148–150.
42. *Ibid.*
43. Jones, *op. cit.,* Vol. 3, pp. 275–280.
44. Freud, *Standard Edition,* Vol. 19, pp. 53–58.
45. *Ibid.*
46. *Ibid.,* Vol. 19, pp. 169–170.
47. *Ibid.,* Vol. 20, pp. 154–155.
48. *Ibid.,* Vol. 21, pp. 134–135.
49. *Ibid.,* Vol. 22, pp. 213–215.
50. *Ibid.,* Vol. 23, pp. 180–182.
51. Jones, *op. cit.,* Vol. 1, p. 5.
52. *Ibid.,* Vol. 1, p. 153.
53. *Ibid.,* Vol. 1, pp. 275–280.
54. Freud, *Standard Edition,* Vol. 14, pp. 289–300.

55. *Ibid.,* Vol. 22, pp. 213–215.
56. *Ibid.*
57. *Ibid.*
58. S. Freud, *Psychoanalysis and Faith* (New York: Basic Books, 1963), pp. 101–102.

15. A Clinical Study of the Role of Hostility and Death Wishes by the Family and Society in Suicidal Attempts

Joseph Richman and Milton Rosenbaum

AUTOBIOGRAPHICAL NOTE

Joseph Richman writes: "My interests and activities for the past thirty years have been devoted to the question of suicide. I trace my interest in the family components to prenatal and postnatal influences. My aunt Hannah, the youngest sister of my mother, committed suicide in 1916, two years before I was born. Hannah had a best friend, Bessie, who felt crushed by the event, but transferred her attachment to my mother. The two became best friends.

"But Bessie never recovered from the guilt and pain. Fifteen years after Hannah's suicide, in 1929, when I was eleven, Bessie committed suicide. I still vividly remember my mother's shocked look when another friend came over and told her the news. Shortly after, Bessie's husband committed suicide. Our family took a special interest in the surviving four children of the couple, who weathered these tragedies with remarkable courage.

"The years passed. The depression of the '30s, World War II and its aftermath during the '40s, and many personal events all became part of my growth and psyche. In 1965 my energies became invested in the study and treatment of suicidal people. I became convinced that working with the families and social network and mobilizing their caring and healing forces was the only way to go for understanding, preventing, and treating suicide. The personal reasons seemed irrelevant. At least, I never thought of them.

"However, on October 5, 1994, Terry Maltsberger phoned and asked that I write something about myself as a preface to the paper Milton Rosenberg and I wrote on the role of aggression and death wishes. As I heard his request, that old memory from 1929, sixty-five years ago, suddenly emerged,

---

Joseph Richman and Milton Rosenbaum, "A Clinical Study of the Role of Hostility and Death Wishes by the Family and Society in Suicidal Attempts." *Israel Annals of Psychiatry and Related Disciplines* 8 (1970):213–231 Reprinted by permission.

with startling visual clarity. That image and the story behind it may be the most fitting preface to my work."

COMMENT

The importance of the family environment as suicide-promoting or suicide-inviting has been documented and richly illustrated by Joseph Richman more than any other writer. In this chapter, written in collaboration with Milton Rosenbaum, the authors show that the family environment is of vital importance, not only in adolescent cases, but in others as well. "It is evident," they write, "that the entire problem of the meaning, function and dynamics of the hostility and death wishes of the significant others, their ambivalent and even loving components, and their place in the multi-faceted problem of suicide is of enormous complexity." That complexity is addressed in this paper, which shows that an effort to understand the riddance impulses in significant others is an essential part of intelligent suicide risk assessment.

The authors further point out that inimical social attitudes within various institutions of contemporary culture, including hospitals, have critical implications for the care of suicidal patients. In the 1990s under "managed care" pressures psychiatric inpatient departments often rush to discharge suicidal individuals before they are fully understood and before potentially life-saving work with ambivalent families can be planned and initiated.

Richman and Rosenbaum have shown that intelligent family intervention is central in preventing suicide. Richman has devoted much of his career to family treatment in suicide cases, and published a distillation of his panoramic experience in the monograph Family Therapy for Suicidal People *(1986).*

REFERENCES

Richman, Joseph. 1986. Family Therapy for Suicidal People. *New York: Springer.*

■

1. THE ROLE OF THE FAMILY

There are many studies documenting the presence of parental loss and broken homes in the backgrounds of persons who later became suicidal (e.g., Jacobs and Teicher, 1967) and of pathology in the current family (e.g., Tuckman and

Youngman, 1964). However, there have been few studies dealing with the dynamics of family interaction in suicidal behavior. The specific ways in which family structure and function are translated into suicidal behavior is the concern of a larger study by the authors which considers role relationships, sexual behavior, communication disturbances, and other areas which are significant within the family and larger social system. In this paper we shall present one aspect of the problem, the handling of aggression within the family and the role of the larger society in perpetuating much of the scapegoating and other suicidogenic phenomena which exist.

Historically, the prevailing attitudes towards suicide have ranged from either a pejorative condemnation, a reasoned tolerance, or an impassioned defense on religious, moral, and philosophical grounds, to a consideration of suicide as a social deviation or psychiatric sickness (e.g., Lecky, 1955). It is only in the relatively recent past that efforts have been made to understand suicide as a meaningful and understandable human reaction to inner and outer events. Concurrent with this humanistic emphasis, there has arisen a phenomenal increase in the study of suicide by clinical and research workers from a variety of biological and behavioral disciplines. The main thrusts have been in the direction of suicide prevention on the one hand and epidemiological and psychosocial studies on the other. These new directions have added much to our knowledge and understanding of the phenomenon of suicide, but we believe that continuous clinically oriented studies based on the individual and family approach are the bedrock of further progress. Hence this report.

As for the specific topic of this inquiry, it is remarkable how little aggression was considered a significant factor before 1917, the date of the publication of Freud's "Mourning and Melancholia," and how prominent this drive has been considered since. (In all this we are referring to the technical and semi-official religious, social and medical writings. Poets and playrights have been presenting the human and hostile side of suicide since at least the time of Sophocles.) Before psychoanalysis there were no studies on aggression and suicide, while the past fifty years has seen a stress upon the vital role of aggression and of the death wish and hate turned against the self. Freud's formulations and observations have been elaborated and systematized by both Freud and other theorists. Menninger (1938), for example, has extended and emphasized the place of aggression and the death instinct in his elegant triad of the wish to kill, the wish to be killed, and the wish to die.

The base of the psychodynamics of suicide has been broadened to include other intrapsychic constellations such as self-punishment, and rebirth and reunion fantasies, as well as a host of psychosocial factors such as object loss, hopelessness and despair, and social isolation. Nevertheless, Freud's original dictum that "no neurotic harbours thoughts of suicide which are not murderous impulses against others re-directed upon himself" (1925, p. 162) is so well known and accepted that the clinician almost routinely raises this basic question in formulating the psychodynamics of his suicidal patient: "Whom did the patient really want to kill or wish dead, or to suffer?" That aggression turned against the self is found frequently in suicidal patients appears to need no further clinical documentation. To quote Farber, "The evidence for the presence of aggression in suicide is overwhelming and widely documented" (1968, p. 34).

Despite the clinical evidence, few research studies have been able to demonstrate a relationship between suicidal behavior and the amount and direction of aggression. Tuckman et al. (1959) found little hostility and much positive affect in their analysis of the emotional content of suicide notes. Vinoda (1966) did report more "general hostility" in patients who had made suicidal attempts and Lester (1967) found that suicidal subjects were more irritable and had more resentment than non-suicidal subjects. However, all these investigators described the suicidal subject as more similar to the controls than different. On the basis of his and other studies, Lester concluded that the suicidal groups did not differ from the controls in either the manner or the direction of aggression and that the entire concept of suicide as an act of inward directed aggression may be erroneous.

Based upon a study of TAT fantasies McEvoy (1963) questioned the hypothesis that suicide is self directed aggression, because of his failure to discover differences between groups. Sakheim (1955) in a study utilizing the Rorschach stated that hostile impulses were not revealed with any greater frequency by his suicidal patients than by the non-suicidal controls. He concluded that suicidal patients are no more hostile than mentally ill patients in general, and reached the rather sweeping conclusion that the psychoanalytic interpretation of suicide as a form of self hatred or aggression towards others turned inward cannot be substantiated. Sakheim and McEvoy evidently consider the Rorschach and TAT to tell not only the truth but the whole truth.

Similarly, those scales for the evaluation of suicidal potential which are based upon a direct clinical assessment of the patient also select variables other than aggressive tendencies for prediction (e.g., Cohen, Motto, and Seiden, 1966). Devries' Suicide Potential Scale (1968), which is based upon the critical incident technique, contains at least three questions dealing with sexual feelings and activities, several on depressive symptoms, many on object loss and social isolation, and only one on aggression ("Sometimes I feel angry all day.").

Our own studies, which include the use of structured interviews and questionnaires, have made us very wary of questionnaire responses which are taken at face value, especially in such a sensitive and complex area as the role of aggression in self destructive behavior. For example, one of our questions is, "Were you angry at anyone at the time of your attempt?" One nineteen-year-old boy denied any disagreements with or anger at anyone and added, "I never get angry."

"Never?" queried the examiner.

"Never," repeated the patient, and then, "I'm afraid to."

The last qualification, of course, suggested a far different interpretation of his "no" than the absence of anger or of the internalization of aggression.

We suggest, therefore, that paper and pencil questionnaires are not the ideal method for studying a phenomenon as complex as "aggression turned within." The very concept of an internalization of aggression implies a process taking place outside of awareness or in a state of reduced consciousness. An individual's responses can therefore only be accepted as data to be analyzed, not facts to be taken at face value.

In addition, all of these research tests and scales examine the problem outside of the actual context. All of them which deal with aggression study the suicidal act only as a function of the patient's own hostility or aggression, thereby eliminating the reciprocity of human interaction and other vital variables in what they are studying.

In the clinical literature, the death wishes present in the patient have been discussed frequently (Menninger, 1938; Furst and Ostow, 1965), but there has been relatively little about the death wishes that may be directed against the patient. Freud, however, emphasized the ubiquitousness of such thoughts in the unconscious of everyone (1925a). You don't have to be suicidal to harbor death wishes.

We have been struck, not only with the problem of aggression in the suicidal person, but with the amount of hostility and aggression which was directed against the suicidal person. Our family studies suggested that aggression was a prominent feature in the behavior of everyone involved in the situation. In addition, we were impressed with the frequency with which family members presented themselves as the victims of their sick, bad, or damaged family member who was suicidal, and their own hostile and rejecting attitudes as justified by society. The social attitudes towards the most suicidal groups were therefore also considered worthy of special consideration.

Subjects

We have interviewed over a hundred suicidal persons together with at least one family member, and have subjected thirty-six of them to a more intensive study. We have done the same for thirty patients who had been admitted for reasons other than a suicidal attempt, such as an acute psychotic break or schizophrenic episode, a depressive state without significant suicidal ideation, behavior disturbances, and anxiety or panic states.

Four of the control subjects admitted to having made suicidal attempts in the past. They were included as controls because their present admission was for other reasons, and our primary concern was with the attitudes and events related to the present situation. There was evidence of concealed suicidal behavior or ideation in the present admission of several controls. For example, a twenty-four-year-old married man with a past history of suicidal and manic behavior entered the hospital because he felt another "nervous breakdown" coming on. He categorically denied any suicidal thoughts or intent. It was only after we had seen him and his family that his wife revealed her husband's private psychiatrist had phoned her recently to warn that her husband was becoming suicidal again. Another patient, a thirty-eight-year-old paranoid woman with the delusion that a lover was sending concealed messages to her through the television set, warned her sister that she would kill herself if the family tried to keep her from him. However, few control patients manifested no suicidal behavior whatsoever. In fact, we were hard put to find controls in whom suicidal thoughts, feelings, impulses or behavior did not play some part in their current decompensation. We seriously question, therefore, whether there are any severely disturbed psychiatric patients who are not significantly suicidal.

Our suicidal subjects ranged in age from eight to eighty-six, and the controls from fourteen to seventy. The educational level in both groups ranged from rudimentary grammar school to college and professional education. The majority of patients in both groups had not completed high school. "Unemployed" was the most frequent occupation of the males, and "unemployed," "housewife," and "clerical" of the females.

Method

Individual and family interviews were conducted with all subjects, and a questionnaire filled out for each subject during the individual interview. This present report is based primarily upon an analysis of parts of the questionnaire responses and the taped family interviews. These interviews and questionnaires covered a wide range of topics, including each person's knowledge and description of the exact events preceding and precipitating the suicidal or disturbed behavior, evidence of aggressive, depressive, and suicidal feelings or acts, social functioning, the presence of various family and personal crises, and many other areas.

The family meetings were open ended ones in which the participants were instructed to talk about the events leading to the hospitalization or requests for treatment. They were conducted with the goal (not always realized or feasible) of minimal intervention from the interviewers.

We realize that our questions and interviews touched upon deep and painful feelings and experiences which are heavily tinged with guilt, blame, and social censure, and that many such feelings and incidents would not be verbalized to a stranger in the course of one interview. Intensive and detailed investigations are needed, during which the patient and his family are given an opportunity to explore, ventilate, and build up confidence in the therapist-interviewer. Our experiences have emphatically convinced us that more thorough and careful case history studies are required at this time, rather than statistical figures, many with built in artifacts. It is understood, meanwhile, that this present report deals with what the informants are conscious of and are willing or able to verbalize.

The findings support the hypothesis that much more aggression, hostility, and rejection is directed towards the suicidal patient by family members than is returned by him, and that this pattern differs from that found in the control patient and his family. For example, the majority of suicidal subjects replied "yes," when asked such questions as "Did you ever feel that they (your family) were fed up with you?" "Did you ever feel they wished you were dead or away?" "Did you yourself ever feel that others would be better off if you were dead or away?" It seemed evident, therefore, that most of our suicidal subjects perceived hostile or rejecting family attitudes.

In the majority of the families we interviewed there was at least one relative who replied yes to such questions as "Did he (the patient) make you feel angry?" "Did you ever feel fed up with him?" "Did you ever feel that he was too much for you to take or to put up with, or that he was too much of a burden?" A significantly lesser number of non-suicidal patients and their relatives replied "yes" to these questions. The differences between the suicidal and control patients is thus found not only in the individual responses but in the patient-family pattern.

In the individual interviews of the suicidal group a mutual feeling of discontent between the patient and his family was apparent. The family was angry at the patient, but he acknowledged much less anger at them. The family was fed up with him and felt he was a burden; the patient agreed that he was a burden and that they would be better off if he were dead or away. Both quantitatively and clinically the responses emphasized the suicidogenic influence of the feeling that the self is not only not needed but is a burden who is causing hardship to others which would be relieved were he out of the way.

These feelings of the suicidal patient have been mentioned in the literature, but their interpersonal character, we believe, has been insufficiently appreciated. Litman and Tabachnick (1968), for example, cite feelings that others would be better off and that they are harming others as one of the unconscious fantasy systems of the individual which plays a role in suicide. Our findings suggest that this may represent a shared fantasy, not only an individual one, and that messages to this effect are communicated to the suicidal person in a usually covert but surprisingly often conscious manner by the significant person or persons in his environment. Any listing of fantasies, therefore, can probably best be understood in the context of the reality situation, especially the current interpersonal, reciprocal dynamics.

Family Interviews

The pattern that has been described in the comparison of the individual interview responses of patient and family tended to be repeated in the family interviews. The suicidal patient was typically either self blaming or else quiet, while the relatives were critical, reproachful, and blaming. There was much communication that the others did feel burdened by him and wished him out of the way, whether these feelings had been acknowledged in the individual interviews or not. In some family groups everyone, including the patient, was quiet, guarded, and covert, with a minimum of verbalized interaction, but with many gestures, glances, warning movements, and other nonverbal indications that a great deal was going on but kept concealed.

Among the less suicidal families the patient was much more often angry and attacking or else not the major focus of blame and condemnation. He was frequently in a hostile alliance with one family member against another, and often the spokesman for a silent partner in a family battle.

In the suicidal group, the more serious the attempt, the greater the denial by both family and patient of any family involvement, often in the face of the eruption of marked disagreements during the family interviews.

An example is that of a forty-year-old physician who was interviewed with his mother and sister. The patient attributed his attempt to vague depressive feelings, with any family involvement denied by all participants. Near the beginning of the interview, however, his sister declared that if everyone said what they really thought there would be an explosion. The mother said this was not so and that there were no disagreements in the family, to which everyone then agreed. Towards the end of the interview the patient described an intense quarrel with his mother because she did not approve of his girlfriend. The mother denied there had been a quarrel and added that her son's statement made her feel *that* small (making a gesture with her fingers). Her son then disqualified his own account and agreed that there were no conflicts or disagreements within the family. This patient also had denied that his near-fatal episode was a suicide attempt or that he harbored any suicidal intentions. He was discharged shortly after the family interview and proceeded to make another serious attempt the day after discharge.

In another case involving a seventy-one-year-old suicidal man, his wife and two children and the patient all denied the presence of disagreements in the family when seen alone. The family interview, on the other hand, consisted mainly of complaints and criticisms by the wife against her husband, while he defended himself weakly and ineffectually while the children sat quietly and reported that the situation was the same at home, although such information had not been forthcoming from them in the individual interviews. There were several cases in which disagreements were denied during the individual interviews, while the family sessions contained lengthy discussions of quarrels that had taken place the day of or the day before the attempt.

It was clear, therefore, that the degree of dissension between family and patient was greater than either reported when seen individually. One sixty-seven-year-old woman and her sister denied any disagreements or any negative feelings at all during their individual interviews. During the family session, however, the patient acknowledged that she felt like an outsider rather than a member of the family. Her sister became exceedingly hurt and upset, said "Wait until the rest of the family hears what you said," and referred to her sister's rather mild complaint for the rest of the hour with implicit and explicit threats of rejection and exposure.

Characteristic of the suicidal subjects was the absence of fighting back when criticized, often with a visible holding in. When challenged as to their acquiescence, a typical retort was, "My mother (father, wife, husband) is ill and I can't upset her (him)." To an even greater degree than in the individual meetings, the family interviews emphasized the degree to which the suicidal patient is the recipient of a considerable degree of aggression from others, but is not free to respond and has to swallow his resentment. As a result he must deal with both his own aggression and that of others, which adds up to a larger quantity, of course, than only his own.

The best descriptions of the operation of death wishes against the suicidal person are to be found in literature. When Anna Karenina's husband found she was ill, for example, he first realized how much he wanted her to die. Although she did not commit suicide until later, the basis of the suicide is here already presented. In Strindberg's *Miss Julie,* the heroine is seduced by a servant, thus placing them both in an untenable position. The man who had just seduced her hands Julie a gun to kill herself. Those who have read *The Sorrows of Werther* may recall that there too the heroine hands the gun to the messenger which Werther had sent in order to kill himself. (Werther was also an example of someone who was expendable.)

What seemed more relevant, however, than any mere quantity of aggression was both the external sanctions against its expression by the suicidal person, and the fear of the magical effect of his aggression by the person. More than one patient verbalized the fear that the person they wanted to express their anger towards would become sick and die. Many patients used the threat of suicide as a manipulative device to control the situation, but more than one relative also utilized the prospect of their own death if a conflict should ensue as a weapon to maintain control or prevent change, but their fantasied death would occur not by their own hands, rather through the badness or fault of the suicidal person. The patient then becomes not only a burden but one who brings death to others.

Death Wishes

Verbalized death wishes and thoughts were implicit or explicit in many statements made by the relatives, and although often voiced jokingly they were voiced with unexpected frequency. Murder and death seemed in the air. There was rarely a family where at least one member, including the patient, did not use the word "kill" during either the individual or family interviews. One mother's first statement after seeing her twenty-four-year-old son in the hospital was, "Next time pick a higher bridge." A depressed man in his seventies said to his wife, "If I had a gun I'd shoot myself." She replied, "I'll buy you a gun." That week he tried pills instead. Many relatives ironically or angrily offered to assist the one who voiced his urge to kill himself. A mother said to her twenty-nine-year-old daughter who had been depressed and withdrawn but not verbalizing her suicidal impulses, "I'll do anything to show my love for you; I'll open the window so you can jump." Another mother told her husband she was concerned about their teen aged daughter and wanted to discuss the situation with him. He became enraged and replied, "If you can't take care of your own daughter why don't you kill yourself." She obligingly swallowed a bottle of aspirins, and after recovery made no further attempts at discussing their children with her husband.

A mother announced to her twenty-eight-year-old daughter, "We'd all be better off if you were dead." An identical statement was made by a father to his seventeen-year-old daughter, adding, "At least we'd know where you are." A thirteen-year-old girl told her mother she had taken several of the mother's tranquilizers as a suicidal gesture. The mother called her a liar, and stated, "If you're a real grown up and mean what you say you'd take the whole bottle." She then placed the nearly full bottle before her daughter and left the house. She returned several hours later, to find the girl in a coma after having proven herself a "real grown up."

These statements were made in the heat of a crisis and family emergency. They were often reported by a significant other in the course of explaining or acknowledging that his anger against the patient had played a part in the attempt. Such acknowledgements, of course, are regarded as potentially corrective and theraputic, rather than as occasions for blame and reproach.

In a perhaps incongruous manner, death wishes may represent an actual concern for the patient. One mother with a suicidal daughter who was brain damaged and physically handicapped denied feeling that her daughter was a burden when she was administered the questionnaire. At the conclusion of the interview, however, she declared, "All I ask is that my daughter die before I do; because she is a burden, let's face it, and who will take care of her." Such statements parallel some of the expressed attitudes of society towards the mentally and physically handicapped and helpless, which are reported later on in this paper, where death wishes are present in a setting of real or assumed compassion and concern. In the above case, the mother's love and concern was genuine, if ambivalent.

Similar observations have been reported in the psychiatric literature. Maddison and Mackay (1966), for example, described the case of a woman who told her husband she had taken twenty sleeping tablets. He responded with "jocular disbelief," and when he could not arouse her the next morning (she was comatose) he left her to go to work. Shneidman and Farberow (1961) described a woman who had made many suicidal threats and attempts, had made out a will the day before, and had an argument with her husband, ending when he walked out. (A large number of presuicidal arguments in our population ended with the other partner walking out.) He returned to find her lying on the floor in the hall, "breathing heavy." He placed a pillow under her head, left the house, and went to a hotel, while his wife perished.

Straker (1958) studied twenty-four patients who had attempted suicide and nine who had succeeded in their attempts. He concluded that the one who makes a serious suicidal attempt wishes to die in order to gratify the hostile wishes of another person with whom the patient is involved. Meerloo (1962) coined the term "psychic homicide" to signal the occurrence of this pattern. As long ago as 1910 Federn stated that "only he who is wished dead by someone else kills himself" (quoted by Maddison and Mackay, 1966). Our family studies indicate that in an attenuated form, this is true of those who make suicidal attempts too.

Such death wishes become particularly potent when the patient has no one to support or side with him. One seventeen-year-old girl ran away with her boy friend and after returning home became involved in a violent altercation with her parents, after which she swallowed her mother's tranquilizers. When seen in the hospital the mother angrily told the interviewer that she would find her daughter's death easier to bear than the strain she was being put under. The daughter reported that her boy friend had acted so ambivalent and hostile that she told him, "If you want me to die why don't you say so?"

In contrast, another patient of the same age and ethnic background also had run away with her boy friend and had become involved in a fight with her parents after returning home. However, she did not take pills, although the conflict was at least as intense as that of the first girl. The differences between the situations were, first, the family did not verbalize or convey death wishes to this girl, at least as far as we know; second, she had an ally in a grandmother with whom she sometimes stayed when the situation became too charged at home, a grandmother who while critical of the girl did not side entirely with the family; and third, her boy friend stood by her. Had the grandmother allied herself completely with the parents and had the boy friend withdrawn or become hostile and blaming, then hers too might have become a suicidogenic situation.

Our perusal of the literature suggests that death wishes by the relatives are reported more often than they are recognized as such by the author. In Stotland and Kobler's *The End of Hope,* for example (1964), the authors quote from the report of a social worker's interview with the mother of "Harry Einston," a patient who subsequently killed himself, that "One interview was so full of death and morbidity in one form or another, including her statement that it would be easier to adjust to her son's death than to his mental illness, that I felt quite concerned about her and her ability to hold together" (p. 114).

Although this appears to us as an accurate and objective account of what we hear regularly in our interviews, the authors present this statement as the most marked example of "The negative attitude of the hospital staff towards the parents" (p. 113). We would speculate that this condemnation is based upon a misunderstanding because the death wish in a suicidogenic situation is communicated by someone who not only is loved by the patient but who loves the patient in return. Marked ambivalence surrounds the anger and death wishes of the family, with the suicidal attempt often representing a response to the non-hostile needs of the significant other.

It might be argued that one should not equate a death wish with the use of the word "dead." However, we must emphasize that much of the communication in our family interviews was non-verbal, and that the verbal message was but one of several ways of communicating such feelings. We must also emphasize that we are not referring to wishes to kill the other person but to messages that the other person do this to himself. "I could kill you" is not a suicidogenic message. "I can't kill you but we'd all be better off if you were dead" is.

It is evident that the entire problem of the meaning, function, and dynamics of the hostility and death wishes of the significant others, their ambivalent and even loving components, and their place in the multi-faceted problem of suicide is of enormous complexity.

2. THE ROLE OF SOCIETY

This section discusses the attitudes of society towards those groups who are known for their high suicide rates. The attitude of society towards suicide itself is well known. Suicide has been condemned as an ignominious and sinful act by the church and state. The suicide's property was confiscated at one time, he was denied the usual church rites, and his body was subjected to shameful and disgraceful practices (Williams, 1957). In the nineteenth century the attitudes of part of society changed from one of condemnation to that of regarding suicide as the outcome of disease. Nevertheless, society's hostility to the act is still evident, as is reflected in the secrecy and shame surrounding a suicide.

The role of society in the genesis of suicidal behavior has also been studied for many years. Durkheim and other sociologists have emphasized that suicide is associated with a breakdown in the integration between the individual and society. We propose that behind this failure of integration lies the hostility and death wishes of society towards the suicidal person.

Among the conditions found significantly related to either attempted or completed suicide are alcoholism, drug addiction, old age, physical and mental infirmity, chronic illness, sexual acting out, and psychopathy. These features were present in the majority of our suicidal cases, few of whom were greeted with open armed acceptance anywhere. In addition, an examination of the literature, as well as years of personal experience and observation, have left little doubt that most of these conditions are the objects of scorn, irritation, and rejection by society—and society most definitely includes the medical profession. Society's communication towards the members of these groups is to go away, disappear, die.

For example, many hospitals refuse to admit chronic alcoholics. In a comprehensive survey of medical practice with alcoholics, Bailey found that "three-fourths of the physicians cannot get these patients admitted to the hospitals with which they are affiliated, under a primary diagnosis of alcoholism" (1968, p. 26). The chronically mentally ill are relegated to what Schmidt called "Democracy's scrapheap." The chronically physically ill, crippled, and maimed are rejected in a more subtle manner, usually characterized as being a burden to themselves. The prevailing attitudes were expressed in the world wide wave of approval that followed the acquittal of Madame Van der Put in Belgium for the murder of her baby who was born deformed as a result of thalidomide (St. John-Stevas, 1964). The psychopath, of course, is the social outcast par excellence. As for the aged, it is virtually taken for granted that they constitute a burden and a nuisance whom everyone, including the old man himself, is hoping will do society a favor and die.

It might be clarifying to anyone who doubts these words to visit some large urban city hospital whose wards are becoming overcrowded with elderly and senile patients. He might also visit certain nursing homes and most state hospitals, or listen in on an argument between admitting physicians from different services over which service should take the senile patient who was dumped into the emergency room by his family, a nursing home, or an ambulance from another hospital. Other societies deal more openly with their aged and infirm. An Eskimo, for example, told the anthropologist Rasmussen of their custom of doing away with old and helpless people. He explained, "And they do this not merely to be rid of a life that is no longer a pleasure, but also to relieve their nearest relations of the trouble they give them" (Leighton and Hughes, 1955).

How different, we wonder, is the attitude of our society. Chesser points out the presence of a "psychological aversion towards the aged, who feel relegated to the scrap heap" (1967, p. 97). The author condemns such attitudes, yet reaches the conclusion that suicide by the aged is justified (with a qualification that is discussed below). He also considers suicide to prevent a painful death in cases of incurable illness "an obviously rational motive" (p. 112). In a similar vein, Gisborne (1928) has presented an extensive list of those persons who should be mercifully put out of their misery by society. He includes the aged, the physically ill, the maimed, the mentally ill, the mentally defective, and the criminal. Chesser condemns the mercy killings of lunatics and incurable patients by the Nazis because their motives were reprehensible, but defends euthanasia in England because it is based upon compassion for suffering. We think, however, that a death wish is a death wish, no matter how sugar coated.

These defenses of suicide in the aged, the ill, the handicapped and so forth are criticized by us for ignoring the role of society, for it is society who feels burdened and does not want the ill person. Pain per se, for example, has not been demonstrably associated with suicide among those so afflicted (e.g., Farberow, Schneideman, and Leonard, 1963). Chesser declared it is often sensible for an aging man to kill himself. It may be significant that he would not say "woman," and perhaps for reasons that are related to the fact that aging women have a relatively low suicide rate and aging men a high one.

The question we have mainly addressed ourselves to is how these existing attitudes of society become concretely translated into suicidal behavior. Our studies indicate that the process can be understood in terms of family dynamics, with the family as the mediator between society and individual behavior.

In our clinical studies we found an impressive number of instances where the family avoided a confrontation with a family crisis related to marriage, moving, the sheer necessity of changing roles with growth or maturity, or other situations which posed a threat to their homeostasis, by blaming the one in the family who was ill, alcoholic, or in some way one of society's outcasts, thus precipitating a situation which was resolved by the suicidal attempt. Confrontation with the more immediate or fundamental sources of strain was thus avoided, as was the taking of steps to change the crisis producing situation. Such processes are subtly supported and encouraged by the corresponding rejecting attitudes of society. A number of examples from our files will be presented.

CASE HISTORIES

Case 1. The Alcoholic. A fifty-three-year-old married man was admitted to the intensive care unit of the hospital in a coma after having ingested thirty sleeping pills. Individual and family interviews disclosed he was an alcoholic and an inadequate personality, while his wife was an oral dependent personality suffering from involutional problems. The attempt was overtly precipitated by a fight with his son, and covertly precipitated by the departure of a daughter from the house who had always assumed the major mothering role in the family. The day after she moved out the younger son beat up the father in the street, after which his wife threatened to leave him, all ostensibly because of his drinking. The patient then went to his room where he swallowed a lethal dose of sleeping pills. The family thus avoided the problem of how to adjust to the trauma of their daughter leaving by displacing their wrath upon the convenient social scapegoat of the drunkard. Uproar replaced coping.

Case 2. The Cripple. Society's attitude is an ambivalent one, and much compassion also exists for the sick and the unfortunate. Pity, however (which is not the same as compassion), can be a potent and often hostile weapon which can quickly change to anger and aversion given the proper pathogenic conditions. This patient was a thirty-year-old single man, a polio victim since the age of seven, who attempted to jump out of a hospital window during an apparent episode of manic agitation and excitement. The overt precipitant was a feeling of helplessness and self disgust after one of his leg braces broke. The covert precipitant was his recent departure to New York from his home in Puerto Rico to seek medical treatment, and the inability of both him and his mother to separate from each other.

The social attitudes prevalent in the family were those of pity and the need to care for a helpless unfortunate. As his brother explained in an individual interview, "Everyone must love him because he's crippled. We have to take care of him." The patient wished for a different role, but his strivings were disapproved of. He was an intelligent man with a good work history in the past. However, when he made efforts to work and establish a social life he was accused of worrying his mother, who became severely anxious whenever he left the house. (This pattern developed after a younger brother had died seven years ago.) Actually, the household was riddled with problems. Nevertheless, the myth was maintained by everyone, including the patient, that any fears, tension, and depression was solely the result of his pitiful existence.

In this case the family's condemnation arose when the patient rebelled against his assigned role of the pitiful cripple, and the family was aided in their efforts to keep him helpless, dependent, and homebound because society, especially industry, did appear uncomfortable with a cripple working for them, and they did want him out of the way.

Case 3. The Sociopath. A twenty-two-year-old married woman with two children, separated from her husband, from a fundamentalist religious background, made a series of suicidal gestures several times a week, usually by cutting her wrists or swallowing a quantity of tranquilizer pills. The suicidal behavior was precipitated by her husband taking legal measures to obtain custody of their two children and place them in the care of his own mother. In the background was her mother's announcement that she was returning to Puerto Rico to live in a few weeks. The mother was a religious fanatic. The patient was a lesbian with an unstable work and social history and a flirting with drug addiction. The mother spent a good deal of time praying for her bad daughter.

In this case the complicity of the mother, the daughter, and society's condemnation of the sociopath was most apparent when the family was seen together.

Case 4. The Handicapped Male. The pathological ambivalence and the appeal to the rejection by society was prominent in the situation of an epileptic young man of twenty-four, also of above average intelligence. When he did get a job he was told by his father that no employer wanted an epileptic and that he should quit before his shameful secret was exposed. When he did not work he was nagged and urged to make something of himself. (This was the patient whose mother had advised him to pick a higher bridge next time.)

Case 5. The Handicapped Female. This was an eighteen-year-old girl, also an epileptic with a paraplegia of unknown origin, who swallowed a variety of objects, including a thermometer, bottle tops, and some small tools. Her mother used her physical and mental condition as a basis for refusing to take care of her at home, while the hospital protested she was capable of self care, and besides, there were no facilities or hospital beds for her.

Case 6. The Hope. Although we have described an unholy alliance between society, the suicidal person, and the immediate family milieu of the suicidal person, we by no means consider this situation universal or irreparable. Many families we saw did not fit into this pattern. One example was a sixteen-year-old girl who ran away from home, then returned and made two suicide attempts with the same pills that her mother had used in *her* attempts.

This family recognized the danger signs and instead of the condemnation of the girl, to which the courts and hospitals are all too often a party, they came to the Mental Hygiene Clinic requesting help.

Discussion

We realize full well, first, that "society" is an abstraction which does not possess the unity or unanimity we ascribe to it; second, that there are forces of love and on the side of life in society for those groups we have been discussing; and third, that the "victims" within these groups are willing victims who exert strenuous efforts to provoke and drive others away. Acknowledging all these important qualifications, our investigations indicate that society presents an attitude of rejection and hostility towards these groups which plays a part in their higher suicide rates and which furnishes a sanction for the family and others to reject, scapegoat, and be hostile towards their members.

An objection may be raised to this theory of the suicidogenic role of society's hostility, on the grounds that many groups who meet with the hostility and rejection of society are not suicidal, such as the Negroes in the United States. We are dealing with this problem more fully in a critique of those theories which ascribe suicide to national and group character. We shall not discuss the questionable validity of the statistics upon which the lower suicide rate among Negroes is based, nor the effect of the closed versus open family system, which we are also dealing with elsewhere. We would like to comment, however, about the "acting out" of aggressive impulses. This feature has been cited as one of the explanations of the low suicide rate among Blacks. What must be examined more closely, however, is the attitude of White society towards such acting out among Blacks. As long as the acting out was confined to the in-group, the White out-group was not overly concerned. There is some evidence, in fact, of subtle encouragement from the out-group in the form of social attitudes indicating that aggressive acting out was a racial characteristic and therefore to be expected.

For example, in a mid-western community several years ago, a group of Negro leaders appealed to the judiciary to sentence Negroes convicted of first degree murder against Negroes to the same maximum as Whites convicted of the same crime against other Whites. The court records indicated that no Negro so convicted was given the maximum sentence (death). If the murder was carried out against a white person then they did receive the maximum sentence. Such procedures by society reward acting out rather than acting in, and in particular acting out against one's own sub-group. The implication is that both aggressive acting out, including homicide, as well as acting in as suicide, may be related to the attitudes and expectations of society.

Implications for Therapy

The social and situational variables in the handling of aggression which we have presented, especially the pattern of rejection and hostility, with covert messages for the suicidal person to disappear or die, may be repeated in the treatment situation, with the therapist as an often unwitting and most certainly unwilling collaborator. In the theraputic situation the doctor is the significant other indeed, combining in his person all the meaningful relationships in the patient's life. The patient, therefore, tries to replicate with this representative of all who are most important to him the destructive suicidogenic situations he is accustomed to.

The patient is also a significant other for the doctor who in addition combines for him all the anxiety-producing problems and responsibilities his profession is heir to. Tabachnick (1961) has emphasized the anger and guilt aroused in the therapist by a suicidal patient. Bloom (1967) reported that in every case of suicide in a psychiatric training center the therapist had withdrawn from or rejected the patient. The suicidal patient arouses the doctor's countertransference feelings and unresolved conflicts as perhaps no other patient.

More than with any other patient, therefore, it is necessary for the therapist to confront himself courageously and recognize his own possible death wishes and desires to be rid of the patient. These reactions may often underlie the decision to hospitalize, for example, rather than a consideration of what is best for the patient. As stated in an earlier paper: "Experiences of my own have led me now always to ask myself the following question: 'Does my concern about the possibility of suicide derive from the patient's clinical condition, behavior, and communications to me all of which I am able to validate by objective fact, or does my concern derive from some desire within myself to be rid of the patient?' " (Rosenbaum, 1967, p. 74).

Such honest self examination by the therapist has been demonstrably salutory and possibly life saving. The interested therapist usually asks, "Who does the suicidal patient want to kill?" In addition, he must also ask, "Who wants him to die?" This could be one person such as the doctor, a friend, a member or members of the immediate social group. It could be the family; it could be society. Or it could be all of these.

Summary and Conclusions

Situational, social, and family aspects of the fate of aggression in suicidal patients was examined. Several research and clinical studies had indicated that such persons are not necessarily possessed of a greater quantity of aggression, nor need they characteristically turn it against themselves at all times and in all situations. We hypothesized that suicidal behavior was associated both with the hostility and death wishes of the family and significant others against the suicidal person, and the hostility of society, which thus lends its approval to the hostility of the more immediate milieu.

To test these hypotheses, individual interviews were conducted with suicidal patients and members of their families, followed by a family interview. A parallel procedure was followed for a group of neuropsychiatric control patients and their families. It was found that in a majority of cases the suicidal patient affirmed that others were angry at him, that he felt he was a burden and that others would be better off if he were dead or away. The majority of the family respondents affirmed that the patient made them angry; they felt burdened by him, and better off if he were dead or away. In several cases death wishes were directly verbalized or acknowledged by family members, either in the heat of anger, or as an admission of their role in the situation. The total amount of such death wishes is undoubtedly larger than was publicly and spontaneously expressed in the course of one interview. The pattern of patient and family responses was different from that of the less (not "non") suicidal controls.

As for the role of society, a survey of the literature as well as clinical observations disclosed markedly negative and rejecting attitudes towards those groups who form the high suicide risks. Our family studies thus pointed to what might be called an isomorphism between societal and individual attitudes, a correspondence between the hostility and scapegoating expressed towards the suicidal person by his family and interpersonal milieu and the attitudes of society towards many of these same persons. The high risk groups are largely those rejected or condemned by society, the aged, the ill, the mentally disturbed, the psychopathic, and the alcoholic. They are the great unwanted, the recipients of hostility and death wishes, expressed either directly or in the recommendations of euthanasia and other compassionate expressions of death wishes. Confronted not only with the aggression and death wishes of those close to them but with those of society in general, they have nowhere to go but the grave. These reflections speculatively suggest that a reduction of hostility by society towards these groups will lead to a more constructive and less suicidal atmosphere in their immediate milieu.

Within the limits of our clinical experiences and studies we find that these social and family aspects of the suicidal situation transcend diagnostic, ethnic, and socio-economic class lines. Our data did not support those studies which declared that aggression is not a factor in suicidal behavior. The data did indicate, however, that this aggression cannot be understood except in the light of the current interpersonal and family dynamics where first, the expression and communication of aggression is one sided and the patient is the recipient of aggression but cannot respond in kind; second, he must deal not only with his own but the accumulated aggression of the significant others in his world; and third, that societal pressures and attitudes contribute to this pattern and are used by the family and others to single the patient out.

For both theraputic and preventive purposes, therefore, the role of not only the patient's aggression but that of the significant others in his milieu should be confronted. The therapist, too, must be alert to the degree to which he may slip into this pattern; and society, meaning all of us, must accept our responsibility for the part we play.

REFERENCES

1. *Bailey, M. B.* A Survey of Medical and Psychiatric Practice with Alcoholics: New York City, *1968. Committee on Alcoholism: New York, 1968. 36 pp.*
2. *Bloom, V. An analysis of suicide at a training center,* American Journal of Psychiatry, *123, 918–925, (1967).*
3. *Chesser, E.* Living with Suicide, *Hutchinson and Co., London, 1967.*
4. *Cohen, E., Morro, J. A., and Seiden, R. An instrument for evaluating suicide potential: A preliminary study.* American Journal of Psychiatry, *122, 886–891, (1966).*
5. *Devries, A. G. Model for the prediction of suicidal behaviour,* Psychological Reports, *22, 1285–1302, (1968).*
6. *Farber, M. L. Suicide and hope: A theoretical analysis. (N. L. Farberow, ed.)* Proceedings of the Fourth International Conference for Suicide Prevention. *Delmar Publishing Co., Los Angeles, 1968.*
7. *Farberow, N. L., Shneidman, E. S., and Leonard, C. V. Suicide among general medical and surgical hospital patients with malignant neoplasms.* Veterans Administration Medical Bulletin, *9, (1963).*
8. *Freud, S. Mourning and Melancholia (1917)* Collected Papers, *Vol. 4, Hogarth Press, London, 152–170, 1925.*
9. *Freud, S. Thoughts for the times on war and death (1915)* Collected Papers, *Vol. 4, Hogarth Press, London: 288–317, 1925a.*
10. *Furst, S. S. and Ostow, M. The psychodynamics of suicide.* Bulletin of the New York Academy of Medicine, *41, 190–204 (1965).*
11. *Gisborne, F. A. W. "The right to die." (In)* Democracy on Trial and Other Essays. *Longmans, Green, and Co., New York: 210–222, 1928.*

12. *Jacobs, J., and Teicher, J. D. Broken homes and social isolation in attempted suicides of adolescents.* International Journal of Social Psychiatry, *13, 139–149, (1967).*
13. *Kobler, A. L., and Stotland, E.* The End of Hope. *The Free Press, New York, 1964.*
14. *Lecky, W.E. H.* History of European Morals. *George Braziller, New York, 1955 (original ed. 1869.) Vol. I, 212–223, 331. Vol. II. 42–61.*
15. *Leighton, A. A., and Hughes, C. C. Notes on Eskimo patterns of suicide.* Southwestern Journal of Anthropology, *11, 327–338 (1955).*
16. *Lester, D. Suicide as an aggressive act.* Journal of Psychology, *66, 47–50, (1967).*
17. *Litman, R. E., and Tabachnick, N. Psychoanalytic theories of suicide. (N. L. Farberow, ed.)* Proceedings of the Fourth International Conference for Suicide Prevention. *Delmar Publishing Co., Los Angeles: 277–285 1968.*
18. *Maddison, D., and Mackey, K. H. Suicide: The clinical problem.* British Journal of Psychiatry, *112, 693–703, (1966).*
19. *McEvoy, T. E. A comparison of suicidal and non-suicidal patients by means of the YAY.* Dissertation Abstracts, *24, 1248, (1963).*
20. *Meerloo, A. M.* Suicide and Mass Suicide. *Grune and Stratton, New York, 1962.*
21. *Menninger, K.* Man against Himself. *Harcourt, Brace, and World, New York, 1938.*
22. *Rosenbaum, M. Recognition of the suicidal individual.* Symposium on Suicide. *(L. Yochelson, ed.) Washington, D.C. The George Washington University, 73–83, 1967.*
23. *St. John-Stevas, N.* The Right to Life. *Holt, Rinehart, and Winston, New York, 1964.*
24. *Sakheim, G. A. Suicidal responses on the Rorschach test. A validation study.* Journal of Nervous and Mental Disease, *122, 332–344, (1955).*
25. *Shneidman, E. S., and Farberow, N. L. Sample investigations of equivocal suicidal deaths. In (N. L. Farberow and E. S. Shneidman, eds)* The Cry for Help. *McGraw-Hill, New York, 118–128, 1961.*
26. *Straker, M. Clinical observations of suicide,* Canadian Medical Association Journal, *79, 473–479, (1958).*
27. *Tabachnick, N. Countertransference crisis in suicidal attempts.* Archives of General Psychiatry, *4, 572–578, (1961).*
28. *Tuckman, J., Kleiner, R. J., and Lavell, M. Emotional content of suicide notes.* American Journal of Psychiatry, *116, 59–63, (1959).*
29. *Tuckman, J., and Youngman. Attempted suicide and family disorganization.* Journal of Genetic Psychology, *105, 187–193, (1964).*
30. *Vinoda, K. S. Personality characteristics of attempted suicides.* British Journal of Psychiatry, *112, 1143–1150, (1966).*
31. *Williams, G. L.* Sanctity of Life and the Criminal Law, *Knopf, McClelland, New York, 1957.*

16. Bondage and Suicide

Robert E. Litman and Charles Swearingen

BIOGRAPHICAL NOTE

Charles Swearingen joined Robert E. Litman in writing this chapter at the beginning of his career. He received his medical degree from Yale, trained in psychiatry in New York at the Albert Einstein College of Medicine Affiliated Hospitals, and in psychoanalysis in Boston, where he is now on the faculty at Harvard and is engaged in private practice.

COMMENT

Suicide in the context of fetishistic masturbation has largely been locked up in the closet of forensic pathology. Confined there, psychoanalytic writers have paid it little attention, and suicidological ones even less. We have chosen to include this review for several reasons.

First, it is a corner of suicide experience that is usually neglected. Patients of this kind, if unusual, are not very rare. As the authors point out, there is a substantial organized sadomasochistic subculture in the United States, less hidden now than in 1972 when this was first published. Literary interest in the "S & M" subculture has been stimulated by the recent disclosure of Michel Foucault's extensive involvement in it (Miller 1993). (Foucault was a prominent French intellectual historian.) While not all those who practice "bondage" are suicidal, it would appear that many are. Litman and Swearingen point this out and describe six cases.

Secondly, we include this paper in the hope of stimulating further interest and clinical study. Few such cases have been studied psychoanalytically. We have scant detailed description of the inner experience of such persons in learned journals. Just as paranoid defenses may defend against suicide (see chapter 12 above), erotization may serve a comparable purpose when self-

Robert E. Litman and Charles Swearingen, "Bondage and Suicide." *Archives of General Psychiatry* 27: (1972):80–85. Reprinted by permission.

destructive behavior is to some extent moderated and symbolically expressed through masturbatory or other sexual activity. Case A in this chapter suggests some component of grandiose excitement, raising the likelihood that orgiastic suicide, or orgiastic suicidal experimentation, may represent manic reaction-formation against intolerable suicide-driving experiences of despair and hopelessness.

Finally, patients in treatment for chronic suicidal disorders often reveal a pattern of sadomasochistic sexual activity. Patients with borderline personality disorder frequently describe ecstatically self-punishing, self-injurious masturbation or other hurtful sexual activity to those psychotherapists whose ears are sturdy enough to hear it. The poetry of Sylvia Plath is full of such themes.

REFERENCES

Miller, Jim. 1993. The Passion of Michel Foucault. *New York: Simon and Schuster.*

Weisman, Avery D. 1967. Self-Destruction and Sexual Perversion. In Shneidman, Edwin S., ed., Essays in Self Destruction. *New York: Science House.*

■

"Bondage" is a well-established category of deviant sexual behavior. It includes practices for erotic pleasure of being humiliated, enslaved, and physically bound and restrained. Life is threatened when, as is common, neck binding or partial asphyxiation forms part of the behavior. In the United States there are yearly about 50 such deaths, sometimes suicide, usually by accident. We report two fatal cases rich in details provided by the now deceased. In addition, we interviewed nine men and three women who responded to a notice in the underground press. Subjects were diverse in character and varied in the details of their bondage behavior. All of the men were isolated, depressed, and oriented toward death. Their masochism was first a challenge, then an invitation to death. When they see psychiatrists (for depression), the sexual problems are minimized.

PSYCHIATRISTS are accustomed to dealing with self-destructive and self-defeating behavior in their patients, and are aware that pain and humiliation can be intimately associated with erotic gratification. This paper will suggest that overt sexual masochism is more widespread and can be more dangerous than current psychiatric literature would indicate. We will report observations on a well-established subculture of masochism, "bondage," in essence the practice for erotic pleasure of being humiliated, endangered, and enslaved; and of being physically bound, restrained, and rendered helpless to a degree that life is threatened. Bondage can be fatal, a mix of suicide and accident.

Coroners and experts in forensic medicine are familiar with deaths by hanging or asphyxiation involving men who seemed to be engaged in autoerotic activity judged by such features as partial nudity, binding of the body and the genitals, pornographic writings and pictures, and special fetishes such as articles of female clothing, leather belts, and chains.[1,2] It should be noted that these cases do not represent medical rarities or forensic curiosities. Stearns[3] reported one or two a year in Massachusetts between 1941 and 1950. In Virginia there were six such deaths in five years.[4] Seven deaths in four years occurred in Fort Worth, Texas.[5] Our attention was directed to bondage deaths by successive Los Angeles County Chief Medical Examiners (Drs. Theodore Curphey and Thomas Noguchi). We know of 25 fatal cases in Los Angeles between 1958 and 1970. Extrapolating from these data we estimate that there are about 50 bondage deaths in the United States yearly.

ILLUSTRATIVE BONDAGE DEATHS

The following two cases are selected for presentation here because each of the now deceased left a handwritten report of what was on his mind.

Case A. This case was certified as an "accident." A 50-year-old actor was found dead in the bathtub strangled by a rope which wound around his neck, looped over the sliding door, and was tied to his left wrist and ankle. Additional ropes and chains were tied around the body and the neck. There was a ball in his mouth with a gag tied over the mouth, scarf over eyes, handcuffs on both wrists, numerous lewd writings—suck, fuck, etc.—on the body. Evidence indicated that he was alone at the time of his death. Apparently the obscene writing and the rope harness had been applied by his own hands. The door was locked from the inside. The apartment contained leather and rubber clothes as well as whips and chains, and an elaborate library of sadomasochistic pornography. The books and periodicals had stories and pictures of men and women bound and gagged in bizarre positions. On a desk in the deceased man's handwriting was a long list of bondage details. Some examples

Hot wax brushed on nipples and genitals
Dildoes
Several 2-inch, flat lathes or short whips

Shaving the genitals
Nipple rings, ear, nose, and penis
Teasing with feathers
The box with a hole for the head
The collar suspended from the ceiling
The buttocks as a pin cushion
Tied by the neck to a tree
Legs spread, hands behind, she sitting on the mouth of her slave
The sexual degrading and abusing of the slave
Directive to masturbate controlled by the whip
Forcing the victim to tie himself
The admission of surrender and acknowledging the mistress by a signature in blood
The taboo and the kneeling
Kissing and sucking the cunt
Put in frame with buttocks as target
Painted in bizarre designs
Walk through the street tied and naked, except for a raincoat
Chained by neck and hand

An investigation revealed that Mr. A dramatized his life experiences to the hilt. He had participated in a variety of bizarre behaviors (Chinese acupuncture, spiritualism, tissue extract therapy for potency, sadomasochism). However, his interest and his library concerning masochism and bondage were of relatively recent development. He had been heterosexual, married many years, then divorced. A girlfriend had participated in some previous bondage scenes with equipment in the apartment, but she had not been with him on the night of death. His finances were good, and he was soon to leave the city to do a film overseas. He had not been visibly depressed, although he had been worried about his health and his failing potency. The coroner's psychiatric consultant inferred that the deceased died accidentally while practicing bondage perversion for auto-erotic pleasure.

Case B. This case was certified as a suicide. In a cheap hotel the maid discovered a 30-year-old man hanging in a closet. The bizarrely costumed body was hanging by its neck by a chain which had been looped around the neck with a small padlock holding the chain in place. The ends of the chain had been placed around the clothes hanger rails on either side of the closet and were brought down to the body where they were attached to a short length of rope which was looped around each leg at the crotch and attached to the ends of the chain by a small padlock on either side. There were two notes. The first note said that he had often in the past masturbated by bringing himself just to the edge of death. He knew of several persons who had died unexpectedly when they lost control of their self-strangulation scenes. This time, however, he meant to go all the way to death. The second note which was less impersonal follows:

"To all who are interested—please be tender when you cut me down. My panty girdles are fastened to my brassieres with safety pins. There are no hooks on the garter belts so you will have to pull them off. I am going to stand on the telephone books on a chair and use 50 feet of rope, truss myself as tightly as possible. I'm putting one pair of panties in my mouth, pulling a nylon over my face, and placing two false rubber breast pads wet over my nose and mouth—two or three turns of rope around my neck over the bar, back around my neck, closing the closet door. I'm going to set fire to the hems of the slips and then bind my hands behind me, then I will kick the phone books away and madly await the end. My body is carefully perfumed and powdered. The nylon slip I stole from the clothes line zippers down and caresses me lovingly. Now I slip the taffeta dress over my head and pull it down over my body. The base makeup starts to change my face into feminine softness, no sign of a beard. It takes ten minutes to put the lipstick on right. Now emerald rings, more jewelry. Now my blond wig transforms me into a woman completely. Now in utter passion I walk about the room, feeling the bite, pull, stretching of bras, garters, panties, all working me up to torture. Standing a chair in the clothes closet, I screw two hook-eyes into the door molding. Next I tie the keys to three padlocks on a string and hang them on a clothes pole at eye level. I put a pair of panties in my mouth that have been soaked in water. Now I pull a stocking down over my head and secure it around my neck with a choker replacing the wig. It certainly makes me look fiendish. I feel fiendish. Now I stand on the chair and deliberately and tightly padlock one end of the chain around my knees. The free end I pull through one hook and pass it around my neck and snap the padlock shut back under the wig. Now I pass the rest of the chain through the other hook and down to my wrists. Because I am just experimenting this time I only wrap the chain but do not padlock it here; reaching back I pull the door closed and hear the lock snap. It is totally black and my blood pounds fiercely. Carefully I work my feet to the edge of the chair and ever so slowly I let my feet slide off. The effect is thrilling. I can't tell where the keys are. I can't find the chair. I can't call for help, and I'm hanging controlled. I can free my hands this time and pull myself up on the chair again. Standing there in that inky darkness I know my next move. Measuring very carefully, I make ready the open lock and end of the chain. I stand on the very top of the chair. Now I strike a match but I'm so nervous it goes out. The next one will do the job though. Quivering with excitement, I just stand and swish the lovely skirts about my legs. I know what I'm going to do next. I'm really terrified by sadistic thrill. It is 9:35 Sunday night and in three minutes I will be dead. I strike the match, reach down and set fire to the gossamer edge of the black nylon slip. Quickly I wrap the chain around my wrists and snap the padlock firmly. In a frenzy of passion, I kick the chair over and my body is spasming at the end of the chain noose. I come wildly, madly. The pain is intense as my clothes start burning my legs. My eyes bulge and I try and reach the keys, knowing I have finally found the courage to end a horrible nightmare life dangerously." End of note.

PSYCHIATRIC LITERATURE

Case vignettes describing the association of transvestism, bondage autoerotism, and death by hanging have been reported by Schechter[6] and Friedman.[7] A typical case was described in some detail by Kronengold and Sterba[8] who emphasized the fetishism and gave a classical psychoanalytic interpretation of the patient's identification with his mother as providing the masochistic content of the perversion, although the essential quality of the fetish was to deny loss of the penis. The above authors emphasized most the identification with the female.

Shankel and Carr[9] described transvestism and hanging episodes in a male adolescent. The first self-hanging episode occurred at age 10 or 11, when he wanted to kill himself because, "I wasn't getting along in school, didn't like being there, and I though my mother didn't want me." In an initial hanging experiment he developed an erection and found the experience exhilarating.

Recently Resnik and Litman reviewed the historical and medical literature on eroticized hangings and attempted to conceptualize various symbolic and physiologic aspects of the syndrome.[10] These authors noted that clinical observations on bondage practitioners are scarce although judging from other evidence, the practices are common.

THE BONDAGE SCENE

There is a flourishing market for pornographic literature on the themes of domination and submission, flagellation and bondage. Typical titles are: *Thongs; Madam Adista; More Tales of Torture Manor;* and *Binding with Briars.* Some of the key images in this kind of pornography are of whips, buttocks, leather costumes, nooses, blindfolds, gags, ropes, shackles, and elaborate torture machines. In Los Angeles there are a dozen stores which have carried this material for years and done a profitable business. Recently relaxed police attitudes have induced many other book stores to add a bondage nook. (We talked with book sellers and attempted to get them to help us interview purchasers of bondage literature, however, the book sellers were not interested in our project.)

In virtually every large metropolitan area there is an "underground newspaper," a "free press," which circulates advertisements appealing to all varieties of sexual interests, including those of sadists and masochists. We indicated our interest in talking with bondage practitioners to the editors of the *Los Angeles Free Press,* an underground newspaper published weekly, with a

Patient Data

Case	Age	Occupation & life style	Sexual orientation	Masochistic behavior	Special fantasy	Pornography	Psychiatric history
1	25	Marginal musician	Single Heterosexual	Much masturbation Binding, mutual spanking	Bound & whipped by women	Major factor	Depression: 3 yr treatment in adolescence
2	26	Successful engineer Employed	Divorced Bisexual	Torture, strangulation to unconsciousness Group beatings	Dog on a leash, total debasement	Not important	Treatment 2 yr Suicide attempt
3	29	Marginal artist Self-employed	Single Homosexual	Masturbation with nooses, self binding	Raped by cowboys	Moderate use	Had treatment: suicide attempt: depression
4	30	Office work, secretary, ticket agent Employed	Exclusively homosexual	Males tie him, threaten him, use nooses, ropes	Foot fetish About to be tenderly murdered	Violent stories, not sexual	None: denies depression or suicide
5	35	Successful commercial artist	Homosexual for years	Tied up, beaten, severe abuse with own group	Thinks of special partners	Moderately important	No therapy: is depressed; made suicide attempt
6	39	Successful engineer Employed	Married Bisexual	Pansexualism Solitary hanging, almost killed self: sex clubs	"Black mass"	Extreme Expensive collection	None: denies depression
7	50	Successful teacher; retired military officer	Married Heterosexual Impotent	Eroticized fear Nooses, hanging Needs danger for orgasm	Leader of imperiled group	Some	None: strongly denies depression or suicide
8	53	Successful businessman	Exclusively homosexual	Tied up and humiliated by male prostitutes: noose symbolic	Tied up in an initiation rite	Extreme	Had treatment twice Now accepts his deviation
9	56	Successful insurance salesman	Married Bisexual	Extreme torture, needles, nooses, whips, etc.	His penis skewered with pins	None	Some therapy: mild depression

circulation of about 90,000. The editors promptly published an illustrated article entitled, "Whips, Chains and Leather." From this article and an advertisement we received about 30 responses, 15 by letter and 15 by telephone. These resulted in face-to-face interviews with nine men and three women. Only the men engaged in the intensive and potentially dangerous masochistic behavior we were trying to study. These nine men were, for the most part, intelligent, verbal, and cooperative. We feel that these volunteer subjects were motivated by loneliness, a wish to share their interests with others, and a need to legitimatize their underground practices. For several there was an element of a cry for help. Our ad offered to pay expenses, but no subject wanted money. Data from these interviews are summarized in the Table. The subjects are all middle class, white men. Most of them have been depressed and suicidal at some time, although not at the present time. All but one of them report a masochistic sexual orientation from early childhood with memories of bondage masturbation fantasies, or experiences of mutual seduction with other children involving ropes and passive submission. Memories of being sexually abused in childhood were not prominent among the subjects. This research revealed no consistent patterns of family interaction or of early traumatic experiences.

The general sexual orientation is toward homosexuality, although many of these men have had heterosexual experiences, and several prefer women. There is a trend toward increasing homosexuality with age, probably because bondage gratifications are more easily obtained in the homosexual world than through contacts with women. There also seems to be a trend with increasing age away from self-immobilization and auto-erotic masturbation toward participation with real partners. Partnerships are facilitated by the underground press. Indeed, many of our callers responded to the ad in a poignant search for other people who might share their deviation. Some of the subjects reported joining clubs for sadists and masochists. Others described call services providing specially trained prostitutes. It seems to us that from the standpoint of threat to life, auto-erotic bondage is a graver danger than bondage with others participating, although occasionally case 9 has come close to being murdered. Case 7 presented himself specifically for the purpose of finding partners to participate with him in hanging experiences which could be pushed to the ultimate threshold of death only when there was someone else present to effect a rescue. He was an expert in how many seconds it would take for ropes of different sizes to cause unconsciousness. "A thin rope around the neck will cause unconsciousness in 15 seconds."

These men reported substantial differences in their attraction to pain, per se, as opposed to psychological humiliation and degradation. Cases 2, 6, and 8 had very intense sexual reactions to scenes or situations of being humiliated. Case 8 said, "I am a masochist who does not like physical pain." He took care to arrange his scenes in such a way that he would not get too badly injured and could call the encounter off if he was in pain beyond "it hurts good." On the other hand, cases 2, 5, and 9 invited severe pain and were in danger of medical injury. Case 7 enjoyed asphyxia, partly for the sensual high, but mainly for the fantasy of great courage in the face of danger. Cases 1 and 3 were involved almost exclusively in masturbation and were looking for experiences with partners.

In every man there was an interaction between fantasy and sensation. For none of them was fantasy alone sufficient to produce orgasm. They needed, in addition, fetish objects and a scenario. Most of them were impotent without these props. Each assigned different values to psychological stimulation on one hand, as contrasted with direct painful or choking stimulation on the other, but both modalities were involved for all. Four of the subjects had found that inhaling amyl nitrite enabled them to prolong masochistic activity and endure more pain. Each of the individuals who used amyl nitrite claimed that it was used universally among masochists.

Concerning the role change from slave to master, about half of these subjects were willing to take the master or sadist role occasionally, but they did it reluctantly and unenthusiastically and only for the purpose of satisfying a partner.

We interviewed three women. For each of them, the involvement in bondage was transient or secondary to a wish to please the sadistic needs of a man. One was a 22-year-old co-ed, who had found spanking enjoyable with a certain boyfriend, but later gave it up happily when she started an affair with another man. The second was the depressed wife of an impotent sociopathic sadist, and she seemed to tolerate his deviant behavior in order to keep them out of further trouble. The third was a successful artist who enjoyed psychologically the feeling of being totally dominated by a masterful man, but who, in fact, had only once submitted to ropes and was turned off by pain.

REPORT OF CASES

Case 2. This 26-year-old well-dressed man at first seemed ill at ease and at a loss for words. Toward the end of the interview he became much more at ease and at the end invited the doctor to participate as an observer in one of his sex scenes which often involve groups. Subject has been beaten with whips, burned with cigarettes, and placed on a block of ice while a noose was tightened around his neck so that as the ice melted, he was strangled. He has been locked in a small box in which he could barely move, which was used as a toilet by others. He speaks with fascinated excitement about danger. He enjoys being blindfolded while he is being abused. He gets particular fascination out of nooses, and several times has been choked to the point of unconsciousness, achieving orgasm by such means. However, a variety of other masochistic activities also lead him to orgasm. He has fantasies about being left alone, tied up, locked in a small box, and he relates these to fantasies about death and dying. However, his favorite erotic fantasy is of being brought on a leash to a party of people dressed in Greek costumes who treat him as a dog. During masochistic orgies he has the competitive feeling that he can stand more pain than anyone else.

This subject remembers very little about his parents or his childhood. He is certain that no one gave him any direct sexual instruction. His first sexual experience was at summer camp with other boys where he took a dominant role. He had heterosexual intercourse in college and married at 19. He says that he has always felt left out of things and inadequate. In college he could not make it in a fraternity. In the army he continued to feel lonely and inadequate and he made one suicide attempt by trying to get himself run over by a truck. He then had two years of psychiatric therapy. During the therapy he recalled having masochistic bondage fantasies during childhood. Even then he had fantasies of being tied up and left alone in a room. He denies that his masochistic sexual inclinations have any influence on his business or social life. However, he was divorced last year. He denies that this still depresses him and then tells the interviewer that he specifically wishes not to talk about things that might depress him. The interviewer has the impression that subject is teetering on the brink of a severe depression with a high suicidal potential.

Case 5. He is a very well-dressed 35-year-old man, a smooth talker, who gives just a hint of being depressed and worried. He denies any present desire to seek psychological or psychiatric help, but he was grateful for an opportunity to discuss sexual matters with an objective listener. He says he is successful in his commercial art work, but masochist thoughts are becoming an all-consuming obsession threatening his work. He was reared in Europe during the war. He remembers homosexual and heterosexual experiences in air-raid shelters when he was about 8 years old. There was mutual masturbation and anal intercourse in which he took the passive role. Pictures of naked men in travel books excite him. In adolescence he had many homosexual relationships in which he was passive. In one attempted heterosexual experience at age 17 he was impotent. He enlisted in the army and had a prolonged affair with an older man, an officer. During those days he was depressed and often thought of suicide. Later he became aware of masochistic fantasies surrounding another older man, but there were no overt masochistic actions. At age 23 during an episode of depression he attempted suicide with sleeping pills. His first overt masochistic actions occurred around age 25. He described ejaculating spontaneously the first time a man offered to spank him with a belt. Having his arm twisted gave him enjoyment. At present he likes to be tied vertically in a door frame and have weights applied to his scrotum or to have electric shocks delivered to his nipples and his penis. He likes to be whipped on the genitals. Occasionally he has tried the sadistic role, but he feels that it is just a game for him and does not give him sexual gratification. He has experimented with being strangled but it has not given him any unique pleasure. He describes himself as a person who keeps his emotions inside and apparently is only able to engage other individuals through the masochistic actions. Recently he has noted that even with quite extreme masochistic behavior he no longer is able to have an ejaculation. This frightens and depresses him.

Case 6. This 39-year-old engineer felt that from early childhood he had no one to turn to. He recalls some depression as a child. He received no sexual instructions from his parents. He remembers masturbation at the age of 12 and having fantasies of being tied up by a woman. At the age of 12 or 13 he recalls tying up a girl and being very excited when she tied him up. He had some sexual experiences with prostitutes around the age of 17, married at age 22, and had normal relationships with his wife. At about the age of 24 he began having more vivid fantasies of oral and anal sexuality and while home from work due to illness, he began to experiment with tying himself up, with watching himself defecate, and smearing himself with excrement. He found that his wife most enjoyed mutual masturbation and this became the main kind of gratification that they had together. On several occasions while alone he would try hanging himself, and on one occasion could not get free and almost died.

He and his wife came to California and have traveled in swinging circles. He particularly enjoys foursomes in which he is forced to perform sexual activities on the other man. He enjoys having his wife dress up in a leather costume and spank him or beat him. He prefers being abused by a woman. He and his wife separated several years ago but came back together, he says, because they were dependent upon each other. In the past two years he has had to turn more and more to the homosexual world in order to get the humiliation and masochistic treatment that he wants. He assumes the passive role in anal intercourse, the active role in oral activities and particularly likes to be tied up and for his partners to wear leather. Often he achieves gratification during these activities by masturbating. He says that pornography is vital to his sex life. He claims not to be depressed at present and to have no suicidal thoughts. He says his job is going very well and he is able to support himself well. His favorite fantasy is of having his wife bring home another man, have intercourse in front of him while he is tied up, and then force him to eat the other man's sperm from her vagina. He has experimented with various kinds of drugs, including LSD and marihuana.

This man is very pleasant, cooperative, and extremely articulate. He gives the impression of pride in having enjoyed all manner of polymorphous activity. He talks about sex and love in a religious way with mystical amorphous metaphysical beliefs. He also describes activities he would like to get into of a ceremonial nature that remind one of the black mass. He gives no evidence of thought disorder and really gives nothing to suggest depression. He does not want treatment at this time but is most eager to join an "encounter" group.

COMMENT

Death Orientation

The outstanding impression created by this group of subjects was that of pervasive loneliness and isolation. We felt that these men were all deeply depressed and death oriented. They fought off the death trend and defended themselves against suicide by their perversions. To quote from Weisman's[11] penetrating study of self-destruction and sexual perversion:

> . . . some patients are self-destructive in order to *preserve* themselves and *triumph* over death. . . . Out of fragments of acts, sensations, organs, meanings, and fantasies, they put together a way of life which condenses conflict into deviant sexual behavior . . . they simulate what is shunned and idealize what is inaccessible . . . what is commonly thought of as degradation or depravity may be for them an inverted image of fulfilling reality. Under these circumstances death may be romanticized. Defeat, pain, and submission are simulated pretexts for ultimate victory, pleasure, and dominance.

A constant death orientation was obvious in all our subjects. Six of the nine gave histories of episodes of serious depression often accompanied by suicide attempts. Of the remaining three who denied depression and suicide, one had a guiding sexual fantasy of being attacked and tenderly murdered; a second had almost killed himself while engaged in solitary hanging masturbation; and a third always needed danger and the closeness of death in order to have orgasm. Eight of the nine have experimented in the past with nooses and strangulation, mostly self-hanging. Apparently self-asphyxiation is a common component added early in the development of the bondage syndrome. Most bondage practitioners know about hanging thrills but are frightened and shy away from the obvious danger to life. Several said they are saving hanging for the ultimate scene or eventual suicide.

The essential element that these men had in common was the erotization of a situation of helplessness, weakness, and threat to life which was then overcome in survival, and there was eventual triumph. Some of the subjects consciously and overtly emphasized the theme of strength and endurance.

For example, case 7 hung himself with the fantasy of being the heroic leader of an imperiled platoon. Mostly, however, they enjoyed fantasies of complete helplessness and destruction but implicit or secretly had the goal of survival which was associated with the orgasm. Often in these men an increase in boredom or depression was signaled by impotence which responded only to increases in the masochistic death-oriented fantasy life and scenes. We felt that these men were reaching out through self-destructive activities for some type of relationship and some type of transcendence beyond their restricted and depressed life styles and personality traits.

The Bondage Syndrome

Taken as a whole, the perversion was in a sense a creative and artistic effort to overcome loneliness, boredom, depression, and isolation. The protagonist here became the producer, director, author, and chief actor in his own dramatic construction. The actual dramatization aspect of this was at a minimum in solitary masturbation and at a maximum when one of these men became the object of attention of a number of sadistic partners. Narcissism was always a prominent feature. Even when there were other people present and participating, the subjects were preoccupied with their own fantasies and their own version of what was going on. Various fetishes were prominent in the form of costumes, ropes, boots, initiation rituals, etc. In addition, partners when they were included participated as part objects or as actors in assigned roles, rather than as recognized people. The subjects really preferred it that way, usually finding new partners and only occasionally maintaining long relationships over time. When married, they had difficulty with their wives, more because of basic personality traits of self-preoccupation than for their peculiar sexual behaviors. Of course solitude held special dangers for these men. While masturbating with bondage apparatus, several had had close brushes with death. When partners were present, the partner would be protective. So there was a premium on being able to secure partners. This played a part in the tendency toward homosexuality since it is easier to find homosexual partners than heterosexual partners in the bondage scene.

We were impressed by the diversity of characters among the subjects, the variety of fetish components, and the intermixture of apparatus, of ropes, of bondage, hanging, of various psychological components, moral discipline, humiliation, pain, and punishment, and of the combinations of homosexuality and heterosexuality. In this group transvestite elements were surprisingly infrequent. Each man had his own special most desired combination of components and could adjust to less optimal circumstances to different degrees. Nearly always the fantasy is more important than the actions, as if the sexual experiences and sexual partners are felt as fragments of experiences and fragments of people held together by imagination like tiles in a mosaic.

In a recent synthesis of work on pornography and perversion, Stoller[12] stated that pornography, as the perverse subject's key daydream, is psychodynamically about the same as his perversion. All of our subjects were aware of the pornographic bondage literature. About one third of them had been strongly influenced by it, they said, and several of them had elaborate, expensive collections. An interesting side-light on this is that from time to time these men would become bored or guilty with their collections and disposed of them only at a subsequent time to renew them. The bondage practitioners confirmed Stoller's concept that there is a congruent pornography for every man's perversion. In addition, about a third of the subjects said they had first discovered important components of their perversion through pornography.

Prevention and Treatment

We were unable to discover any consistent history of specific traumata in childhood or any typical family pathology. Apparently the choice of deviant pattern is unique for each subject and is dependent on complex determinants which might only be reconstructed by an intensive series of depth interviews. Disturbances in core family relationships, impairment in gender identity development, poor ego development, and specific conditioning experiences are all involved. Typically the subjects had few memories of childhood relationships. The details were meager and stereotyped. All of them saw themselves clearly as male in gender, but there was a strong feminine identification as well. Intertwined with masochistic attitudes was a stubborn streak of indomitable endurance, a challenge to death, and finally an invitation and welcome to death. The notes of the two deceased cases A and B illustrate these attitudes most clearly.

We would recommend to parents that bondage experiments and hanging experiments by younger boys are dangerous and should be discouraged. If such behavior persists a psychiatric consultation is recommended. Further publicity should be given to the dangerous consequences for adolescents and older persons of erotic practices involving partial asphyxiation by nooses, gags, plastic bags, binding devices, or gas inhalation. Such activities are especially dangerous to life when carried out in solitude.

As Marmor[13] pointed out in an unusually clear review, normal and deviant sexual behaviors are defined by the value systems of society. It is easily possible to imagine social institutions which would reward these erotic martyrs given suitable social settings. At present, however, society tends to view bondage practitioners with distrust and condemnation. They, in turn, feel guilty and ashamed, and in their previous contacts with psychiatrists have sought help for anxiety symptoms, for depression, and for marriage problems, but had minimized the importance of their sexual deviations.

At the time they talked with us, two of the nine subjects strongly denied any psychiatric disorder, any history of depression, or any need for treatment. The others, however, acknowledged that they had had periods of depression and three had made suicide attempts. Case 3 said of himself that both his father and grandfather had committed suicide and there was a strong likelihood that he would do the same. Friends tell case 9 that he is sure to get himself killed by some of the psychopathic sadists that he visits. Case 7 may easily die accidentally in his experiments with hanging. Case 6 came within seconds of accidentally hanging himself during masturbation in the past, but now seems to be protected by his partnership arrangements. The majority have had some psychiatric treatment, and while only one of them asked for or was interested in more treatment at the present time, it is probable that several will seek psychotherapy in the future.

We felt that each of these men would benefit from treatment emphasizing real personal relationships to offset the overwhelming loneliness, inadequacy, and fragmentation which they have in common. In our past experience, a combination of individual and group therapy extending in time over several years has been most helpful for patients who were sexually deviant, isolated, depressed, and self-destructive.[14]

REFERENCES

1. *Ford R: Death by hanging of adolescent and young adult males.* Forensic Sci *2:171–176, 1957.*
2. *Mant KA:* Forensic Medicine. *Chicago, Year Book Medical Publishers, Inc, 1960.*
3. *Stearns WA: Cases of probable suicide in young persons without obvious motivations.* Maine Med Assoc J *44:16–23, 1953.*
4. *Chief Medical Examiner, Richmond, Va:* Accidental Strangulation During Perverse Sexual Activity, *bulletin No. 38, 1955.*
5. *Gwozdz F: The sexual asphyxias.* Forensic Sci Gaz *1:2–3, 1970.*
6. *Schechter M: The recognition and treatment of suicide in children, in Shneidman*

ES, Farberow NL (eds): Clues to Suicide. *New York, McGraw-Hill Book Company Inc, 1957, pp 131–142.*

7. *Friedman P: Sexual deviations,* Amer Handbook Psychiat *29:489–613, 1959.*
8. *Kronengold E, Sterba R: Two cases of fetishism.* Psychoanal Quart *5:63–70, 1936.*
9. *Shankel W, Carr A: Transvestism and hanging episodes in a male adolescent.* Psychiatric Quart *30:478–493, 1956.*
10. *Resnik HLP, Litman RE: Erotized repetitive hangings. Read before the winter scientific meeting of the American Academy of Psychoanalysis, 1970.*
11. *Weisman AD: Self-destruction and sexual perversion, in Shneidman ES:* Essays in Self-Destruction. *New York, Science House, 1967, pp 265–299.*
12. *Stroller R: Pornography and perversion.* Arch Gen Psychiat *22:490–499, 1970.*
13. *Marmor J: "Normal" and "deviant" sexual behavior.* JAMA *217:165–170, 1971.*
14. *Litman RE: Interpersonal reactions involving one homosexual male in a heterosexual group.* J Group Psychother *4:440–449, 1961.*

17. Attempted Suicide and Self-Mutilation in Adolescence: Some Observations from a Psychoanalytic Research Project

Maurice Friedman, Mervin Glasser, Eglé Laufer, Moses Laufer, and Myer Wohl

COMMENT

This paper brings together many themes familiar to those experienced in the intensive psychotherapy of patients with borderline personality disorder, and sheds much light on the identity diffusion so characteristic of this group. It applies, therefore, not only to adolescents, but to a large group of patients whose intense ambivalence toward their mothers reflects a repudiation of identification with them. Many adolescent girls hate their femaleness, repudiate their genital impulses, disavow their bodies, and attack themselves physically in order to resist feminine sexual identification.

To a considerable extent, Maurice Friedman and his colleagues offer a bridge between earlier and later psychoanalytic contributions. Their central formulation follows Sigmund Freud's description of melancholia (1915), and echoes Karl Menninger's remark that in suicide an adolescent attempts to destroy the parents' most treasured "possession," the patient's disavowed body (see chapter 2 above).

The problem of body repudiation, closely related to the out-of-body experiences common to the borderline group, has been discussed more extensively by Moses Laufer in another paper (1968). Laufer wrote, "A breakdown that manifests itself in the form of suicide or attempted suicide is an aggressive attack on the internalized parent and at the same time is an attack on the person's own body, which at that moment is experienced as separate from the

---

Maurice Friedman, Mervin Glasser, Eglé Laufer, Moses Laufer and Myer Wohl, "Attempted Suicide and Self-Mutilation in Adolescence: Some Observations from a Psychoanalytic Research Project." *International Journal of Psycho-Analysis* 53 (1972):179–183. Reprinted by permission.

rest of oneself and as not belonging to oneself" *(p. 124). "It was as if puberty had suddenly changed the body into an enemy" (p. 126). His assertion was illustrated with case examples.*

John T. Maltsberger (1993), in reviewing disturbances of integration of body-image with the rest of the self-representation in suicidal states, extended these observations beyond adolescents and showed their applicability to suicidal patients across the diagnostic spectrum.

This chapter laid the groundwork for Jack Novick's 1984 discussion of the "suicide sequence" in adolescence (see chapter 33 below).

REFERENCES

Freud, Sigmund. 1915. Mourning and Melancholia. Standard Edition, *14:239–260.*

Laufer, Moses. 1968. The Body Image, the Function of Masturbation, and Adolescence. Psychoanalytic Study of the Child *23:114–137.*

Maltsberger, John T. 1993. Confusions of the Body, the Self, and Others in Suicidal States. In Leenaars, Antoon, ed., Suicidology: Essays in Honor of Edwin S. Shneidman. *Northvale, N.J.: Jason Aronson.*

■

IN THIS PAPER we shall describe some of our findings and express some of our views on the role the developmental process of adolescence plays in the determination of acts of attempted suicide or self-mutilation carried out in adolescence. The paper is based strictly on the clinical material drawn from the psychoanalytic treatment of a number of adolescents who have carried out such acts. Beyond our interest in trying to understand these pathological forms of behaviour is our aim to investigate them in the context of our wider study of mental breakdown in adolescence.

We were influenced in making the choice of such patients for study by the observation that the act of *consciously and intentionally* attacking one's own body with a view to injury or death rarely occurs before adolescence. We take this observation to indicate that changes in mental functioning in adolescence make it possible for the individual to direct his aggression towards himself in these extreme ways. We have regarded such a focus of interest as of particular importance, since we know that one of the fundamental tasks the ego is faced with in adolescence is the mastery of the revived instinctual drives. While a certain amount is known about this in regard to sexuality, little attention has been specifically paid in analytic thinking to the vicissitudes of the aggressive drive during adolescence and its part in this developmental process.

It would be appropriate here to mention briefly the structure and methods of our research project. All the patients whose material is utilized in our study are in five-times-a-week psychoanalytic treatment. In discussing, at the diagnostic stage, whether an adolescent was suitable for our study, we found that we were often faced with material which we could not understand and which sometimes left us uncertain as to whether to regard the adolescent in question as psychotic or not. We decided that we would only include cases in whom we could detect no *sustained* psychotic process and in whom it was only after puberty that severe psychopathology became manifest. We also decided that, in order to be included, the adolescent must have had a conscious wish to kill or mutilate himself *and to have put this into action:* it was not enough that he had thoughts of killing or mutilating himself, however intense his feelings may have been. We paid careful attention to their wish for treatment and their external circumstances so as to ensure, as far as possible, that they would remain in treatment.

It is not possible to condense the descriptions of our patients into one conglomerate, 'typical' picture since their manifest features vary widely and they fall into different categories of diagnosis (insofar as the classical categories can be applied to adolescents). One patient, for example, has a very full and active social life with her contemporaries, while another has no intimate friends and seldom participates in social activities. One patient comes from a psychologically sophisticated family with liberal standards of morality, while another's parents are uneducated and hold strict, narrow, moral views. Diagnostically, some of our patients are so seriously disturbed as to make us wonder if they were not basically psychotic, while others seem to fall firmly within the neurotic range of disturbance. However, we consider that the decision to kill oneself goes so completely contrary to what we assume to be the ego's efforts to perpetuate life that we begin with the assumption that suicide attempt is *always* a sign of severe pathology.

The ages of our patients at the time of starting treatment ranged between 14 and 19. We have had ten patients in analysis, seven girls and three boys. Three of the patients (two girls and a boy) were included in the study because of their self-mutilatory acts, such as deep cuts on the legs, self-burning with steam, and horizontal razor-blade cuts along the upper eyelids.[1] None of these patients has attempted suicide.

Each analyst writes a weekly report on his patient and this is circulated to the other members of the group. The group meets weekly to discuss each patient in turn and to evolve theoretical ideas about such matters as the psychopathology of the patients, technique, aspects of the countertransference, and so on.

Our study has been in progress for three years but since none of the analyses has been completed, the findings we present make no claims to being conclusive or exhaustive. We shall try to indicate where the views we put forward are substantially supported by case material, where our views are held more tentatively and where we feel we cannot yet fully explain what we have observed.

Psychoanalysts generally agree that one of the crucial changes that must take place over the course of adolescence if the individual is to achieve psychic maturity is the detachment of the libidinal tie from the original objects (Blos, 1962; Frankl & Hellman, 1963; Freud, 1958; Harley, 1961). One of our main hypotheses is that the failure of this process plays a significant part in the determination of the suicide attempts or acts of self-mutilation. Normally, this libidinal detachment is achieved through a process similar to mourning (Freud, 1958) and this detachment makes it possible for the adolescent to cathect new, non-incestuous objects. However, in the adolescent patients we have been studying we found that they were unable to give up the libidinal tie to their mothers: each patient appeared to have reacted to his or her internal move towards breaking this tie as if such a break would result in an unbearable loss. Instead of the normal mourning-like process developing, our patients reacted with a state akin to melancholia.[2]

In each of our patients we observed that the nature of the relationship to the mother has been a markedly ambivalent one, in which intensely hostile feelings, amounting at times to death wishes (felt to be omnipotent), exist side by side with equally intense loving feelings. A more careful study of the libidinal tie led us to see that it is narcissistic in character. A further characteristic which we observed in our patients is the presence of a severe, relentless, primitive superego.

As we have tried to understand it, the loss (which the move towards libidinal detachment implies) is regarded by our patients as, on the one hand, a confirmation of their omnipotent death wishes and, on the other hand, as a threat to the vital libidinal supplies. The object, i.e. the mother, is thus not given up but retained through introjection with the resulting intrapsychic situation of melancholia as described by Freud (1917). As mentioned above, our patients are characterized by low self-esteem, excessive self-criticism and intense guilt. Our analytic work has shown us that it is precisely those features which seem to have been established through narcissistic identification with their mother which are so harshly and constantly attacked by their superegos. It is these considerations which have led us to the view that our patients' suicide attempts involved an attack on the internalized object and that this object was invariably the mother. For example, Rita, an 18-year-old girl, who came to treatment six months after taking 60 of her antidepressant tablets, cannot bear anything in herself that she identifies as being related to her mother. She hates herself for being preoccupied with her bowels because her mother has the same preoccupation; she hates herself for having to eat compulsively and her mother is overweight. She thought that her analyst disliked her, giving as a reason that she was Jewish, but she herself hates her mother for insisting on her complying with Jewish customs.

A second line of determination of the suicide attempt has suggested itself to us from further study of the ongoing relationship of our patients to their original objects, particularly in regard to their aggressive feelings. So far, most of the material we have in this regard comes from the girls in treatment and their aggressive feelings appear to be mainly directed towards their mothers. The fathers of these girls come into the material much less and when they do, they feature mostly as helpful and friendly, but insignificant in their lives. We suspect this to be highly defensive against the oedipal feelings involved but though we have some corroborative material, the relationship to the father has not yet fully come under analytic scrutiny.

One striking feature of these girls' relationship to their mothers is expressed in an unremitting need not to 'give in' to their mothers. Maureen, for example, a 15-year-old who took 23 of her father's 'heart tablets', would be literally unable to do her homework, even when she wanted to, when her mother nagged her to do it. This need manifested itself in the treatment as an obstinate resistance, in which complying with the analytic rule or allowing the treatment to have an effect was felt to be such a 'giving in'.

We consider this need not to 'give in' to be a defence against the regressive, passive, masochistic, homosexual wishes in relation to the mother, who is felt as a very powerful, frightening (active) person who will overwhelm them. The gratification of these unconscious wishes would imply castration and abnormality. The girls therefore react with the intense aggressiveness which we have observed them to feel and show towards their mothers. In this respect, we have noted that the mothers behave in a way which can drive their daughters to intense fury with open expression of death wishes and subsequent intense guilt. But we have not yet been able to clarify the respective contributions of mother and daughter to this intense interaction.

Such a defensive use of aggression against these regressive wishes increases the problem of controlling aggression which all adolescents face. The bodily changes which take place from puberty onwards make the carrying out of such death wishes a realistic possibility. In addition, the adolescent sees her body becoming like that of her powerful mother, that is, there is an intensification of her bodily identification with her mother. These factors, taken together with the regressive features we have already mentioned, lead, we think, to their feeling their aggression to be omnipotent. Our patients have given conscious expression to such a belief—their rational judgement notwithstanding—as well as the belief that the only way in which they can protect the mother is to actually be with her. For example, Maureen, after criticizing her mother angrily in a session, expressed great uneasiness and her concern to get home as quickly as possible. These adolescents are thus in a cleft stick: if they left their mothers (in order to avoid attacking and killing them), they could no longer protect them from their omnipotent death wishes.

This seems to lead to an internalization of aggression as an attempted solution: we have already mentioned that all our patients are strongly self-denigratory and we have noted that many of them suffer from psychosomatic conditions (Hartmann et al., 1949). And so we think this is another way in which our patients have become vulnerable to making a suicide attempt. The precipitating factor along this line of determination is an event which is taken to confirm the reality of the omnipotence of the girl's death wishes, namely an injury or illness actually occurs to the mother. We were initially impressed by just how many of the patients' mothers had this feature. Maureen's mother, for example, suffered from sciatica (she found her mother's complaints unbearable) and, shortly before Maureen's suicide attempt, her mother was taken to hospital. During her analysis, her analyst sustained an injury and she could not rid herself of the feeling that she was somehow responsible.

The considerations we have been using Maureen to illustrate have led us to two further meanings of the suicide attempt, namely (1) destroying the body, regarded by the adolescent as the instrument through which actual expression can be given to the wish to kill the mother, and (2) turning the feeling of helplessness in the face of the aggressive and sexual urges into one of omnipotence (echoing their frequent use of turning passive into active).

We consider that it is the dynamic state of affairs that we have so far been discussing, i.e. the nature and consequences of the adolescent's tie to the mother, which goes some way towards explaining something which we have observed as an invariable feature in all our patients, namely a constant underlying fear of 'abandonment'.[3] We could observe this fear as a prominent feature in the transference and as a constant expectation in all their relationships. A major resistance, for example, which we found in many of our patients, was an intense struggle against any emotional involvement with the analyst for fear of abandonment, which they believed to be inevitable. Furthermore, we found that an experience which the adolescent felt to be such an abandonment (or the threat of imminent abandonment) could be seen to have occurred in the period immediately preceding the suicide attempt: for example, a mother hospitalized, a rejection by a boy-friend or a girl-friend, a quarrel between the parents. So invariable a feature did we find this to be in our patients that we were led to consider whether the suicide attempt was not, from this viewpoint, a turning of passive (being left) into active (leaving). Certainly, in the behaviour of our patients generally, they made widespread use of this mechanism. Viewing this fear of abandonment in terms of the intrapsychic situation described above, we would understand it to be, ultimately, the ego's fear of abandonment by the superego (Freud, 1923). As we view it, the suicide attempt or act of self-mutilation is determined by a collection of factors; the experience of 'abandonment' acts as a triggering-off mechanism in that it confirms the adolescent's fear of destroying the object and hence his source of any possible libidinal gratification.

So far, we have been discussing the lines of determination of the suicide attempts and self-mutilatory acts which derive from the adolescent's instinctual ties to the mother. We now turn to a further line of determination which derives from the alteration in the adolescent of his relationship to his own body. With the arrival of puberty, the individual, as we know, should seek sexual gratification via the now maturing genitals and he must therefore come to feel that he no longer wants the intimate physical attention he experienced from his mother in childhood. This is because he is no longer, as he was in latency, able to keep repressed the sexual fantasies that would be stimulated by intimate physical contact with her. The imperative need to avoid intimate physical contact with the mother is intensified by the adolescent's feeling that his body itself is the source of the urges to genital behaviour.[4] Normally, masturbation brings incestuous fantasies to consciousness but *in a disguised way* and the adolescent feels able to control these fantasies. With some of our patients, however, these urges are felt to be constantly threatening to overwhelm the ego. Certain regressive fantasies insist on intruding into consciousness and these adolescents seem compelled to live them out repetitively in a way in which the body is actively involved; that is to say, these adolescents are unable to contain their fantasies in masturbation.[5]

Thus Carol, whose central masturbation fantasy was to see herself overpowered and raped by a much older man, felt compelled to hitchhike, asserting she enjoyed it very much. She recognized the dangers involved, but this did not deter her. After some time she was picked up by a 'pervert' who forced her to participate in a perverse sexual act. A short time later she attempted suicide, feeling, amongst other things which we shall not elaborate here, that she 'must' die because there was no other way of ridding herself of her body.

Many of our patients have talked of hating their bodies intensely and of how they feel *forced* by their bodies to have these fantasies and carry out these acts. From this point of view, we were led to consider that the suicide attempt was aimed at destroying the body, felt to be the source of these urges. At the time of the suicide attempt, the adolescent seems to experience his body as separate from himself and not as belonging to himself: 'dying means killing the body but not necessarily killing the mind' (Laufer, 1968). The fantasy of death also contains the idea of profound peace—the longed-for freedom from these bodily urges and the associated fantasies, a removal of tormenting consciousness, release from the persecutions of the superego and, at the same time, narcissistic equilibrium. We have found that in our patients there is no concept of the reality of death and when confronted by it, they react with panic. For example, Alan, aged 19, who attempted suicide by taking a mixture of mercuric cyanide, became very frightened and ran for help when he felt the sudden, severe, burning sensation in his abdomen. In describing this event in his analysis, he said that the awful burning sensation terrified him—it felt to him as if he were really dying.

In this context, we are awaiting further material to confirm a distinction which we believe we have been able to identify between self-mutilation and attempted suicide: in attacking the body with the aim of mutilating oneself, the unconscious fantasy is of destroying the genitals seen as the source of the urges; through displacement, whichever *part* of the body is attacked then represents the genitals; in the suicide attempt, it is the *whole body* which is attacked as the source of the urges. While a state of calm *precedes* the actual suicide attempt, in self-mutilation the patients describe this state of calm as *following* the act. We believe this state of calm might be understood as a relief that, despite the injury, the genitals are safe. That the self-mutilatory act is also regarded by such patients as a 'removal' of the source of the urges and an act of self-punishment—both ideas serving to pacify the superego—

can be seen from the fact that this relief is always felt to be the result of 'letting the badness out'. The resemblance to orgasm is striking, but our clinical data are not sufficient to confirm this. In our weekly meetings, we repeatedly found that the clinical material led us to speculate that the suicide attempt and self-mutilatory act represent the primal scene fantasies of the patients. The particular way the adolescent chooses to make the suicide attempt or act of self-mutilation represents the enactment of that adolescent's primal scene fantasy and in this enactment he plays both the active and passive partner of the fantasy. However, this is not yet confirmed by our clinical material and we present it as, what is for us, an important speculation.

SUMMARY

In this paper we have attempted to trace how the developmental tasks of adolescence play a crucial role in the determination of the suicide attempts and acts of self-mutilation that our patients have carried out: we elaborated on our ideas about how the need to break the tie to the original objects results in a melancholic-like reaction and how the acquisition of a sense of ownership of the body leads to the need to destroy or mutilate the body because it is regarded as the source of regressive sexual and aggressive urges and the means of their gratification. However, a full metapsychological explanation of the meaning of attempted suicide and self-mutilation in adolescence, especially in regard to genetic considerations, still requires further clinical study.

NOTES

1. Anna Freud, in a personal communication, has drawn our attention to the fact that these cases might more properly be described as carrying out acts of self-*wounding* rather than self-mutilation, since the latter term implies the depriving, usually by cutting off, of a limb or organ; this has not occurred in any of the patients under study.

2. We have chosen to use the term 'melancholia' to avoid confusion between the affect and the psychopathological condition when the term 'depression' is used and because the reaction we have observed so closely resembles that described by Freud (1917).

3. We use the word 'abandonment' to indicate the individual's feeling of being completely alone emotionally, totally cut off from libidinal supplies and frightened of being overwhelmed by their own aggression. It is of interest to us to note that Pao (1969) places similar emphasis on the issue of abandonment in reference to self-

mutilation, although we have not found, as he did, screen memories of early traumatic experiences of being abandoned.

4. We regard this as a complex process involving as it does somatic sensations, bodily changes, parental identifications and other such factors; and we also consider that this attitude is determined differently in boys and girls. But because of the need for brevity, we simply describe here the outcome, which is what the adolescent experiences.

5. These ideas have been more fully elaborated by Laufer (1970).

REFERENCES

Blos, P. (1962). On Adolescence. *New York: Free Press of Glencoe.*

Frankl, L. & Hellman, I. (1963). A specific problem in adolescent boys: difficulties in loosening the infantile tie to the mother. Bull. Philadelphia Assn. Psychoanal. *13, 120–129.*

Freud, A. (1958). Adolescence. Psychoanal. Study Child *13.*

Freud, S. (1905). Three essays on the theory of sexuality. S.E. *7.*

Freud, S. (1917). Mourning and melancholia. S.E. *14.*

Freud, S. (1923). The ego and the id. S.E. *19.*

Harley, M. (1961). Some observations on the relationship between genitality and structural development at adolescence. J. Am. Psychoanal. Assn. *9. 434–460.*

Hartmann, H., Kris, E. & Loewenstein, R. M. (1949). Notes on the theory of aggression. Psychoanal. Study Child 3–4.

Laufer, M. (1968). The body image, the function of masturbation, and adolescence: problems of the ownership of the body. Psychoanal. Study Child *23.*

Laufer, M. (1970). Psychoanalytic studies of seriously disturbed adolescents: with notes on certain forms of regressive fantasies and technique. (Unpublished manuscript.)

Pao, P.-N. (1969). The syndrome of delicate self-cutting. Br. J. Med. Psychol. *42, 195–206.*

18. Countertransference Hate in the Treatment of Suicidal Patients

John T. Maltsberger and Dan H. Buie, Jr.

BIOGRAPHICAL COMMENT

John Maltsberger was raised in Texas and Dan Buie in Kansas. They met when they began their psychiatric training at the Massachusetts Mental Health Center in Boston and both were strongly influenced by the late Elvin Semrad. Both are practicing psychoanalysts. This paper was the first of several collaborations that arose from their experiences with suicidal patients during the course of residency training. Close friends, they were puzzled and troubled when a supervisor commented that it was shameful to entertain angry feelings against sick, depressed patients. Quietly checking the matter out first with each other, later with fellow trainees and a few trusted older colleagues, they decided to bring it out into the daylight.

Maltsberger has written widely on suicidal subjects. Buie has collaborated with Gerald Adler in producing a number of significant papers on patients with borderline psychopathology, and is a training analyst at the Boston Psychoanalytic Society and Institute.

COMMENT

Though the importance of countertransference in psychoanalytic and psychotherapeutic treatment had long been appreciated, this article first drew detailed attention to the critical role therapists' hate responses (malice and aversion) play in treating (or mistreating) suicidal patients.

At the time it was published hate responses to difficult patients were often treated as shameful, indicative of immaturity in trainees, not to be spoken of between self-respecting colleagues. Since that time the inevitability of therapists' aversive feelings has become accepted. Discussion of the subject has opened up and it is now a common matter for review in supervision and

---

John T. Maltsberger and Dan H. Buie, Jr., "Countertransference Hate in the Treatment of Suicidal Patients." *Archives of General Psychiatry,* 30 (1973):625–633. Reprinted by permission.

consultation. Appreciation of therapists' narcissistic vulnerability has deepened (see chapter 29 below). Countertransference acting out by inpatient treatment teams is now more widely appreciated as a contributor to suicide especially in borderline patients (Kullgren 1985; Rosenbluth and Silver 1992).

REFERENCES

Kullgren, Gunnar. 1985. Borderline Personality Disorder and Psychiatric Suicides. An Analysis of Eleven Consecutive Cases. Nordisk Psykiatrisk Tidsskrift *39:479–484.*

Rosenbluth, Michael, and Silver, Daniel. 1992. The Inpatient Treatment of Borderline Personality Disorder. In Handbook of Borderline Disorders, *Silver, Daniel and Rosenbluth, Michael, eds., Madison, Conn.: International Universities Press.*

■

The countertransference hatred (feelings of malice and aversion) that suicidal patients arouse in the psychotherapist is a major obstacle in treatment; its management through full awareness and self-restraint is essential for successful results. The therapist's repression, turning against himself, reaction formation, projection, distortion, and denial of countertransference hatred increase the danger of suicide. Such antitherapeutic stances, their recognition, and the related potential for constructive or destructive action are the subject of this paper.

COUNTERTRANSFERENCE is inevitable in all psychotherapies. Taken in the broader sense of the term, it comprises the therapist's emotional response to his patient's way of relating to him, and to transference which the therapist may form in relation to his patient. Some of the therapist's countertransference response may specifically arise from the way the patient behaves in the specific therapeutic relationship, and some of it may stem from the disposition of the therapist to react in certain ways either to all patients or to patients of a certain type.[1]

When the countertransference is fully conscious it can stimulate introspection in the therapist, can usually be controlled, and can direct his attention to details of his patient's behavior, the meaning of which might otherwise remain obscure. Otherwise, when unconscious, countertransference may generate well rationalized but destructive acting out by the therapist. These facts are well known to experienced therapists and various authors have described them in detail.[2–21]

While inevitable in all psychotherapies, countertransference is likely to be particularly intense in the treatment of "borderline" and psychotic patients, especially those who are prone to suicide.[18] Repeated experience has taught that borderline and psychotic patients have great difficulty with aloneness, hostility, and sadism. Klein[22] has described the mechanism of projective identification encountered in such individuals, and Kernberg,[23–25] their personality organization and primitive defenses. Searles[26] has emphasized the cannibal instincts as well as the role of an attacking, raging posture as a defense against sadness. The contributions of Winnicott[27] and Guntrip[28] have helped better to understand the aloneness, separation, and fears of abandonment that torture such patients. While no review of this complex subject can be attempted here, we take it as understood that the transference hate manifested by borderline and psychotic suicidal patients relates to a deep sense of abandonment (or expectation thereof), an intense craving for yet horror of closeness (it threatens annihiliation through engulfment), and various defensive operations that tend to alienate them from others.[18]

Transference hate disposes these patients to act in a variety of ways that will inevitably stir up countertransference hate. In this paper we will examine countertransference hate as it is experienced in working with them. We will describe the components of this hate—malice and aversion—along with the ways in which they are generated and how they may be usefully or deleteriously managed.

COMPONENTS OF COUNTERTRANSFERENCE HATE

Countertransference hate, like all hate, is a mixture of aversion and malice. The aversive component is the one fundamentally most dangerous to the patient and is often not clearly distinguished from the sadistic (malicious) aspects of countertransference hate. Sometimes the aversion is experienced more consciously while the malice is muted; this will give rise to a sense of inner fear and foreboding, while the patient seems abominable. When aversion is mixed with malice in the form of disgust, the patient seems loathsome.

But whether the patient is the object of punishing, torturing impulses, or whether he is abominated or loathed, it is the aversive impulse that tempts the therapist to abandon the patient. The therapist's malicious impulses, on the other hand, imply a preservation of the relationship, for the exercise of cruelty requires an object; one cannot kill or abandon another and continue to torment him.

Suicidal patients tend to evoke the sadism of others; often they can only maintain object ties in the sadomasochistic mode, and these they usually tolerate reasonably well and for long periods of time. Suicidal crises are likely to arise when the torture is given up and withdrawal takes place. Undesirable and destructive as a sadomasochistic relationship may appear, it is better than no relationship at all.

To live out one's countertransference malice in relation to a patient is antitherapeutic and unacceptable. But even more undesirable is the living out of one's aversion, because then a suicide is likely to be precipitated. Paradoxically, most therapists find the component of lesser danger, malice, more painful to tolerate than the component with lethal potential, the dangerous urge to abandon. In fact, there is a temptation to resort to abandonment of the patient in order not to acknowledge, bear, and place in perspective the countertransference malice.[21] While the impulse to torment and torture will often be felt in some degree along with the impulse to abandon the relationship, in a great number of circumstances there is a reciprocal relationship between the intensity of the aversive impulse and the incapacity to tolerate conscious sadistic wishes.

THE TRANSFERENCE ONSLAUGHT

Transference hate operates against the therapist consciously, preconsciously, and unconsciously, and to support and justify it as well as to bear it, the patient employs a reciprocating system of provoking and projecting. Hate in itself, when intense, is difficult to bear. When felt toward a needed and cared for person, such as the therapist, it gives rise to a severe sense of worthlessness and primitive guilt (superego anxiety).[29] As to the unbearable quality of feeling hatred, Hendrick[30] long ago pointed out that there was an economic gain in the defense of projection. He speculated that projection accomplished a division of the mental representations of a hostile impulse, and that while the sum total of hostility in the experience "I hate him and he hates me" is the same as in the experience "I hate him," the hostility experienced as one's own is less. Put more simply one might say that the patient feels less id anxiety when, by projection, he can share the responsibility for his hatred with others. Projection also offers the advantage of reducing superego anxiety by means of the formula, "You hate me so my hate for you is justified."

Because projection is so useful in attenuating id and superego anxieties, patients attempt to validate it in whatever ways they can. While provocative behavior appears in the transference as a displacement of hate from primary objects, it also serves to render the transference a credible here and now experience. Sometimes in order to obtain sufficient evidence the patient attempts to arouse hate in others through the seductive and inductive conduct known as provocation.[19,20,31] Provocations occur directly and indirectly, verbally, and in other behavior. Often they are highly inventive, persistent, and effective. Lying behind some emotionally neutral or even positive statement of the therapist the patient may claim to perceive evidence of concealed hate and contempt. If nothing of the doctor's verbal content lends itself to plausible misinterpretation, then the patient is likely to think he hears suppressed rage in the tone of voice, or sees it in some accident of posture or a casual gesture. Remarkable about human psychology is the fact that virtually nobody, including psychotherapists, subjected to sufficient provocation of this sort, can respond without some degree of irritation. For this the patient unconsciously waits so that he can prove his point. The irritation, once provoked and once detected, the patient will adduce as proof that he is hated by his therapist.

Provocation can take the form of direct verbal devaluation of the therapist. In one way or another the patient conveys through language his contempt for the therapist as a person. Often enough the therapist is openly discredited. If the patient can obtain some information about the therapist's personal life (perhaps there has been a divorce, or a child has suffered from emotional problems), it will be called forward as evidence that the doctor is personally destructive and too troubled himself to be a good psychiatrist. There may be a direct disparagement of his physical appearance (especially if there is some out of the way feature or another), of race ("kike," "nigger," "WASP"), of his taste of clothing, of his profession ("headshrinker"), of his education, training, or skill. Should the doctor have lost a previous patient through suicide, this fact will not escape the patient as an opportunity for devaluative sadistic incitement.

Provocations may take the form of direct action, sometimes involving physical assault on the person of the physician, or destruction of his personal property. We know of one case in which a patient, rationalizing her behavior on the grounds that she had "a right to know," broke into her psychiatrist's home and ransacked all his papers and personal correspondence in quest of case notes of her treatment. There may be frequent telephone calls at predictably inconvenient hours. We know of two instances in which different women patients telephoned suicide threats at the moment they correctly guessed their doctors would be sitting down to Christmas dinner. "Anonymous" telephone calls may be made, or the patient may tarry in the vicinity of the therapist's office or home, keeping all his doings under vigilant scrutiny. Such patients have been known to make suicide threats directly to the children of the therapists. Of course, such conduct requires limit setting, but the patient will try to find some hate in the doctor's manner.

Suicidal patients may also employ indirect means to provoke a countertransference hate to substantiate their projections. These indirect provocations, which often have other determinants as well, gradually tend to exhaust the endurance of the therapist. An acrid example is the muteness of the patient who remains silent, hour after hour, possibly with a faint smile of hauteur on his face. Akin is the patient who reduces the therapeutic hour to a repetitive, ritual recital of material without affect in an unconscious effort to bore the doctor, or to reduce him to a state of impotent anger. Repeated hypochondriacal complaining can have as a part of its purpose to accuse the physician and to evoke his anger. Constant confounding and forgetting of such matters as appointment hours or fee payment may have the same unconscious purpose. When the smooth and uninterrupted progress of the psychotherapy is precious to the therapist, he will be likely to develop countertransference reactions of an angry nature to all these kinds of disruptive activity.

THE LETHAL POTENTIAL OF THE TRANSFERENCE ONSLAUGHT

In neurotic patients there is a fundamental presumption of trust and relatedness. To be abandoned by all and to abandon all others are often entertained as fantasies, but are not real options for action. In borderline and psychotic cases, however, the circumstances are otherwise. Such patients express fundamental questions about the basic worth, integrity, and reliability of people. When suicidal, their faith in the worth, integrity, and reliability of others is so precarious that they must threaten to quit this world by physically removing themselves from it.

Only in suicidal and homicidal cases is de facto destruction of all relatedness, physical and mental, a stark possibility. The risks are real in fact; they are not imaginary. This aspect makes the treatment relationship far more than a transference investigation; it is a unique encounter on which everything, at least for the patient, may pivot. The reality outcome depends on the transference and its management. The risk to life and limb involved enormously heightens the importance and the burden of countertransference hate. The question is not only whether the therapist can influence the quality of the patient's future life, but whether there will be any future life at all. While we do not believe it is possible to treat any patient without countertransference, and, in the case of suicidal patients, without countertransference hate, clearly the discharge of countertransference hate in the therapeutic relationship is noxious and sometimes fatal for the patient.

NARCISSISM AS A SPECIAL TARGET OF THE TRANSFERENCE ONSLAUGHT

There are points of attack in all of us the striking of which is likely to evoke counterattack. Assaults upon self-esteem characteristically arouse ire, and in the day to day work with a suicidal patient, the therapist may expect many hits in that direction. The best attitude is one of expectant open waiting for the first manifestations of hate; one should assume he will feel provoked rather than to take it for granted that one is proof against taking such pricking personally.

The most common points of vulnerability at which the patient may shoot his arrows are those areas of unrealistic narcissistic self-over-estimation (or overaspiration) that are to some extent universal among beginning psychotherapists.[32] Repeated strikes against these targets are sure to induce countertransference rage. At the beginning of the treatment, when the patient is full of magical hopes and expectations, the therapist will be idealized, as he may from time to time later. To the extent that the therapist is infected with lingering omnipotent attitudes, he will mistake the patient's wishes for realistic expectations and vainly imagine he has the obligation and the power to meet them. This, of course, he will be unable to do, and will before long find himself feeling helpless, guilty, and wishing himself far from his patient.

Chanticleer, Chaucer's learned and ambitious cock, was tempted to ousting his father by the treachery of Russell the Fox and in an effort to do so shut his eyes with the unfortunate result that he was carried off by the throat. The unwary psychotherapist may also be carried away if he believes his powers greater than they are because when the patient reproaches him for his failure, there will be a crisis of countertransference rage, and a danger of regressive anal and oral sadistic acting out.

As experienced therapists know, the three most common narcissistic snares are the aspirations to heal all, know all, and love all. Since such gifts are no more accessible to the contemporary psychotherapist than they were to Faust, unless such trends are worked out in the physician, he will be subject to a sense of Faustian helplessness and discouragement and tempted to solve his dilemma by resort to magical and destructive action.

There is no universal remedy, and though in all medical specialties the young physician is prone to expect of himself that he should be more helpful to the patient than he can, perhaps the psychiatrist is particularly prone to expect of himself that he should be all healing for two reasons. One of them is that in psychotherapy the means of "healing" is the person of the physician. His own personality is the therapeutic tool, and for this reason the means of treatment are more difficult to separate from the self than is the case in surgery or medicine, in which the means involve instruments and drugs. The psychiatrist is therefore prone to confuse the limitation of his professional capacity to heal with his sense of personal worth. Furthermore, the physician-patient relationship is more intense and the patient's expectations for therapeutic magic have a greater impact. In psychotherapy, change comes slowly in small increments, and the process is not only terribly slow from the patient's perspective but from the physician's as well. This adds to the frustration of those who are ardent to heal.

Suicidal patients are surprisingly quick to recognize in a therapist any lingering magical expectation that he personally should provide a panacea. If his self-respect depends on production a "cure," it is here that the patient will be likely to attack. The patient will be strongly motivated not to improve in order to convince the physician that he is worthless. The professional self-respect of any physician, whether psychotherapy, surgery, or pediatrics is his calling, must depend on the best exercise of his skills according to the best knowledge available to him, and not according to "cures," if he is to feel happy and confident in his work.

The initial period of work with a suicidal patient, especially if the patient is a woman and the therapist a man, may be marked by the patient's explicitly declaring in an erotic way that she is convinced that he only and nobody else can help, that she thinks he will understand what others have not. The patient expresses her hopes for the relationship in this way. If the therapist vaunts in himself similar omnipotent hopes—that he should be the panacea for depression and suicidal troubles—then both the patient and the therapist will soon be feeling hopeless, for the successful treatment of such patients requires the recognition of magical expectations as burdensome problems that lead to inevitable disappointments.

Patients commonly expect that the therapist should be able to "know" what is being thought and felt without being told. The expectation for omniscience is of course as magical as the expectation for panacea, but parallel self-expectations are found in some therapists who entertain magical attitudes about intuition and sensitivity. The mark of a skilled and experienced psychiatrist is that he does not "play his hunches" beyond a certain point and that his intuitions about a patient are constantly under examination in the context of the clinical data. Indeed, it is characteristic of a seasoned clinician that if asked to justify a "hunch," he will be able to do so at once by reference to the clinical data. In contrast to this is the tendency to play clairvoyant and to follow one's "empathic sense" as to whether a patient is suicidal or not. To do so is to open the door to countertransference acting out of an omniscience fantasy in the name of empathy and intuition. The error can be fatal.

A further pitfall in the omniscience department lies not in the belief that one does in fact "know," but in the expectation of oneself that if one were a good psychotherapist one *would* know, somehow, even without data, but by intuition. Just as the self-expectation that one should somehow help every patient at once by some magic can lead to a sense of helplessness when the patient reproaches one for providing no succor, so can the expectation that one should "know," even without being told.

The third trap is the expectation held by some therapists that they should love all, that they should respond lovingly to all aspects of the patient. It is, of course, true that psychiatrists care about their patients, and their caring is vital to treatment, especially when the patient is suicidal. Being a caring therapist is also appropriately a part of professional self-esteem. Without exception the transference of borderline and psychotic suicidal patients will involve denouncement of the therapist as a cold uncaring person. Reality testing sometimes fades sufficiently to convert these accusations into near delusional or actually delusional beliefs. Insignificant matters concerning the therapist's demeanor are seized upon, exaggerated, and distorted to prove that his disposition is harsh and selfish. The onslaught can promote outrage in the therapist. Since threat of suicide is intensified during this kind of transference, the therapist will also be frightened, and the imposition of fear further stimulates countertransference rage. The more experienced the therapist, the more he has taken pains to extend himself to the patient, the more liable he will be to this reaction.

With experience most psychiatrists gain perspective on their hopes to be all-loving, and their vulnerability to attacks on this aspect of their self-esteem is much reduced. However, certain therapists are heavily invested in an image of themselves as unfalterably all-encompassing in their love for the patient. The nature of their investment is narcissistic, and they may extend themselves remarkably, even frantically, to preserve it. They are in fact highly vulnerable to attacks on their disposition to lovingness. Once their defenses are breached by the onslaught, they are pervaded by a sense of helplessness and depression, closely followed by retaliatory malice and aversion.

DEFENSIVE POSTURES AGAINST COUNTERTRANSFERENCE HATE

The personality organization of the psychotherapist is usually such that the feelings involved in hate for a patient are most inconsistent with self-esteem. We conceive ourselves to be compassionate, caring, and nonjudgmental, and often predicate our professional self-respect on not being rejecting, punitive, sadistic, murderous, and disgusted with patients. An able therapist cannot permit himself to behave according to such feelings, but neither can he afford the illusion that he differs from other human beings and has no id. Perhaps the intolerance for hating patients accounts in part for the paucity of countertransference literature relating to treatment of suicidal patients. It would explain the tendency to treat these countertransference phenomena as unclean or bad when they are discussed. Enlightened acceptance of one's own hate reactions is not sufficient to ensure against acting on them to the patient's detriment. All therapists, seasoned and unseasoned, find hating a distressing experience, and all are inclined unconsciously to mobilize defenses against it. It might, therefore be helpful at this point to survey five defense postures, the function of which is to protect from full countertransference awareness.

1. Repression of Countertransference Hate

The therapist who needs to remain unconscious of his feelings may find himself having difficulty in paying attention to what the patient is saying. There is a tendency to daydream about being somewhere else doing something else with someone else. Subjectively, the therapist may be aware of some anxiety and restlessness, or possibly he may find himself drowsy. He may feel bored. While this defense offers little scope for direct acting out of the unconscious or preconscious hostility, the therapist may well convey his aversion to the patient by yawning, glancing too often and too obviously at his clock, or by other signs of inattention, conveying nonverbally the message to his patient, "I do not want to be with you." When this defense is in play, the therapist is unable to weigh what the patient is doing to arouse his hostility, and to what extent his reaction is intruding in the work.

2. Countertransference Hatred Turned against the Self

This response is frequently encountered in the inexperienced or beginning psychotherapist but sometimes, too, in the more seasoned. He is filled with doubts as to his capacity to be helpful to the patient, wonders if he has the potential to become good at such work, and thinks perhaps he should give up psychiatry and apply for training in neurology or another specialty. The therapist may wonder if he himself is not deeply sick, and he may experience ideas of self-punishment, degradation, or possibly suicide. Subjectively, there is a sense of inadequacy, helplessness, and hopelessness. While this state of affairs can lead to giving up the case because one feels incompetent, thereby expressing the underlying aversion through action, the patient more often will suffer because the therapist deals with his malice by taking a masochistic stance, allowing to pass unchallenged the patient's efforts to devaluate and dismiss him as an uncaring and incompetent person unworthy of trust and confidence. The hateful transference is likely to remain uninterpreted. This is particularly true when the patient is unconsciously pouring out material the intent of which is to degrade both the therapist and himself, but which the therapist cannot recognize and interpret because he is warding off his own hostility. This is an avoidance device often employed by those who are guilty about their own hostilities, and tend to punish themselves for it. There is an unconscious tendency to turn the encounter with a hostile patient into a penance.

3. Reaction Formation, or, Turning Countertransference Hatred into Its Opposite

The therapist under such circumstances is likely to find himself preoccupied with being very helpful to the patient, too solicitous about his welfare and comfort. The doctor's daydreams may involve somewhat omnipotent ideas of rescuing the patient, either from his illness or from influences and persons in life that the therapist believes, correctly or not, to be destructive. He feels an anxious urgency to cure and to help. The potential for action when this defense is employed has two vectors. The therapist will be prompted to intervene in other relationships on the patient's behalf; this is at best nontherapeutic (the patient is not respected sufficiently to be given responsibility to order his own life) and often it is antitherapeutic, since it heightens the omnipotent transference expectation that the therapist will act at all times on the patient's behalf like an indulgent mother. Such tampering may even destroy relationships without which the patient may be quite isolated. Reaction formation in the therapist may also lead him to fear suicide excessively even in circumstances where there is little realistic hazard. Excessive use of restrictions and hospitalization may then follow, again fostering omnipotent transference expectations for ever present care and protection even when these are not needed. A therapist dominated by reaction formation cannot take necessary reasonable risks and in general cannot help the patient with his rage at not being cared for and gratified as much as he would wish.

4. Projection of Countertransference Hatred

Projected countertransference hostility is usually experienced as a dread that the patient will carry out a suicidal act. It operates according to the formula, "I do not wish to kill you, you wish to kill yourself." While reaction formation against hatred leads to a subjective sense of anxious solicitude, projection is likely to be accompanied by dread. The therapist may become preoccupied with fantasies about his patient's potential for acting out even though there are no objective reasons for such concern. Often enough his worry will be limited to thoughts that the patient will certainly commit suicide no matter what; there will usually be a tendency to take such a possibility "personally" and to feel helpless. This kind of preoccupation is usually accompanied by some degree of fear (the consequence of projected malice), and with a sense of aversion, i.e., the patient seems abominable. Projection of the countertransference anger at this level is often difficult to recognize fully, especially when it is taking place where objectively the patient is giving indications that indeed suicide is an imminent possibility. At such times it may be difficult for the therapist to decide how much of his concern is coming from the objective possibilities in the clinical situation, and how much from his own hostile impulses. We have found that when the therapist's affect is intense, it is safest to assume that substantial countertransference is at work. Sometimes the fantasy will not involve thoughts of outright suicide, but others which imply final breaking off of the relationship, such as the patient's running away (the aversion impulse is projected). When projection is operating in this way, three paths for clinical error lie open. One of them is that the countertransference hostility will be acted out against the patient by the imposition of unnecessary external controls (possibly enforced hospitalization) that will indeed provoke the patient to suicidal acting out and lead to disruption of the therapeutic alliance. The therapist may also err by recognizing in himself a countertransference rage and closing his eyes to the objective need for protective measures for fear that to take them would only be "acting out" on his part. The third possibility for error is that the therapist will give up the case and reject the patient when in fact the situation is not really "hopeless."

Whereas it is unlikely that most therapists will form a complete countertransference projection leading to the conviction that the patient is preparing to attack him or murder him unless there are objective indications that this is so (and suicidal types sometimes do have homicidal potential), fantasies that the patient poses a threat to one's safety or reputation can give a clue to homicidal impulses being awakened in the therapist, and require a careful examination of the objective facts in the clinical data, not only for the sake of the therapist, but for the patient. In such circumstances the stage is set for the rupture of the relationship. Projection of this sort operates according to the formula, "I do not wish to kill you, you wish to kill me."

The suicidal patient who for long periods of time remains mute is particularly prone to become the target of projected countertransference hate. Quite correctly the physician may conclude that the patient's silence is an expression of hostility the purpose of which is to ward off a fearsome relationship and to set the therapist's efforts at naught. The hazard lies in "taking it personally." The patient's silence makes it impossible to know just what fantasies are being entertained, but more than one therapist, sitting in frustrated silence, has felt that the patient is making him a helpless prisoner and torturing him as the cat the mouse, or the spider the fly. In short, to sit for hours with a rejecting mute patient who continues to be suicidal is likely to evoke primitive sadistic countertransference fantasies. Particularly if the patient betrays similar impulses (and usually he will), a situation exists in which the therapist's countertransference hate can be projected *and the projection perfectly validated by the clinical material.* Thus, a situation can arise in which ego boundaries are blurred, the patient projecting his hatred onto the therapist and the therapist his onto the patient, without either being conscious of what is going on. Each will be perfectly convinced that he is the undeserving victim of the hatefulness of the other, but only the patient will be correct. The therapist would be correct also were it not for the fact that he has chosen to bear what the relationship requires in electing to treat such a patient. The therapist is simply the object of the necessary and inevitable hate of his patient, but out of choice, and in that sense he is not in fact a victim.

Implicit in what has been said is that before countertransference acting out can take place, the therapist must first arrive at the position in which his hatred for the patient seems reasonable. Real countertransference action implies that the clinical facts are not in accord with the preparedness to act, and that for action to occur, some aspect of the real clinical situation must be out of perspective in the therapist's mind. Projection is one route to a loss of perspective. Distortion and denial are additional ways to the same end.

5. Distortion and Denial of Reality for Validation of Countertransference Hatred

Usually this involves devaluation of the patient in some way. This frequently is suggested in a preparedness to see the patient as a hopeless or bad case or as a dangerous person. On the affective level the therapist may experience indifference, pity, or anger at the patient, but does not have a feeling of empathic understanding or basic respect. Under such circumstances the patient may well be sent away, either by premature interruption of psychotherapy, transfer to other psychiatrists or institutions, or by premature discharge from a protecting hospital environment.

When countertransference hate is projected and the projection validated, whether by distortion of clinical facts or selective inattention to the facts (denial is really another purposive form of reality distortion), the therapist is employing defenses like those of the patient. Just as the patient seeks to repudiate the relationship by projection, denial, and distortion, a similar pattern often can be seen operating in the therapist at moments of countertransference crisis. The patient unconsciously sets the stage so that the therapist may experience a subjective sense of being attacked if he is not on guard. Like the patient, the therapist feels in danger, perhaps as the patient once was in danger from his rejecting and unsatisfactory mother.

The various defenses and the associated fantasies, affects, and potentials for acting out are summarized in the Table.

THE REGRESSIVE RESPONSE

Defensive reactions to countertransference hate are at best ways of easing the therapist's state of mind and at worst means of facilitating calamitous acting out. Malicious or sadistic behaviors constitute the first steps down the regressive path of countertransference acting out and for that reason will be discussed first. Certainly this sort of activity is thoroughly antitherapeutic. But

Economy of Countertransference Hate

Defense	Therapist's conscious fantasy	Affect experienced	Potential for acting out
None, exercise of caring, restraint	Murder, torture and rejection	Hate	Little
Repression of hate	Wish to be elsewhere, difficulty in concentrating on what patient says	Restlessness, anxiety, drowsiness; little affect experienced toward patient; empathically not in touch	Tendency to watch clock, be impatient, to convey indirectly a mild rejection
Turn hate against self	Impulse to give up; fantasies of self-devaluation, degradation, possibly of suicide	Sense of worthlessness and hopelessness; active sense of inadequacy	Refer patient elsewhere; accept devaluation from patient masochistically and without investigation
Turn hate into its opposite (reaction formation)	Wish to rescue the patient from his plight	Sense of anxious solicitude, an urgency to help and cure	Meddlesome intervention in the patient's affairs; too frequent enquiry into patient's suicidal impulses, plans
Projection of hate	The patient is about to kill himself; the patient will kill me	Fear, some hatred	Rejection of the patient; attempts to control suicidal behavior by imposing controls
Distortion and denial	The patient is beyond help	Indifference, pity, resignation to failure	Rejection of the patient
Sudden breakdown of defense	Death of patient and therapist, utter disaster	Intense fear, rage, and helplessness	Flight, immobilization

farther down the way are the deeper regressions that involve impulses not to torture and punish, but to destroy. Therein lie the great dangers for the patient. These more profound regressions will be taken up in their turn.

Sadism, a 19th century epoynm, is less satisfactory a term than *bloodthirst,* a word current in English for 300 years. The more technical term does not so directly connote the appetite for injuring and hurting. The older word also refers the appetite to the oral cavity, so that it is fairly specific for those forms of cruelty originating from primitive impulses to bite, suck out to depletion, tear, chew up, and devour. A similar specific word for anal sadistic impulses seems to be lacking in our language. We have torment, tantalize, and tease, as well as smutch, domineer, and beat. But the essence of anal sadism—to render a person helpless and then to dirty and injure him and to enjoy his agony—is not captured in any word. Perhaps torture comes as close as any.

The tendency for sadomasochistic patients to give and seek pain is only an exaggerated expression of the universal potential for fascination and delight in suffering. Not only is it evident in war, in prison, in school, but also in the cinema of the ferocious. Audiences relish scenes of bloody mutilation juxtaposed with the most brutal sexual degradation. The same potential for ecstasy in agony lies in the psychotherapist, and a tendency to regress to the level of primitive struggle will be aroused in him when the patient makes him feel helpless or futile.[20] At such moments the patient is likely to become unconsciously equated in the therapist's mind with the adversary mother of his anal stage; he will be tempted into a fight to "show her who is boss." When the therapist is drawn into a fight, the patient plunges into a hating, panic-like frame of mind in which survival or annihilation seems to be the issue. To the extent that the therapist's struggle is on the level of who will control and administer a beating to whom, his regression is to the anal sadistic level. But because the patient is likely to see the contest in terms of annihilation through engulfment or abandonment, for him the threat is one of oral punishment.[33] His threats against the therapist are to destroy himself and abandon the therapist, and he fears bloodthirsty retaliation of a similar kind. In order to cast the patient in the role of a dirty witch adversary complementary to the anal sadistic excitement he experiences, the therapist will have to distort these clinical facts and cannot see his patient as a person in a psychotic or near psychotic panic, in dread of death. Instead he sees the patient as a nasty person spitefully intent on thwarting all of his plans and efforts. When both patient and therapist are drawn into a contest of wills, each devaluating the other by projection, the torture drive and the bloodthirst will dominate their relationship. The therapeutic battle will then be lost because the therapist has given up his own weapons, reason, clear thinking, and caring. He has changed sides, as it were, and joined the patient in destruction.

Unconscious masochistic trends may also be activated in the therapist as he attempts to deal with the primitive aggression of his patients. Under the guise of being loving and tolerant, he may allow the patient to attack and punish him in a way which frightens the patient and deepens his guilt. Often such masochistic acting out is also turned to the service of keeping malice out of mind.

It is hard for most student psychiatrists to appreciate that they cannot only seek out such punishment from patients, but also that they may actually invite it and provoke it. Sometimes such behavior is rationalized by the argument that the patient was never permitted the expression of anger as a child, and that almost unlimited hateful display should be tolerated because it is a necessary "abreaction." Under the spell of such an illusion some therapists have even permitted patients to smear them with feces for periods of time, quite unaware that they were satisfying their own craving for degradation, and further burdening a psychotic patient by inviting him to do the degrading. Much more frequent are those therapists who permit hour after hour of verbal threats and degradation in the "therapy session," making little effort to interrupt the stream of abuse and to direct the patient's attention to what he is doing and why. The therapist who too much needs to make himself an "innocent and loving victim" is likely to be insufficiently active when a patient launches a sadistic attack.

In some instances the therapist may suffer from a masochistic character attitude that leads him to select such patients in the first place to fulfill his need for suffering and abuse.

While sadistic acting out against a patient is sometimes relatively easy to rationalize, the therapist who is well able to tolerate the conscious and physical manifestations of angry and sadistic affect, i.e., he who does not have to rely on isolation or other defenses to ward off such feelings, will be able to attend to his own state of emotional excitation. This means for most people a sense of muscular tightness and tension; especially the abdominal muscles may feel tense, and there may be a tendency rhythmically to tighten the musculature of the jaws, buttocks, and anal sphincter. Sometimes there are sensations of sexual arousal. There may be a sense of tingling in the buttocks or anus, and at the same time a sense of fullness in the chest and head. Subjectively, there may be a sense of righteous indignation. If the therapist can tolerate it he may experience lively impulses to attack the patient, beat him, cut him, or mutilate him where others would experience anxiety. Able psychotherapists monitor themselves even for slight degrees of such responses and use them as indicators that the patient is in danger of evoking an antitherapeutic response.

The kind of countertransference acting out that is more likely to result in suicide involves the therapist's unconscious impulses to kill the patient. These pertain not to the anal struggle for control but to the therapist's more archaic oral craving to be loved exclusively, and to the primitive rage that is aroused when that wish is frustrated.

As the suicidal patient's demands for total love and succor mount, the psychotherapist may worry more and more that his patient will commit suicide. This particularly occurs when the therapist has invited a rapid development of primitive transference from his patient by participating with him in the fantasy that the physician can provide what the patient so desperately craves, i.e., the experience of being loved as a small infant is loved. No psychotherapist can be a Madonna, but many have aspired to be. If the physician unconsciously aspires to the impossibility of being all loving, all caring, all giving, he subtly may be drawn into a relationship in which he tries to provide what the patient seems so much to need. When the psychiatrist tries to meet his patient's longings to be mothered in such a way, usually he longs to be cared for in a similar way himself, and by becoming a Madonna, he enjoys vicariously the patient's experience of being a totally secure, totally loved infant. Just as the patient expects the psychiatrist to love him, so it may develop that the psychiatrist begins to yearn for a return of love and gratitude from the patient for whom he attempts such understanding, care, and forbearance. Should the patient early in the relationship have been lavish in praise, or otherwise warmly responsive, the physician, like Chanticleer, may have been early lulled into the belief that his powers to heal and help were very superior indeed, and that he deserved the love that a little child might give its mother.

Dread of suicide increases as the patient's inevitable transference rage begins to appear; the therapist becomes an object of intense hatred. If the therapist has made promises for perfect mothering, tacitly or overtly, the danger of suicide indeed may be greater than it would be had the transference been correctly managed.

But the dread of suicide may also conceal the therapist's wish to kill his patient. This problem arises when the therapist has formed a narcissistic countertransference in which he has come to expect infantile loving regard from the patient. It is then that he is likely to experience his patient's abrupt eruption of transference hate as a deprivation of the love to which he has unwittingly become addicted. The therapist's dread of the patient's suicide is under such circumstances a countertransference dread of abandonment by *his* mother; he longs for her but hates her because of the way in which she treats him, as an unworthy child, rejecting him and all his best efforts, threatening to go away forever.

When the patient rejects the therapist and at the same time directs against him his cannibalistic rage, to the extent that the therapist regresses under the impact of the narcissistic shock, he will feel what the patient feels. Both will become bloodthirsty, both excited by the primitive sadism of the oral phase, and the temptation of the therapist will be to chew up the patient. An even greater danger exists in that the aversive element of primitive hate may at this juncture come into play. Whether originating in the bloodthirsty oral craving to kill and devour, or in the anal impulse to expel and reject a worthless object, the patient is in danger of actual abandonment. This is a moment of genuine suicide danger. Recognition of murderous impulses against the patient at the peak of suicidal threatening may forewarn the therapist that such a crisis is impending and enable him to avoid it. A breeding transference-countertransference storm can be recognized before the winds of rage begin to blow, however. Efforts by the patient to cast the therapist into the role of a succoring Madonna and a warm, nostalgic response in the therapist, are as sure a signal as a dropping barometer and a calm sea are to a sailor. At this point, if the therapist can recognize the impossibility of such hopes both for himself and for the patient, gentle interpretation or clarification of the patient's impossible expectations and a more realistic demeanor in the therapist may make the coming disturbance easier to manage.

THE THERAPEUTIC RESPONSE

The best protection from antitherapeutic acting out is the ability to keep such impulses in consciousness. Full protection, however, requires that the therapist also gain comfort with his countertransference hate through the process of acknowledging it, bearing it, and putting it into perspective. Guilt then has no place in his feelings, and the therapist is free to exert a conscious loving self-restraint, in which he places a higher value on the emotional growth of his patient than he does on his own tension discharge. At the proper time, the patient can be shown how his behavior leads to an attacking or rejecting response in others. In other words, the suicidal patient's repetition compulsion to involve others in relationships of malice and ultimately to be rejected is signalled in the therapist's countertransference hate. In time it can be interpreted and worked at, provided the therapist, by accepting, tolerating, and containing the countertransference, does not join the patient in repeating his past instead of remembering it.

THE RESULT OF THE CONTEST

Very few patients are incapable of developing the trust and making the compromise necessary to set aside the attitude of hate and the option of suicide. These few may, under the intense impact of the transference rage, bring about a state of affairs in which the therapist has no choice but to give up the case. This may come about when the patient cannot confine his onslaughts to the target of the therapist's narcissism or other noncritical areas, but extends the attack to the physician's person by physical assault, or to his other relationships. Rarely the patient may be so determined to provoke a rejection that in fact he gives the psychiatrist the choice of withdrawing or being destroyed. To persist in the treatment of a patient where there are substantial risks of this order is to fall into the ultimate snare of one's own narcissism, namely, the unrealistic belief that one is physically invulnerable.

However, experience leads us to believe that optimism is appropriate for the treatment of by far the large majority of borderline and psychotic suicidal patients. The most important problem in treatment is the considerable emotional demand the undertaking from time to time places on the therapist. When the therapist has the motivation, skill, and strength to deal with the transference-countertransference burden such a patient stirs up, good results are most often obtained. When the onslaught of the transference is met not with narcissistic overweaning and regressive acting out, when the therapist can maintain the relationship in an appropriately interested way, the patient has a chance to acknowledge his transference for what it is, to learn to bear the intensity of his craving and rage, and put them into perspective. The patient may exchange his impossible narcissistic dreams for real relationships once he finds their fulfillment is not necessary for survival. This exchange can come about as he internalizes his therapist as a good object, tried and tested through the fire of the treatment and found trustworthy. Increasingly, he uses the therapeutic relationship to grow and to accept life in the real world for what it is—something less than a narcissistic paradise but populated with other people who can reliably offer some love, if not total gratification.

REFERENCES

1. *Reich A: On counter-transference.* Int J Psychoanal *32:25–31, 1951.*
2. *Berman L: Countertransference and attitudes of the analyst in the therapeutic process.* Psychiatry *12:159–166, 1949.*
3. *Cohen MB: Countertransference and anxiety.* Psychiatry *15:231–243, 1952.*
4. *Heimann P: On counter-transference.* Int J Psychoanal *31:81–84, 1950.*
5. *Heimann P: Countertransference.* Br J Med Psychol *33:9–15, 1960.*
6. *Kernberg OF: Notes on countertransference.* J Am Psychoanal Assoc *13:38–56, 1965.*
7. *Little M: Countertransference and the patient's response to it.* Int J Psychoanal *32:32–40, 1951.*
8. *Little M: Countertransference.* Br J Med Psychol *33:29–31, 1960.*
9. *Money-Kyrle RE: Normal countertransference and some of its derivations.* Int J Psychoanal *37:360–366, 1956.*
10. *Orr D: Transference and countertransference: A historical survey.* J Am Psychoanal Assoc *2:621–670, 1954.*

11. *Racker H: The meanings and uses of countertransference.* Psychoanal Q *26:303–357, 1957.*
12. *Savage C: Countertransference in the therapy of schizophrenics.* Psychiatry *24:53–60, 1961.*
13. *Searles H: The schizophrenic's vulnerability to the therapist's unconscious process, in* Collected Papers on Schizophrenia and Related Subjects. *New York, International Universities Press, 1965.*
14. *Tower LE: Countertransference.* J Am Psychoanal Assoc *4:224–255, 1956.*
15. *Weigert E: Counter-transference and self-analysis of the psychoanalyst.* Int J Psychoanalysis *35:242–246, 1954.*
16. *Winnicott DW: Hate in the counter-transference.* Int J Psychoanal *30:69–74, 1949.*
17. *Winnicott DW: Countertransference.* Br J Med Psych *33:17–21, 1960.*
18. *Chase LS, Hire A: Countertransference in the analysis of borderlines. Read before the Scientific Meeting of the Boston Psychoanalytic Society and Institute, Boston, March 23, 1966.*
19. *Adler G: Valuing and devaluing in the psychotherapeutic process.* Arch Gen Psychiatry *22:454–461, 1960.*
20. *Adler G: Helplessness in the helpers.* Br J Med Psychol *45:315–326, 1972.*
21. *Semrad EV:* Teaching Psychotherapy of Psychotic Patients. *New York, Grune and Stratton, 1969.*
22. *Klein M: Notes on some schizoid mechanisms, in Riviere J (ed):* Developments in Psycho-Analysis. *London, Hogarth Press, 1952.*
23. *Kernberg OF: Structural derivatives of object relationships.* Int J Psychoanal *47:236–253, 1966.*
24. *Kernberg OF: Borderline personality organization.* J Am Psychoanal Assoc *15:641–685, 1967.*
25. *Kernberg OF: Treatment of borderline patients, in Giovacchini PL (ed):* Tactics and and Techniques in Psychoanalytic Therapy. *New York, Science House Inc, 1972.*
26. *Searles H: The psychodynamics of vengefulness, in* Collected Papers on Schizophrenia and Related Subjects. *New York, International Universities Press, 1965.*
27. *Winnicott DW:* Collected Papers. *New York, Basic Books, 1958.*
28. *Guntrip H:* Schizoid Phenomena, Object-Relations, and the Self. *New York, International Universities Press, 1968.*
29. *Freud A:* The Ego and Mechanisms of Defense. *New York, International Universities Press, 1946.*
30. *Hendrick I: Ego development and certain character problems.* Psychoanal Q *5:320–346, 1936.*
31. *Murray JM: Narcissism and the ego ideal.* J Am Psychoanal Assoc *12:477–511, 1964.*
32. *Sharaf MR, Levinson DJ: The quest for omnipotence in professional training.* Psychiatry *27:135–149, 1964.*
33. *Buie DH, Adler G: The uses of confrontation with borderline patients.* Int J Psychoanal Psychother *1:90–108, 1972.*

19. The Influence of Suggestion on Suicide: Substantive and Theoretical Implications of the Werther Effect

David P. Phillips

BIOGRAPHICAL NOTE

When David Phillips was a Harvard freshman, Talcott Parsons introduced him to Émile Durkheim's theory of suicide. That summer, when Phillips was reviewing epidemiological literature on breast cancer, a medical researcher named Hutchison asked what he had been studying. Full of uncritical pride Phillips mentioned Durkheim. Hutchison asked what evidence supported Durkheim's hypothesis, and, on hearing it, pronounced himself unconvinced. "I was startled by this medical iconoclast, who had so crassly attacked one of the sociological gods," Phillips writes. "I spent the next few years trying to find evidence that would point unequivocally toward Durkheim's theory and would not simultaneously support a host of competing explanations of suicide. After about sixty attempts I gave up. George Bernard Shaw has observed that much of education consists of unlearning *what you have been taught. I finally acquired an education and began to look at non-Durkheimian factors that might influence suicide."*

One of the factors he pursued was imitation, or suggestion. Though Durkheim had believed imitative factors had no effect on the suicide rate, a dictum accepted for seventy-five years, Phillips showed he was wrong. Studying patterns of increasing suicide associated with the publicity suicide receives in the media, he proved the importance of imitation, and named it "the Werther Effect." Goethe's novel The Sorrows of Young Werther *describes the suicide of its heart-broken hero, a martyr to love. Its publication in 1774 triggered a wave of suicides and alarmed Europe.*

David P. Phillips, "The Influence of Suggestion on Suicide: Substantive and Theoretical Implications of the Werther Effect." *American Sociological Review* 39 (1974):340–354. Reprinted by permission.

Phillips, a professor of sociology at the University of California (San Diego), continues to study the relationships among culture, society, psychology, and death by suicide and other causes. "I have presented evidence," he writes, "suggesting that people are able to postpone dying briefly until they have reached important symbolic occasions. In addition, I have found evidence suggesting that persons who are pessimistic about their prognoses die earlier than would otherwise be expected."

COMMENT

Though Durkheim dismissed the epidemiological importance of suggestion as a factor influencing suicide rates, reports of epidemics of suicide alarmed Europeans early in the nineteenth century at the pitch of the Romantic Movement. The English boy-poet Thomas Chatterton (1752–1770), poor and starving, swallowed arsenic and died at the age of eighteen. Alfred Victor de Vigny's sensational Chatterton, *dramatizing this tragic episode, was followed by a doubling of the French suicide rate between 1830 and 1840. Goethe's autobiographical* The Sorrows of Young Werther *was an enormous popular success, and it provoked imitation suicides in sufficient numbers to alarm the authorities (Fedden 1938; Alvarez 1970; Colt 1991).*

Phillips observes that "the dearth of studies linking suicide and suggestion is somewhat puzzling, in view of the general importance ascribed to contagion and suggestion in other areas of sociology." He systematically examined fluctuations in suicide rates after the publication of suicide reports in newspapers and empirically showed that suicides increase after these reports, and increase according to the intensity of the publicity. This work has stimulated numerous other parallel studies and has obvious importance for the news media to the extent they are interested in suicide prevention. It offers grounds for a strong argument against romanticizing and idealizing suicide victims when schools and other close communities must deal with such tragedies.

REFERENCES

Alvarez, A. 1970. The Savage God. *New York: Random House. (See especially pp. 201–213.)*

Colt, George Howe. 1991. The Enigma of Suicide. *New York: Summit Books.*

Fedden, Henry Romilly. 1938. Suicide: A Social and Historical Study. *London: Peter Davies.*

■

This paper shows that suicides increase immediately after a suicide story has been publicized in the newspapers in Britain and in the United States, 1947–1968. The more publicity devoted to a suicide story, the larger the rise in suicides thereafter. The rise in suicides after a story is restricted mainly to the area in which the story was publicized. Alternative explanations of these findings are examined; the evidence indicates that the rise in suicides is due to the influence of suggestion on suicide, on influence not previously demonstrated on the national level of suicides. The substantive, theoretical, and methodological implications of these findings are examined.

Two hundred years ago, Goethe wrote a novel called *The Sorrows of the Young Werther,* in which the hero committed suicide. Goethe's novel was read widely in Europe, and it was said that people in many countries imitated Werther's manner of death. According to Goethe, "My friends . . . thought that they must transform poetry into reality, imitate a novel like this in real life and, in any case, shoot themselves; and what occurred at first among a few took place later among the general public. . . ." (Goethe, quoted in Rose, 1929:xxiv.) Widespread imitation of Werther's suicide was never conclusively demonstrated, but authorities were sufficiently apprehensive to ban the book in several areas, including Italy (Gray, 1967), Leipzig, and Copenhagen (Rose, 1929).

More than one hundred years after *Werther* was written, Durkheim (1897) reviewed research linking suicide and suggestion (e.g., Tarde, 1903) and found no conclusive evidence relating imitation and the social suicide rate. Durkheim acknowledged that imitation might influence a few persons in the immediate vicinity of a well-known suicide, but he asserted that imitation does not affect the national level of suicides. He conceded that a few suicides might be precipitated by suggestion but he felt that these would probably have occurred eventually even in the absence of suggestion. Students of suicide have tended to follow Durkheim rather than Goethe or Tarde; and in the eighty years since *Suicide* was published, the influence of suggestion on suicide has seldom been studied. The comprehensive *Bibliography on Suicide and Suicide Prevention, 1897–1970* (Farberow, 1972) which includes several thousand items, does not list the words "suggestion," "imitation," or "contagion" in its index.

In his book reviewing the literature on suicide, Lester (1972) found seven studies on suggestion or imitation, and he devoted a chapter to describing them. Lester noted that the results of some studies were inconclusive (Motto,

1967), contradictory (Crawford and Willis, 1966; Seiden, 1968) or could be explained by processes other than imitation (Weiss, 1958; Kreitman et al., 1969). Motto (1967) hypothesized that suicide rates should fall during newspaper strikes because during those periods, potential suicides would find no publicized suicides to imitate. Motto examined the suicide rates in seven cities undergoing newspaper strikes and found no evidence to support his hypothesis. Crawford and Willis (1966) studied six pairs of suicides and found evidence of imitation in three pairs and no evidence in the remaining three. Seiden (1968) examined five suicides during a one-month period in Berkeley, and felt that imitation was not involved. Weiss (1958) noted that sometimes a widower (or widow) attempts suicide on the anniversary of his spouse's death. This phenomenon might result from imitation, but it might also result from a grief that becomes overwhelming on the anniversary of a partner's death. Kreitman et al. (1969) noted that attempted suicides had an unusually large number of suicidal friends. This result might indicate that persons imitate their friends' suicides, or that suicide-prone persons select each other as friends. In conclusion, Lester (1972:188–9) observed, "On the whole, therefore, contagion and suggestibility effects are equally difficult both to document and to rule out. . . . Clearly, the analysis of this topic is at too early a stage for reliable conclusions to be drawn." Thus, prior to the present study, no investigation that I know of has systematically and empirically demonstrated that suggestion affects the national level of suicide.[1]

The dearth of studies linking suicide and suggestion is somewhat puzzling, in view of the general importance ascribed to contagion and suggestion in other areas of sociology (Blumer, 1955; Cantril, 1963; Toch, 1965; Klapp, 1969; Lang and Lang, 1961). Furthermore, Cantril, Toch and Klapp have claimed that anomic individuals are unusually suggestible, and many students of suicide have claimed that anomic individuals are prone to suicide. If both these claims are correct, then individuals prone to suicide should also be suggestible.

In this paper, I will use American and British statistics to show that the number of suicides increases after the story of a suicide is publicized in the newspapers.[2] It seems appropriate to call this increase in suicides "the Werther effect," after Goethe's hero. I will show that this effect is probably due to the influence of suggestion on suicide. Contrary to Durkheim's assertions, the Werther effect is manifested on a national and sometimes on an international scale; furthermore, it is not necessarily produced by those who would have committed suicide anyway, even in the absence of a publicized suicide to imitate. The Werther effect is interesting for substantive and for theoretical reasons. These will be discussed after the effect has been demonstrated.

INCREASE IN NATIONAL SUICIDES AFTER A PUBLICIZED SUICIDE

A list of postwar suicides publicized in the newspapers was generated from *Facts on File,* a general index to world news. The *New York Times Index* was then used to determine a subset of particularly publicized suicides, namely, those appearing on the front page of the *New York Times.* The *New York Times* was used because it is the only U.S. daily newspaper with a large circulation (averaging about 700,000, 1950–1970) and an index covering the entire postwar period. Later in this investigation, the *New York Daily News* (the most popular U.S. newspaper), the *Chicago Tribune,* and the *London Daily Mirror* will also be examined.

National postwar suicide statistics are available for each month during the period 1946–1968. These statistics can be used to determine the effect of front-page suicides during the period 1947–1967. If front-page suicides stimulate a rise in national suicides, this increase can be detected by a technique developed in an earlier paper (Phillips and Feldman, 1973). The use of this technique can be illustrated in the case of Daniel Burros, a leader of the Ku Klux Klan who committed suicide on November 1, 1965, when the newspapers revealed that he was Jewish. In the month after Burros' death, November of 1965, 1,710 suicides were recorded. There were 1,639 suicides in November of the previous year (1964) and 1,665 suicides in November of the subsequent year (1966). The average, $(1{,}639 + 1{,}665)/2 = 1{,}652$, can be taken as an estimate of the number of suicides expected in November of 1965, under the null hypothesis that Burros' death had no effect on national suicides. It can be seen that this method of estimating the expected number of suicides controls for the effects of the seasons on suicide and for the existence of linear trends over time in the level of suicide. Because the observed number of suicides in November 1965 (1,710) is greater than the number expected (1,652) there was a rise in suicides just after Daniel Burros killed himself.[3]

In general, the above procedure was used to estimate the effect of front-page suicides. However, in some instances, the following modifications were required.

1. Burros' suicide occurred in November of 1965, and November of 1964 and 1966 were used as control months to estimate the effect of Burros' death.

However, if another front-page suicide had occurred in November of 1966 it would be inappropriate to use this as one of the control months. Instead, November of 1967 would be a more appropriate choice.

2. If Burros' suicide had been discussed on November 30, 1965 instead of on November 1, it would be inappropriate to seek the effects of Burros' death in November; instead, December would be a more appropriate choice. In general, if the *Times* discussed a front-page suicide late in a month (after the 23rd), the month after the *Times* story was examined. The 23rd was chosen as a cut-off point because it was arbitrarily assumed that the effect of a front-page story would last only two weeks. This implies that a front-page story will have its major effect primarily in the month of the story, if the story appears on or before the 23rd of the month. Otherwise, the greatest effect of the front-page story will be in the month after the story.

Although these procedures seem plausible, they are also somewhat arbitrary. It is therefore worth noting that, in general, the Werther effect still appears when different procedures are followed, for example, if the 15th is used as a cut-off point, rather than the 23rd.

Table 1 gives the number of U.S. suicides observed after a front-page suicide, and the number expected under the null hypothesis that front-page suicides have no effect on the level of national suicides. It can be seen that suicides increase after twenty-six front-page stories, and decrease after seven of them. Given the null hypothesis the probability of twenty-six or more suicide peaks out of thirty-three is .00066 (binomial test, $p=.5$ $n=33, \times \geqslant 26$).[4]

In the next section, I will show that the Werther effect is probably caused by the effect of suggestion on suicide.

POSSIBLE CAUSES OF THE WERTHER EFFECT

In attempting to determine the causes of the Werther effect, I will first show that the available evidence is consistent with the effect of suggestion on suicide. Then I will show that some other plausible explanations of the Werther effect are inconsistent with the available data.

Timing of the Werther Effect with Respect to Newspaper Stories on Suicide

If the Werther effect is caused by the publicizing of suicide stories, then the rise in the national suicide level should occur only *after* each suicide story

Table 1. Rise in the Number of U.S. Suicides after Suicide Stories Publicized on Page 1 of the New York Times

Name of publicized suicide	Date of suicide story	Observed no. of suicides in mo.[a] after suicide story	Expected no. of suicides in mo. after suicide story	Rise in U.S. suicides after suicide story: observed—expected no. of suicides
Lockridge, author	March 8, 1948	1510	1521.5	−11.5
Landis, filmstar	July 6, 1948	1482	1457.5	24.5
Brooks, financier	August 28, 1948	1250	1350	−100.0
Holt, betrayed husband	March 10, 1949	1583	1521.5	61.5
Forrestal, Ex-Secretary of Defense	May 22, 1949	1549	1493.5	55.5
Baker, professional	April 26, 1950	1600	1493.5	106.5
Lang, police witness	April 20, 1951	1423	1519.5	−96.5
Soule, professor	August 4, 1951	1321	1342	−21.0
Adamic, writer	September 5, 1951	1276	1258.5	17.5
Stengel, N.J. police chief	October 7, 1951	1407	1296.5	110.5
Feller, U.N. official	November 14, 1952	1207	1229	−22.0
LaFollette, Senator	February 25, 1953[b]	1435	1412	23.0
Armstrong, inventor of F.M. Radio	February 2, 1954	1240	1227	13.0
Hunt, Senator	June 20, 1954	1458	1368.5	89.5
Vargas, Brazilian President	August 25, 1954	1357	1321.5	35.5
Norman, Canadian Ambassador	April 5, 1957	1511	1649.5	−138.5
Young, financier	January 26, 1958	1361	1352	9.0
Schupler, N.Y.C. councilman	May 3, 1958	1672	1587	85.0
Quiggle, Admiral	July 25, 1958	1519	1451	68.0
Zwillman, underworld leader	February 27, 1959	1707	1609	98.0
Bang-Jensen, U.N. diplomat	November 27, 1959	1477	1423	54.0
Smith, police chief	March 20, 1960	1669	1609	60.0
Gedik, Turkish Minister	May 31, 1960	1568	1628.5	−60.5
Monroe, filmstar	August 6, 1962	1838	1640.5	197.5
Graham, publisher; Ward, implicated in Profumo Affair	August 4, 1963	1801	1640.5	160.5
Heyde & Tillman,[c] Nazi officials	February 14, 1964	1647	1584.5	62.5
Lord, N.J. Party chief	June 17, 1965	1801	1743	58.0
Burros, KKK Leader Morison, war critic	November 1, 1965 November 3, 1965	1710	1652	58.0
Mott, American in Russian jail	January 22, 1966	1757	1717	40.0
Pike, son of Bishop Pike	February 5, 1966	1620	1567.5	52.5

Name of publicized suicide	Date of suicide story	Observed no. of suicides in mo.[a] after suicide story	Expected no. of suicides in mo. after suicide story	Rise in U.S. suicides after suicide story: observed—expected no. of suicides
Kravchenko, Russian defector	February 26, 1966	1921	1853	68.0
LoJui-Ching, Chinese Army leader	January 21, 1967	1821	1717	104.0
Amer, Egyptian Field Marshall	September 16, 1967	1770	1733.5	36.5
				1298.5

[a] For rules determining the month to be examined, see text.
[b] All February statistics have been normed for a month of 28 days.
[c] The suicides of Heyde and Tillman were discussed in the same suicide story.
Source of suicide statistics: U.S. Department of Health, Education, and Welfare, Public Health Service, *Vital Statistics of the U.S.,* Yearly Volumes, 1947–1968.

appears. One cannot check this prediction as precisely as one would wish because U.S. suicide statistics are not tabulated by day of occurrence, only by month. Nonetheless, these monthly suicide statistics allow us to determine approximately whether suicide levels rise before or after suicide stories.

Figure 1 gives the rise in suicides in the month *before* the suicide story appears, in the month *when* it appears,[5] and in the months *thereafter.* As predicted, suicide levels are not higher than expected in the month before the stories appear; but they are considerably higher than expected in the month of the story and in the month thereafter. In these two months, the number of excess suicides is 2,034 (1275 + 759). This is an average of 58.1 (2,034/35) excess suicides per suicide story.

Of course, it is conceivable that some excess suicides in the month of the suicide story occur before that story appears. It is possible that suicides increase early in the month of a suicide story even though that story appears later in the month. This is unlikely, however, because of the following evidence. If suicides rise only *after* a story appears, then stories appearing late in the month should elicit a relatively small rise in suicides in the month *of* the story, and a relatively larger rise in suicides in the month *after* the story. Conversely, stories appearing early in the month should elicit a relatively large rise in suicides in the month of the story, and a relatively smaller rise in suicides in the month after the story.

These predictions are consistent with the available data: Stories appearing on or before the 15th of the month elicit a total rise of 636 suicides in the month of the story and in the month thereafter. Ninety-eight percent of this rise (624/636) occurs in the month of the story. In contrast, stories appearing

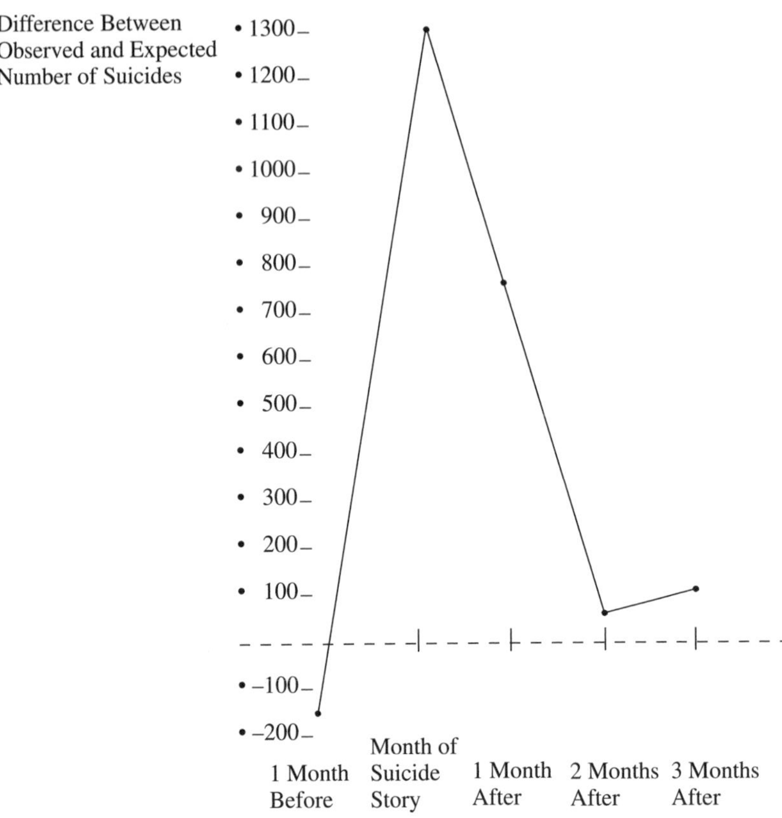

Figure 1: Fluctuation in the Number of Suicides, before, during and after the Month of the Suicide Story

after the 15th of the month elicit a rise of 1,398 suicides in the month of the story and in the month thereafter. Only forty-seven percent of this rise (651/1398) occurs in the month of the story.

Variation in the Size of the Werther Effect according to Amount of Newspaper Publicity

If the Werther effect is due to the influence of newspaper publicity on suggestible potential suicides, then the more publicity given to a story of suicide, the larger should be the rise in suicides after the appearance of that story. Thus, for example, the more days a suicide story appears on the front page, the larger should be the rise in suicides after that story appears.

Unfortunately, it is difficult to check this prediction with *New York Times* stories because the *Times* devoted more than one day of front page space to only three suicides.[6] However, the *New York Daily News,* the most popular daily newspaper in the U.S., can be used for this purpose. The thirty-five suicide-stories on page one of the *New York Times* can be divided into five categories, according to the number of days they appear on the front page of the *New York Daily News.* Table 2 shows that, as predicted, the more days a story appears on the front page of the *News,* the larger the average rise in suicides after that story appears. The five categories in this table (0 day, 1 day, etc.) would be ranked in the predicted order by chance .0083 (1/120) of the time.

Table 2 implies that suicides increase more after stories publicized in the *Times* and in the *News* than they do after stories publicized in the *Times* alone. On the average, suicides rise by 22.03 in the month after stories publicized by the *Times* alone (those in category 0). Suicides increase an average of 51.3 after stories publicized in both the *Times* and the *News* (stories in categories 1–4). Of course, this result would be expected if the Werther effect is related to newspaper publicity.

Coverage in the *Times* and in the *News* might also be related to the size of the Werther effect in another way. If this effect is caused by the suggestive influences of newspaper publicity, then suicides that receive a great deal of publicity in New York City, but very little elsewhere, should elicit large

Table 2. Size of the Suicide Rise after a Suicide Story by Number of Days Devoted to the Story on the Front Page of the New York Daily News

Number of Days on Page 1 of the News	0[a]	1[b]	2[c]	3[d]	4[e]
Average rise in U.S. suicides after each suicide story[f]	25.26	28.54	35.25	82.63	197.5

[a]The following suicide stories carried in the *New York Times* fall in this category: Lockridge, Baker, Lang, Soule, Armstrong, Hunt, Vargas, Norman, Zwillman, Gedik, Smith, Graham, Heyde, Tillman, Morrison, Kravchenko, Amer, Lo Jui-Ching.

[b]This category includes: Landis, Brooks, Forrestal, Stengel, Adamic, Feller, LaFollette, Bang-Jensen, Lord, Burros, Mott, Pike.

[c]This category includes Holt and Young.

[d]This category includes Schupler and Ward.

[e]This category includes Monroe.

[f]Ward and Graham died on the same date, August 4, 1963. Half the rise in suicides in August, 1963, has been credited to Ward, and half to Graham. A similar procedure has been followed for Heyde and Tillman, who died on February 14, 1964, and for Burros and Morrison, who died on November 1 and November 3, 1965.

Source of suicide statistics: U.S. Department of Health, Education, and Welfare, Public Health Service, *Vital Statistics of the U.S.,* Yearly Volumes, 1947–1968.

Table 3. The Percentage Rise in Suicides in New York City and in the Rest of the Country after Suicide Stories Publicized Mainly in New York City

	Percentage rise in suicides $\left(\frac{\text{Observed-Expected}}{\text{Expected}} \times 100\right)$	
Suicide story	In New York City	In remainder of U. S.
Adamic	8.62	1.04
Stengel	13.33	7.97
Schupler	25.58	4.50
Lord	4.58	3.27

Source of New York City suicides statistics: New York City, Department of Health, *Vital Statistics.*

Source of U. S. suicides statistics: U. S. Department of Health, Education, and Welfare, Public Health Service, *Vital Statistics of the U.S.*

increases in New York City suicide levels, and smaller increases in other parts of the United States. Unfortunately, suicide stories which grip the imagination of the New York public almost always interest the rest of the country as well. Only four suicides are publicized on page one of the *Times* and the *News* but are not publicized on the front page of the *Chicago Tribune,* one of the largest U.S. newspapers outside New York City.[7]

Table 3 shows that after each of these four publicized suicides, the proportional rise in New York City suicides is greater than the proportional rise in the rest of the country. This result would occur by chance .062 of the time (Wilcoxon's matched pairs signed rank one-tailed test). This result is not statistically significant at the .05 level but is very nearly so. Consequently, one might find it instructive to collect additional data to examine the problem more extensively. If suicide stories generate a rise in suicides mainly in the area where they are most publicized, then two predictions can be made:

1. Suicide stories publicized in the U.S. but not in Great Britain should elicit larger rises in American suicides than in British suicides.
2. Suicide stories publicized in Britain should elicit larger rises in British suicides than stories not publicized in Britain.

The most popular British daily newspaper, *The London Daily Mirror* (Newspaper Press Directory), was used as an indicator of the publicity given to a suicide story in Britain. It was assumed that a story covered by the *Mirror* received wide publicity in Britain, and that a story not covered by the *Mirror* received little or no publicity in Britain. Copies of the *Mirror* are available from 1956 in the Library of Congress. Table 4 indicates which of

Table 4. Percentage Rise in Suicides in the U.S. and in Britain (England and Wales) after Suicide Stories always Publicized in the U.S. and Occasionally in Britain, 1956–1967

Suicide story	Publicized in Britain	Percentage rise in U.S. suicides: $\frac{\text{Observed-Expected}}{\text{Expected}} \times 100$	Percentage rise in British suicides: $\frac{\text{Observed-Expected}}{\text{Expected}} \times 100$	Difference between percentage rise in U.S. & percentage rise in Britain, after suicide stories not publicized in Britain
Norman	No	−8.40	−2.63	−5.77
Young	No	.66	−11.77	12.43
Schupler	No	5.36	.11	5.47
Quiggle	No	4.69	−1.09	5.78
Zwillman	No	6.09	−5.52	11.61
Bang-Jensen	No	3.79	−10.03	13.82
Smith	No	3.73	−8.59	12.32
Gedik	No	−3.72	−13.23	9.51
Monroe	Yes	12.04	9.83	
Ward	Yes	9.78	17.26	
Heyde and Tillman	No	3.94	6.60	−2.66
Lord	No	3.33	−9.88	13.21
Burros and Morrison	No	3.51	−6.75	10.26
Mott	No	2.33	−.85	3.18
Pike	No	3.35	12.04	−8.69
Kravchenko	No	3.67	8.67	−5.00
Lo Jui-Ching	No	6.06	−2.06	8.12
Amer	No	2.11	−3.96	6.07

Source of U.S. suicide statistics: U. S. Department of Health, Education, and Welfare, Public Health Service, *Vital Statistics of the U.S.*

Source of British suicide statistics: Great Britain, General Register Office, *The Registrar General's Statistical Report for England and Wales.*

the suicide stories on the front page of the *New York Times* (1956–1967) were also on the front page of the *Mirror.* Table 4 also gives the size of the proportional rise in suicides after each suicide story, in the United States and in England and Wales.

As predicted, American suicides generally rise more than British suicides after a suicide story publicized in the U.S. but not in Britain. This result is significant at .005 (Wilcoxon matched pairs signed ranks test, one tail). On the average, British suicides decreased by 2.72% after suicide stories not publicized in Britain. In contrast, suicides increased an average of 13.54% after the two stories that did appear on the front page of the *Mirror.* These two, which are the most heavily publicized of all the stories in Table 4, produce the first and third largest rises in British suicide in that table. A result as extreme as this one would occur less than .025 of the time by chance

(Mann-Whitney two sample U-Test). Thus, as predicted, the stories publicized in Britain produce significantly larger rises in British suicides than stories not publicized there.[8]

SOME POSSIBLE ALTERNATIVE EXPLANATION OF THE WERTHER EFFECT

The data I have presented are consistent with the idea that the Werther effect is caused by newspaper publicity and suggestion. However, one might prefer a more conventional explanation of the Werther effect if this explanation were also consistent with the data. Three such conventional explanations will be suggested and examined in turn.

Possible Influence of Bereavement on the Werther Effect

Several investigators have found that the suicide rate of bereaved persons is higher than expected soon after their bereavement. MacMahon and Pugh (1965) found that the risk of suicide is high in the four years after the death of a spouse and particularly high in the first year. Bunch and Barraclough (1971) found that suicides tend to kill themselves close to the anniversary of the death of their fathers. Other studies on the effects of bereavement on suicide are reviewed by Rushing (1968) and by Lester (1972).

MacMahon and Bunch did not show that suicides increase within a month after bereavement, but such an increase is certainly consistent with their findings. Thus, because of these and other studies, one might well claim that the Werther effect results from bereavement at the occurrence of publicized suicides.

It is probable that dying persons are most likely to elicit widespread intense grief if they have been widely known and admired for some time. Most persons whose suicides were reported on the front page of the *Times* were not widely known until they killed themselves; in addition, many were in trouble with the law and thus not likely to be admired by the general public. Consequently, it is difficult to believe that these persons could elicit sufficient grief to increase the national level of suicides.

The "bereavement explanation" can also be evaluated more empirically by examining the level of suicides after the deaths of U.S. Presidents. In general, Presidents are among the most famous and admired persons of their day. If the Werther effect is caused by grief at a publicized death, then U.S. suicides

Table 5. Fluctuation in U.S. Suicides after Deaths of U.S.[a] Presidents,[b] 1900–1968

President	Date of death	Observed number of suicides in the month after[c] the presidential death	Expected number of suicides in the month after the presidential death
Harrison	March 13, 1901	292	297
McKinley	September 14, 1901	314	311.5
T. Roosevelt	January 6, 1919[d]	764	627.5
Taft	March 8, 1930	1514	1515.5
Coolidge	January 5, 1933	1673	1550
F. Roosevelt	April 12, 1945	1219	1307
Kennedy	November 22, 1963	1664	1637.5
Hoover	October 20, 1964	1758	1753.5

[a]Data for 1933–1968 are for the U.S.; from 1903 to 1932, data are for the U.S. death registration states, which consisted of all states whose statistics met certain standards of accuracy; prior to 1903, data are for the U.S. death registration area, which included all the death registration states and the cities with accurate statistics that were not in death registration states.

The number of death registration states and the size of the death registration area have changed over time as the statistics of localities improved. These increases must be corrected for before one can draw valid inferences about the fluctuation of suicides after presidential deaths. The method of correction used for the figures in this table can be illustrated with the statistics examined for Coolidge's death: suicides in January, 1932, 1933, 1934. The death registration states included Texas in 1933 and in 1934, but *not* in 1932. In order to make the death registration states of 1933 and 1934 comparable with the death registration states of 1932, Texas suicides were excluded from the analysis of 1933 and 1934 data. A similar correction procedure was followed for other presidential deaths.

[b]Because the necessary data are unavailable, one cannot calculate the fluctuations in suicides for presidents who died before 1900, after 1968, or for Cleveland, Harding, and Wilson.

[c]See text for rules determining the month to be examined.

[d]Data for the control years 1918, 1944 exclude suicides of the armed forces. This small bias slightly increases the chances of finding a rise in suicides after the death of Presidents T. and F. Roosevelt; hence, the bias favors the bereavement explanation.

Sources of data: U.S. Department of Commerce, Bureau of the Census, *Mortality Statistics,* yearly volumes, 1900–1936. U.S. Department of Health, Education, and Welfare, Public Health Service, *Vital Statistics of the U.S.,* yearly volumes, 1937–1968.

should increase significantly after Presidential deaths. Furthermore, Presidential deaths should generally elicit a much larger rise in suicides than is elicited by the more obscure and less admired persons in Table 1.

These predictions are not confirmed by the data. Monthly suicide statistics are available for many of the years 1900–1968. These statistics enable us to calculate the number of suicides after eight Presidential deaths. Table 5 shows that the level of suicides increases after five Presidential deaths, while it decreases after three Presidential deaths. If Presidential deaths have no effect on the level of suicide, one would observe five or more rises out of eight, .363 of the time. Consequently, there is no statistically significant tendency for suicides to increase after Presidential deaths. On the average, suicides rise by 24.81 after a Presidential death; yet they rose by more, 37.0, after the less famous, less admired suicide stories in the *Times.* These data are not consistent with the notion that suicides rise after front-page suicide stories because of the grief elicited by these stories.

Prior Conditions May Cause Both the Front Page Suicides and the Rise in Suicides Thereafter

A prior change in social conditions might produce the association between a front page suicide and a rise in national suicide levels. Perhaps the social integration of the society declines and thus produces a general increase in publicized *and* unpublicized suicides.

This explanation seems implausible for two reasons.

1. If prior conditions create a wave of suicides of which the front page suicide is merely a publicized example, one would expect the front page suicide to occur some time during the suicide wave. In fact, however, this does not happen: The front page suicide does not seem to occur during the suicide wave, but before it.
2. The "prior conditions" explanation implies that there is no causal link between the characteristics of front page suicide stories and the rise in national suicide levels. If no such link exists, it is difficult to explain the observed association between the publicity given to a suicide story and the rise in suicide levels thereafter. Until these two difficulties are resolved, the "prior conditions" explanation remains implausible.

Misclassification of Deaths as a Cause of the Werther Effect.

Suicides can be misclassified in various ways, but only one of these (to be called "type A") is capable of producing the Werther effect. It is possible that a front page suicide story affects the suggestible mind of the coroner rather than the mind of the potential suicide. After reading the suicide story, he may be unusually likely to classify an ambiguous death as a suicide instead of as an accident or homicide.

If the Werther effect is caused by this "type A" misclassification, then accidental and homicidal poisonings should decrease after a suicide story by as much as suicidal poisonings increase, because the coroner "shifts" deaths from accidents and homicides into the category of suicides. Similarly, accidental and homicidal firearm deaths should decrease by as much as suicides by firearms increase, and so on for other modes of suicide like falls and strangulation. In a sequel to this paper, I will examine extensively the covariation of suicides, accidents, and homicides. Space does not permit such an examination here. At the moment, it is sufficient to note that I have found no evidence for that particular type of misclassification (type A) capable of producing the Werther effect.

I have now examined three alternative explanations of the Werther effect.[9] None of these explanations seems consistent with the data. At present, the best available explanation of the Werther effect is that it is caused by suggestion. In the next sections, the sociological importance and usefulness of the Werther effect will be evaluated.

DURKHEIM AND THE WERTHER EFFECT

We recall that Durkheim felt the effects of suggestion on suicide are unimportant for three reasons. First, he claimed, suggestion has only a local effect on suicide. A person's suicide may influence those in his immediate vicinity, but the national suicide level does not respond to suggestion. Secondly, those who are prompted by suggestion to commit suicide would have done so anyway, but perhaps a little later. And thirdly, even on the local level, the effect of suggestion is small, being limited to a few individuals. Each of these claims can be examined in turn.

1. The evidence contradicts Durkheim's claim that the effects of suggestion are only local. We have seen a nationwide increase in suicides in the U.S. and in Great Britain after a suicide story is publicized. Indeed, after some suicide stories, like Marilyn Monroe's or Stephen Ward's, the increase in the suicide level is international.

2. Durkheim also claimed that suggestion serves merely to precipitate a suicide a little sooner than it would otherwise have occurred. If Durkheim is correct, then the peak in suicides after a front-page suicide story should be matched soon afterwards by an equally large dip in suicides, this dip being caused by suicides "moving up" their deaths by a month or two. Referring to Figure 1, we see that no such dip can be found in the months immediately after the rise in suicides. Thus, front page suicide stories do not seem to precipitate suicides by a month or two, although suicides may be precipitated by a somewhat larger period. Figure 1 is consistent with three alternative hypotheses: (a) The excess suicides after a suicide story would have killed themselves anyway, but several months or several years later; (b) The excess suicides would not have killed themselves if the suicide stories had not occurred; (c) A third hypothesis, combining the two previous ones, is also

possible: Newspaper suicide stories precipitate some suicides, and create others. Pending future research, one cannot discriminate between these three hypotheses.

3. Durkheim is partly correct in maintaining that suggestion has only a small effect on suicide: Some suicide stories elicit small rises in national suicides; however, other suicides stories elicit much larger rises. On the average, the U.S. suicide level increased by only 2.51% after the suicide stories publicized in the *New York Times*. This increase is somewhat larger, 3.27%, after stories appearing in the *New York Daily News*, a newspaper with more than twice the circulation of the *Times*. The rise in British suicide levels is still larger, 13.54%, after stories appearing in the *London Daily Mirror*, which has more than twice the circulation of the *Daily News*.[10] The largest increases in British and American suicides occurred after the deaths of Marilyn Monroe, the actress, and Stephen Ward, the British osteopath involved in the Profumo affairs. In the United States, suicides increased by 12% in the month after Marilyn Monroe's death and by 10% in England and Wales. In the two month period following Miss Monroe's death, there were 303 excess suicides in the U.S. and sixty excess suicides in England and Wales. Thus, Marilyn Monroe's death alone seems to have elicited 363 (=303+60) excess suicides in two countries (and other countries may also have experienced a rise in suicides). In the month after Dr. Ward's death, British suicides rose by 17%, while American suicides increased by 10%. In the two-month period after Dr. Ward's death, there were 104 excess suicides in England and Wales and 198 excess suicides in the United States, for a total of 302 suicides.

Considering that the observed increases in suicides after all front-page stories represent more than two thousand "excess" suicides, one might be a little callous in claiming that these increases are unimportant. But for sociologists, the Werther effect is probably more important for its theoretical implications. These will be discussed in the next section.

SOME THEORETICAL RELATIONSHIPS BETWEEN SUICIDE, SUGGESTION, SOCIAL MOVEMENTS, AND ANOMIE

Sociologists have long believed Durkheim's proposition that anomic individuals are susceptible to suicide. The findings I have reported suggest that this proposition needs to be elaborated: Anomic individuals may be particularly susceptible to suicide when the notion of suicide has been heavily publicized.

The link between anomie and susceptibility has also been discussed in the literature on collective behavior, and this fact suggests some interesting relationships between the literature on suicide and the literature on collective behavior.

Studies of suicide and of collective behavior indicate that anomic persons are susceptible to solutions to their anomie. But the former studies indicate that anomic persons are susceptible to suicide as a solution, while the latter studies show that they are susceptible to certain social movements which aim to reduce anomie. For example, persons who find no meaning in life are thought to be susceptible to religious and political movements, which provide them with coherent belief systems that reduce their anomie (Kornhauser, 1959; Cantril, 1963; Toch, 1965; Klapp, 1969). Persons without friends are considered susceptible to advertisements from lonely hearts clubs (Toch, 1965:93–8) or to "befriending" groups like the Samaritans (Fox, 1968) and may join them to counter their intense isolation. Alcoholics, who are often isolated, may be susceptible to the appeals of Alcoholics Anonymous as a collective solution to their problems. Persons with incurable diseases may be susceptible to the appeals of faith-healing cults or of other religious groups (Toch, 1965:120). The lonely, the alcoholic, and the incurably ill are also susceptible to suicide (studies on these topics have been reviewed by Lester, 1972). Thus, people suffering anomie and its associated problems seem to be susceptible both to suicide and to certain social movements that relieve anomie. This suggests a conclusion seldom proposed in the literature on suicide: Committing suicide or joining certain social movements may be alternative solutions to the general problem of anomie or to the specific problems, like alcoholism, associated with it.[11] A person who finds no meaning in life may kill himself; but, on the other hand, he may join a religious or political movement that provides him with meaning. An intensely lonely person may "choose" suicide as a solution to his loneliness or he may instead join a movement like the Samaritans that provides him with companionship. Alcoholics may kill themselves or join Alcoholics Anonymous; terminal cancer patients may commit suicide or join faith-healing cults.

If suicide and social movements are sometimes alternative solutions to the problem of anomie, then some interesting questions are raised. Why do some anomic individuals "choose" suicide, a degenerative, individual solution to their problems, while other anomic persons choose regenerative collective solutions like social movements? Social movements are often regarded as drastic solutions to life's problems, to be taken only when conventional institutional solutions are unavailable or inadequate (Cantril, 1963:16; Lang and Lang, 1961:492; Wilson, 1973:32–84). Suicide is an even more drastic solution than joining a social movement and perhaps is chosen only when appropriate anomie-reducing movements are unavailable or inadequate. If so, then the following predictions should hold: In any given location, the introduction of an anomie-reducing social movement should lower the suicide rate of that location, because some potential suicides have been diverted from the more drastic solution of suicide to the less drastic one of joining a social movement.[12] Suicides in a region should decrease after a revival movement begins to recruit members there. Similarly, the growth of Wallace's "American Party" or of Thurmond's "Dixiecrats" should be accompanied by a fall in suicides, especially in the areas where these movements were most successful. This predicted drop in suicides actually occurs, as will be shown in a sequel to this paper. One would also predict that anomic persons who join a social movement should be less likely to kill themselves than anomic persons who do not join a movement. For example, alcoholics who join Alcoholics Anonymous should be less likely than other alcoholics to kill themselves; and persons with terminal cancer should be less likely to kill themselves if they belong to a faith-healing cult than if they do not. Finally, anomic persons who are committed to one movement should have a lower suicide rate than anomic persons who are less committed and continually switch allegiance from one movement to another.

Although suicide may generally be a less attractive solution than joining a social movement, in some special circumstances the two solutions may be equally attractive. In this case, the choice of suicide over an alternative may depend on (1) the relative amount of publicity given to the alternative and to suicide and (2) the type of publicity given to the alternative and to suicide. Earlier in this paper, I predicted and found that the more publicity given to front-page suicides, the more suicides increase in the area where the publicity occurs. The converse predictions should also hold: The more publicity given to an alternative to suicide, the more the suicide rate should decrease. For example, if these arguments are correct, during the election of a Pope, when much publicity is given to Catholicism, suicides should decrease.

The type of publicity devoted to suicide or to an alternative should also affect the suicide rate. Studies of suggestion (reviewed in Lang and Lang, 1961:255–89) indicate that a model is more likely to be imitated if he is prestigious and if his circumstances are thought to be similar to those of the imitator. If these conclusions can be generalized to include the imitation of suicide, then the following predictions should hold: When the amount of publicity given to a suicide is controlled for, the more prestigious the publicized suicide, the more it should be imitated. Thus, for example, Secretary Forrestal or Marilyn Monroe should be imitated more often than less prestigious suicides with equivalent publicity. Controlling for the amount of publicity devoted to a suicide story, one might also expect that persons who are the most similar to the front-page suicide should be the most likely to imitate it. Thus, for example, Americans should imitate the front-page suicide of an American more often than the front-page suicide of a foreigner. Furthermore, Americans like Mott or Quiggle who killed themselves abroad under exotic circumstances should be imitated less often than Americans who killed themselves at home in familiar circumstances. Finally, well-known female suicides should affect women more than men; while the opposite should be true for well-known male suicides; famous white suicides should affect whites more than blacks; the suicides of the old should be copied more often by the old than by the young; and so on.[13] Clearly, the theoretical relationships between suicide, social movements, suggestion, and anomie need to be further explored.[14]

NOTES

1. Subsequent to Lester's review, Motto (1970) examined an eighth U.S. city (Detroit) undergoing a newspaper strike. He found that male suicide rates went up during the period of the strike, while female suicide rates went down. He concluded from this that newspaper strikes produce a drop in suicides (at least among females). One might just as well have concluded that newspaper strikes produce a rise in suicide rates (at least among males). Even if one supposes with Motto that the newspaper strike did indeed "produce" the drop in female suicides, this need not imply that the drop occurred because suicides were not publicized during the period. Besides having no suicides reported in the paper, Detroit changed in many other ways during the strike; perhaps some of the other changes in Detroit produced the drop in female suicides.

2. Some authors (for example, Meerloo, 1968:82–90; Motto, 1967) have noted in passing that suicides increased after Marilyn Monroe's death, but they were not prompted by this observation to examine systematically the suicide level after many publicized suicides.

3. One might wish to examine the increase in the suicide rate in the month after the story, rather than the increase in the number of suicides. Unfortunately, one cannot indulge this wish because the necessary data are lacking. To calculate the suicide rate in the month after a story, one would need monthly population figures; and these are generally unknown, or estimated only.

4. This probability, calculated from the binomial distributions ($p = 5 \times \geqslant 26$; $n = 33$), holds only if one assumes independence among the thirty-three successive suicide rises. Because of the logic of statistical testing, one can never prove that these

thirty-three rises are mutually independent. The most one can do is test for dependence amongst the thirty-three observations and, if one finds none, assume independence amongst them. Accordingly, the Von Neumann test for serial correlation (Von Neumann et al., 1941) was used to test for dependence; no evidence of dependence was found and independence was assumed. The Von Neumann test was originally designed for observations drawn from an underlying normal distribution, and one cannot assume that my observations are drawn from such a distribution. However, Phillips and Chase (1969) have shown statistically that the Von Neumann test can be used for other distributions as well. For a more detailed discussion of the problem of dependence, see Phillips (1970).

Another, related problem must also be considered before the binomial test can be applied meaningfully to the results in Table 1. Exactly the same suicide data are used to determine whether suicides rise after Burros' death and to determine whether they rise after Morrison's death. Obviously, it would be inappropriate to count the same suicide rise twice in determining the statistical significance of my findings, because this would make the statistical significance artificially high. Hence, for the purposes of significance testing, the Burros and Morrison suicide stories have been treated as one story; and the rise in suicides after Burros and Morrison killed themselves has been counted only once. For similar reasons, the Graham and Ward suicide stories, which occurred on the same date, have been treated as one story only. Thus, although there are thirty-five suicide stories described in Table 1, they have been treated as thirty-three stories to ensure that the statistical significance of the results in Table 1 is not artificially high.

5. The total number of excess suicides in the month of the suicide story (1,275) is not equal to the sum of the excess suicides listed in Table 1 (1,298.5). This is because, in Table 1, the number of excess suicides was calculated sometimes for the month after the suicide story, and sometimes for the month of the story, depending on whether the story appeared late or early in the month.

6. These were Ward, Forrestal and Schupler, who received two, three and three days of coverage, respectively. On the average, the number of national suicides increased 100.3 in the month after each of these three committed suicide; while suicides increased by 33.2 after each of the remaining front-page suicides listed in Table 1. One would expect this result if the Werther effect is caused by suggestion.

7. The assumption that these four suicide stories were relatively unpublicized outside of New York City becomes even more plausible when we learn that all four suicides died in the New York City area and that three of the four were minor local political figures (Stengel, Lord, Schupler) unlikely to excite national interest. However, the fourth suicide (Adamic) did have some national reputation as a writer.

8. In this study, I have found no conclusive evidence that the means used by the publicized against the "suggestion hypothesis." However, failure to imitate one aspect of the front-page suicide need not imply that the front page suicide is imitated in no respect whatever.

9. A fourth, minor, alternative explanation might also be mentioned here. Beginning in 1968, a new disease category was introduced: "Injuries undetermined whether accidentally or purposely inflicted." This new category tended to reduce the number of deaths reported as suicides in 1968, because some of the deaths that would have

been recorded as suicide were instead recorded as "Injuries undetermined" in 1968. This tendency for reported suicides to be decreased in 1968 affects our analysis of the rise in suicides after two suicide stories (Amer and Lo Jui-Ching). Amer's case will serve as an illustration. Amer killed himself in September, 1967; and the number of U.S. suicides in September of 1967 was high compared with the number in September 1966 and 1968. This result could occur because the number of suicides in September of 1967 was unusually high, or because the number of suicides in September of 1968 was unusually low, following the introduction of the new disease category "Injuries undetermined." Similarly, the apparent rise in suicides after Lo Jui-Ching's death might also be explained as an artifact of the new category introduced in 1968. The introduction of this category cannot explain the suicide rise after the remaining thirty-one stories in Table 1, because the rise in suicides after these thirty-one stories was not calculated with 1968 data.

At present, one cannot determine whether the introduction of the new category in 1968 explains away the entire rise in suicides after the deaths of Amer and of Lo Jui-Ching. Some of the suicide rise after their deaths may be due to imitation, and some may be due to the introduction of the new category. But even if one assumes that the rise in suicides after their deaths is entirely due to the new category, the results in Table 1 are still statistically significant. Eliminating Amer and Lo Jui-Ching from the analysis of Table 1, we have thirty-one suicide stories; U.S. suicides increased after twenty-four of these stories and decreased after seven. This result is significant at .0017 (one-tailed binomial test, $p=.5$; $X \geqslant 24$; $n=31$).

10. On the average, the persons whose suicides are publicized in the *Daily News* or in the *Daily Mirror* are perhaps more prestigious than persons whose suicides are publicized in the *Times*. At the present stage of the investigation, one cannot separate the effects of a suicide's prestige from the effects of the publicity given to his death. Consequently, one cannot be certain that the response to the *Daily Mirror* stories is greater than the response to the *Times* stories because the former newspaper has a much larger circulation than the latter.

11. The relevant literature bears only indirectly on the notion that some social movements may be alternatives to suicide. Perhaps Fox (1968) has come closest to suggesting that joining a social movement (the Samaritans) may be a substitute for suicide. But even Fox did not appear to generalize his discussion to include other social movements. Farberow (1968) has suggested the formation of groups to promote "the reestablishment of feelings of belonging" in the potential suicide. But the groups he envisaged were to be formed through group psychotherapy, not through social movements. Stengel (1968) has noted that a suicide attempt may be a potential suicide's plea to be reintegrated into the group. But Stengel did not consider the social movement as one way to achieve reintegration.

12. Toch (1965:124) cites the example of a woman who felt ready to gas herself, then met a member of the Seventh Day Adventists and became a member herself. In general, Toch and other students of collective behavior do not explore the notion that committing suicide may be an alternative to joining certain social movements. See the brief comments of Toch (1965:15–16) and of Wilson (1973:36) on this issue.

13. These predictions cannot be tested with confidence until many more suicide stories have been collected and their effects examined. Some of the predictions

discussed cannot be checked with data from monthly suicide tables, because these are not subclassified by race, sex and age. However, these predictions can be checked with data taken directly from death certificates, which provide more detail on the characteristics of each suicide.

14. One might also try to generalize this discussion to other behaviors that might be influenced by suggestion and might be alternatives to suicide. For example, Henry and Short (1954) have claimed that homicide may be an alternative to suicide in certain circumstances. If Henry and Short are correct, and if homicide is affected by suggestion, then the following predictions should hold: (1) homicides should increase after a publicized homicide story (see Berkowitz and Macaulay [1971] for evidence of this increase), (2) homicides should decrease after a publicized suicide story, (3) suicides should decrease after a publicized homicide story.

REFERENCES

Benn Brothers Ltd. Newspaper Press Directory. *London: Ben Brothers, Ltd.*

Berkowitz, L. and J. Macaulay. 1971. "The contagion of criminal violence." *Sociometry 34 (June):238–60.*

Blumer, H. 1951. "Collective behavior." *Pp. 167–222 in A. M. Lee (ed.), Principles of Sociology. New York: Barnes & Noble, Inc.*

Bunch, J. and B. Barraclough. 1971. "The influence of parental death anniversaries upon suicide dates." *British Journal of Psychiatry 118 (June):621–6.*

Cantril, H. 1963. The Psychology of Social Movements. *New York: John Wiley & Sons, Inc.*

Crawford, J. P. and J. H. Willis. 1966. "Double suicide in psychiatric hospital patients." *British Journal of Psychiatry 112 (December):1231–5.*

Durkheim, E. 1951. Suicide. *Tr. by J. A. Spaulding and G. Simpson. New York: The Free Press.*

Facts on File, Inc. Facts on File. *New York: Facts on File, Inc.*

Farberow, N. L. 1968. "Group psychotherapy with suicidal persons." *Pp. 328–40 in H. L. P. Resnik (ed.), Suicidal Behaviors. Boston: Little Brown and Company.*

———. *1972.* Bibliography on Suicide and Suicide Prevention. *Washington: Government Printing Office.*

Fox, R. 1968. "The samaritans." *Pp. 405–17 in H. L. P. Resnik (ed.), Suicidal Behaviors. Boston: Little, Brown and Company.*

Gray, R. 1967. Goethe: A Critical Introduction. *Cambridge: Cambridge University Press.*

Great Britain. General Register Office. The Registrar General's Statistical Review of England and Wales. Annual Volumes.

Henry, A. F. and J. F. Short. 1954. Suicide and Homicide. *Glencoe: Free Press.*

Klapp, O. E. 1969. Collective Search for Identity. *New York: Holt, Rinehart & Winston, Inc.*

Kornhauser, W. 1959. The Politics of Mass Society. *New York: The Free Press.*

Kreitman, N. et al. 1969. "Attempted suicide in social networks." *British Journals of Preventive and Social Medicine 23 (May):116–23.*

Lang, K. and G. E. Lang. 1961. Collective Dynamics. *New York: Thomas Y. Crowell Co.*

Lester, D. 1972. Why People Kill Themselves. *Springfield, Ill.: Charles C. Thomas.*

MacMahon, B. and T. Pugh. 1965. "Suicide in the widowed." *American Journal of Epidemiology 81 (January):23–31.*

Meerloo, J. A. M. 1968. "Hidden suicide." *Pp. 82–9 in H. L. P. Resnik (ed.) Suicidal Behaviors. Boston: Little Brown and Company.*

Motto, J. A. 1967. "Suicide and suggestibility." *American Journal of Psychiatry 124 (August):252–6.*

———. *1970.* "Newspaper influence on suicide." *Archives of General Psychiatry 23 (August):143–8.*

New York City Department of Health. Annual Report. *New York: Department of Health.*

New York Times Publishing Company. The New York Times Index. *New York: The New York Times Publishing Company.*

Phillips, D. P. 1970. Dying as a Form of Social Behavior. *Unpublished doctoral dissertation. Princeton University.*

Phillips, D. P. and G. A. Chase. 1969. "On the robustness of the Von Neumann test." *Technical Report Number 115. Johns Hopkins University, Department of Statistics.*

Phillips, D. P. and K. A. Feldman. 1973. "A dip in deaths before ceremonial occasions: some new relationships between social integration and mortality." *American Sociological Review 38 (December):678–96.*

Rose, W. 1929. "Introduction." *Pp. i–xxix in J. W. von Goethe, the Sorrows of Young Werther. Tr. by W. Rose. London: Scholastic Press.*

Rushing, W. A. 1968. "Individual behavior and suicide." *Pp. 96–121 in J. P. Gibbs (ed.), Suicide. New York: Harper & Row.*

Seiden, R. H. 1968. "Suicide behavior contagion on a college campus." *Pp. 360–7 in N. L. Farberow (ed.), Proceedings of the Fourth International Conference on Suicide Prevention.*

Stengel, E. 1964. Suicide and Attempted Suicide. *Baltimore: Penguin Books.*

Tarde, Gabriel. 1903. The Laws of Imitation. *New York: Holt.*

Toch, H. 1965. The Social Psychology of Social Movements. *Indianapolis: The Bobbs-Merrill Company, Inc.*

United States Bureau of the Census. Mortality Statistics. *Yearly volumes, 1900–1936. Washington: Government Printing Office.*

United States Public Health Service. Vital Statistics of the United States. *Yearly volumes, 1937–1968. Washington: Government Printing Office.*

Von Neumann, J., et al. 1941. "The mean square successive difference." *Annals of Mathematical Statistics 12:153–62.*

Weiss, E. 1958. "The clinical significance of the anniversary reaction." *General Practitioner 17:117–19.*

Wilson, John. 1973. Introduction to Social Movements. *New York: Basic Books.*

20. Treatment of the Suicidal Character

Donald A. Schwartz, Don E. Flinn, and Paul F. Slawson

BIOGRAPHICAL NOTE

When Donald A. Schwartz was director of the Division of Adult Psychiatry at the University of California (Los Angeles) in 1971, a series of inpatient and recently discharged outpatient suicides alarmed the staff of the Neuropsychiatric Institute. Associated with him at the time were Don Flynn (director of Outpatient Services) and Paul Slawson (director of Evaluation and Treatment Services).

A suicide seminar chaired by Edwin Shneidman was organized for staff, students, and faculty. A number of papers grew out of this seminar, including this one. A special subgroup of patients were identified for whom suicidal living-on-the-brink had become a means of obtaining special nurture and support from others, and who seemed to grow worse when treated conventionally.

COMMENT

By the time this paper was first published there was a growing clinical appreciation that just as acutely suicidal patients suffering from melancholic depressions are different from those patients with chronic suicidal character problems, their treatment needs differ. With the passing of time, prolonged inpatient hospitalization has become increasingly impossible for economic and political reasons. As a result the requirements for clear differentiation between the two groups have become more pressing; outpatient management with minimal hospital respite is now the general rule. These authors sketch a lucid outline for intelligent outpatient care, and address the need to take calculated risks with chronic suicidal characters if they are ever to establish themselves as autonomous adults.

Donald A. Schwartz, Don E. Flinn, and Paul F. Slawson, "Treatment of the Suicidal Character." *American Journal of Psychotherapy* 28(1974): 194–207. Reprinted by permission of the Association for the Advancement of Psychotherapy.

The reader may suspect, as do the editors, that "existential despair" as described in this paper is in fact a portmanteau into which a number of different phenomena have been packed. Many young patients, especially university students, tend to philosophize (intellectualize) their suicidal preoccupations. In the United States and Europe much of the current argument in favor of "rational suicide" comes out of the same bag. "Existential" suicidal thinking commonly masks depression in narcissistically wounded patients whose capacity for deep object-relatedness has either not fully developed (as in adolescence) or is characterologically deficient. Therapeutic attention to these matters commonly leads to an abandonment of interest in suicide, however plausible the philosophic arguments have seemed beforehand. Those who wish to study a case report wherein an actual suicide was rationalized and permitted are referred to Binswanger (1944–1945).

REFERENCES

Binswanger, Ludwig. 1944–1945. The Case of Ellen West, an Anthropological-Clinical Study. In May, Rollo, Angel, Ernest, and Ellenberger, Henri F., eds., Existence: A New Dimension in Psychiatry and Psychology, *Mendel, Werner M. and Lyons, Joseph, trans. New York: Basic Books, 1958.*

■

In certain patients suicidality is not a symptom of another psychiatric disorder, but a central element of character structure. Treatment approaches that are effective in acute, symptomatic suicidal states may actually increase the long-term suicide risk in such patients. Special treatment techniques are needed for patients with suicidal characterology.

INTRODUCTION

Whatever it may be for the person who is dead, suicide is generally a multidimensional tragedy for the survivors. It evokes grief, shame, guilt, and anger, at least. Often, it magically imposes a deep fear for their own potential suicidality upon children of the person who has committed suicide. The physician who had cared for the suicidal person does not escape the burden of emotion. He, too, must confront his own anxiety, anger, guilt, and impotence in varying degrees. If the person was under psychiatric care, the physician's burden may include his own or others' expectation that he should have been able to predict and avert the risk of suicide (1). Courts have sometimes added to those expectations by holding that physicians and other mental health personnel have a duty, in certain cases, to prevent suicide (2).

The risk of suicide is often the impetus to psychiatric hospitalization. It is presumed that the hospitalization itself will diminish the risk by providing surveillance and physical restraint, if necessary, to prevent self-destruction. Thus, the suicide of a hospitalized patient evokes an even greater sense of concern in the minds of those who contemplate it. This may lead to special policies designed to prevent suicide in those inpatients at risk for it. It may eventuate in a situation where prevention of suicide takes precedence over all other treatment efforts. The suicide of a hospitalized patient has a major impact on the general policies and procedures of the hospital, not only with respect to other suicidal patients, but also patients for whom suicide had not appeared to be a significant issue.

This paper arises from an ongoing examination of staff attitudes related to suicide and suicide prevention at a university medical center. A multidisciplinary group meets on a weekly basis for discussion of a variety of clinical and theoretical issues connected with death and suicide. The discussions are wide ranging but focus especially on staff attitudes, philosophies, and treatment strategies and tactics applicable to suicidal patients. The authors of this paper are a part of that group. Out of our shared interests in hospital management of suicidal patients, we have also been meeting separately from the rest of the group. Our focus has been on suicides committed by patients who are in the hospital or on authorized or unauthorized absence from the hospital, and the effects of such suicides on staff attitudes and hospital management policies. This paper deals with the problems in treatment and management of patients for whom suicidality is a central element of life style.

DEATH, SUICIDE AND THE PHYSICIAN

Death is the ongoing enemy of the physician, and it always waits in the wings. He may not often face death directly and imminently in his practice, but he lives with the awareness of its omnipresence. It has been suggested by Kasper (3) and others that the fear of death and the wish to master it are potent motivators of people who enter into careers in medicine. In fact, of course, the physician never masters death but only postpones it. The only form of control over death which men possess is the power to choose it actively rather than to await it passively. As Feifel (4) states it, "If living leads inevitably to death, then death can be fended off by not living." Suicide represents the closest approach to the active mastery of death. People who have attempted suicide and survived often voice such fantasies of mastery in retrospect. In fact, achieving magical control over a potential disaster by causing it to happen is a frequent occurrence in everyday life. One is most likely to slip up in carrying out an act of skill in proportion to one's conscious preoccupation with the possibility of making an error. Patients and nonpatients who have experienced such events are usually able to recall the conscious feeling of relief which occurred after they fumbled. It was as if they had escaped from the position of intolerable waiting for an event over which they had no control. Bakan suggests (5) that the ability to will to die is magically equated to its reverse: the ability to will to live forever, that is, to be immortal.

Additional evidence bearing on this matter comes from the response of patients who have learned that they have fatal diseases. It is not late in the course of such illnesses, when physical suffering has become greatest, that suicidal preoccupation is most common. It is when they first learn that they have such a disease that rumination about suicide is most common. The suicidal preoccupation of such patients appears to be in response to their anxious uncertainty about when and how death will occur rather than a reaction to pain and impairment. It is not that suicide *attempts* are frequently made at that point in the course of a fatal illness. What is significant is that suicide is thought about so commonly, and that patients can report so often the conscious idea of suicide as an active mastery over their impending deaths. The GAP Report on *Death and Dying* (6) suggests that the frequent repetition of thoughts which imply a mastery over death is one method of binding death anxiety. That comment restates in this specific area what is generally accepted about the binding of anxiety by repetitive acts or thoughts which symbolize mastery over that which is feared. Since commission of suicide is a form of mastery over death, rumination about suicide may sometimes be a successful method of binding death anxiety, rather than a sign of special suicide risk.

Physicians, whether because they have undue concerns about their own death or for other reasons, are not known for their comfortable and mature attitudes about death. The GAP Report (6) has documented in detail the discomfort which physicians have with the issue of death in their patients, a matter also dealt with by Litman (1) and Kasper (3). If there is nothing he can do about the patient's illness and impending death, the physician most frequently vacates the scene and leaves the nurse and the clergyman to sit with the dying patient and waiting family. In other situations, the unwillingness of physicians to deal directly with their patients' death anxiety and suicidal preoccupation has been perceived by patients as rejection and disinterest. McKegney and Lange described this as it was seen by some chronic hemodialysis patients (7).

Assuming that physicians have problems in their feelings about death which impair their effectiveness, one may reasonably conclude that something is needed to counterbalance those difficulties if physicians are to be maximally helpful to patients for whom death is a contingency. In fact, little has been done in the education and training of most physicians to help them face and overcome their difficulties in this area. Yet there is little reason to assume that specific teaching and training is unnecessary in this area. There are no data to indicate that clinical experience alone modifies physicians' attitudes toward death or increases their capacity to deal with it.

In the case of psychiatric education and training, though the physician is taught how to recognize a suicide risk, he is less often helped to recognize his own attitudinal distortions in the area of death and suicide. Psychiatrists are taught how to manage the suicidal patient more than they are helped to develop the capacity to examine the suicide issue therapeutically in the conflict-free spheres of their own egos. The suicide rate for psychiatrists is reported to be higher than for physicians in general (8). If we can use those rates as any indication of capability or incapability to deal rationally with issues of death and suicidality, then we might conclude that the characterology of physicians and especially of psychiatrists works against their capability to deal rationally with such matters.

We have spoken so far about physicians. There is less evidence about the attitudes and problems of other health personnel in connection with death and suicide. The authors have some impressionistic evidence from the comments of nurses that they too are sometimes directed toward their profession by wishes to control death. But nurses generally are constrained to deal directly with death far more than are physicians. In fact, the delegation to nurses of the responsibility for "being with" the dying patient may provide them with experiences of "mastery by repetition" which significantly improve their ability to deal rationally with death. This is not true for psychiatric nurses whose exposure is generally to the threat of death in the suicidal patient rather than to death itself. Only a small percentage of suicidal patients actually commit suicide, so psychiatric nurses face the prospect of death many times and the actuality seldom. Repetitive experience of an event may promote mastery of it. But repetitive threat of an event without its actual experience is more likely to produce anxiety about it than mastery. Thus, the nature of the work of psychiatric nurses holds little promise of experiential revision of any problem attitudes they may have about death and suicide.

A DILEMMA IN SUICIDE PREVENTION

In short, then, one might expect that the major personnel of psychiatric hospitals are not optimally suited by predisposition, training, or experience to deal with the issue of suicide in a rational and objective fashion. Recent court decisions and the widespread use of the doctrine of *res ipse loquitur* in some jurisdictions have additionally complicated the psychiatric treatment of the suicidal patient in the hospital. Legal pressures summate with emotionally charged attitudes in dictating the prevention of suicide at virtually any costs. In a sense, this is not irrational. It is certainly a fact that nothing of a remedial sort can be done for a person who has committed suicide. On the other hand, Kubie (9) has suggested that "We must ask whether we want to prevent every suicide if such an effort will render us therapeutically impotent." In some cases, it appears that the price of continuing emphasis on suicide prevention may be an increase in the risk of ultimate suicide. To put it another way, the only method of reducing the long-term risk of suicide may be one that risks its short-term commission.

ASSESSMENT OF COMPARATIVE RISKS

Let us illustrate this point by starting with an analogy. In mothering, one is forced constantly to make choices which involve the comparison of risks. One can protect a child against infectious diseases by the maintenance of a sterile environment in the nursery, if one is willing to pay the price of diminished human contact. A study in a hospital for the mentally retarded (10) reviewed changes in mortality rates over time. One factor which appeared related to decreasing mortality rates was the degree of interpersonal contact allowed the newly admitted child. It had been the policy to keep children isolated from others at first, to keep down exposure to infectious agents. When this policy was changed and greater contacts with family and other children were permitted, mortality rates decreased rather than increasing.

Again, one must decide when to let a young child climb on the jungle gym. One can reduce the number of falls he will have by making him wait until he is older and better developed. But the price of this protectiveness is that the falls he has to take when learning later may be from greater heights because he is strong enough to climb higher; moreover, others will not supervise him so closely because he is older and they will assume he needs less supervision. If waiting has retarded his muscular development, his clumsiness may impair his relationships with other children and his own sense of self-esteem.

Still again, one can protect a child from the risk of being run down by forbidding him to cross streets. But the longer one does so, the longer one puts off the child's development of the judgment and skills needed to cross streets safely. The child is then required to learn how to cross streets safely at an age when it is expected he should already know how, with the consequence of less protection from others and more likelihood of carelessness by the child who is trying to "act his age."

To move closer to the specific topic at issue, one may look at the older adolescent with an impulse disorder. Psychiatrists frequently are confronted by families who have overprotected a child and saved him from the consequences of his behavior. In his continuing and finally desperate search for limits, the child has behaved more and more self-destructively, requiring more and more desperate measures of rescue by the parents. In the process of all this, the adolescent has abandoned his own responsibility for his life. At that point, the psychiatrist is asked what the parents should *now* do. If he responds that they need to withdraw some of their responsibility for the child's life and that he needs to develop some of his own, they will object that unless they save him, he will destroy himself. Or they may withdraw too much responsibility or do so too precipitously, thus inviting a piece of gross self-destructive behavior by the child and demonstrating without the need for words that it would be wrong to permit the child more responsibility for his life.

If a situation has gone for enough in this direction, then the risk of self-destruction may be a very serious one. One may, nevertheless, feel justified in taking such risks if the only alternative is to continue the previous process to the point that disaster is no longer a risk but a certainty. In situations like that, legal and emotional concerns intrude: the therapist who recommends a course with 40% risk takes a 40% chance that he will be blamed for the consequences. To take the safe way out and let the family continue on its prior path may entail an 80% risk of disaster to the family but no risk to the therapist, since he has not taken the responsibility of pushing for a change in family policy.

THE SUICIDAL CHARACTER

The group of patients described above have developed a life style characterized by risk-taking behavior of an increasingly self-destructive nature. Being ego-syntonic and an integral part of their life style, this behavior is a characterological problem rather than part of a symptomatic disorder. Most commonly, it would be classified as an impulse disorder but there is no specific category of diagnosis into which it fits neatly. Its central characteristic is its self-destructiveness and Shneidman might conceive of it as a subintentioned form of suicidality (11). Although not marked by a conscious intent of suicide, it is a form of suicidal character problem.

In some patients with more overt suicidal intent the self-destructiveness is characterological rather than symptomatic. They have developed a life style in which frustration and anger in response to deprivation of narcissistic supply evokes overt suicidal impulse or behavior. We have become so used to conceiving of overt suicidality as symptomatic behavior that it is difficult to conceive of it as a characterological manifestation. But one sees a certain number of patients for whom the suicidal impulse and behavior (even to the overt attempt) have become an element of life style, something ego-syntonic rather than ego-alien. Suicidal behaviors in such patients are chronic elements of general interpersonal transactions rather than the results of the breakdown of normal ego defenses in response to unconscious conflicts.

The treatment and management of such patients is most difficult, especially in the hospital setting. Hospitals have developed methods of management and treatment which are effective with persons who present an acute, symptomatic suicide risk. Because of medicolegal factors as well as for other reasons, hospitals are expected to behave in nurturing ways in the interests of preventing suicide. The more suicidally the patient behaves, the more parental will the hospital staff become. Once the suicide risk subsides, the hospital can relax its precautionary style. But for the characterologically suicidal person, the risk may not abate. In fact, the mothering behavior may enhance suicide risk, since it creates a secondary gain for suicidal behaviors. As we will attempt to show below, the suicidal characterology may be a result of repeated transactions in which suicidality has come to evoke mothering. (Seymour Perlin [personal communication] conceives of this kind of eventuality as a "toxic side effect" of psychotherapy.)

Apart from the hypothesized dynamics in this kind of situation, the maintenance of focus on the patient's suicidality can act as an obstruction to his coming to deal with the problems underlying his suicidality and his life problems in general. Constant preoccupation with suicide may actually act to increase the risk of it. Wooley and Eichert looked at changing rates of both suicide and escape in The Sheppard and Enoch Pratt Hospital during the 1930s (12) and found a decreasing incidence over time for both of those actions. They attributed this in part to a decrease in special precautionary measures over that period. They concluded that such special measures act to increase suicide or escape by focusing attention on those actions.

THE LETHALITY-RESPONSIVE COMMUNITY

The characterologically suicidal person relates to others in large measure in the context of his suicidality. He does not do this with all others, of course, but with an increasingly large group of others whom he has collected. Some of them may also suffer from the lethal character structure, but others are simply people prone to the helping/supportive role. These others form what may be thought of as a lethality-responsive community, to which the characterologically suicidal person relates himself as to a good mother. They are constantly aware of him *as a suicidal person,* tuned in to that dimension of his personality as a sleeping mother is tuned to the pitch of her crying infant.

THE MOTHERING RESPONSE

The lethality-responsive community responds to suicidal behavior with mothering attention. The need for such mothering response, then, comes to evoke behavior which implies suicidality. For the person in acute and painful despair, desperately needful of mothering, lethality (the terms "lethal" and "lethality" are used here as synonymous with suicidal and suicidality) becomes the admission ticket to fulfillment of that need. A mothering response to regressive behavior relieves the immediate distress and lends some strength to the patient. It does so at the cost of having "rewarded" the regressive behavior, that is, it is a prominent secondary gain. In assessing the value of such mothering responses, we need to compare the advantages of the short-term support provided with the disadvantages of the secondary gain.

This is a comparison which we make fairly often in medicine. We hospitalize patients even though immobilization enervates them if we feel that the seriousness of the illness justifies the undesirable side-effects of bed rest. On the other hand, we mobilize patients rapidly after most surgery in spite of the pain and discomfort that rapid mobilization causes, because the rapidity of healing and the general health benefits of early mobilization more than compensate for the discomfort. We try to keep depressed patients working, even if at low efficiency, while treating them, because work activity shortens the duration and severity of depressive illness. But we may hospitalize a patient even at the risk of his losing his job permanently if we feel he may commit suicide or do something else severely destructive.

The use of anaclitic therapy for certain severe physical illnesses is based on the conviction that the employment of short-term mothering will lead to ultimate strengthening and recovery which will terminate the need for the mothering behavior. In the treatment of some acute psychotic illnesses, comparable mothering techniques are used in the short range. But the intent behind this technique is that it will *ultimately decrease* the demand for mothering behavior.

MOTHERING AND LETHALITY

The importance of mothering in the management of the suicidal patient is that suicidality evokes such anxiety that we tend to respond in a mothering way without the usual assessment of long-term and short-term contingencies. Moreover, the imminent risk of suicide does not permit either time or calmness in which to assess risks; and the wrong guess may end the opportunity entirely. We are not so skilled for the most part that we can make long-range predictions of behavior on brief assessment of an acutely distressed person. Thus, there are many justifications for the employment of immediate mothering responses to lethal people.

As mentioned earlier, suicidality is often a manifestation of an acute symptomatic illness. In such cases, the lethality will diminish as the person recovers. Whatever regression may have been promoted by the mothering response in such patients, it is small compared to the great regression of the illness itself. As the latter regression dissipates in the process of recovery from the illness, the interactions related to suicidality and mothering generally diminish and disappear also. If the illness has been brief enough, the patience and endurance of the hospital staff have not been exhausted by the need to maintain the mothering stance of special care; patient and staff are usually in a mutually positive relationship to each other.

Problems arise when the suicidality is the product not of acute symptomatic illness but of a long-term lethal character structure upon which has been superimposed the tumult of a crisis. The crisis response in such a situation may look much like an acute symptomatic illness and if this is the first such episode which has led to psychiatric attention, psychiatrists and others will generally approach it as they would a lethality-manifesting acute illness. What happens in such cases is that the crisis state passes but we are left with a characterologically lethal person whom we come to recognize more and more clearly as chronically suicidal. By this time, if the patient is hospitalized in a teaching setting or if he can afford long-term private hospitalization, patient and staff may be mutually engaged in the lethality-mothering bind, and unable to extricate themselves from it.

In such a case, one must re-evaluate the treatment plan and consider how to ameliorate the lethal character structure. Most often this will entail decreasing the mothering response: lessening surveillance and other regression-promoting measures. But this will evoke in the staff the same anxiety that is evoked in the parents of impulsively destructive adolescents: that is, the anxiety over whether lessened mothering may permit actual suicide.

Since long-term maintenance of special measures of surveillance are distressing to the staff who have to carry them out, the relaxation of such measures creates another problem. The staff often feel guilty at taking less of a mothering role, as though they were depriving the patient of some help out of their own selfishness.

SUICIDES BY HOSPITALIZED PATIENTS

Nothing in the foregoing discussion should be taken to mean that characterologically suicidal people are not really suicidal. They may be highly lethal at times and many do commit suicide. Thus, precautionary and mothering measures are not relinquished because of low lethality but because of the concern that their continuance would increase long-term lethality. There are real risks in making judgments of the kind we are considering, since measures which may very well decrease long-term lethality may lead to an unnoticed increase in immediate lethality sufficient to provoke suicide.

Probably few things distress the staff more than the suicide of one of their in-hospital patients. Because of the relative frequency of the threat of such suicide plus its relative infrequency of actually occurring, most hospital staff members have inadequate mastery of their feelings about suicide. The personal factors in the psychiatric staff which may make them even more uncomfortable about suicide have been mentioned earlier. Apart from such dynamic issues, there is the simple feeling of failure which staff members experience in the face of the suicide of one of their patients. One cannot prevent every suicide, but that fact does not spare from guilt and pain those who have tried and failed. Even if the death has not resulted from the kind of risk-taking described above, an actual suicide from any cause generally has the effect of making all staff lean away from taking risks with patients' lethality.

There is a tendency in all situations to try most vigorously to prevent things which have already happened. This is done by applying one's efforts to other situations since it is obviously too late to apply them to the situation already past. The success of that kind of approach depends on the similarity of the past situation to future ones. Measures instituted after a suicide are subject to that contingency. If the preventive measures to be applied could be expected to be pertinent to future suicides, their application would be greatly desired. However, a review by the authors of 11 consecutive suicides by patients in or only briefly discharged from one hospital reveals that the circumstances of each case differed from those of the cases preceding so much that measures taken to prevent one episode would not have prevented those which followed. In many cases the measures suggested to be applied to prevent future suicides would not even have prevented the suicide which had already occurred.

In another setting a twenty-year old man hanged himself on a hospital ward after returning from a court hearing at which he was committed to a rehabilitative facility for treatment of heroin addiction. It was suggested then that every patient who returns to the hospital from court should be seen for evaluation of his mental status. Not only were there no other suicides or attempts by people in that particular situation before or since; it was also found in the course of investigating the case at hand that the patient *had* been seen after return from court. He had talked with the nursing staff who knew him fairly well *and* he had been seen by his own doctor who talked with him about the court action and his feelings about it. None of them felt that he was suicidal at the time. Yet the act took place within a half hour or so of those contacts.

After several suicides by hospitalized patients, one facility decided to establish a special unit on which would be placed all patients who were on suicidal observation. But none of the patients whose suicides had precipitated the establishment of the special unit had been on suicidal observation at the time of their suicides. There is no way of determining whether the existence of the special unit prevented suicides which might have occurred otherwise; but we can say fairly certainly that it would *not* have prevented the suicides which led to its establishment.

The foregoing discussion may sound nihilistic, as though it were being proposed that there is no use doing anything to try to prevent suicides. It is not our intention to convey that attitude. We believe strongly that all suicides of patients in treatment should be looked at most closely for possible clues which were missed, and for procedures which may have contributed to the suicides in any way. Such investigations may turn up situations which increase the risk for future suicides even though they may not have been contributory to the one under investigation. Obviously, such situations should be corrected. But we believe equally strongly that changes in procedures should be labeled clearly as either relevant or irrelevant to the suicide which has just happened. The feelings of distress and guilt that staff members feel after the suicide of one of their patients are great enough. They should not be unwittingly aggravated by policy or procedure changes which may be assumed to be indicative of blame for the past event when they are really being carried out solely for future safeguarding. Carelessness in this regard will increase the anxieties of the staff in the management of patients who are suicide risks and may inappropriately enhance mothering responses toward patients who might be harmed by them.

MANAGEMENT OF THE SUICIDAL CHARACTER

The significance of all this for the topic at hand is that the suicide of an in-hospital patient gravely affects the management of other suicidal patients at that hospital. The staff reactions to suicide are only one element in that, but they are an important element, and they interact with other elements of the matrix. For instance, other patients may react with criticism of the staff or a lack of trust in the staff's judgment and capability. They may ask "Why didn't you save him?" If staff guilt is significant, then their reactions will lead to reinforcement of the patients' concern and accusations, thus further raising patient and staff anxiety. Periodically a court finds a hospital and its staff liable for the suicide of a patient (2).

Such court judgments have generally occurred in cases where suicide risk was not considered in spite of clear evidence that it should have been, or where the patient was known to be suicidal and was not prevented from committing suicide. Where the issue of suicide was considered by the physician but where he misjudged the seriousness of the threat, courts have generally held him blameless. In other words, courts have not required of physicians that they be always right, but only that they *act in consonance* with their best judgment. Even if the circumstances of the court cases differ from the circumstances of the case at hand, the effect of court judgments on hospital staff members is a further reinforcement of the inclination to return to mothering with a suicidal patient whom one had been attempting to wean.

The management of the person for whom suicidality has become a way of life requires a willingness to take risks and an acceptance of the fact that one cannot prevent all suicides. Those are two qualities which not all therapists have. Once one has concluded that the only way to strive toward the ultimate reduction of lethality is to accept the risk of suicide in the interim, one next needs to determine to what degree the patient and the other people important in the patient's life are ready to accept those risks and to share the responsibility for treatment. It is crucial that the patient know he is expected to accept a major share of the responsibility for his own life. The temptation to relinquish this responsibility to the therapist and to others is always strong. The person with a suicidal character structure has become used to letting himself fall toward death as a means of coercing others to catch him. He must be helped to recognize that the treatment plan will gradually remove some of those catching arms, leaving him with increasing responsibility for not letting himself go.

The successful management of this kind of patient requires the exercise of great judgment and some caution. There are patients who must be mothered for a time lest they not be able to go on living otherwise. Or there may be times in the course of gradual life style change when temporary regression leads to a need for temporary return to mothering of the patient. And there are instances when the anxiety of the staff is so great that the therapist may need to permit, for a time, more mothering than he feels is really necessary.

A review by the authors of detailed investigations of some in-hospital suicides revealed that often the crucial clue to the impending suicide was known to a family member or friend but was not communicated to the hospital staff. Sometimes a transaction between the patient and a family member or friend seems to have been the trigger for a suicide. In order to prevent such contributions to suicide, one needs to maintain a link for communication with those people who are significant to the patient. Moreover, in many cases one needs to make those others aware of the risks that are felt to be inevitable in the treatment program. This is especially important in the case of adolescents' parents and patients' spouses. The "significant others" are significant allies in a good treatment program for this kind of patient. The responsibility for taking risks of suicide is a lonely burden of the therapist. But it is good to have the support or at least the understanding of the reasons for the risk-taking by the family (or close friends if there is no family or if the family is estranged).

Existential Despair

The aim of treatment of the suicidal person is to reverse the process by which suicidality has become reinforced and enhanced. The responsibility for one's own life must be gradually reaccepted. But acceptance of the responsibility for one's own life is not identical with a decision to go on living. In marital treatment, one often seeks to help couples who have not been speaking to each other. Sometimes when such a couple is helped to communicate, what they say to each other is that they want a divorce. A person who is helped to assume responsibility for his own life may not choose to continue living.

Beginning with Kierkegaard, especially in *The Sickness unto Death* (13), and continuing with the more modern existentialists, there has developed the notion of "existential despair." Existential despair needs to be differentiated from depressive illness, which may also contain a quality of despair. Depressive illness is a symptomatic disorder, experienced as ego-dystonic, having an onset and a course as do all symptomatic disorders. Existential despair may be an ego-alien aspect of a symptomatic disorder but it is sometimes an ego-syntonic despairing outlook on life, in which one feels hopeless of meaningful existence, rejecting of intimacy or close love relationships, and alienated from the life around.

Existential despair, thus, may be a life style problem as well as symptomatic. But the existentially despairing life style is not the same thing as what we have called the suicidal character. The latter is a different kind of life style problem, in which the basic interpersonal mode is the use of self-abandonment to evoke nurturance. The suicidal character type is that form of the generally dependent character type in which suicidal threat is the specific device by which succorance is coerced from others. The existentially despairing character implies an abandonment of the wish for or hope of nurturant response.

It is our experience that a certain number of those patients we see in the setting of a university teaching hospital are young people suffering from chronic existential despair. They do not necessarily exhibit the suicidal character, but occasionally they do. When these two traits coexist, they present a special challenge to those who would hope to treat these patients. Those who are not able to find something which justifies the retention of life will eventually relinquish it. That is another risk that the therapist must accept if he hopes to work with suicidal characterology. It is often possible to help a person recover from acute or chronic psychiatric illness, but the "cure" of the existentially despairing life style is not something psychiatry has learned.

SUMMARY

Suicide prevention in the hospital setting is generally undertaken in situations in which the patient's lethality is acute and time-limited. The techniques developed for such patients may not be well adapted to the management of *chronic* suicide risk. Some patients suffer from a suicidal character structure in which lethality is not so much symptomatic as it is a way of life. In the person with a suicidal character the need for mothering is expressed as suicidality. The mothering response may avert the suicidal impulse but it does so at the expense of reinforcing the suicidal character structure. Management and treatment of persons with a suicidal character structure entails taking short-term risks in the interests of achieving long-term reduction of suicidality. It requires a long-term commitment to a program of gradual character modification with respect to the use of suicidality as a means of coercing nurturance from others.

REFERENCES

1. *Litman, R. E. When Patients Commit Suicide. In* The Psychology of Suicide, *Shneidman, E. S., Farberow, N. L., and Litman, R. E., Eds. Science House, New York, 1970.*
2. *Litman, R. E. Medical-Legal Aspects of Suicide. In* The Psychology of Suicide, *Shneidman, E. S., Farberow, N. L., and Litman, R. E., Eds., Science House, New York, 1970.*
3. *Kasper,* A. *M. Fantasy of Mastery of Death. In* The Meaning of Death, *Feifel, H., Ed. Blakiston Division, McGraw-Hill, New York, 1959.*
4. *Feifel, H. Attitudes Toward Death in Some Normal and Mentally Ill Populations. In* The Meaning of Death, *Feifel, H., Ed. Blakiston Division, McGraw-Hill, New York, 1959.*
5. *Bakan, D. Suicide and Immortality. In* The Nature of Suicide, *Shneidman, E. S., Ed. Jossey-Bass, San Francisco, 1969.*
6. Death and Dying: Attitudes of Patient and Doctor. *GAP Reports, Vol. 5, Symposium No. 11, Mental Health Materials Center, New York, 1965.*
7. *McKegney, P. F. and Lange, P. The Decision to No Longer Live on Chronic Hemodialysis.* Am. J. Psychiat., *128:267, 1971.*
8. *Blachly, P. H., Disher, W., and Roduner, G. Suicide by Physicians.* Bull. Suicidol-

ogy, *N.I.M.H., National Clearinghouse for Mental Health Information, Dec. 1968, pp. 1–18.*

9. *Kubie, L. S. Multiple Determinants of Suicide Attempts (Editorial).* J. Nerv. Ment. Dis., *138:3, 1964.*
10. *Tarjan, G., Brooke, C., Eyman, R., Suyeuasu, A., and Miller, C. R. Mortality and Cause of Death in a Hospital for the Mentally Retarded.* Am. J. Publ. Health, *58:1891, 1968.*
11. *Shneidman, E. S.* Deaths of Man. *Quadrangle/New York Times Book Co., New York, 1973, pp. 81 ff.*
12. *Wooley, L. F. and Eichert, A. H. Notes on the Problems of Suicide and Escape.* Am. J. Psychiat., *98:110, 1941.*
13. *Kierkegaard, S. (1849).* The Sickness unto Death. *Princeton University Press, Princeton, N.J., 1954.*

21. Hopelessness and Suicidal Behavior

Aaron T. Beck, Maria Kovacs, and
Arlene Weissman

BIOGRAPHICAL NOTE

Aaron Beck, a Yale Medical School graduate, received his psychiatric training at the Cushing Hospital in Massachusetts, and later graduated from the Philadelphia Psychoanalytic Institute. Now professor of psychiatry at the University of Pennsylvania, Beck, in addition to his contributions to the study of suicide, has been a major contributor to the development of cognitive therapy, especially of depression. He is director of the Center of Cognitive Therapy in Philadelphia.

COMMENT

This paper describes what was perhaps the most important empirical demonstration of a central clinical tenet in the decade in which it was published: that hopelessness *is more highly characteristic of suicide than depression. Hopelessness, commonly found as a feature in depression, identifies the depressed patients at highest risk. In the same research described here Beck and his colleagues devised the Beck Hopelessness Scale, now widely used not only as a research instrument, but as a screening device in many clinical settings (Beck, Weissman, and Lester 1974).*

Jan Fawcett and co-workers in Chicago showed sixteen years later that hopelessness observed at the time of hospital admission was more predictive of those suicides occurring a year or more after discharge than those in the immediate post-discharge months (see chapter 38 below).

Aaron T., Beck, Maria Kovacs, and Arlene Weissman, "Hopelessness and Suicidal Behavior." *Journal of the American Medical Association* 234 (1975):1146–1149. Reprinted by permission.

REFERENCES

Beck, A. T., Weissman, A., Lester, D., and Trexler, L. 1974. The Measurement of Pessimism: The Hopelessness Scale. Journal of Consulting and Clinical Psychology *42:861–865.*

■

The relation of hopelessness to levels of depression and suicidal intent was explored both psychometrically and clinically. The results of an investigation of 384 suicide attempters support previous reports that hopelessness is the key variable linking depression to suicidal behavior. This finding has direct implications for the therapy of suicidal individuals. By focusing on reducing the sources of a patient's hopelessness, the professional may be able to alleviate suicidal crises more effectively than in the past.

THE PHENOMENON of suicide presents a puzzle to students of psychopathology as well as to the lay public: what mysterious force drives a person to violate one of the most hallowed notions of human nature—the "survival instinct"? Of the multitude of explanations by various writers, few seem to ring true or have even minimal empirical support.

Conventional wisdom has often attributed suicidal attempts to an individual's hopelessness, that is, his desire to escape from what he considers an insoluble problem. The recorded history of suicides among the Jews of antiquity, among the ancient Greeks and Romans, and during the Middle Ages contains many anecdotes of suicide based on the belief of being trapped in an impossible situation.[1]

Another historical paradigm stresses suicide as a symptom of impaired reason due to mental disorder or as a specific disease, sui generis. Since the 18th century, this psychopathological model of suicide has been paralleled by a statistical-sociological approach that relates suicide to environmental and demographic factors such as population density, socioeconomic class, degree of social integration, and national ideologies.[2,3]

The most popular thesis among psychoanalytically oriented psychiatrists and psychologists has been the conception that suicide is the result of hostility turned against the self. This retroflected hostility theory of suicidal behavior reaches its ultimate expression in the elaboration of the death instinct.[4]

During the past decade, the thinking of suicidologists has largely shifted to the view of suicide as "a cry for help."[5] This conception of suicidal behavior has been dramatized by the growth of suicide prevention centers, crisis intervention centers, and emergency telephone "hot lines." These fresh theoretical and practical approaches to the problem of suicide, however, have not been supported by any empirical evidence. In fact, recent studies have questioned whether or not these newer agencies have perceptibly affected the suicide rate.[6]

Similarly, the concept of retroflected hostility has been challenged. A variety of experimental and correlational studies of depressed suicidal patients, conducted by Beck and his colleagues,[7] have failed to confirm the internalized aggression conception. Moreover, these studies provided the framework for Beck's formulation of suicidal behavior as related to cognitive distortions.

On the basis of long-term psychotherapy of 50 depressed suicidal patients, Beck[8] noted:

> The suicidal preoccupations . . . seemed related to the patient's conceptualization of his situation as untenable or hopeless. He believed he could not tolerate a continuation of his suffering and he could see no solution to his problem: The psychiatrist could not help him, his symptoms could not be alleviated, and his various problems could not be solved. The suicidal patients generally stated that they regarded suicide as the only possible solution for their "desperate" or "hopeless" situation.

Beck's thesis of suicidal behavior incorporates two themes that occur in the historical survey of suicide; namely, the concepts that *hopelessness* is the catalytic agent and that "impaired reason" plays an important role in most cases of hopelessness and, consequently, in suicidal behavior. The main thrust of Beck's argument is that the suicidal behavior of the depressed patient is derived from specific cognitive distortions: the patient systematically misconstrues his experiences in a negative way and, without objective basis, anticipates a negative outcome to any attempts to attain his major objectives or goals.

A number of preliminary operations were necessary before Beck's formulation of suicidal behavior could be empirically tested. Because of the amorphous and contradictory terms used by various investigators to designate and classify suicidal behavior, a new nosology was prepared by a committee of the Center for the Study of Suicide Prevention.[9] The new classification is based on the quantification of intent in three major categories: completed suicide, attempted suicide, and suicidal ideation. The rationale and utility of this system was subsequently supported in a systematic study.[10]

The testing of the hopelessness hypothesis of suicidal behavior also required the development of methodologically sound measures of suicidal intent and hopelessness. Suicidal intent was conceptualized in terms of the relative weight of the patient's wish to live and his wish to die, his psychological deterrents against yielding to suicidal wishes, and the degree to which he has transformed his suicidal wishes into a concrete plan or actual act oriented to death. The reliability and validity of the instrument to measure suicidal intent among suicide attempters were established in a number of studies.[11,12]

Similarly, the concept of hopelessness was operationalized by the development and systematic testing of an instrument to measure this construct.[13] Paralleling Stotland's[14] formulation, hopelessness was conceptualized in terms of a system of cognitive schemata that share the common element of negative expectations.

In a pilot study of 67 suicide attempters, Minkoff et al[15] found that hopelessness was a more sensitive indicator of suicidal intent than depression per se. This study also demonstrated that the often-observed relationship between depression and suicidal intent was based on their joint attachment to a moderator variable—hopelessness. Furthermore, suicide attempters who were not depressed showed a substantial correlation between hopelessness and suicidal intent. Working at a different research center, Wetzel[16] replicated the findings of Minkoff et al.[15] In addition, he found that hopelessness was the mediating variable between depression and suicidal intent among patients who had planned, but had not actually carried out a suicidal attempt ("ideators").

The present study was designed to test the reliability of findings of Minkoff et al by investigating a much larger sample of suicide attempters and by employing clinical indexes of depression and hopelessness, in addition to the psychometric instruments used in the pilot study.

SUBJECTS AND METHODS

Data were collected from 384 suicide attempters admitted to two large metropolitan hospitals. The sample was composed of 160 men and 224 women, who ranged in age from 17 to 63 years, with a mean age of 30.2 years. The mean years of education was 10.9. Demographic data are presented in Table 1.

Of 250 patients who attempted suicide by ingestion of some dangerous substance, 222 used coma-producing drugs. Cutting or piercing instruments were employed by 66 persons. The rest used a variety of other methods such

Table 1. Demographic Characteristics of 384 Suicide Attempters

Variable	% of suicide attempters	
	Men	Women
Age, yr		
≤35	70.0	77.2
>35	30.0	22.8
Race		
White	59.4	45.1
Nonwhite	40.6	54.9
Marital status		
Single	50.6	35.7
Married	12.5	19.6
Cohabitating	3.8	8.1
Divorced or separated	28.7	33.9
Widowed	4.4	2.7
Religion		
Protestant	31.8	42.9
Roman Cotholic	43.1	29.4
Jewish	3.8	3.1
Atheist	1.3	2.7
Agnostic	5.6	6.3
Other	14.4	15.6
Psychiatric diagnosis		
Schizophrenia	28.8	23.2
Depressive disorders	45.0	54.0
Other	26.2	22.8

as jumping, gas inhalation, and drowning; 28 persons had used more than one method.

Each patient was seen twice within 48 hours of admission to the hospital. On the basis of a psychiatric interview, an experienced clinician completed the Suicidal Intent Scale (SIS),[11] a comprehensive schedule that covers the objective circumstances related to the suicidal attempt as well as the patient's self-report of his attitudes, plans, and expectations relevant to suicide at the time of the attempt. In addition, the clinician rated each patient on a scale from 0 (none) to 8 (severe) for intensity of depression and hopelessness.

A psychological technician independently administered and scored the Beck Depression Inventory (BDI)[17] and the Hopelessness Scale (HS),[13] which were used as the psychometric means of measuring the intensity of depression and hopelessness, respectively.

Table 2. Mean Suicidal Intent Scores for Levels of Depression and Hopelessness (N=384)

	Depression (BDI)	
Hopelessness	Low (0–23)	High (24–63)
Low (0–9)	$\bar{X}=11.5$ (n=164)	$\bar{X}=12.1$ (n=69)
High (10–20)	$\bar{X}=14.8$ (n=25)	$\bar{X}=15.7$ (n=126)

RESULTS

For the entire sample, the mean score on the BDI was 23.6, with a standard deviation of 11.9; the mean HS score was 9.0, with a standard deviation of 6.1; and the mean SIS score was 13.2, with a standard deviation of 5.9.

The data were analyzed by dividing the sample into two roughly equal groups on the basis of the median scores for both hopelessness and depression. The mean SIS scores for the four paired groups were computed (Table 2). A two-way (hopelessness by depression) analysis of variance for unequal sample numbers disclosed a highly significant main effect for hopelessness ($P<.001$), while neither the main effect for depression nor the hopelessness-×depression interaction was significant. As the data in Table 2 indicate, irrespective of whether the BDI scores were high or low, the groups with the high hopelessness scores had the higher mean intent scores.

A correlation matrix was computed for age and for BDI, HS, and SIS scores. Previous findings that the BDI, HS, and SIS are significantly correlated were corroborated (Table 3). As expected, the correlation between SIS and HS was significantly higher than that between SIS and BDI (Hotelling $t=2.19; P<.05$).

When partial correlations were computed, it was found that the correlation of SIS with HS (holding BDI constant) decreased from .38 ($P<.001$) to .24 ($P<.001$), while the correlation of SIS with BDI (holding HS constant) decreased from .30 ($P<.001$) to .06 (nonsignificant.).

These results confirm a previous finding by Minkoff et al that the association between depression and suicidal intent is primarily due to hopelessness as a common source of variance. Depression (BDI) has a bearing on suicidal intent (SIS) only by virtue of its association with hopelessness (HS). For the present data, hopelessness accounts for 96% of the association between depression and suicidal intent.

Table 3. Intercorrelations for Age and Three Psychometric Measures of Attempted Suicides

Variable	Age	Depression (BDI)	Hopelessness (HS)	Suicidal intent (SIS)
Total sample (N = 384)				
Age	1.00	0.02	−0.04	0.08
BDI	—	1.00	0.71*	0.30*
HS	—	—	1.00	0.38*
SIS	—	—	—	1.00
Schizophrenic subjects (n = 98)				
Age	1.00	−0.01	0.03	0.05
BDI	—	1.00	0.75*	0.17
HS	—	—	1.00	0.30†
SIS	—	—	—	1.00
Depressive subjects (n = 193)				
Age	1.00	0.07	−0.07	0.10
DBI	—	1.00	0.70*	0.32*
HS	—	—	1.00	0.39*
SIS	—	—	—	1.00

* $P<.001$.
† $P<.01$.

The clinical ratings of hopelessness and depression, which were obtained independently of the psychometric assessments, showed the same pattern of relationship to SIS scores as the HS and BDI. Clinical evaluations of hopelessness were more closely related to suicidal intent ($r = .50$; $P < .001$) than were the ratings of depression ($r = .27$; $P < .001$). As with the scores on the psychometric scales, the correlation between hopelessness and suicidal intent (controlling for depression) remained significant ($r = .47$), while the correlation between depression and intent (controlling for hopelessness) decreased to nonsignificance ($r = .09$). In addition, the ratings correlated significantly with the corresponding psychometric instruments (HS with ratings of hopelessness, $r = .66$, $P < .001$; BDI with ratings of depression, $r = .46, P < .001$).

To assess whether or not the nosological category may differentially affect the hopelessness-depression-intent interrelationship, separate analyses were done for the two major diagnostic groups in the sample: schizophrenia (n = 98) and depressive disorders (n = 193). The schizophrenics had a mean SIS of 12.3; mean BDI, 22.2; and mean HS, 7.6. In the depressive disorders group, the mean SIS was 14.2; mean BDI, 23.9; and mean HS, 9.3. The differences in means between the diagnostic groups and between each group and the total sample were not significant.

As the data in Table 3 indicate, the correlations among BDI, HS, and SIS scores were of similar magnitude for the schizophrenic and depressive groups. For both of these groups, the SIS scores correlated more highly with the HS than with the BDI, although the differences did not quite reach significance.

To assess whether or not the BDI-SIS and HS-SIS correlations for the two diagnostic groups were spuriously inflated in the same manner as found in the total sample, partial correlations were computed. When the effect of hopelessness (HS) was held constant, the association between intent (SIS) and depression (BDI) decreased close to zero for both diagnostic groups ($r = -.06$ for schizophrenics and $r = .08$ for depressives). In other words, hopelessness inflates the correlation between suicidal intent and depression just as much for schizophrenics as it does for depressives. Thus, irrespective of diagnosis, the construct of hopelessness (or negative expectations) appears to be a primary feature in suicidal intent.

COMMENT

The results of this study replicate and extend the preliminary findings of our research unit.[15] There is now consistent evidence that hopelessness accounts for the relationship between depression and suicidal intent. Whether measured psychometrically or clinically, hopelessness, defined operationally in terms of negative expectations, is a stronger indication of suicidal intent than is depression itself.

Several clinical studies have demonstrated the statistical relationship between suicidal behavior and hopelessness. A study by Harder[18] of the case histories of 11 depressed women who killed or tried to kill their children and then attempted suicide showed that these patients regarded their homicide-suicide plans as the only way out of what seemed to be an impossible situation. Bjerg,[19] in a systematic study of suicide notes, reported that in 81% of the notes there was a theme of "the person's seeing himself as having a desire . . . which could not, cannot, or will not be fulfilled."

Farnham-Diggory[20] found that, compared to nonsuicidal patients, the suicidal patient sees his future as highly constricted. Similarly, Ganzler[21] reported that, although three different psychiatric groups described their current life situations in negative terms, only the suicidal group rated the future negatively.

A great deal of experimental evidence has accumulated regarding the depression-hopelessness-suicide interrelationship. In a factor analysis of the

BDI, Pichot and Lempérière[22] isolated a factor with high loadings for only two items: hopelessness (.40) and suicidal wishes (.34). Cropley and Weckowicz[23] also extracted a factor whose major loadings were on hopelessness (.53) and suicide (.57). In a study of 254 suicide attempters, Beck and Lester[24] obtained factors similar to those found in previous studies, adding more weight to the hypothesis that hopelessness is highly related to suicidal behavior.

In another constructive replication of the study by Minkoff et al,[15] Kovacs et al. found hopelessness to be a significantly better indicator of both the intensity of current suicidal ideation and the extent of a patient's aversion to life than was depression. The analyses also suggested a specific behavioral sequence: hopelessness leads to attenuated desire to live, which leads to increased current suicidal ideation. In addition, N. Farberow, PhD (written communication, February 1974), and J. Motto, MD (written communication, December 1973), have reported that hopelessness is one of the best predictors of completed suicides.

Although many workers have pointed to depression as a danger sign of possible suicide,[26–29] this knowledge seems to have little impact on the understanding of suicidal behaviors. Furthermore, emphasis on the relationship between depression and suicide has often left workers at a loss in explaining such self-destructive behaviors in clinically nondepressed individuals. The current findings have removed the puzzle by pinpointing hopelessness as the missing link between depression and suicidal behavior.

The implications of this finding for therapy of suicidal individuals are important. The cognitive and attitudinal phenomena of hopelessness are important target symptoms in treating suicidal individuals. The clinician is more likely to "get a hold" of the situation by targeting in on the patient's hopelessness rather than by dealing with his overt self-destructive acts. By focusing on reduction of a patient's hopelessness, the professional may also be able to alleviate suicidal crises more effectively than in the past.

In addition, the "hopelessness" formulation of suicidal behavior has provided the rationale for active cognitive and behavioral approaches directed at correcting the pervasive misconceptions inherent in such an attitude. The techniques for cognitive-behavioral treatment of suicide have been described elsewhere.[30] When the negative expectations are related to various reality factors in life, the current findings might help to identify a starting point for professionals whose ultimate goal is constructive social change.

REFERENCES

1. *Rosen G: History in the study of suicide.* Psychol Med *1:267–285, 1971.*
2. *Durkheim E: Le Suicide:* Étude de Sociologie. *J A Spaulding, G Simpson (trans), Glencoe, Ill, Free Press, 1951.*
3. *Maris RW:* Social Factors in Urban Suicide. *Homewood, Ill, Dorsey Press, Inc, 1969.*
4. *Menninger K:* Man Against Himself. *New York, Harcourt Brace Jovanovich, Inc, 1938.*
5. *Farberow NL, Shneidman ES (eds):* The Cry for Help. *New York, McGraw-Hill Book Co, Inc, 1965).*
6. *Lester D: The myth of suicide prevention.* Compr Psychiatry *13:555–560, 1972.*
7. *Beck AT:* Depression: Clinical, Experimental, and Theoretical Aspects. *New York, Hoebner Medical Division, Harper & Row Publishers, Inc, 1967.*
8. *Beck AT: Thinking and depression: I. Idiosyncratic content and cognitive distortions.* Arch Gen Psychiatry *9:324–335, 1963.*
9. *Beck AT, Davis JH, Frederick CJ, et al: Classification and nomenclature, in Resnik HLP, Hathorne BC (eds):* Suicide Prevention in the Seventies. *Department of Health, Education, and Welfare, 1973, pp 7–12.*
10. *Beck AT, Beck R, Kovacs M: Classification of suicidal behaviors: I. Quantifying intent and medical lethality.* Am J Psychiatry, *to be published.*
11. *Beck AT, Schuyler D, Herman I: Development of suicidal intent scales, in Beck AT, Resnik HLP, Lettieri D (eds):* The Prediction of Suicide. *Bowie, Md, Charles Press, 1974, pp 45–56.*
12. *Beck R, Morris J, Beck AT: Cross-validation of the Suicidal Intent Scale.* Psychol Rep 34:445–446, 1974.
13. Beck AT, Weissman A, Lester D, et al: The measurement of pessimism: The Hopelessness Scale. J Consult Clin Psychol *42:861–865, 1974.*
14. *Stotland E:* The Psychology of Hope. *San Francisco, Jossey-Bass, Inc, 1969.*
15. *Minkoff K, Bergman E, Beck AT, et al: Hopelessness, depression, and attempted suicide,* Am J Psychiatry *130:455–459, 1973.*
16. *Wetzel RD: Hopelessness, depression, and suicide intent.* Arch Gen Psychiatry, *to be published.*
17. *Beck AT, Ward CH, Mendelson M: An inventory for measuring depression.* Arch Gen Psychiatry *4:561–571, 1961.*
18. *Harder J: The psychopathology of infanticide.* Acta Psychiatr Scand *43:196–245, 1967.*
19. *Bjerg K: The suicidal life space, in Shneidman ES (ed):* Essays in Self-Destruction. *New York, Science House, Inc, 1967, pp 475–494.*
20. *Farnham-Diggory S: Self-evaluation and subjective life expectancy among suicidal and non-suicidal psychotic males.* J Abnorm Soc Psychol *69:628–634, 1964.*
21. *Ganzler S: Some interpersonal and social dimensions of suicidal behavior.* Dissertation Abstracts *28B:1192–1193, 1967.*
22. *Pichot P, Lempérière T: Analyse factorielle d'un questionnaire d'auto-évaluation des symptomes dépressifs.* Rev Psychol Appl *14:15–29, 1964.*

23. *Cropley AJ, Weckowicz TE: The dimensionality of clinical depression.* Aust J Psychol *18:18–25, 1966.*
24. *Beck AT, Lester D: Components of depression in attempted suicide.* J Psychol *85:257–260, 1973.*
25. *Kovacs M, Beck AT, Weissman A: Hopelessness: A powerful predictor of suicidal behavior. Read before the American Association of Suicidology, Jacksonville, Fla. 1974.*
26. *Dorpat T, Boswell JW: An evaluation of suicidal intent in suicide attempts.* Compr Psychiatry *4:117–125, 1963.*
27. *Pokorny AD: Suicide rates in various psychiatric disorders.* J Nerv Ment Dis *139:499–506, 1964.*
28. *Kessel N: Self-poisoning, in Shneidman ES (ed):* Essays in Self-Destruction. *New York, Science House, Inc, 1967, pp 345–372.*
29. *Lester G, Lester D:* Suicide: The Gamble with Death. *Englewood Cliffs, NJ, Prentice-Hall, Inc, 1971.*
30. *Beck AT, Greenberg RL: Cognitive therapy with depressed women, in Franks V. Burtle V (eds):* Women and Therapy: New Psychotherapies for a Changing Society. *New York, Brunner/Mazel, Inc, 1974, pp 113–131.*

22. 5-HIAA in the Cerebrospinal Fluid: A Biochemical Suicide Predictor?

Marie Asberg, Lil Träskman, and Peter Thorén

COMMENT

Though efforts to understand mental illness in the laboratory began in the nineteenth century, advances in understanding the boichemical basis of depression have occurred primarily in the past thirty years. Plasma cortisol levels, the dexamethasone suppression test, imipramine binding on platelets, thyroid function tests, dopamine, and the hypothalamic-pituitary-adrenal axis are all under examination. No avenue has aroused greater interest or shown greater promise, however, than the investigation of the serotonin system.

This paper investigates suicidal behavior in depressed patients with correlation to the spinal fluid levels of 5-hydroxyindoleacetic acid (5-HIAA), a breakdown product of serotonin, and shows that patients with low 5-HIAA levels are significantly more likely to attempt suicide, and to use more violent means.

Later investigators have corroborated the findings of Marie Åsberg and her colleagues. Subsequent studies indicate that lowered 5-HIAA levels are most significantly correlated with violent attempts (van Praag 1982; Banki and Arato 1983; Åsberg et al. 1986; Maris 1986; Roy and Linnoila 1990).

REFERENCES

Åsberg, M., Nordstrom, P., and Traskman-Bendz, L. 1986. Biological Factors in Suicide. In Suicide, *Roy, A., ed. Baltimore: Williams and Wilkins.*

Banki, C. M., and Arato, M. 1983. Amine Metabolites and Neuroendocrine Responses Related to Depression and Suicide. Journal of Affective Disorders 5:*223–232.*

Maris, R., ed. 1986. The Biology of Suicide. *New York: Guilford Press.*

Marie Åsberg, Lil Traskman, and Peter Thoren, "5-HIAA in the Cerebrospinal Fluid: A Biochemical Suicide Predictor?" *Archives of General Psychiatry 33* (1976):1193–1197. Reprinted by permission.

Roy, A., and Linnoila, M. 1990. Monoamines and Suicidal Behavior. In Violence and Suicidality, *van Praag H. M., Plutchik, R., and Apter, A., eds. New York: Brunner/Mazel.*

Traskman, L., Åsberg, M., Bertilson, L., and Sjostrand, L. 1981. Monoamine Metabolites in CSF and Suicidal Behavior. Archives of General Psychiatry 38:*631–636.*

Van Praag, H. M. 1982. Depression, Suicide, and the Metabolism of Serotonin in the Brain. Journal of Affective Disorders *4:275–290.*

■

The incidence of suicidal acts was studied in 68 depressed patients and related to the level of 5-hydroxyindoleacetic acid (5-HIAA) in the cerebrospinal fluid. The distribution of 5-HIAA levels was bimodal. Patients in the low 5-HIAA mode (below 15 ng/ml) attempted suicide significantly more often than those in the high mode, and they used more violent means. Two of the 20 patients in the low mode, and none of the 48 patients in the high mode died from suicide.

THE FREQUENCY of suicide is high in psychiatric patients,[1,2] particularly in those suffering from depressive illness.[3–5] But only a minority of depressed patients commit or attempt suicide.[6] Additional risk factors for suicidal behavior have mainly been sought among demographic, sociocultural, and psychological variables.[7] The biological concomitants of psychiatric illness and their possible relationship to suicidal behavior have hardly received any attention at all, with a few notable exceptions. In 1965, Bunney and Fawcett[8] found exceptionally high levels of urinary 17-hydroxycorticosteroids in three patients who subsequently committed suicide. Bunney et al[9] have subsequently replicated their original findings in a larger patient group, and in 1974 Krieger[10] found a similar association between plasma cortisol levels and suicide.

Among the biological concomitants of depression, alterations in serotonin turnover have been in focus for several years.[11,12] Evidence for the role of this neurotransmitter in depressive illness is derived, inter alia, from findings of low levels of serotonin in brains from suicide victims[13–15] and low levels of its metabolite, 5-hydroxyindoleacetic acid (5-HIAA), in the cerebrospinal fluid (CSF) of depressed patients.[16–18]

We have studied the levels of 5-HIAA in CSF from 68 depressed patients and found that the distribution of metabolite levels was bimodal.[19,20] The bimodality could not be explained by factors known to influence the levels of

5-HIAA in CSF, such as age, sex, or previous medication. This suggested the existence of a biochemical subgroup within the depressive disorders, characterized by a low level of 5-HIAA in the CSF. Within this subgroup, the concentration of the serotonin metabolite appeared to be related to the illness, since there was a negative correlation between 5-HIAA in CSF and the severity of depression.[20]

Two of the 68 patients in this study have subsequently committed suicide. Both belonged to the subgroup with low 5-HIAA levels in CSF. We therefore decided to compare the incidence of suicidal behavior in the two 5-HIAA modes. Suicidal acts were not registered in the research protocols, and we were forced to rely on ordinary case notes. These are known to be an unreliable source of information, but we considered it unlikely that a suicide attempt would escape attention, and there was no risk of bias, since the clinicians were always unaware of the 5-HIAA levels.

PATIENTS

Consecutive depressed patients without signs or symptoms of schizophrenia, organic brain disease, or abuse of alcohol or other drugs were considered for the study. Those who were still severely or moderately depressed after an observation period in the hospital of a minimum of five days were rated on the Diagnostic Inventory developed by Gurney and co-workers.[21] Those patients diagnosed as depressed on the inventory and who agreed to a lumbar puncture after having had the nature and aim of the procedure explained to them (n = 68) were included in the study.

During the washout period, no drugs were given except for barbiturates or nitrazepam for night sedation when needed, and occasional doses of diazepam or oxazepam to control severe anxiety.

The conditions of the first 43 patients (sample 1) were classified as "endogenous" or "reactive" depressions (n = 27 and 16, respectively) according to clinical criteria.[22] The Diagnostic Inventory was used to classify the following 25 patients (sample 2) into endogenous (n = 17), or reactive (n = 8). Sample 1 consisted of 11 men and 32 women with a mean age of 56.8 ± SD 14.6 years. In sample 2, there were eight men and 17 women. An upper age limit of 65 years was used, and the mean age was 46.4 ± 14.2 years.

The project was cleared by the Ethical Committee of the Karolinska Institute.

METHODS

Severity of Depression

At the end of the observation period, all patients were rated for severity of depression. In sample 1, the modified Cronholm-Ottosson rating scale (CORS) for depression[23] was used. The reliability for two co-trained raters was 0.97 (Spearman rho, $P<.001$). In sample 2, a recently developed, comprehensive psychopathological rating scale (CPRS) was used (Åsberg et al, unpublished data). This scale measures a wider range of psychopathology. Severity of depression was assessed on a subscale, which had an interrater reliability of 0.92 ($P<.001$). Ratings of suicidal thoughts are included in both scales and were also analyzed separately.

Lumbar punctures were performed by a standardized technique at the end of the washout period. The CSF was collected in the early morning, before the patients had risen and after at least eight hours of fasting and bedrest. With the patient in the sitting position, 13 ml CSF was drawn with a fine, disposable needle. Except for occasional headache, there were no complications from the lumbar punctures. After centrifugation, the samples were immediately frozen in 2-ml aliquots in silanized glass tubes and stored at −20 C until analyzed.

5-HIAA determinations were performed according to the mass fragmentographic method developed by Bertilsson et al.[24] In addition to the specificity inherent in mass spectrometric techniques, the use of deuterium-labeled 5-HIAA as an internal standard assures a high degree of precision. The standard deviation is less than 2% above 20 ng 5-HIAA per milliliter and less than 7% below this level.

Suicidal Acts

The case notes of all patients were searched independently by two psychiatrists for evidence of suicidal acts. All acts of deliberate, self-inflicted injury, regardless of the lethality risk involved, were included as suicidal attempts whenever there was evidence that the subject himself had thought there was a risk of dying. Thus, the ingestion of three nitrazepam and three barbiturate tablets by an 88-year-old woman was included, since she stated that she had intended to die and regretted that she had not taken more. Plans or preparations that did not lead to an act, either because they were interrupted or otherwise, were not included. This applies for instance to a middle-aged man who was found by his wife, very drunk and with a bottle of sleeping pills in front of him, after he had filled the bathtub with water. Excluded also was a young woman who went swimming at 5 AM with the vague intention of drowning herself. Instead, she swam to a nearby island where she was taken care of by passersby a few hours later. These three were the only cases where the designation presented any difficulty.

All case notes that contained references to a suicidal act during the index illness period were then reviewed by a third psychiatrist, who was unaware of the results of the chemical analyses. The attempts and the completed suicides were rated for medical risk and intent on two simple three-point scales.

Statistical Analysis

Nonparametric methods[25] were used for the analysis of rating data. Chi-square with Yates correction for continuity was used for the four-field tables unless n was less than 20, when the Fischer exact probability test was used.

RESULTS

5-HIAA in CSF

The distribution of 5-HIAA was bimodal (Fig. 1). The deviation from normality was significant ($\chi^2 = 19.76$, *df* 9, $P = .020$). Twenty patients (29%) had levels below 15 ng/ml and thus fell into the lower mode.

The median ratings for severity of depression and suicidal thoughts did not differ significantly between the two modes (Table 1).

Suicidal Acts

Fifteen patients, four men and 11 women, had tried to commit suicide during the index illness period. Data about these patients and the methods they used are found in Table 2.

Neither age nor sex, diagnostic category, previous attempts, rated severity of depression, or rated suicidal thoughts differed significantly between those who had attempted suicide and those who had not (Table 3).

Suicidal Acts in Relation to 5-HIAA in CSF

Eight patients in the low 5-HIAA mode (40%) and seven in the high mode (15%) had made one or more suicide attempts during the index illness period

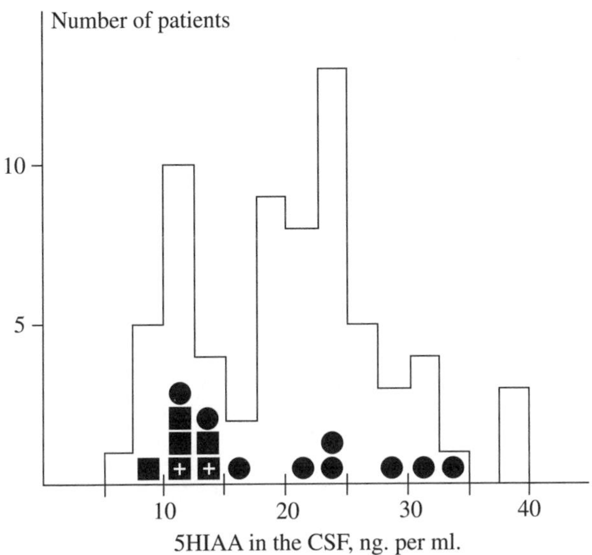

Figure 1: Suicidal acts in relation to 5-HIAA in CSF. Suicidal attempts with sedative drugs (circles); attempts with other means (squares). Patients died from suicide (crosses).

(Fig. 1). The difference between the modes is significant ($\chi^2 = 3.93$, $P = 0.48$). Five patients in the low mode and one in the high mode tried to commit suicide *after* admission to the hospital, also a significant difference ($\chi^2 = 6.59$, $P = .010$). Six patients in each mode had made a suicide attempt prior to admission. The difference, although not significant, is in the expected direction ($\chi^2 = 1.89$, $P = .169$). Two patients in the low mode and none in the high mode died from suicide ($\chi^2 = 2.06$, $P = .151$).

Table 1. Ratings of Psychopathology in Patients with Low (<15 ng/ml) and High (≥15 ng/ml) Levels of 5-HIAA in CSF

	Sample 1 (CORS)			Sample 2 (CPRS)		
Rated Variable	Low 5-HIAA (n = 14)	High 5-HIAA (n = 29)	z*	Low 5-HIAA (n = 6)	High 5-HIAA (n = 19)	z*
Severity of depression (median)	13.25	12.50	1.03, NS	24.00	23.00	0.32, NS
Suicidal thoughts (median)	1.25	1.00	1.78, NS	1.00	1.00	0.25, NS

* According to the Mann-Whitney U-test.

Table 2. Suicidal Acts

Patient	Diagnosis*	Sex	Age, yr	5-HIAA/CSF, ng/ml	Ratings† Depression	Suicidal risk	Metods‡
1	E	M	52	12.1	15	1.5	Several attempts prior to admission; medical intervention not needed. *After release* from hospital, he tried to hang himself after taking 15 barbiturate tablets, but the rope broke.
2	R	F	47	14.6	10	0	Took 10 ml of husband's insulin while he was at work. Deeply comatose when found.
3	E	F	73	23.6	12	1.5	Took unknown number of sedative tablets while husband away. He was alarmed when she did not answer the telephone, returned home, and found her unconscious. Fully awake next day.
4	E	F	88	32.0	15.5	1.5	Took three nitrazepam and three barbiturate tablets. Slightly drowsy.
5	R	F	54	21.0	13.0	2	Took 200 mg of nortriptyline hydrochloride (20 tablets). Slightly drowsy.
6	R	F	38	23.1	12.0	1.5	Several attempts during earlier periods of illness. Took unknown number of barbiturate tablets and hid in the family's garage. Unconscious when found after a few hours. Awake next day.
7	E	F	48	13.3	10.5	0.5	Took unknown number of methaqualone tablets while *on leave from hospital* (a few weeks after lumbar puncture). Two days in intensive care unit.
8	E	M	60	12.1	10.0	1	Gas poisoning two days *after release* from hospital. Family away; accidentally discovered by an adult son. Unconscious when taken to hospital. Awake after a few hours.
9	R	F	51	17.4	5	0	Took 20 barbiturate tablets. Fully awake next day. Admitted to psychiatric clinic one month later.
10	E	M	23	7.7	31	2.5	Tried to hang himself in the garage, but the rope broke.
11	E	F	52	34.2	21	2	Took 20 barbiturate tablets and went to sleep; husband soon noticed her snoring and took her to the hospital. Awake next day.

Patient	Diagnosis*	Sex	Age, yr	5-HIAA/CSF, ng/ml	Ratings† Depression	Suicidal risk	Metods‡
12	E	F	47	29.8	32.5	2.5	Took 100 barbiturate tablets *after release* from the hospital and hid outdoors. Circulatory collapse and ventricular fibrillation when hospitalized, but eventually recovered.
13	E	F	60	11.7	25.0	1.5	Overdose of sedatives prior to admission. No medical attention. Left hospital against medical advice and subsequently drowned herself.
14	R	F	23	12.4	23.0	0.5	Took 25 tablets of an anticholinergic preparation (told her boyfriend, who took her to the hospital).
15	R	M	46	13.6	9.75	0.5	Several attempts during previous periods of illness and also prior to index admission. Several months *after release* from the hospital he took unknown number of tricyclics and sedatives and drowned himself in the bathtub.

*E = endogenous depression; R = reactive depression.
†According to the CORS (range 5.0–19.5 in the entire material) in first nine patients; CPRS (range 9.75–32.5 in entire material) in the remainder.
‡Unless otherwise stated, suicide attempt immediately preceded hospitalization.

The combined risk-intent ratings tended to be higher in the low 5-HIAA mode (medians 4 and 2, respectively; Mann-Whitney U = 15.5, NS). Nine patients took overdoses of sedative drugs only; six used other methods, such as hanging or drowning. All those who used the more violent methods belonged to the low 5-HIAA group (Fischer exact $P = .006$).

COMMENT

In this selected sample of depressed patients, a low level of 5-HIAA in the CSF was thus a "predictor" of suicidal acts. The nature of the intervening variables between suicidal behavior and the concentration of a serotonin metabolite in lumbar CSF is, however, far from clear.

The interpretation of the biological significance of 5-HIAA concentrations in lumber CSF raises a number of questions that are still largely unresolved.[26] The relative importance of the many factors that may contribute to individual variability of lumbar CSF 5-HIAA in man is not well known. There is,

Table 3. Comparisons between Suicide Attempters and Nonattempters

	Attempters (n = 15)	Nonattempters (n = 53)	Statistical analysis
Age (mean ± SD)	50.8 ± 16.5	54.3 ± 14.5	$t = 0.81$, NS
Men (number of patients)	4	15	$\chi^2 = 0.04$, NS
Reactive depressions (number of patients)	6	18	$\chi^2 = 0.02$, NS
Suicide attempts during previous illness periods (number of patients)	2	12	$\chi^2 = 0.18$, NS
Severity of depression (CORS; median)	12.00	13.00	$z^* = 1.15$, NS
Suicidal thoughts (CORS; median)	1.50	1.00	$z^* = 0.32$, NS
Severity of depression (CPRS; median)	24.00	23.50	$z^* = 0.32$, NS
Suicidal thoughts (CPRS; median)	1.75	1.00	$z^* = 0.99$, NS

* According to the Mann-Whitney U-test.

however, evidence (recently summarized by Garelis et al[27]) that the concentrations of the serotonin metabolite in lumbar CSF to some extent reflect the turnover of the parent amine in the central nervous system. In man, the evidence is largely indirect and based on the alterations of CSF 5-HIAA caused by substances known to interfere with serotonin turnover. Especially suggestive are perhaps the quantitative relationships observed between the concentrations of the serotonin precursor, tryptophan, and 5-HIAA after tryptophan loading,[28] and those between the decrease in 5-HIAA and serotonin uptake blocking activity in patient plasma during treatment with the tricyclic antidepressant, clomipramine hydrochloride (Åsberg et al, unpublished data).

Among the other factors that are likely to contribute to the variability in CSF 5-HIAA, the capacity of the active transport mechanism that removes the metabolite from CSF to blood and the rate of flow of CSF may be important.[27,29,30] We have attempted to reduce variability in the latter factor by strict standardization of the lumbar puncture procedure and by always removing roughly the same amount of fluid, but have made no attempt to interfere with the transport mechanism.

The active transport of 5-HIAA can be blocked by means of probenecid, and many investigators[31–35] have used the probenecid technique in order to reduce individual variability in the egress of the metabolite from CSF. The probenecid-induced accumulation of 5-HIAA in CSF may reflect the rate of synthesis of the metabolite more closely than baseline levels, provided the blockade is complete and there is no other interference with indolamine turnover. With the dosages of probenecid usually employed, the blockade is, however, often subtotal and there is quite a strong correlation between the concentrations of 5-HIAA and probenecid in the CSF (which in turn vary widely between individuals receiving similar dosages).[36,37] Although this variability may be reduced by pharmacokinetic dosage monitoring[38] or by using extremely high dosages of probenecid,[39] we have not been convinced that the gains with the probenecid technique would outweight the inconveniences to the patients.

The correlation between severity of depression and concentration of 5-HIAA in our low 5-HIAA group of patients[20] would also seem to support the validity of baseline estimates of the metabolite. This finding is particularly interesting in view of the evidence that some of the 5-HIAA in lumbar CSF is derived from the spinal cord, rather than from the brain.[40,41] It might mean that an alteration of serotonin turnover is depressive illness also involves cord neurons, or that the contribution from the brain is large enough to be reflected in lumbar CSF.

The interpretation of a possible association between alterations of serotonin turnover and suicidal tendencies raises still more formidable questions. Because of our limited knowledge of what functions serotonin neurons subserve, and how they interact with other neuronal systems, any attempt at a comprehensive explanation would almost certainly be premature. It is interesting, though, that among those functions where serotonin neurons are thought to play a role, several, such as sleep, aggressive behavior, and pain, are also affected in depressive illness.

Aggressive behavior and pain appear especially interesting in relation to suicidal behavior. Experimentally induced reduction of serotonin synthesis leads to increased sensitivity to pain in test animals.[42] Experiences of physical pain have been associated with suicidal ideation in depressed patients.[43] Aggressive behavior induced by social isolation of rats or mice is accompanied by a reduction of serotonin synthesis, which does not occur in animals who fail to develop aggressive behavior.[44] The relation between suicide and aggressive behavior is obvious, and an increased hostility is also one of the main differences between depressed patients who attempt suicide and those who do not.[45] In this context, the preference for more active and "violent" suicidal methods among our low 5-HIAA patients is suggestive.

It is also possible that the low level of 5-HIAA is not directly related to depressive and suicidal behavior, but rather an epiphenomenon to other, more important, processes. Serotonin turnover is, for instance, affected by experimental stress in animals.[46,47] Corticosteroids also appear to interfere with serotonin turnover[47,48]—an interesting finding in relation to the reports of increased corticosteroid levels in plasma and urine from suicidal patients.[8–10]

The clinical value of 5-HIAA determinations as an indicator of suicidal potential remains to be proved. It should perhaps be pointed out that a highly specific and precise analytical method (such as mass fragmentography) is probably necessary to demonstrate the bimodal distribution of 5-HIAA. It does not seem to have emerged in investigations where conventional spectrophotofluorometric methods were used to assess baseline 5-HIAA (although van Praag and Korf[49] have demonstrated a tendency to a bimodal distribution of probenecid-induced accumulation of the metabolite). It is obvious that a somewhat larger methodological error might easily have filled the narrow gap between the two modes in the distribution (Fig. 3).

In many countries, suicide ranks as one of the major causes of death in the productive years.[50] The feeling that it could, and should, be prevented has motivated an impressive amount of research that has proved beyond doubt that sociocultural and psychological factors play a major role in the complex phenomenon of self-destruction. The present investigation, albeit of a preliminary nature and based on a comparatively small sample, indicates that it may prove worthwhile to take biological issues into consideration in attempts to understand, and perhaps ultimately prevent suicide.

NONPROPRIETARY NAMES AND TRADEMARKS OF DRUGS

Nitrazepam—Mogadon.
Clomipramine hydrochloride—Anafranil.
Methaqualone—Aqual, Quaalude, Sopor, Tuazole.

REFERENCES

1. *Temoche A, Pugh TF, MacMahon B: Suicide rates among current and former mental institution patients.* J Nerv Ment Dis *138:124–130, 1964.*
2. *Rorsman B: Suicide among Swedish psychiatric patients.* Soc Psychiatry *8:140–144, 1973.*
3. *Dahlgren KG:* On Suicide and Attempted Suicide. *Lund, Sweden, Ph. Lindstedts universitetsbokhandel, 1945.*

4. *Pokorny AD: Suicide rates in various psychiatric disorders.* J Nerv Ment Dis *139:499–506, 1964.*
5. *Barraclough B, Bunch J, Nelson B, et al: A hundred cases of suicide: Clinical aspects.* Br J Psychiatry *125:355–373, 1974.*
6. *Guze SB, Robins E: Suicide and primary affective disorders.* Br J Psychiatry *117:437–438, 1970.*
7. *Waldenström J, Larsson T, Ljungstedt N: Suicide and attempted suicide, in* Skandia International Symposia. *Stockholm, Nordiska Bokhandelns Förlag, 1972.*
8. *Bunney WE Jr, Fawcett JA: Possibility of a biochemical test for suicidal potential.* Arch Gen Psychiat *13:232–239, 1965.*
9. *Bunney WE Jr, Fawcett JA, Davis JM, et al: Further evaluation of urinary 17-hydroxycorticosteroids in suicidal patients.* Arch Gen Psychiatry *21:138–150, 1965.*
10. *Krieger G: The plasma level of cortisol as a predictor of suicide.* Dis Nerv Syst *35:237–240, 1974.*
11. *Lapin IP, Oxenkrug GF: Intensification of the central serotoninergic processes as a possible determinant of the thymoleptic effect.* Lancet *1:132–136, 1969.*
12. *Coppen A: Indoleamines and affective disorders.* J Psychiatr Res *9:163–171, 1972.*
13. *Shaw DM, Camps FEA, Eccleston EG: 5-hydroxytryptamine in the hindbrain of depressive suicides.* Br J Psychiatry *113:1407–1411, 1967.*
14. *Pare CMB, Yeung DPH, Price K, et al: 5-hydroxytryptamine, noradrenaline and dopamine in brainstem, hypothalamus and caudate nucleus of controls and of patients committing suicide by coal-gas poisoning.* Lancet *2:133–135, 1969.*
15. *Lloyd KG, Farley IJ, Deck JHN, et al: Serotonin and 5-hydroxyindoleacetic acid in discrete areas of the brainstem of suicide victims and control patients, in Costa E, Gessa GL, Sandler M (eds):* Serotonin: New Vistas. *New York, Raven Press, 1974, pp 387–397.*
16. *Ashcroft GW, Crawford TBB, Eccleston D, et al: 5-hydroxyindole compounds in the cerebrospinal fluid of patients with psychiatric or neurological diseases.* Lancet *2:1049–1052, 1966.*
17. *Dencker SJ, Malm U, Roos B-E, et al: Acid monoamine metabolites of cerebrospinal fluid in mental depression and mania.* J Neurochem *13:1545–1548, 1966.*
18. *Coppen A, Prange AJ Jr, Whybrow PC, et al: Abnormalities of indoleamines in affective disorders.* Arch Gen Psychiatry *26:474–478, 1972.*
19. *Åsberg M, Bertilsson L, Tuck D, et al: Indoleamine metabolites in the cerebrospinal fluid of depressed patients before and during treatment with nortriptyline.* Clin Pharmacol Ther *14:277–285, 1973.*
20. *Asberg M, Bertilsson L, Ringberger V, et al: "Serotonin depression"—A biochemical subgroup within the affective disorders?* Science *191:478–480, 1976.*
21. *Gurney C, Roth M, Garside RF, et al: Studies in the classification of affective disorders: The relationship between anxiety states and depressive illness.* Br J Psychiatry *121:162–166, 1972.*
22. *Cronholm B, Ottosson JO: Experimental studies of the therapeutic action of electroconvulsive therapy in endogenous depression.* Acta Psychiatr Scand *35 (suppl 145):69–101, 1960.*

23. *Asberg M, Kragh-Sørensen P, Mindham RHS, et al: International reliability and communicability of a rating scale for depression.* Psychol Med *3:458–465, 1973.*
24. *Bertilsson L, Atkinson AJ Jr, Althaus JR, et al: Quantitative determination of 5-hydroxyindole-3-acetic acid in cerebrospinal fluid by gas chromatography-masspectrometry.* Anal Chem *44:1434–1438, 1972.*
25. *Siegel S:* Nonparametric Statistics for the Behavioural Sciences. *New York, McGraw-Hill Book Co Inc, 1956.*
26. *Baldessarini RJ: The basis for amine hypotheses in affective disorders.* Arch Gen Psychiatry *32:1087–1093, 1975.*
27. *Garelis E, Young SN, Lal S, et al: Monoamine metabolites in lumbar CSF: The question of their origin in relation to clinical studies.* Brain Res *79:1–8, 1974.*
28. *Ashcroft GW, Crawford TBB, Cundall RL, et al: 5-hydroxytryptamine metabolism in affective illness: The effect of tryptophan administration.* Psychol Med *3:326–332, 1973.*
29. *Moir ATB, Ashcroft GW, Crawford TBB, et al: Cerebral metabolites in the cerebrospinal fluid as a biochemical approach to the brain.* Brain *93:357–368, 1970.*
30. *Post RM, Kotin J, Goodwin FK, et al: Psychomotor activity and cerebrospinal fluid amine metabolites in affective illness.* Am J Psychiatry *130:67–72, 1973.*
31. *Roos B-E, Sjöström R: 5-hydroxyindoleacetic acid (and homovanillic acid) levels in the cerebrospinal fluid after probenecid application in patients with manic-depressive psychosis.* Pharmacol Clin *1:153–155, 1969.*
32. *Sjöström R, Roos B-E: 5-hydroxyindoleacetic acid and homovanillic acid in cerebrospinal fluid in manic-depressive psychosis.* Eur J Clin Pharmacol *4:170–176, 1972.*
33. *van Praag HM, Korf J, Puite J: 5-hydroxyindoleacetic acid levels in the cerebrospinal fluid of depressive patients treated with probenecid.* Nature *225:1259–1260, 1970.*
34. *van Praag HM, Korf J: Serotonin metabolism in depression: Clinical application of the probenecid test.* Int Pharmacopsychiatry *9:35–51, 1974.*
35. *Goodwin FK, Post RM, Dunner DL, et al: Cerebrospinal fluid amine metabolites in affective illness: The probenecid technique.* Am J Psychiatry *130:73–79, 1973.*
36. *Korf J, van Praag HM: Amine metabolism in the human brain: Further evaluation of the probenecid test.* Brain Res *35:221–230, 1971.*
37. *Sjöström R: Steady state levels of probenecid and their relation to acid monoamine metabolites in human cerebrospinal fluid.* Psychopharmacologia *25:96–100, 1972.*
38. *Sjöström R: Diagnosis of manic-depressive psychosis from cerebrospinal fluid concentration of 5-hydroxyindoleacetic acid, in Costa E, Gessa GL, Sandler M (eds):* Serotonin: New Vistas. *New York, Raven Press, 1974, pp 369–375.*
39. *Perel JM, Levitt M, Dunner DL: Plasma and cerebrospinal fluid probenecid concentrations as related to accumulation of acidic biogenic amine metabolites in man.* Psychopharmacologia *35:83–90, 1974.*
40. *Bulat M, Živković B: Origin of 5-hydroxyindoleacetic acid in the spinal fluid.* Science *173:738–740, 1971.*

41. *Živković B, Bulat M: 5-hydroxyindoleacetic acid in the spinal cord and spinal fluid.* Pharmacology *6:209–215, 1971.*
42. *Lytle LD, Messing RB, Fisher L, et al: Effects of long-term corn consumption on brain serotonin and the response to electric shock.* Science *190:692–694, 1975.*
43. *von Knorring L:* The Experience of Pain in Patients with Depressive Disorders. *Umeå University Medical Dissertations, Umeå, 1975.*
44. *Valzelli L: 5-hydroxytryptamine in aggressiveness, in Costa E, Gessa GL, Sandler M (eds):* Serotonin: New Vistas. *New York, Raven Press, 1974, pp 255–263.*
45. *Weissman M, Fox K, Klerman GL: Hostility and depression associated with suicidal attempts.* Am J Psychiatry *130:450–455, 1973.*
46. *Rosecrans JA: Effects of acute stress on forebrain 5-hydroxytryptamine metabolism and pituitary adrenal function.* Eur J Pharmacol *9:170–174, 1970.*
47. *Curzon G: Relationships between stress and brain 5-hydroxytryptamine and their possible significance in affective disorders.* J Psychiatr Res *9:243–252, 1972.*
48. *Richter D: Tryptophan metabolism in mental illness, in Himwich HE, Kety SS, Smythies JR (eds):* Amines and Schizophrenia. *New York, Pergamon Press, Inc, 1967, pp 167–179.*
49. *van Praag HM, Korf J: Endogenous depressions with and without disturbances in the 5-hydroxytryptamine metabolism: A biochemical classification?* Psychopharmacologia *19:148–152, 1971.*
50. *Mortality and morbidity trends, 1962–1972,* WHO Chronicle *29:377–386, 1975.*

23. Aloneness and Borderline Psychopathology: The Possible Relevance of Childhood Development Issues

Gerald Adler and Dan H. Buie, Jr.

BIOGRAPHICAL NOTE

Gerald Adler trained in psychiatry at the Massachusetts Mental Health Center after graduating from the Columbia University College of Physicians and Surgeons in New York. Important influences in his early training were Ives Hendrick and Elvin Semrad. After graduation from the Boston Psychoanalytic Institute he became a training analyst and has published a large number of articles and books dealing with the psychology and treatment of patients with borderline personality disorder.

COMMENT

This paper concentrates our attention on affect as a central phenomenon in suicide. Emil Kraepelin (1904) was directing attention to suicide as a complication of depressions at the turn of the century, and Sigmund Freud (1915) showed the importance of hate turned against the self. But the force of other emotional states as suicide-driving, and the incompetence of some patients to modulate and moderate anxiety and depression, began to be noticed by psychoanalysts after the close of World War II (Zetzel 1949, 1965). Here intolerable aloneness, *a reflection of unmodulated separation or abandonment anxiety, at the core of the suffering of patients with borderline personality disorder, is discussed as a suicide-inviting therapeutic challenge.*

This paper foreshadowed the subsequent demonstration of the high incidence of suicide attempts in panic states (see chapter 37 below) and antici-

---

Gerald Adler, and Dan H. Buie, Jr., "Aloneness and Borderline Psychopathology: The Possible Relevance of Child Development Issues." *International Journal of Psycho-analysis 60*(1979):83–96. Reprinted by permission.

pates Edwin S. Shneidman's discussion of "psychache" as central to suicide (see chapter 40 below).

REFERENCES

Freud, Sigmund. 1915. Mourning and Melancholia. Standard Edition of the Complete Psychological Works of Sigmund Freud, *14:237–260, Strachey, J., ed., London: Hogarth Press.*

Kraepelin, Emil. 1904. Lectures on Clinical Psychiatry, *Johnstone, T., ed., London: Baillière, Tindall and Cox. (This English translation from the German was reprinted in facsimile in 1968 by the Hafner Publishing Co. in New York.)*

Zetzel, E. 1949. Anxiety and the Capacity to Bear It. Reprinted in The Capacity for Emotional Growth, *London: Hogarth Press, 1970.*

———*. 1965. On the Incapacity to Bear Depression. In Schur, M., ed.* Drives, Affects, and Behavior, *vol. 2. New York: International Universities Press.*

■

IN OUR psychoanalytic and psychotherapeutic efforts at definitive characterologic work with borderline patients, we have observed a core experiential state of intensely painful aloneness. This feeling state often includes a sense of inner emptiness together with increasing panic and despair; over time these patients develop a concomitant desperate hopelessness that this feeling will ever be alleviated. When we view borderline patients on a spectrum extending from psychotic to more nearly neurotic experience, we find that those closer to psychosis experience this aloneness more frequently and more intensely. It appears as a major vicissitude in their attempts to form dyadic relationships, including those with their therapists or analysts. We find that this experience of aloneness is characteristic of borderline patients and is an intrinsic aspect of a fundamental personality defect which we feel is the consequence of a developmental failure. We believe this defect occupies a position of major importance when we consider the nature of the character changes which definitive treatment must involve.

A notable aspect of the borderline patient's experience with aloneness is his relative or total inability to maintain positive fantasies or images of sustaining people in his present or past life. At these times the patient often states that he has no fantasies at all; at other times he has fantasies, but they consist of unsustaining or disruptive negative memories and images of the people who are important to him. Common to both experiences is his inability to feel himself, in fantasy, to be involved with a figure who sustains. Our observations of this state have been made in the context of a treatment approach which utilizes the basic principles of psychoanalysis and psychoanalytic psychotherapy, i.e. in the setting of a working alliance, and analysis of transference and resistance along with encouragement of fantasy exploration. This treatment method is derived from the vast literature of psychoanalytic work with neurotic patients and recent contributions by Anna Freud, Kohut, Kernberg, Balint, Guntrip, and Winnicott, which have stressed extension of this treatment approach to patients struggling with more primitive issues and ego states.

In this paper we shall discuss aloneness in borderline patients, define the ways in which it becomes manifest, and elaborate the affectivecognitive qualities of one particular developmental line which appears to bear strongly on the ultimate vulnerability to, or freedom from, unbearable aloneness. We shall also discuss some therapeutic implications of our formulations about this developmental line.

A significant literature has accumulated over the past ten years defining agreements and disagreements about patients who are labelled borderline. Grinker (Grinker, Werble & Drye, 1968), in his research study, has described four groups of borderlines along a continuum from near psychotic to near neurotic. Kernberg (1967) has emphasized a stable aspect of personality organization in borderlines and has detailed its descriptive, genetic, structural, and dynamic qualities. One of Kernberg's major contributions has been the elucidation of an important defence, splitting, along with its origins in unsatisfactory object relations early in life. Frosch's (1970) contributions stress the transient reality-testing problems of borderlines and their reality-sense difficulties. Chase (Chase & Hire, 1966) has emphasized feelings of abandonment as critical to borderline patients.

This literature has contributed to our formulation of borderline patients as people with a relatively stable personality organization who are particularly vulnerable to feelings of abandonment and aloneness, which are precipitated in the context of dyadic relationships (Adler, 1972, 1973, 1975; Adler & Buie, 1972, Buie & Adler, 1972). In order to alleviate or prevent aloneness, intense needs to be held, fed, touched, and ultimately to be merged together, are mobilized in these patients within a dyadic relationship; when these felt needs are not fulfilled, intense rage ensues. Borderlines are exquisitely sensitive to evidence of rejection; the latent and chronic aloneness they feel is compounded by aloneness which follows their destructive rage. In addition, they fear the closeness they long for, partly because the merging they want brings the threat of mutual destruction, and partly because they fear their inevitable destructive fury. They utilize primitive defences: projection, projective identification, splitting, and primitive idealization. The result of all these factors is an instability in their relationships, which readily become unrealistic, intense, demanding, chaotic, and terrifying. This entire complex of vulnerability, needs, fears and defences must be addressed in definitive therapeutic work with borderlines.

We wish to emphasize that the borderline patient can arrive at the subjective experience of aloneness by a variety of psychodynamic routes; each one requires therapeutic attention. Three such routes are commonly recognized: (1) Rage at the sustaining object when it is insufficiently available or insufficiently able to fill the patient's need, can be annihilatory in intent and intensity. Under these circumstances the borderline, as one patient put it, 'stomps' the therapist out of his mind. (2) At times the need for sustenance is so urgent that the borderline is impelled to use the most primitive mode of internalization, that of incorporation, as Meissner (1971) defines it. Incorporation is experienced in terms of ideas and impulses to eat the sustaining object or be eaten by it, or to absorb or be absorbed. The inherent difficulty with the incorporate mode of internalization in persons who have achieved self-object differentiation, as borderlines have, is that it is experienced as threatening the loss of the object and/or the loss of the self. In order to preserve the object and the self, the borderline, at the times of his most intense incorporative wishes, must distance himself from the needed person. But the protective psychological distance he imposes between himself and the object is experienced as the very isolated state of aloneness out of which the drive for incorporation originated. (3) Grief is felt by borderlines as unbearable sadness in the same way that Semrad (1969) describes it as intolerable for psychotics. Like psychotics, they utilize gross denial to avoid the sadness; this denial removes from awareness all trace of the object representation or introjection of a lost sustaining object. Absence of the therapist, at certain times, threatens such sadness and mobilizes denial of this order. But the subjective experience of aloneness is the result of this denial.

Our clinical and supervisory experiences have convinced us that there exists a fourth, more fundamental, determinant of aloneness in borderlines. We have invariably been confronted with episodes of aloneness which have often been the most unbearable, the most hopeless, for the patient. When explored in the context of a good working alliance, we have been told that this particular aloneness feels more basic in their total life experiences, more like a given primary. For example, one patient who expressed this opinion of her most unbearable aloneness, traced the experience as far back as a memory from childhood. Her mother had in fact been unable most of the time to be empathically together with her daughter. The patient recalled lying in her crib pervaded by a desperate aloneness; she did not, however, call out, because she knew no one would come. It was notable that in this memory there was no imago of any person and no hope that she would arouse anyone.

The concept of an aloneness which consists simply of the absence of the sustaining object or an affective memory (introject) of it has received little attention from analysts and psychotherapists who treat borderline patients. The reason may possibly lie in the absence of a theoretical framework which admits the possibility of such a phenomenon. In psychoanalytic metapsychology, personality development is viewed as a moulding process in which innate potentials progressively emerge and are shaped or limited by interactions with persons in the environment. The concept of primary narcissism (Freud, 1914) still occupies an important place in standard metapsychology, and from that viewpoint the infant is considered innately endowed with self-love and belief in entitlement to gratification of his wishes and needs. Kernberg's contributions (1966, 1967, 1968) belong in this framework. He conceives the borderline condition to be most basically rooted in failures of 'oral gratification'. These failures lead to a rage (not aloneness) which requires perpetuation of 'splitting' in order to manage it. This view, along with other views formulated in the same metapsychological context, allows the conception of an ungratified and enraged infant who can feel alone as part of the three well known dynamics listed above. It does not, however, allow for the fourth possibility: an aloneness which is potential in all infants because they necessarily must rely on objects for psychological and physical supplies which are essential to their psychic and physical survival. (It is survival in addition to oral gratification that is at stake.) Failure of sustenance from the object threatens survival, and on a psychological level, it is failure of the 'holding environment' (Winnicott, 1960a) which initiates a sequence which has been documented by such observers as Bowlby (1969) and the Robertsons (1971), one which begins with protest and ends in detachment. We would add that the endpoint, when this situation persists too long, is a fundamental long-standing aloneness. Although aloneness is multiply determined, as we have outlined, this most fundamental aloneness is the subject of our study. If this aloneness constitutes too much of the infant's experience, he will be unable to negotiate development of libidinal object constancy (Fraiberg, 1969; A Freud, 1960), i.e. as an adult he will not be able to maintain a sense of soothing contact with sustaining introjections because the introjects will be unstable and subject to loss through a form of structural regression. Temporary loss of sustaining introjects brings the same experience of aloneness as did the serious failures of the holding environment during infancy.

This theoretical concept of a fourth form of aloneness is implicit in the work of many authors. It is beyond the purview of this paper to take them all into account. We will instead draw upon a few: Fraiberg (1969), A.-M. Sandler (1975), Piaget (1937), Bell (1970), Mahler (1971), Mahler et al. (1975), Bowlby (1969), the Robertsons (1969, 1971), M. Tolpin (1971), and Winnicott (1953, 1960a, 1960b) in order to make explicit the theoretical understanding of aloneness which they contain.

We will formulate this understanding as an aspect of a particular affective-cognitive line of development which both Fraiberg and A.-M. Sandler have delineated. Fraiberg utilized Piaget's six stages in the sensori-motor development of an object concept to clarify the infant's formation of recognition and evocative memory in relation to its mother. Piaget's stages III to VI trace the development of early memory capacity. In stage III (ages 5–8 months) a baby will make no attempt to retrieve a toy hidden behind a pillow even though the toy is placed there while the baby is watching. Apparently no memory for the object exists. In stage IV (ages 8–13 months) the infant will look for the toy which has been hidden behind something while he is watching. He has gained the capacity to remember an object for a few seconds. With stages V (13–18 months) the infant will pursue and find a toy that has first been placed behind one pillow, then removed and hidden behind a second: however, the child must *see* the movement from one place to the other. If the second hiding is done by sleight of hand, he makes no effort to search beyond the first hiding place. Not seeing the changes in the object's location, he apparently loses his image of it. Finally, with stage VI (at 18 months) the infant will continue to look for the toy even when the second hiding is done without his seeing it. Piaget concludes that only when the child reaches stage VI does he possess a sustained mental representation of the object as retaining permanent existence despite the fact that it leaves the field of his perception. At stage IV (8–13 months) the child can recognize an object, i.e. follow it and retrieve it when it is hidden within his view, but two more stages and at least five more months must be traversed before the child gains the capacity to remember that the toy exists even though he fails to find it where he first expects and for a moment it seems to be lost. In Fraiberg's (1969) words, 'in the absence of perceptual cues or any sign, he can evoke the image of the absent object and pursue it' (p. 31). This magnificent achievement coincides with others, such as symbolic thought, increasingly complex speech, deferred imitation of other people, and the beginning of imaginative play.

Fraiberg relies on this work of Piaget (1937) on the permanence of the object concept to formulate two kinds of memory: recognition memory and evocative memory. The memory of the infant at stage IV is so impermanent that the toy cannot be looked for under a second pillow even when observed to be placed there; Fraiberg designates this phenomenon as recognition memory. With recognition memory, the object can be recognized when presented and can be remembered for a few moments but its image cannot be evoked unaided. With the achievement of stage VI (the end of the sensori-motor stage) the object no longer must be present, or recently present for the child to summon up its mental image. Fraiberg designates this stage VI capacity as evocative memory. As A.-M. Sandler (1975) states: 'It is only by the end of the sensori-motor stage, by about 18 months, that we can even begin to speak of the baby's world having acquired permanence, substantiality and solidity, independent of the actions and immediate experience of the subject' (p. 367). Fraiberg's, A.-M. Sandler's and Piaget's utilization of these experimental data also expands Freud's (1925) discussion about 'the capacity to bring before the mind once more something that has once been perceived, by reproducing it as a presentation without the external object having still to be there' (p. 237), i.e. evocative memory capacity.

Translating these formulations into a discussion of infants and their mothers, we can postulate that the toddler who becomes lonely and anxious when his mother is away too long and who has an evocative memory capacity can utilize a fantasy or image of his mother which can serve for a time as a source of comfort. A baby with only recognition memory cannot evoke the memory of mother when she has gone away. Instead he is inclined to cry in a way that we empathically perceive as expressing helplessness, abandonment, and rage. The achievement of solid libidinal object constancy requires at least another year or two. It is relatively fragile in the 18-month-old child and readily lost at least transiently if he is stressed by too long a period of separation. Furthermore, we know that recently achieved capacities or 'structures' are especially vulnerable to temporary disintegration; so it seems reasonable to expect that the toddler is particularly prone to a breakdown of evocative memory capacity when experiencing a relative inadequacy of 'good enough mothering' (Winnicott, 1960b).

We now have evidence that the optimal development of recognition and evocative memory depends upon the child's interaction with its environment, especially the quality of the relationship with his mother. Bell's (1970) important study suggests that those children who seem to have had the most positive maternal experience (1) develop the concept of person permanence, e.g. for mother, before object permanence, e.g. for a toy, and (2) achieve earlier mastery of the stages of permanence for both persons and objects. In contrast, mothers who seem rejecting had children who tended to develop object permanence before person permanence and were delayed when compared to the former group in achieving the highest stage of permanence for both objects and persons. Thus, affective cognitive development, i.e. person permanence, can be separated from cognitive development for non-libidinally invested objects and both developmentally seem related to experiences within the mother-child dyad. Clinically in adult patients aspects of these phenomena may be applicable to experiences with borderline patients in which they can transiently lose an evocative memory of their therapist and yet retain this evocative memory capacity in other areas of their life.

Achievement of the capacity for evocative memory is a major milestone for a child and a most significant step in his developing capacity for autonomy. No longer does he depend so fully upon the presence of actual people for comfort and support. Instead he has acquired some capacity to soothe and comfort himself with memories and fantasies of real people and his interactions with them. Prior to the development of evocative memory capacity, another method of attaining soothing comfort is utilized by the child through transitional objects (Winnicott, 1953), e.g. his blanket, which help him experience soothing aspects of his mother without turning to mother herself. Tolpin (1971) describes how the child uses the transitional object to recreate the all-soothing mother at a time when he is too old to be comforted in the cuddly way he has been in the past. It is interesting, and in our opinion significant, that transitional objects come into use at approximately the age of six months and are given up largely by the end of the second year. The beginning approximates that of stage IV, i.e. recognition memory; normally transitional objects are no longer necessary when stage VI is achieved, i.e. with the capacity for evocative memory. One might say that the transitional object serves as an external activator which helps evoke certain qualities which it shares in common with mother, e.g. softness. For the infant with only recognition memory capacity, the presence of the transitional object is necessary in order to activate and maintain an affectively charged memory of the soothing mother. When evocative memory is achieved the transitional object is no longer necessary, for these memories of mother and the child's interaction with her are a part of the child. In the language of the present paper, we would say that the experiences involved in the use of the transitional object are adequately remembered at stage VI. The little child can soothe himself in the same way through the use of his evocative memory of his libidinally charged experiences with persons, things, and activities, including those involved with the old transitional object. However, there is a very sensitive balance in the mother-child relationship for the child's development of evocative memory capacity and his ability to utilize the transitional object in this development. The 'good enough mother' as described by Winnicott (1960b), must be available often enough for the child to be able to use the transitional object effectively to aid in the development of evocative memory capacity. In addition, when partial development of evocative memory capacity is achieved, the adequate support and presence of the good enough mother makes it possible for the child to utilize the transitional object to strengthen further the developing evocative memory capacity. The positive development of evocative memory capacity and the ability to utilize a transitional object go hand in hand in the development of solid person and object permanence. In contrast, when there is an absence or disruption of good enough mothering, a reverse of this positive developmental line occurs. The child who is too stressed by relative or absolute maternal deprivation may have an evocative memory development which is extremely vulnerable; for such a child the use of the transitional object may become desperate and unsuccessful in what may seem like a rapid downhill spiral.

We emphasize the acquisition of evocative and recognition memory capacities and the utilization of the transitional object during this process because we feel that this developmental line may possibly be relevant to a major developmental defect in borderline patients, and therefore an important issue to be addressed in any treatment approach. *We believe that adult borderline patients have not achieved solid evocative memory in the area of affective object relationships and are prone to regress in the area of object relations to recognition memory or earlier when faced with certain stresses.* These stresses, which may be a sudden trauma, usually involve actual losses of important people, or the real or fantasied loss of support from them. Lengthy separations themselves tend to lead to a functional regression toward recognition memory in these vulnerable patients.

Clinically we have found that this regression very often occurs in response to the rage that these patients experience when there is a real or fantasied loss of relationships or adequate support. This experience of rage is usually the essential feature that precedes the borderline decompensation and which leads to the intense feelings of aloneness and panic. It is this rage in borderlines along with the developmental vulnerability we have been defining that leads to a loss of higher levels of evocative memory formation and the regression to recognition memory or earlier levels (e.g. stage III) with feelings of aloneness and panic. In attempting to define the varieties of rage in adult borderline patients we have found the Robertsons' work (1969, 1971) with children conceptually useful. Their studies also highlight the experiences we have been describing: regression from evocative to recognition memory and the breakdown of the capacity to utilize transitional objects.

The Robertsons describe, in their film (1969) and commentary (1971), a 17-month boy, John, who was left in a residential nursery for nine days while his mother was having a baby. John had had a good, healthy relationship with his mother. Although the staff of the nursery to whom John was entrusted cared about children, no one staff member took responsibility for any one particular child. Moreover, the staff came and went with changing shifts and days off. The other children were chronically institutionalized there and had become expert in aggressively getting as much as possible from the inconstant staff. John, with his background of good individual mothering, attempted repeatedly to reach out to various staff members for the consistent individual care he needed. The changing staff was even more inadequate for John's needs because the other children effectively intruded with demands for a staff member's attention which otherwise would have gone to John. Over the nine days John changed from a friendly child to one who cried and struggled to return home when his father visited. Later he grew alternately sad and forlorn, then angry; finally he withdrew into apathy, ate little, and could be reached by no one who tried to comfort him. He took solace, often desperately and with inadequate results, only in a large teddy bear. On the ninth day his parents came to take him home. The Robertsons described his reaction as follows:

> At the sight of his mother John was galvanized into action. He threw himself about crying loudly, and after stealing a glance at his mother, looked away from her. Several times he looked, then turned away over the nurse's shoulder with loud cries and a distraught expression. After a few minutes the mother took him on her knee, but John continued to struggle and scream, arching his back away from his mother and eventually got down and ran crying desperately to the observer. She calmed him down, gave him a drink, and passed him back to his mother. He lay cuddled into her, clutching his cuddly blanket but not looking at her.
>
> A few minutes later the father entered the room and John struggled away from the mother into the father's arms. His crying stopped, and for the first time he looked at his mother directly. It was a long hard look. His mother said, 'He has never looked at me like that before' (p. 293).

We shall return to John later to discuss other aspects of our thesis. But first let us clarify John's rage experience and its possible relationship to the kinds of rage that occur with adult borderline patients.

When we evaluate the childhood literature and attempts to apply an understanding of childhood rage reactions to rage in adult patients we shall postulate two varieties of rage that occur in response to feelings of abandonment: (1) recognition memory rage and (2) diffuse primitive rage.

Recognition memory rage applies to the child who, in his mother's too prolonged absence, has regressed to Piaget's stage IV, designated by Fraiberg as the stage of recognition memory. His loss of his mother's real presence leads to a rage at her followed by a loss of her comforting image. With her continued absence he finally withdraws into quiet despair. When his mother eventually reappears, his recognition does not bring joy. Instead all the rage over abandonment is remobilized and attached to her image. He hates and rejects her, much as borderline patients are wont to do; he might make extended attempts to ignore her, in the manner of the schizoid patient. However, he maintains a recognition memory capacity for her.

Diffuse primitive rage applies to the little child who regresses beyond stage IV, i.e. to a loss even of recognition memory. Characteristically his rage is much more diffuse and not confined to his mother; discharge is much less controlled, and panic is a prominent element. To heal the trauma, such a child may need his mother continuously, for he has lost recognition memory for her and requires prolonged physical and visual contact with her in order to know that she exists. Of course, her presence will evoke diffuse anger and rejection for a long time, but her very consistent presence including her empathic tolerance for his anger and rejection is essential if he is to reestablish the peace-giving equilibrium that is promoted by regaining the recognition and evocative memory capacities for her.

It seems to us that continued intense rage itself is a central contributor to the more extensive regression from recognition memory rage to diffuse primitive rage. The little child who experiences recognition memory rage is inclined, especially when exposed to his mother or father for tantalizingly brief intervals, to experience an ever-towering rage of a kind which can only be called annihilatory. Annihilatory rage toward the parents has the effect of destroying the parents in the child's fantasy, of smashing them and ejecting them out of his fantasy life, so to speak. This experience very much escalates his sense of abandonment and has the effect of further destroying his memory of them, i.e. of propelling his regression back to stage III or even earlier, and can leave him with a feeling of intense desperate aloneness and panic.

The stage of recognition memory rage is a higher developmental level than that of diffuse primitive rage. With recognition memory rage, the child (or adult) can actively blot out the image of an important person at whom he is angry even though he recognizes that person. In addition, he might utilize the defence of identification with the aggressor, angrily rejecting an important person for the fantasies of rejection or real rejections he has incurred from that person. In contrast, diffuse primitive rage is a much more uncontrolled, objectless, panicky state that does not include these defences.

When we examine John's nine-day separation from his mother in the context of the work of Piaget, Fraiberg, Winnicott, and Tolpin, we can postulate that at 17 months, John was well on his way towards an evocative memory capacity; however, the loss of his mother for nine days without adequate replacement precipitated a regression which the Robertsons (1971) and Bowlby (1969) would describe as movement from protest to despair to detachment. After many efforts to get the care he needed from the nursing staff, he was reduced to crying and temper tantrums, then sulking and finally withdrawal. Intermittently he turned to a large teddy bear with which he tried desperately to evoke an experience of being soothed. In our framework, it appears to us that John regressed from a nearly achieved capacity for evocative memory to an earlier level of development: recognition memory and nearly exclusive reliance on a transitional object. His inability to be comforted and the look he finally gave his mother can be understood as representing recognition memory rage. When John recognized his mother, the rage he had earlier manifest, before regression to stage IV, came bursting forth: he gave her a 'long hard look', then resolutely turned away from her and clutched his blanket. This recognition memory rage also seems to include active avoidance of her and an identification with the aggressor. The same kind of rage, with detachment and tantrums, continued through the first weeks after he returned home. In the Robertsons' paper, John is contrasted with other children of his age who were placed in foster homes where the needs of the child were well understood and met; for them such regressive behaviour was minimal.

The vulnerability of children to deficiencies of good enough mothering extends beyond the first year of life clearly into the second year and even later. For borderline patients the developmental issues of the second year may be particularly crucial and partially determine the degree to which later borderline vulnerabilities may become established (Mahler, 1971; Mahler et al., 1975; Adler, 1975; Masterson, 1976).

Mahler's contributions to the literature on early childhood development especially clarify the vulnerability of toddlers to inadequate or unavailable mothering. She describes important changes which begin to occur in the toddler at about 15 months of age. These children previously could explore their environment with confidence and vigour, returning to their mothers only in times of need for food, comfort, or 'refueling' when tired or bored. However, at about 15 months of age their skillful locomotion can carry them far away from mother; other skills they acquire mean that they can dispense with some of her ministrations. Acquiring stage VI of sensorimotor development not only allows the permanence of object concept and evocative memory but also brings clearly to the toddler's attention the fact of psychological separateness from his mother. These developments—individuation, in Mahler's language—inexorably bring about a greater degree of separation than he can tolerate. He now becomes increasingly concerned about his mother's exact whereabouts. His behaviour alternates between stout independence and clinging, and in his mother's absence he becomes restless and concerned. At times he wants his mother to fulfil all his needs magically. Mahler has called this interval between 15 and 25 months the rapprochement sub-phase. During this time the child is particularly sensitive to the physical and emotional presence or absence of mother; he has renewed difficulty in leaving her, especially when compared to the ease with which he would toddle away towards new explorations in Mahler's preceding 'practising' sub-phase. During the rapprochement sub-phase, much is demanded of the mother's flexible empathic responsiveness to her child's varying and contradictory needs because children at this stage are particularly vulnerable to inadequate empathic maternal responses. When we consider 17-month-old John in the light of Mahler's observations, we can hypothesize that he lost his mother early in the rapprochement sub-phase, a time when he especially needed her empathic responses. The fact of her loss in this sub-phase may account for a portion of the devastating intensity of his reaction and regression, even though he was separated from her only for nine days. This review of contributions by Piaget, Fraiberg, Bell, Mahler, and the Robertsons suggests that permanent vulnerability to loss of supportive persons and pathological need for nurturance in adult life can be the result of traumatic experiences during the infancy and toddler periods of development. In a follow-up report over several years, the Robertsons (1971) describe how John reacted for a while with rejection of his parents alternating with destructive outbursts of angry demandingness. When Mrs. Robertson visited to gather follow-up information, this regressive behaviour exacerbated more markedly. Irritability and over-sensitivity to his mother's absences continued for some time. At the age of 4½ John was observed to be a happy lively child, but heightened concern about losing his mother continued, and every few months he had bouts of unprovoked aggression towards her. In reviewing these data, Anna Freud (1969) concluded that traumatic separations which appear brief from an adult's viewpoint can cause permanent severe vulnerability when they occur at critical times in the child's development and in the absence of support by adults who are empathically available as 'good enough mother' substitutes.

The case of John represents the effects of acute traumatic loss. It is equally clear, we think, that sub-acute traumata as well as chronic failure of good enough mothering will exert the same kind of effects on development. Our clinical experiences suggest that it is especially the chronic failure of good enough mothering during the child's early individuation, i.e. the second year of life, that eventuates in the psychopathological constellation in the adult which we would call the borderline personality.

We have presented this detailed formulation of the borderline patient's vulnerabilities because we feel that they must be directly addressed in any treatment plan, and, of course, in a discussion of the process of change in psychotherapy. However, we are very aware that we have had to oversimplify a complex field which contains many important contributions to which our concepts can be related.

Otto Kernberg's (1966, 1967, 1968) significant work illustrates this complexity. He has brought clarity to a confusing literature and has provided a rich multidimensional view of borderline personality organization. His definition of such defences as splitting, projective identification, primitive idealization, denial, omnipotence and devaluation as basic to borderline patients can add a further dimension to our understanding of evocative memory concepts. As Kernberg states, splitting keeps libidinally determined affects and self and object images apart from those which are aggressively determined. Utilizing the concept of splitting to clarify the development of recognition and evocative memory capacities, we can postulate that recognition and evocative memories are not necessarily pure, accurate images for the child of, e.g. mother. The child's perceptions are coloured by positive and negative affects and experiences which become part of these memories. Therefore, when we study the developmental line of evocative memory capacity, we have to consider how positively and negatively charged memories which grow out of splitting, projections, and projective identifications are reconciled. The highest development of evocative memory capacity must include the synthesis of positive and negative affects and memories into an evocative memory of the parent as someone the child both loves and hates yet maintains his libidinal attachment in a real, sustaining relationship. The capacity to maintain a libidinal attachment to an object while experiencing frustration (defined as object constancy by Anna Freud, 1960) depends upon this internal synthetic capacity. The maturing evocative memory of mother is one in which loved and hated images are synthesized into a coherent remembered image that functions as an internal source of sustenance, i.e. splitting no longer functions as a major defence at the point that high level evocative memory capacity has been achieved.

THERAPEUTIC IMPLICATIONS

When we discuss the clinical implications of our formulations, we emphasize again that aloneness is often a central experience for these patients. It usually begins to become manifest gradually in the transference unless the patient comes to treatment in such a regressed state that the panic of aloneness is already with him. The patient usually becomes aware of feelings of aloneness as he gradually finds the therapist to be a good sustainer, or soother. The therapist need not make direct efforts, for the patient senses that the reliable capacity to sustain is an inherent part of the therapist's personality. The patient relinquishes some of the defensive distancing which he has maintained in various ways to some extent in all relationships. Because he needs it, and sometimes because he has a tenuous trust that is worth the risk, the patient allows himself to depend on the therapist for sustenance of the holding-soothing variety. As he does so, the extent of his felt need which corresponds to the extent of his felt need which corresponds to the extent of his vulnerability to feeling abandoned, comes forcefully to his attention. To varying degrees this need feels overwhelming and uncontrollable as his dissatisfaction emerges that the therapist cannot gratify the intensifying longings that occur in the treatment. Usually it begins as an aimless, joyless sense of something missing from his life in the intervals between therapeutic sessions. Ultimately it develops into episodes of emptiness, preceded and accompanied by a rage which may not be conscious and therefore not verbalizable, felt within himself and in the surrounding environment—an emptiness often called aloneness. And when this experience is intense and accompanied by conscious or unconsciousness rage, it brings panic. We find that this escalating experience almost always centres around being away from the therapist; it reaches such proportions in an uncontrollable way because the patient finds himself unable to remember the soothing affective experience of being with the therapist especially as his anger increases. Sometimes he cannot even remember what the therapist looks like. We would say that he behaves as if he has largely lost evocative memory capacity in this sector of his life.

The therapeutic task is to provide the patient with an interpersonal experience over time which will allow him to develop a solid evocative memory for the soothing, sustaining relationship with the therapist. Clarification, interpretation and sometimes confrontation (Buie & Adler, 1972) are necessary in order for the patient to gain understanding of his frightening experience and make intelligent use of the therapist's help. Then, most crucial, is the provision by the therapist of adequate support to keep the experience of aloneness within tolerable bounds as the underlying issues, including the patient's rage, are examined. Brief telephone calls to augment a faltering evocative memory are often necessary. At times a patient may need to phone briefly several times a day simply to re-establish on a feeling level that the caring therapist in fact exists. When evocative memory fails more completely, extra appointments are necessary. If the failure is extensive, a period of hospitalization with continuance of therapy hours is crucial.

As described, the overwhelming rage of the borderline patient often is the precipitant of the regression to the aloneness we have been defining. Clinically the therapist must constantly assess the patient's capacity to tolerate this rage before the inevitable regression to recognition memory or an even earlier stage occurs. Activity by the therapist that defines these issues, clarifies the meanings and precipitants of the rage, and puts it into terms the patient can discuss, at the same time demonstrates the therapist's availability, caring, concern, and reality as a person who has not been destroyed by the patient (Winnicott, 1969; Adler, 1975). The therapist's repeated empathic assessment of his need to define the issues around the patient's rage while simultaneously demonstrating his own survival and existence supports the patient's faltering evocative and recognition memory capacities. Here too, hospitalization may be required when the therapist's activities in this area are insufficient to stem the sometimes transient overwhelming regression into desperate aloneness.

In the 1974 Tufts Symposium on Psychotherapy the treatment of a borderline man was described in a paper by Buie. Certain details of that case can be recalled now to illustrate the problems of evocative and recognition memory loss in the borderline. The patient's history was characterized by frequent separations of weeks to months from his mother, beginning prior to the age of 2. It was her practice to send him away to a relative in a distant state when for various reasons she found it inconvenient to care for him herself. Even when with him, she was emotionally inconstant, and the relative who took care of him was affectively rather remote. During his early adolescent years, and at other times, he was able to establish periods of closeness to his mother largely by serving her narcissistic needs. When he left home for college he became depressed. This depression turned into panic when he discovered that he could not remember his mother's face (we would say he lost his evocative memory capacity for his mother and may have also used avoidance defences to keep from thinking about her and about his rage at her). He was panicked with aloneness and sought treatment at the school clinic. There he received three years of therapy of an ego-supportive highly directive nature. He reconstituted emotionally, but no work was done with his problems with aloneness; any manifestation of dependency was discouraged by the therapist. After graduation he successfully worked in a distant city for a few years, then returned for graduate studies. His old therapist had left the area, and the patient found himself escalating into an angry and suicidally desperate depression over his absence. He began therapy anew, this time along the lines we have been describing. For a two-year period he struggled with his inadequate evocative memory as his anger in therapy emerged. He increasingly felt that outside his therapy hours the therapist did not exist. The aloneness was intolerable, and he turned to dangerous levels of drinking and sexual activity in an effort to deal with his emptiness and panic. His problem with remembering his therapist was clarified repeatedly, and the patient was encouraged to use the telephone and extra appointments as previously described. He was able to utilize this help and managed his aloneness a little better through re-establishing an affective sense of the presence of the remembered therapist between sessions.

While this particular patient did not require it, there are other ways available to the therapist for helping the borderline patient maintain contact with an affective memory of the therapist during absences. It is one which seems developmentally specifically indicated, namely the transitional object, which is so important to the infant during the time between his recognition of separation from mother and his acquiring the use of evocative memory as a way of maintaining a sense of her soothing presence. Transitional objects specific to the therapist can be useful at these desperate times, such as the therapist's phone number on a piece of paper, a gift (perhaps a book), or the monthly bill (which the patient may carry in his wallet for weeks at a time). During vacations a card with the therapist's holiday address and phone number usually are not used in order actually to contact the therapist but are carried as activators of memories of the absent therapist just as the blanket is used as an activator for remembering the feel of mother by the infant who has as yet acquired only recognition memory. Fleming (1975) recently described how, in retrospect, she became aware that asking a patient to monitor his thoughts while he was anxious over weekend separations was a way of helping him evoke her image. We know of several patients who have spontaneously kept journals about their therapy. Through communicating with their journals they activated the feelings associated with being with the therapist.

We shall digress from this patient for a moment longer to recall that some borderlines will transiently lose not only evocative but also recognition memory. The patient we have been describing could always recognize the therapist once he heard his voice or saw him, that is, he could regain the affective recognition memory of, and sense of support from the therapist. But some borderline patients regress to the point that even when they are with the therapist they are unable to feel, i.e. to 'recognize' his supportive presence—this occurs despite the fact that they can identify the therapist as a person. We also have noted that when covering a colleague's borderline patient during the colleague's vacation, our primary, often sole task is to help the patient retain evocative memory of the absent therapist through talking about details of the patient's experience with him.

To return to the student patient, we have not yet described in detail the role of rage in his therapy. It complicated his use of recognition and evocative memory greatly. This patient would conduct his life in a fairly stable manner outside of therapy for long periods of time, although he felt chronically moderately depressed. Then on meeting the therapist for a specific session he would experience a fury expressed as cold, rejecting rage at the therapist. This rage increased his aloneness, so that he felt himself alone in the middle of a desert, hopelessly stranded. The problem for him was that his rage seemed to destroy his affective memory of the therapist. During this time he dared not look at the therapist because he felt the rage in his glance would shatter the therapist's head as if it were made of glass. He was then prone to regression outside the therapy hours to the level of diffuse primitive rage. Believing that the therapist did not exist, he engaged in dangerous sexual practices which discharged this rage as much as it served to gain some transient substitute supplies. In this state of diffuse rage he drank, but not enough to account for loss of psychomotor control; then he drove with purposeful recklessness, crashing his car into the steel siding of a bridge. He was absolutely clear in his mind about the intensity and diffuseness of his rage and its origin in his inability to feel that his therapist existed at all.

Therapeutic work with recognition memory rage and diffuse primitive rage utilizes clarification, interpretation and confrontation as well as the offers of additional support already described. If these measures are not effective, hospitalization is required until the rage, at least temporarily, is sufficiently resolved.

Frosch (1970) and Chase (Chase & Hire, 1966) believe that helping the borderline patient experience and examine his rage is itself basically therapeutic. We agree with the importance of the patient's experience that his therapist survives his rage (Adler, 1973, 1975; Buie & Adler, 1972). It does seem to be necessary, as Winnicott (1969) wrote, in order for the patient to gain the capacity to 'use an object'. However, in our opinion, the primary reason the rage of the borderline must be experienced and analysed is that the patient and the therapeutic relationship both survive long enough so that the patient can develop full and stable use of his nascent capacity for evocative memory of the sustaining affective relationship with the therapist. We believe that the innate developmental line that leads to evocative memory capacity is mobilized towards maturation once the issues that led to fixation or regression are addressed, whether in the child or adult. For the patient whose development is advanced enough to be called borderline, it is only a matter of sufficient time in an adequately holding and insight-providing relationship for him to be able to correct the defect which is basic to his psychopathology. As one patient stated at a point during which he felt held and sustained in therapy, the experience for him was one in which 'the abandoned child has its due'. By this he meant being sustained through a sufficiently long affective re-living of old issues with his therapist; this included a reconstructive insight-oriented approach.

In the repeated working with the anger that arises secondary to the inevitable frustrations that occur in psychotherapy, we would add that a benevolent cycle is set in motion through gaining increments of evocative memory for the sustaining therapist. With each such gain, the basic cause of anger with the therapist is diminished, and as the anger diminishes, the regressive pressure exerted by the anger on evocative and recognition memory is decreased.

The recognition memory—evocative memory framework can be a useful way of defining issues in the process of change in psychotherapy. It can be utilized to monitor a major task in psychotherapeutic work: the goal of helping the more primitive patient achieve a solid use of evocative memory which is relatively resistant to regression. Once the capacity for affective evocative memory for important relationships is firmly established, the patient has reached the neurotic spectrum of problems. During the vicissitudes of the process of this therapeutic work, the patient can shift from the borderline to narcissistic character continuum. For many narcissistic characters, the capacity to form stable mirror and idealizing transferences (Kohut, 1971) implies a relatively well-developed evocative memory of aspects of the therapist and the patient's relationship with him between sessions.

Patients in the narcissistic character disorder spectrum, many of whom have achieved secure evocative memory capacity, can utilize the safety of the therapeutic holding environment to allow the experiencing of mirror or idealizing transferences with varying degrees of merger with the therapist. The evocative memory capacity of transference aspects of the therapist between sessions permits a relatively stable treatment setting to continue. In contrast, the borderline patient's defective evocative memory capacity can lead to a treatment experience in which the patient's frightening desperation, aloneness, and fury can surface with potential real dangers to the patient and the continuation of the treatment.

The pathway that leads to the capacity to be comfortable by oneself involves the increasing ability to have fantasies (both conscious and unconscious) about positive experiences of oneself with important people in one's life, and to be able to summon up these fantasies when under stress, e.g. faced with a relative or real loss, or loss of a position of esteem.

We have observed a major shift in borderline patients as evocative memory capacity becomes more permanent. Patients who have felt only fury and hardly any positive feelings for parents will gradually begin to remember shared experiences, e.g. with a mother, with sadness. This sadness may also be experienced after the therapist's vacation, instead of the previous fury, numbness, or sense of aloneness. Sustained sadness is only possible with a stable evocative memory capacity. At that point a person no longer experiences aloneness. Sustained memories of positive experiences and disappointments are related to issues of loneliness and longing, and belong to the neurotic and normal spectrum of experiences. When the former borderline patient experiences this true sadness, he is beginning a particularly painful aspect of mourning work. It includes acknowledging, bearing, and putting into perspective (Semrad, 1969) not only what was missing in childhood parental relationships, but also childhood and later disappointments in narcissistic idealizations. Finally he has to face how much was lost in the aloneness of his adult years because he had defensively destroyed or avoided mutually gratifying relationships.

SUMMARY

The experience of intense painful aloneness is a common event in the lives of borderline patients, especially those closer to the psychotic spectrum. This experience is defined as an intrinsic aspect of the borderline personality defect and consists of a relative or total inability to remember positive images or fantasies of sustaining people in the patient's present or past life, or being overwhelmed by negative memories and images of these people.

The development of borderline aloneness is related to a possible developmental failure, defined by Piaget, Fraiberg, and A.-M. Sandler. These workers describe the child's development of object permanence and evocative memory capacity (Piaget's sensori-motor stage VI). We postulate that a major borderline vulnerability is the tenuous achievement of the capacity for affective object permanence and its regressive loss to recognition memory or earlier when under specific stresses. We relate our hypotheses to possible empathic parental failures during the substages of separation-individuation, especially the rapprochement sub-phase.

The treatment implications of our formulations are discussed, with an emphasis on the clarification of the need for the therapist's availability and the use of transitional objects during times of the patient's loss of his affective cognitive capacities. These regressive experiences often emerge as a core transference manifestation during psychoanalytic therapy with borderline patients, and often become the basis of significant therapeutic work.

REFERENCES

Adler, G. (1972). Helplessness in the helpers. Br. J. Med. Psychol. *45, 315–326.*

Adler, G. (1973). Hospital treatment of borderline patients. Amer. J. Psychiat. *130, 31–36.*

Adler, G. (1975). The usefulness of the "borderline" concept in psychotherapy. In J. E. Mack (ed.), Borderline States in Psychiatry. *New York: Grune and Stratton.*

Adler, G. & Buie, D. H. Jr. (1972). The misuses of confrontation with borderline patients. Int. J. Psychoanal. Psychother. *1, 109–120.*

Bell, S. M. (1970). The development of the concept of object as related to infant-mother attachment. Child Develpm. *41, 292–311.*

Bowlby, J. (1969). Attachment and Loss, *vol. 1. London: Hogarth Press.*

Buie, D. H. Jr. (1974). Paper presented at Ninth Annual Tufts Symposium, April 1, 1974.

Buie, D. H. Jr. & Adler, G. (1972). The uses of confrontation with borderline patients. Int. J. Psychoanal. Psychother. *1, 90–108.*

Chase, L. S. & Hire, A. W. (1966). Countertransference in the analysis of borderlines. Read before The Boston Psychoanalytic Society and Institute. March 23, 1966.

Fleming, J. (1975). Some observations on object constancy in the psychoanalysis of adults. J. Am. Psychoanal. Assn. *23, 743–759.*

Fraiberg, S. (1969). Libidinal object constancy and mental representation. Psychoanal. Study Child *24.*

Freud, A. (1960). Discussion of Dr. John Bowlby's paper. Psychoanal. Study Child *15.*

Freud, A. (1969). Film Review: John, seventeen months: nine days in a residential nursery. Psychoanal. Study Child *24.*

Freud, S. (1914). On narcissism: An introduction. S.E. *14.*

Freud, S. (1925). Negation. S.E. *19.*

Frosch, J. (1970). Psychoanalytic considerations of the psychotic character. J. Am. Psychoanal Assn. *18, 24–50.*

Grinker, R. R. Sr., Werble, B. & Drye, R. C. (1968). The Borderline Syndrome. *New York: Basic Books.*

Kernberg, O. (1966). Structural derivatives of object relationships. Int. J. Psycho-Anal. *47, 236–253.*

Kernberg, O. (1967). Borderline personality organization. J. Am. Psychoanal. Assn. *15, 641–685.*

Kernberg, O. (1968). The treatment of patients with borderline personality organization. Int. J. Psycho-Anal. *49, 600–619.*

Kohut, H. (1971). The Analysis of the Self. *New York: Int. Univ. Press.*

Mahler, M. S. (1971). A study of the separation-individuation process and its possible application to borderline phenomena in the psychoanalytic situation. Psychoanal. Study Child *26.*

Mahler, M. S., Pine, F. & Bergman, A. (1975). The Psychological Birth of the Human Infant. *New York: Basic Books.*

Masterson, J. F. (1976). Psychotherapy of the Borderline Adult. *New York: Brunner/Mazel.*

Meissner, W. W. (1971). Notes on identification. II. Clarification of related concepts. Psychoanal. Q. *40, 277–302.*

Piaget, J. (1937). The Construction of Reality of the Child. *New York: Basic Books, 1954.*

Robertson, James & Robertson, Joyce. (1969). Film: John, Seventeen Months: For Nine Days in a Residential Nursery. *Britain: Concord Films Council: U.S.A.: New York Univ. Films.*

Robertson, James & Robertson, Joyce. (1971). Young children in brief separation: a fresh look. Psychoanal. Study Child *26.*

Sandler, A.-M. (1975). Comments on the significance of Piaget's work for psychoanalysis. Int. Rev. Psycho-Anal. *2, 365–377.*

Semrad, E. V. (1969). Teaching Psychotherapy of Psychotic Patients. *New York: Grune & Stratton.*

Tolpin, M. (1971). On the beginnings of a cohesive self: an application of the concept of transmuting internalization to the study of the transitional object and signal anxiety. Psychoanal. Study Child *26.*

Winnicott, D. W. (1953). Transitional objects and transitional phenomena. In Collected Papers. *London: Tavistock, 1958.*

*Winnicott, D. W. (1960*a*). The theory of the parent-infant relationship. In* The Maturational Process and the Facilitating Environment. *New York: Int. Univ. Press, 1965.*

*Winnicott, D. W. (1960*b*). Ego distortion in terms of true and false self. In* The Maturational Process and the Facilitating Environment. *New York: Int. Univ. Press, 1965.*

Winnicott, D. W. (1969). The use of an object. Int. J. Psycho-Anal. *50, 711–716.*

24. Suicide, and the Hidden Executioner

Stuart S. Asch

AUTOBIOGRAPHICAL NOTE

"For many years before I wrote this paper I had been curious and intrigued by the phenomena associated with suicide," Stuart S. Asch *writes. "I am aware of current thinking and the role played by serotonin in the causation of suicide, but the basic fantasies which are probably always associated with the drive have not been completely investigated. As a psychoanalyst I know full well the current thinking that eschews dynamics and involves itself solely with phenomenology. I persist, however, in believing that the fantasies associated with suicide expose deeper levels of understanding.*

"This paper (written actually in 1978) was an attempt to describe an unconscious fantasy concerning suicide. . . . The 'passive victim' of suicide, even in its ostensible violent forms, has always fascinated me. . . . Yukio Mishima has long been an intriguing persona for me. The dramatic suicide of such a 'larger than life' man preoccupied me during the five or so years between his flamboyant and carefully stage-managed death and my paper. His suicide was a clear, true-to-life example of the thesis of this paper."

The first twenty-eight years of Asch's psychiatric career were spent at the Mt. Sinai Hospital and School of Medicine in New York, where he was promoted to professor. Then he joined the staff at the Payne Whitney Clinic, Cornell University, New York Hospital. He was trained in psychoanalysis at the New York Psychoanalytic Institute.

COMMENT

"The fantasy I will elaborate upon is a response to an object loss with an effort to enlist or force the significant object to act as an actual or imagined executioner," Asch begins. B. D. Lewin (1950) had identified three compo-

Stuart S. Asch, "Suicide, and the Hidden Executioner." *International Review of Psychoanalysis* 7(1980):51–60. Reprinted by permission.

nents of what he called the manic triad *thirty years before this chapter appeared: the wish to eat, the wish to be eaten, and the wish to sleep. This was a deeper elaboration of Karl Menninger's three wishes in suicide: the wish to kill, the wish to be killed, and the wish to die (see chapter 2 above). Asch takes up the second of Lewin's components, the wish to be eaten, but in fact addresses much more in the suicidal unconscious. His theme is the recruitment of others in rationalizing and making suicide possible.*

To date little attention has been paid to the fact that many suicides aim at dissolving self-object boundaries toward the fusion with someone else. The "someone else" is often symbolically represented in fantasies of fusion with the sea, the earth, or the vastness of nature. This theme appears in cases of provoked murder, and it is the principal motif *of Melville's* Moby Dick *(Murray 1951, 1967). Though suicidal patients are rarely clinically hypomanic, psychodynamically they often play out Lewin's explication of the manic unconscious in their deaths.*

Asch goes further and addresses the importance of self-object confusion in suicide (Maltsberger 1993) and implies the importance of projective identification in the transference-countertransference exchanges of suicidal patients in psychotherapeutic treatment (Ogden 1979). Suicidal patients commonly distort and project in psychotherapy in order to convince themselves they are hated and rejected in order to render suicide plausible.

This dense paper is outstanding in its development of older psychoanalytic themes as they apply to suicide, and in anticipating later elaborations that help us understand what transpires in the minds of suicidal patients.

REFERENCES

Lewin, B. D. 1950. The Psychoanalysis of Elation. *New York: Psychoanalytic Quarterly.*

Maltsberger, John T. 1993. Confusions of the Body, the Self, and Others in Suicidal States. In Leenaars, A., ed., Suicidology: Essays in Honor of Edwin Shneidman. *Northvale, N.J.: Jason Aronson.*

Murray, Henry A. 1951. In Nomine Diaboli. New England Quarterly *24:435–452.*

———. 1967. Dead to the World: The Passions of Herman Melville. In Shneidman, E., ed., Essays in Self-Destruction. *New York: Science House.*

Ogden, Thomas H. 1979. On Projective Identification. International Journal of Psychoanalysis *60:357–373.*

■

ALTHOUGH there is a voluminous literature on suicide, it concerns itself mainly with the externals—phenomenology, sociological factors, and evaluations of suicide prevention centres. Studies on the intrapsychic conflicts expressed in a suicide act are much less common; these fall into two groups.

One group attempts to provide a systematic and dynamic classification of the specific suicide methods employed. They suggest that each form of suicide—shooting, drowning, jumping, etc.—can usually be found to have its own unconscious meaning (Freud, 1920; Zilboorg, 1936; Oberndorf, 1948, p. 190). The second group of papers which attempt to formulate common dynamic elements in the psychopathology of suicide is quite small. It is with this still insufficiently explored area that the present report deals.

I will attempt to elucidate a specific unconscious fantasy that seems basic to at least one group of suicides, and is possibly an element common to the unconscious motivation of most suicides. The many other disturbances of ego functioning that are seen in the suicidal patient are independent of this thesis and will not be discussed. Because of the difficulties in obtaining sufficiently detailed data on this subject from patients in formal analysis, I will draw on my experience with patients in psychoanalytically oriented psychotherapy, work with psychotic patients, and depth interviews with hospitalized patients; I will attempt to correlate these findings with certain cultural phenomena and with the writings of creative individuals.

The fantasy I will elaborate upon is a response to an object loss with an effort to enlist or force the significant object to act as an actual or imagined executioner. Such suicides attempt restitution by establishing a regressed masochistic relationship whose determining unconscious fantasy is an oral submission to the object—'to be eaten' (Lewin, 1950, p. 104), to be 'tenderly murdered' (Litman & Swearingen, 1972), and 'seduction of the aggressor' (Loewenstein, 1957). I will illustrate the pertinent autistic meanings of such acts by describing several unusual and dramatic suicides with which I am familiar.

Before discussing this specific suicide fantasy in more detail, it may be helpful to review those aspects of the mental life of the suicidal depressive with which we are already familiar.

The classic concepts of depression leading to suicide still derive from the formulations presented by Freud (1917) in his paper, 'Mourning and Melancholia'. The loss of an ambivalently cathected, narcissistic object leads to an identification with this object so that part of the self-representation comes to stand for the object. The aggressive aspects of the ambivalent drives originally directed towards the object are now directed towards the part of the self-representation that has been identified with the lost object. As a result, part of the self now becomes the victim of the aggressive part of the ambivalence, initially experienced as self-criticism and ultimately expressed in the suicide act itself.

As analytical theory evolved, this earlier model of 'aggression directed against the self' became more sophisticated. The development of the dual instinct theory gave new status to the role of aggression in ambivalence, and helped to clarify some of the confusion surrounding the phenomenon of masochism. The introduction of the structural theory explicated the role of the superego, already hinted at in the 1917 paper. Jacobson's (1964) work on the development of the separate images of the self and the object world, and then Mahler's (1968) elucidation of both the meaning and genetic basis of the 'narcissistic object choice,' has made it possible to extrapolate from Freud's deceptively simple formulations of 1917.

One of the many values of Mahler's exposition of the vicissitudes of the early symbiotic relationship of mother and child has been to make clear how in the child's mind his self-representation is never fully distinguished from the object representation of the mother. The degree to which this *combined* image tends to be transferred to the representation of a new object determines the degree to which the individual still treats the new object as if it were part of himself—in Freud's older terminology the degree of 'narcissistic investment' in this object. Clinically, one measure of the individual's original failure to separate and individuate is the extent to which new objects *continue* to represent symbiotic/narcissistic object choices. Much of the meaning of the usual suicidal act can be understood once we recognize that there is frequently a double aim of first cleansing the self, and then uniting (actually *re*-uniting) with an omnipotent love object.

It is the second part of the suicide fantasy, the aim of fusion, with which this paper is concerned. The mental content of the depressed suicide is usually preoccupied with self-critical thoughts. (Either *he* is no good, or the criticism is limited to a specific part of the self-representation as being no good.) Although his suicidal aim may be *in part* to punish the self, its primary goal is to cleanse, to rid the self of the 'bad part': 'the act, successful or not, is fundamentally an attempt at exorcism' (Alvarez, 1972, p. 110). He is then purified, either through the punishment or the removal of the bad part by the suicidal act. Now he can be loved by the significant object once again.

Variations of these aims are frequent. For example, it appears likely that with the more psychotic patient, the fusion fantasies are more significant and may even be conscious, e.g. the common fantasies of becoming a part of God, of entering the secret kingdom, etc. It is clinically important to recognize that such individuals can commit suicide without the depressed mood and self-criticisms of the usual suicide (Asch, 1966).

Similar motivations are sometimes found as part of a group process, without psychosis. To the extent that they are shared *mores* rather than idiosyncratic autistic fantasies, they may be part of a common 'reality', as in an organized religion. The early Christians welcomed death and even provoked their own martyrdom in order to reach God before they might be overly tempted to sin. (It was not until St. Augustine's teachings in the fifth century that the church came to consider suicide as a sin.) The 'altruistic' suicides in Durkheim's (1951) classification include this group. We would similarly include the Buddhist monks who immolate themselves. Inevitably the argument is advanced that certain suicides are 'realistic', i.e. appropriate ways of dealing with some inevitable and unacceptable reality. Examples of terminal cancer patients, or of the suicide of whole troops of soldiers in early history when facing defeat (and torture) are often presented (e.g. the Masada experience). While the suicide of the cancer victim may be in fact a realistic solution to an irreversible reality, we have become sufficiently familiar with the mental processes of such patients still to be able to discern elements of the familiar fantasy of getting rid of a painful aspect of oneself and finding 'peace' by dissolving into a blissful sleep.

The unconscious determinants of such aims are not difficult to discern. The helpless, passive role is shifted to an active 'identification with the aggressor', 'fate' is thwarted, the cancer is cheated of its death power. Since the fantasy includes getting rid of the pain, the sick part is eliminated and the purified self is left to 'rest peacefully'. Aggression directed towards 'fate' or the family remains a major element in all suicides. Although the anger is often obscured by the act, it may be overt. As an example, a man who had been ill for some time was told after several operations for a painful cancer that the malignancy could no longer be contained. He then committed suicide. However, more than just this 'reality' would be needed to explain his choice of method—shooting himself through the head in his living room, to be found by his family with the walls and furnishings splattered with tissue and blood.

The sense of helplessness has often been emphasized as the contral core of depression. It is often the most obvious symptom and experienced so painfully by the patient that many analysts have accepted uncritically Bibring's

(1953) concept that depression is produced by a primary ego state of helplessness. However, Bibring offers no explanation of why this primary state of helplessness occurs. It seems to me to be more valid clinically to view this as a reactive helplessness, as the *conscious* affective response to an *unconscious* submission to the special passive masochistic role I have been describing.[1]

THE SUICIDAL FANTASY

The category of suicide of which I am writing deals with both the form and content of the fusion fantasy. Examination often reveals certain elements in such fantasies that appear with some regularity. The conflict over the internalized ambivalently loved object is externalized—displaced and projected onto outside objects:

A. Specific psychic structures are externalized and anthropomorphized.
B. The protagonist views himself passively as a victim (a role he may either seek out or resist).
C. The fantasy involves two people.

With the delineation of these elements, the suicidal act can be understood as the acting out of a fantasy in which the bond between two people is recaptured through regression to a sado-masochistic relationship in which the suicide views himself as the 'passive victim' of an externalized superego (Menninger, 1936).

A. Externalization of the Intrapsychic Conflict

The suicide's aim is to resolve his intrapsychic conflict. He does this by first externalizing some or all of the depressive constellation. The displacement and projection of the various elements of the superego/self-representation tension help to explain the multiple forms of suicide we see clinically (Asch, 1966). With externalization of the ambivalently cathected lost-object part of the self-representation (the introject), the victim of the punitive superego becomes an outside object. As an example, child abuse, battering and assault, or even murder can be understood as an acting out of this kind of displacement. The infant represents the bad part of the self and is the victim of the batterer's (almost always the mother) punitive superego impulses (Asch, 1968).[2]

It is possible and even useful to make further discrete distinctions in the understanding of some of the ancillary phenomena of depression. For example, if the main object of the self-criticism (the hated part) is conceptualized as a part of the body image, the ideation may be manifest in hypochondriasis (Asch, 1966). At times conflict may be acted out with overt attacks on the pertinent part of the physical body, sometimes resulting in actual self-mutilation, i.e. partial suicide. This phenomenon is painfully apparent in those psychotic patients who attempt to get rid of their genitals which have come to represent the 'bad introject', while at the same time the self-castration serves as a punishment for their evil sexual impulses.

Example:

A 16-year-old girl was hospitalized following several suicide attempts. Her most recent self-destructive act had been an attempt to cut out her heart with a knife. The girl was intensely and erotically attached to her father, a ship's engineer whose travels had kept him away from home for much of her life. During several sessions it was possible to relate the suicidal urges to a sequence of seductive play by father, followed by his departure on an extended voyage. Her verbal productions gradually made it clear that in her psychotic thinking, the beating engine of her body, the pulsating heart deep in her chest, had concretely (and *consciously*) come to represent the beating and pulsing of the ship's engines deep in the 'heart' of the ship (her words) where she pictured her father staying.

The familiar and often unstable balance between suicide and homicide is another demonstration of this phenomenon. Stekel (who later committed suicide) is quoted in Friedman's (1967) minutes of the 1910 Vienna Conference on suicide: 'No one kills himself who did not want to kill another, or at least wish death to another'. The final choice of act depends on whether the ultimate victim is internalized (oneself in a suicide) or externalized (the hated image displaced onto an outside person in a homicide). Jacobson (1971) claims that the tendency to externalize conflicts, to act out, and to employ external objects as an aid for failing defences is typical of latent psychotics. This is quite possibly an explanation for the curious phenomena of suicide pacts, which serve acting out *both* roles as the individual kills himself together with the object.[3]

B. The Wish to Be a Passive Victim

Although suicide is unfortunately a familiar enough phenomenon, the importance of the passive aims in the fantasy may not have been sufficiently emphasized. So often the suicide seems to be insisting that he be seen as the *victim* of circumstances, fate, etc. Similar passive submission is part of many cultures. The Mohammedans, for example, ritualize this process of submitting to fate in their attitude towards the Koran, 'It is written'. In addition to its defensive function of turning the impulse against the self, I suggest that such passivity is often a primitive way of re-establishing, in fantasy, a lost (or threatened) object relationship.

The participant in a game of Russian roulette will often name *fate* as his partner who will decide if he lives or dies. The power of life or death, the role of executioner, is thrust onto fate with the implicit thought 'I will *force* fate to make the choice between bullet or empty chamber for me'. Or, in the arena more familiar to our profession, fate is 'forced' to decide if the patient will be found before his sleeping pills take their lethal effect. It becomes clear that eventually fate will be forced to embrace his victim and accept the executioner's role. In our therapeutic work with such patients, the analytic task is to reconstruct gradually the specific hidden by the abstraction; to uncover the object the patient has chosen fate to screen; to trace out the genetic origins of the object he has chosen as his executioner.

It may help to clarify further the suicide's passive aims by examining what seem to be analogous fantasies often associated with creativity.[4] As with the suicide, the active creative role is conflicted, and both libidinal and aggressive drive derivatives are defended against through passivity. The creative individual often experiences his work as being produced *for* him, to some degree outside of his control (e.g. the final structure of the benzene ring 'appeared' to Kekulé, its discoverer, in a dream). The Greeks anthropomorphized this concept through the Muses whose gifts are passively taken in, 'inspired', and accepted by the artist. The artist's forbidden aggressive and covetous impulses to steal from the gods are defended against with the use of passive fantasies. I suspect that the denigration we so often hear applied to some artistic work as being 'too derivative' is part of a reluctance to tolerate in others their stealing from the gods. The myth of Prometheus, who stole the fire of the gods for man, is a version of the cautionary tales told to children: One must not steal from the gods (or from our parents, of course), or our livers (or other valuable parts) will be torn out.

C. Dyadic Element in Suicide

Many suicides become more understandable if one assumes as a constant the fantasy of two people being involved. Loewenstein (1957) has already described a similar fantasy device in masochism, 'what is characteristic for the masochist's enjoyment of suffering and humiliation is a tacit but essential pre-requisite: namely, that the sexual partner participate in the sexual scene or masturbatory fantasy'. Obsessional manoeuvring to modify aggressive drives occasionally results in such elaborate suicidal dramas that they can be useful to illustrate this thesis.

Two clinical examples:

Several years ago, I was asked to provide a psychiatric explanation for a medical examiner's case of an unusual suicide. A 19-year-old boy had fatally shot himself on a rubber raft drifting out to the ocean. After apparently paddling out to the open sea from the bay, he had succeeded in tying himself up so that he was forced to lie with his left breast facing the muzzle of a gun he had previously tied to the raft. A clock had been wired to the gun trigger, but with its face turned away so that he was unable to see the time. In addition, he had connected a tube to the inflated portion of the raft, attached in such a way that it would be severed by the shot at the instant the bullet entered his heart. It seemed reasonable to assume that the intention was to be shot while he was a passive, helpless victim, not even knowing *when* the gun would be fired. This shot would perforate the raft which would then sink and he would be swallowed up by the open sea and disappear. Once having set up the apparatus, he played no further active role.

The plan worked well enough, up to a point. The shot was fatal but the hole in the raft inadvertently sealed itself over with a loose flap of rubber. Although the raft and its grisly burden were carried out to the ocean it did not sink and was sighted by a police helicopter and brought back. The arrangements were so elaborate, the victim's position so helpless, it was understandable that even the medical examiner's office initially suspected murder rather than suicide (i.e. accepting the victim's implicit fantasy as real). This man had succeeded to a fair degree in sufficiently altering reality to fit his *probable* fantasy of being a passive victim and to implicate some unknown person as his murderer. (An additional macabre feature that could not be readily explained was that he painted everything black—the raft, the paddles, the clock, the gun, even his clothes and himself. Dr P. Luloff has suggested this was inspired by a suicidal rock song of the period, 'Paint It Black' sung by the Rolling Stones, that contains many elements found in this case.)[5]

A second clinical example required less reconstruction and speculation since the suicide attempt failed and it was possible to get confirming data from the patient. This young man, who worked as a hospital orderly, succeeded in setting up an elaborate I.V. drip of barbiturates into his own arm. The apparatus was activated by a small mechanical pump that automatically fed him the drug slowly but continually. The patient was discovered quite fortuitously and recovered. Thus, it was possible to discover that the stimulus for the suicide was a homosexual rejection. The suicide was set in motion—provoked—by the lover's desertion. The suicidal act through its accompanying fantasy, re-involved the lover, having him infuse the patient passively with a special fluid. On a deeper level, I would infer that the suicide fantasy in common with many similar, more familiar homosexual fantasies, involved manipulating the lover to fuse and merge with his victim.

It has been mentioned above that the silent partner in the suicidal act derives from the object relationship that originally had been internalized. An ego ideal derived from an identification with a masochistic parent tends to perpetuate similar submissions and sufferings in order to be loved (Asch, 1976). By externalizing the conflict, with re-projection of both the primitive and ego ideal elements of the superego, moral masochism is avoided. Instead of experiencing the painful affect of guilt as a result of internal conflict, the external object is allowed to attack. As we have seen, 'fate' becomes the executioner; 'death' takes over.

It may help to conceptualize this hierarchy of superego stability or autonomy by schematizing it as follows: an autonomous, mature superego can be discerned in a fully integrated conflict, as for example in the conscious decision, 'I would like to smoke a cigarette (or have that extra dessert) but *I* don't think I should so I won't'. *Partial* autonomy is revealed by these thoughts: 'I want to smoke (or eat more) but part of me makes me feel guilty', or, 'A little voice says I shouldn't'. And finally, with minimal internalization, '*They* will punish me, think less of me, if I give in to these temptations'. The 2-year-old child who cautions himself out loud, 'Johnny mustn't touch this' as he approaches the parents' precious vase in the living room, has not yet fully internalized the parental prohibitions. He still derives these prohibitions from outside himself, and by saying it out loud to himself, he is at the same time trying to keep his parents with him.

In some masochistic perversions, the relationship to externalized superego elements is more easily recognized because the chosen partner is *required* to act out his role. This is in contrast to the moral masochist whose intrapsychic conflict remains internal. The masochist avoids Prometheus' punishment for having stolen the fire from the Gods by provocation—until the object 'gives it to you'. He gets what he wants without taking Prometheus' route and stealing. In this way he can avoid either destroying the object (in fantasy) with his aggressive act, or feeling the guilt associated with an active role. At the same time the need for punishment is similarly satisfied. Litman & Swearingen (1972) have described a series of patients with masochistic perversions who would require an *actual* partner to hurt them; fantasy was not enough. One of their patients had the 'guiding sexual fantasy of being attacked and tenderly murdered'.

Freud's (1917) 'criminal out of a sense of guilt' similarly tries to force an outside agent to play the role of punisher. Such patients do this with the hope that the external agent will be less severe than their internal oppressive conscience. These criminals commit crimes in order to be punished, to alleviate guilt over unconscious infantile aggressive impulses towards the parent. However, one can also recognize the additional aim of forcing the object into a sado-masochistic relationship. This fantasy frequently appears in the therapy of depressed patients at some point. Any idea that the analyst is withdrawing some of his support, or not proffering enough 'love' results in the familiar (implicit or explicit) blackmail: 'Unless you do such and such (see me more often, don't take this vacation, etc.), I will commit suicide'. The implication is clear. 'If I commit suicide, it is because you have failed me. You are my executioner.' The analyst as executioner has become both the externalized manifestation of the punitive part of the superego and also, perhaps more importantly, the parent of infancy, the ambivalently loved lost object.

In his play, 'After the Fall', Arthur Miller (1964) re-enacted with painful verisimilitude, the burden of the ambivalent conflict for the person onto whom the suicide has forced responsibility. The wife in the play is a recurrently depressed woman who has made multiple suicide attempts with pills. Each attempt has followed a clear warning to the husband. Each time her life has depended on his rescuing her by calling on medical aid and instituting heroic life saving measures. The audience is involved in sharing with the protagonist the last such episode when the wife has overdosed, once again, and again has left it up to the husband to decide whether or not to get help. This time, after an agonizing internal battle, the husband refuses to accept his assigned role and she dies. Tarachow (1960) discussed a similar theme as found in the New Testament. During the Last Supper, Jesus prophesies that one among the group will betray him. He then puts his 'sop' (the unleavened bread soaked with wine) directly into Judas' mouth indicating that *he* will be his betrayer. Tarachow states, 'Jesus, as Father, bids Judas, as son, to kill and eat him'. Once the object *is* provoked successfully, once he has 'accepted the sop', he is perceived to have accepted the role of the original hated-and-loved rejecting object. The suicide can now proceed, with the fantasy that the object is bound to him regressively in a sado-masochistic fusion. Straker (1958) has even suggested that the suicide wishes to die in order to gratify the hostile wishes of another person with whom he is involved. Federn (1929) (who was himself a suicide much later) said, 'Only he who is wished dead by someone else kills himself.'[6]

In our psychotherapeutic work with suicidal patients, the therapist is always vulnerable to being provoked into negative counter-transference attitudes. The suicidal patient evokes such a response and then seizes upon it to justify his acting out: 'a decisive factor in the successful suicide attempt appears to be the implied consent or unconscious collusion between the patient and the person most involved in the psychic struggle' (Straker, 1958). In one of Freud's case histories (1920) just such a sequence is described. A young girl is walking with her homosexual partner when they meet her father. Enraged, he gives her a 'murderous look', and she responds by flinging herself over a railroad parapet in a serious but unsuccessful suicide attempt. Freud remarks that she 'fell' through her father's fault. In the German, it is pointed out, there is a play on the word *neiderkommen* which means both 'to fall' and 'to be delivered of a child'. Despite the defensive function of her homosexuality, the daughter has succeeded in achieving what was forbidden. By provoking her father's 'murderous look' she has forced him to become at once her impregnator, lover and executioner.

Several years ago, I supervised the therapy of a malignantly suicidal girl of 27 during several of her many hospitalizations.[7] Her father, a pharmacist, had committed suicide with cyanide when she was 13. Within a week of *his* suicide, she made her own first attempt by taking all the pills in her medicine cabinet, and was comatose for several days. Since then she had made repeated serious attempts each time a relationship was about to end.[8] The patient was finally hospitalized following one such attempt and was worked with intensively. Had the malignant identification with the dead father (who also had had seven close relatives who committed suicide) not been a sufficiently imposing therapeutic obstacle, the mother was a chronically depressed alcoholic, and at best an unreliable nurturant figure. In the transference, the patient was never fully convinced that her therapist was a reliable or consistent object. Each time it was felt that she might be managed on an out-patient basis because a 'good' relationship with her therapist seemed to have been established, she made another suicide attempt. Finally, all looked well and when even she overtly agreed, a discharge date was arranged. On that morning she presented her doctor with a gift of a box of chocolates (namely: the sop to Judas), went to the regular morning group on the ward where she extolled his virtues, and then collapsed. Apparently she had stolen an enormous amount of drugs the night before and took them just before she gave the doctor his gift. She was saved only by heroic measures and spent several days in the respirator, but then tried suicide again just before transfer to another hospital. I had been able to follow her path for a while before I lost track of her; each attempted discharge from each hospital was associated with a serious suicide attempt.

The patient had been constantly searching for an antidote to the depressive pre-oedipal mothering objects, using multiple affairs with faceless people, and a clutching transference. But each time she *had* to prove these objects were not reliable, she had to justify her rage at the original object and, therefore, needed to provoke rejection. This explains the attempt to force the therapist into the mould of the lost introject—to set up the therapist as executioner—('see, you *too* are like all the others. You *say* you are different, but you are just like father, mother, etc. You too disappoint me'). Thus, suicide becomes a justified murder of the introject—'dying someone in effigy'; 'Employing the strange human capacity to merge, or interchange, or even confuse oneself and the object' (Stone, 1971). It is both a suicide *and* an execution directed by the therapist.

Hara Kiri is perhaps the most familiar cultural ritualization of this process of forcing the object to become the 'beloved executioner' (Tarachow, 1960). The act gratifies both libidinal and aggressive drives, and encompasses both active and passive aims. While usually an act of overt submission to the object's implicit order to die, Hara Kiri often includes a more or less covert aim of shaming the object. (This is similar to the less lethal 'potlatch' ceremony of the Kwakiutal Indians of the Northwest [Klineberg, 1940, p. 84] who shame their wrongdoers through a ritual in which they give them all their possessions.)

Hara Kiri is one of the varieties of suicide that is not necessarily associated with overt depression, and guilt feelings are usually not manifest. Shame is the main affect involved and the suicidal act seems to have the aim of exorcizing the shameful part in order to regain face, be purified and once again be worthy of love by the object. The relationship between the external object and the shameful introject is even more apparent when the Hara Kiri victim throws his extirpated viscera at his object (Tarachow, 1960), establishing the union by contaminating him with the shameful parts. The ritual developed in a culture in which suicide was, until recently, socially acceptable. 'No one circle in the Inferno will boast of greater density of (Japanese) population than the seventh to which Dante consigns all victims of self-destruction' (Nitobe, 1974, p. 123). Seward (1973), in his book on Hara Kiri, quotes from Lord Redesdale, secretary to the British Consulate in Japan in 1868. He describes the role of the 'Kaishaku' whose responsibility it is to carry out the ritual of decapitation after the suicide has completed his own disembowelling. 'In what other country in the world does a man learn that the last tribute of affection which he may have to pay to his best friend may be to act as his executioner?' (p. 19).

Yukio Mishima (1966), the Japanese writer, describes just such a suicide in his short story 'Patriotism'.[9] The piece illustrates all the elements described above. The opening paragraph is worth reading in full, not only for the beauty of the sparse informative writing, but also for the 'sphincter morality' that dictated Mishima's controlled presentation of violence:

> On the 28th of February 1936 (on the third day, that is, of the February 26 incident), Lt. Shinji Takeyama of the Kre Konal Transport Bn.—profoundly disturbed by the knowledge that his closest colleagues had been with the mutineers from the beginning, and indignant at the imminent prospect of Imperial Troops attacking Imperial Troops—took his officer's sword and disembowelled himself in the 8-mat room of his private residence in the 6th block of Aoba-cho, in Yotsuja Ward. His wife, Reiko, followed him, stabbing herself to death.

The suicides are preceded by an intensely erotic love scene which Mishima intentionally juxtaposes in the reader's mind.

> Thus, so far from seeing any inconsistency or conflict between the urges of his flesh and the sincerity of his patriotism, the lieutenant was even able to regard the two as part of the same thing (p. 102).

As has been mentioned, acts of Hara Kiri have a notable lack of manifest guilt or depression, and in fact the preparations for the ritual suicide in the story are associated with euphoria, heightened self-esteem and even sexual arousal.

The externalization of the inner psychic conflict with the displacement onto Death as the ambivalently loved object, and the 'tender murder' are seen in the following passage, as the lieutenant is waiting for Reiko to finish her bath and join him:

> Was it death he was now waiting for? Or a wild ecstasy of the senses? The two seemed to over-lap, almost as if the object of his bodily desire was death itself (p. 103).

The fantasy that he is the passive victim takes over:

> Despite the effort he had himself put into the blow, the lieutenant had the impression that someone else had struck the side of his stomach (p. 112).

The 'executioners' take shape in his mind as he distorts the image of his white-robed wife watching him, 'a vision of all those things he had loved and for which he was to lay down his life—the Imperial household, the Nation, the Army flag. All these . . . were presences observing him closely with clear and never faltering eyes' (p. 111).

It was perhaps progressively inevitable that Mishima would finally commit suicide similarly a few years later in 1970. In his typically dramatic fashion, he had several trusted members of his private army kidnap the Commandant of a regiment of the Japanese Army and then forced him to assemble his troops in the barracks courtyard. On a balcony above them, Mishima began a prepared speech to castigate and shame them for not living up to his ideals. Then, before the eyes of these troops and with his closest friends at his side observing him (as in his story), he plunged the sword into his abdomen and disembowelled himself. He then gave the signal and his most beloved companion, who had stationed himself alongside, cut off his head.[10]

SUMMARY

The suicidal patient often has an unconscious fantasy of himself as a willing but passive victim in a submissive dyadic relationship with 'Death'. Death, or Fate, serves as a screen for the original ambivalently loved lost object, the early parental imago. The fantasized 'passive' role of the suicide is compared with the creative individual's need to experience *his* work as 'inspired'—placed inside him by some magical figure.

It is possible to recognize in many suicidal fantasies a double aim: of first cleansing the self to get rid of the bad parts, and then uniting (actually re-uniting) with the original ambivalently loved object. The 'realistic' suicide of the terminal cancer patient is shown to have similar motivations.

Through externalization of the depressive conflict, the suicide victim supports his fantasy of being swallowed up and fusing with the object by manipulating him into the role of covert executioner. The projection and displacement of various intrapsychic elements of the tension between the superego and the self-representation (the 'introject') can result in a multiplicity of clinical forms—murder, child battering, hypochondriasis, mutilation and finally suicide. Both clinical and literary examples are given.

The management of the frequent 'blackmailing' of the therapist by the suicidal patient is discussed.

Bibring's concept of Depression as produced by a primary state of helplessness is disputed and an alternative explanation offered.

Hara Kiri is presented as a prototypical suicide. Details from the work and death of Yukio Mishima are used as illustrations.

NOTES

1. The conflict over this passive, submissive acceptance of being swallowed up by Death (or whoever personifies Death) is not always responded to with helplessness.

Some of the more assertive forms of suicide can be easily understood as defences against such a surrender. They can be seen as an expression of the need to re-affirm one's omnipotence, to have control over one's life and death, as with Dylan Thomas' (1957) exhortation to his dying father, 'Do not go gentle into that dark night'. This may well be one of the motivations for suicide in the fatally ill (see above), 'in the suicidal act the self, too, regains a feeling of power, and achieves a final, though fatal, victory' (Jacobson, 1971, p. 231).

In the bloody aftermath of the Cuban revolution, where hundreds fell before the Castro firing squads, it was striking to note how many victims, when granted a final wish, chose to give their executioners the fatal order to fire. They controlled their final fate, and perhaps thereby denied their helplessness.

2. There is good evidence that almost all child battering begins in the post-partum period, most likely as part of the mother's post-partum depression (Asch, 1974).

3. There is almost no literature in this area. Ernest Jones' 'Dying Together' (1911, 1912) is the only analytic or psychiatric study of this phenomenon and is unfortunately mainly inferential from a newspaper article.

4. Orgel (1974) elaborated on the connexion between suicide and creativity in his studies on the poet Sylvia Plath, a celebrated suicide.

5.

Paint It Black

I see a red door and I want it painted black
No colours any more I want them to turn black
I see the girls walk by dressed in their summer clothes
I have to turn my head until my darkness goes
No more will my green sea turn a deeper blue
I could not foresee this thing happening to you
If I look hard enough into the setting sun
My love will laugh with me before the morning comes
I wanna see your face painted black, black as night
Don't wanna see the sun flyin high in the sky
I wanna see the sun blotted out of sky black as coal,
I see a line of cars and they're all painted black
With flowers and my love both never to come back
I see people turn their heads and quickly look away
Like a new-born baby it just happens every day
I look inside myself and see my heart is black
I see my red door and I want it painted black
Maybe then I'll fade away and not have to face the facts
It's not easy facing up when your whole world is black

6. This quote is incorrectly attributed by Stengel (1960) to the 1910 Vienna Conference on Suicide which Federn didn't even attend. The actual quote is from an

article by Federn (1929) in the same issue of the journal in which he also reported on the second Vienna Suicide Conference of 1918.

7. I am indebted to Dr. Richard Scharf for the details of this case history.

8. We know that the death, especially suicide, of a close relative around the oedipal or puberty period statistically increases enormously the probability of suicide in later life (Zilboorg, 1937). In one study (Moss, 1963), it was claimed that 75% had suffered a dramatic death or suicide in the family before the end of adolescence.

9. Dr Jules Glenn originally pointed out the relevance of this story to the present topic.

10. Actually, this friend, the Kaishaku, was too inept to carry out *his* part of the ceremony successfully and the beheading of Mishima was finally finished by a second 'back-up' friend (Nathan, 1974).

REFERENCES

Alvarez, A. (1972). The Savage God. *New York: Random House.*

Asch, S. S. (1966). Depression: three clinical variations. Psychoanal. Study Child *21.*

Asch, S. S. (1968). Crib deaths: their possible relationship to post-partum depression and infanticide. J. Mt. Sinai Hosp. *35, 214–220.*

Asch, S. S. (1976). Varieties of negative therapeutic reaction and problems of technique. J. Am. Psycho-anal. Assn. *24, 383–407.*

Asch, S. S. & Rubin, L. J. (1974). Post-partum reactions: some unrecognized variations. Amer. J. Psychiat. *131, 870–874.*

Bibring, E. (1953). The mechanism of depression. In P. Greenacre (ed.), Affective Disorders. *New York: Int. Univ. Press.*

Durkheim, E. (1951). Suicide. *Glencoe, Illinois: Free Press.*

Federn, P. (1929). Selbstmordprophylaxe in der analyse. Z. Psychoanal. Pad. *3, 379–389.*

Freud, S. (1969). Some character-types met within psycho-analytic work. S.E. *14.*

Freud, S. (1917). Mourning and melancholia. S.E. *14.*

Freud, S. (1920). Psychogenesis of a case of homosexuality in a woman. S.E. *18.*

Freud, S. (1923). The ego and the id. S.E. *19.*

Friedman, P. (1967). On Suicide. *New York: Int. Univ. Press.*

Jacobson, E. (1964). The Self and the Object World. *New York: Int. Univ. Press.*

Jacobson, E. (1971). Depression. *New York: Int. Univ. Press.*

Jones, E. (1911). On 'dying together'. In Essays in Applied Psychoanalysis. *London: Hogarth Press, 1951.*

Jones, E. (1912). An unusual case of 'dying together'. In Essays in Applied Psychoanalysis. *London: Hogarth Press, 1951.*

Klineberg, O. (1940). Social Psychology. *New York: Henry Holt.*

Lewin, B. (1950). The Psychoanalysis of Elation. *New York: W. W. Norton.*

Loewenstein, R. M. (1957). A contribution to the psychoanalytic theory of masochism. J. Am. Psychoanal. Assn. *5, 197–234.*

Litman, R. & Swearingen, C. (1972). Bondage and suicide. Archs. Gen. Psychiat. *27, 80–85.*

Luloff, P. Personal communication.

Mahler, M. S. (1968). On Human Symbiosis and the Vicissitudes of Individuation. *Vol. 1. New York: Int. Univ. Press.*

Menninger, K. (1936). Purposive accidents as an expression of self-destructive tendencies. Int. J. Psycho-Anal. *17, 6–16.*

Miller, A. (1964). After the Fall. *New York: Viking Press.*

Mishima, Y. (1966). Patriotism. In Death in Midsummer. *New York: New Directions Publishing Co.*

Moss, L. (1963). Current psychoanalytic understanding of suicide—symposium. New York Medicine *197, 214–236.*

Nathan, J. (1974). Mishima. *Boston-Toronto: Little, Brown & Co.*

Nitobe, I. (1974). Bushido: The Soul of Japan. *Rutland, Vermont and Tokyo, Japan: Charles E. Tuttle Co.*

Oberndorf, C. P. (1948). Which Way Out. *New York: Int. Univ. Press.*

Orgel, S. (1974). Fusion with the victim and suicide. Int. J. Psycho-Anal. *55, 531–538.*

Seward, J. (1973). Hara-Kiri: Japanese Ritual Suicide. *Rutland, Vermont and Tokyo, Japan: Charles E. Tuttle Co.*

Stengel, E. (1960). Old and new trends in suicide research. Brit. J. Med. Psychol. *33, 283–286.*

Stone, L. (1971). Reflections on the psychoanalytic concept of aggression. Psychoanal. Q. *40, 195–244.*

Straker, M. (1958). Clinical observations of suicide. Canad. Med. Assoc. J. *79, 473–479.*

Thomas, D. (1957). The Collected Poems of Dylan Thomas. *New York: New Directions James Laughlin.*

Tarachow, S. (1960). Judas, the beloved executioner. Psychoanal. Q. *29, 528–554.*

Zilboorg, G. (1936). Differential diagnostic types of suicide. Arch. Neurol. Psychiat. *35, 270–291.*

Zilboorg, G. (1937). Considerations on suicide, with particular reference to that of the young. Amer. J. Orthopsychiat. *7, 15–31.*

25. The Devices of Suicide: Revenge, Riddance, and Rebirth

John T. Maltsberger and Dan H. Buie, Jr.

COMMENT

This paper addresses the suicidal patient's confusion between himself and others, and in this sense follows Stuart S. Asch (chapter 24 above). Edith Jacobson (1964, 1971) alluded to this phenomenon, and John T. Maltsberger (1993) has come back to it more recently. With this disturbance in reality sense—that survival is possible even after destruction of one's physical self (the body is believed to represent something alien)—conscious (psychotic) and unconscous fantasies about the nature of death can come into deadly play.

The belief that to die is to become nothing often conceals a wish for deep sleep and fusion. Suicide can represent magical passage into another life (flight rebirth) while punishing and abandoning those who disappoint in this one.

We include this chapter as a help in the treatment of suicidal patients. Interpretation, clarification, and reality testing of fantastic beliefs about death can make suicide less attractive to patients who harbor them.

REFERENCES

Jacobson, Edith. 1964. The Self and the Object World. *New York: International Universities Press.*

———. *1971.* Depression. *New York: International Universities Press.*

Maltsberger, John T. 1993. Confusions of the Body, the Self, and Others in Suicidal States. In Leenaars, A., ed., Suicidology: Essays in Honor of Edwin Shneidman. *Northvale, N.J.: Jason Aronson.*

John T. Maltsberger and Dan H. Buie, "The Devices of Suicide: Revenge, Riddance, and Rebirth." *International Review of Psychoanalysis* 7(1980): 61–72.

■

THAT SOMEONE is destroyed in the act of suicide fixes attention at once. Freud (1915) had noticed this when he pointed out the role of murder in melancholia. It is a fact so self-evident, so gruesome, that psychoanalytic writers on the subject have, for more than fifty years, concentrated on aggressive components. They have tended to see suicide as self-execution, or punishment. They have treated it as the ultimate hateful act set against the self.

Execution suicide is a fairly well understood phenomenon. The unwavering, unforgiving self-contempt of psychotic depressive patients is manifest in verbal expressions of loathing, in hatred of body, in self-mutilation, and, ultimately, in killing.

Some writers have shown nevertheless that suicide may occur for purposes other than punishment. There are those who are fascinated with death, who perceive it as a peaceful refuge, who see self-destruction as the transportation there. For others, death in suicide is the achievement of a magical omnipotent moment, the triumph over necessary human limitations. For most people who destroy themselves, it is probable that self-destruction is an aim, but not the total aim. The fuller, if fantastic, intention is to preserve the essence of oneself for a better life beyond the magical passage of death (Morse, 1973).

The only suicides which will be discussed in this paper are those which can be described as the consequences of psychopathology. Of altruistic, patriotic, or 'rational' suicides, we have no experience, but tend to agree with Voltaire, who wrote to his friend Marriott, 'Not that suicide always comes from madness. There are said to be occasions when a wise man takes that course; but, generally speaking, it is not in an access of reasonableness that people kill themselves'.

The patients from whom these theories and inferences are drawn include a series who successfully committed suicide a number of years ago and who were studied at the Massachusetts Mental Health Center in Boston. Others include psychotic and borderline patients treated by the authors and their colleagues in recent years, as well as those described in the literature.

Suicide is a phenomenon which occurs in a variety of diagnostic groups of which the psychotic depressions are the most egregious in the older literature. The frequency of suicide among borderline, schizoid and schizophrenic individuals recently has attracted increasing attention. The fantasies involved, the purposes implied, and the mental mechanisms involved in suicide, however, do not lend themselves to classification by diagnostic category.

Hendrick observed forty years ago that in no group except for frank psychotics is the capacity for tolerating and effecting introjections so faulty as in schizoid individuals; they are unable to solve their anxiety problems as others do by internalization (Hendrick, 1936). Many such people commit suicide as a consequence of this failure, as we will show; Meissner's recent review of the theory of internalization helps to formulate the difficulties which beset the processes of introjection and identification (Meissner, 1970, 1971, 1972). Why these patients experience such difficulty in achieving necessary mental structure we do not know, and it is quite possible that, in part, the explanation is hereditary. In the cases we have studied, however, disturbances in the mothering relationship are frequent. These difficulties are of the kind that disrupt the developmental step of separating and tolerating separateness from the mother with reasonable comfort. Suicide is a phenomenon of disturbed internalization, an effort to cope with hostile introjects, and to cope with the absence of those comforting inner presences necessary for stability and mental quiet. This we will show in the following discussion.

We intend to survey the principal purposes and fantasies expressed in suicide. The destructive or hate causes come first, not only because they are the most easily discernible and attention arresting, but because they have historically taken first place.

An examination of the hate aspects of suicide allows the wishes expressed in such an act to be divided into two groups. Malicious or revenge wishes constitute the first group. In the second group are riddance wishes, which underlie fantasies of annihilation or destruction (Maltsberger & Buie, 1974).

SUICIDE FOR REVENGE AND PUNISHMENT

That suicide can express a wish to punish others has been recognized for many years. Would-be suicides often daydream of the guilt and sorrow of others gathered about the coffin, an imaginary spectacle which provides much satisfaction. While the contemplation of such a scene is a pleasure in itself, the patient may also consciously entertain the illusion that after the act of suicide he will be present as an unseen observer to enjoy the anguish of those who view his dead body. Such an illusion may be held with such intensity that it supersedes reality in emotional value and forms the basis for action. Dying in such a case may mean killing the body, but not necessarily the mind. Zilboorg (1936) has described spite suicides of this sort, commenting that the patients do not necessarily exhibit depressive symptoms, but may be sadistic, cold and sarcastic.

Menninger (1933) has pointed out that to destroy something dear to another person is an effective means of attack, and that the greatest hurt a mother can endure is to see her child tortured or killed. He points out that when a child, piqued at some reproach or denial, takes his own life, he takes it also from his parents. 'He robs them of their dearest possession knowing that no other injury could possibly be so painful to them.'

The need to punish oneself can also lead to suicide when the demand is for the most extreme deprivation. Just as spite directed outward may prompt a person to abandon others in an act of self-destruction, it may, if turned against the self, require that the victim be deprived of relationships with others. In less global forms the need for self-inflicting pain may find its expression in self-mutilation.

Other individuals may erotize pain, suffering and helplessness, elaborating complex sexual rituals in which torture, hanging and asphyxiation lead to orgasm at the point where death seems imminent. Death is sometimes the result of such masochistic practices. Such deaths properly should be classed as suicides, not accidents, because of the sexual fascination and longing for ecstatic death they evince, even though time after time these victims interrupt their activities just before the lethal moment.

The erotization of death is plain in a case described by Litman & Swearingen (1972), for instance, in which the patient achieved orgasm by being choked unconscious, and delighted in the fantasy of being abandoned while tied up and locked in a small box, a situation he associated with death and dying, obviously symbolic of a coffin.

The craving for punishment in association with sexual activity is frequently associated with guilt for incestuous wishes. Psychoanalytic study of a high proportion of patients reveals minor masochistic trends in adolescent masturbatory fantasies, wherein intercourse is permitted only if some punishment is inflicted. More deeply pathological individuals may personify death as an oedipal lover, so that the punishment of execution is imposed at the moment of imaginary incest (Hendin, 1961; Hoyle, 1968). One woman became enamoured of making and handling nooses which symbolized her father's penis, and death, her sexual union with him (Rizutto, 1978).

SUICIDE FOR RIDDANCE OF AN ENEMY

Punishment fantasies are not enough to bring about suicide except in some psychotic cases. Punishment implies the continuation of a relationship, a state of affairs to which an outright suicide would put an end. Hate, including self-hate, implies not only punitive impulses, but aversive ones as well, and in many suicides the self-aversive force is intense. The wishes expressed include punishment but also the wish for riddance.

Clinical work with suicidal patients reveals case after case in which the patient has never been able to achieve comfortable self-integration, but suffers continually a kind of divided inner life, in which the weak and helpless patient feels himself to be under the constant contemptuous scrutiny of an alien yet inner presence. This relentless scorn and the efforts to resist it are exhausting. At times this presence may become sufficiently contemptuous of the self so as to demand an execution, and the spent self may hopelessly acquiesce.

Freud's original description of this inner division referred to an identification's taking place between the ego of the melancholic and the person of a lost object, with the result that the love and hate directed originally towards the object are now turned around upon the ego of the patient. Afterwards he evolved the structural hypothesis, introducing the superego as a specialized derivative of the ego formed by identification with the parents.

Since 1923 the theory of the ego has expanded, and a special theory of the *self* as distinct from the ego has begun to be elaborated. That the term *ego* has been used in a variety of ways, by Freud and others, was pointed out by Hartmann (1950), who distinguished between the self as one's own person and the ego as a psychic system. Within the ego lie *representations of the self* as well as *representations of objects*. These representations may be conscious or unconscious, and they may or may not correspond to the objectively real nature of the actual self or the actual objects.

Before going further into the matter of riddance in suicide, we wish to be clear about certain terms. By *self* we mean the total of one's own person, physical and mental, as distinct from other persons (objects) outside oneself. Included in the self is the mind and the body of the subject.

Following Hartmann (1939), we would see the mind as consisting of an internal world and an inner world. By *internal world* we denote Freud's mental apparatus of the ego, the id, and the superego; that basic structure of the mind most of which lies beyond the reach of subjective self inspection.

The operation of this internal world is responsible, however, for a subjectively more accessible territory. The internal world presents to the perceptual, observing eye of the ego, the *inner world.* This is the mental zone wherein pictures of oneself interacting with others may be 'seen', moving through immediate experience, fantasy, memory, and dream. We take it to be roughly equivalent to the *representational world* of Sandler & Rosenblatt (1962), who have compared it to the visible stage of a theatre. The theatre, which contains the stage, 'would correspond to aspects of the ego, and the various functions such as scene shifting, raising or lowering the curtain, and all the machinery auxiliary to the actual stage production would correspond to those ego functions of which we are not normally aware.

'Whereas the characters on the stage correspond, in this model, to self and object *representations,* their particular form and expression at any one point in the play correspond to self and object *images'* (p. 134). A self or object *image* is the view of oneself or another at a particular time in a specific situation, remembered, perceived, or imagined. *Representations* (of self or objects) are more enduring schemata than images, constructed by the ego out of the multitude of realistic and distorted images which the individual has had at different times.

Not all object or self images are accessible to the inner eye of conscious inspection. Neither are all aspects of self and object representations available to conscious awareness. Some images, parts of some representations, may be unconscious, and many others distorted. The self and object representations provide the material for all the ego's adaptive and defensive functions, and they are shaped by these functions. Rapaport (1967) says that the inner world, and, by implication, the representations which people it, lie in the force field of the internal world; selective omissions and shapings therefore occur that are the work of the internal world (psychic apparatus). It follows that what one perceives on the inner world's stage may differ from the world of external reality not only at moments of fantasy or dream, but at other times, too, depending on the capacity of the ego for reality testing.

In summary, one may refer to the inner world as a substructure of the ego, that place which is partly available to the ego's 'observing eye'. The self representations and object representations are the contents of this substructure.

The subjective sense of oneself as a continuing individual discrete from objects is the complex consequence of a balancing of self and object representations, memories, perceptions, and affects by the ego. It would not appear to depend on one structure only, but is the result of a dynamic balance of energies, libidinal and aggressive, between a variety of structures. This sense of identity implies that the mature ego is able to keep self and object representations separate, and at the same time to relate them to each other, in fantasy to be sure, but always under the ultimate domination of the reality principle. The *sense of self* is therefore the subjective, conscious consequence of balanced structures, representations, and affects related to and under the control of the ego.

Jacobson (1954, 1964) has suggested that a more precise formulation of the phenomena, observed in melancholia would require us to say that the libido and the aggression which are turned back in the direction of the self after object loss are cathected onto the *self representation* and *not onto the system ego at large.* She further comments that in psychosis, self and object images become fused in ways that completely disregard realistic differences between the self and the object. Thus it becomes possible for the melancholiac to hate and accuse himself as though he were the love object, and for the schizophrenic to be quite sure he is somebody else.

Our observation of suicidal patients has convinced us that they commonly suffer from gross disturbances in the sense of self, and that their aversive struggles are played out between different part-representations of the self. The following note, written by a 23-year-old woman, will illustrate the point.

These last few days were a death-like existence. I am so tired I just want to sleep. My mind, oh, my mind, it's sick. I feel as if I am sinking and I can't call for any help but death. I don't seem to feel as though I want to die. It's like another person telling me what to do. I feel as though my mind isn't connected to my body, and it seems to refer to me as 'you', as in 'Die,' you fool, die'. I feel as though there are two of me, and the killer is winning. When my death comes, it won't be suicide. It's that someone has murdered me. While I am writing this letter, it's like the other part is laughing at me and calling me a fool for writing this nonsense, but it's how I feel. I know it must sound confusing to you, but this is the only way I can express myself. I wish I could have told you many of my confused feelings, but I feel as though you won't understand and believe me and then the other part takes over and goes into therapy for me. I want to destroy that part of me, but I cannot seem to separate myself in therapy to do it, while it's trying to kill me, I'll kill myself and take it with me. You have done your best to help me, but I just couldn't help myself. I'm so tired I can't fight any more. I wish I could tell someone now, but they can't help me, even worse is they won't understand, oh—if they only would understand, it would mean so much, but nobody has ever understood me so how could I expect someone to now. I took those pills before, it was to kill the other part of me, but I really won't die, I'll just wake up and things will be different. That's how I feel tonight, that I'm not really going to die, and the other one is and I don't know how to explain that to you. I seem to be contradicting myself, but I am writing as I feel. So if you are confused, just think of how I must feel. I have used the term Robot to you, it's like someone is hurt up in my head and is using my eyes as windows and controlling me and my actions. Last week during ward meeting when the people were talking, it was like the voices weren't coming from them and I had to keep looking at their mouths to be sure. I can't even explain that one, it's too hard and you wouldn't understand anyway. I don't know why the hell I'm telling you this anyway, it sounds like a bunch of shit all thrown in together. If you think I'm looking for pity through this, you're crazy, because it won't do me any good, for where I'm going I need pity like I need another problem. Well that's it, so have a good laugh. It's on me.

The patient calls attention to the fact that she does not experience mind and body as connected, and that her self-experience is that of two selves, not one. There is the 'me' which wants to live, and the 'killer', which the patient experiences as alien to her self, yet a part of herself nevertheless. It should be noted that both the 'me' and the 'killer' are bent on murder.

The 'killer' as a representation in the patient's inner world appears not to have the quality of an object representation, but to be experienced as a part of herself, i.e. as an inhabitant of her body. It must therefore be understood as a component of the self representation even though it is experienced at the same time as alien.[1]

This state of affairs can be explained by the theory that the patient's self representation divides into two parts. One portion of the division is designated 'me' by the patient, and to it belongs the representation of her mind. The other portion which she calls 'killer' sets itself over against the 'me' portion and seems to control her body. The 'killer' refers to 'me' contemptuously and orders 'me' to die. It seems to commandeer the patient's body for periods of time (the therapy sessions), a hurt alien which has taken over the body and operates it like a robot.

The patient's subjective sense of self remains with the 'me' representation, while 'killer', though connected with the patient's body representation, is experienced as non-self. 'Killer' is therefore a composite creature which, in many respects, resembles an external object, genetically derived from hostile introjects. It is now half expelled by this self division, and it is highly cathected with hate. But it has no body of its own, borrowing its corporeity from a portion of the patient's fragmented self representation. The 'killer', as it were, steals its physical being from the patient herself. The patient splits off her body representation from her self representation and binds it to the 'killer' in order to contrive a physical presence which she may attack.

The struggle evident in this suicide is not just a case of the 'killer' against the 'me'. 'Me' is bent on destroying 'killer' in self-defence, under the force of the psychotic fantasy that an attack on the patient's own body, now integrated with the representation of 'killer', will not result in the end of the

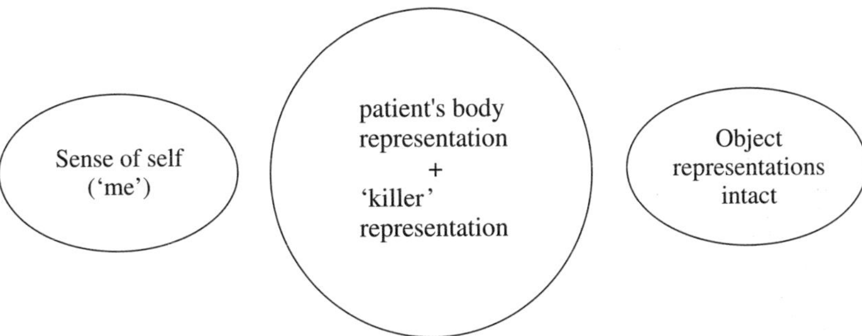

Figure 1: Splitting of self. Representation in suicide, with fusion of body representation with hostile alien presence.

self. 'Me' says the 'other one' will die, not she herself. When the representation of the body becomes separated from the representation of the thinking and feeling 'me' (both are integrated in a cohesive, non-psychotic self representation), the body representation may become fused with the representation of a hostile object, which opens the way to suicidal self-attack.

This model is congruent with the Freudian explanation of melancholic suicide; the hostile inner presence, killer, represents the hated yet loved object, which has become identified with the self (ego). It goes further, however, in suggesting that in some suicides the self representation splits and that the patient's body representation fuses with a representation of the intolerable object. This is represented schematically in Figure 1.

Obviously there are resemblances between this pattern of suicide and certain persecutory phenomena in paranoid conditions (Waxberg, 1956). There, too, we encounter an intolerable persecutory presence which probably again arises from an introjected intolerable early object relationship, possessing the permanency of a mental structure, but not portrayed in the inner world as close to the centre of the self representation. In paranoid cases this hostile representation is capable of more complete externalization than is the case in suicide, so that it may be experienced as a completely alien hallucinatory enemy, or assigned to some object in the form of a persecutory delusion. Here the carping, criticizing enemy does not remain bound to the patient's body representation. It is, once internalized, not experienced as a part of the self, but as belonging to another, real or imaginary. This implies that the hostile inner presence has been split from the self representation, and fused with an object representation within the mind of the paranoid individual. This is represented in Figure 2.

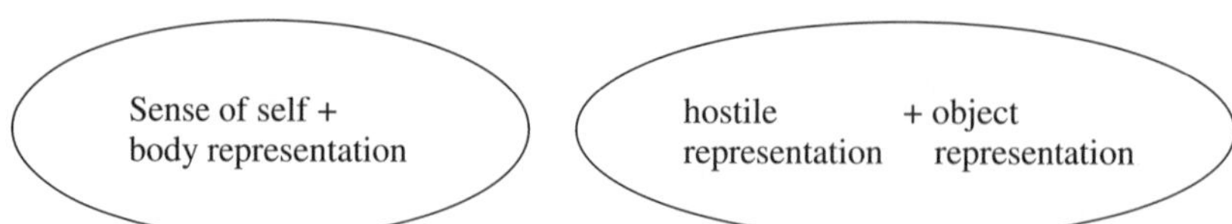

Figure 2: Limited splitting of self representation in paranoid cases, in which hostile representation only is fused with an object representation. Experienced as a persecution from outside.

Less pathological states occur in which a hostile presence is experienced as a part of the self, albeit as an unpleasant, burdensome part. In these states the patient suffers from a chronically nagging and disapproving conscience. He may be annoyed by such unwelcome baggage, fully appreciating that the relentless perfectionistic or omnipotent demands emerging therefrom are unfair and unrealistic. Such a conscience may be experienced as comparatively alien to the self, although the patient readily admits that his conscience is indeed a part of himself. In these cases the critical presence is integrated, however loosely, into the self representation, and recourse to splitting and externalizing is not had.

In any case, both suicide and the murderous attack carried out by a paranoid individual under the influence of a persecutory delusion can be understood as arising from the wish to be rid of an intolerable part of the self, a part which has a developmental history, has a mental structure, is incompletely identified with the self, is highly charged with the energy of hate, and which is represented on the stage of the inner world as an intolerable and exhausting enemy who will either kill or be killed.

We have observed at least one instance in which the patient gave up a persecutory psychosis only to become acutely suicidal. It was as though the intolerable presence of which he sought to be rid had moved closer, across the line dividing the self from the object world, and into the patient, where the angry struggle continued and suicide resulted.

A parallel clinical phenomenon which even more immediately reflects the shift between externalization to internalization has been described by Havens (1962), in which the hallucinatory voice is experienced as drawing closer to the patient's ear as recovery from psychosis occurs, until it moves inside the head, and ultimately is experienced not so much as an alien at all, but as one part of the self addressing the other. In some cases of visual hallucination the body of the patient seems to be fused with that of someone else.

If the subjective sense of oneself is the consequence of a balance of mental

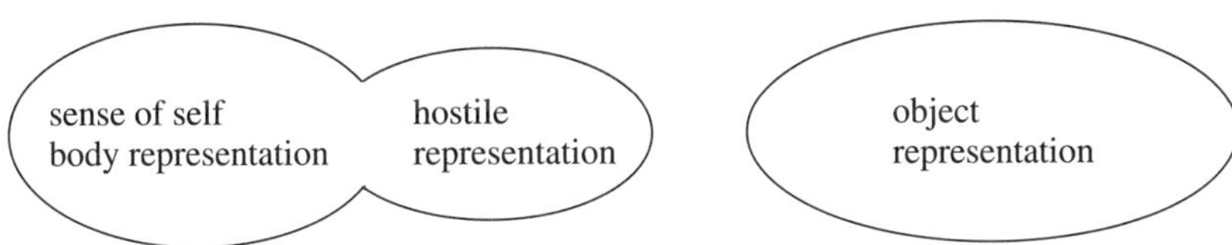

Figure 3: Hostile representation poorly integrated with self representation but nevertheless bound to it. Experienced as an annoying, nagging conscience.

energies between various structures, including those of the inner world, and not on the integrity of any one structure there, it would follow that in psychotic states the sense of the self may organize around a fragment of the self-representation (the body or mental self image of the moment), or even around an object image.

It would also follow that psychotherapeutic intervention which promotes the restructuring of self and object representations may lead to an improved sense of self as the dynamic balance between the various representations shifts. Such a reshaping of the inner world may lead to ego strengthening as the internal world is built up by the identifications which may follow.

Hendrick (1936) has suggested that the economic gain in projection lies in the fact that there is less anxiety associated with being hated by an object than with the idea that the object will retaliate the subject's unprojected hostility. Projection permits a division of the mental representations of the hostile impulse. Incomplete identification, in which a part of the hostility is assigned to an introject held apart from the core of the ego, and a part accepted as originating from the victimized self, may serve a similar purpose. As Hendrick observed, the sum of the total hostility involved in the experience, 'I hate him and he hates me', is the same as that in the experience, 'I hate him', but the intensity is less. Complete identification with the hated introject would break down this division and give rise to overwhelming murderous anxiety as the introject draws closer to the ego core and identification is threatened.

Suicide can be understood as an effort to rid oneself of intolerable hostile impulses originating from within, through attributing them to an inner enemy. Understood in this way, the act can best be understood as an effort to get rid of a part of oneself, but not as an act of total self-annihilation. Total self-annihilation may be the consequence of suicide; it is not primarily the intention in fantasy.

Although suicidal patients may say that they wish to end it all, and, when questioned, even say that in death they would be 'nothing', close examination of the clinical material often reveals that there is a fantasy that life, however transformed, will continue in a better, more peaceful way, beyond the grave.

DEATH AS NOTHING

Nothing is a term of negation, implying the absence of matter, time and space. When a suicidal patient expresses the fantasy that he will through death become nothing, we cannot rest with his manifest statement, but look to the unconscious meaning of the state of being nothing, or *no thing.* The conception of having no physical being is as much an abstraction as the sphinx or the griffin, creatures of the imagination compounded from disparate bits of experience, but not corresponding to anything in the outward world. The 'state' of being nothing lies completely outside human experience. There is no such *state.*

A sphinx is a composite lion and woman. What are the components of 'nothingness'? It can be defined in terms of the conglomerate of the negatives of daily experience, i.e.:

1. The opposite of perceptive capacity is insentience.
2. The opposite of consciousness is unconsciousness.
3. The opposite of physical being is incorporeity.
4. The opposite of having a place in the stream of time is timelessness.

These negatives taken together would allow us to define the hypothetical state of nothingness as a state of insensate, unconscious, bodiless timelessness. But nothingness so conceived remains a *state of being.*

When somebody begins to long actively to '*become* nothing', one may reasonably assume that the abstraction of nothingness has taken on a symbolic meaning, and that some components of the abstraction have become equated with the instinctual aim of an unconscious drive. That a drive operates, we may be sure, because pseudo-nothingness is *desired.* Sometimes the desire is clinically observed in the form of a deep nostalgic yearning. At other times, desire is expressed in terms of surcease from pain, but however expressed, some balancing and weighing of life and death on the scales of pleasure-unpleasure is always detectable.

If this desire is investigated, the clinician may discover that the patient craves the restful oblivion of peaceful sleep. Sleep, of course, really has nothing to do with death. The tendency to equate death with sleep is nevertheless both ancient and universal. The Greeks believed that Hypnos, the god of sleep, and Thanatos, that of death, were brothers. *'Requiescant in pace',* we wish the dead. Keats in the sonnet *To Sleep* calls upon the 'embalmer' of midnight to 'seal the casket of his soul' so that he may escape from a burrowing, mole-like conscience.

While nothingness as an experience is beyond human grip, the oblivion of easeful rest is known to all. It belongs to some of the sleep of adulthood. Pleasant oblivion to surroundings, to perception, to time, to separateness from the greater world outside and the people who populate it is the experience of a sleeping, satiated infant. We believe that this is the state suicidal patients wish to recapture. In their inner world the self representation tends to fuse with the image of the madonna of infancy. By becoming one with her the suicidal patient hopes to taste again the omnipotent, timeless, mindless peace of his baby origins, far from the wearisome hostile inner presences of his miserable adulthood.

The oral erotic value of suffering and death is often evident when the symbolic meaning of a suicidal act is deciphered. Some patients wish to be devoured by their mothers. One woman expressed this idea symbolically in the fantasy of being crushed by a subway train; the clatter of the wheels was associated with the sound of gnashing teeth. Death by being consumed in flame may have a similar meaning, just as the yawning grave may symbolize a mouth (Arlow, 1955).

Mythology offers many examples of ambivalent mother-witches who devour their children only to give them birth again. The Hindu goddess Kali is an excellent example. The earth which swallows all and from which all life emerges has always been seen as feminine in mythology. The great agricultural goddesses of antiquity were not only the divinities of fecundity, but of death, birth and re-entry into the maternal womb.

Not the earth only, but its waters, are common maternal symbols, the words wave and vulva arising from the same Indo-Germanic root, *vel-*. Symbolization of birth and motherhood by the earth and water are not only commonplace in folklore, but repeatedly occur in the dreams and fantasies of patients.

Since in suicide, as in all death, the body returns to the earth, mixing with it so as to become indistinguishable in the course of time, it is not surprising that for many patients death becomes a symbolic means for reunion with the mother of infancy, and a passage of rebirth.

REBIRTH FANTASIES

The fantasy of being born again is ubiquitous in mythology and religion. A comparison of various beliefs and stories reveals the recurrence of certain themes that are parallel to the daydreams of suicidal patients.

Osiris is torn to pieces through the treachery of Set. The fragments of his body are cast into the Nile. In the waters, his penis is swallowed by a fish and carried to a distant land, where the god is reincarnated and reunited with Isis, his sister-wife.

Christ is mutilated and killed. His dead body is placed within the earth (a tomb), from whence he descends into hell, and then ascends into heaven, reincarnated and transformed in new life.

Jonah is cast into the sea. While there is no physical death in this story, he is in immediate danger of it. In the depths of the sea he is swallowed by a fish, only to be spit out later on shore, if not physically reborn, morally and spiritually so.

These and other myths portray common elements of escape from lives of suffering and struggle through physical death. They involve swallowing by a fish or the sea, or burial in the earth. A reincarnation follows, into a life in which great difficulties are overcome and hope is restored in a new beginning.

If fantasy is a trial in thought at problem solving, myth can be seen as the collective expression of commonly shared fantasies. In suicidal patients one encounters three fantasy elements which are also recognizable in myths of death and rebirth. They are the equation of death with the bliss of dreamless sleep, the vision of death as becoming 'nothing', and the view of death as a passage into a new world.

In fantasy, myth, and in fact, to die is to lose the discreteness of one's own body. The dead body is destroyed either through decay or artificially through burning. The result is the same—the physical part of the self which defines us as separate individuals is dissipated into components which rapidly become indistinguishable from the earth, the air and the water. Religions insist, of course, on the indestructability of the individual soul, and while the suicidal patient as much as anyone may entertain the unconscious expectation of being born again, his fascination with death lies not only in the hope of a resurrection. To die is for him to become nothing, to lose all sense of identity and separateness, and to be one with mindless nature. Death is in itself a kind of new life, a fusion with the universe.

Such fantasies of transcendental 'nothingness' are suggested in the literature of most religions, most notably in the Vedic literature of India. The phenomenon of Nirvana is understood as the union of the soul of an individual (Atman) with the universal soul of the universe (Brahman), unseen, immaterial, immanent, ineffable, in which every semblance of individual consciousness and self-object differentiation disappears. The following hymn to Brahman expresses this sense (as does R. W. Emerson's poem, 'Brahman').

Thou art the dark butterfly
Thou art the green parrot with red eyes,
Thou art the thunder cloud, the seasons, the seas.
Without beginning art thou,
Beyond time, beyond space.

One thou art, one only.
Born from many wombs,
Thou has become many
Unto thee all return . . .
Whoever finds thee
Finds infinite peace.

Thou, womb and tomb of the universe,
And its abode . . . (Swetaszatara Upanishad)

The following case will help map out the common territory between religion and suicide.

A 29-year-old woman developed a severe depression with active suicidal impulses. She withdrew from friends, could not work, and intensely wanted to die. Winter weather fascinated her. The wind and snow 'call me out of myself,' she said. She wanted to fuse with them.[2] Sometimes she yearned to be a bird borne up on the wind, and thirsted for the freedom which she imagined death would bring. At other times, she insisted that more than anything else she wanted to be 'nothing'. She was much burdened by a sense of 'emptiness' and 'blackness'. Sometimes it seemed to her as though she would be swallowed up into a deep abyss or vortex, and it was impossible for her to endure the darkness of her room without a lamp burning.

The patient's early childhood had been a difficult one. When she was 3-months-old, the family took in an orphaned baby who was soon sent away. A second orphan baby followed immediately and died in its crib. When the patient was 3 her brother, 5 years older, accidentally drowned. After this, her mother became depressed, withdrew, and the maternal grandmother took over the mothering. The patient, shy as a child and adult, formed few other attachments, and lost her grandmother at the age of 17. She taught at a school briefly, and later lived in a commune of women.

In the course of her treatment, she became aware not only of the wish to become one with wind and snow, but also of the wish to lie in a snow-covered grave with her grandmother as once they had nestled together between white sheets.

Later yet, as the patient was able to be more consciously aware of aggressive and sexual impulses hitherto warded off from consciousness, she was able to identify the wind with her passions, its freedom and caprices symbolizing the wish to live them out uninhibited and without guilt. And if a storm of wind stood for a rage or a moment of sexual abandon, the snow personified qualities of gentleness and purity.

Into the wind the patient had projected unconscious instinctual impulses which she longed to satisfy but which were the source of great guilt. She described herself as 'a volcano' as she became increasingly conscious of her impulses. To die, becoming one with the wind, would mean achieving the gratification, sexual and aggressive, she so much desired, but could not permit, so long as she was trapped with her cruel superego, that inward enemy which suicide would destroy.

Into the snow were projected qualities of gentleness and warmth, recognizable as components of her ego ideal, derivatives from loving experiences with the dead grandmother. To die and to fuse with the pure snow would mean final escape from frightening and repudiated sexual and aggressive forces, reunion with the grandmother by becoming her in death.

The fantasies described here plainly represent strivings not only to join and be with the lost grandmother, but to *become* her. The fantasy is not only of restitution, but of identification in death. Later in her treatment the patient recalled childhood experiences in which her body seemed to blur into that of her grandmother. She became frightened that she might fuse into the body of her therapist, which she, at the same time, wished she could do. She recalled a horror of 'bear hugs' in childhood, and a dread of darkness associated with swirling dark waters and her mother's mouth.

Just as the beauty of nature was unconsciously associated with images of the good mother-grandmother, the 'blackness' and 'emptiness' which troubled her we came to understand as derivatives from unconscious images of the bad mother. The patient drew a series of pictures in which she first showed herself, a tiny stick figure, about to topple into the mouth of an abyss. This reminded her of her fear of the dark. Later the abyss was replaced by an obese bad mother, clutching the patient to herself in a greedy 'bear hug', while the little stick figure struggled to get away, in terror of being drawn into the vast dark hollowness which she believed was contained inside the mother's huge hulk. She was afraid of fusing, of being engulfed. These fears appeared in the transference as well and were available for reality testing and working through.

Suicide for this patient can be seen as a flight from a 'bad nothing', the empty void of the devouring and engulfing mother imago with which the patient dreaded to fuse. It further represents a flight to the 'good nothing', the external world of snow and wind, linked in memory to the living grandmother, arising from the imago of a loving madonna.

Into her diary the patient had copied some of Psalm CXXXIX:

> Where can I escape from thy spirit?
> Where can I flee from they presence?
> If I climb up to heaven, thou art there;
> If I make my bed in Sheol, again I find thee.
> If I take my flight to the frontiers of the morning
> or dwell at the limit of the western sea,
> even there thy hand will meet me
> and thy right hand will hold me fast.
> If I say, 'Surely darkness will steal over me,
> night will close around me'.
> Darkness is no darkness for thee
> and night is luminous as day;
> to thee both dark and light are one.

Suicidal individuals struggle not only with the problem of ill-integrated hostile introjects, but also lack well-integrated identifications with good introjects. To be without such identifications is to lack the necessary structure to maintain reasonable self-respect. Furthermore, without appropriate comfort-giving identifications, it is not possible to rest easy when alone unless the structural deficiency is compensated for, either by another person who provides narcissistic support, or by sufficient distortion of the external world so that a grandiose self-view is maintained (Hendrick, 1940).

Kohut (1966, 1968) and Tolpin (1971) have described the development of those parts of the self which are necessary for narcissistic balance, i.e. the capacity to experience solitude in tranquillity, and to bear the vicissitudes of separation and loss. Through the process of transmuting internalization, the experience of the comfort-giving mother is introjected, and ultimately built into the very core of the self (ego) by the process of identification. In some patients, such as the woman just described, this internalization did not adequately take place in the course of development. Without essential comforting internalizations and beset by hostile introjections, they remain in a state of precarious narcissistic balance. They are often vulnerable to suicide in the face of object loss or failure of the distortion system used to support a grandiose self-view.

The suicidal patient finds the state of adult separateness a source of constant anxiety, the consequence of developmental failures specifically in the phase of separation from his mother. Were death seen as a perpetual state of the same wretched solitude, the continuation of the chronic affective misery of daily living, such individuals would never seek it. Indeed, many people, imagining death to be a perpetual isolation, have a horror of it. The suicidal patient, however, sees death not as a separation, but as its opposite, union and fusion with the great mother, leading to infinite peace (Friedlander, 1940).

Suicide can be understood as a regressive quest to restore the state of primary narcissism, one aspect of which is the sense of oceanic omnipotence. Zilboorg (1936) emphasized the grandiose aspects of suicide.

Failed identification with the comfort-giving mother not only renders a patient vulnerable to intolerable feelings of aloneness, but opens the way to extraordinarily intense feelings of helplessness as well. In normal individuals the narcissistic shock that results from the loss of some physical or intellectual power is manifested by a sense of anger and grief accompanied, however, by the awareness that one has not been rendered utterly helpless and worthless. Is this resilience related to the fact that in early childhood, when one was comparatively weak and incompetent, comfort was at hand, and love was consistently offered? We believe so.

When childhood powerlessness and early incompetence were endured more or less alone, without the necessary narcissistic succour, the adult may be ill equipped to ensure the loss of his powers later. We have studied one patient whose lifelong excellent (if highly narcissistic) adaptation deteriorated into a suicidal crisis when old age brought a loss of physical and mental prowess. He felt that suicide was a way to 'beat the game' and to escape the dependency and incompetence of the senility he imagined for himself with such horror.

We have had no opportunity to study a so-called 'rational' suicide, carried out to avoid the anticipated ravages of incurable illness. It may well be the case, however, that those who accept such illnesses and live out their lives to the last moment, however helpless and painful, have had happy infancies, with helping and caring mothers who made a frightening and overpowering world somehow bearable, and taught the first lessons of hopeful endurance.

Suicide can be understood as an effort to deal with failures in internalization. The hating introject, poorly integrated and always alien in some degree, calls out for the execution of an evil self. The perpetual menace of the hating introject may prompt the self to attack in order to be rid of a persecutor. Death may itself become personified as the comfort-giving mother, as may that dark oblivion which waits beyond the grave.

From life, a desert of intolerable inner aloneness and helplessness, the patient turns to death in flight from inner persecutors, in quest of rebirth into the arms of a comfort-giving mother. It is the paradox of suicide that the victim, finding inner death in life, seeks inner life in dying.

SUMMARY

Since Freud, suicide has been commonly understood as an attack intended to destroy an inner presence. While this is usually so, suicide may often serve the purposes of revenge, punishment, flight from a persecutor, reunion with the mother of early infancy, and is often accompanied by fantasies of escape and rebirth. The inter-relationships of such fantasies with common religious and mythical ideas is discussed, as well as the fragmentation of the self representation and the psychotic merging of its parts with the representations of objects.

NOTES

1. The quality of alienation suggests that the 'killer' derives from an introject, highly cathected with aggressive energy. It is important to distinguish between this hostile representation, an actor on the stage of the patient's inner world, from the introject which gives rise to it; the introject is a part of the deeper structure of the mental self which has been called the internal world. It is true that representations of self or objects have a status as mental structures inasmuch as they comprise the contents of a substructure of the ego, but these contents are not of the same order as the introjects.

2. A similar fantasy is found in the short story, "Silent Snow, Secret Snow," by Conrad Aiken (1950).

REFERENCES

Aiken, C. (1950). Silent snow, secret snow. In The Short Stories of Conrad Aiken. *New York: Duell, Sloan & Pearce.*

Arlow, J. (1955). Notes on oral symbolism. Psychoanal. Q. *24, 63–74.*

Freud, S. (1915). Mourning and melancholia. S.E. *14.*

Friedlander, K. (1940). On the 'longing to die'. Int. J. Psycho-Anal. *21, 416–426.*

Hartmann, H. (1939). Ego Psychology and the Problem of Adaptation. *New York: Int. Univ. Press, 1958.*

Hartmann, H. (1950). Comments on psychoanalytic theory of the ego. In Essays on Ego Psychology. *New York: Int. Univ. Press, 1964.*

Havens, L. L. (1962). The placement and movement of hallucinations in space: phenomenology and theory. Int. J. Psycho-Anal. *43, 426–435.*

Hendin, H. (1961). Suicide: psychoanalytic point of view. In N. Farberow & E. Schneidman (eds.), The Cry for Help. *New York: McGraw-Hill.*

Hendrick, I. (1936). Ego development and certain character problems. Psychoanal. Q. *5, 320–346.*

Hendrick, I. (1940). Suicide as wish fulfilment. Psychiat. Q. *14, 30–42.*

Hoyle, J. (1968). Sylvia Plath. A poetry of suicidal mania. Lit. & Psychol. *18, 187–203.*

Jacobson, E. (1954). Contribution to the metapsychology of psychotic identifications. J. Am. Psychoanal. Assn. *2, 239–262.*

Jacobson, E. (1964). The Self and the Object World. *New York: Int. Univ. Press.*

Kohut, H. (1966). Forms and transformations of narcissism. J. Am. Psychoanal. Assn. *14, 243–272.*

Kohut, H. (1968). The psychoanalytic treatment of narcissistic personality disorders: outline of a systematic approach. Psychoanal. Study Child *23.*

Litman, R. E. & Swearingen, C. (1972). Bondage and suicide. Archs. Gen. Psychiat. *27, 80–85.*

Maltsberger, J. T. & Buie, D. H. (1974). Countertransference hate in the treatment of suicidal patients. Archs. Gen. Psychiat. 30, 625–633.

Meissner, W. W. (1970). Notes on identification. I. Psychoanal. Q. *39, 563–589.*

Meissner, W. W. (1971). Notes on identification. II. Psychoanal. Q. *40, 277–302.*

Meissner, W. W. (1972). Notes on identification. III. Psychoanal. Q. *41, 224–260.*

Menninger, K. A. (1933). Psychoanalytic aspects of suicide. Int. J. Psycho-Anal. *14, 376–390.*

Morse, S. (1973). The after-pleasure of suicide. Brit. J. Med. Psychol. *46, 227–238.*

Rapaport, D. (1967). A theoretical analysis of the superego concept. In M. M. Gill (ed.), The Collected Papers of David Rapaport. *New York: Basic Books.*

Rizutto, A. M. (1978). Personal communication.

Sandler, J. & Rosenblatt, B. (1962). The concept of the representational world. Psychoanal. Study Child *17.*

Toplin, M. (1971). On the beginnings of a cohesive self. Psychoanal. Study Child *26.*

Waxberg, J. (1956). Study of attempted suicide in psychotic patients: a dynamic concept. Psychiat. Q. *30, 464–470.*

Zilboorg, G. (1936). Differential diagnostic types of suicide. Archs. Neurol. Psychiat. *35, 270–291.*

26. Psychotherapy with Suicidal Patients

Edwin Shneidman

BIOGRAPHICAL NOTE

Edwin Shneidman is professor of thanatology (emeritus) at the University of California, Los Angeles. In the 1950s he co-directed the Los Angeles Suicide Prevention Center, and in the 1960s, he was chief of the Center for the Study of Suicide Prevention at the National Institute of Mental Health, Bethesda, Maryland. He has served as visiting professor at Harvard and at the Ben Gurion University in Beersheva; research associate at the Massachusetts General Hospital (Boston) and at the Karolinska Hospital (Stockholm); and fellow at the Center for the Advanced Study in the Behavioral Sciences, Stanford University. In 1968 he founded and served as first president of the American Association of Suicidology. He is the author of Deaths of Man, Voices of Death, The Definition of Suicide, *and* Suicide as Psychache, *as well as the forthcoming* The Suicidal Mind. *Further, he has served as editor or co-editor of a dozen books on death and suicide, and he has written 160 chapters and articles, mostly on these topics. He is the recipient of the American Psychological Association Award for Distinguished Professional Contributions to Public Service.*

COMMENT

While emphasizing the importance of transference in treating suicidal patients, Shneidman points out that extraordinary measures are often desirable and life-saving in working with them. In the current era, when hospitalization is often not available for extended periods, interventions with the family, associates, and the patients' academic and work environments can make an

---

Edwin Shneidman, "Psychotherapy with Suicidal Patients." In Karasu, T. B., and Bellak, L., eds., *Specialized Techniques in Individual Psychotherapy*. New York: Brunner/Mazel, 1980, pp. 305–313 (This article was reprinted in *Suicide and Life-Threatening Behavior,* 11(1981):[149]341–[156]347.) Reprinted by permission.

important difference in recruiting life-preserving support. He wisely emphasizes the importance of consultation in treating these patients.

■

It seems logical that before we consider what the psychotherapy of a suicidal person ought to be that we have some common understanding of the suicidal state itself. Of course, everybody agrees that suicide is an enormously complicated term, encompassing a wide variety (and different ranges) of dysphoria, disturbance, self-abnegation, resignation, terror-cum-pain—to mention but a few inner states that are involved. . . .

Suicide is the human act of self-inflicted, self-intended cessation (i.e., the permanent stopping of consciousness). It is best understood as a bio-socio-psychologico-existential state of malaise. It is obviously not a disease and just as obviously a number of kinds of trained individuals other than physicians can help individuals who are in a suicidal state.

If we are to escape many of the current somewhat simplistic notions of suicide (especially those which totally equate a disease called suicide with a disease called depression), then we need to explicate what the suicidal state of mind is like. Our key source in this can be the ordinary dictionary—eschewing any nomenclature of technical and, especially, technically diagnostic terms. In the dictionary there are words, e.g., angered, anguished, cornered, dependent, frustrated, guilty, helpless, hopeless, hostile, rageful, shamed, that will help us in our understanding. For us, in this chapter, two less common (but ordinary) dictionary words—*perturbation* and *lethality*—will be the keystone words of our understanding.

Perturbation refers to how upset (disturbed, agitated, sane-insane, discomposed) the individual is—rated, let's say, on a 1 to 9 scale. Lethality refers to how lethal the individual is, i.e., how likely it is that he will take his own life—also rated on a 1 to 9 scale.

At the outset, I need to indicate what kinds of suicidal states I am talking about in order to indicate what kinds of psychotherapy are appropriate for them. We can arbitrarily divide the seriousness (or risk, or lethality, or suicidality) of all suicidal efforts (actions, deeds, events, episodes)—whether verbalizations (ordinarily called threats) or behaviors (ordinarily called attempts)—into three rough commonsense groupings: low, medium and high. In this chapter, I shall focus on the suicidal events or deeds of *high* lethality, where the danger of self-inflicted death is realistically large and imminent; what one might ordinarily call high suicide risks. Of course, a suicide act (deed, occurrence, event, threat, attempt) *of whatever lethality* is always a genuine psychiatric situation and should be treated without any iatrogenic elements. Thus, in the treatment of the suicidal person there is almost never any place for the therapist's hostility, anger, sardonic attitudes, daring the patient, or pseudo-democratic indifference.

By focusing solely on the *psychotherapeutic* approaches to high suicide risks, it should be obvious at the beginning that this chapter is a moiety—omitting entirely (and advertently) the lively areas of treatment suicidal individuals receive by means of chemical, electrical or institutional modalities.

Theoretically, the treatment of an acutely highly suicidal person is quite simple: It consists, almost by definition, of lowering his lethality level; in practice, this is usually done by decreasing or mollifying his level of perturbation. In short, we defuse the situation (like getting the gun), we create activity of support and care around the person, and we make that person's temporarily unbearable life just enough better so that he or she can stop to think and reconsider. *The way to decrease lethality is by dramatically decreasing the felt perturbation.*

Working intensively with a highly suicidal person—someone who might be assessed as 7, 8 or 9 on a 1 to 9 scale of lethality—as distinguished from someone of moderate or low lethality, is different from almost any other human encounter, with the possible exception of that of working intensively with a dying person—but that is another story. Psychotherapy with an intensely suicidal person is a special task; it demands a different kind of involvement. The goal is different—not that of increasing comfort, which is the goal of most ordinary psychotherapy, but the more primitive goal of simply keeping the person alive. The rules are therefore different, and it follows (or rather precedes) that the theoretical rationale is different.

At this juncture, I wish to make a distinction among *four* psychologically different kinds of human encounters: conversation (or "ordinary talk"); an hierarchical exchange; psychotherapy or a "professional exchange"; and, finally, clinical suicidology or working psychologically with a highly lethal person.

In ordinary talk or conversation, the focus is on the surface content (concrete events, specific dates, ordinary details); on what is actually being said; on the obviously stated meanings; on the ordinary interesting (or uninteresting) details of life. Further, the social role between the two speakers is one in which the two participants are essentially equal. Each participant has the social right to ask the other the same questions which he or she has been asked by the other. The best example of ordinary talk is two friends conversing with one another.

In a hierarchical verbal exchange the two participants are socially, and hence psychologically, unequal. This difference may be imposed by the situation, such as the exchange between a military officer and an enlisted person, or it may be agreed to by the two involved parties, such as between a physician and a patient. In either instance, the two are not psychologically equal. For example, an officer or a physician can ask an enlisted person or a patient, respectively, certain personal questions to which a rational response is expected, that the person of "lower status" could not ask the other person in return without appearing impertinent or aberrant. Yet most of the talk is still on the surface, concerning the real details of everyday life.

In a professional psychotherapeutic exchange the focus is on feelings, emotional content and unconscious meanings, rather than on what is apparently being said. The emphasis is on the latent (between-the-lines) significance of what is being said more than on the manifest and obvious content; on the unconscious meanings, including double-entendres, puns, and slips-of-the-tongue; on themes that run as common threads through the content, rather than on the concrete details for their own sake. Perhaps the most distinguishing aspect of the professional exchange (as opposed to ordinary talk) is the occurrence of transference, wherein the patient projects onto the therapist certain deep expectations and feelings. These transference reactions often stem from the patient's childhood and reflect neurotic patterns of reaction (of love, hate, dependency, suspicion, etc.) to whatever the therapist may or may not be doing. The therapist is often invested by the patient with almost magical healing powers, which, in fact, can serve as a self-fulfilling prophecy and thus help the interaction become therapeutic for the patient. In this paragraph, the use of the words therapist and patient already implies that, of the two parties, one has tacitly agreed to seek assistance and the other has agreed to try to give it. The roles of the two participants, unlike those in a conversation, are, in this respect, not co-equal. A therapist and a patient could not simply exchange roles.

In working as a clinical suicidologist with an individual who is highly suicidal, the focus is again different. In this situation, the attention is primarily on the lethality. Most importantly, what differentiates this modality of therapy from any other psychotherapy is the handling of the transference feelings. Specifically, the transference (from the patient to the therapist) and the countertransference (from the therapist to the patient)—especially those positive feelings of affection and concern—can legitimately be much more intense and more deep than would be seemly or appropriate (or even ethical) in ordinary psychotherapy where time is assumed to be endless and where it is taken for granted that the patient will continue functioning in life.

Working with a highly suicidal person demands a different kind of involvement. There may be as important a conceptual difference between ordinary psychotherapy (with individuals where dying or living is not *the* issue) and psychotherapy with acutely suicidal persons as there is between ordinary psychotherapy and ordinary talk.

The main point of working with a lethally-oriented person—in the give-and-take of talk, the advice, the interpretations, the listening—is to increase that individual's psychological sense of possible choices and sense of being emotionally supported. Relatives, friends and colleagues should, after they are assessed to be on the life-side of the individual's ambivalence, be closely involved in the total treatment process. Suicide prevention is not best done as a solo practice. A combination of consultation, ancillary therapists and the use of all the interpersonal and community resources that one can involve is, in general, the best way of proceeding.

Recall that we are talking about psychotherapy with the highly suicidal persons—not one of low or even medium lethality. With this in mind—and keeping in mind also the four psychological components of the suicidal state of mind (heightened inimicality, elevated perturbation, conspicuous constriction of intellectual focus, and the idea of cessation as a solution)—then relatively simple formula for treatment can be stated. That formulation concentrates on two of the four psychological components, specifically on the constriction and the perturbation. Simply put, the way to save a highly suicidal person is to decrease the constriction, that is, to widen the range of possible thoughts and fantasies (*from* the dichotomous two—either one specific outcome or death—*to* at least three or more possibilities for admittedly less-than-perfect solution), and, most importantly—without which the attempt to broaden the constriction will not work—to decrease the individual's perturbation.

How does a psychotherapist decrease the elevated perturbation of a highly suicidal person? Answer: by doing anything and almost everything possible to cater to the infantile idiosyncrasies, the dependency needs, the sense of pressure and futility, the feelings of hopelessness and helplessness that the individual is experiencing. In order to help a highly lethal person, one should involve others; create activity around the person; do what he or she wants done—and, if that cannot be accomplished, at least move in the direction of the desired goals to some substitute goals that approximate those which have been lost. Remember that life—and remind the patient of this fact (in a kindly but oracular way)—is often the choice among lousy alternatives. The key to functioning, to wisdom and to life itself is often to choose the least lousy alternative that is practicably attainable.

Taken down to its bare roots, the principle is: To decrease lethality one puts a hook on perturbation and, doing what needs to be done, pulls the level of perturbation down—and with that action brings down the active level of lethality. Then, when the person is no longer highly suicidal—then the usual methods of psychotherapy (which are not the subject for this chapter) can be usefully employed.

As to how to help a suicidal individual, it is best to look upon any suicidal act, whatever its lethality, as an effort by an individual to stop unbearable anguish or intolerable pain by "doing something." Knowing this usually guides us as to what the treatment should be. In the same sense, the way to save a person's life is also to "do something." Those "somethings" include putting that information (that the person is in trouble with himself) into the stream of communication, letting others know about it, breaking what could be a fatal secret, talking to the person, talking to others, proferring help, getting loved ones interested and responsive, creating action around the person, showing response, indicating interest, and, if possible, showing deep concern.

I conclude with an example—actually a composite of several actual highly suicidal persons I have known.

CASE STUDY

A young woman in her 20s, a nurse at the hospital where I worked, asked me pleadingly if I would see her teenage sister whom she believed to be highly suicidal. The attractive, younger woman—agitated and tearful but coherent—told me (in the privacy of my office) that she was single, pregnant and determined to kill herself. She showed me a small automatic pistol she had in her purse. Her being pregnant was such a mortal shame to her, combined with strong feelings of rage and guilt, that she simply could not "bear to live" (or live to bear?). Suicide was the *only* alternative, and shooting herself was the *only* way to do it. Either she had to be unpregnant (the way she was before she conceived) or she had to be dead.

I did several things. For one, I took out a sheet of paper and—to begin to "widen her blinders"—said something like, "Now, let's see: You could have an abortion here locally." ("I couldn't do that.") It is precisely the "can'ts" and the "won'ts" and "have to's" and "nevers" and "always" and "onlys" that are to be negotiated in psychotherapy. "You could go away and have an abortion." ("I couldn't do that.") "You could bring the baby to term and keep the baby." ("I couldn't do that.") "You could have the baby and adopt it out." ("I couldn't do that.") "We could get in touch with the young man involved." ("I couldn't do that.") "We could involve the help of your parents." ("I couldn't do that.") and "You can always commit suicide, but there is obviously no need to do that today." (No response.) "Now first, let me take that gun, and then let's look at this *list* and rank them in order and see what their advantages, disadvantages and implications are, remembering that none of them may be perfect."

The very making of this list, my professional and nonhortatory and nonjudgmental approach already had a calming influence on her. Within 15 minutes her lethality had begun to deescalate. She actually rank-ordered the list, commenting negatively on each item, but what was of critical importance was that suicide, which I included in the total realistic list, was now ranked third—no longer first or second.

She decided that she would, reluctantly, want to talk to the father of her child. Not only had they never discussed the "issue," but he did not even know about it. But there was a formidable obstacle: He lived in another city, almost across the country and that involved (what seemed to be a big item in the patient's mind) a long distance call. It was a matter of literally seconds to ascertain the area code from the long distance operator, to obtain his telephone number from information, and then—obviously with some trepidation and keen ambivalence for her—to dial his number (at university expense), with the support of my presence to speak to him directly.

The point is not how the issue was practically resolved, without an excessive number of deep or shallow interpretations as to why she permitted herself to become pregnant and other aspects of her relationships with men, etc. What is important is that it was possible to achieve the assignment of that day: to lower her lethality.

In general, any suicidal state is characterized by its transient quality, its pervasive ambivalence, and its dyadic nature. Psychiatrists and other health professionals are well advised to minimize, if not totally to disregard, those probably well-intentioned but shrill writings in this field which naively speak of an individual's "right to commit suicide"—a right which, in actuality, cannot be denied—as though the suicidal person were a chronic univalently self-destructive hermit.

A number of special features in the management of a highly lethal patient can be mentioned. Some of these special therapeutic stratagems or orientations with a highly lethal patient attend to or reflect the *transient, ambivalent* and *dyadic* aspects of almost all suicidal acts.

1. A continuous, preferably daily, monitoring of the patient's lethality rating.
2. An active out-reach; being willing to deal with some of the reality problems of the patient openly, where advisable; giving direction (sans exhortation) to the patient; actively taking the side of life. It relates to befriending and caring.
3. Use of community resources including employment, Veterans Administration (when applicable), social agencies, and psychiatric social work assistance.
4. Consultation. There is almost no instance in a therapist's professional life when consultation with a peer is as important as when he is dealing with a highly suicidal patient. The items to be discussed might include the therapist's treatment of the case; his own feelings of frustration, helplessness or even anger; his countertransference reactions generally; the advisability of hospitalization for the patient, etc.
5. Hospitalization. Hospitalization is always a complicating event in the treatment of a suicidal patient but it should not, on those grounds, be eschewed. Obviously, the quality of care—from doctors, nurses and attendants—is crucial. Stoller, discussing one of his complex long-range cases, says: ". . . there were several other factors without which the therapy might not have succeeded. First, the hospital. The patient's life could not have been saved if a hospital had not been immediately available *and a few of the personnel familiar with me and the patient.*"[1]
6. Transference. As in almost no other situation and at almost no other time, the successful treatment of a highly suicidal person depends heavily on the transference. The therapist can be active, show his personal concern, increase the frequency of the sessions, invoke the "magic" of the unique therapist-patient relationship, be less of a *tabula rasa,* give "transfusions" of (realistic) hope and succorance. In a figurative sense, I believe that Eros can work wonders against Thanatos.
7. The involvement of significant others. Suicide is most often a highly charged dyadic crisis. It follows from this that the therapist, unlike his usual practice of dealing almost exclusively with his patient (and even fending off the spouse, the lover, parents, grown children), should consider the advisability of working directly with the significant others.

For example, if the individual is married, it is important to meet the spouse. The therapist must assess whether, in fact, the spouse is suicidogenic; whether they ought to be separated; whether there are misunderstandings which the therapist can help resolve; or whether the spouse is insightful and concerned and can be used by the therapist as an ally and co-therapist. The same is true for homosexual lovers, for patient and parent, etc. It is not suggested that the significant other be seen as often as the patient is seen, but that other real people in the suicidal patient's life be directly involved and, at the minimum, their role as hinderer or helper in the treatment process be assessed.

8. Careful modification of the usual canons of confidentiality. Admittedly, this is a touchy and complicated point, but the therapist should not ally himself with death. Statements given during the therapy session relating to the patient's overt suicidal (or homicidal) plans obviously cannot be treated as a "secret" between two collusive partners. In the previous example of the patient who opened her purse and showed me a small automatic pistol with which she said she was going, that day, to kill herself, two obvious interpretations would be that she obviously wanted me to take the weapon from her, or that she was threatening me. In any event, I told her that she could not leave my office with the gun and insisted that she hand her purse to me. She countered by saying that I had abrogated the basic rule of therapy, namely that she could tell me anything. I pointed out that "anything" did not mean committing suicide and that she must know that I could not be a partner in that kind of enterprise. For a moment she seemed angered and then relieved; she gave me the gun. The rule is to "defuse" the potentially lethal situation. To have left her with a loaded gun would also leave her with a latent message.
9. Limitation of one's own practice to a very few highly lethal patients. It is possible to see a fairly large number of moderate and low-rated lethal patients in one's patient load, but one or two *highly* lethal patients seem to be the superhuman limit for most therapists at any given time. Such patients demand a great deal of investment of psychic energy and one must beware of spreading oneself too thin in his or her own professional life.

Working with highly suicidal persons borrows from the goals of crisis intervention: not to take on and ameliorate the individual's entire personality structure and to cure all the neuroses, but simply to keep him or her alive. That is the *sine qua non* without which no human being can function—and no therapy would have meaning.

NOTES

1. Robert J. Stoller. *Splitting*. New York: Quadrangle Books, 1973.

27. Psychotherapy and Suicide

Herbert Hendin

BIOGRAPHICAL NOTE

Thirty of Herbert Hendin's professional articles and five of his eight books, the most recent of which is Suicide in America, *have dealt with the problem of suicide. He has won numerous prizes and awards for his work, including a special award from the American Scandinavian Foundation for his study of suicide in Scandinavia, and the Louis I. Dublin Award of the American Association of Suicidology for "distinguished contributions to our understanding of suicide."*

Herbert Hendin is professor of psychiatry at New York Medical College; he was the first president, and is now the executive director, of the American Suicide Foundation, an organization that funds research, education, and treatment programs in the prevention of suicide. He has recently completed a study of assisted suicide and euthanasia in the United States and in the Netherlands, which was published in Issues in Law and Medicine *(July 1994) and will shortly appear, expanded into a book,* Doctors, Patients and the Final Cure.

Hendin lives in New York with his wife, Josephine Hendin, a professor of English at New York University. Their older son Neil is a graduate student at Harvard majoring in electrical engineering; their younger son Erik is completing college at Drew University as a behavioral science major.

COMMENT

Hendin identifies and discusses the tendency of suicidal patients to make others responsible for whether they live or die, and shows how this lethal trend can be managed in psychotherapy. Suicidal patients tend to involve unwary therapists in their games of Russian roulette and tangle them up in their ambivalence about living and dying (see also chapter 9 above). Omnipo-

---

Herbert Hendin, "Psychotherapy and Suicide." *American Journal of Psychotherapy* 35(1981):469–480. Reprinted by permission.

tent self-expectations and countertransference vulnerabilities prompt some therapists to involve themselves in ongoing rescue operations that invite suicide as patients descend in a cascade of suicidal activity. Attempts to treat these patients by increasing efforts at management and control are not enough, and, when injudicious, can be suicide-inviting.

■

Psychotherapy can be successful with suicidal patients if the therapist does not reduce therapy to management and control of the patient; understands the ways in which the patient uses his potential death as part of his adaptation; and avoids specific countertransference pitfalls. Case examples are provided.

IN REVIEWING articles written in the past thirty years on the treatment of suicidal individuals one is struck with how often the word "management" is used synonymously with therapy. Such articles are usually guides designed to help the therapist outmaneuver the potentially suicidal person. They contain a series of recommendations of a practical nature such as "Make every effort to have firearms and potentially lethal medications removed from the home of the suicidal patient," "Control carefully the prescription of potentially lethal drugs," "Advise the family to be watchful," and so forth.[1–6]

Such precautions and warnings seem reasonable, but in practice they reflect a state of mind and a way of relating to suicidal patients that often make treatment unsuccessful. Since many suicidal patients are themselves preoccupied with management and control, therapy can become a contest with the suicidal patients usually obtaining their pills if they really want them, and the therapist reassuring himself that he has taken all possible precautions. All the precautions and all the management may result in encouraging one of the most lethal aspects of the suicidal individual, that is, his tendency to make someone else responsible for his staying alive.

In most articles the approach to therapy itself is usually based on similar attempts at manipulation. In a widely recommended article on the subject it is suggested that the therapist encourage the patient to believe that his current mood will pass; hold out hope by telling the patient of others who felt as he does and have gotten better; point out that actual suicidal behavior will interfere with treatment; indicate that the treatment cannot help the patient if he is dead; and remind the patient of his feelings for his spouse, children, or pets.[1]

Encouraging a suicidal patient to live for the sake of the therapy, the therapist, or his family is a reinforcement of what many such patients already feel, that is, that they are only living for the sake of others. Such feelings are more apt to encourage suicide than prevent it.

The warning issued in one form or another in most articles on the treatment of suicide is "No form of treatment is effective with a dead patient." A list of criteria for evaluating suicidal risk is likely to follow. In some cases the list is basically an evaluation of the degree of the patient's depression based on his mood, energy, performance—socially and vocationally—and degree of anxiety. A series of danger points may be listed: When the patient is on pass from the hospital, when he first goes home, when stress in his life increases, to name a few examples. Such a list usually includes the clinically axiomatic warning, going back to Manfred Bleuler, that a lessening of depression often precedes a suicide attempt. In other words, if the patient remains depressed be wary and if he is getting less depressed be even more wary.

These articles reiterate in some form or another an injunction, for "constant monitoring" to ascertain suicidal risk. They recommend that a judgment of increased risk should invariably be accompanied by more intensive management measures—hospitalization, medication, more medication or new medication, and electric shock. What such articles fail to include is any statement as to how lacking in evidence we are that such measures are effective in preventing suicide.

In any case it would be better for the therapist working in or out of a hospital to recognize that he is not likely to keep alive by surveillance, incarceration, or any form of precaution a patient who is determined to kill himself. The best chance for helping the patient lies in understanding and helping him with the problems that are making him suicidal, including most specifically the way in which he uses the threat of death.

THERAPIST'S ANXIETIES

A therapist who is threatened by the fact that a patient may kill himself while under his care is in no position to be a therapist to the patient. The rationalization that emergency measures are necessary to prevent suicide and make therapy possible serves to conceal the fact that emergency measures, reflecting the therapist's anxiety, often make therapy impossible.

Only in psychotherapy does the nature of the suicidal individual's involvement with death and self-destructiveness become fully apparent. The therapist's own attitudes toward death, dying, and suicide, however, become almost as important as the patient's in determining the outcome. Fear of the responsibility for suicidal patients is a conscious motivation leading many therapists to avoid treating them. Among therapists who do treat suicidal patients, anxiety over a patient's possible death often serves unwittingly to deaden their perceptions. Such anxiety is as apt to derive from guilt or a fear of being blamed for the death as it is from any excess of compassion or empathy. Although suicide is a life-or-death matter for the patient, once the therapist begins to see the success of therapy as a life-or-death matter to his own self-esteem, his efforts are apt to be futile.

Suicidal patients, although they may deaden themselves to much else in life, are usually perceptive about such anxieties on the part of a therapist. Since so many of them (including those who eventually kill themselves) have learned to use the anxiety they can arouse in others about their death in a coercive or manipulative way, they will usually test the therapist to see if they can do the same thing with him. If the therapist meets unreasonable demands in response to death threats, the situation usually repeats itself with escalation of the demands and increasing angry dissatisfaction if they are not met. Unless these character attitudes and expectations of the patient are explored and understood, the therapist is apt to go into bondage to the patient—with bad results.

One therapist was coerced into calling a patient every morning for a year because of an implicit threat that if the therapist did not call, the patient might kill herself. This particular patient eventually did, despite the calls, leaving the therapist feeling both troubled and betrayed. Had more effort been spent in challenging and understanding the patient's attempt to structure how and in what manner the therapist was to show interest, rather than gratifying the patient's demands, the therapy would have had more chance of success.

THERAPEUTIC INTERACTION

The suicidal person often makes conditions for life: if you don't save me I'll die; if I can't make you happy I'll end my life. Such attitudes are central to the patient's involvement with suicide; if their emergence does not arouse excessive anxiety on the part of the therapist, he is in a position to explore them to therapeutic advantage.

Case 1. A successful, forty-eight-year-old executive, whose wife had left him after years of an unhappy marriage, became depressed, began drinking heavily, and was suicidal. Although his wife seemed satisfied with the new life she was making for herself, he insisted he would not rebuild his own life until he knew she was happy. A dream he had when he was concerned about my leaving on vacation opened up some of the meaning of his wife's leaving him. He dreamed that his father had died and he was annoyed that his two brothers had not consulted him over the funeral arrangements. The dream helped make him aware that his response to his wife's leaving was centered around the issue of control—who determined the circumstances of separation or loss was as central to him as the loss itself. His need to set the conditions under which he would be happy was an outgrowth of his inability to determine the conditions of her happiness.

Therapy helped him to become aware of how much his response originated in fear of severing an unhappy relationship with his mother. He had felt frightened and despondent over his inability to influence her lack of interest in him, but had also felt responsible for her unhappiness. As he perceived the interconnections and origins of his need to control his relationships with his wife, his mother, and with me, and was able to use this insight constructively, his depression lifted, his excessive drinking stopped, and he was no longer suicidal. He was once again able to be productive at work although his difficulties in forming a close and satisfying relationship with a woman remained.

Case 2. One young man had shot himself in the heart—the bullet grazed his heart, pierced his lung, and came to rest close to his spine. He came into treatment telling me that he would give me six months to make him less lonely, isolated, and depressed before killing himself. This kind of ultimatum, whether given to a therapist, a lover, or to oneself is designed not merely to bring about the end but to kill whatever relationship comes before it. This young man was treatable only when we focused on the way in which he tried to make our relationship one in which he would be dead and therefore challenge or resist any efforts to bring him back to life. Life is not, as it seems, or as the individual often says, unbearable *with* depression, but may sometimes be inconceivable *without* it.

Sometimes the conditions the patient wishes to set in therapy include involving the therapist actively during a suicide attempt. A therapist's own inclination to see himself as the savior or rescuer of the suicidal patient can be responsible for perpetuating suicidal behavior, particularly in young people.

Case 3. One young woman had made five suicide attempts in her past therapy. She would call her therapist during her attempts and manage to have him come to one hotel or motel after another to save her. He dealt with his irritation with her behavior by a fierce determination to save her and pride in being her rescuer. His willingness to do so seemed to intensify the severity of her attempts. After her last attempt, which she was lucky to survive, her parents, her therapist, and the patient agreed on the need for some change in therapy.

This young woman came from a family where little interest, affection or attention was paid to her. She had learned to use illness or suicide attempts coercively to gain attention. She felt secure only when she was able to use crises to control the interest and attention given to her, and she had to learn to value affection of any other kind.

Despite progress in her therapy it seemed likely that she would eventually test me, as she had her parents and her prior therapist, with her coercive use of the threat of suicide. She did. She called one evening from a motel in the suburbs just after swallowing some sleeping pills. I told her to go to a nearby hospital and to have them call me. My knowledge of her and her progress made me feel that this decision was reasonably safe and necessary. Yet I was considerably relieved when the hospital called after having pumped out her stomach. She came in for her next appointment initially angry with me for not coming to her rescue, but this was the end of her suicide attempts and the beginning of a dramatic over-all therapeutic improvement. There is a risk in being misunderstood in relating such an incident. A therapist must know a patient well and have extensive experience in order to make such a decision. But there is a greater risk in allowing to leave unchallenged the widespread misconception that a therapist does such a suicidal patient a service by allowing himself to become a constant savior. A therapist in such a coercive bondage, no matter how well intentioned, is of little use to a patient.

THERAPY WITH OLDER SUICIDAL PATIENTS

If suicidal young people arouse rescue fantasies in therapists, older people who are suicidal are more apt to arouse irritation and to be dealt with by medication or hospitalization without psychotherapy. Many make the unwarranted assumptions that little can be done with psychotherapy for older people in general and even less for older people who are suicidal.

Many older people who are suicidal have, despite their problems, demonstrated varying degrees of adaptive capacity throughout a lifetime. Past proven adaptive capacity is probably a better indicator than age in determining the prognosis in psychotherapy.

Case 4. A sociology professor of sixty became suicidal after a stroke left him almost completely paralyzed on the left side. He was depressed, enraged, and unable to tolerate the decline in his physical and mental abilities. He told me, "When you came out to see me I watched you like a hawk. You can move your left arm and left leg and envy and anger just swells up in me." He became impossibly irritable with his wife and step-children, although he had had a good relationship with them previously. He was aware of being enraged by their ability to come and go as they pleased in contrast to the restrictions imposed by his own incapacity.

His past life had made him particularly vulnerable to what had happened. He had grown up with a powerful need for self-sufficiency and control that was fostered by his mother's indifference. A great deal of his self-esteem was tied up with his teaching. He was seen as the best teacher in his department, frequently received accolades for his performance, and was nominated several times for special teaching awards. His wife confirmed that the majority of his students would say that he was the best teacher they ever had.

He had had a recurrent dream during the last five years. He is teaching a class, then begins to move his arms like wings and rises to the top of the room where he flies around the room and then out the window and over some tall trees. He then becomes afraid of the height. In talking about the dream it is clear that he does get "high" on teaching and on the admiration and awe of his students.

His wife had treated him with similar awe and respect. Indeed she continued to do so. His own self-esteem was so tied to receiving admiration for his performance, knowledge, and ability to control situations that he could not conceive of his wife's continuing to love him in his partly disabled condition. As a result he became increasingly critical of her in a manner that was bound to push her away.

During a session when he related to me several instances in which he had helped to resolve some friction between two attendants in the hospital, I had responded positively to what he had done. He immediately replied that he used to be so much more capable. He compared any current achievement in a derogatory way to his past abilities. This attitude became a central issue in his therapy and as soon as he was able to change his mood improved.

Even more critical was a passive, resigned attitude he had toward his progress in rehabilitation therapy in particular and toward his life in general. He wanted greater mobility within the hospital grounds, yet he did not request such privileges. He was passive about caring for himself, waiting for his wife to visit to help him button his shirt. His passivity was in marked contrast to his prestroke behavior. When his behavior was pointed out, he became quite angry. The word "passivity" irritated him, but also challenged him, and he began doing everything for himself, becoming remarkably agile with his walker. He would begin many subsequent sessions by letting me know how much he had accomplished and how wrong I had been to see him as passive. His ability to resume a satisfactory relationship with his wife and children also became a challenge to him, which in time he met.

Case 5. A fifty-five-year-old man who had built up his own accounting firm had come home from work ten years earlier to find his wife and only son—a boy of fourteen—had drowned. They had been visiting his wife's parents and he had asked his in-laws to make sure that his wife and child did not sail alone in a small boat he owned. They had done so anyway with the result that the boat overturned in rough water.

Two weeks after their death, this man turned on the ignition of his car in his closed garage with the intention of suicide. He would have succeeded if his neighbors had not seen him pulling into the garage without any lights going on subsequently in the house. They became suspicious and rescued him just in time.

In the ten years that followed the deaths of his wife and son and his suicide attempt, this man became progressively alcoholic. He gave up his business and worked on and off at menial jobs, some of which he lost because of his drinking. Contrary to the popular belief that people drink to forget, he claimed the he did not think of his wife and son except when he was drinking. He had broken off with his in-laws, blaming them for what had occurred. His anger at them permitted him to avoid facing his anger toward his wife for not listening to him or his own guilt over having bought the boat for his son.

He had a recurrent dream during his drinking episodes. He was on a roof top (a place where he often drank) and two rats were trying to climb up the drain pipe to get up to the roof. He was pushing them down with a stick. His associations indicated that the two rats were his wife and son—rats for having abandoned him, rats because what had happened continued to gnaw away at him.

Despite his ten-year history of alcoholism and suicide attempts he made excellent progress in psychotherapy. When he was freer of the emotions that bound him to the death of his family, when he was able to feel entitled to live, his past ability to enjoy work and to care for other people were strengths that were soon in evidence.

Case 6. Prior to the past few years when the loneliness and depression caused by her unhappy marriage had made her suicidal, a sixty-five-year-old woman who had come to this country from Austria had had a successful working career and a good relationship with her son (who lived in another state) whom she had raised virtually without help from her husband. Her situation was complicated because she viewed her unhappy marriage as just punishment for having left her mother and sister who later died in concentration camps.

In response to a question as to why she stayed with her husband if she was so unhappy with him she spoke of her childhood, telling first about her father who was killed in World War I when she was two, while her mother was pregnant with her sister. Her mother and the two daughters went to live in a household headed by her mother's bachelor brother, an Austrian newspaper publisher, and by the patient's grandmother. Her mother was something of a servant in the household, and, although they were treated well, they were all conscious of the need not to offend her uncle and her grandmother. She seemed to be indicating that her fear of being uncared for and abandoned had a long history.

She then went on to tell me that she is frequently preoccupied with the question of why she was spared when her mother and sister died. She feels that maybe God spared her in order to punish her—that she was destined to live an unhappy life ending up in suicide. She had one dream years ago which she regards as the most significant dream of her life:

Her sister, dressed as monk, was behind barbed wire and was trying to hand her a letter. She never gets to know what was in the letter. The monk's outfit suggested death to her, the barbed wire the concentration camp. The letter appeared to be a message from her sister, perhaps an answer to the question she had always wanted resolved as to why she lived and they died. What she appeared to need and had never received from her sister was permission to enjoy her life, permission that would free her from her sense that she had no right to live or was destined to live unhappily.

At first this patient needed the therapist to give her the permission to live that she had vainly and recurrently sought in her dreams of her dead sister. Even before the loss of her mother and sister, and despite her intelligence and ability, she had never felt entitled to shape the circumstances of her life. Since childhood, after her father's death, she and her family were dependent on her uncle's permission for every decision they wished to make. The major decision she had made independently—to leave Austria—saved her life, but left her feeling guilty for having survived.

As she came to understand the relation of her past life to her present situation, she was able to make a satisfying life for herself apart from her husband. She moved to where her son lived, became more involved with him, his wife, and her grandchildren, and was able for the first time in years to take a trip by herself to visit old friends in Vienna.

Case 7. Even in older patients where the past adaptive capacity has been poor, psychotherapy can make suicide much less likely. A fifty-six-year-old man who suffered from chronic schizophrenia and nearly killed himself while a patient in the hospital is a case in point. Dependent on, but abused by, first his mother and then his two wives, he was unable to function on his own.

In the hospital he was treated primarily with medication for his anxiety with the dosage increased whenever he seemed more upset. His periods of disturbance were considered to be due to the vicissitudes of his schizophrenia and usually resulted in the hospital restricting his freedom to leave the ward because of the fear that he might kill himself. His response in turn was to become only more agitated.

When seen in psychotherapy it soon became evident that all his disturbed periods were triggered by episodes in which he felt rejected or abandoned by the hospital staff or by his brothers and sisters who refused to visit him in the hospital. His sensitivity to such rejection was great, but his agitated response and attempts at suicide only occurred when the staff's response to his difficulties was restriction, seclusion, or more medication rather than empathy with what he was feeling. When such empathy was provided in psychotherapy he changed from a nonfunctioning, angry, depressed suicidal individual to an active and productive member of the hospital community.

COUNTERTRANSFERENCE PROBLEMS

Since many suicidal patients have been in psychotherapy at the time of their suicide, researchers have sought to examine such cases systematically to see what might have gone wrong. Wheat[7] did a retrospective study of therapeutic interaction in the cases of thirty patients who committed suicide during or after hospitalization. He emphasized three factors in attempting to explain these suicides: (1) the refusal of the therapist to tolerate infantile dependency so that the therapist conveyed to the patient an expectation of mature behavior exceeding the patient's capacity; (2) discouragement on the part of the therapist about the progress of treatment; and (3) an event or environmental crisis of overwhelming importance to the patient unrecognized by the therapist or beyond the control of the therapeutic situation such as the refusal by the family of the last patient to respond to his requests that they visit him in the hospital.

"All of these processes," Wheat writes, "can lead to a breakdown in the therapeutic communication resulting in the patient's feeling abandoned or helpless, thus setting the stage for the disastrous result of suicide." Bloom,[8] in a similar review of known suicides in treatment at a psychiatric training center, identifies as significant precipitants rejecting behavior on the part of the therapist, including verbal and facial expressions of anger, premature discharge of the patient, reduction of frequency of psychotherapeutic sessions, and lack of availability of the therapist.

Lowenthal[9] complains of a lack of empathy on the part of therapists treating suicidal patients. He lists a number of factors as responsible: The potential for guilt is greater if the therapist is close to a patient; shame over a potential suicide being a reflection on the therapist's capacity or competence; and most important the therapist's inability to come to terms with suicidal impulses in himself or in his patients as a possibly reasonable alternative to life's dilemmas. He implies that only a therapist who has seriously contemplated suicide can properly empathize with a suicidal patient. He provides no evidence for this conclusion, but is content to state his admiration for the empathy with suicidal patients which A. Alvarez expresses in his book on suicide, *The Savage God,*[10] an empathy which Lowenthal believes stems from Alvarez having made a serious suicide attempt.

Although having been personally involved with a problem may be of aid in the treatment of others, providing the therapist has satisfactorily resolved it, it does not guarantee greater insight or empathy. I have seen many suicidal individuals, including therapists, who attempt suicide without gaining either insight into themselves or greater understanding of their own or others' desire for suicide. Case studies by suicide prevention centers suggest that counsellors who are not depressed or suicidal, but are reasonably happy with their own lives, do best with suicidal patients.

I have long been impressed, however, by the fact that most articles on suicide, including Lowenthal's, seem more comfortable with abstractions than with people; they usually do not present a single suicidal individual with a view toward conveying a sense of the quality of the person's life or wish to die. Such articles stand in startling contrast to articles on virtually any other clinical problem. The absence of such case descriptions does bespeak the distance and lack of empathy about which Lowenthal complains.

Maltzberger [sic] and Buie[11] in a fine article on the subject of therapy with suicidal patients (flawed only by the absence of any case illustrations) deal with many of the harmful countertransference reactions aroused in therapists by suicidal patients, particularly those who are borderline or psychotic. By their primitive attacks on the therapist, ranging from attempts to frustrate his therapeutic efforts to expressions of contempt for him as a person, such patients are often able to arouse "countertransference hatred." "The three most common narcissistic snares," they write, "are the aspirations to heal all, know all and love all . . . such gifts are no more available to the contemporary therapist than they were to Faust." The attack by the suicidal patient, who may sense the therapist's vulnerability, can lead to destructive reactions in the therapist varying from malice to aversion.

Maltzberger [sic] and Buie go on to point out that the therapist's repression of these reactions may lead him to lose interest in the patient or to reject the patient as hopeless. Conversely, projection of countertransference hatred taking the form of "I do not wish to kill you, you wish to kill yourself," leads to the therapist's paralyzing preoccupation with the danger of suicide by the patient. Reaction formation to such countertransference feelings can contribute to oversolicitousness, exaggerated fear of suicide, fantasies of rescue, and overprotection of the patient.

Lesse[12] has pointed out that experience and competence as well as self-knowledge are vital if the risks in treating suicidal patients are to be minimized. He pointed out the necessity for competent supervision if inexperienced residents are to treat seriously suicidal patients.

In the past fifteen years I have been consulted on numerous occasions by therapists who wished help in understanding a patient's suicide attempts or suicide and their reactions to this behavior. In most cases, the problem was the therapist's failure to understand what was going on in the interaction between the patient and therapist, rather than any basic lack of concern for the patient. In fact, a major therapeutic difficulty often stems from the therapist's assumption that by simply supplying a care and concern that had been missing in the patient's life, that is, by not being rejecting, he will somehow give the patient the desire to live. Often the patient's hidden agenda, however, is an attempt to prove that nothing the therapist can do will be enough. The therapist's wish to see himself as the suicidal patient's savior may blind the therapist to the fact that the patient may have cast him for the role of executioner.[12]

Case 8. For example, one young woman jumped in front of a train and lost both her legs when her therapist was about to leave on a vacation. On the day she jumped she called a local TV station to tell them that at 8 P.M. a man—she gave her therapist's last name without indicating that he was treating her—would push a girl in a pink dress in front of a train at a particular station. Her warning was not heeded and at 8 o'clock, dressed in a pink dress, she jumped.

She considered she had "died" when her father left the family when she was eight or nine. She was preoccupied with death throughout her adolescence. She could recall the death scene in many novels, vividly recalling Anna Karenina's suicide in front of a train. Her relationships with men had been painful recapitulations of the earlier rejection by her father—and one unhappy love affair had been followed by a suicide attempt.

The following dream concerning her present suicide attempt made her wish to die more understandable. She was in a long, narrow tunnel and could see a light at the end of it. She walked toward the light, and there she saw a man and a woman standing over a manger. In her associations to the dream, the tunnel suggested to her the subway, where she had jumped with the train coming out of the tunnel and into the lighted platform area. Moving from the darkness of the tunnel and into the light she saw as like being born. The child in the manger was both the Christ child and herself. She particularly identified with the sense that the crucifixion reunited Christ with his Father. She saw her life as having been set on a course in which gratification of her fantasies was only possible through her death. One can see how much she accomplished in her death fantasy. She is reborn, is a boy, is reunited with her father and, finally, is omnipotent. For a patient with such fantasies the thought of dying has a very strong appeal.

The grandiosity expressed in the dream of a rebirth as Christ is a common feature in the psychodynamics of suicide. It reflects the illusion of omnipotent mastery that suicide may provide, as well as suggesting the profound narcissistic injury that underlies the need for such grandiosity.

This young woman's therapist had tried to be available in the way that her father was not. He was uncomfortable with the way in which the patient had actually incorporated him into her suicidal fantasies but did not realize till later that she was determined to perceive him—like her father—as responsible for her death while binding him to her through death. She structured the relationship this way and used his leaving on vacation as an excuse for her suicide attempt. Even in the way in which she tried to kill herself, she appeared to be asking him to rescue her, but in fact was trying to make sure that he could not, and that he would be blamed for her death.

When seen in consultation after her suicide attempt she was still interested in punishing her therapist. She suggested that I should write up her case being sure to include her therapist's name. At the same time she behaved as if she had accomplished a rebirth. And paradoxically in her new life as a cripple with vastly reduced expectations she made a much better adjustment than she had previously. One suspects that her need for self-punishment may in some way have been permanently satisfied by the self-inflicted injury. (Her response to the incapacity that followed her suicide attempt was paralleled by the suicide attempt of a man who had shot himself in the head as a college student, blinded himself, but survived. When I met him twenty-five years later he insisted his life had been changed for the better by the experience and had published a book detailing the transformation.)

Successful therapy cannot be conducted with the suicidal patient unless the therapist understands the ways in which the patient uses his potential death as part of his adaptation. Such knowledge may minimize the risk of suicide, but therapy requires that the therapist be able to accept and live with some risk. As Schwartz, Flinn, and Slawson[13] point out, "the only method of reducing the long-term risk of suicide may be one that risks its short-term commission."

As we have seen, suicidal patients often use the threat of suicide as a means of controlling the behavior of others. This is true of those who eventually kill themselves and those who do not. Szasz[14] points out correctly that many therapists respond to the patient's need to control with their own need to control. In order to avoid the risk of suicide, they coercively hospitalize the patient. Although hospitalization and involuntary commitment of the suicidal patient are subjects requiring separate treatment, it should be noted here that ultimately, in or out of a hospital, successful psychotherapy cannot be conducted by a "policeman."

Psychotherapy with an experienced therapist is the treatment of choice for seriously suicidal patients. It should be supplemented by psychotropic drugs when necessary to relieve severe depression or paralyzing anxiety. Seriously suicidal patients are either too depressed, too withdrawn, or too fragile to tolerate the anxiety that is generated in the psychoanalytic process. Yet most suicidal patients, like most of the individuals discussed in this article, can work psychodynamically in psychotherapy and should be given the opportunity to do so.

SUMMARY

In contrast to most current strategies for treating suicidal patients, which consist largely of intensive measures for management and control, psychodynamic psychotherapy is described as a potentially highly effective method of treatment for this patient population. Elaborating the thesis that successful therapy cannot be conducted with suicidal patients unless the therapist understands the ways in which the patient uses his potential death as part of his adaptation, several specific countertransference issues which often prevent such understanding are discussed. Numerous case examples are provided which illustrate approaches to successful psychotherapy with young, middle-aged, and elderly suicidal individuals.

REFERENCES

1. *Mintz, R. Psychotherapy of the Suicidal Patient.* Am. J. Psychother., *15:348, 1961.*
2. ———. *Some Practical Procedures in the Management of Suicidal Persons.* Am. J. Orthopsychiatry, *36:896, 1966.*
3. ———. *Basic Considerations in the Psychotherapy of the Depressed Suicidal Patient.* Am. J. Psychother., *25:56, 1971.*
4. *Shein, H., and Stone, A. Monitoring and Treatment of Suicidal Potential within the Context of Psychotherapy.* Comp. Psychiatry, *10:59, 1969.*
5. ———. *Psychotherapy Designed to Detect and Treat Suicidal Potential.* Am. J. Psychiatry, *125:141, 1969.*
6. ———. *Psychotherapy of the Hospitalized Suicidal Patient.* Am. J. Psychother., *22:15, 1968.*
7. *Wheat, W. Motivational Aspects of Suicide in Patients during and after Psychiatric Treatment,* South. Med. J., *53:273, 1960.*
8. *Bloom, V. An Analysis of Suicide at a Training Center.* Am. J. Psychiatry, *123:918, 1967.*
9. *Lowenthal, U. Suicide—The Other Side: The Factor of Reality among Suicidal Motivations.* Arch Gen. Psychiatry, *33:308, 1975.*
10. *Alvarez, A.* The Savage God: A Study of Suicide, *Weidenfeld, Nicholson, London, 1972.*
11. *Maltzberger [sic], J., and Buie, D. Countertransference Hate in the Treatment of Suicidal Patients.* Arch. Gen. Psychiatry, *30:625, 1974.*

12. *Lesse, S. The Range of Therapies in the Treatment of Severely Depressed Suicidal Patients.* Am. J. Psychother., *29:308, 1975.*
13. *Schwartz, D., Flinn, D., and Slawson, P. Treatment of the Suicidal Character.* Am. J. Psychother., *28:194, 1974.*
14. *Szasz, T. The Ethics of Suicide.* Antioch Review, *31:7, 1971.*

28. Suicide in Chronic Schizophrenia

Alec Roy

BIOGRAPHICAL NOTE

Alec Roy recalls that he wrote the two papers included here during his lunch hours at the Clarke Institute of Psychiatry, Toronto. He reviewed records, extracted data, and, in connection with his schizophrenia paper, moved along the rows of records looking to match suicide victims with control patients of the same sex, age, and diagnosis. "It took a long time matching controls," he writes.

His paper on the family history of suicide taught him the value of computerized data base analysis.

COMMENT

Unlike most of the contributions in this volume, this report is comparatively clinically remote. It is nevertheless of importance to those who treat such patients, because suicide in schizophrenia is different from suicide in patients with major depressive illness, alcoholism, and different, too, from suicide in patients with borderline personality disorders.

Depression is an important feature in schizophrenic suicide. It has been our observation that depression is frequently overlooked in this population; such patients are often not forthcoming, and may not complain of depression in the ordinary way. Too often busy inpatient psychiatrists treat the psychosis and miss the despair. Depression in schizophrenia is usually not difficult to detect when one inquires closely. When present, it needs to be treated vigorously.

One component of depression in such patients is especially easy to miss unless it is actively inquired after—psychic anguish, or psychache. *(See Chapter 40 below). The schizophrenic patient who sits quietly and uncommu-*

Alec Roy, "Suicide in Chronic Schizophrenia." *British Journal of Psychiatry 141 (1982):171–177. Reprinted by permission.*

nicatively in the ward may show no outward signs of agitation or other distress, but may, if asked, confess to a level of anguish so intense as to be almost unbearable. Affectively the patient may experience a sense of profound, harrowing aloneness that is not relieved by the usual neuroleptic drugs he is likely to be receiving. In these instances anti-depressant drugs or electroconvulsive treatment, especially if accompanied by empathic supportive psychotherapy, can bring substantial relief and prevent suicide.

There is evidence to suggest that schizophrenic suicide often takes place during comparatively non-psychotic periods when the patient develops some grasp of the devastation his illness has wrought. When the patient sees his aspirations for success at work and love hopelessly shattered he may decide to commit suicide and suffer no longer (Drake et al. 1989).

It follows that schizophrenic patients must be especially suicide vulnerable, and most in need of supportive, empathic care, as psychosis fades and hospital discharge approaches.

REFERENCES

Drake, Robert E., Gates, Charlene, Whitaker, Anne, and Cotton, Paul G. 1989. The Suicidal Schizophrenic. In Jacobs, Douglas, and Brown, Herbert N., eds., Suicide, Understanding and Responding. *Madison, Conn.: International Universities Press.*

■

A matched controlled study of 30 chronic schizophrenic suicides is presented. Eighty per cent were male and committed suicide at a mean age of 25.8 years after a mean duration of illness of 4.8 years. Significantly more of the suicides had a chronic relapsing schizophrenic illness; 23.3 per cent committed suicide while in-patients, and 50 per cent of the out-patients committed suicide within three months of discharge from in-patient care. Significantly more of the suicides had a past history of depression (56.6 per cent), were depressed in the last episode of contact (53.3 per cent), had their last admission for depression or suicidal ideation (55.2 per cent) and were unemployed (80 per cent).

SCHIZOPHRENIC ILLNESS carries with it an increased risk for suicide. In a 20-year follow-up study of 500 schizophrenics admitted to the Phipps

Clinic at Johns Hopkins Hospital, Rennie (1939) found that 11 per cent of the 100 schizophrenics who had died had committed suicide. In England, Markowe et al. (1967) found that of 100 chronic schizophrenics first treated in the mid 1950s, 6 had committed suicide over the 10-year follow-up period. Winokur et al. (1975) found that at 30 to 40 years follow-up, 10 per cent of the 170 schizophrenics hospitalized in Iowa City between 1934 and 1944 had killed themselves. Using the records of the Houston Veterans Administration Hospital, Pokorny (1964) calculated that the suicide rate for male schizophrenic patients was 167 per 100,000 per year compared with the then U.S. national rate of about 10 per 100,000 per year. Miles (1977) reviewed all the available follow-up studies and estimated that 10 per cent of schizophrenics died by suicide, and that approximately 3,800 schizophrenics committed suicide per year in the United States.

Little is known, however, about the causes of suicide in schizophrenia. Since 1968 an audit has been routinely carried out when a psychiatric patient of the Clarke Institute of Psychiatry, Toronto, is known to have committed suicide. Thirty chronic schizophrenic patients of the Clarke have committed suicide between July 1968 and June 1979. Twenty-six of these 30 suicides met DSM-III diagnostic criteria for chronic schizophrenia (duration 2 years or more), while 4 met the criteria for subchronic schizophrenia (duration 6 months to 2 years) (APA, Diagnostic and Statistical Manual of Mental Disorders, 1978).

The aim of this study was to compare chronic schizophrenics who committed suicide with those who did not, and to try to determine risk factors for suicide in chronic schizophrenia.

SUBJECTS AND METHODS

Each of the 30 subchronic or chronic schizophrenic suicides was matched for sex, age (within 7 years) and type of schizophrenia (undifferentiated or paranoid) with the next patient who had presented at the Clarke, had been diagnosed as suffering from schizophrenia, and met DSM-III criteria for subchronic or chronic schizophrenia. The patients were not matched for social class, marital status or whether Canadian or foreign born in order to allow any potential differences between the groups to emerge.

All these charts, which included the reports from other psychiatric hospitals, were examined and data extracted. Social class was determined using the occupation of the head of the household of the family of origin and the classification of occupations of Goldthorpe and Hope (1974). Depressive disorder was only recorded if it met the criteria of DSM-III for a depressive episode.

The suicide and control groups were compared for potential social and psychiatric risk variables for suicide. The social variables examined included marital status, whether Canadian or foreign born, social class, religion, parental loss due to death of a parent, separation of or from parents for at least one year before 17 years of age, whether or not the patient was living alone or was unemployed at the time of suicide. The psychiatric variables examined included psychiatric disorder or suicide in a first degree relative; a history of a past suicide attempt, past psychiatric admission, past psychiatric treatment, and past depression and treatment for depression. In the last episode of psychiatric disorder, whether admitted, depressed and whether or not treated for depression (by antidepressant drugs or ECT) were recorded.

RESULTS

Within the group of suicides significantly more of the suicides were male: 24 of the 30 compared with 6 females ($P<0.05$). Sixteen of the 24 males had chronic undifferentiated schizophrenia compared with 1 of the 6 female suicides ($P<0.04$), 5 of whom had chronic paranoid schizophrenia compared with 8 of the 24 males ($P<0.04$).

The mean presenting age at the Clarke for the total 30 suicides was 24.8 years ($SD \pm 6.2$). For the 24 male suicides, the mean ages of onset of the illness and presentation at the Clarke were 21.0 and 23.3 years compared with 22.5 and 23.7 years for their controls (no significant differences). For the 6 female suicides, the mean ages of onset and presentation at the Clarke were 26.4 and 30.8 years compared with 30.8 and 33.1 years for their controls (no significant differences).

The mean duration of treatment at the Clarke for the total 30 suicides was 2.9 years ($SD \pm 2.7$). For the male suicides the mean total length of illness was 4.8 years compared with 5.9 years for their controls ($t=0.83$, no significant difference). The male suicides were treated at the Clarke for a significantly shorter period of time than their controls: 2.8 years compared with 4.4 years ($t=1.77$, d.f. 46, $P<0.05$). For the female suicides the total length of illness was 9.8 years compared with 9.3 years for their controls (no significant difference, $t=0.18$), the length of time treated at the Clarke was 4.4 years compared with 7.2 years for their controls (no significant difference, $t=1.39$).

Table 1. Ages, by Sex, for Suicides

	Men n = 24	Women n = 6	Significance
Age illness began	21.0	26.4	P <0.01
Age presented at Clarke	23.3	30.8	P <0.005
Total length of illness	4.8	9.8	P <0.02

The male suicides began their illness at a significantly earlier age, presented at the Clarke at an earlier age and had a shorter duration of illness before suicide than the female suicides (Table I).

Nine of the 30 suicides (8 men) committed suicide using firearms, 7 by throwing themselves under a subway train, 6 by jumping (all men), 3 by overdoses (2 women), 2 by hanging and 3 by unknown methods.

Social Variables

Eighteen of the 30 suicides were Canadian born and 12 foreign born compared with 16 and 14 respectively of the 30 controls (no significant differences). Fifteen of both groups were middle class and 15 working class (no significant differences). There were no significant differences between the groups for religious background. None of the 30 suicides had physical disease compared with 1 of the controls (no significance difference). Eleven of the 30 suicides had parental loss before 17 years of age compared with 14 of the controls (no significant difference).

Marital Status

Only 3 of the 30 suicides (10 per cent) were married and 25 (83.3 per cent) were single compared with 5 (16.6 per cent) and 21 (70 per cent) respectively of the controls (no significant differences). Two of the 6 female suicides were divorced compared with none of the 24 male suicides ($P<0.03$). Four of the female suicides were married or divorced compared with 1 married male suicide ($P<0.002$).

Unemployment

Twenty-four of the 30 schizophrenic suicides (80 per cent) were unemployed compared with 17 of the controls ($P<0.05$); 4 of the 6 female (66 per cent) and 20 of the 24 male (83.3 per cent) suicides compared with 1 and 16 of their respective controls (no significant differences).

Living Alone

Fourteen of the 30 (46.6 per cent) in both groups were living alone, 4 of the 6 females (66 per cent) and 10 of the 24 (41.7 per cent) male suicides compared with 1 and 13 of their respective controls (no significant differences).

Psychiatric Variables

Neuroleptics

Twenty-six of the 30 patients in both groups were receiving neuroleptics up to either the time of the study or transfer to another hospital (in 4 controls) or loss to follow-up. Amongst the four suicide patients not receiving neuroleptics, one was managed by a private practitioner, and amongst the four controls not receiving neuroleptics, one refused to take medication.

To compare the groups all the neuroleptic dosages were converted to equivalent daily doses of chlorpromazine. The 5 of the 6 female suicides on neuroleptics were receiving an equivalent mean daily dosage of chlorpromazine of 880.0 mg compared with the equivalent mean daily chlorpromazine dosage of 508.3 mg of the 6 female controls ($t = 1.0907$, no significant difference). For one male the daily dosage of his neuroleptic was unknown. The 20 male suicides on a known dosage of neuroleptics were receiving an equivalent mean chlorpromazine daily dosage of 597.5 mg compared with the 812.5 mg of the 20 male controls receiving neuroleptics ($t = 0.6363$, no significant difference). For the total 25 suicides receiving neuroleptics in known doses, the mean equivalent daily dosage of chlorpromazine was 654.0 mg compared with the 742.3 mg of the 26 controls ($t = 0.3220$, no significant differences).

Course of Illness

Significantly more of the suicides had a chronic schizophrenic illness with acute exacerbations (Table 2). Secondly more of the controls had a chronic illness with few acute exacerbations. Only two of the 24 male suicides had an illness with a chronic course with few acute exacerbations compared with 10 of the 24 male controls ($P < 0.009$). All 6 female suicides had a chronic

Table 2. Course of Illness

	Suicide n=30	Control n=30	Significance
Subchronic	3	1	NS
Chronic	2	13	P <0.001
Subchronic with acute exacerbation	1	1	NS
Chronic with acute exacerbation	24	15	P <0.01

illness with acute exacerbations compared with 3 of the 6 female controls (no significant difference).

Psychiatric Status at Time of Suicide

Twenty-seven of the 30 suicides were in active treatment at the Clarke at the time of suicide—one was seen only once for an assessment, one was managed by a private practitioner and one had dropped out of follow-up care.

Seven of the 30 committed suicide (23.3 per cent) while in-patients, while an eighth committed suicide after admission to hospital day care from outpatient care; all 8 were male. Only one committed suicide in hospital—by jumping.

One suicide patient was never admitted and it was not known when the patient seen once for assessment was an in-patient. Of the 20 who committed suicide after changing from in-patient to out-patient status, one died the next day, another 4 days later, a third 10 days later, a fourth of the 20 (25 per cent) after 2 weeks, a fifth and sixth after a month (30 per cent). Ten of the 20 (50 per cent) had committed suicide within three months, 13 of the 20 (65 per cent) within six months, and 18 of the 20 (90 per cent) within a year of changing from in-patient to out-patient care.

Family History of Psychiatric Disorder

Two of the 30 suicides had a first degree relative who had been treated for depression by a psychiatrist compared with 2 of the 30 controls; 1 had a first degree relative who had committed suicide compared with 1 of the 30 controls (no significant differences). One of the 30 suicides had drug or alcohol dependence (meeting DSM-III criteria) compared with 3 of the 30 controls (no significant difference).

Previous Suicide Attempt

Twelve of the 30 suicides (40 per cent) had made 26 previous attempts at suicide (mean 2.2 attempts) compared with 25 previous attempts by 11 of the 30 controls (36.6 per cent) (mean 2.1 attempts)—no significant differences.

Suicidal Behaviour and Schizophrenic Symptoms

In 2 of the 30 suicide patients (6.6 per cent) it was reasonably certain that they had committed suicide (one by jumping and one by hanging) as a consequence of persistent auditory hallucinations instructing them to kill themselves. However, this was not significantly different from the controls, two of whom had attempted suicide as a consequence of auditory hallucinations.

Depression

Significantly more of the suicides than the controls had in the past both been diagnosed by their psychiatrists as suffering from a depressive episode (meeting DSM-III criteria) and treated in the past for depression with either antidepressants or ECT (Table 3). Seventeen of the 30 suicides (56.6 per cent) had had a past depressive episode, and 14 of the 30 suicides (46.6 per cent) had been treated with antidepressants or ECT for depression.

Table 3. Psychiatric Variables

	Men			Women			Total		
	Suicide n=24	Control n=24	Sig.	Suicide n=6	Control n=6	Sig.	Suicide n=30	Control n=30	Sig.
Psychiatric history:									
Psychiatric disorder in first degree relatives	6	3	NS	2	2	NS	8	5	NS
Past depressive episode	14	4	P <0.003	3	1	NS	17	5	P <0.001
Past treatment for depression	10	7	NS	4	0	NS	14	7	P <0.05
Previous suicide attempt	10	10	NS	2	1	NS	12	11	NS
Number of admissions	3.9	3.3	NS	5.3	3.2	NS	4.2	3.3	NS
Last episode:									
Depressed in last episode	13	4	P <0.007	3	0	NS	16	4	P <0.001
Treated for depression in last episode	7	5	NS	2	1	NS	9	6	NS

In their last period of psychiatric contact, 16 of the 30 suicides (53.3 per cent) had been diagnosed by their psychiatrists as suffering from a depressive episode (meeting DSM-III criteria) compared with 4 controls (13.3 per cent)—$P<0.001$.

Psychiatric Admissions

Twenty-three of the 24 male suicide and control groups had had admissions to psychiatric wards. The 23 male suicides had had a total of 95 psychiatric admissions (mean 4.1 admissions) compared with a total of 79 psychiatric admissions for the 23 male controls (no significant difference, $t=0.78$). The 6 female suicides had had a total of 32 psychiatric admissions compared with a total of 19 admissions for the 5 of the 6 female controls who had an admission (no significant difference). Thus the total group of 30 suicides had had 127 psychiatric admissions (mean 4.2 admissions) compared with 98 psychiatric admissions of the total 30 control (mean 3.3 admissions)—no significant difference.

Reasons for All In-Patient Admissions at the Clarke

One suicide and 2 control patients were never admitted anywhere and 2 suicides and 3 controls never had an admission at the Clarke. Table 4 shows the reason for admissions to the Clarke for the 27 suicides' 86 admissions (mean 3.2 admissions) compared with the 25 controls' 60 admissions (mean 2.4 admissions)—no significant difference.

In the suicide group, 34 of the 86 admissions at the Clarke (39.5 per cent) were for schizophrenic symptoms plus either a depressive syndrome or suicidal ideation, impulses or attempts or for a depressive episode alone. These admissions were not accounted for by a small subgroup as 19 of the

Table 4. Reason for All Admissions to the Clarke

	Suicide n=86	Control n=60	Significance
1. Schizophrenic symptoms plus depressive episode	15	4	P <0.05
2. Schizophrenic symptoms plus suicidal	18	7	NS
3. Depressive episode	1	1	NS
4. 1, 2, and 3 together	34	12	P <0.009
5. Situational crisis	7	1	NS
6. Schizophrenic symptoms only	45	47	NS

Table 5. Reason for Last Admission

	Suicide n=29	Control n=28	Significance
1. Schizophrenic symptoms plus depressive episode	7	2	NS
2. Schizophrenic symptoms plus suicidal	8	3	NS
3. Depressive episode	1	2	NS
4. 1, 2, and 3 together	16	7	P <0.02
5. Situation crisis	3	2	NS
6. Schizophrenic symptoms only	10	19	P <0.01

27 suicides (70.3 per cent) had such an admission to the Clarke at some time compared with 10 of the 25 controls (40 per cent) ($P<0.03$).

Reasons for Last In-Patient Admission

In 2 of the suicides and 3 of the controls their last admission had not been at the Clarke, but their subsequent out-patient care was at the Clarke and summaries were in the chart. Table 5 shows the reason for the last admission for all these patients.

For 16 of the 29 suicides (55.2 per cent) their last admission had been precipitated by having become depressed or having suicidal ideas or impulses compared with 7 of the 28 controls (25 per cent)—$P<0.02$. In 4 of the suicides, 3 men and 1 woman, the last admission had been precipitated by a suicidal attempt compared with 5 of the controls, 4 men and 1 woman (no significant difference).

Management during Last In-Patient Admission

In order to compare the management of both groups in the same hospital, 2 suicides and 3 controls for whom their last admission had been at a hospital other than the Clarke, and the 1 suicide and 2 control patients who were never admitted, were omitted. The total length of time of the last admissions at the Clarke for these 27 suicides was 164 weeks (mean of 6 weeks) compared with the total 166 weeks (mean of 6.6 weeks) for the 25 controls (no significant difference). The risk of later suicide was noted in the case summary of 6 of the suicides compared with 5 of the controls (no significant difference). The management variables both before and during the last admission showed no significant differences between the suicides and their controls. During their last admission 15 of the suicides received social case work,

7 day care after admission and 6 vocational rehabilitation compared with 11, 7 and 8 respectively of the controls (no significant differences). When earlier admissions at the Clarke were examined, 11 of the suicides received social case work, 5 day care after admission, and 9 vocational rehabilitation compared with 6, 4 and 6 respectively of the controls (no significant differences).

Frequency of Out-Patient Appointments

Two control patients were never admitted, one went absent without leave and 4 were transferred as in-patients to other hospitals, and another was referred to a private practitioner. Thus 22 controls, 18 men and 4 women, were followed up at the Clarke after their last admission for a mean length of 28.9 months (range 1 month to 10 years) which was significantly longer than the mean 6.4 months (range 1 day to 2½ years) from changing from in-patient to out-patient care to suicide for the 20 suicides who experienced this ($t=2.72$, d.f. 40, $P<0.005$).

Fourteen suicides and 22 controls were seen long enough as Clarke out-patients after changing from their last in-patient status for a pattern of attendance to have become established. Five of these suicides were seen more frequently than monthly, 5 monthly and 4 less frequently compared with 11, 5 and 6 respectively of the controls (no significant differences).

DISCUSSION

This study confirms the previously reported male preponderance of suicide in schizophrenia. Warnes (1968) reported 16 schizophrenic patient suicides between 1962 and 1964 at the Douglas Hospital in Montreal; 13 of them were men (81.2 per cent). In the United States, Rennie's (1939) follow-up study showed that of the 11 per cent of the schizophrenics who committed suicide, 7 per cent were male and 4 per cent female. Tsuang (1978) found in Iowa that suicide was a significant factor in the long-term outcome only for male schizophrenics and clustered near the beginning of the follow-up period. From Norway, Noreik (1975) in a follow-up study of first admission schizophrenics reported that only 1 of 399 females (0.25 per cent) committed suicide in the first five years compared with 15 of 524 males (2.86 per cent) $P<0.001$.

The schizophrenic men began their illness at a significantly younger age and killed themselves after a significantly shorter duration than the women. This may account for the sex difference in marital status, significantly more of the women being married or divorced, and type of schizophrenia—significantly more of the males having chronic undifferentiated and more of the females paranoid schizophrenia. Seeman (1981) reviewed the evidence that females develop schizophrenia at a later age than males. All 6 women had a chronic relapsing illness with a non-significant greater mean number of admissions than the men—5.3 versus 4.1, but the women had their admissions over twice the length of illness of the men.

The possible role of neuroleptics in schizophrenic suicide has been a controversial point. Cohen et al. (1964) found no significant difference between schizophrenic suicide and control groups either for treatment with chlorpromazine (22 of the 40 suicides and 16 of 40 controls) or in the daily dosage; in both groups the mean daily dosage was over 300 mg. However, in 1968 Warnes compared phenothiazine dosage in 16 schizophrenic patient suicides with 16 chronic schizophrenic patients who had shown past suicidal behaviour. He found that 'significantly more control subjects were on a higher dosage than the experimental group'. However, in the study reported here there were no significant differences between the groups for numbers receiving neuroleptics or mean equivalent daily dosages of chlorpromazine.

In Cohen et al.'s study, 55 per cent had attempted or threatened suicide and 6 of the 16 suicides (37.5 per cent) reported by Warnes had made a previous suicide attempt and a further 6 had suicidal ruminations. Shaffer et al. (1974) considered that the number of previous suicide attempts was a predictor of eventual suicide in schizophrenia. From this study it appears that probably neither a past suicide attempt nor the number of attempts are helpful long-range predictors of eventual suicide in schizophrenia (40 per cent of the suicides versus 36.6 per cent of the controls).

Persistent auditory hallucinations may lead some chronic schizophrenics to commit suicide (Levy and Southcombe, 1953; Falloon and Talbot, 1981). This was thought to be the case in 2 suicides here.

Depression occurs in a substantial percentage of chronic schizophrenic patients. Amongst a consecutive series of 100 chronic undifferentiated schizophrenics who presented and were managed at the Clarke from the start of their illness, 39 per cent were treated for depression by antidepressants or ECT over the first six years, and amongst a similar series of 100 chronic paranoid schizophrenics, 30 per cent had a depressive episode over the first six years of illness (Roy, 1980; 1981). Knights et al. (1979) found that 54 per cent of a group of chronic schizophrenics experienced depressive symptoms over a six-month period and 27 per cent were prescribed antidepressant drugs. Falloon et al. (1978) reported a one-year drug trial and noted that 18 of the 48 schizophrenic patients (37.5 per cent) suffered significant episodes of depression and that depression was the principal reason for readmission to hospital. Warnes reported that 12 of his 16 schizophrenic suicides (75 per cent) had a 'hopeless awareness of their own pathology', and 4 (25 per cent) had been treated with antidepressants or ECT. Levy and Southcombe (1953) found depressive features in 6 of 23 (25.2 per cent) in-patient paranoid schizophrenic suicides. In this study, 17 of the 30 schizophrenic suicides (56.6 per cent) had had a past depressive episode and 14 (46.6 per cent) had past treatment for depression with antidepressants or ECT. The high frequency of a depressive syndrome (53.3 per cent of the suicides) confirms Cohen et al.'s finding that during their last hospitalization 28 of their 40 schizophrenic suicides (70 per cent) were rated as moderately or severely depressed compared with 15 of the 40 controls (38 per cent) ($P<0.01$). In over half of the suicides here (55.2 per cent) their last admission had been due to depression or suicidal impulses. Thus it is particularly the chronic schizophrenic patient who is admitted because of depression or suicidal impulses who is at risk for suicide.

The risk of suicide for psychiatric patients after leaving a mental institution was estimated to be 34 times as great as in the general population (Temoche et al., 1964). In Cohen et al.'s study, 18 of the 40 schizophrenics (45 per cent) committed suicide in hospital while 22 of the 40 (55 per cent) committed suicide 'outside the hospital while the patient had been on a pass, AWOL, trial visit, or recent discharge status'. In Warnes' study, 8 of the 16 (50 per cent) killed themselves while in-patients, '4 had left against advice, 2 were recently discharged and 2 were in foster homes'. In Pokorny and Kaplan's study (1976), 15 of 29 schizophrenics (51.7 per cent) committed suicide within a month of changing from in-patient to out-patient care. Similarly, in this study it was the schizophrenic who had been admitted who was at risk and it was particularly after changing back to out-patient care that suicide occurred—30 per cent within the first month and 50 per cent within three months.

Social isolation is frequent amongst both general population and psychiatric patient suicides (Dublin, 1963; Barraclough et al., 1974; Flood and Seager, 1968). In this study, 90 per cent of the suicides were unmarried and 46.6 per cent were living alone, although comparable figures were found in the controls. However, there was a significant difference for unemployment, 80 per cent of the suicides compared with 56.6 per cent of the controls.

This study suggests that there are risk factors for suicide in chronic schizophrenics. These include being young, male, having a chronic relapsing illness, having been depressed in the past, being currently depressed, being admitted for depression or suicidal ideas, and having recently changed from in-patient to out-patient care and being unemployed.

REFERENCES

American Psychiatric Association Task Force on Nomenclature and Statistics (1978) Diagnostic and Statistical Manual of Mental Disorders. *Washington, DC: American Psychiatric Association, pp C9–C12, E13, E14.*

Barraclough, B., Bunch, J., Nelson, B. & Sainsbury, P. (1974) A hundred cases of suicide. British Journal of Psychiatry, *125, 355–73.*

Cohen, S., Leonard, C. V., Farberow, N. L. et al. *(1964) Tranquillizers and suicide in the schizophrenic patient.* Archives of General Psychiatry, *11, 312–21.*

Dublin, L. (1963) Suicide: A Sociological and Statistical Study. *New York: Ronald Press.*

Falloon, I., Watt, D. & Shepherd, M. (1978) A comparative controlled trial of pimozide and fluphenazine decanoate in the continuation therapy of schizophrenia. Psychological Medicine, *8, 59–70.*

——— *& Talbot, R. (1981) Persistent auditory hallucinations: coping mechanisms and implications for management.* Psychological Medicine, *11, 329–39.*

Flood, R. & Seager, C. P. (1968) A retrospective examination of psychiatric case records of patients who subsequently committed suicide. British Journal of Psychiatry, *114, 443–50.*

Goldthorpe, J. H. & Hope, K. (1974) The Social Grading of Occupation: A New Approach and Scale, *pp. 134–43. New York: Oxford University Press.*

Knights, A., Okasha, M., Salih, M. & Hirsch, S. (1979) Depressive and extrapyramidal symptoms and clinical effects: A trial of fluphenazine versus flupenthixol in maintenance of schizophrenic out-patients. British Journal of Psychiatry, *135, 515–23.*

Levy, S. & Southcombe, R. (1953) Suicide in a state hospital for the mentally ill. Journal of Nervous and Mental Disease, *117, 504–14.*

Markowe, M., Steinert, J. & Heyworth-Davies, F. (1967) Insulin and chlorpromazine in schizophrenia: a ten-year comparative study. British Journal of Psychiatry, *113, 1101–6.*

Miles, P. (1977) Conditions predisposing to suicide: a review. Journal of Nervous and Mental Diseases, *164, 231–46.*

Noreik, K. (1975) Attempted suicide and suicide in functional psychoses. Acta Psychiatrica Scandinavica, *52, 81–106.*

Pokorny, A. (1964) Suicide rates in various psychiatric disorders. Journal of Nervous and Mental Diseases, *139, 499–506.*

——— *& Kaplan, H. (1976) Suicide following psychiatric hospitalization.* Journal of Nervous and Mental Disease, *162, 119–25.*

Rennie, T. A. C. (1939) Follow-up study of five hundred patients with schizophrenia admitted to the hospital from 1913 to 1923. Archives of Neurology and Psychiatry, *42, 877–91.*

Roy, A. (1980) Depression in chronic paranoid schizophrenia. British Journal of Psychiatry, *137, 138–9.*

——— *(1981) Depression in the course of chronic undifferentiated schizophrenia.* Archives of General Psychiatry, *38, 296–300.*

Seeman, M. (1981) Gender and the onset of schizophrenia: neurohumoral influences. Psychiatric Journal of the University of Ottawa, *6, 136–8.*

Shaffer, J., Perlin, S., Schmidt, C. & Stephens, S. (1974) The prediction of suicide in schizophrenia. Journal of Nervous and Mental Disease, *159, 349–55.*

Temoche, A., Pugh, T. & MacMahon, B. (1964) Suicide rates amongst current and former mental institution patients. Journal of Nervous and Mental Disease, *138, 124–30.*

Tsuang, M. T. (1978) Suicide in schizophrenics, manics, depressives and surgical controls: a comparison with general population suicide mortality. Archives of General Psychiatry, *35, 153–5.*

Warnes, H. (1968) Suicide in schizophrenia. Diseases of the Nervous System, *29, 35–40.*

Winokur, G. & Tsuang, M. T. (1975) The Iowa 500: Suicide in mania, depression and schizophrenia. American Journal of Psychiatry, *132, 650–1.*

29. The Abandoned Therapist

Dan H. Buie, Jr.

COMMENT

After surveying some of the narcissistic vulnerabilities of therapists nine years earlier, Dan H. Buie, Jr., returns to the subject to write about another: therapists' needs to derive soothing and closeness from their work with patients in order to ward off their own feelings of separation anxiety, depression, and rage (see chapter 18 above). This short paper reflects a deepening appreciation of the importance of psychotherapists' *personal balance as a factor necessary for favorable outcome in the treatment of suicidal, as well as other, cases.*

The excerpts to which the author refers belong to an article by Edward Shapiro (1982), of which "The Abandoned Therapist" is a discussion. In Excerpt I, a fragment of a interview with the parents of Mary (a hospitalized adolescent), the father ruefully recalls how as a child his daughter had steadily rejected physical demonstrations of affection. Though she pushed him away night after night, he insisted on kissing her goodnight anyway, though she repeatedly rejected him and pulled the covers over her head.

The excerpt referring to Fred B. is a case description from the same paper. Fred was a sixteen-year-old schizoid adolescent, chronically suicidal, most recently admitted to the hospital for attempting to hang himself. Fred was aloof, detached, unrelated, and sullen. In family sessions the mother was tearful, guilty, and ineffectual. The father seemed brusque and insensitive. In short, the family was profoundly disconnected from the patient. Fred's therapist, rejected and warded off by the patient, experienced a dream that made it clear that certain parts of the family's interaction were being unconsciously re-experienced in the countertransference. Self-analysis of the dream was followed by significant forward progress in this case.

Dan H. Buie, Jr., "The Abandoned Therapist." *International Journal of Psychoanalytic Psychotherapy* 9 (1982):227–232. Reprinted by permission.

REFERENCES

Shapiro, Edward R. 1982. The Holding Environment and Family Therapy with Acting Out Adolescents. International Journal of Psychoanalytic Psychotherapy *9:209–226.*

■

It is presupposed that the central motivation of psychotherapists is to derive a secure holding environment from the patient. The most fundamental need of human beings is the allaying of separation anxiety. As parents use their children to maintain an inner sense of security, the unresponsive child will cause the parent significant depression and anxiety. The parallel of the therapist's and parent's position with the patient/child is explored.

PSYCHOTHERAPISTS become psychotherapists out of a need to be sustained, and they look to patients to provide them with a holding environment that sustains them. Other motivations play a part in becoming a psychotherapist, but this one is central. Specifically, the therapist hopes, consciously or unconsciously, to be relieved of his sense of aloneness; prior to his own therapy or analysis he is unable, however, to conceive of the possibility of achieving for himself a comfortable sense of security as an autonomous human being. Instead he implicitly hopes that in meeting his patient's needs his own need for the kind of sustaining togetherness that mitigates depressive aloneness will be fulfilled. Even when his own treatment is successfully completed, he continues to yearn for comforting closeness with his patients, but his yearning is less a need and more simply a wish. Thus therapists remain vulnerable to using their patients this way, but the more mature they become and the more experienced they are, the less pressing is the need or wish, and the more likely it is that they will observe it in perspective before it grows troublesome.

The sicker spectrum of patients, including schizoid, borderline and some narcissistic personalities, are especially vulnerable to aloneness; they require a holding environment that supplies them with sustaining togetherness, e.g., from their parents and their therapist. When they are able (as much of the time they are not) to accept this caring togetherness, the parent or therapist who is allowed to give it experiences the pleasure of participating in the patient's state of peaceful security. The provider (parent or therapist) and the recipient (patient) both partake of the essential quality of the holding dyad, which is a feeling of close, soothing togetherness that allays separation anxiety. For the therapist this is the relief he has always sought. For the parent it is likewise palliative against the depression that was left unhealed by too much abandonment at the hands of his own parents. Both parent and therapist then share in common a need to gain an inner soothing security against their own separation anxiety through participating in a holding environment, which the patient/child makes possible by accepting, with implicit gratitude, the soothing togetherness that they offer him.

Separation anxiety—aloneness—precipitates states of depression and panic of such quality as to threaten subjectively the survival of the self. The most fundamental psychological need of human beings is, therefore, the allaying of separation anxiety, either through use of other persons or through use of one's own developed autonomous resources. When another person is elected to allay one's separation anxiety, failure or threat of failure by that person to do so elicits remarkable aggression and deep hostility. Mary's father (Excerpt I) needed her to accept his love in order that his aloneness might be soothed, but she was unresponsive and rejecting, fighting off his goodnight kisses and not allowing herself to be held. He was threatened with too much aloneness and responded with aggression and anger. His adaptability must be credited for salvaging something for himself and his daughter. He did not reject her in his rage. Instead he turned his aggression and hostility into years of persistence in kissing her goodnight, thus maintaining, probably to the benefit of both of them, a holding environment of sorts.

Inherent in parenthood is the need to use children for maintaining an inner sense of security (as well as worth and hope) and this need persists, silently in fortunate cases, throughout life to some degree. Quite apart from psychopathology, parents could be expected to react to an unresponsive or rejecting baby and child with significant depression and separation anxiety, along with aggression and hostility. If this child at some point becomes a patient, the psychotherapist would need or wish to use him as a resource for security in a similar way and would be vulnerable to reacting to rejection with similar anxiety and anger. The parallel of the therapist's and parents' positions in relation to the patient/child lends itself to direct empathic understanding of the parent's experience with their child. This was evident in the excerpt involving Fred B. and his parents. Although the therapist responded with anger at the abandoning parents, in empathic accord with the patient's anger with them, he also was aware of being angry with Fred for subjecting him to the same kind of rejection that he inflicted on the parents. The example invites closer attention, which in turn requires speculation in the service of making a general point.

Despite their pathologies and limitations, Fred's parents loved him; although defended against it, with help they could also acknowledge their yearning and hopelessness about his loving them. They had not been able to prepare him for their absences through the years, because to do so would have meant painfully acknowledging that they yearned to be truly important to their son. This acknowledgment would have threatened them with despair and aloneness to whatever extent they believed he did not need them. To the extent they believed that he did need and love them, it would have threatened to precipitate the grief "over what had been lost in past family relationships" that finally came to light in family therapy. They could not have stood this grief outside a therapeutic holding environment. They loved and needed Fred, then, and even though they could not acknowledge it, they needed Fred to love and need them.

Unlike their other children, Fred rejected his parents overtly, not only in the form of obliqueness, indirectness, suspiciousness, and a detached stance toward them, but also by means of the most hateful possible punishment and rejection—repeatedly threatening to deprive them of their child by suicide, on one occasion violently. In the face of their need for him, they must have responded with separation anxiety and murderous rage. The excerpt does not tell us about these feelings in the parents and how they managed them. Undoubtedly they used various defenses to avoid awareness, especially of hating Fred. To what extent did their struggle with these feelings lead to further guilt, helplessness, and incompetence in relating to him? To what extent was their unpredictable cancelling of appointments, about which the father was very defensive, a means both of expressing and avoiding their rage? To what extent was their cancelling an evidence that an adequate holding environment had not been established for them?

The forces of need (e.g., for a closeness with Fred that would quiet his own residual separation anxiety) were operating in the therapist also. He may not have elected Fred to serve that purpose on first meeting. It probably happened slowly as Fred initially responded to the therapist's efforts to engage him in discussions. As Fred allowed himself to be "held" by the therapist, the therapist came to depend somewhat on holding him in order to feel better held himself. Then came relentless behaviors, now directed at the therapist, of the sort that the parents had suffered. Fred once expressed his angry, assaultive rejectingness by putting out a live cigarette on the palm of his hand in front of the therapist. Open rejection was displayed in silences as well as lateness and nonattendance of therapy. The therapist began to feel disconnected, hopeless, and confused, rather like the parents had come to feel.

In this setting Fred's therapist had a dream, ". . . in which he was profoundly identified with Fred and in a rage at the B. parents who had gone off unpredictably leaving him alone." One can guess the ways this dream deepened understanding of Fred's rage with his parents and the parent's rage with Fred. Self-analysis yielded insight into two countertransferences, both traced to the same genetic roots in the therapist's having been too much abandoned by his own parents. One countertransference was expressed in the manifest content: the therapist was enraged with the B. parents. In part this rage derived from empathy with Fred; in part it was the therapist's rage with his own parents displaced onto Fred's. This insight must have enhanced the therapist's understanding of the intensity and quality of Fred's rage, as well as relieved the therapeutic situation of some inappropriate anger toward the B. parents.

The other countertransference was contained altogether in the latent content of the dream and was the more powerful stimulus for the dream. It consisted of rage with Fred for threatening the therapist's sense of security. Fred's rejecting behavior stirred the therapist's repressed feelings and memories about the abandonment by his own parents, which had formed the basis for his ongoing wish to use Fred and other patients to feel secure. This latent content was disguised in the manifest content by using the B. parents to stand, by displacement, for his own parents and also to stand, by displacement, for Fred himself. Rage at his own parents and at Fred could be focused then on the B. parents. Analysis of the dream allowed recognition of countertransference rage with Fred, which, in turn, provided the therapist access to better understanding of the B. parents. It became apparent that they must be enraged with Fred for reasons similar to the therapist's, and their need for Fred and rage with him must similarly be based on childhood experiences that resembled the therapist's.

It is important that the therapist analyzed his dream so completely. He discovered that, in order to preserve hope for secure togetherness with Fred, he had been displacing his anger with Fred onto Fred's parents. Without this insight the crucial parallel between his countertransference experience with Fred and the B. parents' experience with their son would have been missed. The parents would have been deprived of empathic and cognitive understanding of their need and rage, and their acting out through abandoning Fred and the treatment would have continued. The therapist's empathic understanding of them, which he undoubtedly shared with the couple's therapist, enabled provision of a more therapeutic holding environment for the parents. This must have alleviated some of their anger and much of their rejecting behavior, diminished their guilt, and helped them to relate more effectively with their son.

CONCLUSION

This is another in a fine series of papers describing Dr. Shapiro's excellent clinical studies of acting out adolescents and their families. The report of clinical work, countertransference, and self-analysis is a courageous one that allows a discussant to engage freely with the material. It provides a context for expressing some opinions about parents, patients, and psychotherapists:

1. Therapists become therapists partly in search for a holding environment that will allay their own separation anxieties.
2. The holding environment that the therapist provides to patients, when it is accepted by patients, serves to hold the therapist as well.
3. The rejecting patient deprives the therapist of holding, thereby precipitating separation anxiety, depression, and rage.
4. Parents similarly have need for a holding environment provided to them by the patient/child's acceptance of their caring, and rejection by the patient/child similarly brings separation anxiety and rage.
5. A natural parallel exists between the countertransference of the therapist and the reaction of parents, and this countertransference is a resource for the empathic understanding of parents that is necessary in order to provide them with a therapeutic holding environment.
6. The therapist, in order to safeguard his dyadic holding environment with the patient from his own reactive hostility, may unconsciously displace his hostility onto the parents; he may then rationalize this defense by declaring it to be a simple empathic response to the patient's rage with his parents because of the rejection he suffers at their hands.
7. Defensive means of avoiding countertransference rage with the patient threaten to undercut the holding environment the therapist could otherwise offer the parents; they also threaten to interfere with the patient's therapy because, to the extent it is kept unconscious, the therapist's hostility with the patient is likely to be expressed in unseen ways.

30. Psychotherapeutic Considerations in the Management of the Suicidal Patient

John Birtchnell

AUTOBIOGRAPHICAL NOTE

John Birtchnell writes from the Institute of Psychiatry, London: "In November 1966 I left my National Health Service post to do a one year full-time training in psychodynamic psychotherapy. In the same year I was awarded an M.D. for a thesis entitled 'Parent Death and Mental Illness.' At the end of that year I was torn between pursuing a career in psychotherapy and pursuing one in research. I was successful in obtaining a clinical research fellowship from the Medical Research Council and that set me on a research career. By the early 1970s, because of my psychotherapy training, I was beginning to have serious doubts about the epidemiological research methods which I was being urged to adopt and I wrote three papers pointing to their limitations (Birtchnell 1973, 1974, 1978). The director of my research unit objected strongly to these papers and would have blocked their publication if he could. At about the same time I began a research project on a series of subjects who had made serious suicide attempts, taking detailed notes about their past and present life circumstances and conducting psychotherapy on them. A paper about the research was included in the Proceedings of the Ninth International Congress of Psychotherapy in Oslo in 1973. This was later reproduced in Psychotherapy and Psychosomatics *(Birtchnell 1975). The director of the unit became increasingly embarrassed about the project, excluded any mention of it from his annual report to the Medical Research Council, and transferred my co-worker to a different location. I worked in the unit until 1982, continuing to include more personal accounts of the study subjects in my research and continuing to receive adverse reports on my work. I also continued to treat*

John Birtchnell, "Psychotherapeutic Considerations in the Management of the Suicidal Patient." *American Journal of Psychotherapy, 37* (1983):24–36. Reprinted by permission of the Association for the Advancement of Psychotherapy.

suicidal patients by psychotherapy, though not as a part of a research project. The [paper reproduced in this volume] was a distillate of my experiences during this period. From 1982 onwards, I worked in a different research unit where my work was more appreciated, but I cannot help thinking that I would have had an easier life had I become a professional psychotherapist."

COMMENT

"The more respectful the therapist is of the patient's right to take his own life, the more open will the patient be about his suicidal intent," says Birtchnell. He asserts that after a period of psychotherapy the patient's suicidal resolve should be respected when it is based on a clear appraisal that his situation is personally intolerable. These bold words will shock many readers; the current ethos *demands the prevention of suicide at all costs. In the face of the general conviction to the contrary, Birtchnell argues that suicide can be rational even in the absence of terminal physical illness.*

Few psychotherapists in the United States possess the sang-froid *to adopt Birtchnell's position; to do so would expose them to legal reprisal should a patient die. Nevertheless, it underscores a central truth voiced by Herbert Hendin (see chapter 27 above): One of the most lethal trends in suicidal patients in their tendency to make others responsible for their survival. Were it possible for more therapists to minimize their proclivity for rescuing action, and to concentrate instead on what in their patients' characters renders them so ready to abandon attachment to life, many treatments might proceed with greater success.*

The narcissistic needs of therapists not to lose a patient to suicide (to avoid abandonment by the patient) have been addressed in the preceding chapter by Dan H. Buie, Jr. Birtchnell implies that it is just such narcissistic concerns that underlie the contemporary ethical demands to prevent all suicides.

The perspective set forth here at least alerts caregivers to the destructive effect of excessive readiness to compel hospitalization. Certainly Birtchnell is correct in asserting that it is preferable that patients "should ask for help in resisting their suicidal urges and not have controls imposed upon them," though this is not always possible.

Successful treatment of suicidal patients, especially those who are suicidal in character organization, must always rest on their re-establishing enough investment in living to surrender their tendency to thrust responsibility for it on others. Birtchnell suggests much that is useful in moving toward that end.

REFERENCES

Birtchnell, John. 1973. How Appropriate Is the Epidemiological Approach to the Investigation of the Familial Causation of Mental Illness? British Journal of Medical Psychology *46:365–371.*

———. *1974. Is There a Scientifically Acceptable Alternative to the Epidemiological Study of Familial Factors in Mental Illness?* Social Science and Medicine *8:335–350.*

———. *1975. The Special Place of Psychotherapy in the Treatment of Attempted Suicide, and the Special Type of Psychotherapy Required.* Psychotherapy and Psychosomatics *25:3–6.*

———. *1978. The Peculiar Problems of Psychiatric Research.* British Journal of Medical Psychology *51:113–118.*

■

Therapists' responses to suicidal patients include: anxiety, increased interest, restraint, irritation, avoidance, denial, and passivity. The psychopathology of such patients includes excessive attachment, regression, dependence, sensitivity to rejection or separation, aggression, low self-esteem and despair. Assessment of suicide risk and involvement of significant others are important aspects of treatment.

> One must approach such a phenomenon as suicide with the greatest caution, for any act that opposes the instinct of life is bound to arouse in us a set of reactions which interfere with a clear and purely rational understanding of the phenomenon itself. Gregory Zilboorg, 1936[1]

A USEFUL ANALOGY may be drawn between our attitudes towards suicide and homosexuality. There are both homosexual and suicidal inclinations in all of us. What disturbs the therapist in both situations is the capacity of the subject to arouse his own latent emotions and perhaps bring them out more strongly. There is always the nagging question "Why can't he be more like the rest of us?" and the wish, either consciously or unconsciously, to "convert" him. Just as abstinent alcoholics derive strength to resist their own alcoholic tendencies with every wayward drinker they pull back from the brink, so too does the therapist's love of life increase with every suicidal patient he deters. This should not, of course, necessarily be the object of therapy any more than keeping a marriage intact should be the object of marital therapy. It is conceivable that, after a period of psychotherapy, the patient's resolve to kill himself may be stronger than ever and that his resolve is based upon a clearer appraisal of his situation. Under such circumstances the therapist should be prepared to accept the patient's decision with good grace.

THE THERAPIST'S REACTION TO THE PATIENT'S INTIMATION OF SUICIDAL INTENT

Mintz suggested that "attitudes towards suicide, held knowingly or unknowingly by the therapist may prevent him from adequately inquiring into the suicidal ruminations of his patient."[2] The therapist is inclined to resort to one or more defensive responses to enable him to cope with the suicidal patient.

Anxiety

At a personal level, apart from the aforementioned arousal of the therapist's own suicidal inclinations, is the idea that a suicide attempt is a form of rejecting behavior. At a professional level is the need to judge correctly how likely it is that the patient will act upon his feelings. Should the patient commit suicide, the therapist may feel he has failed as a clinician. He may fear the disapproval of his colleagues, the coroner's accusing finger, and unfavorable publicity.

Some psychiatrists play safe every time and invariably take precautionary action; there are, however, therapeutic rewards to taking a calculated risk, which is why many therapists do so. More often than not the patient is aware of the therapist's anxiety, and the more anxious the therapist appears to be the more likely is the patient to believe himself capable of self-destruction. The patient feels insecure if he is aware that he can easily frighten his therapist. Mayer[3] stressed the importance of conveying to the patient that his reputation "is in no way dependent on the patient's getting better or even of his staying alive." This is, of course, not entirely true. It is, however, important not to appear intimidated and to emphasize to the patient that he, not the therapist, should be the one to decide whether he lives or dies.

Increased Interest

Henderson[4] includes the expression of suicidal intent and making suicidal attempts among what he terms care-eliciting behaviors. Patients readily become aware of the intensification of the caring attitude in the therapist following their expression of suicidal intent. Therapists, like husbands or parents, almost instinctively become more caring towards someone they fear they may be going to lose. The therapist should become alerted to this possibility and make a determined effort not to allow such a response to show. Lest this may cause bewilderment in the patient he should explain that he genuinely does care about the patient but that he will care neither more nor less if the patient gives expression to his suicidal feelings.

Restraint

The concept of restraint is closely related to that of suicide prevention. The word "prevention" has more than one connotation: preventing fires is not the same as preventing someone from lighting a fire. The psychotherapist mostly prevents suicide by the offer of a trusting relationship; rarely does he physically restrain the patient. Restraint is also something to do with the incomprehensibility of suicide. Freud[5] wrote:

> So immense is the ego's self-love, which we have come to recognise as the primal state from which instinctual life proceeds, and so vast is the amount of narcissistic libido which we see liberated in the fear that emerges at a threat to life, that we cannot conceive how the ego can consent to its own destruction.

It was once believed that one could not commit suicide unless the balance of one's mind was disturbed, though exactly what that involved was never clearly defined. There is, of course, ample evidence that at various times in history in various cultural groups, people have indulged freely in suicide. The justification for much restraint of suicidal individuals is that ultimately the balance of their mind will be restored and the suicidal urge will pass.

Restraint is also related to censorship: you stop people doing something you would rather they would not do. It is often quite difficult to refrain from intervening when someone is intent on doing something which you cannot bear to witness—like being cruel to animals. Bernard Williams, the Cambridge (England) philosopher, in a lecture to British Samaritans, likened suicide to emigration and has drawn a parallel between those who actively try to prevent people committing suicide and those totalitarian regimes that impose restrictions on people leaving the country. He, too, maintains that the only justification for restraint is a conviction that in time the person will change his mind. An important question is, how long does one wait? The picture is complicated by the fact that aiding and abetting a suicide is still a criminal offence. If you let a patient free, knowing that he intends to kill himself, are you assisting him to do it?

Restraint is restricting the mobility of the individual and depriving him of the responsibility for his actions. It is not unlike, and sometimes amounts to, imprisonment. Initially he may respond with resentment and protest; subsequently he may become subdued, resigned, and accepting. After a prolonged period of restraint a person finds it difficult to resume responsibility for his actions and he may even come to like decisions being made for him. It is an important principle of psychotherapy that patients should actively determine their own futures and should be discouraged from seeking direction from the therapist. It is preferable, therefore, that they should ask for help in resisting their suicidal urges and not have controls imposed upon them.

Irritation

Patients who make suicide attempts are accused of attention or sympathy seeking. Feeling that they have "cried wolf" once too often, long-suffering relatives are prone to respond with: "Why don't you make a proper job of it next time?" or "Stop beating about the bush and get on with." Such remarks are sometimes interpreted by the patient as confirmation of what he had long suspected, that they really do want him out of the way. He then feels he has permission to make a more serious attempt. Doctors and nurses in general hospitals often make clear their intolerance of suicide attempters, accusing them of wasting time or taking up beds of which genuinely ill patients are more deserving. Such responses, however, are not uncommon among psychiatrists and even psychotherapists. Andriola[6] observed that therapists who accuse their patients of "playing games" or "shilly-shallying" strip them of any remaining shred of hope and encourage them to kill themselves. The trivial attempt may be a way of saying: "If things go on like this I might as well kill myself." If this is so, it is important for the therapist to convey that he has registered the extent of the patient's despair but, at the same time, to tactfully point out that this might not be the most effective way of bringing about the desired change.

Avoidance

Suicidal patients, like psychotic patients, are frequently kept at a distance and "handled with kid gloves." This has largely to do with an irrational fear of them, almost a fear of contamination, causing both suicidal and psychotic patients to feel even more estranged from people. A similar defense is to "medicalize" the problem and to want only to know about the illness from which the patient is suffering. By this means the therapist conveys to the patient that the suicidal urge is a manifestation of the illness, that it has nothing to do with the patient himself. If the patient can allow the doctor to eliminate the illness he will find that his suicidal urge has gone away.

Related to this approach is to consider the suicidal urge solely as a symptom. The psychiatrist asks the patient whether he feels that life is worth living; whether he feels like putting an end to it all. Once the patient has answered yes, the symptom has been elicited, and the psychiatrist wishes to know no more. He has no inclination to experience the full blast of the suicidal feeling, believing perhaps that the closer to the surface it is brought the more likely is the patient to act upon it.

A case could be made for giving the patient the opportunity to accept and own his suicidality, to give free emotional expression to it, perhaps even to enact suicide in a kind of psychodrama. This opportunity the patient will probably welcome; but before he is prepared to do this he will need assurance that he is not going to be certified or locked up, however strongly he expresses his suicidal feelings. So often patients feel that admitting to being suicidal is equivalent to a criminal confessing his guilt.

Denial

Denial represents a step beyond even avoidance, and because it is so extreme a reaction it can have fatal consequences. People in eminent positions are sometimes allowed to commit suicide, despite previous intimations that they may do so, because no one is prepared to acknowledge the seriousness of their plight. Suicidal doctors are sometimes similarly ignored by their colleagues. Denial is so strong in these circumstances because of role rigidity. The eminent person is the figurehead towards whom everybody looks for guidance. The doctor is the well one who treats those who are unwell. The eminent person and the doctor find it as difficult to ask for help as others do to offer it. Conceivably this reaction can also occur when the therapist has reason to identify with a patient due to some similarity of life situation.

Passivity

Passivity has also to do with the doctor's or therapist's role behavior. It is conventional for the transaction between therapist and patient to take place in the therapist's office, at appointed times, for specified periods. The therapist maintains a posture of unruffled calm, listening with interest and conveying appropriate concern. For the suicidal patient, this is sometimes insufficient. His problem is, "Nobody cares whether I live or die" and he becomes plagued with the question, how much does his therapist care? He askes, "Would he see me if I didn't pay him? Would he see me at an inconvenient time? Would he come to rescue me if I were dying?" Patients sometimes complain, "You only see me because it's your job to do so." It is a well-established principle that patients should not be allowed to manipulate their therapists, though why this is of such vital importance is never made clear.

People often make suicide attempts when they feel let down or rejected by a significant other person. They are kept alive by finding themselves able to transfer cathexis on to the therapist. Under these circumstances it is hard for them to accept the impassive attitude of the therapist as an adequate replacement for the love of the significant other. It may therefore be necessary for the therapist to extend himself more than he is normally inclined to do in order to convince the patient that he is human.

ASPECTS OF THE PSYCHOPATHOLOGY OF SUICIDAL INDIVIDUALS

It is pertinent now to review some of the more salient characteristics of suicidal individuals and to outline methods of coping with them.

The Need for Attachment

The person who makes a suicide attempt is in a kind of emotional limbo: he has severed his ties with life and his affectional bonds with all significant others. This is an intensely painful state which is hard to bear for long. The pain is relieved by alcohol or other sedative drugs, which is what makes the overdose so tempting. On emergence from unconsciousness the pain returns. At such times rather than offer further sedatives it is preferable for the therapist to offer himself as a source of comfort. Actual physical contact in the form of a reassuring hug may help to consolidate the attachment.

It is important for the therapist to realize the intensity with which the patient clings to him in this kind of situation, and to accept that he has become the patient's reason for living. Once the bond has formed, as with imprinting, it is difficult to pass the patient on to someone else either by referral to an outpatient clinic or through hospital admission. Continuity of care is essential. Initially, at least, it is necessary for the therapist to present himself as a constant, warm, attentive, tolerant, sympathetic, understanding person. As the patient re-establishes relationships with friends and relatives such indulgence may be relaxed.

Regression

The attachment of the suicidal patient to the therapist is reminiscent of that of the newborn infant to its mother. Mintz[2] has observed that the patient may even be unable to walk or leave the bed and proposed that the "concept of regression is a clinically useful one in attempting to understand changes in many suicidal patients." A state of regression in an adult is not an easy condition to witness and the therapist must beware of his own inclination to avoid or terminate it for unsound reasons. Regression may manifest itself in an excessive preoccupation with sleeping, feeding or the ingestion of drugs, petulance, and the abandonment of adult rationality in favor of drive-dominated, impulsive behavior. Some patients speak in a childish voice, spend money irresponsibly, drive recklessly, become involved in fights, and do damage to property.

Dependence

Suicidal behavior is a common feature of the dependent personality. Dependent individuals respond to stress by adopting the posture of helplessness, clinging, asking to be told what to do, and wanting to be looked after. This is antitherapeutic, since the object of therapy should be to enable the patient to become more responsible for his behavior. Just as the overprotective parent does his child no good by continuously sheltering him from danger, so the therapist does no service to his patient by too readily responding to his cries for help. Schwartz et al.[7] wrote: "The suicidal character type is that form of the generally dependent character type in which suicidal threat is the specific device by which succorance is coerced from others." They proposed that management of such persons entails taking a short-term risk by resisting responding to suicidal threats as a means of modifying their life style over a period of time.

Tabachnick,[8] who considered the suicide attempter to be "often a person who is more than usually dependent in a rather infantile manner," believed that such a person was afraid to express his irritation or anger towards frustrating objects because he was afraid that a lack of dependent support might ensue. An appropriate therapeutic attitude might therefore be to encourage him to dare directing his aggressive feelings outward, initially on to the therapist and subsequently towards relevant family members.

It is probable that the suicidal individual has never progressed beyond what Mahler[9] has termed the symbiotic relationship to the parent, that is, a relationship which does not permit either parent or child to feel a truly separate being. For such a person adult relationships become a replication of this, and in marriage neither partner feels free to develop a separate identity. Attempts to do so by one generate anxiety in the other.

Sensitivity to Rejection or Separation

Richman[10] has described separation as "the major precipitant for seriously suicidal behaviour" and Litman[11] observed that suicide during therapy most often occurred during periods when patient and therapist were separated. This is what Bowlby[12] has termed "anxious attachment." In this state the subject may exhibit dramatic fluctuations in mood which are directly related to his estimation of the success he is having in his relationships with the therapist or significant others. He is liable to react with dejection to reprimands or mildly critical remarks. Failure of a relative to keep a promise to phone can cause him to plummet into a state of intense gloom, with the emergence of further suicidal preoccupation or attempts. Evidence of positive feeling, such as a loving letter, can bring about immediate amelioration of despair. It is important, therefore, for the therapist, as far as he is able, to be punctual for appointments and true to his word.

The suicidal individual has experienced what he considers to be rejecting behavior by others on many occasions. Each time it has hurt and he has resolved never to entrust himself to another person again. He goes on trying and repeatedly getting hurt. With each failed relationship his hold on life becomes progressively more tenuous.

Ambivalence

It is the ambivalence of the suicidal patient that imposes such a strain upon the therapeutic relationship. He is ambivalent towards the world, towards living, towards significant others, and, therefore inevitably, towards the therapist. He is half resentful and half grateful for being brought back to life. He listens to the therapist's arguments, observes his efforts to be understanding, experiences the warmth that is offered him, knowing that he always has the option to turn away and go back to death. He tries the patience of the therapist by not keeping or turning up late for appointments, making telephone calls at inconvenient hours, requiring extra time, needing emergency appointments, not co-operating with treatment and, in general, playing hard to get. He consoles himself with the thought that he cannot lose because he is not much interested in staying alive anyway: if he accumulates debts or commits criminal offences he is making it more difficult for himself to become re-established in life. He knows that by killing himself he can wipe the slate clean and render the whole business irrelevant. In a sense the therapist has no right to object to the punishment doled out to him by the suicidal patient because, in the patient's eyes, he had no need to get involved in the first place. Why did he not just let him die?

The thought that sustains the therapist throughout the struggle is that the patient is not as determined to die as he is making out. Though the patient does not show it, he is gradually being worn down by the therapist's persistence and though partly amused by the efforts of the therapist, he is secretly appreciative. The therapist stands as a representative of humanity and by warming to the therapist the patient is warming to the world.

Aggression

Maddison and Mackay[13] expressed the opinion that "underestimation of the patient's aggressiveness, whether this be due to the clinician's inexperience or to his own personal defence structure, is the largest single factor responsible for errors of judgment in these cases." Certainly a recurrent theme in the histories of suicidal patients is this overt or covert anger expressed against those in their past and present who have not responded to their demands for affection. Mintz[2] warned that the therapist "may not adequately realize that the anger or hostility the patient is expressing towards him would be expressed towards any person attempting treatment. In his own insecurity, the therapist may take the patient's castigations personally, and his own behavioral response may iatrogenically complicate the treatment process." Draper[14] went so far as to suggest that the therapist may be actually in danger "should a rageful psychotic transference continue in development."

It is well established that violent behavior is frequently directed at those who are most dearly loved.[15] Parents batter their children and husbands batter their wives. Aggression is often generated by the nonreciprocation of affectionate overtures and it would almost seem that the aggressor hopes to evoke loving responses by his hostility. It would be inappropriate here to deal at great length with the extensive literature which conceives of suicidal behavior as a "miscarried aggressive act directed towards an important figure in the patient's life."[16]

Opinions differ as to how best to deal with the aggression of the suicidal patient. Mintz[2] has advised that until the patient can become aware of his hostility and can gain control over such behavior it may be desirable to attempt to limit the degree of anger aroused in the patient. Richman[10] proposed that it is "better to permit and control its expression in therapy than to suppress or avoid it." His rationales for this were (1) ". . . that rage is often so intense and the pressure so great that need for sheer discharge is called for" and (2) ". . . if not expressed in the office, aggression will be expressed at home under less controlled conditions." Mayer,[3] in general agreement with this point of view, pointed out that "the therapist may convince the patient, perhaps for the first time, that he can be accepted in spite of his rage and hatred." She considered this sometimes to be a turning point in therapy.

Low Self-Esteem

To varying extents the suicidal individual believes himself to be better out of the way, since he has nothing to offer and causes unhappiness to those around him. Breaking down this negative self-image is one of the most difficult aspects of the treatment of the suicidal patient. What complicates the therapist's task is the patient's realization that if he is convinced that he has worth he will have to stay alive. He therefore continues to court disaster and to throw up his failures as further evidence of his worthlessness.

The first principle of treatment is to behave in a respectful way towards the patient and to be appreciative of his positive features. Related to this is to reveal to him, by providing appropriate feed-back, the effect that his habitual attitudes have upon other people. Next, it is important to point out to him the discrepancy between his various attributes and his own conception of these, reminding him of the objective evidence of his worth which he chooses to ignore. Finally, it is necessary to discover the origin of his low opinion of himself which is likely to be based upon unfavorable parental attitudes towards him. It is likely that he carries around within him their assessment of him and applies it indiscriminately to present situations. Some form of assertiveness training may be desirable to combat this.

Despair

The suicidal patient is obsessed with the hopelessness of his situation, the meaninglessness of life, and the pointlessness of going on. This attitude has a contagious quality and may induce a similar attitude in the therapist who is himself overcome by an overwhelming sense of failure at his inability to lift the patient out of this pessimistic state. One almost reflex response to this is to try to cheer him up, to try to convince him that things are not so bad and to point to this or that area of his life where things look brighter. Staying with the despair is more likely to bring about an intense catharsis which may have the effect of dislodging the patient from his immobile posture. If, for instance, the despair can be converted into anger, he may be motivated to act upon the anger.

Another response to despair is, of course, to want to do something, such as institute or change a treatment regime, admit the patient to hospital or pass him on to another therapist. Action out of a sense of impotence is rarely effective. The patient, suspecting that the therapist is just going through the motions, feels even more disheartened. In fact, an attitude of constant acceptance may be sufficient to maintain a despairing patient over a protracted period of time.

GENERAL THEMES IN THE TREATMENT OF THE SUICIDAL PATIENT

The Role of the Significant Other

Fawcett et al.[17] have shown that the suicide risk is highest among those who have the greatest difficulty in relating to others and emphasized the need to identify "specific facets or manifestations of this paucity of relating." Fellner[18] has described the suicide attempt as a "direct outcome of an interpersonal conflict situation with a specific, psychologically important figure."

Maddison and Mackey[13] observed that "the psychiatrist will find on numerous occasions that his therapeutic efforts with the primary patient are opposed by the overt or covert hostile destructive behavior and attitudes of the specific important figure to whom the patient is relating." They pointed to the need to sometimes hospitalize the patient as a means of temporarily interrupting this pathological relationship. Richman and Rosenbaum[19] observed that the suggestion by relatives that the subject should kill himself "occurs with remarkable frequency" and Richman[10] remarked that therapists are sometimes shocked by the "raw destructiveness and directness of the expression of death wishes by relatives." Examples are occasionally quoted in the literature of one member of a partnership delaying seeking help, following a suicide attempt, in the conscious or unconscious hope that this may prove fatal. Maddison and Mackey[13] further warn that relatives "cannot always be trusted to remove from the patient's orbit all significant instruments of suicide." Tabachnick[8] proposed that suicide attempts arise when dependency needs are not met. This is especially liable to occur when two excessively dependent individuals are married to each other. "Often," he said, "we infer a kind of race to see who will use the weapon of suicide first." Litman et al.[20] also observed that "often both of the partners in the dyad are potentially suicidal."

Involvement of the Significant Other in Therapy

Sometimes, of course, the significant other has departed from the scene and the suicide attempt represents a bid to effect a reversal of this state of affairs. As the initial first-aid treatment of the attempter is the establishment of a close bond with the therapist, the significant other, quite reasonably, will feel that the therapist and attempter are allied against him and this may thwart attempts to resolve the conflicts which gave rise to the attempt. It is important for the significant other to feel that he has an ally: it is therefore desirable to introduce a second therapist. It is important, too, that he should be given the opportunity to express more openly his murderous feelings towards the attempter and the consequent guilt. A useful arrangement is to involve both partners and both therapists in combined therapy sessions, while still affording each the opportunity to have individual sessions. Frequently several family members are involved. For this reason Richman involves the entire family in therapy, relying heavily upon "the healing forces of the family itself."

Assessment of Suicide Risk and the Need for Hospitalization

There is no absolute quantity of suicidality in any one patient: he may be highly suicidal one minute and not suicidal the next. The more respectful the therapist is of the patient's right to take his own life, the more open will the patient be about his suicidal intent. An orthodox psychiatrist, inclined to view the patient as a case of depression, is likely to have the most difficulty eliciting suicidal tendencies and be the least successful in modifying them. A therapist who has established a strong, holding relationship is capable of sustaining a patient with powerful suicidal urges. In fact, a patient with a close, trusting relationship with his therapist will spontaneously ask for help if his suicidal urges become hard to resist.

Only rarely should compulsory admission to hospital be resorted to. The most compelling reason would be the inaccessibility of the patient on account of psychosis; the profoundly depressed patient with feelings of hopelessness, guilt or unworthiness is best treated in hospital; so, too, is the patient who had experienced recent serious loss. Assessment of significant others may be as important as that of the patient. If it is suspected that strongly malevolent forces exist within the patient's family he is safer on neutral territory.

Treatment Failures

Maddison and Mackey [13] allude to "the special learning which may be derived from close study of those patients who successfully commit suicide after adequate clinical appraisal during hospitalisation or during the course of outpatient psychotherapy." Reports of such cases rarely appear in the literature, for if therapists are liable to respond emotionally to their patients' reference to suicide they are likely to be profoundly affected by the actual suicide of one of them. Since during a prolonged course of treatment no therapist has been free from the experience of negative feelings towards the suicidal patient it would seem almost inevitable that part of his reaction to the patient's suicide is self-blame. It is important that the opportunity should be available for him to make adequate emotional expression of this to a supervisor. If the therapist has been closely involved with the patient over a period of time he will also pass through a period of grief.

Whether or not a report is published it is important that a full-scale psychological post mortem be carried out in order to reveal such errors of judgment the therapist may have been responsible for and also to piece together the pressures which ultimately caused the patient to take his life.

SUMMARY

The management of the suicidal patient is complicated by (1) the emotions expressed and the demands made by the patient, (2) the therapist's own responses, and (3) the influence of significant others. The therapist may be required to make himself available and to become personally involved to a greater extent than is usual.

The suicidal patient has a tendency to involve himself in symbiotic relationships from which it is difficult for either partner to become detached without generating anxiety in the other. The degree to which the therapist indulges the patient in his dependency needs or encourages him to act responsibly is a matter of fine clinical judgment.

The unwillingness of the suicidal individual to entrust himself to others causes him to become ambivalent towards both the therapist and life itself. The hostile, even murderous attitude of family members may require his temporary removal from them and necessitate their involvement in his treatment.

REFERENCES

1. *Zilboorg, G. Suicide among Civilised and Primitive Races.* Am. J. Psychiatry, *92:1347, 1936.*
2. *Mintz, R. S. Psychotherapy of the Suicidal Patient. In* Suicidal Behaviors, Diagnosis and Management, *Resnik, H. L. P., Ed. J. and A. Churchill Ltd., London, 1968.*
3. *Mayer, D. A Psychotherapeutic Approach to the Suicidal Patient.* Br. J. Psychiatry, *119:629, 1971.*
4. *Henderson, A. S. Care Eliciting Behaviour in Man.* J. Nerv. Ment. Dis., *159:172, 1974.*
5. *Freud, S. Mourning and Melancholia (1917). In* Standard Edition of the Complete Psychological Works of Sigmund Freud, Vol. 19. *The Hogarth Press and the Institute of Psycho-Analysis, London, 1917.*
6. *Andriola, J. A Note on the Possible Iatrogenesis of Suicide.* Psychiatry, *36:213, 1973.*
7. *Schwartz, D. A., Flinn, D. E. and Slawson, P. F. Treatment of the Suicidal Character.* Am. J. Psychother., *28:194, 1974.*
8. *Tabachnick, N. Interpersonal Relations in Suicidal Attempts.* Arch. Gen. Psychiatry, *4:16, 1961.*
9. *Mahler, M. S.* On Human Symbiosis and the Vicissitudes of Individuation, Vol. 1: Infantile Psychosis. *International Universities Press, New York, 1968.*
10. *Richman, J. Family Therapy of Attempted Suicide.* Fam. Process, *18:131, 1979.*
11. *Litman, R. E. Suicide as Acting Out. In* The Psychology of Suicide, *Shneidman, N. L., and Litman, R. E., Eds. Science House, New York, 1970.*
12. *Bowlby, J.* Attachment and Loss. Vol. 2: Separation, Anxiety, and Anger, *The Hogarth Press and the Institute of Psycho-Analysis, London, 1973, pp. 211–26.*
13. *Maddison, D. and Mackey, K. H. Suicide: The Clinical Problem.* Br. J. Psychiatry, *112:693, 1966.*
14. *Draper, E. A Developmental Theory of Suicide.* Compr. Psychiatry, *17:63, 1976.*
15. *Payne, J. The Roots of Violence and Symbolism in Childhood and Adolescence. In* Symbols and Sentiments, *Lewis, I. M., Ed. Academic Press Ltd., London, 1977.*
16. *Moss, L. M. and Hamilton, D. M. The Psychotherapy of the Suicidal Patient.* Am. J. Psychiatry, *112:814, 1956.*
17. *Fawcett, J., Leff, M. and Bunney, W. E. Suicide: Clues from Interpersonal Communication.* Arch. Gen. Psychiatry, *21:129, 1969.*
18. *Fellner, C. H. Provocation of Suicidal Attempts.* J. Nerv. Ment. Dis., *133:55, 1961.*
19. *Richman, J. and Rosenbaum, M. A Clinical Study of the Role of Hostility and*

Death Wishes by the Family and Society in Suicide Attempts. Isr. Ann. Psychiatry, *8:213, 1970.*

20. *Litman, R. E., Shneidman, E. S. and Farberow, N. L. A Suicide Prevention Centre. In* Current Psychiatric Therapies, *Vol. 1, Masserman, J. H. Ed. Grune and Stratton, New York, 1961.*

31. Prediction of Suicide in Psychiatric Patients: Report of a Prospective Study

Alex D. Pokorny

BIOGRAPHICAL NOTE

Following psychiatry training in the U.S. Army, Dallas, and Topeka, Alex D. Pokorny arrived at the Veterans' Administration Hospital in Houston in 1949 where he remained until 1973, as chief of the Psychiatric Service from 1955 on.

As a result of the occasional suicides that occurred in the hospital and the subsequent "boards of inquiry," Pokorny began to assemble lists and files on all aspects of suicidal behavior. This gradually led to a number of studies. He soon found that some of his earlier work was limited because initial information from patient records was often incomplete or slight. He decided to carry out the prospective study that led to this chapter.

The thread that runs through most of Pokorny's work is that suicide (like most human behavior) is not predictable. The contrary presumption is common to many clinicians, and to courts of law.

COMMENT

This is probably the most clinically remote paper in this book, but we include it because it is an adroitly intelligent report with an important clinical message: suicide cannot be predicted *with the means we have at hand. There is no known suicide "tag" (no psychological test, clinical technique, or biological marker) sufficiently specific and sensitive to enable prediction.*

Prediction of suicide is somewhat different from the assessment of suicide

---

Alex D. Pokorny, "Prediction of Suicide in Psychiatric Patients: Report of a Prospective Study." *Archives of General Psychiatry 40* (1983):249–257. Reprinted by permission.

risk. Suicide prediction *refers to the foretelling of whether suicide will or will not occur at some future time, often many months, based on the presence or absence of a specific number of defined factors, within definable limits of statistical probability.* Suicide risk assessment, *a clinical activity, refers to the establishment of a clinical judgment of risk in the very near future, based on the weighing of a very large mass of available clinical detail. From time to time confused clinicians conclude that because suicide cannot be predicted, clinical risk assessment is a chimerical pursuit, and that one might as well toss a coin. Risk assessment carried out in a systematic, disciplined way (Maltsberger 1992) is more than a guess or an intuition (Motto 1989, 1992). The best clinical risk assessment is a reasoned, inductive process, and it is a responsibility that we cannot escape. It is a necessary exercise in estimating probability over short periods. But the fact remains that suicide prediction is beyond our reach.*

REFERENCES

Maltsberger, John T. 1992. The Psychodynamic Formulation: An Aid in Assessing Suicide Risk. In Maris, Ronald W., Berman, Alan L., Maltsberger, John T., and Yufit, Robert I., eds., Assessment and Prediction of Suicide. *New York: Guilford Press.*

Motto, Jerome A. 1989. Problems in Suicide Risk Assessment. In Jacobs, Douglas, and Brown, Herbert N., eds., Suicide, Understanding and Responding. *Madison, Conn.: International Universities Press.*

———. *1992. An Integrated Approach to Estimating Suicide Risk. In Maris, Ronald W., Berman, Alan L., Maltsberger, John T., and Yufit, Robert I., eds.,* Assessment and Prediction of Suicide. *New York: Guilford Press.*

■

A prospective research study attempted to identify persons who would subsequently commit or attempt suicide. The sample consisted of 4,800 patients who were consecutively admitted to the inpatient psychiatric service of a Veterans Administration hospital. They were examined and rated on a wide range of instruments and measures, including most of those previously reported as predictive of suicide. Many items were found to have positive and substantial correlations with subsequent suicides and/or suicide attempts. However, all attempts to identify specific subjects were unsuccessful, including use of individual items, factor scores, and a series of discriminant functions.

Each trial missed many cases and identified far too many false positive cases to be workable. Identification of particular persons who will commit suicide is not currently feasible, because of the low sensitivity and specificity of available identification procedures and the low base rate of this behavior.

THIS REPORT is based on two assumptions: (1) Suicide is an undesirable event; (2) suicide in patients should be prevented if possible. Although each of these points is arguable, these are the positions from which physicians in the medical system generally work.

METHODS OF SUICIDE PREVENTION

There are three basic approaches to preventing suicide in patients. The first is to physically prevent the act, by locking patients up, watching or restraining them, removing harmful objects, etc. This has been the traditional approach with patients on suicidal precautions. However, these precautions are all somewhat demeaning and infantilizing, and they pit the treatment staff against the patients to see who can outwit the other. There are also practical limits to the number of persons who can be kept under such precautions and to the duration of enforcement.

The second approach is to remove the distress or dysphoria that is feeding the suicidal urge. This goal might be achieved by social changes, medication, psychotherapy, or other treatment or rehabilitative measures. Such an approach has the advantage of placing the treating team and the patient more nearly on the same side, both fighting the "disease," distress, or discomfort. Unfortunately, not all distress, dysphoria, or misery can be removed.

The third possibility is to instill some ethical or moral barriers to the act of suicide, making such behavior less "available" to the patient. It is questionable whether this can be done in adulthood, after suicidal behavior or preoccupation has already appeared. It may work only if taught or instilled during childhood.

Each of these three approaches requires considerable time and individual attention. It is not feasible to apply them to whole populations or even sizable subsets of whole populations. We need to apply them to those persons who will almost certainly commit suicide unless prevented. Hence, there is a pressing need for "prediction" of suicide, i.e., identification of the persons who will commit suicide unless stopped.

EARLIER STUDIES

The relationship of various characteristics to suicide or suicide attempts has been the subject of hundreds of published studies. Most of them have been correlational in nature and have identified "significant" relationships. Many have claimed to be "predictive of suicide," which has almost always meant that a subgroup was identified that had a suicide rate significantly greater than the base rate or the rate of a comparison group.

The research findings on suicide between 1882 and 1969 were summarized in a 1972 book by Lester.[1] Although that book concludes that research into suicide tends to be repetitious, uninspired, and sterile, it provides a good summary of the demographic, sociologic, psychopathological, and other characteristics related to suicide.

Another useful review, focusing on prediction of suicide, is a 1974 book edited by Beck et al.[2] In it, a chapter by Diggory[3] notes the limitations of prior prediction efforts and strongly recommends the use of multiple regression methods. The book includes a review of the suicide prediction "scales" in use at that time.[4]

Another excellent review of the topic was published in 1972 by Brown and Sheran.[5] It summarized information on predictive signs based on a person's attributes, behavior, and surroundings. Brown and Sheran concluded that results of such research are equivocal and that it is not possible to predict suicide at *useful levels* from single signs, psychological tests, specially devised tests, clinical judgments, or special scales. They urged researchers to put more stress on subgroupings, interactions, and duration of indicators.

Murphy[6] reviewed these same issues in 1972 and illustrated the impracticality of available suicide predictors, using hypothesized data and data from previously published reports. He then sidestepped the issue to a degree by arguing that if the treatment offered is relatively innocuous and appropriate in its own right, the issue of false-positive predictions is not a serious one. He acknowledged, however, that if the required "treatment" was long-term hospitalization, too many false positives would be impractical.

MacKinnon and Farberow[7] stressed the difficulties in identifying specific cases, because of low base rates and the error rate of our prediction "instruments." They presented a simulated exercise in prediction of suicide with a hospital population, using an imaginary instrument having idealistically low false-positive and false-negative rates of 1%. Even under these circumstances, only 20% of the predictions of suicide would be valid (true positives).

Because any currently conceivable prediction instrument or scheme would perform more poorly (with more inherent error), the actual results would be far worse.

PREVIOUS WORK BY AUTHOR

The present study was based in part on my earlier studies of suicidal behavior, which were carried out at the Houston Veterans Administration Medical Center (VAMC).[8–11] One study[9] derived suicide rates for diagnostic groupings, all strikingly higher than the current U.S. suicide rate of 10/100,000/yr and the calculated expected rate of 22.7/100,000/yr for male war veterans, in Texas.

Another study followed up 618 patients who had initially been seen in psychiatric consultation for suicide attempts or threats, preoccupation, or ideation.[10] Of that group, 615 were successfully traced for a period averaging 4.6 years, and 21 (3.4%), all male, had committed suicide. By computing man-years of risk for each case and summing these results by categories, the following suicide rates were derived: all 615 subjects, 740/100,000/yr; male suicidal patients, 786/100,000/yr; suicide attempters, 805/100,000/yr; suicide threateners, 710/100,000/yr; and patients with suicidal ideas, 704/100,000/yr. The period of greatest risk was the first two years after the initial suicidal behavior; during the first three months, the incidence of suicide was almost 1% of the entire group. It was concluded that suicide attempts, threats, and ideas were strong indicators of future completed suicide, stronger than the psychiatric diagnostic grouping. Male patients who had shown suicidal behavior had about 35 times the expected suicide rate.

Another study investigated the matter of suicide rates in veterans generally,[11] to see whether war veterans were significantly more suicidal than the general population. My colleagues and I examined the absolute and relative suicide rates in three groups: Texas men, Texas male veterans, and male former psychiatric inpatients of the Houston VAMC. Suicide rates in veterans did not differ from those in the general population for persons of the same age and sex, but suicides in veterans tended to occur at an earlier age.

RATIONALE FOR CURRENT PROJECT

The study reported herein was designed as a definitive test of whether, in a high-risk population, the particular persons who would later commit suicide could be identified at a practical or feasible level, i.e., without too many false positives. The population consisted of all patients admitted to an inpatient psychiatric service, a group already shown to have a suicide rate nine times that in the general population of the same age and sex.[11] The project was designed to include, in each patient's admission workup, inquiries regarding most of the previously reported "predictors" of suicide.

There are several general problems in research on completed suicide: (1) suicide is a rare event, so there are few positive cases; (2) subjects are not available for direct study after committing suicide; (3) retrospective data are likely to be distorted; and (4) when observers encounter a strong indicator (such as the statement, "I am going to kill myself today"), they immediately attempt to prevent a suicidal outcome, which, from a research standpoint, weakens the relationship of predictor to outcome.

My colleagues and I attempted to avoid some of these problems, as follows. By enrolling a very large number of subjects, we ensured that even such a rare event as suicide would occur in a reasonably large number of cases. To further increase the probability of having cases of suicide within the population, the study used a sample of subjects known to have a high suicide rate, namely, psychiatric inpatients.

The study was prospective. This meant that the subjects were alive and available for study at the time of intake, and also that the distortion found in retrospective data could be avoided.

We had no solution for the fourth problem.

Our "solutions" introduced three new problems. First, to follow up so many cases is a formidable task, although with a VA sample this was facilitated through use of the elaborate and comprehensive VA records system.

Second, the need to include a large number of subjects meant that multiple raters had to be used, which very probably introduced greater variability and more error into the ratings.

Third, the need to process so many cases necessarily limited the time that could be spent with any individual subject. This required the streamlining, abbreviation, and selection of items from the large number of available rating instruments and scales.

SUBJECTS AND METHODS

We assembled and developed a set of rating instruments, using items from established rating scales and incorporating most of the items that have been shown to predict higher rates of suicide. These were applied to 4,800 patients consecutively admitted to the psychiatry inpatient service of the Houston VAMC. Informed consent was obtained from each subject after the nature of the procedures had been explained. All 4,800 subjects were followed up for the duration of the study, to identify subsequent instances of (1) actual suicide, (2) suicide attempts or suicidal ideation leading to rehospitalization, (3) behavior or events that might have served as "alternatives to suicide" (including accidental death, death from cirrhosis, death as homicide victim, hospitalization for psychosis, and rehospitalization for alcoholism, or drug abuse), and (4) death from any cause. This article reports only subsequent suicides and suicide attempts. The data collected were analyzed through item-by-item analysis in terms of prediction of completed suicide and also by grouped or summary scores for the various rating instruments. The good predictor items were then combined into predictor scales by various techniques, including discriminant function analysis.

Sample

The sample included all consecutive "first admissions" (defined as the first admission to occur after the start of the project) to the nine psychiatry inpatient wards of the Houston VAMC. The service included two alcoholism wards and one drug-abuse ward, so these two disorders were well represented.

A "high-risk" subsample, about 15% of the total sample, was also selected for study, according to a formula using conventional indicators of increased suicide risk, such as history of attempted suicide, presence of depression, or being widowed or divorced. The 21 items making up this formula were selected on the basis of previous reports, many based on studies of the general population. It was recognized that "conventional" indicators of high suicide risk for the population at large might not apply in the same manner to a population of psychiatric patients.

The subsample subjects were given additional interviews and ratings, as a second screening, to see whether this additional information might help identify future suicides. These additional ratings were too time-consuming to be used with the entire sample of 4,800 patients.

Rating Instruments

The selection of items and scales was based on the following considerations:

1. Those items that had proved to be good predictors in previous VAMC

studies[8–11] were assembled into structured interview and rating forms, to be completed by the physician examining the patient immediately after admission and by a research clerk who reviewed and abstracted all prior hospital and claims records.

2. Ratings reported in the literature[1,2,5] as predictive of suicide were also performed; these included standard demographic items, items from the scales of Tuckman and Youngman[12] and Cohen et al.[13] and ratings of depression.

3. The Brief Psychiatric Rating Scale (BPRS),[14] with 24 items added for greater breadth of coverage, was administered as a general assessment of psychopathologic condition.

4. The Nurses' Observation Scale for Inpatient Evaluation (NOSIE)–30[15] was used to assess behavior and symptoms observed by nursing personnel.

In addition, the "high-risk" subsample, about 15% of the entire group, answered a 94-item questionnaire containing the Zung Depression Scale,[16] the Rosenberg Self-Derogation Scale,[17,18] the Brief Michigan Alcoholism Screening Test (MAST),[19] a drug-abuse identification scale, and portions of scales intended to rate anxiety, somatization, general state of health, subjective life expectancy, and attitudes toward death. Additionally, a research social worker interviewed each patient and completed several ratings. For suicide attempters and ideators, the appropriate Beck intentionality scales were completed, along with the Beck hopelessness and depression scales.[20,21]

Raters

The research social worker did all of the additional ratings in the high-risk group. The regular ward physician performed the examination and completed the BPRS. The NOSIE-30 was completed by the ward nursing staff. The records review was done by a research clerk. Each of the raters was given initial training in completion of the rating forms, followed by continual supervision by the investigators.

Follow-up

All 4,800 patients were followed up for a period of four to six years (mean, five years), using several sources of data. Instances of completed suicide and death from any cause were identified by (1) word of mouth, (2) local newspaper stories and obituary columns, (3) information from VA officials, (4) monthly report of death certificates for veterans in Texas, and (5) a yearly search of the VA national record system. These sources are listed in order of increasing completeness, but decreasing immediacy. We used all of these systems to be able to follow up completed suicide instances as soon after the event as possible.

We also studied records of admission to any VA hospital to identify patients rehospitalized for suicide attempts or suicidal ideation.

For each identified case of suicide, we interviewed relatives or associates of the patient, but those data will not be presented in this article.[22]

RESULTS

Sample Characteristics

Some of the principal characteristics of the sample were as follows:

Characteristic	No. of Patients
Sex	
M	4,691
F	109
Race	
Black	1,162
Nonblack	3,638
Marital status on admission	
Single	1,034
Married and together	1,900
Married but separated	566
Widowed	124
Divorced	1,157
Not determined	19
Diagnosis on admission	
Affective disorder	518
Schizophrenia	834
Alcoholism	1,618
Drug abuse	721
Neurosis	400
Personality disorder	428
Organic brain syndrome	281
Age at admission, yr	
<20	98
20–29	1,332

30–39	711
40–49	1,375
50–59	1,039
60–69	178
≥70	67

The diagnoses, collapsed into seven principal groups, were those made by the admitting ward physician, according to *DSM-II* criteria. Because one goal of the project was to see whether suicide could be predicted by the results of a thorough psychiatric examination by treatment staff at time of admission, we used the admission diagnosis as the official diagnostic grouping, even though other sources of information might have indicated some other diagnostic category.

Follow-up

The U.S. death rate from all causes has been about 900/100,000/yr in recent years (just under 1% dying annually). The death rate for persons with heart disease has been about 350/100,000/yr; for those with malignant neoplasms, about 170/100,000/yr; and for those with stroke, about 100/100,000/yr. The death rate from suicide has been around 12/100,000/yr. The age- and sex-adjusted suicide rate for all veterans, however, is about 23/100,000/yr.[11] These death rates should be kept in mind as standards against which the reported suicide rates can be evaluated.

During the five-year follow-up period, we identified 67 suicides within the total group of 4,800 subjects, as well as 179 subsequent suicide attempts. This yields a suicide rate of 279/100,000/yr, about 12 times the expected rate for veterans. The high-risk group, which included 803 subjects, had 30 subsequent suicides, giving a suicide rate of 747/100,000/yr, about 32 times the expected rate for veterans.

The 67 suicides occurred fairly evenly throughout the four to six year follow-up period. This observation may appear to contradict the usual finding that most suicides occur soon after release from the hospital. However, many of these subjects were readmitted to the hospital, often more than once. The important duration is the time elapsed since *last* discharge from the hospital. Analyzed in this way, the 67 cases were grouped as follows: five suicides occurred when the patient was still in the hospital; ten, within one to seven days after release; six, within eight to 30 days; eight, within one to three months; 12, within three to six months; six, within six to 12 months; eight, within one to two years; and the other 12, within two to six years after last discharge from the hospital. Excluding the five occurring in the hospital, 16 (26%) occurred within one month and 36 (58%) within six months of hospital discharge, a pattern that resembles the usual experience.

The length of time between last release from the hospital and completed suicide was cross-tabulated against race, age at time of initial admission, marital status, and diagnosis. No striking or significant relationships were observed.

Of the 21 items making up the formula for selecting the "high-risk" subsample, ten turned out to be significant predictors: Eight of these related to current or past suicidal behavior, one was a diagnosis of affective disorder, and one was not being black (data available from National Auxiliary Publications Service [NAPS]).

Suicide Rates

Table 1 shows the age breakdown of the patients who committed suicide and of the total sample. The distributions resemble each other; they are bimodal with peaks in the 20- to 29-year and 40- to 49-year periods. (This age distribution, of course, reflects that of U.S. war veterans in general.) The 20- to 29-year-old group was slightly overrepresented in suicides, but the difference was not statistically significant. In these atypical, high-risk subjects, all of whom had psychiatric disorders requiring hospitalization, the usual principle that suicide rates in men increase progressively with age did not seem to apply. Evidently this "indicator," like many others that are valid in the general population, no longer applies when the rate of suicide is increased greatly; other and stronger risk factors overcome the effect of age.

The bimodal distribution may also represent the recently observed tendency for younger age cohorts in the United States to have higher suicide rates at *all* ages. Within each age cohort, however, suicide rates still increase with age. Combining all age groups results in a bimodal distribution with a first peak in the 20s.[23–25]

The bimodal age distribution shown in Table 1 was used as a basis for several comparisons. One involved the method of suicide, comparing those under age 40 years with those 40 years old or older at the time of the index admission date. There were no significant differences.

Table 2 shows the number of suicides by diagnostic group, for the total group and for age subgroups. The distributions show an over-representation of patients with affective disorder and schizophrenia in the completed suicide

*Table 1. Incidence of Subsequent Suicides by Age at Admission**

Age, yr	Total Sample, % (N=4,800)	Suicides, No. (%)
10–19	2	2 (3)
20–29	28	25 (38)
30–39	15	9 (13)
40–49	29	15 (22)
50–59	21	15 (22)
60–69	4	1 (1)
≥70	1	0 (0)
Total	100	67 (99)

*The mean follow-up period was five years. The χ^2 test yielded no significant differences when the 10- 19-year-old and 60- to 79-year-old categories were collapsed into adjoining groups.

group ($\chi^2=24.5$, $P=.001$). All of the drug-abuse–related suicides were in the younger group, whereas most of the alcoholism-related suicides were in the older group.

Table 3 gives the same information on diagnostic categories, but expressed as rates. It also gives the total number of deaths from all causes in each diagnostic group. As expected, the death rate for patients with organic brain syndrome was very high, as was the death rate in the alcoholic group. However, the death rate for *all* diagnostic groups was high (2,758/100,000/yr, compared with about 900/100,000/yr for the general U.S. population).

Table 3 also shows that the suicide rate for the total group of 4,800 subjects was 279/100,000/yr, or about 12 times the age- and sex-adjusted rate for male veterans. The completed suicide rate was highest in the affective disorder

Table 2. Incidence of Suicide by Diagnosis and Age Group

Diagnosis	Total sample, % (N=4,800)	Suicides, No. (%)	Age at admission to project, yr	
			<40, No. (%)	≥40, No. (%)
Affective disorder	11	18 (27)	11 (31)	7 (23)
Schizophrenia	17	19 (28)	12 (33)	7 (23)
Alcoholism	34	15 (22)	2 (6)	13 (42)
Drug abuse	15	7 (10)	7 (19)	0 (0)
Neurosis	8	3 (4)	1 (3)	2 (6)
Personality disorder	9	4 (6)	2 (6)	2 (6)
Organic brain syndrome	6	1 (1)	1 (3)	0 (0)
Total	100	67 (98)	36 (101)	31 (100)

*Table 3. Incidence of Death and Suicide by Diagnostic Category**

	Total deaths		Suicides		
Diagnosis	No.	Rate/ 100,000/yr	No.	Rate/ 100,000/yr	% of total deaths
Affective disorder (n=518)	59	2,278	18	695	30.5
Schizophrenia (n=834)	65	1,559	19	456	29.2
Alcoholism (n=1,618)	334	4,129	15	187	4.5
Drug abuse (=721)	49	1,359	7	194	14.3
Neurosis (n=400)	30	1,500	3	150	10.0
Personality disorder (n=428)	21	981	4	187	19.0
Organic brain syndrome (n=281)	104	7,402	1	71	1.0
Total (N=4,800)	662	2,758	67	279	10.1

*The mean follow-up period was five years.

group, but the schizophrenic group was a close second. Table 3 also gives the percentages of deaths that were suicides; for affective disorders and schizophrenia these percentages were about 30%.

Table 4 shows the suicide rates for several special groups. All of the patients who committed suicide were male. The rate for nonblack men was about three times that for black men. The rate for single men was the highest, whereas the marital-status group with the lowest rate was "married and together." Our a priori "high-risk" group had a suicide rate of 747/100,000/yr, compared with 185/100,000/yr in the rest of the sample—a ratio of 4.04:1. Therefore, our high-risk formula *did* identify a group with a signifi-

*Table 4. Incidence of Suicide by Subgroup**

Group	No. of subjects	No. of suicides	Suicide rate/ 100,000/yr
Total sample	4,800	67	279
"High-risk" subsample	803	30	747
Rest of sample	3,997	37	185
Women	109	0	0
Men	4,691	67	286
Nonblack	3,549	60	338
Black	1,142	7	123
Single	1,008	23	456
Married	1,860	17	183
Separated, widowed, or divorced	1,823	27	296
Reason for admission			
Suicide attempt	188	16	1,702
Other	4,612	51	221

*The mean follow-up period was five years.

*Table 5. Incidence of Suicide by Diagnosis and Subgroup**

	Affective disorder	Schizophrenia	Alcoholism or drug abuse	Other diagnoses	Total
Total sample					
Suicides/subjects, No.	18/518	19/834	22/2,339	8/1,109	67/4,800
Rate	695	456	188	144	279
Male subjects					
Suicides/subjects, No.	18/498	19/804	22/2,308	8/1,081	67/4,691
Rate	723	473	191	148	286
Nonblack male subjects					
Suicides/subjects, No.	17/429	15/507	21/1,786	7/827	60/3,549
Rate	793	592	235	169	338
High-risk male subjects					
Suicides/subjects, No.	14/200	6/119	7/266	3/194	30/779
Rate	1,400	1,008	526	309	770
Nonblack, high-risk male subjects					
Suicides/subjects, No.	13/187	4/94	7/245	2/171	26/697
Rate	1,390	851	571	234	746

*The mean follow-up period was five years. Rates are given as suicides per 100,000 subjects per year.

cantly greater probability of suicide. Finally, patients admitted for a suicide attempt had a subsequent suicide rate of 1,702/100,000/yr. On the average, nearly 2% of this group completed suicide during each year of follow-up. This is high as suicide rates go, but in terms of the feasibility of predicting individual cases, it is still relatively low.

Table 5 shows the five-year suicide rates for other special groups. (Some of these rates may have quite broad confidence limits when the base is only a few hundred subjects.) The risk increases progressively as the various lower-risk groups are subtracted, except that in the high-risk subsample the rates do not increase (rather, they drop slightly) when the black subjects are removed. Again this illustrates the general point: although the racial distinction is significant in the general population, and even in our total sample, it no longer applies in the high-risk subsample, with its much higher suicide rate.

Cross-Tabulations

Each item from the rating instruments was cross-tabulated against suicide, suicide attempt, or absence of these behaviors during the follow-up period.

For the total group of 4,800 subjects there were 153 such cross-tabulations, and 51 showed statistically significant relationships (data available from NAPS). Items that were strongly associated with subsequent suicide included diagnoses of affective disorder or schizophrenia, history of suicide attempt, having been placed on suicide precautions, overt evidence of depression, complaints of insomnia, and presence of guilt feelings, along with 45 others.

The same type of comparison was made for the total group of 4,800 subjects using 12 factor scores derived from the BPRS and NOSIE-30 rating scales. Both the patients who later committed suicide and those who attempted it were rated high on the depression factor. The suicide attempters (but not those who actually committed suicide) rated high on the "personality disorder" and "irritability" factors. The completed suicide group rated low on "social interest."

The suicide groups were not differentiated significantly from each other or from the rest of the sample when cross-tabulated with eight other factor scores: the BPRS factors of "schizophrenia," "somatic symptoms," "deterioration," and "organicity" and the NOSIE-30 factors of "social competence," "personal neatness," "manifest psychosis," and "retardation."

For the 803 high-risk subjects, there were additional ratings and evaluations; those items were examined in 106 additional cross-tabulations, of which 20 showed significant relationships (data available from NAPS). With most of these items, the suicide completers and attempters deviated from the rest of the sample in the same direction, but this was not always true. For example, in response to the item, "I have an urge to do harmful, shocking things," the attempters answered *true* more often than did the rest of the sample, but the actual suicides deviated significantly in the other direction.

The additional ratings given to the high risk group also yielded ten summary scores (data available from NAPS). Three of them showed significant differences between the two groups. Two of these (the drug-abuse and self-derogation scores) were high in both suicide attempters and completers, whereas one (the impulsivity score) was elevated only for the attempters.

Seven other summary scores did not differentiate significantly between groups. These were the total scores on the Brief MAST, the internalization-externalization score, the authoritarian score, the score on the Rosenberg "Favorable Self-Presentation" factor,[17] the guilt score, the anxiety score, and the total score on the Zung Self-Rating Depression Scale.[16]

Clearly, we were able to differentiate the groups using any one of a large number of items and summary scores. We had been interested in whether the suicide completers would resemble the suicide attempters. Since the work of Stengel and Cook,[26] it has generally been held that the two groups are basically different, though overlapping. We found, however, that in most respects the two suicidal groups were similar, that is, they were mostly related to the same predictors, and generally in the same direction. Therefore, at least for this population of mostly male adult veterans, suicide attempters do not differ sharply from suicide completers. However, a minority of items did relate differently: a prior diagnosis of personality disorder was common in patients who later attempted suicide but not in those who actually succeeded, and the same relationship applied to projection of blame and drug dependency. Therefore, though for the most part the two behaviors involved similar subjects, the suicide attempters did show more personality disorder-related traits, along with such traits as manipulativeness and hostility.

Of the 281 individual items and factor or summary scores looked at by cross-tabulations, 78 showed statistically significant relationships to subsequent suicide or suicide attempts, almost one of every three predictors examined.

Hence, we did find numerous significant relationships. We confirmed the findings of numerous previous studies by identifying many of the same indicators or "predictors." This kind of information is useful in making clinical judgments; it provides a background for treatment decisions. This is the same kind of information used in patient management in many areas of medicine; physicians make use of trends and correlations to make the best choice of moves, to "play the odds." This approach helps us to adopt a treatment policy that should lead in the long run to the largest proportion of correct decisions. The task is quite different, however, when we attempt to predict for each particular case.

Stepwise Discriminant Analysis

We applied the technique of stepwise discriminant analysis (Statistical Package for the Social Sciences) in an attempt to select, from this long list of significantly related items and scores, some weighted combination of variables that could successfully identify at a practical level the patients who would later commit or attempt suicide. As items for use in the discriminant analysis, we chose those that had shown the strongest relationships when looked at individually. Sixty variables were initially selected in this way.

The number of variables was further reduced by running "trial" discriminant function analyses with 20 variables at a time, and selecting for the final analysis the 20 items with the highest F values in the one-way analysis of variance between groups. For the discriminant analysis, only those variables were retained whose partial multivariate F ratios were larger than 1.00.

Four discriminant function analyses were performed. In two analyses we attempted to discriminate patients who committed suicide from all the others; this was done separately for the total group of 4,800 subjects and for the high-risk subgroup of 803. The other two analyses, again for both groups, attempted a three-way discrimination: completed suicide *v* suicide attempts *v* others. There was some loss of cases in these analyses because of incomplete information.

The first discriminant function analysis was applied to the entire sample and employed the following variables:

	Discriminant Coefficients
History of suicide attempt	−.62
Diagnosis of affective disorder or schizophrenia *v* other	−.33
Single, widowed, or divorced *v* other	−.38
Having been on suicidal list at any VA hospital	−.34

The standardized canonical discriminant function coefficients are given.

The program was first instructed to disregard prior information concerning the low rate of suicide in the population, ie, to assume equal base rates. That procedure yielded the following results:

	Prediction		
Actual Outcome	**Suicide**	**Other**	**Total**
Suicide	35	28	63
Other	1,206	3,435	4,641
Total	1,241	3,463	4,704

This procedure correctly identified 35 of the 63 subsequent suicides (55.6%), but at the cost of 1,206 false-positive predictions. Of the 1,241 subjects identified as suicides, only 2.8% were identified correctly. Overall, only 73.81% of the cases were classified correctly.

When the program was instructed to use the actual base rates (67 suicides in 4,800 subjects), the results were as follows:

	Prediction		
Actual Outcome	**Suicide**	**Other**	**Total**
Suicide	0	63	63
Other	1	4,640	4,641
Total	1	4,703	4,704

The total percentage of cases classified correctly this time was 98.64%. However, a simple prediction that *no one* would commit suicide would have led to a slightly higher percentage.

We also performed a discriminant analysis using only the high-risk subjects, which made available a larger number of predictor items and scores. The following variables were used:

	Discriminant Coefficient
History of attempted suicide	.52
Suicidal ideation	.19
Diagnosis of affective disorder or schizophrenia	.27
Recent history of physical violence	−.25
Social interest	.30
Urge to do harmful, shocking things	.45
Fear of losing control	.51
Feeling remorseful	.43
Tendency to become impatient	.34
Sense of being a failure	−.39
Feeling downhearted and blue	.31

When the program was set to disregard the base rates, the results were as follows:

	Prediction		
Actual Outcome	**Suicide**	**Other**	**Total**
Suicide	21	8	29
Other	164	550	714
Total	185	558	743

In this high-risk subgroup, the program performed somewhat better in that 72.4% of the actual suicides were correctly identified. However, only 11.4% of the 185 classified by the program as suicides were classified correctly. Overall, 76.8% were classified correctly.

When the program was instructed to use the actual base rates, the analysis yielded the following results:

	Prediction		
Actual Outcome	**Suicide**	**Other**	**Total**
Suicide	0	29	29
Other	0	714	714
Total	0	743	743

This time, the classification results were the same as if we had simply predicted that no one would commit suicide; 96.1% were classified correctly.

We followed a similar procedure in attempting to separate the suicide completers from the attempters and from the rest of the sample (data available from NAPS). Using the total sample of 4,800 patients, 20 of the 63 suicide completers (31.7%) were identified correctly, as were 63 of the 174 attempters (36.2%). Again, there were a large number of false-positive predictions.

The same procedure was applied to the 803 high-risk subjects (data available from NAPS). When the program was set to disregard base rates, suicide completers and attempters were identified fairly well, but at the cost of many false-positive identifications. When the program was instructed to use actual base rates, the prediction was extremely conservative, with no subject predicted to commit suicide (thus yielding no true- or false-positive results).

Discriminant analysis was clearly inadequate in correctly classifying the subjects. For a disorder or event as rare as suicide or suicide attempts, our predictive tools and guides are simply not equal to the task.

The general situation regarding the usefulness of a "test" (which could just as well be a suicide prediction scale, a formula, or a discriminant function) is covered thoroughly and clearly in a book by Galen and Gambino.[27] Table 6 is adapted from their book and presents the standard definitions of true positives, false positives, etc, as used in a screening situation. Galen and Gambino define *sensitivity* and *specificity* (paraphrased by them as "positivity in disease" and "negativity in health") as follows:

$$\text{Sensitivity} = \frac{\text{TP}}{\text{TP}+\text{FN}} \times 100$$

$$\text{Specificity} = \frac{\text{TN}}{\text{FP}+\text{TN}} \times 100$$

where TP indicates true positive; FN, false negative; TN, true negative; and FP, false positive.

Galen and Gambino also define the predictive value of a test result, as follows:

$$\text{Predictive Value} = \frac{\text{TP}}{\text{TP}+\text{FP}} \times 100$$

They stress that predictive value is highly dependent on base rates or prevalence rates of the disorder and define the efficiency of a test as the percentage

*Table 6. Predictive Value of a Test When Applied to Healthy and Diseased Populations**

	Patients with positive test result	Patients with negative test result	Total
Patients with disease	TP	FN	TP + FN
Patients without disease	FP	TN	FP + TN
Total	TP + FP	TN + FN	TP + FP + TN + FN

*Adapted from Galen and Gambino.[27] TP indicates true-positive classification; FP, false-positive; TN, true-negative; and FN, false-negative.

of cases classified correctly. (Sensitivity, specificity, and predictive value are properly *population* measures; the corresponding measures derived from a *sample* are estimates of population values.)

We applied these formulas to the results of the first discriminant analysis, given earlier (total sample, base rates disregarded). As already noted, the "test" for suicide provided by that discriminant function was not very sensitive; only 35 of the 63 subjects who actually committed suicide were correctly identified. Using the formulas, we found its sensitivity to be 55.5%, its specificity 74.0%, its predictive value, 2.8%, and its efficiency, 73.8%. In everyday language, by applying our "test" for suicide, we correctly identified just over half of the 63 suicides, but at the cost of 1,206 false-positive identifications. We classified over one fourth of our subjects as suicidal and still only predicted just over half of the actual suicides. It is not particularly helpful to concentrate our special efforts on one fourth of the entire group. This level of case identification will not permit any meaningful redirection of effort, because it is simply not feasible to maintain one fourth of psychiatric inpatients on "suicidal precautions" indefinitely.

Handpicked Predictors

I also assembled a "suicide prediction test" by hand, combining five items that were significantly related to suicide: being in the high-risk group, being nonblack, having a diagnosis either of affective disorder or schizophrenia or of alcoholism or drug abuse, having any marital status other than married and together, and being male. Subjects with all five characteristics had a suicide rate of 1,020/100,000/yr, certainly a high rate compared with that of the general population. When this new "formula" was used as a classification tool, 15 of the 67 completed suicides were identified correctly, but there were

*Table 7. Predictive Value of a Positive Test Result at Three Prevalence Levels**

Specificity, &	Sensitivity, % 50	70	90	95	99
	A. Prevalence, 1/100,000				
50	0	0	0	0	0
70	0	0	0	0	0
90	0	0	0	0	0
99	0	0	0	0	0
99.9	0	1	1	1	1
	B. Prevalence, 10/100,000				
50	0	0	0	0	0
70	0	0	0	0	0
90	0	0	0	0	0
99	0	1	1	1	1
99.9	5	7	8	9	9
	C. Prevalence, 500/100,000				
50	1	1	1	1	1
70	1	1	1	2	2
90	2	3	4	5	5
99	20	26	30	32	33
99.9	72	78	82	83	83

*Adapted from Galen and Gambino.[27] Numbers indicate predictive values, given as percentages. See text for further explanation.

279 false-positive predictions. The (estimated) sensitivity was therefore less than half as good as that of the discriminant function formula, but the specificity was much improved. The predictive value of a positive (completed suicide) score had increased to 5%, and the efficiency was increased to 93%, but neither gain was clinically significant or useful.

In their book, Galen and Gambino provided a useful set of tables showing the interaction between test sensitivity, specificity, and disease prevalence in influencing the predictive value of positive test results.

Table 7 gives selected information from their more detailed tables. When the prevalence is as low as one per 100,000, even at the unrealistically high levels of 99% sensitivity and 99.9% specificity, the predictive value of a positive test is only 1%.

Table 7 gives the corresponding percentages for a situation in which the prevalence is ten per 100,000, approximately the incidence of suicide in the general population. Again, if both the sensitivity and specificity were 99%, the predictive value of a positive test result would be only 1%.

Given a prevalence of 500 per 100,000, approximately the incidence of suicide found in the population of hospitalized psychiatric patients used in this study, a test with 99% sensitivity and 99% specificity would have a positive predictive value of only 33% (Table 7). An actual test, however, is more likely to have only about 50% sensitivity and 90% specificity, reducing the predictive value of a positive test result to only 2%.

Artificial Manipulation of Base Rates

Because of the powerful effect of the low base rates in predicting suicide, we ran a series of discriminant functions, using the same predictors, while artificially increasing the proportions of completed suicide cases in the sample. This was done by leaving in the 67 completed suicide cases, but progressively reducing the size of the "other" group by randomly subtracting subjects from it. The size of the "other" group was set so that the proportions of suicide cases would be approximately 0.01, 0.05, 0.1, 0.2, 0.3, 0.4, and 0.5 (as there was always some loss of cases because of incomplete data, these proportions were only approximated). The results of this series of discriminant function classifications, with the program instructed each time to use actual base rates, are shown in Table 8.

This Table shows how our "test" for identifying future suicides would perform if this behavior were less rare. Section A describes the actual situation, and the resulting classification is the same as shown earlier. The subsequent sections of the Table, B through G, show how the discriminant function procedure would perform if completed suicides occurred in a progressively larger proportion of the sample (as shown in the third column). The (estimated) sensitivity improves steadily, but even in section G the procedure identifies only two thirds of the cases. In conditions B through F, too few of the suicides are identified to make discriminant analysis a very helpful procedure. The false-positive classifications are less of a problem under these artificial conditions; in conditions B through G, the true positives outnumber the false positives, mostly by a 2:1 ratio. The predictive value of a positive prediction does not change appreciably in conditions B through G, and the percentage correctly classified drops steadily. We could probably live with condition G, as two thirds of the suicide cases are identified, and the number of false-positive predictions is small enough that it might be feasible to treat them all as "suicidal."

This procedure demonstrates that low base rates are not our only problem, but that the "test" or case-identifying procedure we are using is also unequal to the task. We need more sensitive and specific tests or predictive instruments. Our study, which incorporated most of the inquiries, ratings, and

Table 8. Discriminant Function Classifications with Progressively Increased Base Rate of Suicide

Sample employed	No.	Prediction, no. Suicide	Prediction, no. Other	Proportion of suicides in sample	Sensitivity, %	Specificity, %	Predictive value of positive result, %	Subjects correctly classified, %
A.								
Suicide	63	0	63	.013	0.0	99.9	0.0	98.6
Other	4,641	1	4,640					
B.								
Suicide	63	8	55	.046	12.7	99.5	57.1	95.5
Other	1,295	6	1,289					
C.								
Suicide	63	9	54	.105	14.3	98.9	60.0	95.5
Other	535	6	529					
D.								
Suicide	66	13	53	.183	19.7	98.3	72.2	83.9
Other	294	5	289					
E.								
Suicide	63	19	44	.290	30.2	94.2	67.9	75.6
Other	154	9	145					
F.								
Suicide	66	24	42	.370	36.4	90.2	68.6	70.2
Other	112	11	101					
G.								
Suicide	63	43	20	.543	68.6	60.4	67.2	64.7
Other	53	21	32					

measurements previously shown to correlate with suicide, failed to come up with an adequate prediction procedure.

COMMENT

We are attempting to identify cases of a low-incidence disorder with a "test" totally inadequate for that purpose, one that yields too many false-positive and false-negative results to make any clinical use feasible.

False Positives

The false positives are a greater problem than false negatives. We might tolerate 50% false negatives; if we could apply a screening test that would correctly identify only half of the future suicides without false positives, that would be very helpful. However, with currently known "tests," to identify the actual suicides, we will also have to make a great many false-positive identifications, labeling up to a quarter of the total group as "future suicides" when only 1% to 5% actually are. From a cost-benefit standpoint, the application of such a "test" is simply not feasible.

False-positive results are a problem with many screening tests. For example, nationwide mass screening of children for heart disease was said to produce much harm from anxiety-producing false-positive identifications.[28] The morbidity in those with false-positive results was greater on follow-up than the morbidity in children with actual organic lesions.

Influence of Base Rates

Galen and Gambino[27] stress the great influence of base or prevalence rates in determining the usefulness, predictive value, and other characteristics of any test or procedure. They point out that tests are typically developed in an artificial situation, in which the sample is so chosen that the incidence of the disorder is around 50%. The tests are then applied to the screening situation, where the incidence may be very low. Nevertheless, a user may naively expect it to perform as well there as during the "laboratory" standardization.

Error in Predictive Tests

There are several possible sources of error in a test. One source may simply be sloppy application of the test, leading to careless mistakes, which can be minimized by greater care, training, supervision, and motivation.

Even if careless error has been removed, there remains an inevitable residual error characteristic of the test. This, however, is composed of two different elements.

First, there is the true chance error in a test, which should be randomly distributed, meaning that a repetition of the same test on the same subjects should make incorrect identifications of *different* subjects, but at about the same rates. Such measurement error can be avoided by repeating the test at least once. If a test has a 10% rate of error, repeating it once should reduce the error to 1%, and repeating it twice should reduce error to 0.1%. This is the logic behind "successive screening" or using two or three different tests designed to measure the same thing.

The second possibility for error lies in the characteristics of a subject that are measured and identified correctly but are in the wrong relation to the predicted state. An example of this condition is a genuine false-positive syphilis test result. The serologic response really *is* reactive, and repeated measurement will repeatedly show it this way. Therefore, repeating the test one or more times is not likely to decrease predictive error.

This type of error applies to many clinical, demographic, and life-history predictors of suicide. For example, an elderly, depressed, and alcoholic man who lives alone and has a history of suicide attempts *is* at increased risk of suicide. If this aggregate of predictors is our "test," then it will predict successfully in some proportion of cases, but wrongly in others. Repeating the test will not change this outcome, as these characteristics remain the same; the procedure will predict wrongly every time. Unfortunately, most of the tests or predictors of suicide fall into this second class, and repeated or successive screenings are therefore of no help.

Limitations of Present Study

In a study such as the one reported here, there is a preset and inevitably limited list of inquiries. Even though we inquired about several hundred items for each subject, the items were from preset lists, so that there was no follow-up of any lead in greater depth. In the usual clinical situation, by contrast, the clinician is free to pursue each lead or clue at length. From a research standpoint, this is undesirable, as it makes every case study almost unique and thus limits discovery of general truths or relationships. Furthermore, the freehand, artistic method of clinical inquiry makes it almost impossible to eliminate bias, suggestion, and the tendency to find what one expects to find.

There is, however, a more hopeful view of the clinical situation with a "suicidal" patient. Diagnosis in clinical practice (in contrast to a prospective research project) typically consists of a sequence of small decisions. For example, in suicide prediction, the first decision might be based on some alerting note or sign, and the decision would be to investigate further.

After further investigation, one might stop, if no additional alerting or confirming indicators were found, or one might decide to explore the situation even further, perhaps to hospitalize, for example. In each case, the decision is not what to do for all time, but rather what to do next, for the near future. In such a situation, the consequences of "false-positive" identifications early on may be relatively minor, and it may be appropriate for physicians to screen in many cases.

Long-range versus Short-range Prediction

The thrust of our project has been long-range prediction of completed suicide during a follow-up period averaging five years. The conclusion is inescapable that we do not possess any item of information or any combination of items that permit us to identify to a useful degree the particular persons who will commit suicide, in spite of the fact that we do have scores of items available, each of which is significantly related to suicide.

Yet, it seems that psychiatrists do know which patients are highly suicidal and, on the whole, do an acceptable job of protecting and treating them. This clinical work is in an entirely different time frame, dealing in minutes, hours, or days. It is commonly recognized that a "suicidal crisis" will pass, with or without a suicide attempt, so that after a few days the risk has abated and it may be safe for the patient to be discharged. Such a time frame has not been included in this research, and it may be that suicide risk on this short-term basis is essentially unresearchable, as it would not be ethical to withhold taking appropriate emergency steps to ensure safety. Furthermore, in considering a time frame of minutes, hours, or days with highly disturbed patients, it is not feasible to obtain detailed quantitative ratings or evaluations of mood, or to determine such things as suicide intentionality or the level of hope or despair.

In this short-term time frame, the concept of prediction may not even apply; rather, one is required to *identify* a suicidal crisis that is already here, a task involving a different set of concepts and clinical skills.

The negative findings of this study have clear implications. The courts and public opinion seem to expect physicians to be able to pick out the particular persons who will later commit suicide. Although we may reconstruct causal chains and motives after the fact, we do not possess the tools to predict particular suicides before the fact.

REFERENCES

1. *Lester D:* Why People Kill Themselves: A Summary of Research Findings on Suicidal Behavior. *Charles C. Thomas Publisher, Springfield, Ill, 1972.*
2. *Beck A, Resnik H, Lettieri D (eds):* The Prediction of Suicide. *Bowie, Md, Charles Press, 1974.*
3. *Diggory J: Predicting suicide. Will-o-the-wisp or reasonable challenge? in Beck A, Resnik H, Lettieri D (eds):* The Prediction of Suicide. *Bowie, Md, Charles Press, 1974, chap 4.*
4. *Litman R, Wold C, Farberow N, et al: Prediction models of suicidal behaviors, in*

Beck A, Resnik H, Lettieri D (eds): The Prediction of Suicide. *Bowie, Md, Charles Press, 1974, chap 10.*

5. *Brown T, Sheran T: Suicide prediction: A review.* Suicide Life Threat Behav *1972;2:67–98.*
6. *Murphy GE: Clinical identification of suicidal risk.* Arch Gen Psychiatry *1972;27:356–359.*
7. *MacKinnon D, Farberow N: An assessment of the utility of suicide prediction.* Suicide Life Threat Behav *1975;6;86–91.*
8. *Pokorny A: Characteristics of 44 patients who subsequently committed suicide.* Arch Gen Psychiatry *1960;2:314–323.*
9. *Pokorny A: Suicide rates in various psychiatric disorders.* J Nerv Ment Dis *1964;139:499–506.*
10. *Pokorny A: A follow-up of 618 suicidal patients.* Am J Psychiatry *1966;122:1109–1116.*
11. *Pokorny A: Suicide in war veterans: Rates and methods.* J Nerv Ment Dis *1967;144:224–229.*
12. *Tuckman J, Youngman W: A scale for assessing suicide risk of attempted suicides.* J Clin Psychol *1968;24:17–19.*
13. *Cohen E, Motto J, Seiden R: An instrument for evaluating suicidal potential.* Am J Psychiatry *1966;122:886–897.*
14. *Overall J, Gorham D: The Brief Psychiatric Rating Scale.* Psychol Rep *1962;10:799–812.*
15. *Honigfeld G, Klett J: The Nurses' Observation Scale for Inpatient Evaluation.* J Clin Psychol *1965;21:65–71.*
16. *Zung WWK: A Self-Rating Depression Scale.* Arch Gen Psychiatry *1965;12:63–70.*
17. *Kaplan H, Pokorny A: Self-derogation and psychosocial adjustment.* J Nerv Ment Dis *1969;149:421–434.*
18. *Kaplan H:* Self-Attitudes and Deviant Behavior. *Santa Monica, Calif, Goodyear Publishing Co Inc, 1975.*
19. *Pokorny A, Miller B, Kaplan H: The Brief MAST: A Shortened Version of the Michigan Alcoholism Screening Test.* Am J Psychiatry *1972;129:342–345.*
20. *Beck A, Weissman A, Lester D, et al: The measurement of pessimism: The hopelessness scale.* J Consult Clin Psychol *1974;42:861–865.*
21. *Beck A, Schuyler D, Herman I: Development of suicide intent scales, in Beck A, Resnik H, Lettieri D (eds):* The Prediction of Suicide. *Bowie, Md, Charles Press, 1974, chap 3.*
22. *Pokorny A, Kaplan H: Suicide following psychiatric hospitalization: The interaction effects of defenselessness and adverse life events.* J Nerv Ment Dis *1976;162:119–125.*
23. *Hellon CP, Solomon MI: Suicide and age in Alberta, Canada, 1951 to 1977: The changing profile.* Arch Gen Psychiatry *1980;37:505–510.*
24. *Solomon MI, Hellon CP: Suicide and age in Alberta, Canada, 1951 to 1977: A cohort analysis.* Arch Gen Psychiatry *1980;37:511–513.*
25. *Murphy GE, Wetzel RD: Suicide risk by birth cohort in the United States, 1949 to 1974.* Arch Gen Psychiatry *1980;37:519–523.*

26. *Stengel E, Cook N:* Suicide and Attempted Suicide. *London, Chapman & Hall Ltd, 1958.*
27. *Galen R, Gambino S:* Beyond Normality: The Predictive Value and Efficiency of Medical Diagnoses. *New York, John Wiley and Sons Inc, 1975.*
28. *Golin M: Medical computer: Master or servant?* Am Med News, *Jan 25, 1980, Impact section, p 3.*

32. Some Difficulties in Assessing Depression and Suicide in Childhood

Erna Furman

AUTOBIOGRAPHICAL NOTE

"During the many years of being a practicing child psychoanalyst and consultant to a residential treatment center for adolescents, depression and suicide were often part of my daily work," writes Erna Furman. "Trying to feel and think with my patients to understand the nature of their distress and unravel its underlying causes proved to be emotionally difficult and intellectually challenging. What my patients taught me, each in his own way, did not fit at all with the general assumptions about these syndromes or with the related professional literature. Suicides were, more often than not, unaccompanied by depression; depressions, though often described and diagnosed as such, repeatedly turned out not to be depressions at all and represented, instead, the surface manifestations of a variety of other pathologies. Developmental factors emerged as very significant, but they rarely included loss of a loved one. Precipitating events were equally crucial, but they almost never included disappointments. The differences between suicidal wishes, attempts, and successes proved to be most important, but their relationship to specific personality factors had been neglected. In short, there were many new findings and many unsolved puzzles.

"Dr. Sudak [Howard S. Sudak, M.D., formerly dean, Case Western Reserve University School of Medicine in Cleveland, now clinical professor of psychiatry at the University of Pennsylvania in Philadelphia, and psychiatrist-in-chief of the Institute of the Pennsylvania Hospital] knew some about my work and thinking and asked me to make a contribution to the planned

Erna Furman, (1984) "Some Difficulties in Assessing Depression and Suicide in Childhood." In Howard Sudak, Amasa B. Ford, and Norman B. Rushforth, eds., *Suicide in the Young*. Boston: John Wright/PSG Inc., pp. 245–258. Reprinted by permission.

book of which he was co-editor. I promised no more than I delivered—a description of the discrepancies between the clinical data and the received wisdom, and an account of my different but as yet incomplete theoretical understanding of the findings. Since that time I learned more but, fortunately, far from everything."

COMMENT

This valuable paper derives from Furman's extensive experience in the psychoanalytic study and treatment of depressed children, and it has much to offer for the treatment of adults. She writes from a developmental perspective and sheds light on those chronically suicidal patients who have little capacity to bear painful affect and who injure themselves as a means to escape it.

Furman emphasizes the importance of "hurting excitement" in the course of latency and adolescence in establishing sadomasochistic fixation, and in preventing the development of bodily self-love as a barrier to self-injury. With clinical and developmental vignettes from the development of children disturbed in these ways, she brings to life what is now becoming empirically established: that chronically suicidal, self-injuring adults have been disproportionately abused, physically and sexually, in growing up (Shearer, Peters, Quaytman, and Ogden, 1990; Links 1990).

Furman suggests how it is that many patients, biological factors aside, are crippled by developmental experiences in forming the capacity to maintain hope in the face of depression or adult narcissistic injury, especially loss. She helps us to understand the phenomenon of hopelessness, now proven to have an important role in suicide (see chapter 21 above; and Zetzel 1965).

REFERENCES

Links, Paul S., ed. 1990. Family Environment and Borderline Personality Disorder. *Washington, D.C.: American Psychiatric Press.*

Shearer, S. L., Peters, C. P., Quaytman, M. S., and Ogden, R. L. 1990. Frequency and Correlates of Childhood Sexual and Physical Abuse Histories in Adult Female Borderline Inpatients. American Journal of Psychiatry *145:1424–1427.*

Zetzel, Elizabeth. 1965. On the Incapacity to Bear Depression. In Schur, M., ed. Drives, Affects, and Behavior, *Vol. 2. New York: International Universities Press.*

■

The focus of this chapter is on three areas: (1) uncertainties in defining and diagnosing nonpsychotic depression prior to adulthood are explored, and the theoretical problems and clinical pitfalls in using a descriptive definition are highlighted and exemplified; (2) some personality factors which allow or compel suicidal actions in children and adolescents are pinpointed, especially the manner in which sadomasochistic fixations and early deficiencies in bodily self-love contribute to self-hurting tendencies; and (3) the relationship between depression and suicide is discussed, when these pathologies do and do not coexist, and how this affects the chances of helpful therapeutic intervention.

UNCERTAINTIES IN DEFINING AND DIAGNOSING DEPRESSION

My interest in assessing and understanding depressed children began in connection with studying parental bereavement in childhood.[1] At that time, a group of child psychoanalysts, affiliated with the Cleveland Center for Research in Child Development and the Hanna Perkins Therapeutic Nursery School and Kindergarten, pooled and researched the psychoanalytic data we had gained from the long-term treatments of 23 children who had lost a parent through death. My colleagues and I decided to focus one aspect of our research work on depression because some of our patients showed depressive symptomatology prior to and/or during periods of their treatments,[2] and because object loss had often been linked with depression in psychoanalytic writings. We found that there was a dearth of data gathered from the analyses of depressed children. The limited available clinical material stemmed from the observations of infants and from diagnostic or brief psychotherapeutic contacts with older children.

Although many authors had addressed the topic, they did not agree upon a metapsychological definition or any aspects of it—the genetic origins, the pertinent dynamic and structural conflicts within the personality, the specific economic investments and shifts of psychic energy, and the adaptational factors. The links between depressive phenomena at different phases in childhood and in adulthood were tentative, mostly theoretical and insufficiently documented. There was not even a generally accepted descriptive clinical definition of depression. In our dismay we took comfort from Sandler and Joffe[3] who found themselves in a similar quandary and introduced their paper on childhood depression by stating, "The research worker who aims to investigate the subject of depression in childhood must inevitably find his task extraordinarily difficult."

Although much has been said and written on childhood depression in more recent years, the basic obstacles to definition, diagnosis and metapsychological understanding of childhood depression are still with us. This chapter will attempt to clarify some of these difficulties with the help of some of my clinical experiences.

I shall adhere to the definition of depression we ultimately used in our study of bereaved children.[2] We decided to exclude depressive psychoses because neither we nor others[3,4] had encountered this illness in children; none of our adolescent patients were psychotic; and we considered psychotic illness not a mere variation or extension of neurotic disturbances but a disease entity with different and additional organic components. We limited ourselves to the terms "depressed," "depressive reaction or response," "neurotic depression," and agreed on a working definition based on descriptive clinical manifestations: A dejected, helpless mood; a restriction of motility; a restriction of interest in the world and in objects; a loss of self-esteem." This definition is close to Bibring's,[5] and is not far from the mainstream of current psychiatric usage.

Difficulties Encountered in Using the Descriptive Definition

Some difficulties with this definition are at once apparent. It does not apply to babies in its exact form. The term "loss of self-esteem" would have to be changed, perhaps to a phrase like "loss of well-being" or "narcissistic depletion." This points up the problem of comparing manifestly depressive phenomena in patients at different phases of personality development. They may all look depressed, but this does not allow us to infer that they suffer from the same affliction, that the same causes are operative, or that their minds cope with them in like manner. The depressed 10-month-old, 4-year-old, schoolchild, adolescent, and adult, may each be dealing with different internal and external factors. Even when the depressive symptoms continue from one developmental phase to another or recur at a later stage, we cannot assume that the patient is still, or again, suffering from the same illness.

We know, for example, that obsessional symptoms in young preschoolers indicate a psychic disorder that is very different from the obsessional neurosis of the latency child or adult, although their rituals and ceremonials may appear identical; we also know that in some instances in which the young schoolchild's and adult's obsessional neurosis is the same in its psychic factors, the child's manifest symptoms may be altogether different due to the defensive externalization and interaction with the parental figures.[6,7] Likewise, the fears of the toddler and the phobias of the older preschooler are psychologically quite differently structured, though manifestly alike,[8] and anxiety attacks, though psychologically identical, typically show themselves in the form of temper tantrums during the preschool years and even during early latency, in sharp contrast to the well-known anxiety symptoms we observe in later phases and adulthood.[6,9]

Further, we know that the 2.5-year-old bedwetter who is still enuretic at age 9 has developed a disturbance that bears little relation to his or her earlier incontinence.[10] In regard to depression, such terms as "underlying depression" or "depressive equivalents"[11] point in this direction, but they do not help us diagnostically. Whether or not a nondepressive symptom wards off or contains a depressive response cannot be ascertained by observation. It can only be revealed and understood in the course of psychoanalysis or, in some instances, psychoanalytically oriented psychotherapy.

Another difficulty with the descriptive definition of depression is that one or another of its parts may be lacking in the manifest clinical picture or may be supplanted by its opposite. For example, instead of restriction of motility we see, not infrequently, hyperactivity or alternation between the two states.[2] Such substitutions confuse clinicians and tempt them to focus on one or another criterion instead of all, or to infer multiple substitutions. When the definition is so loosely applied, it may lead us to include a considerable variety of disturbances under the heading of "depression" instead of helping us to refine our diagnostic accuracy.

In my work as consultant to several social agencies and treatment centers, for example, the following cases were presented with a diagnosis of "depression": A prepubertal girl refused to attend school, often remained in her room, and seemed to gain little pleasure from activities and social contacts. Closer scrutiny revealed that her "restricted motility and restricted interest in people and activities" was primarily due to a severe phobia. In a second case an older adolescent boy complained that he could not get up in the morning and was always quite late for school; did not complete his assignments in spite of repeated extensions; tended to absent himself from home and described himself as depressed. Detailed investigation and coordination of information showed that his apparently "slowed down activity," "lack of interest in work," "distance in relationships" and "depressed affect" were due to a psychopathic disturbance. He lived by his instinctual pleasures (e.g., excitement with a pile of pornographic magazines interfered with his getting up on time) and he manipulated his environment to escape responsibility. Even his faked self-professed "depression" served that end and had misled two psychiatrists into prescribing antidepressant medication for him.

Many disturbed adolescents, with mixed long-standing pathologies, exacerbated by internal developmental conflicts and external stress, present real puzzles to the clinician and do not readily fit into diagnostic categories. It is easy to misread their primitive instinctual excesses and drug abuse as defense against depression, and their feelings of guilt and inadequacy as a confirmation of it; to attribute their lack of phase-appropriate investment in ego functions and activities to depressive restriction; and to regard their difficulty in pursuing and achieving success to dejection and helplessness.

The depressive affect, often viewed as the cornerstone of the descriptive syndrome, poses its own special diagnostic problem, even when the patient is not trying to "con" us. Always present is the potential discrepancy between the clinician's observation and the patient's experience. One of our parentally bereaved children, 8-year-old Jim,[2] had frequent "depressed" periods which were of concern to his family. He would sit motionless, stare for hours with a dejected facial expression, withdrawn into himself and unresponsive to the approaches of his surroundings. In his analysis it was a surprise to find that Jim did not *feel* depressed at all at these or other times. He was totally apathetic and felt nothing. In his case, the apathy turned out to be a defense against sadness and painful memories, but apathy, a poorly understood phenomenon in itself,[2] does not necessarily represent a defense against sadness or against depression. When we observe apparently "depressed" infants, however, we cannot, in contrast to Jim, correct our impression with the help of their verbalized analytic material and may be off the mark. Even older children do not always recognize, observe and share their own feelings during diagnostic interviews and therefore with them, too, our perception of their affective experiences may be erroneous.

Perhaps the most common difficulty in assessing the patient's affect is the easy confusion between feeling sad and feeling depressed. The depressed feeling is marked by dejection, helplessness and hopelessness, and it is accompanied by lowered self-esteem. None of these are characteristic of sadness. Sadness occurs in relation to an internal or external loss. Though the loss is acknowledged, the loving investment of the mental representations of self and object is maintained and what was lost is actively longed for. The depressed feeling may or may not be attributed to a specific inner or outer loss but tends to spread and encompass all the psychic experiences. What is lost is internally surrendered and the self is thereby diminished. The investment of the mental representations is depleted and even inner restoration is given up as hopeless. Hence, the depressed person feels impoverished, while the sad person feels unhappy but relatively rich.

Experiences in Understanding the Psychic Mechanisms of Depression in Childhood

Our work with depressed bereaved children showed only one characteristic shared by all, namely their depressive response, in each instance, represented an unconscious defense against the affect of sadness and/or its true content. Some of the children were weepy during their depressed periods but attached their feeling to a displaced content; some realized neither their sadness nor its cause, its ideational content. Their depression lifted when the analytic work revealed the hitherto unconscious sadness and related content, and enabled them to be aware of being sad and of what they were really sad about.[2] If these children had been treated in a supportive psychotherapy, perhaps to bolster their self-esteem, or if they had been given antidepressant medication, their pathological defenses against the unconscious affect and content would have been reenforced rather than diminished. This may have produced a temporary improvement in their depressive symptoms but would not have helped them in the long run, because the unconscious factors would have continued to be active and forced the personality once again to resolve the inner tensions with the help of pathological compromise formations.

As to the underlying causes of our patients' depression, I may add that the unconscious content was not their parental bereavement, their loss of the love object. Instead it was a variety of internal and external experiences.[2] Unfortunately, our data were not ample enough to formulate a coherent theory about the metapsychological aspects of depression or to construct its developmental line in childhood and to relate it to adult depression.

This brief mention of the underlying causes of depression brings us to a group of children who, as a rule, clearly exhibit all the aspects of the descriptive clinical depressive syndrome, but are rarely diagnosed as depressed. I am referring to dying children—either children whose death is actually imminent or who suffer from potentially fatal illnesses. I have worked with such children over many years, sometimes directly in psychotherapy, sometimes indirectly as consultant to child-life workers in several pediatric hospitals.[12]

The professional staff, including mental health professionals, and the parents usually deny both the child's depression and its content, i.e., the child's approaching death. They tend to view the patient as uncooperative, resistant, stubborn, lazy, self-willed, spoiled, manipulative, overly sensitive to pain and discomfort, and/or they attribute his or her behavior to neurotic factors. My findings suggest that the dying or fatally ill child, at a certain point in the course of the disease, senses his or her deterioration, consciously or unconsciously. I am not implying that these children were told about their condition or that they have a specific concept of death. Rather, they register from internal bodily signals the waning of life's energy, the decrease of pleasure in bodily and mental functions.

Dying children of all ages have been observed to show depressive symptoms and to experience relief from them, depending on whether their parents and other caring adults could accept and understand their depleted, realistically helpless state, and could respect and meet their special needs at that critical time. When the caring adults do not recognize and accept the child's status but intrude upon him or her with demands for responsiveness and activity and interfere with the child's attempts to preserve any remaining sense of well-being by imposing painful stimuli which are intended to better or cure the disease, the child is left alone with an excessive internal burden. He or she withdraws, becomes inactive and dejected and reacts to external demands with irritation or lack of response.

By contrast, when the caring adults accept the child's dying or potentially dying state, share and understand his or her sense of dying, protect the child from excessive stimulation and help maintain minimal comfort, the child's depression subsides. He or she becomes able, often to a surprising extent, to utilize remaining energies for the pleasurable investment of people and activities. With the help of the adult's shared awareness and acceptance of his or her dying state, the child can then also bear his or her own sense of dying, at times keeping it in conscious awareness and at times finding relief from it by means of unconscious defense mechanisms. It seems impossible for the child to employ such helpful defenses unless the adults are fully aware of the child's condition.

The experiences with dying depressed children may give us a pointer toward comparable states at the beginning of life—in earliest infancy, where perhaps primitive forerunners of later, more complex depressive reactions, originate.

UNCERTAINTIES IN LINKING SUICIDE AND DEPRESSION

It is not uncommonly held that depression and suicide are directly proportional, i.e., the more depressed a patient is, the more likely is he or she to commit suicide. In addressing the topic of suicide I shall, as with depression and for the same reasons, exclude psychoses.

Children in prepuberty, adolescence and, more rarely, in latency who are clinically depressed may indeed be suicidal, but there are also many depressed youngsters who neither endanger nor harm their bodies. Depressed patients may think about dying and wish they were dead but this does not necessarily lead them to bring it about or to do it. Even healthy youngsters, especially in adolescence, *think* about death and perhaps most, if not all, have at one or another time *wished* they were dead, in despair, in anger, or with fascination. It seems to me that the potential for suicide is not directly related to the depressive response but to other personality factors which may or may not be present along with the depression. Suicide attempts and/or suicidal behaviors occur also in children and adolescents who are not manifestly depressed or whose pathology includes only some depressive features.

What then are the personality factors that allow or compel suicidal actions? Here, I find myself in a quandary. To clarify and substantiate my findings and tentative conclusions requires detailed data gathered from the work with individual patients. I do not lack such data. They derive from a few patients seen in daily psychoanalytic sessions over a period of years, and from more extensive but more superficial experiences as consultant to outpatient agencies and residential treatment centers, and to child-life workers who see such youngsters in the hospital following admission for suicide attempts. Unfortunately, I am unable to use any of these data for reasons of confidentiality and of concern lest revealing their material exacerbate the patients' disturbance. I therefore have to limit myself to generalities and a few diluted vignettes. It is my hope, nevertheless, that the reader will bear with me and that those who work with such patients may recognize, or be alerted to, similar circumstances in their experiences and will be able to follow my thinking.

The Role of Primitive Excitement and Aggression in Self-Hurting

The manifest events that the patients, and others, often view as the precipitating cause of the suicide attempt tend to be stressful but not of overwhelming proportions. For example, they include difficulties or failure at school, rejection by a boyfriend or girlfriend, parents leaving town temporarily, or contacts with family members who live elsewhere and are usually absent, such as a divorced parent or the parent of a child in placement. Quite often, the events would contain pleasure for other people; for example, impending graduation from high school, prospects of going away to college, success in being accepted at the school or job of his choosing, parties and outings with peers.

Only closer scrutiny reveals that these events were experienced, not only in terms of hurt feelings, loss of love, humiliation, fear of losing the loved ones and/or proof of inadequacy or guilt, but that they, or something associated with them, also excited the patient and unleashed intolerable impulses. In some instances genital sexual feelings and homo- or heterosexual activities were actually experienced but, even when this is the case, it is not this excitement which directly contributes to the suicidal attempt. The developmentally more advanced genital feelings and experiences either stimulated concurrent, more primitive sadomasochistic impulses or proved so threatening to the personality that it regressed defensively to such a more primitive level. It is this primitive sadomasochistic excitement which contributes to the danger of self-damage, because in it violence and mutual hurting provide gratification and death may take the place of surrender or orgasm.

Suicidal youngsters often act out these exciting doing-and-being-done-to fantasies. They provoke attacks, insults, rejections and humiliations or they perceive and misconstrue the words and behavior of others in these terms even when the reality does not warrant it. Sometimes they exhibit their excitement by means of exaggerated or unrealistic tales of woe and usually succeed in involving their audience by evoking pity or guilt or anger at the presumed perpetrators of cruelty to the patient. For example:

A 16-year-old boy provoked his teachers by not completing his work, then experienced their grant of extensions as humiliating torture, their ultimate deadline as an attack, and finally forced his school into suspending him, their supreme cruelty. He was quite unaware how, at the same time, he had hurt and upset his teachers and rendered them helpless.

A 17-year-old girl aggressively seduced her boyfriend into intercourse and deceived him by telling him that she was using contraceptives. She then experienced pregnancy, abortion, and the boyfriend's hurt withdrawal as torture, and masochistic punishment to which she surrendered.

A 13-year-old boy withdrew into stoic silence after his mother's criticism of his inconsiderate behavior and provoked her to tears with his refusal to have anything to do with her. In his treatment he similarly rejected the therapist and tried to provoke her to intrude upon him with aggressive questioning or to berate him for his lack of cooperation. His fantasies revealed that he was preoccupied with a hurting interaction between them.

Relationships with therapists tend to be drawn into all aspects of the hurting excitement. They are tortured and humiliated as the patient makes them anxious and helpless. They are perceived as tormentors and forced to take active "punitive" steps, and they are put into the position of the participating audience as patients reveal their excited distressing experiences or subject them to silent imperviousness. The patients who are most seriously driven to self-hurting and suicide may not share their difficulties or involve their therapists manifestly at all. They appear cooperative and may even feign improvement while they actively prepare for suicide. Casual acquaintances who are in no position to help such patients may receive signals of the impending danger, but the therapists are kept in the dark and receive their own sadistic punishment when they suddenly learn of the patients' suicides.

I am not implying that the patients are aware of their pathological excitement, contained in their behavior and/or fantasies, or that they consciously manipulate their relationships to gratify it. On the contrary, these manifestations are largely defensive and serve to protect them against the internally perceived danger of sadomasochistic masturbatory activities and fantasies centered on the infantile parental figures. Unfortunately, the defense is not always successful because the interactions with others also stimulate excitement so that they may create a vicious cycle.

Many of these patients are very afraid of being alone because this increases the threat of masturbation. This is one reason for their distress at being left by love objects or at being uninvited to participate in peer activities. Many suffer from sleep disturbances or escape into sleeping. Their reported masturbation often includes self-hurting practices and fantasies of being beaten, tortured or humiliated and of inflicting such suffering on the loved ones. The suicidal act may represent several aspects of the internal struggle—defense and gratification.

The primitive, raw, unattenuated aggression, attached to their sadomasochistic sexual life, often invades other aspects of these patients' personalities. It may manifest itself in breakthroughs of temper outbursts, physical violence and sarcasm, in their periodic lack of care for themselves and their possessions, and in their inability to protect their interests and to allow themselves to achieve and enjoy success. It may also rage at them from within, berating and belittling them in the form of lowered self-esteem and in the form of a harsh conscience which does not serve as an integrated inner monitor and guide but viciously "beats up" on them, meting out cruel punishments. In this way the doing-and-being-done-to excitement is reenacted within the psychic scenario. This aspect of the inner conflict may also lead to suicide.

Origins of Sadomasochistic Pathology

Where does such an intense sadomasochistic sexuality come from and why is the aggression that accompanies and coexists with it so unattenuated? We know, of course, that these manifestations are a normal part of toddler development and do resurface in prepuberty and early adolescence, along with other infantile impulses.[6,13] In our patients, however, they are not only unusually intense but so pervasive that they take precedence instead of subsiding. The personality is unable to progress to more mature genital functioning with considerate object relationships and modulated expression of aggression. When we have opportunity to observe the development of such difficulties long term in early childhood, and/or to explore it psychoanalytically in retrospect, we find that the crucial fixation points occurred in the preschool years, that their manifestations, for example, in the form of sadomasochistic masturbatory fantasies and activities, were relatively contained during latency, and then intensified in adolescence when the increased strength of the developing impulses could no longer be matched by the ego's resources of control and defense.

The early intensification of these impulses and the child's inability to resolve and overcome them during the preschool years may be due to a variety of factors. Among the patients I have worked with, pathology in the early parent-child relationships proved most important. In some cases there was marked ambivalence toward the child, manifested in a great deal of physical punishment, sadistic verbal humiliation, exposure to the parents' sadomasochistic relationship with each other and to their sexual activities. The young child perceived such sexual activities as violent fights which, in his mind, coalesced with the sadomasochistic interactions he experienced in daytime. With other patients, the most significant factor was the mothering person's inability to be sufficiently and consistently available and to protect the child from harm during the crucial early years. This resulted in overwhelming experiences at the hands of substitute caretakers or others outside the family. In some cases important contributory factors were repeated early medical and surgical treatments. These were experienced as sadistic attacks to which the patients had to submit without protest.

In all these situations the toddler's and young preschooler's affectionate bonds proved too weak or too inconsistent to outweigh, fuse and modify his or her aggression in the relationship to the loved ones. The child could not achieve the necessary measure of drive fusion that allows the personality to progress to and master subsequent developmental phases without undue interference from earlier levels; to surpass the sadomasochistic impulses; and to develop consideration for others and kindness to oneself in spite of mixed feelings.

The worst intensification of sadomasochistic pathology in later phases occurred in those patients whose vulnerable areas were again stimulated by interactions with the parental difficulties at such a later time because these interplays stirred or repeated the early pathology. For example, a father who had sadistically humiliated and beaten his boy in early childhood was once again drawn into teasing and belittling him in puberty as well as regaling him with florid tales of his (the father's) sexual exploits. The father's behavior unconsciously excited and infuriated the son, intensified his already present homosexual sadomasochistic fantasies, and interfered with his progressive sexual development and his age-appropriate task of transferring his emotional investment from the parent to new love objects outside the family.

I am not suggesting that these were not caring and concerned parents. Nor did they and their children lack love and affection which can indeed exist side by side with the disturbed features merely because the fusion between love and aggression is inadequate. The parents were completely or largely anaware of their pathology and of its impact on the growing child. A number were well-functioning families, in good social and economic standing, with admirable achievements in their professional or business pursuits. They were eager to do well by their offspring and often supportive of their intellectual and athletic activities.

The Role of Bodily Self-Love as a Barrier to Self-Injury

The persistence of intense, unfused early aggression in its sexualized sadomasochistic form and in its invasion of self-esteem and conscience is not, however, the only important factor contributing to suicidal actions. More important still is the difficulty which already precedes and later interacts with the toddler pathology—namely, an insufficient, loving self-investment of the infant's own body image during the first and second years of life.[14]

Usually, by the middle of the first year, babies have experienced enough pleasurable well-being that they can begin to build an idea of a primitive limited bodily self whose sense of comfort they want to preserve. They do not chew and bite themselves, they protest vigorously when they are hurt, they seek and accept comfort and welcome feeling good again. In short, they like their bodies and like to keep them feeling good. During the subsequent early years, the images of self and mother become increasingly differentiated and the inner image of the bodily self comes to include all parts of the body. The child's own pleasurable bodily experiences, together with the mother's loving ministrations, protection from harm and comfort of pain, help to build the liking of one's body, help it to take a firm hold and to create a lasting barrier against self-injury.

During toddlerhood, we commonly see indications that children are still struggling to take this developmental step; for example, when they turn down mother's food, mess their pants, or provocatively dash into the street to hurt and enrage mother, they show that they have not yet sufficiently differentiated themselves from her to appreciate that they are causing more harm to themselves than to her, and that their fun in engaging her in an excited tug-of-war outweighs their pleasure in being kind to themselves. The mother may facilitate progressive development by pointing out the reality and by not becoming a party to her toddler's provocation, or she may perpetuate and confirm his or her infantile gratifications by responding to the toddler at his or her level.

In some instances infants cannot complete these crucial developmental steps. It may be due to physical distress from illness or treatments which the mother is unable sufficiently to alleviate, or it may be due to deficits in handling, such as meeting the infants' needs in a way that prevents pleasurable gratification, failing to comfort them enough at times of bodily stress, or not protecting them from harm. When the parent actually inflicts hurt on children's bodies through rough care, in anger, excitement, or by way of punishment, such children cannot develop a proper liking for their bodies. They identify with the parental mistreatment of their bodies and may even come to enjoy and seek pain and discomfort in pathological gratification instead of avoiding and protesting such experiences. Early signs of such a development can be seen in not complaining when hurt, not seeking help and comfort, delay in learning to avoid common dangers, repeated injuries, accident proneness, self-hurting "comfort" habits, such as headbanging, violent scratching, hair pulling, injurious masturbatory activities, and in provocations to physical attack and punishment.

Children's failure to develop their protective bodily self-love is paralleled by a failure in the concomitant step of differentiation between self and object. When their raw and/or sexualized aggression is directed against themselves, it may therefore also represent aggression to the parental figures, vengeance upon them, or excited violent interaction with them. The more shaky and inadequate the earliest loving bodily investment, the more prone are patients to self-damaging and suicidal actions, with or without pathological admixture from later phases. This includes not only active self-hurting but passive inability to care for themselves, which can be just as life threatening.

The patients I worked with showed, in each instance, a considerable interference in the early development of liking their own bodies and consistently striving to protect them. Their psychological, though not their physiological pain barrier was inadequate to maintain self-preservation and, under stress, failed to protect them from self-injury when later impulses and conflicts drove them to it. The vulnerable substructure of their personality constituted an acute suicidal danger when it combined at the early level with strong sadomasochistic tendencies, poor self and object differentiation and inadequate fusion of aggression, and was later augmented by the adolescent increase in impulses, by conflicts inherent in achieving emotional independence, and by environmental stresses which strained already limited means of mastery and/or further stimulated existing pathology. These factors may be present in a variety of nonpsychotic personality disturbances. They may or may not accompany a depressive reaction. The extent to which they are inherent in the personality structure determines the suicidal risk in depressed youngsters.

Whenever a patient's depression or other disturbance occurs in the context of such early pathology, the therapeutic task is extraordinarily difficult and, at best, limited. By contrast, depressed patients who show no or minimal signs of weakness at the described early levels are often able to utilize psychological treatment that can help them to uncover and master the unconscious psychic contents.

For purposes of clarity, these statements are very concise and definite. This may be misleading because the reported findings are actually quite complex, with intricate individual ramifications. Thus, these conclusions are tentative and may need to be modified in the light of further clinical data.

REFERENCES

1. *Furman E:* A Child's Parent Dies. *New Haven, Yale University Press, 1974.*
2. *Furman E: Observations on depression and apathy, in Furman E (ed):* A Child's Parent Dies. *New Haven, Yale University Press, 1974, pp 184–197.*

3. *Sandler J, Joffe WG: Notes on childhood depression.* Int J Psychoanal *1965;46:88–96.*
4. *Anthony J, Scott P: Manic-depressive psychosis in childhood.* J Child Psychol Psychiatry *1960;1:53–72.*
5. *Bibring E: The mechanism of depression, in Greenacre P (ed):* Affective Disorders. *New York, International Universities Press, 1953, pp 13–48.*
6. *Freud A:* Normality and Pathology in Childhood. *New York, International Universities Press, 1965.*
7. *Furman E: Some aspects of a young boy's masturbation conflict, in Marcus IM, Francis JJ (eds):* Masturbation from Infancy to Senescence. *New York, International Universities Press, 1975, pp 185–204.*
8. *Freud A: Fears, anxieties, and phobic phenomena.* Psychoanal Study Child *1977;32:85–90.*
9. *Freud A: The symptomatology of childhood: A preliminary attempt at classification.* Psychoanal Study Child *1970;25:19–44.*
10. *Katan A: Experience with enuretics.* Psychoanal Study Child *1946;2:241–256.*
11. *Toolan JM: Depression in children and adolescents.* Am J Orthopsychiatry *1962;32:404–415.*
12. *Furman E: Helping children cope with dying.* Archives Foundation Thanatology *1981;9:3.*
13. *Freud S: Three Essays on the Theory of Sexuality, 1905* The Complete Psychological Works of Sigmund Freud, *standard ed. London, Hogarth Press, 1953, vol 7, pp 125–243.*
14. *Hoffer W: Development of the body ego.* Psychoanal Study Child *1950;5:18–23.*

33. Attempted Suicide in Adolescence: The Suicide Sequence

Jack Novick

AUTOBIOGRAPHICAL NOTE

"My first contact with suicide was abstract, philosophical, and part of the avant-garde atmosphere of coffee houses in Montreal where I obtained my B.A. in literature from McGill University in 1955," writes Jack Novick. *"This romanticized view of suicide as an existential choice, a challenge to bourgeoise morality and established religion, continued during my stay in New York where I pursued graduate studies in clinical psychology at New York University and discussed issues of life and death with Black Mountain poets and painters at the Cedar Bar. Suicide became real and lost its romantic, rebellious aura during my years in London where I trained as a child analyst at the Anna Freud Center and as an adult and child analyst at the British Psychoanalytic Institute. A large number of my cases, during training and after, were suicidal. This initial clinical experience was exponentially increased during my eight years of work at the Brent Consultation Centre, a walk-in service for adolescents, and at the Center for the Study of Adolescence, where I participated in an analytic research project on adolescent suicide.*

"Both these centers were organized and directed by Moses and Eglé Laufer. The paper reprinted in this book acknowledges my debt to these two dedicated psychoanalysts and refers to the research done.

"I returned to the United States in 1977 as chief psychologist and associate professor at the Children's Psychiatric Hospital, Department of Psychiatry, University of Michigan School of Medicine. I became a supervising psychoanalyst at the Michigan Psychoanalytic Institute and a training and supervising analyst at the New York Freudian Society. But I continued by clinical and research interest in suicide.

Jack Novick, "Attempted Suicide in Adolescence: The Suicide Sequence." In Howard Sudak, Amasa B. Ford, and Norman B. Rushforth, eds., *Suicide in the Young*. Boston: John Wright/PSG Inc., 1984, pp.115–137. Reprinted by permission.

"With Kerry Kelly Novick I have studied a range of self-destructive behaviors in children, adolescents, and adults. We believe that suicide and depression occur in the context of sadomasochistic pathology with the delusion of omnipotence as a core fantasy."

COMMENT

Experiences in the treatment of seven adolescent suicide-attempters (their attempts had been dangerous) led Novick to infer a pattern, or sequence, which typified them. The critical psychopathology in each derived from incapacity to achieve adolescent separation from their mothers, and the resultant morbid attempts to master the developmental problem led to a descent into suicide.

Novick's findings are useful in understanding not only adolescents locked in this difficulty, but pertain as well to many adults in their twenties and thirties who suffer from chronic suicidal character pathology, of which a singular aspect is the tendency to make the therapist responsible for whether the patient lives or dies.

Novick acknowledges his indebtedness to colleagues at the Centre for Research into Adolescent Breakdown in London, some of whom collaborated in another chapter included in this book (see chapter 17 above).

■

This chapter reports psychoanalytic research on seven adolescents who had each made at least one serious suicide attempt, and presents a replication of the findings using the psychoanalytic material of another adolescent suicide case. The investigation demonstrated that attempted suicide in adolescence is not an impulsive act but the end point in a pathological regression. In each of the cases the suicide attempt appeared in the context of severe, long-standing disturbance; depression, feelings of abnormality, and suicide thoughts had been present for a long time. The regression started, in each case, with the experience of failure in the attempt to separate from mother. Age-appropriate sexual impulses were experienced by these adolescents as hostile separation and a sadistic oedipal triumph. Subsequent events led to regressive intensification of a sadomasochistic tie to mother and displacement of the experience of rejection and anger from mother to another person. Following displacement, guilt was no longer an inhibiting factor and the suicide plan was put into action. At the time of the attempt, all the adolescents denied the reality of death and thought of suicide as a positive, brave action producing multiple results. The importance of elucidating the elements of the suicide sequence in the treatment of suicidal adolescents is discussed.

SOON AFTER her 18th birthday, Mary drove her car down a steep embankment. The car was completely destroyed, Mary suffered severe internal injuries and nearly died. After recovering from major surgery, she told her psychiatrist that she had intended to kill herself. I saw Mary and her parents soon after she left the hospital. Near the start of the interview mother said, "I refuse to feel guilty," and remained fairly silent, as did Mary, for the rest of the session. Father, a tall, tree-trunk of a man, did most of the talking and the women nodded assent when I looked at them for additional comments. The whole family referred to the suicide attempt as "the accident," and apparently viewed it as an impulsive, rebellious bit of behavior to be appropriately punished and not repeated. The parents had insisted that Mary use her college savings toward paying for a new car as this would help impress her with the unacceptability of her actions.

Mary was the second of two children, with a brother three years older. The elder child had always rebelled, fought with the parents and failed at school, whereas Mary was seen as a high-achieving person who had always done well at school and was well behaved. She was said to have had many friends, to have played on the school teams and in general to have been well adjusted and happy, with a secure future in the professional career she had chosen. The parents said that they were completely surprised by the event. It was totally out of character and they could see no reason why she had done it. Even when I saw Mary alone she had little to add to our understanding of her serious suicide attempt. She claimed that she too had no idea why she had done it, and said that while driving she had suddenly felt that it would be better if she were dead. She was having difficulty with her superior at work, and felt unjustly criticized by her but, at the same time, felt that she was not doing well enough. The referring psychiatrist had ruled out psychosis or a major biological depression, a view that concurred with my assessment and that of another psychiatrist I had called in for a second opinion and a drug consultation. So why had she made a serious suicide attempt? What was the risk of a further attempt? What was the treatment of choice?

When I recommended four-times-per-week psychoanalysis, father went back to the referring psychiatrist to ask, "What kind of nut is Novick? Are they still doing psychoanalysis?" Aside from his personal issues, which were then addressed, he did well to ask about psychoanalysis. Psychoanalysis is not commonly used with adolescents and almost never with suicidal young people.

There is a vast literature on suicide and attempted suicide, for, as Baechler comments, "It is probable that suicide is the most unremittingly studied human behavior."[1] Except for the epidemiological data on suicide and attempted suicide which underscores the increasing incidence of the problem, the vast literature offers little assistance to the clinician.[2–4] Given the nature of the topic, it is understandable that there are few studies based on clinical case material, but even research into attempted suicide in adolescence has relied almost entirely on demographic data, interview data obtained immediately subsequent to the event, and sometimes on clinical material obtained from brief interventions with suicidal adolescents. Hurry[5] and Kernberg[6] provide notable exceptions to the meager clinical literature on the topic.

The value of psychoanalysis as a research technique has often been questioned by those outside the field, and of late the research value of psychoanalysis has been put under very severe test by sophisticated arguments from within. Without entering into these stimulating and controversial issues, such as natural versus humanistic science, the search for meaning (hermeneutics) versus the explication of general scientific laws, nomothetic versus idiographic science, narrative versus historical truth, etc., this writer will present a research project on attempted suicide in adolescence conducted by analysts using five-times-a-week psychoanalysis both as a method of treatment and as a method of investigation. Mary's material is used to illustrate and amplify the research findings. (Mary is the pseudonym of a young woman seen in analysis while she was attending university in England. I would like to thank Mary for permission to use material from the first three years of our work together.)

METHODS

It is now almost ten years since my colleagues and I began to summarize the results of a research project based on the psychoanalysis of adolescents who had attempted suicide. This report, completed in 1976, has not been published in toto as yet, but brief descriptions, summaries and references to this research have appeared in the literature.[5,7–10] Subsidized, five-times-a-week psychoanalysis was offered to nonpsychotic adolescents who had made medically serious suicide attempts. We were thus excluding those who made suicide threats, where the attempt did not require medical intervention to save the person's life, or where an ongoing psychotic process obscured the issue of intentionality.

The final sample consisted of seven adolescents, three females and four males ranging from 14 to 19 years of age. Analysts wrote detailed weekly reports on each case. These reports were circulated to the other members of the group, and all the analysts met weekly for two hours to discuss each patient and to evolve a conceptual and technical approach to the topic. We started with the assumption that attempted suicide in adolescence is always a sign of severe pathology. There are many who tend to romanticize suicide; to see it as an expression of free will. One of the current best sellers in France is a book on techniques of suicide. Alvarez[11] traces the differing attitudes toward suicide and the attraction suicide has for the young and the creative. However, in an earlier study on adolescents who came to a walk-in center my colleagues and I[12] found that adolescents who had made a serious suicide attempt showed more signs of current disturbance, a history of greater childhood disturbance, and a higher incidence of parental disturbance than the nonsuicidal adolescents who had come for psychological help. The psychoanalytic project on attempted suicide further confirmed this finding as each of the seven subjects proved to have been severely disturbed from childhood on.

The same was true in Mary's case. Near the end of her first year of analysis, Mary was attending college but did nothing more than study for her courses. She lived at home, totally dependent on her mother for everything from shopping to laundry. She turned down all offers of friendship and spent weekends and evenings alone in her room. When she was not studying, she stayed up late at night rearranging the furniture or spending hours trying to decide which side of the desk to put her pencils on. She sat silently at meals, hardly said anything to her father, and spoke only when asked direct questions. She was 19 years old, fully developed sexually but always dressed in bib overalls, sneakers and loose-fitting sweatshirts. She wore her hair closely cropped and looked like a young boy. Her inhibited behavior and strange appearance were the overt signs of her disturbance; I was more concerned about the continuing danger that she might either kill herself or suffer a psychotic breakdown and have to be hospitalized.

Nevertheless, at this point in her treatment her father, under pressure from mother, told Mary that he and mother were very pleased with her progress, that they felt she was now a "normal girl," that she seemed to be doing well and perhaps she should think of stopping her analysis or at least cutting down. They were intelligent, college-educated, professional people. Defenses, of course, have no respect for class or intellectual distinctions. Gross denial of pathology was the hallmark of this family, and a major focus of analytic work was Mary's view that only she knew that the story of her being a normal child from a normal family was untrue. It she were to reveal to anyone how disturbed she and her mother had been, and still were, terrible consequences would ensue. It is risky to base an assessment of parental pathology on the patient's distortions of memory and the selective acuity of projections, but Mary's description of mother as "weird" probably comes close to the mark. Mother's barely concealed hostility to her daughter and her extreme obsessionality were evident during my meetings with the parents, and over the years the family had completely acceded to her pathological concerns with cleanliness and security.

Most striking, however, was mother's inability to tolerate the slightest sign of hostility. In her constant preoccupation with defending against both her own hostility and that of others mother seemed completely out of touch with Mary's ordinary needs. This could be seen in many examples from current and past behavior and also in Mary's identification with an inattentive, unresponsive, affectless mother. Mary told me that she had always considered herself as neuter, neither male nor female. Although signs of severe problems in sexual identity had appeared at puberty, including serious menstrual dysfunction of probable psychogenic origin, Mary's identity problem was more basic. As we learned from the analytic work, her choice was not between male and female but between life and death. Neuter did not refer to gender identity but to existence. Repeatedly, in treatment, Mary's response to stress was to "tune out, go blank, become a zombie." We came to call this "a little suicide" and she said that she could remember long periods of time, going back to childhood, when she would function like a robot, with no feelings. "When I tune out," she said, "it's as if I'm not there." Mary's memories of childhood showed signs of a lifelong difficulty in experiencing and maintaining feelings of pleasure in achievement. She had what Krystal[13] has referred to as "anhedonia"—we called it the "big deal" response. She would work with enormous energy out of a near panic that she would fail. When she achieved her A or A+, she would feel a brief period of relief and then say to herself "big deal" and forget about her accomplishment. The disturbance in her ability to tolerate and experience affect and her feeling of being a "robot, a zombie" are typical signs of a post-traumatic reaction which have led me to hypothesize that infantile trauma is part of Mary's history.

THE FOCAL RESEARCH

It does not require the effort and power of psychoanalysis to demonstrate that attempted suicide represents a breakdown in normal adolescent development and appeared, both in Mary and in the other adolescents in our research, in the context of severe, long-standing disturbance. As important as this finding may be, a psychoanalytic project should be able to tell us much more about attempted suicide in adolescence. An immediate obstacle, one shared by most psychoanalytic research projects, related to the volume of material generated by psychoanalysis. We devised a method, called "focal research," in part as a response to the challenge of dealing with large amounts of data. The weekly reports on each case contained many references to suicide. Most of these suicide references related to the actual attempt, some were threats or plans for further attempts and some were intellectualized comments on the nature of death. Each suicide reference was extracted from the weekly reports and put on a separate piece of paper. It was noticed that these comments varied in frequency, and the focal research was an attempt to study both the content and the context in which these suicide thoughts appeared. Examples of such comments, taken at random from each of the seven cases, are as follows:

Female Case #1:	"I had told my school friends that I wanted to kill myself but they didn't believe me."
Female Case #2:	"When I took the tablets I felt nobody cared for me."
Female Case #3:	"It may sound paradoxical but I think of suicide as my lifeline. Suicide is my way out. Without it I would become dependent on life."
Male Case #4:	"Suicide people don't really believe they will die."
Male Case #5:	"I always feel that it is something I might try again. I'm frightened of doing it again and frightened of the pain but it's something I can't give up."
Male Case #6:	Patient reported that while at his parents' home for the weekend he had made a trial run, taking six aspirins to see if he could swallow them one after the other. The next day he tried to kill himself.
Male Case #7:	"I think I must have been in a mad, insane mood. I can't even remember what happened or how I came to turn the gas on, so I think I must have been crazy."

On the same page as the extracted comment, note was made of the immediate context, the larger context and, finally, space was allotted for speculations. The immediate context included proximal interventions by the analyst, the patient's material and affective state prior to and subsequent to the suicide thought and such events as an upcoming vacation, a weekend break, etc. The larger context referred to events which took place over a span of time, such as the developing and predominant transference relationship, emerging changes within the patient, shifts in defenses and the increasing dominance of certain phase-specific dynamics. The section on speculations allowed the analyst to associate freely to the material and to see whether certain hypotheses could be borne out by subsequent material. In doing the focal research analysts worked in pairs, each abstracting the suicide comment and content on the other analyst's case. A pilot study using pairs of analysts working independently on one case showed almost perfect agreement on the abstracted suicide items and on the immediate context for the emergence of these suicide thoughts. Surprisingly, there was also very high agreement between the analysts on the larger context for the emerging suicide thoughts.

As a further measure of the reliability of the findings, two measures of internal consistency were used. Each analyst wrote a detailed metapsychological portrait of the case in treatment. The sections and subheadings of this portrait were based on Anna Freud's metapsychological profile[14] as extended for adolescents by Laufer.[15] The analyst who was doing the focal research could then check the dynamic picture emerging from the focal research with the metapsychological profile written by the analyst of the case, and, finally, the analyst of the case would evaluate the focal research findings for consistency with his own clinical view of the case.

RESULTS

An immediate and striking finding of the focal research was the extent to which significant bits of information concerning the actual suicide attempt were not available until well into the analysis. For each case an enormous amount of additional information emerged during the course of analysis compared to what was elicited by direct questions soon after the suicide attempt. Often, the new information came in response to an interpretation, especially a transference interpretation. In an earlier publication[10] this writer referred to one of the seven cases, a 19-year-old who had claimed that his suicide attempt was precipitated by a rejection from the university of his choice. Near the end of his first year of analysis, my interpretation of his attempt to force me to reject him led to his remembering that he had applied to the university knowing that the deadline had passed. Similarly, in Mary's case the meager information available soon after the suicide attempt was considerably augmented by memories recovered following analytic intervention. For example, she recalled, in the third year of her analysis, that the car she had smashed was her mother's; mother had loved the car and Mary had hated it.

The focal research provided two sets of information: (1) suicide thoughts (which include memories of the actual attempt, attitudes and fantasies about suicide, etc.) and (2) the context in which these thoughts emerged. We hypothesized that the thoughts and memories did not emerge at random but related to specific dynamic patterns discernible in the immediate and larger context of the flow of material. We found in all seven cases that suicide thoughts emerged in relation to: (1) fear of or feeling of abandonment, (2) fear of or wish for engulfment, and (3) fear of or guilt over what were felt to be omnipotent, aggressive wishes toward mother. The details of this finding and many others of the suicide research such as distinctions between a suicide act and a suicide thought and the multidetermination of such thoughts and acts await the publication of the full report, but in this chapter the author wishes to present another of the major findings of the focal research, *The suicide sequence.* Material from the case of Mary, who was seen subsequent to the study, will be used in an attempt to test the reliability of the findings and exemplify the steps in the suicide sequence.

THE SUICIDE SEQUENCE

Mary and her parents viewed her suicide attempt as an impulsive act, out of character with a previous well-functioning personality and precipitated by some person or event outside the immediate family. This characterization of the suicide attempt is similar to the one presented by the adolescents in the research project and is not an unusual view. In a recent syndicated newspaper article (*Ann Arbor News,* May 7, 1981, Dallas [AP], Leigh Shirley) the reporter wrote of a 16-year-old boy who had shot himself with his father's favorite shotgun. Father described him as "popular, played football, just a normal, teenage kid." This view of adolescent suicide has attained the power of a myth, and one of the major findings of the focal research was to contradict this myth. In every case we found a consistent sequence of psychological steps leading to a suicide attempt. In a previous publication the suicide sequence was summarized as follows: "The suicide attempt in each of the cases was not a sudden act but the end point in a pathological regression."[10]

The focal research enabled us to combine the memories of the suicide attempt with the dynamic context for the recall of these events to arrive at a first approximation of the steps in the regressive sequence leading to the suicide attempt. Bearing in mind all the limitations and controversies concerning the accuracy of reconstructions the author would like to present the steps in the sequence and use the material from Mary's case to test the findings. The numbered sections in this text refer to the steps in the sequence as described in the unpublished report.[16]

1. For a considerable period prior to the suicide attempt, the adolescents had felt depressed, sexually abnormal, and had suicidal thoughts. The focal research shows that depression and feelings of sexual abnormality can coexist with suicidal thoughts without in themselves motivating the act of suicide.

When Mary reached puberty her feelings of nonexistence were expressed as feelings of sexual abnormality. She frequently constructed mental lists of "impossibles." The order of "impossibles" changed during our work together, but for years the top three remained unaltered—sex, marriage, and babies. Much later in the analysis she admitted with embarrassment that during junior and senior high school she sometimes had fantasies about boys, thought of talking to certain boys but was sure that they would find her "weird and unattractive." Mary was potentially an attractive young woman and as the analysis progressed and she gathered courage to take charge of her own body, there were times when she allowed herself to be quite feminine and pretty. It was evident, however, that from early puberty on she had felt sexually abnormal and incapable of becoming a mature, sexual woman.

Regarding feelings of depression preceding the suicide attempt, Mary reported that she had been "feeling bad" for at least four years. Her father, a professional, had accepted a position in another part of the country and Mary had to leave her friends and her school. She said that she had felt "bad" ever since and had never been able to make the kind of friends she had before the move. "Feeling bad" was Mary's term for an undifferentiated state of dysphoria; as she slowly became able to differentiate and verbalize her feelings, she could talk about her anger at her parents, especially her father, for not having considered her feelings or her needs and for never having talked to her about the move.

As to preexisting morbid fantasies and suicidal thoughts, the material revealed that for many years Mary had been preoccupied with thoughts of death and dying. Father traveled frequently and since childhood Mary had worried that he might die. She was surprised when she had reached her 18th birthday and realized that she had never thought of herself as being 18. She felt this indicated that she probably thought she would not live to be 18.

Some aspects of her memories regarding the actual attempt are still unclear, but there is evidence for a preexisting suicide plan from another source. The year after the start of treatment, just before the anniversary of her suicide attempt, Mary was in a state of visible anguish and "feeling bad." She was spending many hours in her room, not sleeping at night, and defending vigorously against conscious awareness of any angry feelings toward her parents. I mentioned the anniversary, the reemergence of suicide thoughts and, when she agreed that such thoughts were in her mind, I asked if she were making concrete plans for such an event. Following extraction of wisdom teeth her dentist had prescribed a powerful pain killer. Mary told me that she had been refilling the prescription for weeks and saving the pills for her next suicide attempt. As we found with the seven adolescents in the project, so, in Mary's case, depression, feelings of sexual abnormality and suicidal thoughts could be present for considerable time without leading to an actual attempt. This finding suggests that there is a more complicated link between depression and adolescent suicide than usually noted in the literature. As will be demonstrated, it requires more than depression and a suicide plan to lead to a suicide attempt. Erna Furman [see chapter 32 above] arrived independently at a similar conclusion.

2. The sequence leading to the suicide act is precipitated in all cases by external events which impose on the adolescents the responsibility of taking a step that represents to them the breaking of the tie to the mother.

In Mary's case the suicide attempt was preceded, first, by her leaving home to go to college and then by her 18th birthday. Both these external events symbolized independence and adulthood, a phase she had never imagined entering. During the course of analysis, many external independent moves were seen to represent for Mary the complete severing of ties to mother, actions which she felt were totally unacceptable. Moving out of her house to a dorm precipitated suicidal thoughts. Going to a party or even imagining buying her own television set was felt by her to be an act of extreme defiance which was followed by suicidal thoughts. In her third year of analysis she planned to return to the city of her childhood home in order to visit her old high school friends. She first arranged a change in her analytic schedule, then went through all the other necessary steps. On her way to the travel agent she realized that this final step would mean that she had done it all without her parents. She knew that she should feel pleased; instead, she felt terrible. "It wasn't right." When I suggested that this was what she might have felt when she was away at college, she recalled a moment of panic when she had realized that her winning a scholarship meant she did not need her parents for anything.

3. In all cases the adolescents fail to make such a step. The external event and the experience of failure make the adolescents conscious of their dependency on their mothers.

In Mary's case the failure which occupied most of the first year of analysis was her inability to stay away at college. The college was highly competitive and she had attained a place and a full scholarship by beating out a long list of female applicants. The college not only symbolized independence from mother but would, in fact, have made her independent since she would not need them for any financial support. During the period of extreme difficulty at college, she felt very close to her mother and appreciative of mother's support. She felt that it was father who wanted her to stay. She left college after six weeks and returned to her parental home. Following the start of analysis, she attended a local college but remained at home and had her mother do everything for her from cooking to laundry. Mary felt totally dependent on mother, would panic at the thought of traveling to a different place without her, and allowed mother to select and buy all her clothes. It was only during her third year of analysis, at the age of 20, that Mary began to allow herself to shop independently. A psychology of will and action must encompass the paradox of adolescent suicide. Mary's behavior underscores the fact that these young people are often incapable of the simplest actions such as buying clothes or going to a party. On the other hand, they are capable of self-destruction, an avenue of activity not open to other young people, even those who are otherwise seriously disturbed.

4. The failure to make the normal adolescent move away from the parent throws the adolescent back into an intense infantile relationship with mother, which on a descriptive level could be termed a sadomasochistic relationship. . . . The female adolescent, terrified of being abandoned by mother, will submit to her and create situations in which she is repeatedly forced to do so. . . .

This summary paragraph from the adolescent attempted suicide study is condensed and requires much amplification. It was an attempt to state as concisely as possible that the preexisting relationship with the mother is very primitive and that failure to separate and become autonomous throws the adolescent back into the primitive relationship.

The analytic material, especially during the periods of repeated suicidal crisis, allowed us to reconstruct the relationship between Mary and her mother prior to the suicide attempt. It had revolved around Mary's total inability to contain the slightest negative thought about her mother. The anger was, as she termed it, a "hot potato." She dealt with her anger mainly by turning it against herself and displacing it onto some other object. Since childhood, anger at her elder brother had been an accepted outlet and often she and mother joined together to criticize and attack him. Prior to the suicide attempt, aggression was displaced onto her father and then onto the superior at work. In the analysis I was frequently the recipient of her displaced aggression. This occurred concomitant with regression to a state of helpless submission in which Mary saw herself as totally inadequate and her mother as perfect.

The state of total submission to a powerful, idealized mother who could do no wrong was epitomized in Mary's hairstyle. Mary wore her hair in a highly unusual style. It was shorter than that of most boys, clipped behind the ears and the back of the neck, a "short back and sides," reminiscent of the style of haircut worn by men in the 1950s. Well into the analysis, in the context of talking about her inhibited exhibitionism, her wish to wear pretty clothes but her fear and inability to do so, I inquired about her hairstyle. I wondered about it and asked if she were aware that it was cut unusually short. She said that her brother and father had said that her hair was very short. Her friends had also said so, but her mother thought it was a good length. Mary then looked at me, smiled ruefully and said, "But she would, you know, since she cuts my hair."

The sadomasochistic battle centered on who owned Mary's body and it could be safely inferred that toilet training was achieved in a traumatizing, unempathic manner. Mary commented on mother's rough, "no nonsense" handling of her niece and said that mother would have been a good animal trainer but a bad child raiser. Mary's fear of making a mess was a focus of considerable work, and links could be drawn between her fear of losing bladder or bowel control and her severe constriction of affect and activity. At one point, when discussing her inability to tolerate ambivalent feelings, she said that she thought such feelings were messy. She said, "I always thought feelings should be neat and tidy."

5. In this state of heightened consciousness of their dependency all sexual and aggressive preoccupations become a source of anxiety. There is evidence in the memories of the external event that these adolescents become at least dimly aware of the incestuous nature of their fantasies.

In Mary's case one could see repeatedly how her extreme dependency and submission served to defend against her primitive rage at mother. However, the dependency intensified her anger, which in turn made dependency more necessary but more unacceptable. As she gradually learned to tolerate her feelings and began to recognize anger directed at her mother, she said often, "If I'm angry at someone else I still have mother, but if I'm angry at mother then I'm all alone." Regarding incestuous fantasies breaking through prior to the suicide attempt, it is evident that the oedipal situation is a source of enormous anxiety for Mary, especially because of the aggression involved in the rivalry. To take a minor example: Mary always performed extremely well at school, but seldom had any pleasure in the results. It was a problem we focused on, and it was linked with her inability to dress in a pretty way, to take pride in herself or to exhibit herself in an appropriate fashion. Following this work, she explained that when she brought back a good grade father was appreciative and seemed to understand the nature of the effort involved and the achievement in the grade. Mother, on the other hand, expressed her pleasure by immediately comparing Mary's high grades with her own academic difficulty when she went to college. Mary felt that there was a rivalry, that mother felt beaten, and then Mary began to wonder if this was why she could take only momentary pleasure in her academic achievements and then dismissed them as "big deal."

Clearer evidence of a link between positive oedipal fantasies and suicide thoughts emerged in what came to be seen as a repeated pattern in which good feelings about me and father emerged in the context of criticism of her mother. When she criticized her mother, she then felt good about me. During one of these periods, she dreamed that she was going on a trip with her father and that her mother had floated off alone in a balloon. There was a period of about two weeks in which she and father shared giggly jokes and teased each other. She worked hard in treatment, and brought much material related to her feeling that her mother was "weird" and unusual. The situation then became unbearable. She began to "feel bad," she refused to talk in treatment, father and I became the "bad guys" and she again became totally dependent on mother and highly suicidal. As I linked this repetitive pattern to the sequence preceding the suicide attempt, she at first denied that there had been any positive feelings for her father. But she then remembered that she had been able to make an important intervention in regard to the father's feelings about the elder brother, an intervention which father still describes as having been enormously important. Further, it seemed that Mary's intervention had altered the balance of forces within the family. It had brought father, Mary, and elder brother close together and excluded mother. Mary had completely forgotten about this event which had happened just before her actual suicide attempt.

As the work progressed, the influence of persisting sadistic sexual theories became explicit and were seen to have had an important influence on Mary's inability to retain positive oedipal fantasies. In her dreams, associations and memories, sex involved intensely sadistic attacks eventuating in death or destruction.

6. The next event in the sequence was the attempt, once again, to break away from their mothers by appealing to another person. The appeal took the form of a suicide

threat. The appeal to the other person is an attempt by the adolescent to get out of a highly dangerous situation, one in which both sexual and aggressive wishes are threatening to break through to consciousness.

As yet, there is no evidence in Mary's case that she had threatened suicide and had appealed to some person outside the family for help. Mary's material both amplifies and clarifies the points in the sequence outlined from the suicide research. Her material indicates that the aborted move to someone outside the family is not simply an emergent step in the sequence but a repetitive pattern that occurs with increasing frequency in the adolescents' frenzied attempt to defend against aggressive feelings toward mother. There is an attempt to break away from the dangerous dependency, but very quickly the person toward whom they turn as an ally comes to be seen as an enemy. Disappointment, hurt and anger toward mother are quickly displaced, and the person who could help them is seen as the person who drives them into a more intense dependency on mother.

This is what I have described in another publication as a "negative therapeutic motivation";[10] when it appears in treatment it becomes a means of displacing failure, blame and anger onto the therapist and intensifying the primitive tie to the again-idealized mother. Did this happen prior to Mary's suicide attempt? Her memory was somewhat fuzzy, but repeatedly in the course of treatment each moment of suicidal crisis—and there were many—was preceded by just such a point in the sequence. Friends who seemed eager to help would be regarded with suspicion and anger. She would be invited away for a weekend and then imagine getting sick so that she would have an excuse not to go. Most ominous, and a sign that suicidal thoughts and wishes were in the forefront, was when I became the "bad guy," when she would come to the session determined not to talk to me, when she deliberately kept things secret. During a session filled with stubborn silence she said, "I feel as if I'm a POW and you're trying to make me talk." It was at these times that my anxiety increased, and I would then tell her of my concern that she was thinking about and intending to kill herself.

The suicide research summarized this section of the sequence as a series of steps of appeal to an outside object to take them away from the intense and dangerous tie to the mother. In Mary's case it was apparent that it was a lifelong pattern of oscillation between mother and nonmother. During the analysis, one could see the oscillation occurring with increased frequency and intensity as, with each return to mother, Mary's anger at her intensified. Displacement as a defense was no longer sufficient. Mary's material revealed reasons for this. Even while locating all the negative feelings on the external object, Mary was aware that she was doing this for mother's sake. In Mary's view, and there seemed to be some justification for this perception, it was mother who could not tolerate separation, mother who could not accept or absorb any aggression or criticism. Mary had been dimly aware of this before but, during analysis, she became conscious of an intense feeling that all her sacrificing of an external life was done for mother. To return to a submissive dependency on mother and still feel unattended to, unappreciated and unloved, intensified her rage even further and led to an ever-increasing frequency of oscillation between mother and nonmother.

7. In the sequence of actual events we now have a breakthrough of aggressive feelings toward mother by both girls and boys. In the case of girls it is a breakthrough of conscious aggressive feelings toward mother accompanied by extreme guilt reactions. The guilt was intensified by an event which confirmed the girls' feelings of omnipotent aggression. The girls experience a conscious choice between killing themselves or killing their mothers. As a result of the breakthrough of aggression, both boys and girls experience a fear of loss of control over their impulses.

For much of the first year of her analysis, Mary denied that she had been angry with her mother before the suicide attempt. However, Mary's repeated pattern of dealing with her anger at her mother during analysis made her aware of how she had distorted her memory of the events prior to the attempt. During her sessions, any remark critical of mother would be followed, at times in the same session, by Mary "feeling bad," becoming highly self-critical, and "tuning out" or "becoming a zombie." She would stop feeling and thinking. A voice in her mind kept saying, "you've said enough, you've gone too far, you better stop now." The next day Mary would be agitated and very anxious about school or angry about something a friend had said. When I pointed out the displacement and the fact that only the day before she had been critical of her mother, she would react with genuine surprise, having completely forgotten that she had said those things about her mother. Eventually, my supposition that this "whitewash" might have occurred in relation to her feelings prior to the suicide attempt brought some confirming material. The most intense and sustained feeling of anger centered on her reactions to her birthdays. Her 18th birthday had occurred a week and a half prior to the suicide attempt; during analysis we saw her reactions to her 19th and 20th birthdays as repeating the reactions before the suicide attempt. Mary and her father had birthdays two days apart, and it was a family custom, initiated by mother, to hold their birthday parties on the same day. This was but one of the many features of her birthday which left Mary feeling unattended to, uncared for and unloved. The birthday celebration and the presents seemed perfunctory, slapdash and performed out of duty rather than caring. This young woman, who had a remarkable memory for academic subjects, could not remember what she had received on her 18th or 19th birthdays. During the analysis, the breakthrough of rage at mother immediately following the birthday was evident, expressed in the analysis and immediately followed by self-criticism, "feeling bad," agitated attempts to displace the anger, and then another suicide crisis in which she was overwhelmed by suicidal wishes and close to putting suicidal plans into action.

In relation to the issue of loss of control, Mary regarded everything in extremes. In her view she had to become a zombie (i.e., totally devoid of wishes), or she would be swept away by impulses and move directly into omnipotent action. In her dreams she never just felt angry but continued to hit until the person was killed. The zombie reaction was termed a "little suicide," and I suggested that she was killing a part of herself. She responded by saying that if she did not kill herself she would kill someone else. Regarding the finding that some external event confirmed the adolescent's fantasy of omnipotent aggression, there was no evidence by the third year of treatment that anything had occurred specifically in relation to mother just before the suicide attempt. What probably did occur was a breakdown in Mary's strenuous denial of mother's severe pathology, her "weirdness," her vulnerability, and the marital difficulties of the parents. When, after an extended period of work, Mary found the courage to confront mother over an incident of intrusive behavior, mother reacted by crying, running away, and not returning for hours. When Mary took charge of her own body, including doing her own hair, moving to her own apartment and in general acting more independently, mother became busy cleaning out the attic and would not come down to greet Mary when she returned for a weekend visit. Mary asked father about mother's behavior and he told her that they were involved in a mother-daughter game. It became evident that the family had for years been playing a more serious game, that of protecting mother and denying her pathology.

8. The adolescent will now feel in a state of intense panic and deadlock. Suicide thoughts which had been present for a considerable period of time will now become the solution. It is considered a positive, brave action. It is a solution to the conflict, a way out of the dilemma. Unable to make the normal adolescent moves, the wish to positive action is transferred to the suicide attempt.

In Mary's case suicide as a positive, brave action and a solution to an insoluble dilemma was addressed from the very beginning and interpreted as such. She confirmed my interpretation and when, for example, I suggested that it would be wise if I kept the pills she had saved for her next suicide attempt, she agreed to give them to me but said that she would hate herself for doing it. It was her only way out. It was a positive action, she said, one she could not think of giving up. She described her suicide attempt as an overpowering surprise to her parents, and it became clear that the attempt represented, in part, an acting out in reverse form of the experience of having been surprised and thus unprepared and overwhelmed. Her parents had been completely taken by surprise; she had kept all thoughts and suicide plans secret from them. During the analysis, I found myself especially uneasy at moments when the suicide crisis seemed to have passed. When I first verbalized my disquiet and my concern that she was thinking of suicide she said, "I was just thinking that this would be a good time to do it—I mean, everyone thinks the worry is over." It became apparent that suicide as an overwhelming surprise was a derivative of what Laufer[17] has termed a "central masturbation fantasy" and, in turn, could be traced to repeated primal scene exposure and a persistent lack of parental protection from other overwhelming experiences. Note, in the chapter by E. Furman [chapter 32 above], the role of parental pathology in the exposure to traumatic situations and "the persistence (in the suicidants) of intense unfused early aggression in its sexualized sadomasochistic form." At another point, Mary agreed that her suicide was an attempt to change her parents and went on to say that she had achieved many of her aims by attempting suicide. For the first time, her parents had paid attention to her and had expressed their love and devotion. In fact, she was in analysis only because of her suicide attempt and the analysis was being supported by her parents.

9. Totally preoccupied with suicidal impulses, the adolescent turns once more to the outside world, not for help but in order to deal with guilt in reaction to aggressive feelings about mother. Material on the suicide event indicates that unconsciously the adolescent provokes a rejection and the focal research shows that they are compelled to do so. There is an unconscious need to take the blame away from mother and put it on some person outside the home. By provoking rejection at the hands of someone else the conscious awareness that the suicide is an aggressive attack on mother is avoided. This is a decisive move because the blame is located on some external object, the guilt no longer acts as an inhibiting factor and the suicide plan is put into action.

In Mary's case we know that consciously she experienced the suicide attempt as due entirely to a difficult relationship with a superior at work. She was critical of this superior and felt criticized by her. She felt that she was not living up to the expectations of the superior, but at the same time this woman had disappointed her. All her feelings of rage, rejection and abandonment had been displaced from mother onto this female authority figure, and consciously the act was precipitated only by her feelings about this female superior. She had been preoccupied with thoughts about her superior, anxiety about work and self-hatred for having failed to remain at college. She had not thought of her parents or brothers nor felt any pangs of conscience for intending to kill herself.

10. Consciously, at the time of the actual suicide attempt, the adolescent saw the event as producing multiple results. It would reassert their control over external events, over people and over their bodies. The world would be sorry for having mistreated them and they would achieve a bodily state where there was no experience of aggressive or sexual feelings.

Mary's fantasies about the effect of her suicide on other people and on her own impulses was a central theme from the beginning of her analysis; various aspects recurred repeatedly in her words, actions, and dreams. Most prominent was the fantasy that by killing herself she would make others "feel bad." She would force them to pay attention to her, to feel sorry for having neglected her and not having paid attention. Their reaction, she imagined, would be one of total surprise and guilt. They would say, "Oh, we never knew, we never suspected."

11. In the memories of the circumstances of the actual attempt there are many details to indicate that the adolescent had experienced an altered ego state, a psychotic state, at the time of the attempt. In all cases the adolescent did not experience any conscious concern or feelings of guilt in relation to their parents. Further, there is a total denial of death as evident in the conscious fantasies that they would not only achieve their aims through the suicide but would be around to observe and to benefit from the changes effected by their deed. This denial of death was related to the ever-increasing regression in which they had given up completely any feelings of ownership of their body; the body was something which did not belong to them. It was a source of unwanted impulses, both aggressive and sexual, something intruded upon, controlled by and belonging to mother. Finally, analysis showed that as part of the ego regression the mother they wish to destroy becomes the mother who wishes them dead, and suicide then is not an attack but a submission to the wishes of mother. Thus, we see that the adolescents not only deny the reality of death but see it as a state of peace and being at one with their mothers.

All this was very true of Mary; in her case projection of her death wishes seemed to fall on very fertile ground. Mary felt that her mother did not like her children, that she wished that she had never had any. As Mary became more observant and more capable of containing these observations and bringing them to treatment, we began to see many things which, as Mary said, "make one think." A particularly vivid example was the following: a psychiatric patient had committed suicide by jumping from a bridge. Within a day of the event, Mary's mother was driving Mary to a shopping center and took a roundabout route which passed over that bridge. Then, according to Mary, mother mentioned casually, as if commenting on the weather, that she had heard a rumor that a psychiatric patient had jumped off that bridge the other day.

12. In many cases the very choice of method will itself be of dynamic significance and not just fortuitous.

In her third year of analysis Mary mentioned that the suicide attempt was made with mother's car, a car which mother loved and Mary hated.

13. Immediately following the suicidal act the adolescent will feel a state of calm, of relief and release from all tensions.

This was true in Mary's case. She felt an enormous sense of relief and total calm while waiting for the ambulance to arrive. She knew that she would not die, she said. She felt that she had finally accomplished something. She had done a powerful, brave thing, something most people could not do. She had shocked everyone and forced them to pay attention to her and now everything would be different.

DISCUSSION

The material from Mary's case appears to confirm the results of the study of seven adolescents who had each attempted suicide. From the psychoanalytic material of Mary's case, we can replicate the finding that the suicide attempt was not a sudden act but the end point of a pathological regression. Suicide thoughts had been present for a considerable period prior to the attempt. The regression started with her experience of failure in the move toward independence from mother. Subsequent events then led to an intensification of her tie to mother and a displacement of the experience of rejection and anger from mother to an external object. Once the experience of rejection and blame was displaced, guilt was no longer an inhibiting factor, and the suicide plan was put into action. At the time of the attempt, Mary thought of suicide as a way to change the external world, mother and self. Suicide was considered a positive, brave action, producing multiple results including the restoration of positive self-regard. Reality of death was denied and the death wish was projected onto mother.

In addition to replicating the findings from the psychoanalytic study of attempted suicide in adolescents, the material from Mary's analysis amplifies some of these findings. Here are summarized some points in the sequence which can be looked at in the somewhat different light cast by the analytic material emerging in Mary's case.

Relationship with mother prior to suicide attempt: The emphasis on the adolescent's fear of abandonment and engulfment, though correct, does not sufficiently emphasize the importance of primitive aggression. In Mary's case it was not rejection or abandonment in themselves which were crucial components, but the omnipotent rage which would break through if these events were to occur. Her intense anxiety consequent upon each developmental step was not primarily a fear of abandonment, but a fear of enjoying and preferring the nonmother to her own mother. This would break down her denial of her mother's pathology and unleash Mary's primitive and omnipotent rage. For example, as a way of saving money mother provided only powdered milk at home. Mary could not remember having had whole milk until she was a school child and then she was shocked and thrown into a panic on finding out how much she loved milk.

Dependency intensifying anxiety: Although it is true in Mary's case that the experience of complete dependence on mother intensified fear of drive expression, especially hostility, her material underscored another, possibly more important reason for the association between increased dependency and heightened anxiety over hostile wishes. Mary experienced her dependency as a giving up for mother. It was "a little suicide" with the same motives of self-sacrifice in order to change mother into a caring, loving mother. Mother's failure to change intensified Mary's primitive rage. Concomitant with defenses against the rage was an ever-increasing self-sacrifice of autonomy and feelings of separate existence which made Mary even more dependent. Suicide was the ultimate sacrifice of a separate self, with the fantasy that this surrender to total dependency would create the wished for "purified pleasure dyad"[10] free of hostility from either partner.

Provoking rejection: Regarding the step in the sequence in which the adolescent provokes rejection, Mary's material emphasized that this was an old pattern of oscillation between mother and nonmother objects such as sibs, father and teachers. For her, there was a lifelong pattern of splitting the ambivalent feelings, displacing negative feelings onto some object other than mother, and thereby retaining the illusion of a purified mother-child dyad. Such a history of intermittent involvement with others might be looked for in other cases.

Projection of death wishes onto mother: Mary's material indicated that her conviction that mother wished her dead was not just a projection but had a substantial basis in reality. Mary's material should make us sensitive to the intense death wishes of mothers of suicidal adolescents. Looking back over the material of the seven suicide cases, including one of my own cases, there is abundant evidence that the intense hostility and death wishes of mothers played an important role in the suicidal behavior of the adolescents. Hurry,[5,8] in her excellent summary of suicide in adolescents and her detailed clinical presentation of one of the suicidal patients from the study, demonstrates the importance of this factor.

Turning the aggression against the self: Although this mechanism in suicide was described by Freud in *Mourning and Melancholia*[18] and noted in an earlier report on the suicide study,[7] insufficient emphasis was placed on this factor in the final summary of the research. In Mary's case the mechanism by which it was accomplished could be seen. It was via an identification with the hated part of the mother that the instinctual vicissitude of turning aggression against herself could not only defend against but also express her hostility towards mother. An important shift in the treatment was when these identifications could become a focus of the analytic work. As one of many examples: mother had put the envelope containing Mary's grade reports in Mary's desk without showing them to father. On the weekend, Mary discovered the grades in her desk and thought to herself that mother did not want father to see the grades. She said to me, "So then I did the same as mother did. I put them back into the desk." She then completely forgot about the grades and about the incident. That weekend she was "feeling bad" and felt angry and critical of herself for not doing what she imagined she should be doing for school.

Affect regression: In cross-validating the regressive sequence with Mary's material I was struck with how much of our work and material centered on the history and vicissitudes of her feelings, especially her anger, toward her mother. In my attempt to conceptualize the material I was stimulated by the highly original views of Orgel[19] and the series of critical papers on affect and trauma by Krystal.[13,20] Orgel postulates that the suicidant, in infancy (6 months to 15 months), has been deprived of a primary love object who could "absorb his waves of aggression." Krystal writes about a progressive response to trauma termed "lethal surrender." Starting with anxiety, it progresses to catatonoid states, aphanisis and potentially to psychogenic death.[13] It would be useful to look at the suicide sequence in relation to its infantile roots and to the sequence described by Krystal.

SUMMARY AND CONCLUSIONS

What answers and general conclusions can we draw from the adolescent suicide study and the cross-validation of the findings using material from Mary's analysis?

First, I believe that we have demonstrated that the "focal research" as described is a fruitful way of handling the vast amount of analytic data and provides, at least for topics such as suicide, a way of replicating and cross-validating previous studies.

The amount of significant data which emerged after the initial interviews and often not until late in the analysis casts serious doubt on those studies that rely solely on interview data subsequent to the suicide attempt. The value of psychoanalysis for obtaining a more complete picture of an event appears to be demonstrated in the study.

Finally, the study demonstrates that suicide is best viewed as the result of a complex interaction of many factors taking place over a long span of time and leading, by a sequence of steps, to this pathological solution.

The findings presented here emerged from a study using psychoanalysis as a research tool. But psychoanalysis is also a therapeutic technique and, as such, this study leads to certain technical suggestions regarding the treatment of adolescents who have made serious suicide attempts. Initially the family, the adolescent, and even the referring person may try to deny the seriousness of the attempt and may speak of it as a one-time occurrence totally out of character with the adolescent's usual good behavior. This should be addressed quickly with the adolescent and the family. The one action these adolescents are capable of is suicide. To the adolescent, suicide represents a positive, powerful solution to all their conflicts and they will be reluctant to give it up. The aggression in the attempt should be verbalized, as this may produce some guilt in regard to the suicide attempt. Without guilt, there is little to stop the adolescent from repeating the attempt. The multiple motives in the attempt and the unreality in the fantasy that the adolescent will actually be around to reap the rewards should be taken up. The lifelong pattern of displacing negative feelings from mother to others may soon become a problem in the therapy. This will be especially true around weekends and vacations. If the adolescents can construe the analyst as the bad object, the one who rejects and abandons them, then they are free once more to kill themselves without guilt.

The finding that a suicide attempt is the end point of a regressive sequence was a major result of the focal research. The author's subsequent work has been influenced by this result and he actively engages the young person in a search for the elements of the suicide sequence. In Mary's case it took almost three years to elucidate the crucial elements of the sequence. In her third year of analysis she could become conscious of the fact that the precipitating event of leaving home meant a sadistic oedipal triumph over mother and, with her integration of this last bit of knowledge concerning the first step in the sequence, the issue of suicide receded to make way for more pressing neurotic conflicts about becoming a mature, adult woman.

To undertake the treatment of an adolescent who has made a suicide attempt is a responsibility that entails a ceaseless struggle. Litman[21] notes that there are references to suicidal symptomatology in all of Freud's published case histories except that of "little Hans." Many of Freud's cases, especially his earlier ones, were adolescents, and Freud's experience with suicidal young people might be one of the factors influencing his shifting views on aggression and his final adoption of the theory of the death instinct. One cannot work with suicidal adolescents without being impressed with the power of their wish to kill themselves. The positive value they put on suicide and the power of this force is caught in a poem by Sylvia Plath, written before she killed herself.

> Dying
> Is an art, like everything else.
> I do it exceptionally well.
>
> I do it so it feels like hell.
> I do it so it feels real.
> I guess you could say I've got a call.

To counter this force, we have to call on all our experience, our tolerance and the support of our colleagues. In 1926, discussing a young patient, Freud said, "What weighs on me in his case is my belief that unless the outcome is very good it will be very bad indeed: What I mean is that he would commit suicide without any hesitation. I shall therefore do all in my power to avert that eventuality."[22]

REFERENCES

1. *Baechler J:* Suicides. *New York, Basic Books, 1979.*
2. *Haim A:* Adolescent Suicide. *New York, International Universities Press, 1974.*
3. *Otto U: Suicidal behavior in childhood and adolescence, in Anthony EJ, Chiland C (eds):* The Child and His Family. *New York, John Wiley & Sons, 1982, vol 7.*

4. *Petzel SV, Riddle M: Adolescent suicide: Psychosocial and cognitive aspects, in Feinstein S, et al (eds):* Adolescent Psychiatry. *Chicago, University of Chicago Press, 1981, vol 9, pp 343–398.*
5. *Hurry A: My ambition is to be dead.* J Child Psychother *1977;4:66–83.*
6. *Kernberg P: The analysis of a fifteen-and-a-half-year-old girl with suicidal tendencies, in Harley M (ed):* The Analyst and the Adolescent at Work. *New York, Quadrangle, 1974.*
7. *Friedman M, Glasser M, Laufer E, et al: Attempted suicide and self-mutilation in adolescents: Some observations from a psychoanalytic research project.* Int J Psychoanal *1972;53:179–183.*
8. *Hurry A: Part II. Past and current findings on suicide in adolescence.* J Child Psychother *1978;4:69–82.*
9. *Novick J: Walk-in clinics for adolescents.* J Child Psychother *1977;4:84–89.*
10. *Novick J: Negative therapeutic motivation and negative therapeutic alliance.* Psychoanal Study Child *1980;35:299–320.*
11. *Alvarez A:* The Savage God. *London, Weidenfield & Nicholson, 1971, p 3.*
12. *Hurry A, Novick J, Laufer M:* A study of 84 adolescents who have attempted suicide. Report to the Department of Health and Social Security, *Center for the Study of Adolescence, London, England, 1976.*
13. *Krystal H: Trauma and affects.* Psychoanal Study Child *1978;33:81–116.*
14. *Freud A: Assessment of childhood disturbances.* Psychoanal Study Child *1962; 17:149–158.*
15. *Laufer M: Assessment of adolescent disturbances: The application of Anna Freud's diagnostic profile.* Psychoanal Study Child *1965;20:99–123.*
16. *Hurry A, Laufer E, Novick J, et al:* Attempted suicide in adolescents. *Center for the Study of Adolescence, Report to Grant Foundation, New York.*
17. *Laufer M: The central masturbation fantasy, the final sexual organization, and adolescence.* Psychoanal Study Child *1976;31:297–316.*
18. *Freud S: Mourning and Melancholia, in* The Complete Psychological Works of Sigmund Freud, *Starchy J (trans), standard ed. London, Hogarth Press, 1957, vol 14, pp 237–260.*
19. *Orgel S: Fusion with the victim and suicide.* Int J Psychoanal *1974;55:532–538.*
20. *Krystal H: The activating aspects of emotions.* Psychoanal Contemp Thought *1982;5:605–648.*
21. *Litman RE: Sigmund Freud on suicide, in Shneidman E (ed):* Essays in Self-Destruction. *Science House, 1967.*
22. *Freud S:* Psychoanalysis and Faith. *New York, Basic Books, 1963, pp 101–102.*

34. Family History of Suicide

Alec Roy

COMMENT

We include this second contribution by Alec Roy, though it is clinically remote, to provide general background information about the importance of family history in suicide. Roy interprets as a genetic phenomenon the fact that patients with a family history of suicide are twice as likely to attempt it as those without such a history.

■

Among 243 patients with a family history of suicide, almost half (118 [48.6%]) had attempted suicide, more than half (137 [56.4%]) had a depressive disorder, and more than a third (84 [34.6%]) had recurrent affective disorder. These 243 patients with a family history of suicide were compared with 5,602 patients with no family history of suicide. A family history of suicide was found to significantly increase the risk for an attempt at suicide in patients with a wide variety of diagnoses: schizophrenia, unipolar and bipolar affective disorders, depressive neurosis, and personality disorders.

AMONG those who commit suicide, a family history of suicide has been noted in a small but meaningful number.[1–4] Explanations include the psychological phenomenon of identification,[5] genetic factors in the transmission of affective and other psychiatric disorders, and genetic factors in the transmission of suicidal behaviors. Kallman and Anastasio[6] in 1947 found no twins concordant for suicide, but, in 1967, data about suicide in twins were reviewed by Haberlandt.[7] Among 149 pairs of twins in which one twin had suicided, there were nine sets of twins in which the other twin had also suicided; all of these twins were found among the 51 monozygotic pairs (18%). In a further five of the 51 monozygotic twin pairs (10%), the other

Alec Roy, "Family History of Suicide." *Archives of General Psychiatry* 40(1984):971–974. Reprinted by permission.

twin had attempted suicide. No dizygotic twin pairs were found in which both twins had committed suicide.

Schulsinger et al[8] examined suicide in the relatives of the 71 adoptees with affective disorder who had suicided in the Copenhagen adoption register study. Substantially more of their biological relatives had suicided than their adopting relatives, although there were no important differences for suicide between the biological and adopting relatives of the affective disorder controls who had not suicided. In a second study, the 57 Copenhagen adoptees without known psychiatric disorder who had committed suicide had substantially more biological relatives who had suicided than the biological relatives of the 57 nonsuicide adoptee controls. There were no suicides among any of the adopting relatives in either group. Schulsinger et al[8,9] suggested the possibility of a genetically determined transmission of suicidal behavior independent of affective disorder, alcoholism, schizophrenia, or other psychiatric conditions associated with suicide, possibly through a biochemical predisposition that manifests itself at times of life stress.

One research group[10,11] found that urinary levels of 17-hydroxycorticosteroids were substantially higher in patients who had attempted or committed suicide, although there have been contradictory reports.[12] Suicide is more likely to be associated with primary depressive disorder and hypothalamic-pituitary adrenal dysfunction than with other types of depressive disorder.[13–16] Asberg et al[17] found a bimodal distribution in the serotonin metabolite 5-hydroxy-indoleacetic acid (5-HIAA) levels in the CSF of 68 depressed patients. Fifteen of the 68 depressed patients had attempted suicide and substantially more of the attempters, and the two who eventually suicided, were in the lower 5-HIAA mode. Brown et al[18] found similar results.

The possible genetic inheritance of suicidal behavior and its relation to depression could be examined further, since from January 1974 a record has been kept at the Clarke Institute of Psychiatry, Toronto, of all those psychiatric inpatients known to have a family history of suicide. The aim of this study was to examine which psychiatric patients with a family history of suicide would themselves have attempted suicide and suffer from depressive disorders when compared with psychiatric patients who did not have a family history of suicide.

SUBJECTS AND METHODS

All charts of psychiatric inpatients at the institute between January 1974 and June 1981 who had a family history of suicide were examined. Excluded were 16 patients with suicide of a third-degree relative, four patients with suicide of a fourth-degree relative, one suicide of a spouse, and five suicides of other nonblood relatives or friends. All these 26 patients were left out of the study completely. A consecutive series of 243 patients with a definite history of suicide in a first- or second-degree relative was thus obtained.

All 243 charts were carefully examined. Data concerning the sex, marital status, social class, age at first psychiatric contact, duration of psychiatric contact, and primary psychiatric diagnosis of each patient were recorded. Whether the patient ever had a depressive episode, diagnosed by a psychiatrist and meeting the *DSM-III* diagnostic criteria for a depressive episode,[19] was noted, as was whether the patient had ever been treated for depression with antidepressant drugs or electroconvulsive therapy (ECT). Whether the patient had ever attempted suicide, the number of attempts, and the methods used were recorded. Suicidal plans or preparations that did not lead to an attempt at suicide, either because they were interrupted or otherwise, were not included. Data about the first- or second-degree relative who had suicided were noted, as was the age of the patient at the time of the suicide of their relative.

The control group was composed of the remaining 5,602 psychiatric inpatients admitted to the institute during the same period who had no family history of suicide. The computerized data base at the institute was used to indicate, by diagnostic groups, the number of these control patients who had attempted suicide. On April 1, 1979, the medical records department at the institute changed from eighth edition of the *International Classification of Diseases* (ICD-8)[20] to the ninth edition (ICD-9).[21] This change had an effect on the coding of cases of affective disorders other than depressive neurosis (which retained the same code 300.4). For the unipolar depression group, ICD-8 codes 296.0 (involutional melancholia), 296.2 (manic-depressive psychosis, depressed type [includes endogenous depression]), and 296.9 (affective psychosis, unspecified) up to April 1979 were combined with the ICD-9 codes 296.1 (manic-depressive psychosis, depressed type) and 296.9 (affective psychosis, unspecified) after April 1979. For the bipolar affective disorder group, the ICD-8 codes 296.1 (manic-depressive psychosis, manic type) and 296.3 and 296.8 (manic-depressive psychosis, circular type and others) up to April 1979 were combined with the ICD-9 codes 296.0 (manic-depressive psychosis, manic type) and 296.2 to 296.8 (manic depressive psychosis, circular type) after April 1979.

The occupation of the head of the household and the classification of occupations of Goldthorpe and Hope[22] were used to determine social class.

Rank order 1 to 22 inclusively was called *middle class* and 23 to 36 was called *working class.*

RESULTS

These 243 patients had 274 suicides among their first- and second-degree relatives. Twenty-six (10.7%) of the 243 patients had two or more first- or second-degree relatives who had committed suicide. Of these 243 patients, 111 were men and 132 were women; 100 were single, 91 were married, and 52 were separated, divorced, or widowed; 87 were working class and 156 were middle class; the mean age at first psychiatric contact was 31.7 years, and the mean duration of psychiatric contact was 7.5 years. The depressive neurosis group had a significantly older mean age of onset of illness (38.7 years) than the bipolar, personality disorder, and schizophrenia groups, (31.8, 26.1, and 24.4 years, respectively) and the alcoholic, unipolar, and other groups were significantly older than the schizophrenic group ($P < .05$). The bipolar and unipolar groups had significantly longer mean durations of illness (12.4 and 12.5 years, respectively) than all the other groups ($P < .05$).

Attempted Suicide

Of these 243 patients with a family history of suicide, 118 (48.6%), 50 men and 68 women, had attempted suicide and had made 252 attempts at suicide. The only significant sex difference for the method used was that seven of the 107 suicide attempts of the 50 men were by hanging compared with one of the 145 attempts of the 68 women ($P < .03$). The 50 men had made 61 of their 107 suicide attempts by overdose, 24 by cutting, and six by jumping compared with the 113, 21, and six attempts, respectively, of the 145 attempts by the 68 women (no significant difference).

Attempted suicide occurred in 15 (45.4%) of the 33 schizophrenic patients, 13 (40.6%) of 32 unipolar depressives, 22 (37.9%) of the 58 bipolar patients, 26 (55.3%) of the 47 depressive neurosis patients, and 33 (68.8%) of the 48 personality disorder patients. Of the 70 patients with suicide in a second-degree relative, 32 (45.7%) had attempted suicide compared with 86 (49.7%) of the 173 patients with suicide in a first-degree relative (no significant difference).

Of the 243 patients with a family history of suicide, 118 (48.6%) had attempted suicide compared with 1,225 (21.8%) of the 5,602 control patients who did not have a family history of suicide ($P < .0001$). Highly significant

Table 1. Patients, by Diagnostic Group, Who Attempted Suicide

Diagnostic group	Second-degree relative suicided		First-degree relative suicided		Second- of first-degree relative suicided		No family history of suicide, no. (%) attempted	*P*
	No. (%) attempted	No. of attempts	No. (%) attempted	No. of attempts	No. (%) attempted	No. of attempts		
Schizophrenia	6/12 (50.0)	11	9/21 (42.9)	17	15/33 (45.4)	28	150/1,114 (13.5)	<.0001
Unipolar	3/9/ (33.3)	6	10/23 (43.5)	18	13/32 (40.6)	24	50/372 (13.4)	<.0001
Bipolar	10/20 (50.0)	23	12/38 (31.6)	25	22/58 (37.9)	48	56/405 (13.9)	<.0001
Depressive neurosis	6/14 (42.9)	12	20/33 (60.6)	33	26/47 (55.3)	45	221/715 (30.9)	<.0001
Personality disorder	7/11 (63.6)	13	26/37 (70.3)	76	33/48 (68.8)	89	328/1,048 (31.3)	<.0001
Alcohol	0/0	0	3/7 (42.9)	3	3/7 (42.9)	3	42/147 (28.5)	NS
Others	0/4	0	6/14 (42.9)	15	6/18 (33.3)	15	378/1,801 (21.0)	NS
Total	32/70 (45.7)	65	86/173 (49.7)	187	118/243 (48.6)	252	1,225/5,602 (21.8)	<.0001

differences were found for the schizophrenic, unipolar, bipolar, depressive neurosis, and personality disorder groups (Table 1). When the 118 patients who had a family history of suicide and who had attempted suicide are added to the 1,225 patients without a family history of suicide who had attempted suicide, a group of 1,343 patients is formed who had attempted suicide. Of these, 118 (8.8%) had a family history of suicide.

Depressive Disorder

Of the 243 patients with a family history of suicide, 32 (13.2%) had a unipolar depressive disorder, 58 (23.9%) had a bipolar affective disorder, and 47 (19.3%) had a depressive neurosis. Thus, 137 (56.4%) of the 243 cases had a primary psychiatric diagnosis of affective disorder and 61 (44.5%) of the patients had attempted suicide. Among the 32 unipolar depressives, all but six had a recurrent depressive disorder. When these 26 patients were added to the 58 with bipolar affective disorder, 84 (34.6%) of the 243 patients had had recurrent affective disorder.

The group with a family history of suicide had significantly more patients with a primary affective disorder diagnosis than the group with no family history of suicide. Among the 243 patients with a family history of suicide, 137 (56.4%) had a primary affective disorder compared with 1,492 (26.6%) of the 5,602 with no family history of suicide ($\chi^2 = 102.5$, $P < .0001$).

Table 2 shows the data for having at some time an illness diagnosed as a depressive episode (diagnosed by a psychiatrist and meeting *DSM-III* criteria) and treatment for depression (by antidepressant medication or ECT). Of the 243 patients with a family history of suicide, 205 (84.4%) had a depressive episode at some time and 165 (67.9%) were treated for depression by antidepressants or ECT. Twenty (60.6%) of the 33 schizophrenic patients had a depressive episode and 13 (39.4%) were treated for depression. Among the 48 personality disorder patients, 37 (77.1%) had a depressive episode and 29 (60.4%) were treated for depression.

Early Loss by Parental Suicide and Later Suicide Attempt

The data about first-degree relatives' suicides were examined for parental suicide only and for the age of the patient at that time. Forty-two had a parent who suicided before the patient was 20 years old; of these, 26 (61.9%) later

Table 2. Diagnosis and Treatment of Depression for 243 Patients with Family History of Suicide

	Second-degree relative suicided		First-degree relative suicided		Second- or first-degree relative suicided	
Diagnostic group	No. depressive	No. treated for depression	No. depressive	No. treated for depression	No. (%) depressive	No. (%) treated for depression
Schizophrenia	5/12	2/12	15/21	11/21	20/33 (60.6)	13/33 (39.4)
Unipolar	9/9	9/9	23/23	23/23	32/32 (100)	32/32 (100)
Bipolar	18/20	14/20	34/38	32/38	52/58 (89.7)	46/58 (79.3)
Depressive neurosis	14/14	12/14	33/33	23/33	47/47 (100)	35/47 (74.5)
Personality disorder	7/11	6/11	30/37	23/37	37/48 (77.1)	29/48 (60.4)
Alcohol	0/0	0/0	7/7	3/7	7/7 (100)	3/7 (42.8)
Others	3/4	1/4	7/14	6/14	10/18 (55.6)	7/18 (38.9)
Total	56/70 (80.0%)	44/70 (62.8%)	149/173 (86.1%)	121/173 (69.9%)	205/243 (84.4)	165/243 (67.9)

attempted suicide compared with 22 (46.8%) of the 47 patients who were older than 20 years when a parent suicided (no significant difference).

However, there was a significant difference when patients were younger than 11 years when their parent suicided. Twelve (75%) of the 16 patients who were less than 11 years old when a parent committed suicide later attempted suicide; of the 47 aged more than 20 years when a parent suicided, 22 (46.8%) later attempted suicide ($P < .05$).

Eventual Suicide

After their initial examination at the institute, seven (2.8%) of the 243 patients with a family history of suicide themselves eventually suicided. Two were women and five were men and three had a first-degree and four had a second-degree relative who had suicided. Five of the seven eventual suicides, two women and three men, had bipolar affective disorder; two had schizophrenia. Two of the five bipolar patients had a first-degree and three had a second-degree relative who suicided. A psychiatric diagnosis was known for only one of the seven relatives who suicided (i.e., schizophrenia in a second-degree relative of one of the two schizophrenic patients). All seven patients who eventually suicided had previously attempted suicide. As a group they had made 18 previous attempts. The five patients with bipolar affective disorder who suicided had made 15 previous attempts at suicide (range, one to seven attempts).

COMMENT

The Clarke Institute of Psychiatry is a postgraduate psychiatric teaching hospital, and the quality of the charts is good. The psychiatric and social work histories are detailed and typed, and records of admissions elsewhere are routinely sent for and filed in the charts. Many of the patients had more than one admission at the institute, which allowed for a reexamination of the history. Finlay Jones et al[23] demonstrated that subjects can reliably recall the fact of early loss of a parent by death, and Barraclough and Bunch[24] showed that subjects can date parental death accurately. However, it may be that some of the many psychiatric residents who took the histories of these 5,845 patients had a bias in collection such that in a depressed patient with a suicide attempt more inquiry might have been made into whether there was a family history of suicide.

There were five main findings in this study. First, almost half (48.6%) of these patients with a family history of suicide themselves attempted suicide. Second, more than half (56.4%) of all the patients with a family history of suicide had a primary diagnosis of a depressive disorder. Third, more than a third (34.6%) of all the patients with a family history of suicide had recurrent affective disorder. Fourth, regardless of the primary diagnosis, the great majority (84.4%) of all the patients with a family history of suicide had a depressive episode meeting *DSM-III* criteria at some time (67.9% were treated for depression with antidepressants or ECT). Fifth, during the 7½-year study, seven (2.8%) of the 243 patients with a family history of suicide themselves committed suicide.

A significantly higher percentage of the patients with a family history of suicide than of the patients with no family history of suicide had attempted suicide (48.6% *v* 21.8%). However, there was no significant difference in the percentages of patients with a first- or second-degree relative committing suicide who had attempted suicide. A significantly higher percentage of patients with a family history of suicide suffered from primary depressive disorders when compared with the patients who did not have a family history of suicide (56.4% *v* 26.6%). Among the patients with primary depressive disorder with a family history of suicide in each of the unipolar, bipolar, and depressive neurosis groups, a significantly higher percentage had attempted suicide when compared with the same groups with no family history of suicide. The same applies in the comparison of the schizophrenic groups. This result supports the following view of Tsuang[25]:

> It seems reasonable to suggest that the genetic factors in suicide may be attributable to the genetic transmission of manic-depression, schizophrenia and alcoholism [and that those] who are at special risk for suicide . . . are those . . . who likewise have a family history of suicide.

The association of affective disorder and attempted suicide in these psychiatric patients with a family history of suicide raises controversial issues. Four of the nine monozygotic twins concordant for suicide in Haberlandt's[7] 1967 twin review came from the Danish Psychiatric Twin Register, and the case histories revealed an affective disorder in the twins or their relatives.[26] Similarly, Zaw[27] recently reported suicide in identical male twins widely separated in time, but in both twins the suicide occurred during a depressive episode. Also, both parents of the twins had been treated by psychiatrists for depression with ECT and antidepressants. The maternal grandmother of the twins had also had inpatient psychiatric treatment for a depressive episode and a paternal great-grandfather and a maternal grandfather had both committed suicide. Dabbagh[28] noted that each suicide in several members of an Iraqui family was associated with depression. In a study similar to this one, Pitts and Winokur[29] found that among 748 consecutive patients admitted to psychiatric institutions, 37 reported a possible or definite suicide in a first-degree relative. In 25 (68%) of these 37 cases, the diagnosis was an affective disorder (56.4% in our study), and the investigators reported that the statistical probability of this distribution occurring by chance was less than .02. When the probable diagnoses in the cases of the first-degree relatives who suicided were considered, in 24 of the 37 patient-relative pairings, both members had affective disorders, and Pitts and Winokur also estimated that 79% of the suicides of the first-degree relatives were associated with probable affective disorder.

There are several studies reporting a strong association between depression and suicidal behavior.[4,30–36] The follow-up studies of the Iowa 500 have revealed that the suicides have occurred mainly among the manic-depressive and schizophrenic patients.[37] Paykel and Dienelt[38] reported a 10% annual rate of attempted suicide in a group of depressed patients. The results of our study indicate that the percentage of patients with depression who attempted suicide in the group with a family history of suicide is high (44% of the 137 patients with depressive disorder) and comparable to the findings of Crook et al,[46] where among 308 depressed psychiatric inpatients, 44% had attempted suicide at some time.

Early parental loss has been shown in several studies to be associated with attempted suicide and with suicidal behavior in depressive illness.[39–43] In our study, significantly more of the patients who had experienced loss of a parent by suicide before the age of 11 years had attempted suicide compared with the patients who had such a loss after 20 years of age.

Murphy and Wetzel[44] reviewed the literature and found that 6% to 8% of those who attempted suicide have a family history of suicide. In our study 8.8% of the total group of 1,343 patients who had attempted suicide had a family history of suicide. Murphy and Wetzel studied 127 patients hospitalized after attempting suicide and found that, when they examined them by psychiatric diagnosis, the personality disorder group had as high a family history of suicide as the affective disorder group. However, since persons with affective disorders form a substantially larger proportion of suicides than persons with personality disorders, they suggested that a family history of suicide in primary affective disorders signifies an increased suicide risk but that such a history in most other psychiatric diagnoses does not. The finding in this study that five of the seven patients with a family history of suicide who eventually committed suicide had a primary affective disorder lends support to that view. It has been well demonstrated by Krietman[45] that approximately 1% of those who attempt suicide go on to commit suicide during the next year. Thus, throughout our mean follow-up period of 3½ years, four to five suicides might well have been expected among the 243 patients in this study, of whom almost half had attempted suicide.

REFERENCES

1. *Haberlandt W: Der Suizid als Genetisches Problem (Zwillings-und Familien analyse).* Anthropol Anz *1965;29:65–89.*
2. *Farberow N, Simon M: Suicide in Los Angeles and Vienna: An intercultural study of two cities.* Public Health Rep *1969;84:389–403.*
3. *Stengel E:* Suicide and Attempted Suicide. *New York, Viking Penguin Inc, 1964.*
4. *Roy A: Risk factors for suicide in psychiatric patients.* Arch Gen Psychiatry *1982;39:1089–1095.*
5. *Perlin S, Schmidt C: Psychiatry, in Perlin S (ed):* Handbook for the Study of Suicide. *New York, Oxford University Press Inc, 1975, chap 8.*
6. *Kallman F, Anastasio M: Twin studies on the psychopathology of suicide.* J Nerv Ment Dis *1947;105:40–55.*
7. *Haberlandt W: Aportacion a la Genetica del Suicidio.* Folia Clin Int *1967;17:319–322.*
8. *Schulsinger F, Kety S, Rosenthal D, et al: A family study of suicide. Read before a meeting of the* Third World Congress of Biological Psychiatry, *Stockholm, July 1981.*
9. *Schulsinger F, Kety S, Rosenthal D, et al: A family study of suicide, in Schou M, Stromgren E (eds):* Origins, Prevention and Treatment of Affective Disorders. *New York, Academic Press Inc, 1979, pp 277–287.*
10. *Bunney W Jr, Fawcett J, Davis J, et al: Further evaluation of urinary 17-hydroxycorticosteroids in suicidal patients.* Arch Gen Psychiatry *1969;21:138–150.*
11. *Bunney W Jr, Fawcett J: Possibility of a biochemical test for suicidal potential: An analysis of endocrine findings prior to three suicides.* Arch Gen Psychiatry *1965;13:232–239.*
12. *Fink E, Carpenter W: Further evaluation of a biochemical test for suicide potential.* Dis Nerv Syst *1976;37:341–343.*
13. *Coryell W, Schlesser M: Suicide and the dexamethasone suppression test in unipolar depression.* Am J Psychiatry *1981;138:1120–1121.*
14. *Carroll B, Greden J, Feinberg M: Suicide, neuroendocrine dysfunction and CSF 5-HIAA concentration in depression, in Angrist B (ed):* Recent Advances in Neuropsychopharmacology. *New York, Pergamon Press, 1981, vol 31:* Advances in the Bio-Sciences, *pp 307–313.*
15. *Beck-Friis J, Aperia B, Kjellman B, et al: Suicidal behavior and the dexamethasone suppression test.* Am J Psychiatry *1981;138:993–994.*

16. *Åsberg M, Varpila-Hannson R, Tamla P, et al: Suicidal behavior and the dexamethasone suppression test.* Am J Psychiatry *1981;138:994–995.*
17. *Åsberg M, Träskman L, Thorén P: 5-HIAA in the cerebrospinal fluid: A biochemical suicide predictor?* Arch Gen Psychiatry *1976;33:1193–1197.*
18. *Brown G, Goodwin F, Ballenger J, et al: Aggression in humans correlates with cerebrospinal fluid amine metabolites.* Psychiatry Res *1979;1:131–139.*
19. Diagnostic and Statistical Manual of Mental Disorders, *ed 3. Washington, DC, American Psychiatric Association, 1980.*
20. International Classification of Diseases, *ed 8. Geneva, World Health Organization, 1968.*
21. International Classification of Diseases, *ed 9. Geneva, World Health Organization, 1977.*
22. *Goldthorpe J, Hope K:* The Social Grading of Occupations. A New Approach and Scale. *New York, Oxford University Press Inc, 1974, pp 134–143.*
23. *Finlay Jones R, Scott R, Duncan Jones P, et al: The reliability of reports of early separations.* Aust NZ J Psychiatry *1981;15:27–31.*
24. *Barraclough B, Bunch J: Accuracy of dating parents' deaths: Recollected dates compared with death certificate dates.* Br J Psychiatry *1973;123:573–574.*
25. *Tsuang M: Genetic factors in suicide.* Dis Nerv Syst *1977;38:498–501.*
26. *Juel-Nielsen N, Videbech T: A twin study of suicide.* Acta Genet Med Gemellol *1970;19:307–310.*
27. *Zaw K: A suicidal family.* Br J Psychiatry *1981;139:68–69.*
28. *Dabbagh F: Family suicide.* Br J Psychiatry *1977;130:159–161.*
29. *Pitts F, Winokur G: Affective disorder: III. Diagnostic correlates and incidence of suicide.* J Nerv Ment Dis *1964;139:176–181.*
30. *Guze S, Robins E: Suicide and primary affective disorders.* Br J Psychiatry *1970;117:437–438.*
31. *Robins E, Murphy G, Wilkinson R, et al: Some clinical observations in the prevention of suicide based on a study of 134 successful suicides.* Am J Public Health *1959;49:888–889.*
32. *Dorpat T, Ripley H: A study of suicide in the Seattle area.* Compr Psychiatry *1960;1:349–359.*
33. *Barraclough B, Bunch J, Nelson B, et al: A hundred cases of suicide: Clinical aspects.* Br J Psychiatry *1974;125:355–373.*
34. *Flood R, Seager C: A retrospective examination of psychiatric case records of patients who subsequently committed suicide.* Br J Psychiatry *1968;114:443–450.*
35. *Myers D, Neal C: Suicide in psychiatric patients.* Br J Psychiatry *1978;133:38–44.*
36. *Robins A, Brooke E, Freeman-Browne D: Some aspects of suicide in psychiatric patients in Southend.* Br J Psychiatry *1968;114:739–747.*
37. *Tsuang MT: Suicide in schizophrenics, manics, depressives and surgical controls: A comparison with general population suicide mortality.* Arch Gen Psychiatry *1978;35:153–155.*
38. *Paykel E, Dienelt M: Suicide attempts following acute depression.* J Nerv Ment Dis *1971;153:234–243.*

39. *Dorpat T, Jackson J, Ripley H: Broken homes and attempted and completed suicide.* Arch Gen Psychiatry *1965;12:213–216.*
40. *Greer S: Parental loss and attempted suicide: A further report.* Br J Psychiatry *1966;112:465–470.*
41. *Greer S, Gunn J, Koller K: Aetiological factors in attempted suicide.* Br Med J *1966;2:463–467.*
42. *Birtchnell J: The relationship between attempted suicide, depression and parent death.* Br J Psychiatry *1970;116:307–313.*
43. *Walton H: Suicidal behaviour in depressive illness: A study aetiological factors in suicide.* J Ment Sci *1958;104:884–891.*
44. *Murphy G, Wetzel R: Family history of suicidal behaviour among suicide attempters.* J Nerv Ment Dis *1982;170:86–90.*
45. *Kreitman N:* Parasuicide. *New York, John Wiley & Sons Inc, 1977.*
46. *Crook T, Rashkin A, Davis D: Factors associated with attempted suicide among hospitalized depressed patients.* Psychol Med *1975;381–388.*

35. Suicidal Behavior in Child Psychiatric Inpatients and Outpatients and in Nonpatients

Cynthia R. Pfeffer, Robert Plutchik, Mark S. Mizruchi, and Robert Lipkins

BIOGRAPHICAL NOTE

Cynthia R. Pfeffer is professor of psychiatry at Cornell University Medical College and chief child psychiatrist (Inpatient Unit) for the New York Hospital Westchester Division. She is a past president of the American Association of Suicidology and of the New York Council on Child and Adolescent Psychiatry.

She is the author of many research publications and books, and holds five major awards from suicidological and child psychiatric groups around the world.

COMMENT

This paper, one of a series of studies by Pfeffer and her colleagues, is a step in an extended effort to characterize suicidal behavior in children and adolescents. Twenty years ago this phenomenon was terra incognita; *no scholar has done more than Pfeffer to map it out and point the way to further investigation. She is, in short, a preeminent pioneer.*

This chapter reports an important finding valuable in recognizing and evaluating whether children are at risk for suicidal behavior—that recent and past depression, recent aggression, and preoccupation with death are significant indicia.

Those who wish for developmental and family information about suicidal children, as well as for richer clinical detail, may consult Pfeffer's books, the bibliographies of which open the door to the literature on suicidal children (Pfeffer 1986, 1989).

Cynthia R. Pfeffer, Robert Plutchik, Mark S. Mizruchi, and Robert Lipkins, "Suicidal Behavior in Child Psychiatric Inpatients and Outpatients and in Nonpatients." *American Journal of Psychiatry* 143(1986):733–738.

REFERENCES

Pfeffer, Cynthia R. 1986. The Suicidal Child. *New York: Guilford Press.*
Pfeffer, Cynthia R., ed. 1989. Suicide among Youth. *Washington, D.C.: American Psychiatric Press.*

■

One hundred one child psychiatric outpatients were assessed using a standard battery of measures to identify factors associated with suicidal behavior. Data on these outpatients were compared to those for psychiatric inpatients and nonpatients previously studied. The frequency of suicidal behavior among the outpatients (24.8%) was less than for a comparable group of inpatients (78.5%) but more than for a comparable group of nonpatients (12%). Four variables—recent general psychopathology, preoccupation with death, and recent and past depression—were significantly associated with suicidal behavior in the three groups of children.

MOST STUDIES of preadolescent suicidal behavior have been conducted using psychiatric inpatients (1–3) and have indicated that suicidal inpatients have more intense depression (1, 2, 4) and experience more extensive and chronic environmental stresses involving losses and separations (3) than do nonsuicidal inpatients. To our knowledge, there has been only one recent systematic study of suicidal behavior among preadolescent psychiatric outpatients (5). Among these 39 outpatients, who were from low-middle to low social status backgrounds, 33% displayed suicidal ideas or had threatened or attempted suicide. The suicidal children had high levels of psychomotor activity, intense preoccupation with death, and parents who had suicidal ideation.

In contrast to these studies of child psychiatric patients, Pfeffer et al. (6) investigated suicidal behavior in children who had no history of psychiatric symptoms. This study of 101 nonpatients indicated that suicidal nonpatients differed from nonsuicidal nonpatients on 11 variables, including depression, introjection as a defense mechanism, and suicidal ideation of the mothers.

These findings suggested the need to investigate whether there are factors consistently associated with suicidal behavior in different populations of children. We attempted to provide this kind of information by studying a large outpatient sample and comparing these children with previously described inpatients (1) and nonpatients (6). The children were matched on selected demographic variables. We examined the question of whether the same life history variables serve as predictors of suicidal behavior in each of these groups.

METHOD

One hundred one children aged 6 to 12 years were consecutively assigned to and completed assessment in the child psychiatric outpatient clinic of a voluntary hospital. The assessment, which included at least two visits with the child and two sessions with the parents, was conducted by the child's therapist, who was a child psychiatry fellow, a psychiatry resident, or a postdoctoral psychology trainee.

The inpatient sample consisted of children consecutively admitted to the inpatient service of the same voluntary hospital. In the previous inpatient study (1), 65 children were evaluated; the current investigation included 106 inpatients. The nonpatient group (6) consisted of 101 children selected by stratified random sampling f:om a roster of school pupils in a large urban community. Stratification was on the basis of age, sex, and racial/ethnic distribution so that these children matched both the inpatient and outpatient samples on these variables. The children and parents gave informed consent.

Table 1 shows the demographic features of the three groups of children. The mean ± SD age of the inpatients was 10.9 ± 1.3 years, of the outpatients was 9.4 ± 1.2 years, and of the nonpatients was 9.7 ± 1.2 years. The groups did not differ from each other on sex, age, or race/ethnicity. In the inpatient and outpatient groups there were no differences in religious affiliation, but in the nonpatient group Catholics predominated. Forty-three percent of the outpatients, compared to 60% of the inpatients and 20% of the nonpatients, came from families in which there had been a parental separation and/or a divorce.

The social status of each patient's father was determined using the Hollingshead Two-Factor Classification (7). The mean ± SD score for the fathers of inpatients, outpatients, and nonpatients, respectively, was 36.2 ± 18.3 (N = 83), 43.9 ± 18.2 (N = 65), and 47.8 ± 15.4 (N = 101) ($F = 10.4$, $df = 2{,}245$, $p < .00001$). These findings must be qualified by the fact that information was not available for many fathers who were separated from the household and for whom no other source of information was available. The fathers of the inpatient children had the highest social status (an average of social status III) and the fathers of the nonpatient children had the lowest (social status IV).

Table 1. Demographic Features of Child Psychiatric Inpatients and Outpatients and of Nonpatients

	Inpatients (N = 106)		Outpatients (N = 101)		Nonpatients (N = 101)	
Item	N	%	N	%	N	%
Social status						
I	18	21.8	3	4.6	7	7.1
II	10	12.0	11	16.9	4	4.1
III	29	34.9	19	29.2	19	19.4
IV	16	19.3	19	29.2	51	52.1
V	10	12.0	13	20.1	20	17.3
Sex						
Boys	81	76.4	68	67.3	71	70.3
Girls	25	23.6	33	32.7	30	29.7
Race/ethnicity						
White	78	73.6	72	71.2	76	75.2
Other (black, Hispanic, Oriental)	28	26.4	29	28.8	25	24.8
Religion[a]						
Catholic	50	49.5	53	57.7	69	68.3
Jewish	25	24.8	19	20.5	7	6.9
Protestant	15	14.9	14	15.2	18	17.8
Other	11	10.9	6	6.6	7	6.9

[a] $\chi^2 = 28.7$, df = 8, $p < .0004$.

Data were collected using specially devised research instruments administered by the child's therapist, who had been trained in the use of the instruments. The current diagnoses for each child were determined by the child's therapist by applying *DSM-III* criteria to the clinical data (excluding scores on the research instruments).

The research instruments comprised a spectrum of suicidal behavior scale, a spectrum of assaultive behavior scale, a precipitating events scale, general psychopathology (recent and past) scales, a family background scale, a child's concept of death scale, an ego functioning scale, and an ego defense scale. For statistical analysis, a mean or total score was determined for each scale. The suicidal behavior scale measures the extent of behaviors during the 6 months before the evaluation. Definitions of the ratings for this scale are in appendix 1. Each subject's score on the spectrum of suicidal behavior scale was coded according to the highest degree of observed suicidal tendency (e.g., subjects who had suicidal ideas and who made suicidal threats were coded as making threats).

The discriminative validity, internal reliability, and interrater reliability of the research instruments have been established previously (1, 2, 5, 6). Furthermore, interrater reliability was reassessed in this study by a clinician experienced in the use of research instruments who reviewed 20 outpatient case history charts, completed the research instruments, and determined the current *DSM-III* diagnosis on the basis of the chart reviews alone. The product-moment correlations representing interjudge reliability for the scales and diagnoses ranged from $r=1.00$ to $r=.70$, findings that were similar to those in our previous report (6).

A correlation matrix was computed comparing ratings on the suicidal spectrum scale to scores on noncategorical variables. Groups were compared on various categorical variables using chi-square tests. Analyses of variance were performed to compare the inpatients, outpatients, and nonpatients on selected variables.

RESULTS

The Spectrum of Suicidal Behavior

Table 2 shows the suicidal behaviors of the children and mothers of the three groups of children. Of the 101 outpatients, 24.8% had suicidal ideas or had threatened or attempted suicide; most cases were limited to either ideas or threats. Although there were significantly more boys than girls in this outpatient sample, there was no significant difference in the distribution of boys and girls along the spectrum of suicidal behaviors. Similarly, there were no significant differences in the severity of suicidal behavior for the inpatient or the nonpatient boys and girls. The suicide methods reported by the outpatients as being part of their suicidal thoughts included jumping from heights, running into traffic, stabbing, wrist cutting, and hanging.

The mean ± SD suicidal behavior score for the inpatients (27 ± 1.3) was significantly greater than that of the outpatients (1.4 ± 0.7) and the nonpatients (1.2 ± 0.5) ($F=98.1$, $df=2, 305$, $p<.00001$). Post hoc analysis by means of the Scheffé test revealed that the mean suicidal behavior score for inpatients was significantly different from that of both the outpatients ($p<.01$) and the nonpatients ($p<.01$) but that there was no difference in mean score between the outpatients and the nonpatients. Approximately 54% of the inpatients, in contrast to approximately 9% of the outpatients and 3% of nonpatients, had threatened or attempted suicide.

There was a significant difference between the suicidal behavior of the mothers of inpatients, outpatients, and nonpatients ($F=4.6$, $df=2, 299$, $p<.01$). Approximately 11% of the inpatients' mothers had attempted suicide

Table 2. Suicidal Behaviors of Child Psychiatric Inpatients and Outpatients, Nonpatients, and Their Mothers

	Nonsuicidal		Suicial ideas		Suicidal threats		Mild suicidal attempts		Serious suicidal attempts		Suicide	
Group	N	%	N	%	N	%	N	%	N	%	N	%
Inpatients (N = 106)	22	20.8	27	25.5	21	19.8	29	27.4	7	6.6	0	0
Boys	18	22.2	17	21.0	19	23.5	21	25.9	6	7.4	0	0
Girls	4	16.0	10	40.0	2	8.0	8	32.0	1	4.0	0	0
Outpatients (N = 101)	76	75.2	16	15.9	8	7.9	0	0	1	1.0	0	0
Boys	55	80.9	8	11.8	4	5.9	0	0	1	1.5	0	0
Girls	21	63.6	8	24.2	4	12.1	0	0	0	0	0	0
Nonpatients (N = 101)	89	88.1	9	8.9	2	2.0	1	1.0	0	0	0	0
Boys	63	90.1	5	7.1	1	1.4	1	1.4	0	0	0	0
Girls	26	83.9	4	12.9	1	3.2	0	0	0	0	0	0
Mothers (N = 302)												
Of inpatients	89	86.4	2	1.9	0	0	1	1.0	10	9.7	1	1.0
Of outpatients	92	93.8	3	3.1	3	3.1	0	0	0	0	0	0
Of nonpatients	75	74.3	21	20.8	5	5.0	0	0	0	0	0	0

and one inpatient's mother had committed suicide; in contrast, no outpatients' or nonpatients' mothers had attempted or committed suicide. Twenty-six percent of the nonpatients' mothers admitted to having suicidal ideas or threats. Data on the fathers are very limited because in most cases the mothers provided information and did not report suicidal behavior in the fathers. Therefore, comparisons of the fathers' suicidal behavior were not carried out.

Diagnoses

Table 3 shows the current *DSM-III* diagnoses for the inpatients, outpatients, and nonpatients. All outpatients and inpatients and 55.5% of the nonpatients were given psychiatric diagnoses. Multiple diagnoses were used for each child and, thus, the number of diagnoses does not total 100%. There was a total of 12 different axis I diagnoses and three axis II diagnoses for all children combined.

Table 3 shows that there were significant differences among the three groups of children on the frequency of occurrence of almost every diagnosis. In general, the inpatients, in contrast to the outpatients and nonpatients, had more serious and chronic psychiatric disorders such as conduct disorder, major depressive disorder, organic brain syndrome, pervasive developmental disorder, schizophrenia, and borderline personality disorder. In contrast, adjustment disorder was the most frequent diagnosis for the outpatients, whereas anxiety disorder was the most frequent diagnosis for the nonpatients.

Table 3. DSM-III*Diagnoses of Child Psychiatric Inpatients and Outpatients and of Nonpatients*

Diagnosis	Inpatients (N=106)		Outpatients (N=101)		Nonpatients (N=101)		χ^2 (df=2)	p
	N	%	N	%	N	%		
Axis I								
Adjustment disorder	11	10.4	43	42.5	3	3.0	58.8	<.00001
Conduct disorder	42	39.6	24	23.7	6	5.9	32.8	<.0001
Attention deficit disorder	14	13.2	21	20.8	3	3.0	14.7	<.0006
Oppositional disorder	0	0	17	16.8	16	15.8	19.5	<.0001
Anxiety disorder[a]	15	14.2	16	15.8	28	27.7	7.3	<.03
Dysthymic disorder	22	20.8	16	15.8	14	13.9	1.9	n.s.
Major depressive disorder	23	21.7	16	15.8	0	0	23.4	<.00001
Mental retardation	9	8.5	8	7.9	0	0	10.8	<.03
Eating disorder	4	3.8	0	0	0	0	7.8	<.02
Schizophrenia	6	5.7	0	0	1	1.0	11.7	<.003
Organic brain syndrome	8	7.5	0	0	0	0	15.7	<.0004
Pervasive developmental disorder	7	6.6	0	0	0	0	10.5	<.03
Axis II								
Specific developmental disorder	35	33.0	41	40.6	15	14.9	17.6	<.0001
Other personality disorder	4	3.8	17	16.8	5	5.0	14.8	<.0006
Borderline personality disorder	47	44.3	11	10.9	0	0	73.1	<.00001

[a] Anxiety disorder included separation anxiety disorder, avoidant disorder, and overanxious disorder for inpatients and outpatients but only overanxious disorder for nonpatients.

The relationship between diagnostic categories and suicidal behavior was also examined. With regard to outpatients, children who were diagnosed as having major depressive disorder ($\chi^2=22.4$, df=3, $p<.0001$), dysthymic disorder ($\chi^2=17.4$, df=3, $p<.0006$), or borderline personality disorder ($\chi^2=8.4$, df=3, $p<.04$) were more likely to show suicidal behavior. Children with specific developmental disorder ($\chi^2=8.8$, df=3, $p<.03$) had less of a tendency to show suicidal behavior. For inpatients, children who were diagnosed as having a major depressive disorder, an adjustment disorder, or a specific developmental disorder were more likely to have a higher risk of suicidal behavior (1). Those inpatients diagnosed as being mentally retarded or schizophrenic were less likely to show suicidal behavior. In the nonpatients, no diagnosis was significantly associated with suicidal behavior (6).

Variables Associated with Suicidal Behavior

Table 4 shows the variables having significant associations with suicidal behavior for the three groups of children. Forty variables were correlated

Table 4. Variables Associated with Suicidal Behavior in Child Psychiatric Inpatients and Outpatients and in Nonpatients

Variable	Correlatin (r) with suicidal behavior[a]		Difference between suicidal and nonsuicidal nonpatients (t)[b]
	Inpatients	Outpatients	
Introjection	.41	n.s.	2.99
General psychopathology, recent	.37	.40	2.48
General psychopathology, past	.34	n.s.	2.00
Preoccupation with death	.28	.21	3.22
Depression, past	.28	.23	2.57
Arithmetic score (WISC-R)	.27		
Total defense score	.24	n.s.	n.s.
Coding score (WISC-R)	.23		
Displacement	.23	n.s.	n.s.
Depression, recent	.22	.38	3.83
Impulse control	.20	n.s.	n.s.
Aggression, recent	n.s.	.28	n.s.
Bender-Gestalt score	n.s.	n.s.	2.86
Mother's suicidal behavior	n.s.	n.s.	2.42
Father's social status	n.s.	n.s.	−2.25

[a] Significant correlations (at least $p<.05$) between these variables and the spectrum of suicidal behavior.

[b] Significant differences (at least $p<.05$) between suicidal and nonsuicidal nonpatients (positive t value indicates that the suicidal nonpatients had higher scores).

with the spectrum of suicidal behavior for the inpatients and the outpatients. Because of the small number of suicidal children in the nonpatient group, t tests were computed between the suicidal and nonsuicidal children for each of the 40 variables.

For the outpatients, recent general psychopathology and recent depression were the two variables correlating the most with suicidal behavior. However, other variables such as recent aggression, past depression, and preoccupation with death were also significantly correlated with suicidal behavior. Variables that were not significantly associated with suicidal behavior in the outpatients included social status, religion, ordinal position in the family, and parental separation.

Of special interest is the fact that recent general psychopathology, preoccupation with death, and recent and past depression were significantly associated with suicidal behavior in all three groups of children. Furthermore, introjection and past general psychopathology were found to be significantly associated with suicidal behavior in two of the three groups of children. The likelihood of these associations occurring by chance in two or three independent groups is extremely small.

DISCUSSION

This study confirmed the presence of reported suicidal behavior as a frequent symptom among child psychiatric outpatients. Approximately 24.8% of the outpatients had suicidal ideas or had threatened or attempted suicide—a finding similar to the 33% prevalence we found in our study of 39 child psychiatric outpatients who were predominantly from low-middle to low social status backgrounds (5).

Our two studies of child psychiatric outpatients have documented a prevalence of suicidal behavior substantially higher than the 7% to 10% reported elsewhere (8–10). The difference in prevalences may be related to different methods of child evaluation. Another possibility is that there has been an increase in nonfatal suicidal behavior among preadolescents, a trend that has been reported in a study of adolescent inpatients (11). That study revealed that the percentage of suicidal adolescents in a group of adolescents was twice that of a group admitted to the same municipal hospital 13 years earlier.

The current study documented significant differences in the severity of suicidal behavior in child psychiatric inpatients, outpatients, and nonpatients. Child psychiatric inpatients had significantly more serious suicidal behaviors than did either outpatients or nonpatients, but the seriousness of suicidal behavior for the outpatients was similar to that for the nonpatients.

The results of this study provide strong support for the association between certain risk factors and childhood suicidal behavior. The fact that four variables—recent general psychopathology, preoccupation with death, and recent and past depression—were significantly associated with suicidal behavior in three independent groups of children is a direct reflection of the magnitude of their influence. This finding concurs with that of Carlson and Cantwell (4), who determined that severity of depression was associated positively with severity of suicidal tendencies. Two variables in the current study—the use of introjection as a defense mechanism and past history of general psychopathology—appear to be risk factors in two of the three groups of children. The identification of similar risk factors in several independent groups of children provides the basis for recognizing a constellation of associated factors that need to be evaluated in all children who are suspected to be at risk for suicidal behavior.

Another consistent finding in all of our samples has been the lack of distinction between boys and girls with regard to severity of suicidal behavior. This finding differs from reports of adolescents and adults, in whom there is a greater tendency for women to exhibit nonfatal suicidal acts but for men to have a greater frequency of suicide (12, 13).

This study revealed important information about the prevalence of psychiatric disorders among child psychiatric patients. Forty percent of the inpatients had a diagnosable depressive disorder, compared to 30% of outpatients and only 14% of nonpatients. Our results, therefore, support the findings of other investigations (14–18) which pointed out that chronic and severe depressive disorders in child psychiatric patients are relatively common and that such disorders are significantly associated with childhood suicidal behavior (3, 4, 9, 19–21). Our findings also suggest that children with psychiatric diagnoses other than depression, such as borderline personality disorder, specific developmental disorder, and adjustment disorder, are vulnerable to suicidal tendencies. The fact that the children with mental retardation and schizophrenia in our study were less likely to exhibit suicidal behavior may be an artifact of the small number of children with these diagnoses.

Our findings have several implications. Since suicidal behavior appears to be a common symptom among child psychiatric patients, all children who are evaluated psychiatrically should be evaluated for suicidal behavior. These data suggest that suicidal behavior in a child may be considered to be a shifting point along a continuum. Since the intensity of suicidal risk can vary with a number of factors, some of which are related to the child's personality (such as ego defenses and concepts and preoccupations with death), previous experience in the child's life (such as loss experiences leading to depression), and stresses of the child's interactions with parents and others who may have suicidal inclinations, the impetus and the nature of treatment will also vary. For example, school children may show certain suicidal indicators on examination and yet not be involved in any therapeutic encounters. However, our results indicate that there is a similarity between severity of suicidal behavior and types of associated risk factors for the nonpatients and the outpatients. Therefore, we conclude that psychiatric assessment of factors such as extent of suicidal ideation, severity of depression, level of psychopathology, and extent of preoccupation with death, is warranted in a child who is known to exhibit suicidal ideas or acts. Furthermore, if the child seems to be unable to handle these factors and/or there does not exist a sufficient support network, the child may be referred for outpatient or inpatient treatment. In many cases, the boundaries between these modes of treatment are not well defined.

Of course, these ideas should be qualified in view of some of the methodological problems involved in carrying out an investigation of this type. For example, data about the fathers of these children often were sketchy and were biased by reports obtained from the mothers. In many cases, because of the father's absence from the home, there was no way of getting independent confirmation. Another problem relates to the issue of infrequent events: in the entire sample, only one parent had actually committed suicide, and eight children and 10 mothers had made a serious suicide attempt. These figures are too small for us to draw any firm statistical conclusions. However, they suggest relevant variables to be explored further.

Our findings support the notion that there are many common elements important to the expression of suicidal behavior in children, regardless of whether the children are inpatients, outpatients, or nonpatients. These common elements, such as recent and past depression, recent aggression, and preoccupation with death, should be routinely considered in efforts to recognize and evaluate whether children are at risk for suicidal behavior.

Appendix 1. Definitions from a Scale Used to Measure Suicidal Behavior in Children

1. Nonsuicidal: No evidence of suicidal ideas and/or behavior that could have caused self-injury or death.
2. Suicidal ideation: Thoughts or verbalization of suicidal intention. Examples: "I want to kill myself"; auditory hallucinations commanding the child to kill himself or herself.
3. Suicidal threat: Verbalization of an impending suicidal act and/or a precursor act which, if fully carried out, could have led to self-harm. Examples: a child says, "I am going to run in front of a car"; a child puts a knife under the pillow in preparation to kill himself or herself; a child stands near an open window and says he or she will jump out.
4. Mild suicidal attempt: Actual self-destructive act that realistically could not have endangered life and did not necessitate intensive medical attention. Example: a child ingests a few nonlethal pills, following which the child's stomach is pumped.
5. Serious suicidal attempt: Actual self-destructive act that realistically could have led to the child's death and might have necessitated intensive medical care. Example: a child jumps out of a fourth-floor window; a child hangs himself or herself.

REFERENCES

1. *Pfeffer CR, Solomon G, Plutchik R, et al: Suicidal behavior in latency-age psychiatric inpatients: a replication and cross-validation.* J Am Acad Child Psychiatry 21:*564–569, 1982*
2. *Pfeffer CR, Conte HR, Plutchik R, et al: Suicidal behavior in latency-age children: an empirical study.* J Am Acad Child Psychiatry 18:*679–692, 1979*

3. *Cohen-Sandler R, Berman AL, King RA: Life stress and symptomatology: determinants of suicidal behavior in children.* J Am Acad Child Psychiatry 21:*178–186, 1982*
4. *Carlson GA, Cantwell DP: Suicidal behavior and depression in children and adolescents.* J Am Acad Child Psychiatry 21:*361–368, 1982*
5. *Pfeffer CR, Conte HR, Plutchik R, et al: Suicidal behavior in latency-age children: an outpatient population.* J Am Acad Child Psychiatry 19:*703–710, 1980*
6. *Pfeffer CR, Zuckerman S, Plutchik R, et al: Suicidal behavior in normal school children: a comparison with child psychiatric inpatients.* J Am Acad Child Psychiatry 23:*416–423, 1984*
7. *Hollingshead AB, Redlich F:* Social Class and Mental Illness. *New York, John Wiley & Sons, 1958*
8. *Lukianowicz N: Attempted suicide in children.* Acta Psychiatr Scand 44:*415–435, 1968*
9. *Mattsson A, Seese LR, Hawkins JW: Suicidal behavior as a child psychiatric emergency.* Arch Gen Psychiatry 20:*100–109, 1969*
10. *Morrison GC, Collier JG: Family treatment approaches to suicidal children and adolescents.* J Am Acad Child Psychiatry 8:*140–153, 1969*
11. *Schneer HI, Perlstein A, Brozovsky M: Hospitalized suicidal adolescents: two generations.* J Am Acad Child Psychiatry 14:*268–280, 1975*
12. *Weissman M: The epidemiology of suicide attempts, 1960 to 1971.* Arch Gen Psychiatry 30:*737–746, 1974*
13. *Eisenberg L: The epidemiology of suicide in adolescents.* Pediatr Ann 13:*47–54, 1984*
14. *Kuperman S, Stewart MA: The diagnosis of depression in children.* J Affect Disord 1:*213–217, 1979*
15. *Carlson GA, Cantwell DP: A survey of depressive symptoms, syndrome and disorder in a child psychiatric population.* J Child Psychol Psychiatry 21:*19–25, 1980*
16. *Carlson GA, Cantwell DP: Unmasking masked depression in children and adolescents.* Am J Psychiatry 37:*445–449, 1980*
17. *Kashani JH, Husain A, Shekim WO, et al: Current perspectives on childhood depression: an overview.* Am J Psychiatry 138:*143–153, 1981*
18. *Kashani JH, Cantwell DP, Shekim WO, et al: Major depressive disorder in children admitted to an inpatient community mental health center.* Am J Psychiatry 139:*671–672, 1982*
19. *Garfinkel BD, Froese A, Hood J: Suicide attempts in children and adolescents.* Am J Psychiatry 139:*1257–1261, 1982*
20. *Kazdin AE, French NH, Unis AS, et al: Hopelessness, depression, and suicidal intent among psychiatrically disturbed inpatient children.* J Consult Clin Psychol 51:*504–510, 1983*
21. *Myers KM, Burke P, McCauley E: Suicidal behavior by hospitalized preadolescent children on a psychiatric unit.* J Am Acad Child Psychiatry 24:*474–480, 1985*

36. Suicide Danger: Clinical Estimation and Decision

John T. Maltsberger

COMMENT

This chapter, a shortened version of the material presented in the book Suicide Risk: The Formulation of Clinical Judgment *(Maltsberger 1986), arose from a series of about thirty successful suicides that the author studied with Dan H. Buie, Jr., at the Massachusetts Mental Health Center in the 1960s. Under the influence of the late Elvin Semrad, the principles of "case formulation" (Whitehorn 1944) were retrospectively applied to the unusually full case records available, and then to a series of suicidal patients still living who were under care at the same institution.*

Buie and Maltsberger were impressed that clinical guessing and intuitional judgments about the level of suicide danger had resulted in some suicides that might have been prevented if the principles they inductively evolved had been employed to form a judgment about the level of risk. Their findings were initially presented in a twenty-four–page pamphlet (Buie and Maltsberger 1983), which was later expanded into Suicide Risk (Maltsberger, 1986) *at the suggestion of New York University Press.*

REFERENCES

Maltsberger, John T. 1986. Suicide Risk: The Formulation of Clinical Judgment. *New York: New York University Press.*

Maltsberger, Buie, Dan H., and Maltsberger, John T. 1983. The Practical Formulation of Suicide Risk. *Cambridge, MA, published by the authors, printed by Firefly Press.*

Whitehorn, J. C. 1944. Guide to Interviewing and Clinical Personality Study. Archives of Neurology and Psychiatry *52:197–216.*

John T. Maltsberger, "Suicide Danger: Clinical Estimation and Decision." *Suicide and Life-Threatening Behavior* 18(1988):47–54. Reprinted by permission.

■

THE CLINICIAN who is faced with the necessity of deciding how much at risk for suicide an individual patient may be is in a quandary. Diagnostic considerations, epidemiological information, a knowledge of common clinical predictors, and even the biological information that is now becoming available are all alerting and helpful, but they are not enough. Even when all such considerations are combined they often will not answer the question: "Is this patient, sitting here with me now, about to commit suicide?" Psychological tests and the increasingly sophisticated suicide rating scales are further clinical aids, but they are still not enough.

The quandary is not resolved by reliance on two common methods often employed for assessing suicide danger: the mental status examination and the examiner's intuition about the patient at hand. Relying on these two approaches gives rise to many preventable suicides, yet in common practice critical decisions about suicide danger are often based on little else.

The common-sense approach, basing assessment primarily on the mental state examination, does not allow for full consideration of several essential factors that influence the danger of suicide, and it leaves out others altogether. Many patients who commit suicide are plainly very depressed, but many others are not. Patients commit suicide when they are not depressed, when they are angry, when they are drunk, when they are delirious, when they are in paranoid panics, and even when they seem to be recovered from the distress that brought them to psychiatric attention in the first place.

This is not to say that the mental state examination does not have an essential part to play in the assessment of suicide risk; it assuredly does. The mental state examination usually allows direct assessment of the degree of the patient's despair, but not always. It will give us the vital if sometimes subtle clues that the patient may harbor a secret psychosis—this through minor concretisms, clang associations, or other indications of formal thought disorder. But alone it is not enough. One may say that in psychiatry and in psychological practice, the mental state examination is analogous to the physical examination. But what physician would base diagnosis and plan treatment on the physical examination alone? Only a poor one. Good doctors attend to the clinical history as well as to physical signs.

So-called "empathic judgment," when taken alone, is a poor method for deciding suicide risk. Many schizophrenic patients do not give clues to arouse our empathic alarm. Yet these patients comprise more than 70% of those who commit suicide on inpatient units. They take us by surprise when they do it, very often because their intent is not suggested to us by mental state or our personal "hunches." Clinical intuition is easily influenced by preconscious and unconscious forces, especially at times when the examiner is under stress. In deciding by intuition whether a troublesome patient needs to be admitted to or discharged from the hospital, aversive countertransference responses outside immediate awareness can color what we feel and spoil our judgment.

THE FORMULATION OF SUICIDE RISK

What is sometimes called the "formulation of suicide risk" offers the clinician a disciplined method for assessing suicide danger that integrates and balances the presenting clinical material from the patient's past history, his present illness, and the present mental state examination. There are five components in case formulation: (1) assessing the patient's past responses to stress, especially losses; (2) assessing the patient's vulnerability to three life-threatening affects—aloneness, self-contempt, and murderous rage; (3) determining the nature and availability of exterior sustaining resources; (4) assessing the emergence and emotional importance of death fantasies; and (5) assessing the patient's capacity for reality testing. These are now examined in more detail.

Assessment of Past Responses to Stress

The patient's past responses to stress can be weighed by a study of his or her past history, with particular attention paid to such moments of challenge as going off to school; adolescent development; disappointments in love, work, or academic life; family strains; deaths of relatives, friends, children, or pets; divorce; and such other hurts and losses as may be discovered. Here the examiner tries to get a grip on what Edwin Shneidman (1985) calls the 10th commonality of suicide—the consistency of lifelong coping patterns. We assume that patients will tend to cope in the future as they have coped in the past. It is not unreasonable to expect that a man who responded to the death of his mother 10 years ago with a depression from which he recovered after some psychotherapy can probably survive the death of a beloved child without becoming suicidal if the positive resources in his psychological field remain unchanged. But if at his mother's death the patient withdrew from others, overdosed, developed an alcohol problem, or manifested a psychosis, there may be trouble in store. Of special interest in assessing coping patterns will be any history of previous suicide attempts, their nature, purposes, and gravity. In addition, the examiner will want to know on whom or on what the patient has relied to keep going in troubled times. The examiner will also want to know whether the patient has been vulnerable to depression in the past, and whether he or she has been prone to abandon hope in the face of trouble—in other words, whether the patient is despair-vulnerable. Despair is much more highly correlated with suicide and serious suicide attempts than is depression.

The study of the life histories of suicide-vulnerable patients shows that they do not reach adulthood with adequately developed capacities to regulate themselves emotionally. Despair-vulnerability is a case in point. What is the difference between the patient who responds to some staggering misfortune with grief and mourning, but never surrendering hope, and another who falls into suicidal despondency when fate gives him some lesser knock? Granted that there may be biochemical differences between those who hope and those who despair, are these differing biochemical dispositions genetic only? An argument can be made that biochemical vulnerability to despair may be at least partly determined by the vicissitudes of personality development in childhood and later. Future research may illuminate neurochemical differences between well-mothered and ill-mothered children. We do not know what neurochemical patterns are laid down in response to early abandonment, physical abuse, unempathic responses to separation panic, repeated humiliations, and scoldings in children.

Children who are genetically and/or emotionally disadvantaged do not build up in themselves a variety of self-regulatory functions necessary for autonomous adult survival. Some of these essential functions, the want of which disposes an individual to suicide, are as follows: the ability to feel real as a separate and discrete person; the ability to moderate anxiety so that it does not crescendo into panic; the ability to feel worthwhile; the ability to control and moderate rage; and the ability to tell the difference between what one wishes or fears and what reality affords—that is, the capacity for reality testing.

Assessment of Vulnerability to Life-Threatening Affects

Shneidman (1985) writes that the third commonality of suicide, its central stimulus, is intolerable psychic pain. Patients who reach maturity with serious self-regulatory deficits are at risk of being overwhelmed with emotional agony unless there is some outside intervention.

The first variety of potentially lethal pain is aloneness, the subjective correlate of utter emotional abandonment. Aloneness is different from lonesomeness; lonesomeness is an experience softened with hope, experienced as limited in time, eased by memories of love and closeness, and attenuated with the expectation of closeness to come again. Aloneness is, in its most extreme form, an experience beyond hope. In the grips of a full flood of aloneness, the patient feels that there has never been love, that there will never be love, and that he or she is dying. This anxiety is the anxiety of annihilation—panic and terror. People will do anything to escape from this experience. The frantic patient in an agitated depression who plucks at the clothes of passers-by, begging for relief, experiences something of aloneness. Edvard Munch's famous picture "The Scream" evokes a slight echo of aloneness in many of us.

The second variety of psychic pain is self-contempt. Self-contempt in the patient close to suicide is different not only quantitatively from ordinary anger at oneself, but qualitatively as well. To be sure, the patient may be deeply and scornfully self-contemptuous. The subjective experience is not only uncomfortable; it burns. Qualitatively it is likely to be different also, because these patients feel subjectively separate from their hating consciences. One patient said he felt that he was trapped in his body at the mercy of a torturer.

Distinct from self-hate but akin to it is the incapacity for self-appreciation. Those with this incapacity feel worthless, valueless, unlovable. It is easier for people to bear the heat of a burning conscience if they feel they have some merit, in spite of all. Those who feel valueless have much greater difficulty standing up against an interior attack because they do not believe they are worth saving.

The third variety of dangerous psychic pain is murderous rage. Patients may bear ordinary anger, but when murderous hate holds sway, the patients are in danger of turning it against themselves, sometimes because their consciences will not tolerate such a feeling without passing a death sentence, but occasionally in order to protect the lives of other people. Such patients feel their control weakening; fearing they can no longer restrain themselves from murder, they commit suicide instead.

Assessment of Exterior Sustaining Resources

It is only by relying on exterior sustaining resources that those vulnerable to suicide can protect themselves from flooding by the deadly affects. Unable to regulate themselves without relying on someone or something outside the core of the self, such patients nevertheless may remain in good equilibrium as long as the necessary resource is consistently and dependably available. It is the loss of the stabilizing exterior resource that is likely to precipitate an affective flood and invite suicide. The past history will commonly give good indications of what kind of resource the individual patient must have in order to maintain emotional homeostasis. Here we turn to Shneidman's (1985) fourth commonality: the stressor, or frustrated psychological needs.

There are three classes of exterior sustaining resources on which patients depend to keep in balance—others, work, and special self-aspects. Most commonly, suicide-vulnerable people depend on others to feel real, to feel separate, to keep reasonably calm, and to feel reasonably valuable. The loss or threatened loss of such a sustaining other can lead to an explosion of aloneness, murderous fury, and self-contempt. Suicide is often triggered by the loss of a parent, a husband, or a wife. Sometimes suicide is precipitated by the death of a beloved pet. I know of one patient who has warded off suicide all her life by the companionship of a series of cats; she insists that all these cats, by now six or seven of them, are really the same original cat of her childhood. They may look slightly different on the outside, but inside each successive cat the spirit of the original lives on. This cat, by continuous transmigration of its soul, remains constant, always loving her, soothing her, valuing her, and keeping her in balance.

Sometimes patients do not depend on others for maintaining equilibrium, but on work instead. I recall one emotionally isolated child from a distant, cold family. Early in his school years he developed a passion for learning. He was an extraordinarily gifted boy and rapidly progressed through elementary grades, high school, university, and graduate study with highest honors. His personal life was always a shambles; others mattered little to him except as conveniences for the meeting of physical needs. His wife said she felt like a ham sandwich. But academically this boy, by now an eminent professor, was a great man. Learning and now teaching were everything to him. It was not surprising that his retirement precipitated a suicide crisis—a crisis that was resolved only when space was made in a colleague's laboratory for some continuing research, and provision was made for the teaching of a seminar.

A third class of sustaining resources is comprised of valued self-aspects. Some part or function of the patient's own body is commonly such a self-aspect; the patient experiences it as not being quite connected to the rest of his devaluated self. One patient, a socially isolated accountant, paranoid and chronically suicidal, was able to live on only because of his passion for jogging. At the end of his daily run he would shower and then stand before a full-length mirror, lost in admiration of what he beheld there—a fine athletic body, the final destruction of which was unthinkable. We may refer to this patient's body as an exterior sustaining resource, because emotionally what he saw in the mirror was not experienced as a part of his central self. Neither did he experience it as quite belonging to the outside. It was for him a transitional object, and a life-sustaining one.

In this aspect of case formulation, it is important not only to identify which of the necessary sustaining resources has failed or threatens to fail, but to assess as well whether or not some important person may not actually wish the patient to be dead. Often enough after suicide has taken place, we will find evidence that a relative has ignored suicide threats or otherwise complied in a patient's death through inaction.

The identification of who or what the patient must have in order to carry on, and the determination of whether that resource is available, threatened, temporarily unavailable, or hopelessly lost, are crucial steps in the formulation of suicide risk. It is the availability of exterior resources that protects the patient from despair. But equally important is the question of whether or not the patient can appreciate, take hold of, and use resources to keep alive. Some patients may be so overwhelmed with pain that they abandon their attachments in the real world and can only think of taking flight. Helping hands may be held out, but the helping hands may not be grasped.

Assessment of Death Fantasies

Assessment of the emergence and emotional importance of death fantasies is the fourth part of formulation in suicide. Though some would disagree, it is my own belief that, at least to the unconscious, there is no cessation in death. Shneidman (1985) lists the act of egression as the eighth commonality, but it seems to me that when patients speak of "putting an end to it all," they are really wishing for something like a deep sleep, a sleep of peace. Sleep is not death, but for millennia people have tended to equate the two. To the unconscious, the egression of death often amounts to an emigration to another land where things will be better. Does not the word "egression" connote a going somewhere? Going out? We may ask, going out to where?

Fantasies of going somewhere, joining somebody, in another life beyond the grave need to be asked for, explored, and assessed. When fantasies of this nature are in fact delusional, or operate with delusional force, the patient may be in danger of suicide. In situations of intense distress, illusions may be so overvalued that they operate with the intensity of delusions. The following case illustrates this point.

Mr. G, a 63-year-old retired office worker, was transferred to a psychiatric inpatient unit after surviving an almost lethal overdose of digitalis. A former alcoholic, the patient had overcome his difficulties and become widely known for his volunteer work. A stroke left him with a thalamic infarction. He experienced great difficulty in urinating. Frequent catheterization became necessary, and his leg brace was commonly wet with urine. The stroke also left him subject to severe attacks of pain in which his hand, arm, and leg felt as though they were being crushed in a vise or pierced with sharp needles—the worst experiences of pain in his entire life. Furthermore, his ailments forced him out of the home he had shared for some years with friends. What he ostensibly found intolerable were physical decay and the suffering for which he could find no relief. He had hoarded digitalis, planning to commit suicide for months, promising himself "escape" when the suffering became too much. But careful examination showed that in fact what made life intolerable was the loss of his pet dog, Fidel.

When asked what he had imagined it would be like to be dead, Mr. G began to cry, and confided that he had hoped Fidel would be there "on the other side" waiting for him. He was careful to point out he had no sense of certainty, but a strong hope, about life beyond the grave. The patient told the examiner about Fidel eagerly, in great detail, weeping all the while as he explained how inseparable they had been. Fidel had accompanied him to banquets, had appeared on the platform with him, had attracted the notice of celebrities. For years, Mr. G had secretly smuggled Fidel into movies. The dog's intelligence had been noted by everyone; the patient and his pet had enjoyed a complete mutual capacity to understand each others' thoughts and feelings. They were the closest of friends.

When Fidel was 13 years old, he developed diabetes and required insulin injections; urinary incontinence followed. On the advice of the veterinarian, the dog was given "euthanasia." After cremation, his ashes were dispersed on a beach where "by coincidence" those of a friend's wife had been scattered before. Mr. G liked to imagine Fidel frisking along beside her, keeping her company. Before this hospital admission, the patient had not seen the connection between Fidel's illness and "euthanasia" and his own incontinence and suicide attempt.

Mr. G's mother had been physically and emotionally abusive; he had relied on his father and brother to raise him. From the age of 14, he was never without a dog, and before that he would leave for school a half hour early in order to "have conversations with four dogs who lived in the neighborhood." When asked if he would have attempted suicide had Fidel remained at his side, Mr. G exclaimed indignantly, "What? Leave Fidel? Never!"

Assessment of Capacity for Reality Testing

Assessment of the patient's capacity for reality testing is the final aspect of the formulation of suicide danger. The foregoing example shows that in a patient caught up in despair—in this instance, the despair of aloneness—fantasies about a better life after death may operate with perilous intensity. It is important not only to inquire about such fantasies or beliefs, but to decide how much psychological distance the patient can place between them and himself.

Patients in profoundly depressed states may not be able to form realistic appraisals of how much they are loved and valued by others. One must ask not only whether the external sustaining resources are available, but whether the patient is able to understand and grasp that fact.

Paranoid patients may also suffer from such disturbances of reality testing that they have grown convinced others who love them are in fact dangerous traitors who want to do them ill, so that correct appreciation of the availability of others is impossible.

CONCLUSION

The formulative approach to assessing suicide risk that I have outlined here (see Maltsberger, 1986, for a fuller development of it) affords a disciplined method for weighing the various vulnerabilities and strengths of patients who threaten to destroy themselves, and a means of assessing and integrating the influences, both interior and exterior, that hold such patients back from or drive them toward self-destruction.

REFERENCES

Buie, D. H., & Adler, G. Definitive treatment of the borderline patient. International Journal of Psychoanalysis and Psychotherapy, *1982,* 9, *51–87.*

Maltsberger, J. T. Suicide risk: The formulation of clinical judgment. *New York: New York University Press, 1986.*

Shneidman, E. S. Definition of suicide. *New York: Wiley, 1985.*

37. Suicidal Ideation and Suicide Attempts in Panic Disorder and Attacks

Myrna M. Weissman, Gerald L. Klerman, Jeffrey S. Markowitz, and Robert Ouellette

BIOGRAPHICAL NOTE

Myrna M. Weissman is a professor of epidemiology in psychiatry at the College of Physicians and Surgeons and the School of Public Health, Columbia University, and chief of the Department in Clinical-Genetic Epidemiology at the New York State Institute. Her current research is on the epidemiology of psychiatric disorders in the community, and the treatment and genetics of affective and anxiety disorders. She holds numerous awards and has published widely. Her husband, Gerald Klerman, with whom she wrote the present chapter, died in 1993.

Respecting the development of this study Weissman writes: "it came about as we were analyzing the data on the Epidemiologic Catchment Area (ECA) study looking at panic disorder and panic attacks and quality of life. We chose the variables that were about quality of life, such as ability to work regularly, perception of physical and emotional health, quality of interpersonal relations, substance abuse. An assessment of suicidal feelings, ideation and attempts were also included. . . . Much to our surprise, panic disorder was associated with high rates of suicide attempts. We had not anticipated that. We then set out to explore this unexpected finding more closely. For example, in a paper by Johnson, Weissman, and Klerman (1990), we looked at the rate of suicide attempts in uncomplicated panic disorder (i.e., without another psychiatric disorder) and confirmed our initial observation of an increased rate of suicide attempts in persons with panic disorder. We are pleased that other investigators have been interested in our results and have followed up our finding in clinical and epidemiologic samples."

Myrna M. Weissman, Gerald L. Klerman, Jeffrey S. Markowitz, and Robert Ouellette, "Suicidal Ideation and Suicide Attempts in Panic Disorder and Attacks." *New England Journal of Medicine* 321(1989):1209–1214. Reprinted by permission.

COMMENT

Older psychiatric textbooks sometimes emphasized that psychomotor agitation was a sign of suicide danger when it occurred in depressed patients. Emil Kraepelin commented that "serious attempts at suicide are in these [anxious] states extremely frequent" (1921, p. 95).

This chapter presents the first empirical demonstration of the importance of panic as a phenomenon that invites suicidal behavior. The authors found that the risk for suicide attempts in panic states could not be explained by the effect of coexisting psychiatric disorders, including affective illness. Indeed, the rate of suicide attempts in subjects with panic disorder was higher than in subjects with major depression.

The findings reported here should make clinical estimation of psychic anguish a regular part of the mental state examination in assessing suicide risk. Weissman and her colleagues have directed attention to the importance of detecting and treating panic attacks in the general medical and surgical population. When severe psychic anxiety occurs in patients who are depressed and are already known to be suicidal, relieving it may protect against suicidal action.

Awareness of this matter recently prompted John T. Maltsberger to ask a depressed young male inpatient about the level of his anxiety, even though on clinical examination he was quiet, slowed, and seemed drowsy. In a whispery monotone he replied, without moving, that he could hardly bear it, that he felt like running screaming down the corridor. The next day, walking in a supervised group of patients from the hospital cafeteria, he jumped in front of a truck and narrowly escaped injury.

Panic, or psychic anxiety, may not be suggested by observations of patients' general appearance and behavior, but it is central to suicide. Edwin Shneidman (see chapter 40 below) asserts that "psychache" is the central cause of suicide, and severe panic, coupled with depressive despair, is a common form of it. Indeed, Jan Fawcett and colleagues (see chapter 38 below) reported that panic attacks and severe psychic anxiety were significantly associated with suicide in their series of patients with major affective disorders.

REFERENCES

Johnson, J., Weissman, Myrna M., Klerman, Gerald L. 1990. Panic Disorder, Comorbidity, and Suicide Attempts. Archives of General Psychiatry *47:805–808.*

Kraepelin, Emil. 1921. Manic-Depressive Insanity and Paranoia, *Barclay, R. M., trans., and Robertson G. M., ed., Edinburgh: E. & S. Livingstone. (This book was reprinted in a facsimile edition in 1987 by the Ayer Co. of Salem, New Hampshire.)*

■

Panic disorder, which is found in about 1.5 percent of the population at some time in their lives, includes recurrent episodes of sudden, unpredictable, intense fear accompanied by symptoms such as palpitations, chest pain, and faintness. Panic attacks, which do not meet these diagnostic criteria fully, are two to three times more prevalent. Since panic symptoms can mimic those of other medical disorders, patients with these symptoms use medical services frequently.

To determine the risk of suicidal ideation and suicide attempts in panic disorder and attacks, we studied a random sample of 18,011 adults drawn from five U.S. communities. Subjects who had panic disorder, as compared with other psychiatric disorders, had more suicidal ideation and suicide attempts, with an adjusted odds ratio for suicide attempts of 2.62 (95 percent confidence interval, 1.83 to 3.74). The odds ratio was 17.99 (95 percent confidence interval, 12.18 to 26.58) when the group with panic disorder was compared with subjects who had no psychiatric disorder. Twenty percent of the subjects with panic disorder and 12 percent of those with panic attacks had made suicide attempts. These results could not be explained by the coexistence of major depression or of alcohol or drug abuse.

We conclude that panic disorder and attacks are associated with an increased risk of suicidal ideation and suicide attempts. Physicians working in general medical settings and emergency departments should be alert to this problem.

THE PURPOSE of this study was to determine the risk of suicidal ideation and suicide attempts in persons with panic attacks or panic disorder who participated in a large community-based study. This question merits the attention of general physicians, who are likely to see such patients in their practice. Since the symptoms of panic disorder mimic those of cardiac, endocrine, and convulsive disorders, patients with such symptoms often come to the attention of general physicians[1,2] and use the services of emergency departments frequently.[3]

Such medical encounters represent an opportunity to include panic disorder in the differential diagnosis and to start specific treatment plans after other medical conditions are ruled out. In a previous paper, we documented the pervasive social and health consequences of panic disorder as compared with major depression.[3] Unexpectedly, we found that the rate of suicide attempts in subjects with panic disorder was higher than that in subjects with major depression. In this report we explore the range of types of suicidal behavior, including suicide attempts, and their risk factors among persons with panic disorder, as well as the more prevalent and milder panic attacks often seen in medical practice.

The differentiation of panic disorder from generalized anxiety and phobias has occurred only in the past decade and has been incorporated into the official diagnostic nomenclature of the American Psychiatric Association in the *Diagnostic and Statistical Manual of Mental Disorders,* third edition (DSM-III).[4–9] As described in the DSM-III[8] and its recent revision, the DSM-III-R,[9] the essential features of panic attacks are recurrent, unpredictable episodes of sudden, intense apprehension or fear. The symptoms may include dyspnea, palpitations, chest pain or discomfort, choking or a smothering sensation, dizziness, feelings of unreality, paresthesia, hot and cold flashes, sweating, faintness, trembling, or a fear of dying or going crazy. The patient may become reluctant to be alone or in public places away from home in the event of another attack (a fear that is termed agoraphobia).

Not all patients who have panic attacks meet the criteria for panic disorder, because the attacks or accompanying symptoms are not always sufficiently numerous. According to the DSM-III, the definition of panic disorder requires the occurrence within a three-week period of three panic attacks, not solely precipitated by exposure to a specific fearful situation. At least four of the symptoms noted above must be present during each attack. Recent community-based epidemiologic studies using the DSM-III criteria have reported that panic attacks are common, with a frequency ranging from recurrent in 3 percent of the population to comparatively isolated in 10 percent.[10] The prevalence of panic disorder over a lifetime has been estimated to be 1.6 to 2 percent, [10–12] with the rate slightly higher in women than in men. The average age at onset is in the mid-twenties.

The cause and pathophysiology of panic disorder remain to be investigated fully, but familial or genetic factors seem to have an important role. The findings suggest a high lifetime risk of panic disorder among first-degree relatives (15 to 20 percent)[13–15] and a higher concordance in monozygotic than in dizygotic twins.[16] These findings have been sufficiently suggestive to warrant studies of a possible genetic linkage.[16–19] Over the past decade, a variety of pharmacologic and behavioral treatments have been introduced and tested in clinical trials.[4–6,20–23]

METHODS

The study sample was derived from the Epidemiologic Catchment Area study of the rates and risks of psychiatric disorders. The Epidemiologic Catchment Area is a series of five epidemiologic research studies performed by independent research teams in collaboration with the staff of the Division of Biometry and Epidemiology of the National Institute of Mental Health. It was based on a random sample of more than 18,000 adults 18 years of age or over, in New Haven, Conn.; St. Louis; Baltimore; Durham, N.C.; and Los Angeles. A full description of the purpose, methods, sampling frame, and prevalence rates can be found elsewhere.[24–26]

Each of the five sites used the Diagnostic Interview Schedule, a highly structured interview designed for use by lay interviewers in the epidemiologic studies that led to the formulation of the DSM-III definitions of the major psychiatric disorders (see Robins et al.[27] for a description of the instrument and Markowitz et al.[3] for a description of the questions about panic disorder). The interviews included information on suicidal ideation and suicide attempts and were conducted by trained lay interviewers in the subjects' homes. The reliability and validity of the Diagnostic Interview Schedule have been reported and discussed.[3]

Statistical Analysis

The sample was divided into four groups. The first group included all subjects who had been given a diagnosis of panic disorder at some time in their lives. The second included subjects who had had panic attacks that did not meet the criteria for panic disorder. The subjects in either group may have had other psychiatric disorders in the past. Because of their relatively high prevalence and because they may be a prelude to the later development of panic disorder, panic attacks were examined separately. The third group consisted of subjects who had had other DSM-III disorders, but not panic disorder or panic attacks—specifically, major depression, dysthymia, bipolar disorder, obsessive-compulsive disorder, schizophrenia or schizophreniform disorders, somatization disorder, alcohol or drug abuse, or antisocial disorder. The fourth group included subjects who had never had any of these disorders, which include the majority of the adult Axis I disorders in the DSM-III. The entire sample in the analysis comprised 18,011 subjects, for whom complete information on suicidal ideation and psychiatric diagnoses was available.

The statistical association between the four dependent variables (three variables for suicidal ideation and one for suicide attempts) and the subjects in the four diagnostic groups was analyzed with tables of cross-tabulations with raw percentages. These tables described the prevalence rates of the disorder according to site and sociodemographic variables and included the actual numbers of persons surveyed and their weighted percentage in the sample. Each subject in the sample had a known probability of selection from the target population. Weights were assigned to each respondent to compensate for undersampling or oversampling in the determination of population prevalence rates.[25]

In addition, logistic regression models were applied. In the first analysis, the only demographic characteristics controlled for in the regressions were age (a continuous variable), socioeconomic status (a continuous variable with a composite score derived from occupational level, educational level, and household income),[25] race (white or nonwhite), marital status (single, married, widowed, or separated or divorced, considered as one category), and site. In the subsequent analysis, the effect of coexisting psychiatric diagnoses (major depression, alcohol abuse, drug abuse, and agoraphobia) was also controlled for, first separately and then together. Comprehensive data on nonpsychiatric diagnoses were unavailable.

Adjusted odds ratios with 95 percent and 99 percent confidence intervals were derived from the logistic regressions after the application of procedures outlined by Mantel and Haenszel.[28] The ratios indicate the strength of the association between the diagnostic groups and the suicide-related variables, with control for demographic, geographic, and diagnostic differences. The statistical significance of the adjusted odds ratios can be judged from the confidence intervals (whether or not the interval includes 1.0).

Logistic regression analyses were also undertaken in order to identify risk factors for suicide attempts within each diagnostic group. The potential risk factors included all socioeconomic and demographic variables, the DSM-III disorders, and the subject's age at the onset of panic disorder or panic attacks.

To interpret the logistic regression findings for the continuous variables (age at onset, age at interview, and socioeconomic status) in the same manner as the dichotomous variables, two points equidistant from the median of the distribution were chosen to compare the effect of that variable, holding all others constant. This method is analogous to one in which the variable is dichotomized and the "high" values are compared with the "low" values, but it allows a more powerful test. This type of analysis presumes a direct (i.e., noncurvilinear) relation between the given continuous variable and the rate of suicide attempts.

RESULTS

Lifetime Prevalence of the Psychiatric Disorders

A total of 254 subjects from all five sites had had a diagnosis of panic disorder according to the DSM-III criteria at least once in their lives when they were interviewed (Table 1)—a weighted mean of 1.5 percent, with highly consistent rates across the five sites (1.5 percent to 1.6 percent). When the subjects with panic disorder were excluded, the remaining 667 had a prevalence of panic attack during their lifetime of 3.6 percent. The rate of panic attack ranged from 2.3 percent to 4.5 percent across sites. When the subjects with panic disorder or panic attacks were excluded, 4857 of the remaining subjects had had another psychiatric disorder (mean weighted prevalence rate, 27 percent; range across sites, 22 to 35 percent), and 12,233 had never had a psychiatric disorder (weighted prevalence rate, 68 percent).

Demographic Characteristics

There were clear differences between diagnostic groups with respect to sex, race, marital status, age, and social class (Table 2). Consequently, these demographic variables were controlled for in the subsequent multivariate analyses in addition to the variable for site (included because of differences in rates between sites), as explained in Methods.

*Table 1. Prevalence Rates of Panic Disorder, Panic Attacks, Other Psychiatric Disorders, and Absence of Psychiatric Disorders among 18,011 Subjects in the Epidemiologic Catchment Area Study, according to Site.**

Site	Panic disorder	Panic attacks	Any other psychiatric disorder	No psychiatric disorder
	Number (prevalence rate)			
New Haven, Conn.	60 (1.5)	190 (4.5)	897 (22)	3,731 (72)
Baltimore	47 (1.5)	128 (3.8)	1137 (35)	1,975 (60)
St. Louis	48 (1.5)	84 (2.3)	852 (27)	1,965 (69)
Durham, N.C.	50 (1.6)	132 (3.6)	1066 (29)	2,561 (66)
Los Angeles	49 (1.5)	133 (3.7)	905 (28)	2,001 (67)
All sites	254 (1.5)	667 (3.6)	4857 (27)	12,233 (68)

*Number of subjects is unweighted, and prevalence rates are weighted to compensate for undersampling or oversampling. Figures for prevalence are cases per 100 in the study population.

*Table 2. Sociodemographic Characteristics of the Four Study Groups.**

	Panic disorder (N=254)		Panic attacks (N=667)		Any other psychiatric disorder (N=4857)		No psychiatric disorder (N=12,233)	
Characteristic	No.	%	No.	%	No.	%	No.	%
Sex								
Male	62	28	175	30	2298	55	4844	45†
Female	192	72	492	70	2559	45	7389	55
Race								
White	179	75	460	73	2910	65	8245	70
Black	51	17	136	16	1352	22	263	18
Other	17	8	61	11	541	13	1246	13
Marital status								
Married	99	51	262	50	2051	50	6059	59†
Widowed	22	6	97	7	621	6	2350	9
Separated/divorced	79	24	179	21	1017	16	1452	9
Single	54	19	128	22	1166	27	2364	23
Age (yr)								
18–24	22	10	66	13	712	21	1420	17†
25–34	79	27	192	31	1330	30	2411	22
35–44	70	29	131	23	768	17	1456	14
45–64	63	30	158	25	1076	24	2700	30
⩾65	19	4	118	7	970	9	4239	17
Socioeconomic status (in quartiles)								
Bottom	54	20	141	18	984	16	2405	15†
Second	80	36	232	36	1793	38	4235	34
Third	76	28	203	34	1390	32	3565	32
Top	41	17	87	12	666	15	1974	18

*Number of subjects is unweighted, and prevalence rates are weighted as described in the note to Table 1.
†$P<0.01$ for all four columns.

Suicidal Ideation and Suicide Attempts

Table 3 shows the frequencies for each of the suicide-related variables, and Table 4 the adjusted odds ratios on the basis of logistic regression. The adjusted odds ratios (with control for demographic variables and site) are shown for each of the six possible pairwise comparisons of the four diagnostic groups. The overall frequencies have a clear gradient, with the most suicidal ideation and suicide attempts among the subjects with panic disorder, followed by the subjects with panic attacks, then by the group with any other psychiatric disorder, and finally by the group with no psychiatric disorder (Table 4). These effects remained after control for age, sex, race, marital status, and socioeconomic status.

Table 3. Frequency of Suicidal Ideation and Suicide Attempts among Subjects in the Four Study Groups.

Variable	Panic disorder	Panic attacks	Any other psychiatric disorder	No psychiatric disorder
No. of subjects	254	667	4857	12,233
			percent	
"Thought a lot about death"	64	51	33	15*
"Felt like you wanted to die"	44	26	14	3*
"Felt so low, thought about committing suicide"	47	35	19	4*
Suicide attempts	20	12	6	1*

*P<0.01 for all four columns.

The subjects with panic disorder or panic attacks were at higher risk for thinking about death, feeling as though they wanted to die, having thoughts of committing suicide, or attempting suicide than the subjects with any other psychiatric disorder or with no disorder (Table 4). For example, 20 percent of the subjects with panic disorder had attempted suicide at some time in their lives, as compared with 12 percent of those who had panic attacks, 6 percent of those with another psychiatric disorder, and 1 percent of those with no disorder. The adjusted odds ratio for suicide attempts among the subjects with panic disorder as compared with the subjects who had had any other psychiatric disorder was 2.62; as compared with those who had had no psychiatric disorder, it was 17.99. Similarly, the odds ratio for a suicide attempt was 1.67 for subjects who had had a panic attack as compared with subjects who had had any other disorder, and 11.50 as compared with those who had had no disorder.

Coexisting Conditions and the Risk of Suicide Attempts

When the effects of the prevalence rates (not shown) of a coexisting major depression at some time in life were controlled for in the logistic regression, the risk of a suicide attempt in the subjects with panic disorder as compared with the subjects with any other disorder changed only slightly (odds ratio, 2.61)—a consistent pattern across all the suicidal variables. Similar analyses (not shown) were conducted with control for coexisting alcohol abuse, drug abuse, and agoraphobia, separately and in combination. The results did not change substantially. The subjects with panic disorder or panic attacks were at a markedly increased risk for suicidal ideation and suicide attempts—an association that could not be explained by the effect of a coexisting psychiatric disorder.

*Table 4. Adjusted Odds Ratios for Suicidal Ideation and Suicide Attempts among the Subjects in the Four Study Groups.**

Variable and comparison	Adjusted odds ratio (95% CI)
"Thought a lot about death"	
Panic disorder vs. panic attacks	1.66 (1.23–2.26)†
Panic disorder vs. any disorder	3.10 (2.36–4.06)†
Panic disorder vs. no disorder	9.28 (7.10–12.14)†
Panic attacks vs. any disorder	1.86 (1.58–2.19)†
Panic attacks vs. no disorder	5.57 (4.74–6.54)†
Any vs. no disorder	3.00 (2.76–3.26)†
"Felt like you wanted to die"	
Panic disorder vs. panic attacks	2.33 (1.70–3.20)†
Panic disorder vs. any disorder	3.90 (2.97–5.14)†
Panic disorder vs. no disorder	22.07 (16.61–29.32)†
Panic attacks vs. any disorder	1.68 (1.38–2.03)†
Panic attacks vs. no disorder	9.47 (7.71–11.62)†
Any vs. no disorder	5.65 (4.95–6.46)†
"Felt so low, thought about committing suicide"	
Panic disorder vs. panic attacks	1.47 (1.07–2.00)‡
Panic disorder vs. any disorder	3.05 (2.32–4.02)‡
Panic disorder vs. no disorder	16.51 (12.47–21.85)‡
Panic attacks vs. any disorder	2.08 (1.73–2.50)‡
Panic attacks vs. no disorder	11.26 (9.28–13.66)‡
Any vs. no disorder	5.41 (4.77–6.13)‡
Suicide attempts	
Panic disorder vs. panic attacks	1.57 (1.04–2.36)‡
Panic disorder vs. any disorder	2.62 (1.83–3.74)‡
Panic disorder vs. no disorder	17.99 (12.18–26.58)‡
Panic attacks vs. any disorder	1.67 (1.27–2.20)‡
Panic attacks vs. no disorder	11.50 (8.37–15.78)‡
Any vs. no disorder	6.86 (5.42–8.72)‡

*Odds ratios are adjusted for age, sex, martial status, race, socioeconomic status, and site. 95% CI denotes 95 percent confidence interval.

†$P<0.05$

‡$P<0.01$.

Risk Factors for Suicide Attempts

Table 5 shows only the risk factors for a suicide attempt that were statistically significant in at least one of the three groups in which a psychiatric disorder had been diagnosed. Within each group, the continuous variables—age at onset, socioeconomic status, and age at interview—were compared at the 25th and 75th percentiles. Women were compared with men, nonwhites with whites, and the presence of coexisting disorders (e.g., alcohol or drug abuse) with the absence of the disorders.

Female sex and coexisting alcohol abuse were associated with an increase in the risk of suicide attempts in all three diagnostic groups. In the group

*Table 5. Risk Factors for Suicide Attempts in the Study Groups with a Psychiatric Diagnosis.**

Risk factor	Panic disorder	Panic attacks	Any other psychiatric disorder
	Odds ratio (95 perent confidence interval)		
Early age at onset of panic†‡	1.83 (1.14–2.93)§	NS	NA
Female	3.03 (1.07–8.55)¶	2.31 (1.05–5.05)¶	5.29 (3.75–7.52)§
Nonwhite	NS	2.21 (1.16–4.17)¶	1.44 (1.08–1.90)§
Low socioeconomic status‡	NS	2.59 (1.52–4.42)§	1.29 (1.01–1.65)¶
Young age‡	NS	3.63 (1.67–7.87)§	1.85 (1.31–2.60)§
Alcohol abuse	3.28 (1.39–7.70)§	3.48 (1.79–6.78)§	2.48 (1.84–3.35)§
Drug abuse	4.03 (1.43–11.33)§	NS	1.68 (1.22–2.31)§
Major depression	NS	2.34 (1.31–4.18)§	2.57 (1.91–3.47)§
Agoraphobia	NS	NS	1.70 (1.24–2.33)§

*NS denotes not significant, and NA not applicable.

†Refers to age at onset of panic disorder in the group with panic disorder and of panic attacks in the group with panic attacks.

‡The conficence interval compares two otherwise identical subjects at the 25th and 75th percentile levels of the particular variables.

§P<0.01.

¶P<0.05.

with panic disorder, women had a risk of suicide attempts 3.03 times higher than that in men. The risk for women was 2.31 times higher in the group with panic attacks and 5.29 times higher in the group with other disorders. In the group with panic disorder, the subjects with a diagnosis of alcohol abuse had a risk of a suicide attempt that was 3.28 times higher than that of the subjects without a diagnosis of alcohol abuse; in the group with panic attacks, the risk for subjects with alcohol abuse was 3.48 times higher, and in the group with any disorder, it was 2.48 times higher.

In the group with panic disorder, the risk of a suicide attempt was also increased by the presence of drug abuse as compared with no drug abuse (a 4.03-fold increase), and by earlier as compared with later age at the onset of panic. The subjects who were in the 25th percentile with respect to age at the onset of symptoms of panic disorder (15 years of age or less) had a 1.83-fold increase in suicide attempts, as compared with the subjects at the 75th percentile (34 years of age or over). As noted in Methods, the effect of age at onset was linear. None of various logarithmic, squared, and square-root transformations of the age at onset fit the data more precisely, nor did the duration of illness (defined as the age at interview minus the age at onset) account for the results obtained. Therefore, we concluded that the younger the subject at the onset of panic disorder, the higher the risk of a suicide attempt.

In the group with panic attack, the risk factors for a suicide attempt were somewhat different from those in the group with panic disorder and were similar to the risk factors found in the group with other psychiatric disorders. Along with sex and alcohol abuse, these risk factors included race (primarily black), lower social class, younger age, and the presence of major depression. In the group with other psychiatric disorders, drug abuse and agoraphobia (and possibly, undetected panic) added significantly to the prediction of suicide attempts.

DISCUSSION

The principal finding of this study is that both panic attacks and panic disorder, as compared with other psychiatric disorders, are associated with an increase in the risk of suicidal ideation and suicide attempts. The increased risk of suicide attempts occurs independently of the presence of coexisting depression, alcohol or drug abuse, or agoraphobia. Although an increase in the risk of suicide has been associated with major depression[3] and alcohol abuse,[29] the association with panic disorder has been noted in only two studies.[30–32] Coryell and associates reported on a study in which 113 psychiatric inpatients with panic disorder were followed for 30 to 50 years and compared with a matched group of patients with major depression.[30,31]1 They found a significant increase in the mortality rate among the patients with panic disorder, primarily because of suicide or cardiovascular disease.

A recent article by Fawcett[32] reported on a prospective study of 955 patients with major affective disorder, some of whom had coexisting panic attacks (but not panic disorder). This study, conducted in five university centers, found that 25 patients had committed suicide during the five-year follow-up; 13 suicides occurred less than a year after admission ("early" suicides). Among the predictors of early suicide was the presence of coexisting panic attacks. Of the 13 patients who committed early suicide, 62 percent had a history of panic attacks (but not panic disorder) at the time of admission, in addition to major affective disorder. The predictors of suicides that occurred in years 2 to 5 of follow-up were those noted previously, including a history of suicidal ideation and the medical severity of previous attempts.

Patients with panic disorder most often seek medical attention from general physicians and use the services of medical emergency departments frequently.[3,33] An examination of the patterns with which patients sought treatment in the Epidemiologic Catchment Area sample found that the subjects with panic disorder were more likely than the subjects with major depression or other psychiatric disorders to seek help for their emotional problems from general medical or psychiatric professionals, or both, and were more likely to use the emergency department.[3] Twenty-nine percent of the subjects with panic disorder used the emergency departments for the treatment of emotional problems, as compared with 12 percent of the subjects with major depression or another psychiatric disorder and 3 percent of those with no psychiatric disorder.

Because panic symptoms are often similar to those of medical illness, patients may be misdiagnosed or have coexisting medical conditions. Beitman et al.[1] have shown that 59 percent of the patients attending a cardiology clinic with atypical chest pain and no arteriographic evidence of coronary artery disease were found to have panic disorder on psychiatric examination. Kahn et al.[34] found that of 35 patients with idiopathic cardiomyopathy who were studied while being evaluated for cardiac transplantation, 83 percent had panic disorder as determined by a routine psychiatric evaluation.

The differential diagnosis is complicated by the frequent association of panic disorder with other psychiatric disorders[35] and the overlap of its symptoms with those of such physical conditions as hypoglycemia, hyperthyroidism, hypoparathyroidism, Cushing's syndrome, pheochromocytoma, temporal-lobe epilepsy, caffeine intoxication, audiovestibular-system disturbance, mitral-valve prolapse, and cardiac arrhythmias, or the physical conditions resulting from the toxic effect of drugs or from withdrawal from drugs such as cocaine, opiates, or over-the-counter decongestants.[2,6]

Patients who have panic symptoms often believe that they are seriously ill or about to die. In such cases, it may be insufficient merely to rule out immediately life-threatening cardiovascular symptoms or other medical conditions. Evaluation and referral for psychiatric treatment should be accompanied by the reassurance that no immediate medical illness is present, and that there is a range of treatments, both pharmacologic and behavioral.[4–6,20–23] The drug treatments are aimed primarily at reducing the panic symptoms, whereas the behavioral therapies address the avoidance behavior that accompanies the disorder.[5,21] Although there is no direct evidence to show that any of these treatments for panic disorder will affect suicidal behavior, there is good evidence that they will reduce the frequency of panic attacks and avoidance behavior.

REFERENCES

1. *Beitman BD, Basha I, Flaker G, et al. Atypical or nonanginal chest pain: panic disorder or coronary artery disease?* Arch Intern Med *1987;* 147*:1548–52.*
2. *Goldberg RJ. Clinical presentations of panic: related disorders.* J Anxiety Disord *1988;* 2*:61–75.*
3. *Markowitz J, Weissman MM, Ouellette R, Lish J. Panic disorder and quality of life.* Arch Gen Psychiatry *(in press).*
4. *Klein DF. Anxiety reconceptualized. In: Klein DF, Rabkin JG, eds.* Anxiety: new research and changing concepts. *New York: Raven Press, 1981:235–63.*
5. *Klerman GL. Overview of the Cross-National Collaborative Panic Study.* Arch Gen Psychiatry *1988;* 45*:407–12.*
6. *Barlow DH.* Anxiety and its disorders: the nature and treatment of anxiety and panic. *New York: Guilford Press, 1988.*
7. *Sheehan DV. Panic attacks and phobias.* N Engl J Med *1982;* 307*:156–8.*
8. *American Psychiatric Association, Task Force on Nomenclature and Statistics.* Diagnostic and statistical manual of mental disorders: DSM-III. 3rd ed. *Washington, D.C.: American Psychiatric Association, 1980.*
9. *American Psychiatric Association.* Diagnostic and statistical manual of mental disorders: DSM-III-R. 3rd ed. rev. *Washington, D.C.: American Psychiatric Association, 1987.*
10. *Weissman MM. The epidemiology of panic disorder and agoraphobia. In: Hales RE, Frances AJ, eds.* Review of psychiatry. Vol. 7. *Washington, D.C.: American Psychiatric Press, 1988:54–66.*
11. *Canino GJ, Bird HR, Shrout PE, et al. The prevalence of specific psychiatric disorders in Puerto Rico.* Arch Gen Psychiatry *1987;* 44*:727–35.*
12. *Wittchen HU. Epidemiology of panic attacks and panic disorder. In: Hand I, Wittchen HU, eds.* Panic and phobias. *New York: Springer-Verlag, 1986:18–28.*
13. *Crowe RR, Noyes R Jr, Pauls DL, Slymen D. A family study of panic disorder.* Arch Gen Psychiatry *1983;* 40*:1065–9.*
14. *Harris EL, Noyes R Jr, Crowe RR, Chaudhry DR. Family study of agoraphobia.* Arch Gen Psychiatry *1983;* 40*:1061–4.*
15. *Noyes R Jr, Crowe RR, Harris EL, Hamra BJ, McChesney CM, Chaudhry DR. Relationship between panic disorder and agoraphobia: a family study.* Arch Gen Psychiatry *1984;* 43*:227–32.*
16. *Torgersen S. Genetic factors in anxiety disorders.* Arch Gen Psychiatry *1983;* 40*:1085–9.*
17. *Pauls DL, Bucher KD, Crowe RR, Noyes R Jr. A genetic study of panic disorder pedigrees.* Am J Hum Genet *1980;* 32*:639–44.*
18. *Hopper JL, Judd FK, Derrick PL, Burrows GD. A family study of panic disorder.* Genet Epidemiol *1987;* 4*:33–41.*

19. *Crowe RR, Noyes R Jr, Wilson AF, Elston RC, Ward LJ. A linkage study of panic disorder.* Arch Gen Psychiatry *1987;* 44:*933–7.*
20. *Johnston DG, Troyer IE, Whitsett SF. Clomipramine treatment of agoraphobic women: an eight-week controlled trial.* Arch Gen Psychiatry *1988;* 45:*453–9.*
21. *Mavissakalian M, Michelson L. Two-year follow-up of exposure and imipramine treatment of agoraphobia.* Am J Psychiatry *1986;* 143:*1106–12.*
22. *Pecknold JC, Swinson RP, Kuch K, Lewis CP. Alprazolam in panic disorder and agoraphobia: results from a multicenter trial. III. Discontinuation effects.* Arch Gen Psychiatry *1988;* 45:*429–36.*
23. *Ballenger JC, Burrows GD, DuPont RL Jr, et al. Alprazolam in panic disorder and agoraphobia: results from a multicenter trial. I. Efficacy in short-term treatment.* Arch Gen Psychiatry *1988;* 45:*413–22.*
24. *Regier DA, Myers JK, Kramer M, et al. The NIMH Epidemiologic Catchment Area Program: historical context, major objectives, and population study characteristics.* Arch Gen Psychiatry *1984;* 41:*934–41.*
25. *Eaton WW, Kessler LG, eds.* Epidemiologic field methods in psychiatry: the NIMH Epidemiologic Catchment Area Program. *Orlando, Fla.: Academic Press, 1985.*
26. *Regier DA, Boyd JH, Burke JD Jr, et al. One-month prevalence of mental disorders in the United States: based on five Epidemiologic Catchment Area sites.* Arch Gen Psychiatry *1988;* 45:*977–86.*
27. *Robins LN, Helzer JE, Croughan JL, Ratcliff KS. National Institute of Mental Health Diagnostic Interview Schedule: its history, characteristics, and validity.* Arch Gen Psychiatry *1981;* 38:*381–9.*
28. *Mantel N, Haenszel W. Statistical aspects of the analysis of data from retrospective studies of disease.* J Natl Cancer Inst *1959;* 22:*719–48.*
29. *Weissman MM. The epidemiology of suicide attempts, 1960 to 1971.* Arch Gen Psychiatry *1974;* 30:*737–46.*
30. *Coryell W. Mortality of anxiety disorders. In: Noyes R Jr, Roth M, Burrows GD, eds.* Handbook of anxiety: classification, biological factors and associated disturbances. Vol. 2. *New York: Elsevier Science, 1988:311–20.*
31. *Coryell W, Noyes R, Clancy J. Excess mortality in panic disorder: a comparison with primary unipolar depression.* Arch Gen Psychiatry *1982;* 39:*701–3.*
32. *Fawcett J. Predictors of early suicide: identification and appropriate intervention.* J Clin Psychiatry *1988;* 49:*Suppl:7–8.*
33. *Shapiro S, Skinner EA, Kessler LG, et al. Utilization of health and mental health services: three Epidemiologic Catchment Area sites.* Arch Gen Psychiatry *1984;* 41:*971–8.*
34. *Kahn JP, Drusin RE, Klein DF. Idiopathic cardiomyopathy and panic disorder: clinical association in cardiac transplant candidates.* Am J Psychiatry *1987;* 144:*1327–30.*
35. *Boyd JH, Burke JD Jr, Gruenberg E, et al. Exclusion criteria of DSM-III: a study of co-occurrence of hierarchy-free syndromes.* Arch Gen Psychiatry *1984;* 41:*983–9.*

38. Time-Related Predictors of Suicide in Major Affective Disorder

Jan Fawcett, William A. Sheftner, Louis Fogg, David C. Clark, Michael A. Young, Don Hedeker, and Robert Gibbons

BIOGRAPHICAL NOTE

Jan Fawcett, M.D., became the Stanley G. Harris, Sr., Professor and chairman of the Department of Psychiatry at Rush-Presbyterian St. Luke's Medical Center in 1972 and was appointed the Grainger Director of the Rush Institute for Mental Well-Being in 1992. Fawcett has pursued clinical studies concerning suicide, violence, psychopharmacology, depression, and alcoholism over the past thirty years. The study included here arose from his participation as principal investigator of the Collaborative Study on the Psychobiology of Depression funded by the National Institute of Mental Health since 1977. It involved the standard diagnosis and prospective follow-up of 954 patients with major affective disorders over the past sixteen years.

COMMENT

Three years before this paper was first published, Fawcett and his colleagues reported their first prospective study of 954 patients with major affective disorders. There they listed the factors that differentiated the twenty-five suicides that had occurred in the first four years of follow-up: They found that hopelessness, loss of pleasure or interest, and mood cycling during the index episode differentiated their group of suicides (Fawcett et al. 1987).

Three years later, thirty-two suicides had occurred in the patient sample under study and the data were reanalyzed. As you see, six features, when present at the index admission, indicated increased suicide risk within a

---

Jan Fawcett, William A. Scheftner, Louis Fogg, David C. Clark, Michael A. Young, Don Hedeker, and Robert Gibbons, "Time-Related Predictors of Suicide in Major Affective Disorder." *American Journal of Psychiatry* 147(1990):1189–1194.

year: panic attacks, severe psychic anxiety, diminished concentration, global insomnia, moderate alcohol abuse, and severe loss of interest or pleasure (anhedonia). Three other features (severe hopelessness, suicidal ideation, and a history of previous suicide attempts) when noted at admission were associated with suicide occurring after one year.

This research, an impeccable prospective empirical investigation, offers information of great clinical importance. The authors offer strong evidence to show that efforts to treat depression and alcoholism are likely to help prevent suicide in the future, which are now generally appreciated. But the importance of psychic anxiety and difficulty sleeping as suicide predictors had been more obscure. This paper shows us that anxiety and insomnia both need therapeutic attention.

REFERENCES

Fawcett, Jan, Scheftner, William, Clark, David, Hedeker, Don, Gibbons, Robert, and Coryell, William. 1987. Clinical Predictors of Suicide in Patients with Major Affective Disorders: A Controlled Prospective Study. American Journal of Psychiatry *144:35–40.*

■

The authors studied 954 psychiatric patients with major affective disorders and found that nine clinical features were associated with suicide. Six of these—panic attacks, severe psychic anxiety, diminished concentration, global insomnia, moderate alcohol abuse, and severe loss of interest or pleasure (anhedonia)—were associated with suicide within 1 year, and three others—severe hopelessness, suicidal ideation, and history of previous suicide attempts—were associated with suicide occurring after 1 year. These findings draw attention to the importance of 1) standardized prospective data for studies of suicide, 2) assessment of short-term suicide risk factors, and 3) anxiety symptoms as modifiable suicide risk factors within a clinically relevant period.

ONE of the most difficult challenges facing clinicians is the prevention of suicide by their patients. Since psychiatric clinicians routinely deal with patients whose diagnoses are associated with a high risk for suicide, the problem of suicide risk assessment and intervention is always a high priority.

Many of our clinical guideposts for distinguishing high-risk patients who commit suicide from the majority of patients have emerged from retrospective studies (1–5). Because of the statistical requirements for larger sample sizes, follow-up mortality studies of suicide usually encompass long intervals; to our knowledge, there are no prospective short-term (1 year) studies of suicide. Most available knowledge concerning risk factors for suicide is based on examining long-term risk (4, 5). Moreover, most studies of suicide with samples large enough for generalization have been retrospective. These retrospective studies have the disadvantage of not allowing for standardized clinical assessments. They were unable to control for the presence of disorder-specific symptoms (i.e., depression, alcoholism, or schizophrenia) that formed the context of the suicide. The retrospective studies also introduce a tendency for hindsight bias in assessing risk because it is known that a suicide occurred. For instance, the fact that a person committed suicide may influence the perceptions of family members concerning the victim's behavior just before death. Another important dimension difficult to measure retrospectively is the time that passed between the clinician's awareness of risk factors and suicide (6).

Ideally, characteristics predicting suicide will identify short-term risk so that life-saving interventions can be made. Characteristics predicting suicide at some time in the distant future may be of relatively secondary importance because they do not define an acute emergency and may even obscure the more acute predictors that indicate something must be done immediately (7, 8).

This report represents an extension of previous work looking at prospective predictors of suicide in a sample of 954 patients with diagnoses of major affective disorders who were admitted to the Collaborative Program on the Psychobiology of Depression (9). The initial report presented a univariate analysis of characteristics of 25 patients who died by suicide over a 4-year follow-up period (10). The current report describes a multivariate analysis of patient characteristics that correlated with the outcome of suicide in our sample over 10 years. We found that discriminant function profiles predicting suicide for the first year of follow-up did not significantly predict suicide over the next 4 years. This led us to investigate the possibility that different characteristics may be observed in patients who are going to commit suicide within 1 year of initial assessment, in contrast to features observed in patients who are going to commit suicide 2–10 years after clinical assessment.

METHOD

Subjects and Procedure

The sample consisted of 954 subjects from the Collaborative Study on the Psychobiology of Depression who met Research Diagnostic Criteria (RDC) for a major affective disorder (9). The study took place at five university centers, where, on admission to the study, all patients were assessed at intake by professional clinical interviewers using the Schedule for Affective Disorders and Schizophrenia (SADS) (11), which included the symptom variables used in the study. The sample included 401 men and 553 women. Their mean age at the time of admission to the study was 38.1 years (range = 17–79), and all of the patients were Caucasian. Of the 954 patients, 569 had unipolar depression (210 with first episodes and 359 with recurrent episodes), 185 had bipolar type I, 114 had bipolar type II, and 80 had schizoaffective disorder (46 bipolar and 34 depressed); in addition, six patients had minor depression.

All patients who completed suicide during the first 10 years of the study were included. The median age of the patients who committed suicide was 36 years (range = 21–73). Treatment of all study patients was administered independent of the study and in usual settings by professionals (privately or in a clinic setting). Treatment was not controlled but was recorded during follow-up visits at 6-month intervals over the 10 years.

Statistical Analysis

The study began taking in patients in January 1978. In 1982, an exploratory discriminant function analysis was performed to compare the symptoms of patients who had committed suicide or made serious attempts with those of patients who had not demonstrated any suicidal activity. The suicide group studied (N = 68) included some patients who had committed suicide or made serious attempts during the index episode before entry into the study. The comparison group was matched in age, sex, and marital status.

The stepwise analysis (which assumed homogeneous variance-covariance matrixes) examined 46 symptom variables hypothesized by three of us (J.F., W.A.S., and D.C.C.) to be associated with suicidal behavior. Twelve of these were found to be effective discriminators.

Because our sample of patients who had committed suicide was small and results of discriminant function analysis are often difficult to replicate, these results were sequestered to await a cross-validation. The inevitable occurrence of more suicides allowed us to determine whether the original 1982 discriminant function predicted subsequent suicides among the surviving patients. In 1986 the discriminant function was applied to the sample to test whether the function could identify a second group of 11 patients who had committed suicide during the first 5 years of the follow-up. In the original 1986 discriminant function analysis samples, 12 of the 14 suicides had occurred within the first year. In the cross-validation sample of 11 more suicides, only one occurred within the first year of follow-up. The original 1982 discriminant function analysis did not predict suicides in the cross-validation sample, which led to the question of whether the instability of the discriminant function was attributable to the fact that most suicides in the initial suicide group in the discriminant function analysis occurred within the first year of follow-up but the opposite was true of the suicides in the cross-validation group.

To test that hypothesis, the data were re-analyzed in 1990 with all 32 suicides divided into two groups reflecting time of suicide. The 13 suicides that occurred within the first year of follow-up were considered short-term suicides, and the 19 suicides that occurred after the first year of follow-up were considered long-term suicides.

We then compared the characteristics of both groups of patients who had committed suicide with those of the patients who had not committed suicide. The 12 characteristics examined (hopelessness, severity of hallucinations, alcohol abuse, panic attacks, loss of interest or pleasure [anhedonia], somatic anxiety, excessive bodily concern, fatigue, phobia, antisocial behavior, subjective stress, and nonreactivity) were drawn from the 1982 discriminant function analysis.

A Kruskal-Wallis analysis of variance (ANOVA) of ranks was used to evaluate the differences between groups because the symptom data exhibited heterogeneous within-group variances and a questionable distributional form that would invalidate a parametric one-way ANOVA. Two characteristics—suicidal ideation detected by the clinical rater and a history of previous suicidal behavior from the SADS interview—were added to this analysis because of their common association with suicide in previous studies, despite the fact that they did not emerge in our previous univariate analyses. Because of the emergence of somatic anxiety and panic attacks in our discriminant function analysis, the SADS item of psychic anxiety was also added to subsequent analyses to explore the possible significance of all anxiety-related items. The presence versus absence of panic attacks in the current episode among short-term and long-term suicide groups and patients who had not committed suicide was compared by chi-square test.

A series of Mann-Whitney U statistics were subsequently applied to compare each of the two suicide groups (short-term and long-term) with the patients who had not committed suicide. These U statistics test pairwise comparisons between each of the suicide groups and the patients who had not committed suicide.

Because the analyses for this study took place over a period of 8 years, new suicides in the sample were reported as the analysis progressed. Thus, we have 14 suicides in the first analysis, 25 in the second, and 32 in the third. These analyses were performed several years apart, and we learned of new suicides occurring in each interval. Instead of examining only the first sample of 14 or the second of 25, we decided that it was most sensible to include any additional suicides in each set of analyses.

RESULTS

Thirty-two (3%) of the 954 patients had committed suicide. Thirteen (41%) of these suicides occurred during the first year of follow-up: three (9%) during the first 3 months and seven (22%) during the first 6 months. Nineteen (59%) of the suicides occurred during follow-up years 2–10.

Previously reported univariate analyses (10) showed that no specific RDC type or subtype of major affective disorder had a significantly higher incidence of suicide than any of the others.

The 1982 discriminant function analysis that selected the 12 characteristics of hopelessness, severity of hallucinations, alcohol abuse, panic attacks, loss of interest or pleasure (anhedonia), somatic anxiety, excessive bodily concern, fatigue, phobia, antisocial behavior, subjective stress, and nonreactivity produced a Wilks's lambda of 0.71 ($p=0.05$) and a canonical correlation of 0.54. It correctly classified 13 (93%) of the 14 suicides despite a relatively high false-positive rate (41%). It also correctly classified 27 (50%) of the 54 nonlethal suicide attempts and 28 (41%) of the 68 patients who did not attempt suicide. The function failed, however, to predict the suicides and suicide attempts that occurred primarily during years 2–5 of the follow-up at better than chance expectation. It correctly classified seven (64%) of the 11 suicides, 53 (66%) of the 80 nonlethal attempts, and 446 (56%) of the 800 patients who did not attempt suicide.

Table 1 shows the results of the ANOVA of seven of the predictive symptoms of suicide plus suicide attempts, suicidal ideation, and psychic anxiety in patients who committed suicide within 1 year after assessment, patients who committed suicide in 1–10 years, and patients who did not commit suicide. There were significant differences among the three groups in many of the symptoms. The results of the Mann-Whitney U statistics comparing the two groups of patients who had committed suicide with the patients who had not committed suicide are given in table 2. Symptoms that were significantly more severe among those who committed suicide within 13 months than among those who did not commit suicide were loss of interest or

Table 1. Chi-Square Statistics for the Kruskal-Wallis ANOVA of Ranks for 954 Patients with Major Affective Disorder Who Did or Did Not Commit Suicide

Symptom	Chi-Square χ^2 (df=2)	p	ANOVA F (df=2, 951)[a]	p
Hopelessness	7.79	0.020	2.34	0.097
Alcohol abuse	5.73	0.057	2.43	0.089
Loss of interest or pleasure (anhedonia)	8.79	0.012	3.74	0.035
Psychic anxiety	6.36	0.042	3.27	0.038
Suicidal ideation	4.48	0.106	2.10	0.123
Suicide attempts	3.03	0.220	1.90	0.150
Obsessive-compulsive features	4.57	0.102	2.97	0.052
Indecisiveness	6.34	0.042	3.57	0.029
Diminished concentration	7.84	0.020	3.11	0.045
Global insomnia	6.58	0.037	2.39	0.096

[a] For suicidal ideation, df=2, 950.

pleasure (anhedonia), psychic anxiety, obsessive-compulsive features, global insomnia, and alcohol abuse.

The symptom (not the disorder) of panic attacks was present at the intake SADS evaluation in eight (62%) of 13 patients who committed suicide within 1 year but only 262 (28%) of 922 patients who did not commit suicide and four (21%) of the 19 patients who committed suicide in 2–10 years. Despite the small number of suicides overall, this result cannot be attributed to chance alone ($\chi=7.43$, df=2, $p=0.024$). These data suggest that the presence of

Table 2. Probability Values for Mann-Whitney U Statistics Comparing 954 Patients with Affective Disorder Who Committed Suicide Within 1 Year (Short-Term) or 2–10 Years (Long-Term) and Patients Who Did Not Commit Suicide

Symptom	Short-term suicide p	Long-term suicide p
Hopelessness	0.463	0.007
Alcohol abuse	0.029	0.372
Loss of interest or pleasure (anhedonia)	0.005	0.223
Psychic anxiety	0.012	0.879
Suicidal ideation	0.613	0.041
Suicide attempts	0.815	0.086
Obsessive-compulsive features	0.063	0.303
Indecisiveness	0.085	0.062
Diminished concentration	0.028	0.078
Global insomnia	0.011	0.765

panic attacks may be another risk factor in short-term suicide (within a year of assessment).

Suicidal ideation, hopelessness, and history of suicide attempts were not significantly associated with short-term suicide but were significantly (or nearly significantly in the case of attempts) associated with long-term suicide. Hopelessness predicted long-term suicides better than short-term suicides, although both suicidal groups had higher mean ratings than the patients who did not commit suicide. It is also notable that two symptoms—diminished concentration and indecisiveness—were marginally significant in predicting both long- and short-term suicides.

DISCUSSION

The variables produced by the first discriminant function analysis, which correctly identified 13 of 14 suicides occurring in the first year following the beginning of the study, did not identify in better than chance fashion the 11 suicides occurring in the 2–10 years after the intake evaluation. This, plus the fact that the variables associated with suicide in the first year did not include the presence of standard predictors such as suicidal ideation and history of previous suicide attempts, led us to look at time from clinical assessment to suicide as a possible basis for the unexpected variables that emerged (i.e., panic attacks, somatic anxiety, and loss of interest and pleasure [anhedonia]) (7, 12).

The effect of treatment on outcome could not be assessed because eight suicides occurred before the first follow-up visit, when the previous 6 months of treatment was recorded, and because treatment was assigned in a heterogeneous fashion with variable compliance, leaving insufficient numbers of patients in each treatment subgroup (especially among the two suicide groups) for meaningful analysis.

This report suggests two neglected aspects of suicide research that may be of importance for the timely identification of patients suffering from major affective disorders and in danger of suicide: prospective study data and the temporal nature of suicide prediction. The two issues are not really separable because prospective measurement is necessary in order to assess the temporal nature of symptom predictors. In this analysis, the mean symptom levels of traditional suicide predictors (suicidal ideation and previous suicide attempts) among patients who completed suicide within 1 year were well below those of the patients who did not commit suicide, but among patients who committed suicide within 2–10 years they were significantly above those of the patients who did not commit suicide. This finding effectively cancels out any simple direct association between suicide ideation or attempts and completed suicide in the total patient sample. This canceling out effect, based on time to suicide, explains why analyses combining short-term and long-term suicides into one group, such as was done in our previously reported univariate analyses (10), did not find suicidal ideation and suicide attempts to be correlates of completed suicide.

The results of our follow-up study suggest that in this sample of patients with major affective disorders, the three symptoms most strongly related to completed suicide within 1 year of assessment were the anxiety-related symptoms of panic attacks, psychic anxiety, global insomnia, diminished concentration, and alcohol abuse. Loss of interest and pleasure (anhedonia) was also significantly more severe in these patients. Hopelessness, a risk factor that reflects a negative affective evaluation of the world, was found to be associated with completed suicide in the studies of Beck et al. (13). We found, however, that hopelessness was significantly more severe in the patients who completed suicide within 2–10 years than in patients who had not committed suicide only when these groups were compared by using the Mann-Whitney U statistic (see table 2). Risk factors that reflect a patient's current or past preoccupation with suicidal behavior (i.e., suicidal ideation expressed to a clinician and previous history of suicide attempts) are related to completed suicide occurring 1 year or more after assessment.

Inspection of the mean incremental differences in SADS ratings of the discriminating items suggests that some of the differences are clinically as well as statistically significant. That is, the mean differences for ratings of psychic anxiety and loss of interest or pleasure (anhedonia) amounted to a full point or more on the 6-point SADS rating scale and were thus observable by clinicians trained to be precise and reliable with their clinical judgments (14, 15). On the other hand, when viewed from the perspective of time to suicide, hopelessness did not discriminate patients who committed suicide within 2–10 years from patients who had not committed suicide by a sufficient magnitude (0.6 units on a 6-point rating scale) to be considered clinically discriminable. However, the mean difference between patients who had committed suicide within 2–10 years and those who had not was significant (see table 2). Since mean differences of single clinical ratings on SADS items were the basis of measurement, it must be stressed that single clinical dimensions of a specific magnitude are not considered diagnostic of suicide, but a pattern of clinical dimensions (e.g., panic attacks, psychic anxiety, anhedonia, and hopelessness) emerges as an important descriptor of a group of patients at high risk for imminent suicide within weeks up to 1 year after clinical assessment.

Suicidal ideation expressed by a patient with a clinical depression in the course of a clinical assessment is generally accepted as a standard indicator of the presence of suicide risk (12). Yet, in this study most of the patients who completed suicide in the first year after assessment did not communicate the presence of suicidal ideation or plans in response to the specific questions of trained, clinically experienced raters. This finding, somewhat at variance with conventional wisdom, may be related to the prospective design of this study and exactly to whom (clinician or significant other) the patient communicates suicidal ideations. It is possible that instead of communicating suicidal ideation or intent to clinicians, who may try to intervene, patients make tangential communications to relatives, the significance of which is understood in many instances only after the suicide (the previous studies of suicidal communication were all retrospective). This would suggest that the clinician should gather the data for suicide risk assessments not only from the patient but also from significant others (16).

Some of the risk factors correlated with short-term suicide may be modifiable through clinical and therapeutic efforts, thus potentially decreasing the likelihood of suicide. The anxiety-related symptoms in particular may be more rapidly amenable to psychopharmacological or psychotherapeutic interventions than other presuicidal depressive symptoms, such as hopelessness and severe anhedonia. We call symptoms that may be responsive to early clinical intervention "modifiable risk factors."

On the basis of our findings, clinical decision making and research about suicide may benefit from conceptualizing clinical assessments in terms of the differences between acute and long-term and modifiable or nonmodifiable risk factors. This time-related, intervention-oriented focus, which is not emphasized in the current literature on suicide prediction, may help the clinician to weigh individual clinical observations more appropriately when making suicide risk assessments and may also point in a useful direction for treatment intervention efforts.

In the present analysis, the modifiable risk factors of short-term risk, such as panic attacks, global insomnia, and high levels of psychic anxiety, appear to be the best indicators of acute suicidal risk in combination with moderate alcohol abuse, severe anhedonia, diminished concentration, and indecisiveness. The clinical observation and treatment of severe anxiety symptoms may be one of the leading priorities for treating the acutely suicidal patient with affective disorder. This finding is similar to a position suggested in Shneidman's more theoretical discussion (17).

In a prospective study of completed suicide by psychiatric patients during the 5 years following hospital admission, Pokorny (6) pointed out that psychiatrists deal with a time frame consisting of "minutes, hours, or days" to define and respond to a "suicidal crisis" period, unlike the frame of months or years used by clinical researchers. What is needed is a better definition of the attributes of an acute suicidal crisis in order to provide a basis for more successful intervention. Short-term risk factors in patients with major affective disorders, such as panic attacks, severe psychic anxiety, and alcohol abuse, in the context of severe anhedonia and hopelessness, may help define the acute suicidal crisis and point to therapeutic interventions that may substantially reduce acute suicidal risk. The emergence of panic and anxiety as short-term risk factors may converge with the finding of Coryell et al. (18, 19) of high rates of suicide in patients with panic disorder. More recently, Weissman et al. (20) have shown a relationship between high rates of suicide attempts and panic disorder. Both of these studies add validity to the importance of severe anxiety symptoms as precipitants of suicide.

The findings of different predictors based on time to suicide in this sample suggest that the long-term suicide patients in this study may have had symptoms similar to those of the short-term group within a year of their suicide. Efforts are being made to test this hypothesis on the basis of data concerning relapse and symptom patterns in the year before suicide in the long-term suicide group. The sample of suicides presented in this report is small relative to the universe of patients who commit suicide. Since the findings derive from a sample of Caucasian patients diagnosed as having RDC major affective disorders, it is unknown if these findings would apply in other risk groups, such as non-Caucasian patients or patients with schizophrenia, alcoholism, or personality disorders, raising questions of generalizability of these findings to clinical practice. Although the age range of the patients who committed suicide was 21–73 and half of the patients were 36 or younger, the effects of differences in age are difficult to assess because of the small numbers of suicides across the age spectrum.

Although the outcome of this limited sample suggests that such traditional risk factors as previous history of suicide attempts and suicidal ideation were not highly predictive of short-term suicide, such factors should not be dismissed in the clinical assessment of suicide risk. Rather, these initial findings should draw the attention of clinicians and research investigators to the following issues: (1) the importance of standardized prospective data for studies of completed suicide, (2) the importance of assessing patients in terms of acute versus long-term suicide risk, and (3) the possible value of anxiety symptoms (panic attacks, psychic anxiety, psychomotor agitation, global insomnia) as precursors of suicide and target symptoms for vigorous treatment efforts. Further studies of patients with major depression will be required to replicate these results. Continued follow-up of patients in the sample who have revealed long-term risk factors is currently underway. Our findings replicate those of other investigators in identifying severe hopelessness as a precursor of suicide but add severe anhedonia as a precursor as well.

REFERENCES

1. *Robins E, Gassner S, Kayes J, et al: The communication of suicidal intent: a study of 134 consecutive cases of successful (completed) suicide.* Am J Psychiatry *1959;* 115*:724–733*
2. *Barraclough B, Bunch J, Nelson B, et al: A hundred cases of suicide: clinical aspects.* Br J Psychiatry *1974;* 125*:355–373*
3. *Dorpat TL, Ripley HS: A study of suicide in the Seattle area.* Compr Psychiatry *1960;* 1*:349–359*
4. *Roy A: Suicide in depressives.* Compr Psychiatry *1983;* 24*:487–491*
5. *Pokorny A: A follow-up of 618 suicidal patients.* Arch Gen Psychiatry *1966;* 14*:1109–1116*
6. *Pokorny A: Prediction of suicide in psychiatric patients.* Arch Gen Psychiatry *1983;* 40*:249–259*
7. *Hawton K: Assessment of suicide risk.* Br J Psychiatry *1987;* 150*:145–153*
8. *Kreitman N: How useful is the prediction of suicide following parasuicide? in* New Trends in Suicide Prevention. *Edited by Wilmotte J, Mendlewicz J. Basel, Karger, 1982*
9. *Katz MM, Secunda SK, Hirschfeld RMA, et al: NIMH Clinical Research Branch Collaborative Program on the Psychobiology of Depression.* Arch Gen Psychiatry *1979;* 36*:765–771*
10. *Fawcett J, Scheftner WA, Clark D, et al: Clinical predictors of suicide in patients with major affective disorders: a controlled prospective study.* Am J Psychiatry *1987;* 144*:35–40*
11. *Endicott J, Spitzer RL: A diagnostic interview: the Schedule for Affective Disorders and Schizophrenia.* Arch Gen Psychiatry *1978;* 35*:837–844*
12. *Murphy G: The prevention of suicide, in* American Psychiatric Press Review of Psychiatry, vol 7. *Edited by Frances AJ, Hales RE. Washington DC, American Psychiatric Press, 1988*
13. *Beck AT, Steer RA, Kovacs M, et al: Hopelessness and eventual suicide: a 10-*

year prospective study of patients hospitalized with suicidal ideation. Am J Psychiatry *1985;* 142*:559–563*

14. *Keller M, Lavori P, Andreasen N, et al: Test-retest reliability of assessing psychiatrically ill patients in a multi-center design.* J Psychiatr Res *1981;* 16*:213–227*
15. *Keller M, Lavori P, McDonald-Scott P, et al: Reliability of life-time diagnoses and symptoms in patients with a current affective disorder.* J Psychiatr Res *1981;* 16*:229–240*
16. *Fawcett J, Leff M, Bunney WE: Suicide: clues from interpersonal communications.* Arch Gen Psychiatry *1969;* 21*:129–137*
17. *Shneidman E:* Definition of Suicide. *New York, John Wiley & Sons, 1985*
18. *Coryell W, Noyes R, Clancy J: Excess mortality in panic disorder: a comparison with primary unipolar depression.* Arch Gen Psychiatry *1982;* 39*:701–703*
19. *Coryell W, Noyes R Jr, House JD: Mortality among outpatients with anxiety disorders.* Am J Psychiatry *1986;* 143*:508–510*
20. *Weissman M, Klerman G, Markowitz J, et al: Suicidal ideation and suicide attempts in panic disorder and attacks.* N Engl J Med *1989;* 321*:1209–1213*

39. Psychodynamics of Suicide, with Particular Reference to the Young

Herbert Hendin

COMMENT

Revisiting an article he had published twenty-eight years previously (Hendin 1963) when little had been published on the psychodynamic aspects of suicide, Herbert Hendin reviews what had been known before, and what further contributions have appeared since. There are eighty-six citations in his bibliography, all but sixteen of which have been published since 1963.

Necessarily condensed (a full treatment of the development of this subject would easily fill a thick book), Hendin's review provides an excellent survey of current psychodynamic understanding of suicide. Those readers who wish to expand their understanding of this subject will find the references an excellent study guide. Many of the articles he cites are included in this volume.

REFERENCES

Hendin, Herbert. 1963. "The Psychodynamics of Suicide." Journal of Nervous and Mental Disease *136:236–244*

■

Objective and Method: *The article reviews the literature on the psychodynamics of suicide, focusing on factors that will help in evaluating and treating the young suicidal patient. Articles published in refereed journals and books and book chapters based on such articles are the source of most of the material. Articles that first brought a new finding to notice are given preference. Methodological limitations*

Herbert Hendin, "Psychodynamics of Suicide, with Particular Reference to the Young." *American Journal of Psychiatry,* 148 (1991):1150–1158.

and contradictions with the data of other studies are pointed out. Findings: *The psychodynamic meaning of suicide for a patient derives from both affective and cognitive components. Rage, hopelessness, despair, and guilt are important affective states in which young patients commit suicide. The meanings of suicide can be usefully organized around the conscious (cognitive) and unconscious meanings given to death by the suicidal patient: death as reunion, death as rebirth, death as retaliatory abandonment, death as revenge, and death as self-punishment or atonement.* Conclusions: *Knowledge of the psychodynamics helps to distinguish which patients with any given diagnosis are at risk for suicide. Such knowledge is essential to the psychotherapeutic treatment of the young suicidal patient. Topics for future research include the role of anxiety in suicide; the capacity to bear hopelessness, rage, and other unpleasant affects without regression; the use of particular defense mechanisms in distinguishing the risk of either suicidal or violent behavior; and the relation of specific psychodynamic conflicts seen in suicidal patients to particular psychiatric diagnoses.*

IN THE PAST few decades, patients with depression, alcoholism, and schizophrenia have been shown to have a high risk of suicide (1–4). More recently, panic disorder has been linked to a high frequency of attempted suicide (5). The vast majority of patients in any of these categories, however, are not suicidal. Nor does suicide seem to be simply a symptom of an underlying diagnostic condition that goes away if the condition responds to treatment. The current revival of interest in the psychodynamics of suicide derives in part from the increasing realization that assigning to a patient a diagnosis that has a high risk of suicide is not in itself an explanation for suicide.

As a consequence, attention has focused on differentiating the factors within any diagnosis that distinguish patients who are suicidal from those who are not (6–10) and on the lethal factors that cross traditional diagnostic boundaries. Contemporary biological research into suicide moves largely from this starting point (11, 12), as does contemporary psychodynamic interest (13).

The high rate of youth suicide has been the subject of particular concern. "Youth" generally refers to the period of transition between adolescence and adulthood, ending at the age of 30 (14). Although the rise in youth suicide since 1958 appears to have peaked now, the rate remains high. There is demographic evidence that the rate of youth suicide is related to the relative percentage of young people reaching adulthood at a particular period, with the recent rise being the result of the maturation of the "baby boom" generation born after World War II (15, 16). Epidemiologists also point to an increase in the incidence of depression among young people during the same period (17). Advances in establishing diagnostic as well as psychosocial factors of vulnerability serve to underline the importance of understanding the psychodynamics of youngsters who are suicidal when the majority of those with comparable risk factors are not.

Psychodynamics, as used in contemporary psychiatry, deals with the quality of interpersonal relations, recurrent conflict patterns, and ultimately, the *meaning* of actions and experiences (18, 19). Such meaning is understood by observing both its affective and its cognitive components.

AFFECTIVE STATE

It is helpful to begin by understanding the affective state or states in which the patient commits suicide, partly because the affective state usually clarifies and structures the cognitive one. Although suicide is often loosely described as an escape, in young patients it is usually an escape from an intolerable affective state. Rage, hopelessness, despair, and guilt are some of the emotions that have been shown to predominate in suicidal patients. The nature and intensity of these affects are indicators that distinguish patients who are suicidal from those who are not (7, 20–24).

Rage

Clinical study of seriously suicidal young, urban black subjects indicated that among this population the problems of suicide, rage, and violence were related (22, 23, 25–28). Suicide was usually the outgrowth of a devastating struggle to deal with conscious rage and conscious murderous impulses originating in early personal exposure to violence. For example, one young man who eventually killed himself had been trapped as a boy in a room with his father, who was engaged in a shootout with the police. The father, although wounded, continued to fire with a small arsenal until he was killed. As a teenager this young man came to admire Hitler's ability to kill millions. He was arrested for violent fights and wrestled with the idea of knifing his mother and brother before attempting suicide. What he found most disturbing about his violent behavior was the loss of control that he experienced when enraged; he thought he might enjoy killing if he could do it in a cool, controlled, detached manner (22, 23).

The origin of youthful rage in a violent family situation (22, 23, 25–28) that produced identification with a parent or parental surrogate who was violent, self-destructive, or both is typical of young black persons of both sexes who commit suicide. They are disturbed by the feeling of being overwhelmed by loss of control over angry homicidal impulses, and what they describe seems to be a fear of ego disintegration. Their concern is less with the consequences of their violence than with the feeling that they cannot predict or control their impulsive rage and that it threatens their capacity to function. Suicide can be a form of control exercised by people who feel torn apart by rage and violence (22, 23).

The interrelation of rage, violence, and suicide is not limited to young black people. Individuals who have killed others have a suicide rate several hundred times greater than those who have not (13, 29). This rate is largely the result of murder followed quickly by suicide, which is more frequent among white people than it is among the black population (29). In a recent review of studies of the relation between suicide and violence (30), it was estimated that about 30% of violent individuals have histories of self-destructive behavior, while about 10%–20% of suicidal persons have histories of violent behavior. Psychological autopsies of young suicide victims indicated that just under one-half of them had histories of aggressive and antisocial behavior, a much higher rate than that of older age groups, while only one-quarter had histories of major depressive disorder, a much lower rate than has been found in older populations (31). With nonviolent patients as well, the open expression of hostility and rage distinguishes depressed patients who are suicidal from those who are not (6).

Hopelessness, Despair, and Desperation

Beck et al. (7) found that the seriousness of suicidal intent was correlated less with the degree of depression than with one particular aspect of depression: hopelessness about the future. They observed high suicidal intent in some patients who showed minimal depression but whose expectations for the future were also minimal. Eighty-nine of 207 patients hospitalized because they were contemplating suicide had high ratings on a measure of hopelessness from the Beck Depression Inventory. In the subsequent 5 years, 14 of the 207 patients committed suicide. Thirteen of these 14 were from the group of 89 who had the high ratings on the measure of hopelessness. A variety of diagnoses were given the patients who ranked high on hopelessness, but one-half were diagnosed as having some form of depression.

Clinicians often use the word "despair" rather than "hopelessness" to convey the emotional state distinguishing suicidal patients from patients who are depressed but not suicidal. Despair has been described as developing from aloneness, murderous hate, and self-contempt (21) or, more generally, as resulting from any state that leads to the individual's "inability to maintain or envision any human connections of significance" (32).

My own experience with a handful of patients seen a few days before their suicides suggests that their affective state was closer to desperation than to hopelessness or despair. Many patients who feel despair or are hopeless about the future are resigned to their situation. Desperation implies not only a sense of hopelessness about change but a sense that life is impossible without such change. Anxiety and urgency are an integral part of this affective state. The importance of these affective elements was confirmed in a recent study by Fawcett et al. (33) of patients with major affective disorder, among whom anxiety was a stronger predictor of short-term risk of suicide than was hopelessness.

Guilt

In a recently completed study of suicide and posttraumatic stress disorder (PTSD) in Vietnam veterans (24), of 100 veterans with PTSD, 19 had made suicide attempts and 15 more were preoccupied with suicide. Guilt about actions committed in combat, usually involving the killing of civilians and most often while feeling out of control, was the variable that best explained their suicidal behavior. These actions had taken place when these men were 19 years of age on average, but their guilt persisted and fueled their suicide attempts and actual suicides. Their nightmares were often filled with images in which they were punished in ways that reflected their actions in Vietnam.

For the vast majority of the suicidal veterans, the actions that had been committed were of such a nature that the postservice guilt, self-hatred, and nightmares of punishment seem understandable and almost inevitable. In a few cases, however, the combat actions were equivocal, and some were combined with guilt about surviving when close friends had not. When things went well at work or in personal relations, the surviving veterans tended to feel they had no right to be enjoying what their friends who died could never enjoy, and they acted in ways that sabotaged their own success.

The guilt seen in Vietnam veterans was usually conscious, but at times it was only suspected from their behavior and became evident when they discussed their dreams, fantasies, and associations. Consciously expressed, excessive or inappropriate guilt is considered to be one of the cardinal symptoms of a major depressive episode. Such guilt may be elaborated in a delusional way, focused on ideas of sin or worthlessness. Depressed patients who are delusional have been shown to be far more likely to kill themselves than those who are not; the delusions have not been found to be the outgrowth of a greater degree of depression (8).

COGNITION AND MEANING

The cognitive component of the meaning of suicide helps clarify the affective aspects of the suicidal act. For example, the guilt of a veteran about his combat actions and his view of suicide as a punishment that he deserves contribute in a complementary way to our understanding of his suicide attempt. As Kernberg (34) aptly pointed out with regard to the affect of hopelessness, "In clinical practice the question is not the patient's general feeling of 'hopelessness' but what, concretely, the patient is hopeless about."

"Cognition" generally refers to conscious ideation, while "meaning" includes both conscious and unconscious affects and perceptions. The meanings of suicide can be usefully organized around the conscious and unconscious meanings given to death by the suicidal patient.

The evidence for determining any such meaning should not be limited to information the patient volunteers or to his or her responses to questions. The meanings of suicide are often unconscious and are best elicited by free association and dreams. Serious suicide attempts usually stimulate dreams; two-thirds of the suicidal patients in a study by Raphling (35) remembered dreams from the period prior to their attempts. Patients who do not recall such dreams will often do so under hypnosis (36). Those who have studied the dreams of patients shortly before or after suicide attempts have found that the dreams were invariably helpful in understanding the motive for suicide (35–38). Eliciting the dreams of suicidal patients is an important part of a psychiatric evaluation (38), much as it is in cases of PTSD. The dreams of acutely suicidal patients are similar to those of patients with PTSD in the minimal extent to which unconscious material is disguised (35).

We have learned that suicidal patients give to death a special meaning, using death in their adaptation to life. A critical aspect of this adaptation is their actual or fantasized use of their own deaths in an effort to control others or to maintain an illusory control over their own lives.

Some of the common meanings given to death by young patients who have committed suicide are death as reunion (36, 39–43), death as rebirth (36, 39–43), death as retaliatory abandonment (36), death as revenge (43, 44), and death as self-punishment or atonement (24, 36, 45, 46).

Rebirth and Reunion

Some suicidal patients cherish fantasies of effecting a rebirth or a reunion with a lost object through suicide. Death is attractive to these patients as more than simply an escape from crises. In a case that I reported previously (36), for example, a young woman jumped in front of a subway train and was severely injured. Her suicide attempt was precipitated by the end of one of her many unhappy and complicated love relationships and by the vacation of her therapist, both of which events she related to the abandonment of the family when she was a child by her father, whom she idealized. In a dream about her suicide attempt, she was in a long, narrow tunnel. In the light at the end of it, she saw a man and woman standing over a manger. In her associations to the dream, the tunnel suggested to her the subway where she jumped and the way in which the train came out of the tunnel and into the lighted platform area. Moving from the darkness of the tunnel and into light brought to her mind the process of birth. She saw the man and woman as her father and mother. The child in the manger was both the Christ child and herself. (She particularly identified with the idea that death united Christ with his father.) She saw her life as set on a course in which gratification of her fantasies was only possible through her death. One can see how much this patient accomplished in her death fantasy. She is reborn into an intact family, is reunited with her father, and, finally, is omnipotent. For a patient with such fantasies, the thought of dying has become more tolerable.

Early in this century, Ernest Jones and Carl Jung recognized the importance of rebirth and reunion fantasies in suicidal patients. Jones (39) suggested that such fantasies had as their prototype the wish to return to the mother's womb, while Jung (40) and his followers emphasized the unconscious need for spiritual rebirth. This dynamic was reemphasized in the 1930s by Zilboorg (41), who wrote that "the drive towards death, always with the flag of immortality in hand, carried with it the fantasy of joining the dead or dying or being joined in death."

Pollock (42), writing several decades later, emphasized the suicidal person's regression to a state in which there is little differentiation of self and object. The suicide victim gives himself or herself up to an undifferentiated "supposedly blissful state of reunion." This state of narcissistic fusion or symbiotic union with a powerful figure is said to overcome the dread of death and accounts for the patient's fantasies of grandiosity and immortality.

Pollock believed that what may seem to be identification of the suicidal person with someone who is dead is simply likely to be "reflective of the wish to reunite with the one from whom the separation occurred" (42). His view is somewhat different from that of Hendrick (47), who described the suicide of depressed persons as the consequence of identification with a lost object, in contrast to suicide—usually by schizoid or schizophrenic individuals—in which identification with someone who is dead is the purpose of dying and represents fulfillment of the identification.

Retaliatory Abandonment

Suicide attempts and the possibility of suicide give some people the illusion of mastery over a situation through their control of their living or dying. This is probably why some of them keep the means for suicide readily available, whether or not they ever attempt to kill themselves.

In a case described previously (36), a college student was seen following a serious suicide attempt, which he barely survived. The attempt was precipitated by his rejection by a male friend to whom he was sexually attracted and without whom he felt life was intolerable. Shortly after the suicide attempt, the patient had a dream in which he was working for the United Nations, where he had an office that encompassed the entire first floor of the UN building. He was interviewing one of his friends who was applying for a position, and after reviewing the friend's qualifications, he finally told him that he did not qualify for the job. This patient accomplished the same goal in the dream and in the suicide attempt: through being the one who rejects or leaves he gains illusory control over an interpersonal relationship. His holding an important position and having a large office in the dream strongly suggest that he also experienced a feeling of omnipotent mastery through death.

Revenge

Freud's view of suicide derived from his observation that depression is an attempt to regain through introjection a lost object that is both loved and hated (48). In depression, the hate originally directed toward the object becomes displaced onto the internalized representation of the object. The hated person, now identified with the self, can be destroyed by destroying the self. In Freud's formulation, suicide expresses a repressed wish to kill an ambivalently regarded lost love object, and thus it is ultimately an act of revenge.

The mechanism was seen as primarily unconscious. Although the depressed Viennese patients described by Freud were not violent, and we still see patients similar to his, hostility is often strikingly conscious when young people use suicide as an expression of revenge toward their parents. Such youngsters usually feel overwhelmed by murderous feelings toward their parents and are even fearful that they may act on them. These feelings may be conscious as well as expressed in dreams. The suicide may be precipitated by some immediate frustration followed by an impulsive response. However, these youngsters, even if they seem to have been functioning well, invariably have histories of being increasingly unable to cope with murderous rage toward their parents.

Such an expression of revenge was the suicide of a 15-year-old girl who was doing well in school, was well liked by her many friends, and was said by her parents to have shown no evidence of problems. She shot herself in the head with a gun belonging to her father after a fight with her parents over their refusal to allow her and a friend to go to an amusement park some distance from their home. Sessions with the parents after her death revealed that there were long-standing problems between the girl and her mother. After the suicide, her grandmother told the parents that the young woman had told her a day or two before the suicide that she dreamed she had killed her mother. Shortly before killing herself, she told a friend that suicide would be a way of getting back at her parents.

Self-Punishment or Atonement

In the classical formulation of suicide as the product of unconscious hostility toward an introjected lost love object, guilt about hatred of the object is the source of the need for self-punishment. In destroying oneself and the object, one accomplishes atonement as well as revenge.

In 1948 in an article on suicide, Elizabeth Kilpatrick (49) wrote, "When we understand narcissism not as love of the self, but as love of the idealized image of the self, we become aware of the gravity of self-hate and alienation which needs to be present." She pointed out that the unconscious idealized self-image is often accompanied by its counterpart, a despised self-image. This view is maintained in contemporary object relations theory, which formulates suicide as an attempt by the superego, with which the good self is identified, to eliminate the bad self (50).

After Bibring (51) in 1953 focused attention on depression as an independent primary affect—"the emotional correlate of a partial or complete collapse of the ego since it feels unable to live up to its aspirations"—greater attention was paid to suicide as a form of punishment or atonement for such failure. Haim (45) in 1974 noted the "peculiarities" in the organization of the "ego ideal" in adolescents who are prone to suicide, describing an "archaic megalomaniacal ego ideal" with a "demand for the absolute" and "absence or inadequacy of reshaping when put to the test of reality." Mack (46), in his description of the life and suicide of an adolescent girl, viewed her suicide as largely the result of an inability to live with an ego ideal affected by early damage and low self-esteem and the impossibility of satisfying her mother's need to fulfill through her the mother's own need for perfection.

Suicide has been mentioned as a self-inflicted punishment by Vietnam veterans guilty about actions in combat. Comparable dynamics are seen in civilian life (perhaps with less frequency today than heretofore) in young people who, having been raised in fundamentalist religious families, are in anguish over their failure to fulfill moral expectations. They tend to regard their drinking, fighting, or other antisocial behavior as sins and to view suicide as a form of expiation. Their dreams in connection with suicide attempts often contain images of hellfire and brimstone (52). In psychotic individuals these ideas are expressed as delusions of sin.

More common in psychiatric practice today are young people who feel they have failed to meet their own and their families' academic, vocational, and social aspirations and have fallen short of matching the achievements of their siblings and peers. Their lives are filled with a sense of failure and humiliation, their dreams frequently center on "having missed the boat" (52), and their suicides are often an expression of self-hatred and a need for punishment. A typical case is that of a 20-year-old patient who committed suicide after he recorded this dream in his diary: "I was back at high school and saw familiar faces. I felt embarrassed and humiliated. They were going on with life. I tried to be incognito but was spotted." In a similar vein he wrote, "When I think of myself as a recovering patient, I am more patient with myself and more willing to change things. When I compare myself to my potential, I mourn."

INTERRELATED MEANINGS

Although these dynamic themes have different significance in different patients, they are not mutually exclusive. Both the dependent and the aggressive aspects of suicide can be active in some patients, as Melanie Klein (53) recognized when she wrote, "In some cases the fantasies underlying suicide aim at preserving the internalized good objects and that part of the ego which is identified with good objects, and also at destroying the other part of the ego which is identified with the bad objects." At times the self-punishment resulting from self-hatred seems to have become an end in itself, but there is usually evidence in suicide of "a double aim of first cleansing the self, and then uniting (actually reuniting) with an omnipotent love object" (54).

Whether the aim is to cleanse or to rid oneself of the "bad part," purification achieved by either exorcism or self-punishment is seen as enabling the individual to hope that he can be loved by a significant object once again.

A theme that may run through the varying psychodynamic meanings of suicide is the perception of suicidal patients, experienced unconsciously and/ or consciously, that they are already dead. Dreams of death, dying, coffins, and burial are frequent in suicidal young people (32, 35), who experience emotional death in their attempts to bury their rage and despair. The preoccupation of some with death is often the climax of having felt emotionally dead for a lifetime (55).

All of the psychodynamic meanings given to death by suicidal patients can be conceptualized as responses to loss, separation, or abandonment. Rebirth and reunion fantasies may be seen as attempts to undo or deny such losses. Becoming the one who leaves is one way to avoid the feeling of having been left. Feelings of rage that are repressed, suppressed, or expressed may derive from the experience of loss. Self-punishment may express guilt at having been responsible for a loss and the fantasy of rapprochement through atonement. Even numbness or deadness and the insistence that one is already psychologically dead may reflect determination not to live without the lost object (13, 56). Although suicidal patients may have in common their use of their own deaths to deal with their losses, the various meanings they give to their deaths account for the variety in the psychodynamics of suicide.

For most suicidal patients, however, a rejection of life usually includes a rejection of the parents from whom it originated (13, 43, 56). The patient is likely to feel in a deep way that he or she was abandoned first (13, 56). In this sense Freud's insight into the relationship of abandonment, loss, and suicide (48) has perhaps the most meaning and has stood the test of time.

Life and growth inevitably mean emotional separation from parents. For suicidal youngsters, separation, loss, and death are often equated, are intolerable, and leave the youngsters feeling desperately out of control of their lives. Suicide can be used to control others or to maintain the sense of control over one's own life. To obtain such control, seriously suicidal youngsters often make their living conditional ("I won't live unless I can get into this particular school," ". . . unless this person will care for me," etc.) (56).

THERAPEUTIC CONSIDERATIONS

The need to use one's death to express desperation, rage, or guilt reflects, among other things, difficulty in using less extreme forms of communication.

Understanding and conveying to the patient what it is that he or she is hoping to communicate by dying can provide crucial relief to the patient and can reduce the short-term risk of suicide.

The affective states and their accompanying death fantasies are often activated by trauma and seem, in part, to be an attempt to resolve a dysphoric state through use of a fantasied or dysfunctional object tie. The patient's own unique psychodynamic constellation of affect, cognition, and meaning is most dramatically prominent immediately before or after a suicide attempt, during what is referred to as a suicidal crisis or episode (14, 57, 58). The same combination of psychodynamic factors is present in suicidal patients during the chronic phases of their illness and is a central element of the individual's psychic life. For example, grandiose fantasies revolving around conquering or controlling death, immortality, or identification with Christ, Hitler, or a UN dignitary are common among suicidal patients. Kohut (59, 60), Kernberg (61), and others have emphasized that such grandiosity usually reflects disturbances in self-esteem and identity formation that occurred early in childhood. The fears of disintegration or identity diffusion that often derive from such developmental disturbances are frequent in borderline or schizophrenic patients who become suicidal, in suicidal veterans with PTSD, and in enraged suicidal patients regardless of their diagnoses. Although the acute threat of disintegration remits as the suicidal crisis is resolved, the underlying identity problems remain, as does the fantasy of resolving them through suicide.

Suicidal patients are unique in their use of the possibility of ending their lives as a way of dealing with both internal conflict and relations with other people. Their use of this possibility colors the transference and countertransference and presents special problems in treatment.

Studies of therapeutic interactions with patients who have killed themselves while in treatment have found that rejection by the therapist was a precipitating factor in many of these cases. Such rejection most often results from the therapist's countertransference anger or hatred, which is often unconscious and often a response to the patient's angry criticisms or demands (62, 63). The patient's threat of dying if his or her demands are not met may lead the therapist to bury awareness of his or her own anger, to feel coerced into obeying such demands, or, conversely, to react punitively to them. Maltsberger and Buie (64) pointed out that the most vulnerable therapists are those whose need to see themselves as able to save any patient renders the possible suicide of a patient narcissistically devastating. Suicidal patients understand the fear they can produce through their death threats and use it in ways that often lead to temporary control over, but eventual rejection by, their therapists as well as others.

Since suicidal patients use their possible death as a way of relating to and controlling the therapist and other people, the psychodynamics underlying their suicidal feelings can be seen in the transference. One young woman, seen following a serious suicide attempt, had persuaded her therapist to call her every morning at 7:00 a.m., threatening that otherwise she would kill herself. Her therapist's anxiety had led him to permit her to act out her fantasy of exercising power over him and over life and death in this manner. Nonetheless, his calling did not prevent an almost fatal suicide attempt.

Early recognition of the role in which the patient is attempting to cast the therapist is critical for progress in treatment. A young man who survived shooting himself in the chest came into therapy saying he would give the therapist 6 months to make him feel better or else he would be dead. The first months of treatment were spent understanding his need to establish a relationship that made the therapist responsible for whether he lived or died (65).

Therapists may be cast in, or may be tempted to play, the role of saviors. Just as often they are cast in the role of executioners (54). They may be incorporated into patients' rebirth or reunion fantasies, and they often become the targets of suicides motivated by revenge. The therapist of the patient who jumped in front of a train, mentioned earlier, had tried to be available to her in ways that her father was not. Afterward, he realized that she had been determined to perceive him as responsible for her death. Immediately before her attempt and afterward, she made an effort to see to it that the therapist would be blamed. By splitting her feelings toward her father, she could perceive her therapist as the destroying father, making it easier to preserve her fantasy of salvation through reunion with her natural father, whom she could idealize as loving.

EARLY EXPERIENCES

Recent work has questioned the observation by Zilboorg (66) a half-century ago that the loss through death of a parent during the patient's childhood was a significant factor in suicide. Barraclough (67) found that loss of a parent in childhood was no more frequent in his sample of subjects who had committed suicide than it was in his control group. He did find, however, that the recent death of a parent or spouse had occurred significantly more frequently among the subjects who committed suicide.

In adolescents the factors of parental death and recent object loss tend to merge, since a parent's death is likely to have been a recent event. In any case, what Zilboorg was observing was the impact of such deaths on his patients, an impact he attributed to the patient's identification with a dead parent. It is possible that for suicidal patients, even if the frequency of parental death is not extraordinary, its impact is greater, perhaps because of such identification.

More recent study of the families of young people who have killed themselves has indicated that suicide or attempted suicide is disproportionately frequent among the first- or second-degree relatives of these youngsters (68). Whether the factor responsible in these cases is genetic or psychosocial is not clear, and the psychological impact of second-degree relatives' suicide or attempted suicide on young people who eventually kill themselves has not been studied.

Maltsberger and Buie have provided us with a broader explanation of the suicidal patient's vulnerability to loss (69). They build on Kohut's postulate that the experience of an empathic, nurturing mother is a prerequisite for the individual's developing soothing introjects and the ability to comfort himself in times of loss (59, 60). Individuals who lack this ability tend to form relationships in which the other person is not viewed independently but is seen instead as an extension of the self. When these patients experience object loss, they feel a narcissistic insult that can lead to depression or anxiety about disintegration, anxiety that Kohut felt "is the deepest anxiety man can experience" (70). Some patients can turn to other people for comfort, but Maltsberger and Buie point out that suicidal patients have difficulty in doing just this. Instead, they are isolated in a paralyzing sense of aloneness—"a state of vacant cold isolation accompanied by varying degrees of terror"—which these authors liken to the infant's experience of separation anxiety (69).

Object relations theory gives a developmental explanation for the self-punitive elements of suicide. Early intrapsychic conflicts are seen as producing a susceptibility to splitting in the patient's self-representation in times of stress. The suicide may then involve the patient's identifying with the good self and punishing the bad self (50).

The question remains as to why some individuals feel that death is the only way to control their sense of fragmentation or express their need for punishment. Studies of the family relationships of suicidal youngsters may provide some clarification. Retrospective studies conducted in the 1960s and 1970s consistently found that suicidal youngsters were alienated from their families in early childhood by parental attitudes of resentment, hostility, and rejection (55, 71–76). A more recent psychological autopsy study of young suicides confirmed that significantly more frequent parental abuse or rejection had been experienced by the suicidal youngsters than by the control group (77).

Whether these parental responses are reactions to the children's behavior or purely the product of the parents' pathology, the recollections of suicidal youngsters repeatedly invoke parental figures who are frustrating, rejecting, or controlling. Some young people may express their distress through such reckless behavior with cars, motorcycles, or drugs that their parents are forced to acknowledge their self-destructiveness. In some cases the child creates such a disturbance in the family that the parents indicate they wish the youngster were out of the family (75).

In other families the parents seem to want the child's presence, but they do not want to be emotionally involved with the child (16, 55, 76). They want the child to be there and not be there at the same time—to be under their control and to gratify their demands, but not to have any independent character or wishes. The youngster may incorporate parental expectations in a mechanical manner but derives little pleasure or satisfaction from fulfilling them. At the same time, these youngsters do not feel free to act in ways that would separate them from their parents. They often make no emotional demands but instead become withdrawn, depressed, and quietly preoccupied with death and suicide (16, 55, 76).

This formulation is confirmed by an English study of adolescents who were treated psychoanalytically after serious suicide attempts (78). It found that the suicide attempts were triggered by the adolescents' "experience of failure in the attempt to separate from the mother." The failure, which was the outgrowth of a long-standing disturbed parent-child relationship, led to an intensification of maternal ties and to displacement of the experience of rejection and anger from the mother to an external object. Displacement of anger away from the mother diminished the guilt that inhibited action, permitting the anger to be expressed in suicide.

Reconstructions of early family experiences of adults have severe limitations, and most of the retrospective studies of the families of suicidal youngsters have not been controlled studies. Retrospective accounts cannot tell us whether family pathology produced the vulnerability to suicide or whether the family problems developed in response to an already disturbed child. Although the opportunity to observe the families of young patients directly may strengthen the validity of family formulations, the patients' own response to separation may also have biological or genetic roots.

FUTURE DIRECTIONS FOR RESEARCH AND TREATMENT

There is much that we do not know. Recent work on the relation of panic disorder and anxiety to attempted suicide and suicide is likely to focus our attention on the role of anxiety as an important affect in suicidal patients regardless of their diagnosis (5, 33). Evidence suggests that the level of anxiety may distinguish borderline (79) and schizophrenic (9, 10) patients who are suicidal from those who are not. As indicated earlier, there is now more definitive evidence that this is true for patients with major depressive disorders (33).

The capacity to bear hopelessness, rage, anxiety, and other unpleasant affects without collapse or regression (80, 81) has attracted little attention from either biological or psychodynamic investigators. This should change. The capacity or incapacity to self-regulate mood states may derive from biogenetic endowment as well as from struggles over the introjection of ameliorative or destructive objects.

Although suicide often appears to be a form of affect regulation in individuals who feel that their lives are out of control, in some cases the dysregulation and the suicide attempt appear to be expressed in an impulsivity akin to that seen in violent behavior (82, 83). The possibility of measuring the use of particular defense mechanisms to differentiate the relative risks of suicidal and violent behavior is attracting investigators. Pfeffer et al. (84) found that introjection and splitting were fundamental defenses in suicidal children, while compensation, projection, and displacement were correlated with assaultive behavior. Apter et al. (85) found that repression was correlated with risk of suicide, and projection and denial were correlated with risk of violence, while denial was negatively correlated with risk of suicide. It will be interesting to see what patterns of defense mechanisms emerge in patients who are both suicidal and violent.

In the past decade, specific psychodynamic conflicts seen in suicidal patients have begun to be linked to particular diagnoses. In addition to the rage toward lost love objects that is observed in patients with depression, other such linkages are conflicts over separation and abandonment in persons with borderline personalities (79), fear of disintegration in schizophrenic patients (9, 10), guilt about combat actions in veterans with PTSD (24), and grief over recent loss in alcoholics (20). It would not be surprising if further evidence of such linkages were found.

An understanding of what is known of the psychodynamics of suicide is valuable and critical in treating suicidal patients. There has long been concern about suicidal patients who do not receive appropriate psychotropic medication or are not hospitalized when necessary. Today an equally common concern involves suicidal patients, in or out of hospitals, who are receiving appropriate medication but inadequate psychotherapy. The hoary example of the patient who kills himself after his depression has lifted in response to medication serves as a reminder that more than depression is involved in suicide. The best treatment currently available comes from understanding the interactive role that diagnosis, medication, and psychotherapy play in the treatment of suicidal patients (86). If the psychotherapy of such patients is to be effective, it must be guided by a knowledge of the psychodynamics of suicide.

REFERENCES

1. *Dorpat TL, Ripley HS: A study of suicide in the Seattle area.* Compr Psychiatry *1960;* 1*:349–356*
2. *Robins E, Murphy GE, Wilkinson RH Jr, Gassner S, Kayes J: Some clinical considerations in the prevention of suicide based on a study of 134 successful suicides.* Am J Pub Health *1959;* 49*:888–899*
3. *Robins E:* The Final Months: A Study of the Lives of 134 Persons Who Committed Suicide. *New York, Oxford University Press, 1981*
4. *Barraclough B, Bunch J, Nelson B, Sainsbury P: A hundred cases of suicide: clinical aspects.* Br J Psychiatry *1974;* 125*:355–373*
5. *Weissman M, Klerman G, Markowitz J, Ouellette R: Suicidal ideation and suicide attempts in panic disorder and attacks.* N Engl J Med *1989;* 321*:1209–1214*
6. *Weissman M, Fox Klerman GL: Hostility and depression associated with suicide attempts.* Am J Psychiatry *1973;* 130*:450–455*
7. *Beck AT, Steer RA, Kovacs M, Garrison G: Hopelessness and eventual suicide: a 10-year prospective study of patients hospitalized with suicidal ideation.* Am J Psychiatry *1985;* 142*:559–563*
8. *Roose SP, Glassman AH, Walsh BT, Woodring S, Vital-Herne J: Depression, delusions, and suicide.* Am J Psychiatry *1983;* 140*:1159–1162*
9. *Drake RE, Gates C, Cotton PG, Whitaker A: Suicide among schizophrenics: who is at risk?* J Nerv Ment Dis *1984;* 172*:613–617*
10. *Drake RE, Gates C, Whitaker A, Cotton PG: Suicide among schizophrenics: a review.* Compr Psychiatry *1985;* 26*:90–100*
11. *Brown GI, Ebert MH, Goyer PF, Jimerson DC, Klein WJ, Bunney WE, Goodwin FK: Aggression, suicide, and serotonin: relationships to CSF amine metabolites.* Am J Psychiatry *1982;* 139*:741–746*
12. *van Praag HM: CSF 5-HIAA and suicide in nondepressed schizophrenics.* Lancet *1983;* 2*:977–978*

13. *Hendin H: Suicide: a review of new directions in research.* Hosp Community Psychiatry *1986;* 37*:148–154*
14. *Klerman GL: Clinical epidemiology of suicide.* J Clin Psychiatry *1987;* 48*(Dec suppl):33–38*
15. *Easterlin R:* Birth and Fortune: The Impact of Numbers on Personal Welfare. *New York, Basic Books, 1980*
16. *Hendin H:* Suicide in America. *New York, Norton, 1982*
17. *Klerman GL (ed):* Suicide and Depression among Adolescents and Young Adults. *Washington, DC, American Psychiatric Press, 1986*
18. *Malan DH:* Frontiers of Brief Psychotherapy. *New York, Plenum, 1976*
19. *Perry S, Cooper AM, Michaels R: The psychodynamic formulation: its purpose, structure, and clinical application.* Am J Psychiatry *1987;* 144*:543–550*
20. *Murphy GE, Armstrong JW Jr, Hemele SL, Fischer JR, Clendenin WW: Suicide and alcoholism.* Arch Gen Psychiatry *1979;* 36*:65–69*
21. *Maltsberger JT:* Suicide Risk: The Formulation of Clinical Judgment. *New York, New York University Press, 1981*
22. *Hendin H: Black suicide.* Arch Gen Psychiatry *1969;* 21*:407–422*
23. *Hendin H:* Black Suicide. *New York, Basic Books, 1969*
24. *Hendin H, Haas AP: Suicide and guilt as manifestations of PTSD in Vietnam combat veterans.* Am J Psychiatry *1991;* 148*:586–591*
25. *Seiden RH: We're driving young blacks to suicide.* Psychology Today *1970;* 4*:24–28*
26. *Frederick CJ: Suicide in young minority group persons, in* Suicide in the Young. *Edited by Sudak H, Ford A, Rushforth M. Boston, John Wright, 1984*
27. *Baker FM: Black youth suicide: literature review with a focus on prevention, in* Report of the Secretary's Task Force on Youth Suicide, vol 3. *Washington, DC, US Department of Health and Human Services, 1989, pp 177–191*
28. *Gibbs JT: Conceptual, methodological and sociocultural issues in black suicide.* Suicide Life Threat Behav *1988;* 18*:73–89*
29. *Wolfgang M: An analysis of homicide-suicide.* J Clin Experimental Psychopathology *1958;* 19*:208–218*
30. *Plutchik R, van Praag HM: Psychosocial correlates of suicide and violence risk, in* Violence and Suicidality: Perspectives in Clinical and Psychological Research. *Edited by van Praag HM, Plutchik R, Apter A. New York, Brunner/Mazel, 1990*
31. *Gould M, Shaffer D, Davies M: Truncated pathways from childhood to adulthood: attrition in follow-up studies due to death, in* Straight and Devious Pathways to Adulthood. *Edited by Robins LM, Rutter MR. Cambridge, Cambridge University Press, 1990*
32. *Lifton R: Suicide: the quest for a future, in* Suicide: Understanding and Responding. *Edited by Jacobs D, Brown H. Madison, Conn, International Universities Press, 1989*
33. *Fawcett J, Scheftner WA, Fogg L, Clark DC, Young MA, Hedeker D, Gibbons R: Time-related predictors of suicide in major affective disorder.* Am J Psychiatry *1990;* 147*:1189–1194*
34. *Kernberg O: Diagnosis and clinical management of suicidal potential in borderline patients, in* The Borderline Patient, vol 2. *Hillsdale, NJ, Analytic Press, 1987*

35. *Raphling D: Dreams and suicide attempts.* J Nerv Ment Dis *1970;* 151*:404–410*
36. *Hendin H: The psychodynamics of suicide.* J Nerv Ment Dis *1963;* 136*:236–244*
37. *Litman RE: The dream in the suicidal situation, in* The Dream in Clinical Practice. *Edited by Natterson J. New York, Jason Aronson, 1980*
38. *Gutheil EA: Dreams and suicide.* Am J Psychother *1948;* 2*:283–294*
39. *Jones E: On "dying together"—with special reference to Heinrich Von Kleist's suicide (1911), in* Essays on Applied Psychoanalysis, vol I. *New York, International Universities Press, 1964, pp 9–15*
40. *Jung CG: The soul and death, in* The Meaning of Death. *Edited by Feifel H. New York, McGraw-Hill, 1959*
41. *Zilboorg G: The sense of immortality.* Psychoanal Q *1938;* 7*:171–199*
42. *Pollock GH: On mourning, immortality, and utopia.* J Am Psychoanal Assoc *1975;* 23*:334–362*
43. *Maltsberger J, Buie D: The devices of suicide: revenge, riddance, and rebirth.* Int Rev Psychoanal *1980;* 7*:61–72*
44. *Menninger K:* Man Against Himself. *New York, Harcourt, Brace, 1938*
45. *Haim A:* Adolescent Suicide. *New York, International Universities Press, 1974*
46. *Mack J:* Vivienne: The Life and Suicide of an Adolescent Girl. *Boston, Little, Brown, 1981*
47. *Hendrick I:* Suicide as wish fulfillment. Psychiatr Q *1940;* 14*:30–42*
48. *Freud S: Mourning and melancholia (1917 [1915]), in* Complete Psychological Works, standard ed, vol 14. *London, Hogarth Press, 1957*
49. *Kilpatrick E: A psychoanalytic understanding of suicide.* Am J Psychoanal *1948;* 8*:13–23*
50. *Kernberg O: A psychoanalytic classification of character pathology.* J Am Psychoanal Assoc *1970;* 18*:800–822*
51. *Bibring E: The mechanisms of depression, in* Affective Disorders. *Edited by Greenacre P. New York, International Universities Press, 1953*
52. *Hendin H:* Suicide and Scandinavia. *New York, Grune & Stratton, 1964*
53. *Klein M: A contribution to the psychogenesis of manic depressive states, in* Contributions to Psychoanalysis: 1921–1945. *New York, McGraw-Hill, 1964*
54. *Asch S:* Suicide and the hidden executioner. Int Rev Psychoanal *1980;* 7*:51–60*
55. *Hendin H: Growing up dead: student suicide.* Am J Psychother *1975;* 29*:327–338*
56. *Hendin H: Youth suicide: a psychosocial perspective.* Suicide Life Threat Behav *1987;* 17*:151–165*
57. *Mintz R: Basic considerations in the psychotherapy of the depressed suicidal patient.* Am J Psychother *1971;* 25*:56–73*
58. *Pfeffer C:* The Suicidal Child. *New York, Guilford Press, 1985*
59. *Kohut H:* The Analysis of the Self. *New York, International Universities Press, 1971*
60. *Kohut H:* The Restoration of the Self. *New York, International Universities Press, 1971*
61. *Kernberg O:* Borderline Conditions and Pathological Narcissism. *New York, Jason Aronson, 1985*

62. *Wheat W: Motivational aspects of suicide in patients during and after psychiatric treatment.* South Med J 1960; 53*:273–278*
63. *Bloom V: An analysis of suicide at a training center.* Am J Psychiatry *1967;* 123*:918–925*
64. *Maltsberger JT, Buie DH: Countertransference hate in the treatment of suicidal patients.* Arch Gen Psychiatry *1974;* 30*:625–633*
65. *Hendin H: Psychotherapy and suicide.* Am J Psychother *1981;* 35*:469–480*
66. *Zilboorg G: Considerations on suicide with particular reference to the young.* Am J Orthopsychiatry *1936; 71*
67. *Barraclough B:* Suicide: Clinical and Epidemiological Studies. *New York, Croom Helm, 1987*
68. *Shaffer D, Garland A, Gould M, Fisher P, Trautman P: Preventing teenage suicide: a critical review.* J Am Acad Child Adolesc Psychiatry *1988;* 27*:675–687*
69. *Maltsberger J, Buie D: The psychological vulnerability to suicide, in* Suicide: Understanding and Responding. *Edited by Jacobs D, Brown H. Madison, Conn, International Universities Press, 1989*
70. *Kohut H:* How Does Analysis Cure? *Chicago, University of Chicago Press, 1984*
71. *Dorpat T, Jackson J, Ripley H: Broken homes and attempted and completed suicide.* Arch Gen Psychiatry *1965;* 12*:213–216*
72. *Greer S: The relationship between parental loss and attempted suicides: a control study.* Br J Psychiatry *1964;* 110*:698–705*
73. *Jacobs J, Teicher J: Broken homes and social isolation in attempted suicides of adolescents.* Int J Soc Psychiatry *1967;* 13*:139–149*
74. *Teicher JD, Jacobs J: Adolescents who attempt suicide: preliminary findings.* Am J Psychiatry *1966;* 122*:1248–1257*
75. *Sabbath JC: The suicidal adolescent: the expendable child.* J Am Acad Child Psychiatry *1969;* 8*:272–289*
76. *Hendin H:* The Age of Sensation. *New York, Norton, 1975*
77. *Shafii M, Carrigan S, Whittinghill JR, Derrick A: Psychological autopsy of completed suicide in children and adolescents.* Am J Psychiatry *1985;* 142*:1061–1064*
78. *Novick J: Attempted suicide in adolescence: the suicide sequence, in* Suicide in the Young. *Edited by Sudak H, Ford A, Rushforth M. Boston, John Wright, 1984*
79. *Perry JC: Personality Disorders, Suicide, and Self-Destructive Behavior, in* Suicide: Understanding and Responding. *Edited by Jacobs D, Brown H. Madison, Conn, International Universities Press, 1989*
80. *Zetzel ER: Anxiety and the capacity to bear it, in* The Capacity for Emotional Growth. *Edited by Zetzel ER. London, Hogarth Press, 1970*
81. *Zetzel ER: On the capacity to bear depression.* Ibid
82. *Peterson LG, Peterson M, O'Shanick GJ, Swann A: Self-inflicted gunshot wounds: lethality of method versus intent.* Am J Psychiatry *1985;* 142*:228–231*
83. *Apter A, van Praag HM, Plutchik R, Sevy S, Korn M, Brown SL: Interrelationships among anxiety, aggression, impulsivity, and mood: a serotonergically linked cluster?* Psychiatry Res *1990;* 32*:191–199*

84. *Pfeffer C, Plutchik R, Mizruchi MS, Lipkins R: Assaultive behavior in child psychiatric inpatients, outpatients, and nonpatients.* J Am Acad Child Adolesc Psychiatry *1987;* 26*:256–261*
85. *Apter A, Plutchik R, Sevy S, Korn M, Brown S, van Praag H: Defense mechanisms in risk of suicide and risk of violence.* Am J Psychiatry *1989;* 146*:1027–1031*
86. *Dulit RA, Michaels: Psychodynamics and suicide, in* Suicide and Clinical Practice. *Edited by Jacobs D. Washington, DC, American Psychiatric Press, 1991*

40. Suicide as Psychache

Edwin S. Shneidman

COMMENT

Edwin S. Shneidman has coined a new word, psychache, *to refer to the mental pain, which, when sufficiently intense, makes life insupportable and forces suicide. He emphasizes the psychological nature of the pain, reminding his readers that whatever biological underpinnings there may be to depression, suicide is a matter of the mind. Its essence does not lie in the neurochemical processes that form its physical matrix and that, when disordered, may trouble it.*

The tendency in psychiatric hospitals and clinics to view suicide as a consequence of depression, schizophrenia, or alcoholism (the three diagnostic groups in which it is most likely to occur) diverts attention from the central psychological *phenomenon of mental anguish. When one's attention skews to treating a diagnosis instead of the patient it is easy to overlook central unendurable subjective experiences.*

In calling attention to the importance of psychache as the central cause of suicide, Shneidman implicitly agrees with the recent demonstration that panic experiences are more highly associated with suicide attempts than is major depression (see chapter 37 above). This underscores the long-held belief that agitated depressed patients, whose mental suffering is profound, are at high risk.

■

AS I NEAR the end of my career in suicidology, I think I can now say what has been on my mind in as few as five words: *Suicide is caused by psychache* (sīk-āk; two syllables). Psychache refers to the hurt, anguish,

Edwin S. Shneidman, "Suicide as Psychache." *Journal of Nervous and Mental Disease* 181(1993):147–149.

soreness, aching, psychological *pain* in the psyche, the mind. It is intrinsically psychological—the pain of excessively felt shame, or guilt, or humiliation, or loneliness, or fear, or angst, or dread of growing old or of dying badly, or whatever. When it occurs, its reality is introspectively undeniable. Suicide occurs when the psychache is deemed by that person to be unbearable. This means that suicide also has to do with different individual *thresholds* for enduring psychological pain (Shneidman, 1985, 1992).

All our past efforts to relate or to correlate suicide with simplistic nonpsychological variables, such as sex, age, race, socioeconomic level, case history items (no matter how dire), psychiatric categories (including depression), etc., were (and are) doomed to miss the mark precisely because they ignore the one variable that centrally relates to suicide, namely, intolerable psychological pain; in a word, psychache.

By its very nature, psychological pain is tied to psychological needs. In general, the broadest purpose of most human activity is to satisfy psychological needs. Suicide relates to psychological needs in that suicide is a specific way to stop the unbearable psychachical flow of the mind. Furthermore, what causes this pain is the blockage, thwarting, or frustration of certain psychological needs believed by that person (at that time and in those circumstances) to be vital to continued life.

Suicide is not adaptive, but adjustive in the sense that it serves to reduce the tension of the pain related to the blocked needs. Murray's (1938) monumental volume *Explorations in Personality* provides a comprehensive list of psychological needs, and their definitions: abasement, achievement, affiliation, aggression, autonomy, counteraction, defendance, deference, dominance, exhibition, harmavoidance, infavoidance, inviolacy, nurturance, order, play, rejection, sentience, succorance, and understanding.

There is an integral relationship between suicide and happiness—or rather the absence of it. Genuine happiness—contrary to the 19th and 20th century materialistic notions that narrowly identified happiness with the mere absence of pain and the presence of creature comforts—has a special magical quality (Spender, 1988). There is a mundane happiness of comfort, pain avoidance, and psychological anesthesia. But genuine, magical happiness has relatively little to do with creature comfort; rather, it is the kind of ecstasy and consuming exuberance that one can experience only in a benign childhood. To the extent that suicide relates to happiness, it relates in people of any age—not to lack of mundane happiness but to the loss of childhood's magical joys.

A principal task for contemporary suicidology is to operationalize (and metricize) the key dimension of psychache. One way to begin is to ask the simple question, "How much do you hurt?" (Kropf, 1990).

One trenchant way to understand any individual is to rank order (or Q-sort) the prepotency among the 20 needs, that is, to define or characterize that individual's personality in terms of his or her weightings among all the needs. This can be done by assigning, for that individual, a number to each need, so that the total sum for the individual adds up to 100. This permits us to rate various individuals (or a single individual over time) by use of the constant sum method. The task is simple and takes only a few minutes. (Try it by rating yourself; then rate a well-known public figure, have colleagues rate that same figure, rate your patients after each session, rate suicidal patients, and rate nonsuicidal patients.)

In relation to suicide, there are, within any individual, two sets of dispositions or sets of relative weightings among the 20 psychological needs. They are: (a) those psychological needs that the individual lives with, that define his or her personality in its day-to-day intrapsychic and interpersonal functioning—the *modal* needs; and (b) those few psychological needs, the frustration of which that individual simply cannot tolerate; the needs that person would die for—the *vital* needs. Within an individual, these two kinds of needs are psychologically consistent with each other. The vital needs come into play when the individual is under threat or duress. This special disposition of needs can be elicited by asking an individual about his precise reactions to the failures or losses or rejections or humiliations—the dark moments—previously in his life.

By means of an intensive psychological autopsy (Shneidman, 1977), it should be possible to identify (or label) every committed suicide in terms of the two or three prepotent needs the frustration of which played a major role in that death. (With 20 needs, we have a possible taxonomy of a few hundred different "types" of suicide.)

The prevention of suicide (with a highly lethal person) is then primarily a matter of addressing and partially alleviating those frustrated psychological needs that are driving that person to suicide. The rule is simple: Mollify the psychache.

In the progression to a suicidal outcome, I believe that we can distinguish seven components. They are:

(a) the vicissitudes of life; those stresses, failures, rejections, and catabolic and social and psychological insults that are omnipresent by virtue of living.

(b) various approaches to understanding human behavior. Suicidal behavior (as is all behavior) is obviously multidimensional, which means, in practice, that its proper explication has to be multidisciplinary. The relevant fields for suicidology include biochemistry (and genetics), sociology, demography-epidemiology, psychology, psychiatry, linguistics, and so on. The reader should appreciate that *this* paper is limited to the psychological approach to suicide, without derogating the importance of other legitimate approaches.

(c) the vicissitudes of life as they are perceptually funneled through the human mind and apperceived (or appreciated) as ecstatic, pleasurable, neutral, inconsequential, or painful. If there is extreme psychache, a necessary condition for suicide is present. "I hurt too much."

(d) the perception of the pain as unbearable, intolerable, and unacceptable, another necessary condition for suicide, in addition to psychache. "I won't put up with this pain."

(e) the thought (or insight) that cessation of consciousness is the solution for the unbearable psychache, still another necessary condition. In a phrase, death is preferable to living, with death as a means of egression or escape. "I can kill myself."

(f) a lowered threshold for enduring or sustaining the crippling psychache, a final necessary condition for suicide. A priori, people with more or less equal amounts of psychache might have radically different overt outcomes depending upon their different thresholds for tolerating or enduring psychological pain. (In life, pain is ubiquitous and inescapable; suffering is optional.)

(g) the suicidal outcome. "I hurt too much to live."

About now, the alert and restive reader might be asking, What about depression? As everyone knows, depression is a serious psychiatric syndrome, well recognized and relatively treatable. But depression is not the same as suicide. They are quite different. For one thing, they have enormously different fatality rates. One can live a long, unhappy life with depression—not true of an acutely suicidal state. Theoretically, no one has ever died of depression—it is not a legitimate cause of death on the death certificate—but many people, too many, have died of suicide. Vast numbers of people suffer from minor and major depressions. Depression seems to have physiological, biochemical, and probably genetical components. The use of medications in treatment is on target. It is, so to speak, a biological storm in the brain. Suicide, on the other hand, is a phenomenological event,

Table 1. Symptoms of Depression: Characterictics of Suicide

Depression*	Suicide
1. Sadness 2. Apathy 3. Loss of appetite or increased appetite 4. Insomnia, or sleeping far more than usual 5. Feeling physically agitated or slowed down 6. Fatigue and lack of energy 7. Feelings of worthlessness or great guilt 8. Inability to concentrate or indecisiveness 9. Thoughts of death or suicide	1. In great psychological pain (psychache) 2. Cannot stand the pain (lowered threshold for suffering) 3. Sees ending life as an escape (death as solution) 4. Sees no possibilities other than death (constriction) 5. May or may not have symptoms of depression (suicide as a mental state)

*The source (for Depression) was *The New York Times*, August 5, 1992 (by permission).

a transient tempest in the mind. It is responsive to talk therapy and to changes in the environment. Suicide is not a psychiatric disorder. Suicide is a nervous dysfunction, not a mental disease. *All* persons who commit suicide—100% of them—are perturbed, but they are not necessarily clinically depressed (or schizophrenic, or alcoholic or addicted or psychiatrically ill). A suicidal crisis is best treated on its own terms. It is a deadly serious (temporary and treatable) psychache (Table 1).

Depression never causes suicide; rather, suicide; rather, suicide results from severe psychache, coupled with dysphoria, constriction of perceptual range, and the idea of death as preferable to life. By themselves, the clinical symptoms of depression are debilitating, but, by their nature, not deadly. On the other hand, severe psychache by itself may be life threatening. Correlating suicide with DSM categories is irrelevant to the real action in the mind's main tent. Depression merits treatment for itself, but then to assert that suicide is essentially depression is either a logical mistake, a conceptual confusion, or a professional gambit. In any case, it is past time to make this correction.

Here, finally, after over 40 years of experience as a suicidologist, is a tight summary of my current beliefs about suicide.

1. The explanation of suicide in humankind is the same as the explanation of the suicide of any particular human. Suicidology, the study of human suicide, and a psychological autopsy (of a particular case) are identical in their goals: to nibble at the puzzle of human self-destruction.

2. The most evident fact about suicidology and suicidal events is that they are multidimensional, multifaceted, and multidisciplinary, containing, as they do, concomitant biological, sociological, psychological (interpersonal and intrapsychic), epidemiological, and philosophical elements.

3. From the view of the psychological factors in suicide, the key element in every case is psychological pain: psychache. All affective states (such as rage, hostility, depression, shame, guilt, affectlessness, hopelessness, etc.) are relevant to suicide only as they relate to unbearable psychological pain. If, for example, feeling guilty or depressed or having a bad conscience or an overwhelming unconscious rage makes one suicidal, it does so only because it is painful. No psychache, no suicide.

4. Individuals have different thresholds for enduring or tolerating pain; thus, the individual's decision not to bear the pain—the threshold for enduring it—is also directly relevant.

5. In every case, the psychological pain is created and fueled by frustrated psychological needs. These needs have been explicated by Murray (1938, chapter 3, pp. 142–242).

6. There are modal psychological needs with which the person lives (and which define the personality) and there are vital psychological needs whose frustration cannot be tolerated (which define the suicide). Within an individual, these two kinds of needs are psychologically consistent with each other, although not necessarily the same as each other.

7. The remediation (or therapy) of the suicidal state lies in addressing and mollifying the vital frustrated needs. The therapist does well to have this template (of psychological needs) in mind so that the therapy can be tailor-made for that patient. Often, just a little bit of mollification of the patient's frustrated needs can change the vital balance sufficiently to save a life.

REFERENCES

Kropf J (1990) An empirical assessment of Murray's personological formulation of suicide. *Unpublished doctoral dissertion. California School of Professional Psychology, Fresno, CA.*

Murray H (1938) Explorations in personality. *New York: Oxford University Press.*

Shneidman ES (1977) The psychological autopsy. In L Gottschalk et al (Eds), Guide to the investigation and reporting of drug abuse deaths. *Rockville, MD: ADAMHA.*

Shneidman ES (1985) Definition of suicide. *New York: Wiley.*

Shneidman ES (1992) A conspectus of the suicidal scenario. In RW Maris et al (Eds), Assessment and prediction of suicide. *New York: Guilford.*

Spender S (1988) Introduction to the second edition. In P O'Connor, Memoirs of a public baby. *New York: W. W. Norton.*

Index